BLACKSTONE'S GUIDE TO

The Human Rights Act 1998

SEVENTH EDITION

John Wadham, Helen Mountfield QC,
Elizabeth Prochaska, Raj Desai

OXFORD
UNIVERSITY PRESS

OXFORD
UNIVERSITY PRESS

Great Clarendon Street, Oxford, OX2 6DP,
United Kingdom

Oxford University Press is a department of the University of Oxford.
It furthers the University's objective of excellence in research, scholarship,
and education by publishing worldwide. Oxford is a registered trade mark of
Oxford University Press in the UK and in certain other countries

© John Wadham, Helen Mountfield QC, Elizabeth Prochaska, and Raj Desai 2015

The moral rights of the authors have been asserted

First Edition published in 1999
Seventh Edition published in 2015

Impression: 1

Published in the United States of America by Oxford University Press
198 Madison Avenue, New York, NY 10016, United States of America

British Library Cataloguing in Publication Data
Data available

Library of Congress Control Number: 2014959480

ISBN 978–0–19–870575–8

Printed and bound by
Lightning Source UK Ltd

Preface to the Seventh Edition

The Human Rights Act 1998 came into force fifteen years ago and has been spoken of by judges as having quasi-Constitutional status. At time of writing, however, its continued existence is in doubt, and its future abolition is now an issue for the May 2015 General Election. There can be no doubt that the Act continues to have a profound effect on domestic law, substantially strengthening the legal protection afforded to human rights in the United Kingdom. Where citizens once had 'negative' liberties—no more than the residue of rights left over after the law had been obeyed—they now enjoy positive freedoms and the power to enforce them. The Human Rights Act has been used to hold the Government and public authorities to account in a multitude of contexts—preventing the indefinite detention of foreign terrorist suspects,[1] broadening the ambit of procedural justice,[2] recognizing the rights of transsexuals to marry someone of their original gender,[3] protecting the right to freedom of speech, even when it offends,[4] ensuring that the state does not retain the DNA records of innocent people.[5] If it was ever a matter of doubt, it is now plain that the Human Rights Act can no longer be regarded as just another statute. Rather it places on an ever-speaking statutory basis an assumption that certain legal norms are fundamental and underpin all other statutory interpretation. Lord Justice Laws placed it in a category of 'constitutional statutes' which include the Magna Carta and the European Communities Act 1972,[6] and the previous Government accepted its status as a 'received part of our constitutional arrangements'.[7] However the number of cases going to the Strasbourg Court has not yet been stemmed (see Chapter 9 for more details), and the decisions of appeal courts in the United Kingdom are often 'overturned' by the European Court of Human Rights:

there have been no fewer than 10 occasions on which the European Court of Human Rights has issued a judgment which is at variance with that which was earlier reached by the House of Lords.[8]

---

[1] *A and ors v Secretary of State for the Home Department* [2004] UKHL 56, [2005] 2 AC 68.

[2] For example, for Iraqi families of those killed in detention by British troops (*R (Al-Skeini) v Secretary of State for Defence* [2007] UKHL 26, [2008] 1 AC 153); for those placed on 'safeguarding' registers (*R (F and Thompson) v Secretary of State for the Home Department* [2010] UKSC 17, [2011] AC 331, 2 WLR 992) .

[3] *Bellinger v Bellinger* [2003] UKHL 21, [2003] 2 AC 467.

[4] *Livingstone v Adjudication Panel for England* [2006] EWHC 2533 (Admin), [2006] LGR 799.

[5] *R (GC and C) v Commissioner of the Police for the Metropolis* [2011] UKSC 21, [2011] 3 All ER 859, [2011] 1 WLR 1230.

[6] *Thoburn v Sunderland City Council* [2002] EWHC 195 (Admin), [2002] 3 WLR 247.

[7] JCHR, *A Bill of Rights for the UK?* 29th Report (2007–2008), HL 165-I, HC 150-I, vol II, Jack Straw Ev 78.

[8] Or the Supreme Court: Brice Dickson, *Human Rights and the United Kingdom Supreme Court* (London: Oxford University Press, 2013) p 374. This figure remains up to date as at 1 September 2014. In 2014, the European Court has so far considered only one case which had previously been considered by the

This can be seen as a positive mechanism of dialogue between national and international law norms, and a valuable part of the new constitutional settlement.[9]

The Act continues to be condemned by the popular press, however, as a 'villains' charter' that privileges the rights of unpopular minorities (often the criticisms concern non-British citizens 'taking advantage' of the Act) over the law-abiding majority, while the judiciary (both from the UK courts and the judges in Strasbourg) is damned for its usurpation of democratic power. These accusations are—at least when the details of the cases are analysed—unwarranted. Despite common misconceptions to the contrary, the Human Rights Act does not allow courts to strike down legislation that violates fundamental rights. Instead, the Act strikes a careful balance between parliamentary sovereignty and judicial oversight that enables the courts only to issue a declaration of incompatibility where a legislative provision is incapable of being read compatibly with Convention rights. Ministers (and Parliament) make the final decision as to whether or not to amend legislation which has been held incompatible with the Convention. Though it is under no legal obligation to do so, Governments usually respond to declarations of incompatibility by changing legislation (albeit generally after an appeal and some delay). But they do not have to do so as a matter of national law: and indeed, in the celebrated impasse over prisoners' voting rights, they have not done so. Consequently, the Supreme Court has held that it would be inappropriate for it to make any further declaration of incompatibility on this subject: the legislature and executive now have the judicial view on this subject and its constitutional role is at an end.[10] Rather than judicial usurpation, this model of rights protection ought to be characterized as healthy democratic dialogue, and it leaves in place the British dualist legal tradition, in which international legal obligations are applied in national courts only if and to the extent they are incorporated into national law by statute.[11] The late Lord Bingham summed up the position in his powerful and eloquent speech in the *Belmarsh* case concerning detention of terrorist suspects:

I do not in particular accept the distinction between democratic institutions and the courts. It is of course true that the judges in this country are not elected and are not answerable to Parliament. It is also of course true that Parliament, the executive and the courts have different functions. But the function of independent judges charged to interpret and apply the law is universally recognised as a cardinal feature of the modern democratic state, a cornerstone of the rule of law itself. The Attorney General is fully entitled to insist on the proper limits of judicial authority, but he is wrong to stigmatise judicial decision-making as in some way undemocratic. It is particularly inappropriate in a case such as the present in which Parliament has expressly legislated in section 6 of the 1998 Act to render unlawful any act of a public authority, including

---

UK Supreme Court. In *McDonald v United Kingdom* (2013) 37 BHRC 130, it agreed with the Supreme Court that the absence of night time assistance for a disabled person violated Article 8 until a revised care-plan held that this was acceptable, but thereafter was within the margin of appreciation.

[9] *S and Marper v UK* (2008) 48 EHRR 1169; *Kay v UK* [2010] ECHR 1322 (21 September 2010); *Hirst v UK* No 2 (2005) 19 BHRC 546, (2006) 42 EHRR 41, though see observations of the Supreme Court in *Chester* (n 10) as to how far this can go.

[10] *R (Chester) v Secretary of State for Justice* [2013] UKSC 63, [2014] AC 271.

[11] See ch 1, para 1.28.

a court, incompatible with a Convention right, has required courts (in section 2) to take account of relevant Strasbourg jurisprudence, has (in section 3) required courts, so far as possible, to give effect to Convention rights and has conferred a right of appeal on derogation issues.[12]

In any event, contrary to some press accusations, the application of the Human Rights Act by the judiciary has been cautious.[13] The approach to section 2 of the Act, which demands that Strasbourg cases are 'taken into account' in interpreting Convention rights, illustrates the restraint with which the judiciary has approached its new powers. In an attempt to avoid being labelled judicial activists, the House of Lords and the Supreme Court have developed the 'no more, no less' approach to Strasbourg cases and arguably frustrated the creation of a progressive domestic rights jurisprudence on interpretation of Convention rights in the British context.[14] It is necessary only to look at those decisions of the House of Lords and Supreme Court that have been re-considered by the Strasbourg Court to see that English courts regularly adopt a narrower interpretation of the Convention rights even than the long-stop Court in Strasbourg.[15]

Despite the judiciary's responsible application of the Human Rights Act, its future is far from assured. The Conservative Party went into the 2010 general election vowing to abolish the Human Rights Act and to substitute it with a 'Bill of Rights'. The Coalition Government then set up a Commission to investigate the creation of a Bill of Rights that incorporates and builds on the European Convention on Human Rights. The Commission failed to reach a consensus on what, if anything, needed to change.[16] However, some members of the Commission expressed concern that the debate in the Commission was moving towards a discussion of removing rights, and particularly towards withdrawing from the Convention.

Fury over the Human Rights Act reached fever pitch again as a result of the long-delayed legislation brought forward to give prisoners the right to vote in line with the decision of the European Court in *Hirst v UK (No 2)* in 2006.[17] The media and many politicians denounced the Convention and called for the United Kingdom to remove itself from the jurisdiction of the European Court. The Government partly responded by using its chairmanship of the Council of Europe to push on with further reforms of the Court to 'rebalance' its relations with national courts. This resulted in the 'Brighton Declaration'[18] and, in turn, two new protocols, the first of which, protocol 15, will impose (amongst other things)

---

[12] *A and ors v Secretary of State for the Home Department* [2004] UKHL 56, [2005] 2 AC 68 at [42].

[13] See the careful analysis in Leigh and Masterman, *Making Rights Real: The Human Rights Act in its First Decade* (London: Hart Publishing, 2009).

[14] See *R (Ullah) v Special Adjudicator* [2004] UKHL 26, [2004] 2 AC 323.

[15] See *Hirst v UK (No 2)* (2006) 42 EHRR 41; *S and Marper v UK* (2008) 48 EHRR 1169; *Kay v UK* App No 37341/06, 21 September 2010. For a more detailed analysis see Brice Dickson, *Human Rights and the United Kingdom Supreme Court* (London: Oxford University Press, 2013), particularly the table at Appendix 3.

[16] The Commission on a Bill of Rights' report, 'A UK Bill of Rights?—The Choice Before Us', 18 December 2012, Ministry of Justice.

[17] (2006) 42 EHRR 41.

[18] High Level Conference on the Future of the European Court of Human Right: Brighton Declaration, 20 April 2012, Council of Europe.

further restrictions on access to the Court and might push the Court to be more 'careful' in its judgments (see Chapter 9 for more details). Although the UK's initial proposals for reform were watered down, pressure for reform has led to a wider ranging review of the long-term future of the Court, the consequences of which are difficult to predict.[19]

Some critics (including the previous Lord Chief Justice, Lord Judge LCJ,[20] speaking extra-judicially) have suggested that the statutory duty to take Strasbourg judgments into account (section 2) should be reworded to give domestic courts greater leeway to ignore even settled Strasbourg jurisprudence. The judiciary has taken note of the political heat surrounding human rights law and recent domestic decisions from the Supreme Court and Court of Appeal suggest increasing judicial willingness to assert the power of the common law to resolve human rights claims.[21] If the Human Rights Act is repealed, we can expect the courts to turn to other sources of protection for fundamental rights.

The latest proposals from the Conservative Party set out a number of proposals for reform which will be included in the Conservative Party manifesto for the 2015 election.[22] More details are set out in Chapter 1 and a draft Bill is due early in 2015. The Conservatives' proposals gave a factually misleading account of recent human rights judgments from the Strasbourg Court, wrongly suggesting, for example, that the Court had banned whole life sentences.[23] The view of two eminent human rights lawyers, which we share, is that the proposals are 'wholly unworkable, legally contradictory and inherently inconsistent'.[24]

The authors hope that the frenzy about human rights leads to a free and informed debate that enhances rather than hinders the development of the law and recognition of the need for a robust legal framework within which human rights norms can be enforced and remedies assured. Finally, they hope the progressive jurisprudence of the European Court remains part of our domestic law and applicants with real grievances continue to have access to the European Court of Human Rights to right their wrongs.

The law is up to date to 1 October 2014 but, where possible, we have included some later material.

Any mistakes in the text—of course—are ours.

John Wadham, Helen Mountfield QC,
Elizabeth Prochaska, and Raj Desai
October 2014

---

[19] See ch 9, para 9.07.

[20] Speech to the Constitution Unit at University College London, reported in the *Guardian*, 4 December 2013.

[21] See *UK Constitutionalism on the march*, Lady Hale (Deputy President of the UK Supreme Court), lecture to the Constitutional and Administrative Law Bar Association Conference, 12 July 2014.

[22] See 'Protecting Human Rights in the UK: The Conservatives' Proposals for Changing Britain's Human Rights Law', 3 October 2014, discussed in ch 1, paragraph 1.56.

[23] See ch 6, para 6.88.

[24] Advice of Tim Owen QC and Alex Bailin QC, 3 October 2014. Available at: <https://www.scribd.com/doc/241813468/Opinion-on-HRA-Repeal>.

Acknowledgements

Since the first edition of this Guide, the list of acknowledgements we ought to make has grown. We remain enormously grateful to everyone with whom we have discussed the Human Rights Act and incorporation of the Convention into domestic law over the past decade. The thanks which we have accorded to those names in previous editions still stand. We owe particular debts, however, to Anna Edmundson who jointly authored the third and fourth editions, to Caoilfhionn Gallagher who was a joint author on editions four and five, and to Christopher Brown for his work on edition six.

In addition, for this edition we wish to thank Professor Philip Leach for his help with Chapter 9, Anna Henry at the Equality and Human Rights Commission, Anthony Fairclough and the Legal Information Team at Matrix Chambers, and other members of Matrix Chambers who have been generous with their knowledge and ideas. At Oxford University Press, Amy Norman has given us assistance and encouragement throughout the writing, copy-editing, and proofing process, and we are very grateful to her.

Contents

Table of Cases

Table of International Instruments

Table of European Legislation

Table of Statutes

Table of other legislation

Table of Statutory Instruments

1

INTRODUCTION

A. INTRODUCTION

The Human Rights Act 1998 has been in force for over a decade, but the notion **1.01** of rights has an historic pedigree. Legal philosophers have grappled with the complex implications of the concept ever since rights first emerged in the Magna Carta.[1] Despite different perspectives on the debate, however, common threads are discernible in the theorists' writings. It is generally accepted that rights contain both a positive ('claim-right') and a negative ('liberty-right') aspect:

status of a right entails that a person is both entitled to stand on his own right *and* to require others to be duty bound to respect it. It means, for example, that when a person asserts his right to privacy, he has a claim right which others are duty bound to respect; and also that he has a liberty right to privacy which entitles him to insist on an entitlement to be let alone.[2]

---

[1] Detailed discussions can be found in: Hart, *The Concept of Law* (Oxford: Clarendon Press, 1961); Dworkin, *Taking Rights Seriously* (London: Duckworth, 1978); Tuck, *Natural Rights Theories: Their Origins and Development* (Cambridge: Cambridge University Press, 1979); Finnis, *National Law and Natural Rights* (Oxford: Clarendon Press, 1979); Raz, *The Morality of Freedom* (Oxford: Clarendon Press, 1986).

[2] Clayton and Tomlinson, *The Law of Human Rights*, 2nd edn (Oxford: Oxford University Press, 2009) 22, citing Dworkin, *Taking Rights Seriously* (London: Duckworth, 1977) ch 7.

1.02   Equally, it is accepted that rights and responsibilities are inextricably linked. In *Rights of Man* Thomas Paine asserted that 'a Declaration of Rights is, by reciprocity, a Declaration of Duties also...whatever is my right as a man, is also the right of another; and it becomes my duty to guarantee, as well as to possess'.[3] For Paine, rights were not purely the preserve of the 'selfish' individual but were vital to a healthy civil society. As we discuss later, the relationship between rights and responsibilities has become a central feature of the debate over the future of the Human Rights Act.

1.03   English lawyers were traditionally sceptical of the idea of human rights as a positive concept. They preferred instead to focus on the negative conception of liberties in which 'freedom' consisted of the residual leftovers after the law had been obeyed.[4] While there was no recognized right of free expression, for example, everyone was free to write or say what they liked provided it was not libellous or slanderous, or in breach of confidence, or contrary to the Official Secrets Act, or in contempt of court, or in breach of statute. However, without positive guarantees of rights enshrined in a written constitution or a human rights instrument, this negative liberty offered little protection against the acts or omissions of public bodies that harmed fundamental rights. When the former Prime Minister John Major proclaimed 'we have no need of a Bill of Rights because we have freedom',[5] he failed to appreciate that government may show 'a more mundane but still corrupting insensitivity to liberty, a failure to grasp its force and place in democratic ideals'.[6]

1.04   English lawyers' perspective on the legal protection of liberty began to change during the rapid development of international human rights in the second half of the twentieth century. After the horrors of World War Two and the Holocaust, the international community framed new covenants explicitly enshrining universal human rights to try to ensure that such atrocities would never occur again. The first major convention that dealt with human rights, the Universal Declaration on Human Rights (1948), recognized civil and political rights as well as economic, social, and cultural rights. In 1966, the UN-sponsored International Covenant on Civil and Political Rights (ICCPR) was opened for signature. In the same year, the International Covenant on Economic, Social and Cultural Rights (ICESCR) was drawn up, but, unlike the ICCPR, the rights contained within it are subject to the availability of resources and the obligations are to be 'progressively realized'. Doubts about the universality and practicability of economic and social rights have been expressed and the nature of the ICESCR accommodates these concerns.[7] A range of other legal instruments aimed at securing key human rights for specified groups of people (including women, ethnic groups, children, and refugees) and at protecting particular thematic rights (for example, the UN Convention against

---

[3] Paine, *The Rights of Man*, 1791 (Oxford: Oxford University Press, 1995) 165.

[4] See *Malone v Metropolitan Police Commissioner* [1979] ch. 344.

[5] Quoted by Lord Irvine, 'The Development of Human Rights in Britain under an Incorporated Convention on Human Rights', Tom Sargant Memorial Lecture, London, 16 December 1997.

[6] Dworkin, 'Devaluing Liberty' (1988) 17(8) Index on Censorship 7.

[7] See Steiner and Alston, *International Human Rights in Context*, 2nd edn (Oxford: Oxford University Press, 2000).

Torture) have since become an integral part of international law. These treaties and conventions articulate a range of different rights that combine the twin concepts of 'positive' and 'negative' rights, and strive to achieve a balance between individuals' rights and their responsibilities.

The development with the most profound impact on English law and, indeed, on international human rights jurisprudence more broadly, has been the European Convention for the Protection of Human Rights and Fundamental Freedoms (Convention). Although British lawyers were responsible for much of the drafting of the Convention[8] and the United Kingdom was among the first signatories in 1950, it was nearly half a century before the Government was willing to 'bring rights home' by incorporating Convention rights into domestic law in the Human Rights Act 1998. The explanation for this reticence lies in part in the constitutional and common law traditions that, many judges and politicians believed, already accorded human rights adequate protection. 1.05

B. HUMAN RIGHTS IN THE UNITED KINGDOM BEFORE THE HUMAN RIGHTS ACT

1. Rights in English common law before the Human Rights Act

Prior to the enactment of the Human Rights Act, Britain was almost alone amongst western democracies in not having a positive guarantee of rights. However, various historic constitutional texts offered the English limited guarantees of particular rights. The Magna Carta, drafted in 1215, introduced the concepts of habeas corpus and trial by jury. The Bill of Rights of 1689 contained some provisions that later appeared in other human rights covenants, including a prohibition on cruel and unusual punishment, but it was principally a part of a political settlement limiting the power of the monarch and did not purport to protect the basic rights of the citizen. 1.06

In the eighteenth and early nineteenth centuries, many ideas that we regard as central to the rule of law—such as a philosophy of liberty and the notion of the freedom of the press—were developed by English thinkers such as Tom Paine, John Locke, and JS Mill. But despite their political writings and contemporary events such as the French Revolution and the American Declaration of Independence, Britain did not adopt a comparable 'Declaration of the Rights of Man'. 1.07

Instead, the English relied upon 'negative' liberty, the most influential exposition of which is contained in Dicey's nineteenth-century theory of residual rights.[9] Dicey's theory holds that individuals may say or do whatever they please provided they do not transgress the substantive law or infringe the legal rights of others. In other words, 'we are free to do everything except that which we are forbidden to do 1.08

---

[8] See Simpson, *Human Rights and the End of Empire: Britain and the Genesis of the European Convention* (Oxford: Oxford University Press, 2004).
[9] Dicey, *Law of the Constitution*, 1885, 9th edn (London: Macmillan, 1950).

by law'. Further, the Crown and other public authorities may not do anything unless they are so authorized by a rule of common law (including the royal prerogative) or statute, and thus may not interfere with individuals' liberties.

1.09   As well as these residual freedoms, Dicey and others (including Blackstone in his *Commentaries on the Laws of England*)[10] identified a separate body of fundamental rights in English common law including those to personal security and liberty, private property, freedom of discussion, and assembly. These were protected by the presumption of legality, which holds that rights cannot be removed by Parliament except by express words. These rights were recognized by the courts as part of the compact between monarch and Parliament and the birthright of the people. Dicey argued that this system worked well, as Parliament, elected by the people, was the only body which could legislate rights out of existence. Dicey's confidence in residual rights has not been borne out by experience.

1.10   The enormous growth in the power of public and quasi-public bodies over the lives of individuals during the twentieth century has diluted the ability of Parliament to scrutinize legislation—if, indeed, it ever had such omnipotence. Since Dicey was writing, the way in which power is distributed in modern society has altered fundamentally. It is no longer accurate to talk of constitutional power being shared between the legislature, executive, and judiciary alone. The imposition of strict parliamentary party-political discipline has meant that the executive's power within the legislature is often unchallenged, and the growth of quasi-public bodies performing privatized functions of government has led to a reallocation of public power among a variety of different constitutional actors.

1.11   In any case, as JS Mill observed in *On Liberty*,[11] democracy is not in itself a guarantee against the tyranny of the majority over unpopular minorities. In the notorious *East African Asians Case*[12] the European Commission of Human Rights (ECmHR) found that the Commonwealth Immigrants Act 1968, passed to stop British passport holders in East Africa who were fleeing persecution in their home countries coming to the United Kingdom, was motivated by racism. Parliament is also prone to legislating to remove fundamental rights as, for example, in the Criminal Justice and Public Order Act 1994, when the newly created offence of 'trespassory assembly' limited individuals' common law right to assemble (one of the fundamental rights identified by Dicey). In a fast-changing society, relying on the incremental development of the common law to protect rights proved unsatisfactory.

2. European Convention rights in the United Kingdom before the Human Rights Act

1.12   The Convention was drafted with significant input from English lawyers.[13] The United Kingdom ratified the Convention in 1951 and recognized the individual right

---

[10] (1765–1769).
[11] (Oxford: Oxford University Press, 1869).
[12] (1981) 3 EHRR 76.
[13] See n 8.

of petition in 1966. Ironically, in light of the UK's contribution to the Convention, the positive guarantees of fundamental rights contained in the international Convention have been found by the European Court of Human Rights (ECtHR) to have been violated by successive British governments in a surprising number of cases.[14] One reason for this was the judiciary's inability to develop English law consistently with the Convention. Under the dualist principles of English law, international treaties ratified by the UK Government, such as the Convention, do not have direct legal effect in domestic courts until they are incorporated into domestic law by an Act of Parliament.

However, before the Human Rights Act came into force—indeed, even before **1.13** the Bill was drafted—it was possible for Convention principles to have an impact on domestic law either indirectly (through judgments against the United Kingdom in Strasbourg that were then implemented by changes in the law), or directly (by developing the common law through legal arguments based on the Convention).

Over the five decades preceding the enactment of the Human Rights Act, the **1.14** Convention indirectly had an increasing impact on the development of the English law. Findings of violations against the United Kingdom led to several changes being made to primary legislation. The Strasbourg Court's judgment in *Sunday Times v UK (No 1)*[15] was an important factor leading to the reform of the law of contempt by the Contempt of Court Act 1981. The violation of the right to respect for private life in Article 8 found by the ECtHR in the telephone-tapping case of *Malone v UK*[16] led to the enactment of the Interception of Communications Act 1985 (provisions now contained in the Regulation of Investigatory Powers Act 2000).

The judiciary was also able to directly consider the provisions of the Convention **1.15** in cases before the domestic courts. The most important pre-Act uses of the Convention were as follows:

(a) as an aid to the construction of legislation in cases of ambiguity, for example in *R v Secretary of State for the Home Department, ex p Brind*.[17] There is a presumption that Parliament does not intend to act in breach of international law (and the specific treaty obligations the UK Government has committed to on behalf of the Crown), so where there is ambiguity in a statute the courts will construe the law consistently with these international treaty obligations;

(b) to establish the scope of the common law where it is developing and uncertain, or where it is certain but incomplete. For example, in *Derbyshire County Council v Times Newspapers Ltd*[18] Article 10 informed the House of Lords' decision that a local authority could not bring an action for libel as it would offend against the freedom of expression protections in the Convention;

---

[14] See the partial list of (pre-incorporation) violations in Hunt, *Using Human Rights Law in English Courts* (London: Hart Publishing, 1997) app 1.
[15] (1979) 2 EHRR 245.
[16] (1984) 7 EHRR 14.
[17] [1991] 1 AC 696.
[18] [1992] QB 770.

(c) to inform the exercise of judicial (as opposed to administrative) discretion. For example, in *R v Khan*[19] the House of Lords held that a trial judge may have regard to the Convention as a material consideration in exercising the discretion conferred by section 78 of the Police and Criminal Evidence Act 1984 as to whether to exclude evidence; and

(d) to inform decisions on EU law taken by the domestic courts. For example, in *Johnston v Chief Constable of the Royal Ulster Constabulary*[20] the European Court of Justice (ECJ) took Articles 6 and 13 into account in determining that the applicant did not have an effective remedy in her sex discrimination case. The ECJ has declared that the general principles of EU law include the protection of fundamental rights. This means that not only should English judges have regard to the Convention when dealing with questions of fundamental rights in EU law, but also that ECJ judgments involving fundamental rights are to be regarded as authoritative when domestic courts grapple with questions of EU law. These issues are discussed in detail in Chapter 5.

1.16 These techniques continue to be important, and are still used in relation to other international treaties that have not been incorporated into English law.[21]

C. THE INCORPORATION OF THE CONVENTION

1.17 The initial justifications advanced by Parliament for not giving full effect to the provisions of the Convention included concerns that the constitutional doctrines of parliamentary sovereignty and separation of powers would be irreparably harmed. In particular, commentators were worried that judges would wield too much power and that difficult societal questions and conflicts of interests would be resolved by judges rather than through political debate by elected MPs. Opponents also argued that it was an unnecessary step given that rights were already adequately protected by the common law, and indeed the incorporation of the 'vague', general principles of the Convention would be a retrograde step for the protection of rights in the United Kingdom as the 'flexibility' of the unwritten constitution would be constrained.

1.18 Over the past 50 years, those views on the incorporation of the Convention into domestic law slowly changed, culminating in the Human Rights Act. Supporters of a Bill of Rights had long argued that the common law safeguards for rights were inadequate and open to attack by politicians in the grip of party politics. They pointed out that the strict party discipline imposed on the parliamentary political parties did not allow for a fully independent legislature, and so a Bill of Rights was needed to deal with what Lord Hailsham called an 'elective dictatorship'.

---

[19] [1996] 3 WLR 162.
[20] [1987] QB 129.
[21] For a more detailed analysis, see Hunt, *Using Human Rights Law in English Courts* (London: Hart Publishing, 1997); Fatima, *Using International Law in Domestic Courts* (London: Hart Publishing, 2005).

Supporters relied, too, on the unavoidable facts that the United Kingdom was one of a handful of western democracies that did not have a written Bill of Rights and that British citizens were forced to undertake a lengthy and expensive route to enforcing their Convention rights in Strasbourg. The debate on a Bill of Rights during this period was not the preserve of one political party or political philosophy. In the late 1940s, the main British protagonists of what became the Convention were Conservatives such as Winston Churchill and Harold Macmillan. Equally, it was the Labour Attlee Government that ratified the Convention in 1951, the Churchill Government that ratified the First Protocol in 1953, and the Labour Government of Wilson that accepted the right of individual petition to the ECtHR in 1966.

In 1968, the publication of the pamphlet *Democracy and Individual Rights* by **1.19** Anthony Lester (now the Liberal Democrat peer Lord Lester QC) marked the beginning of the debate that led eventually to the Human Rights Act. Lester suggested that incorporating the Convention was only a first step for enshrining human rights guarantees but would be no more than an interim measure. In subsequent years, the issue of incorporating the Convention was debated a number of times from a variety of political perspectives. An important step forward was made in 1974, when Sir Leslie Scarman (later the cross-bench peer Lord Scarman) wrote of the need for an instrument to challenge the sovereignty of Parliament and to protect basic human rights which could not be adequately protected by the legislature alone. Scarman was in favour of entrenchment. He believed that only by making a Bill of Rights superior to the machinations of Parliament could such fundamental rights be protected.[22]

The Labour Party National Executive Committee unveiled a *Charter of Human* **1.20** *Rights* in 1975. This document advocated an unentrenched Human Rights Act. This proposal was regarded as insufficient by many who considered that such an Act would offer inadequate protection to individual interests against the growing power of the state. In particular, many Conservatives (including Sir Geoffrey Howe (now Lord Howe), Lord Brittan, and Roy Jenkins (the late Lord Jenkins)) preferred the concept of a Bill of Rights with entrenched clauses that would prevent even Parliament from granting the executive excessive power over the lives of individuals.

Lord Wade as a Liberal in 1976 moved a Bill in the House of Lords **1.21** which proposed to entrench the Convention as a part of all existing legislation and to make it an entrenched part of all subsequent enactments unless Parliament specifically legislated otherwise. Lord Wade and Lord Harris continued to be the chief advocates for a Bill of Rights in the Lords. In 1978, a House of Lords Select Committee examined the arguments for and against legislation to incorporate the Convention and create a Bill of Rights. However, traditional constitutional views prevailed, particularly a concern about the idea of judges deciding 'human rights' cases. The fear was that this would remove the judiciary from its

---

[22] Lord Scarman, *English Law—The New Dimension*, Hamlyn Lectures, 26th Series (London: Stevens, 1974).

traditionally impartial role, supposedly beyond politics, and embroil it in (party) political questions.

1.22   After John Smith became leader of the Labour Party in 1992, there was a clear shift in Labour Party policy. The Labour Party Conference in October 1993 adopted a two-stage policy supporting the incorporation of the European Convention of Human Rights to be followed by the enactment of a domestic Bill of Rights. The Labour Party planned to entrench Convention rights by the use of a 'notwithstanding clause' procedure. This was similar to the Canadian Charter of Rights and Freedoms, and would have led to the Convention overriding domestic law unless Parliament expressly provided for it to apply notwithstanding that it would violate the instrument. The conference also advocated the establishment of a human rights commission to monitor and promote human rights. Tony Blair MP (shortly before he became leader of the Labour Party) set out his views in the *Guardian* and reaffirmed the need for strengthened incorporation and the idea of a 'notwithstanding clause'.[23]

1.23   Lord Lester of Herne Hill continued his human rights work in the Lords by introducing a Bill in November 1994. The Bill did not receive support from the Conservative Government. Particular aspects of the proposed Bill were criticized by the Law Lords, but significantly they supported incorporation in so far as it allowed UK judges to interpret human rights domestically.

1.24   In December 1996, Jack Straw MP and Paul Boateng MP published a Consultation Paper, *Bringing Rights Home*, setting out the Labour Party's plans to incorporate the Convention if it won the election due in 1997. Whereas the 1993 policy had advocated incorporation to be followed by a second stage in the form of a home-grown Bill of Rights, the Consultation Paper deferred the second stage, and the five key issues posed by the paper concerned only the incorporation of the Convention. In May 1997, Labour won a landslide victory on a manifesto which included a commitment to incorporate the Convention into domestic law. The debate then turned to how the Convention should be incorporated, and in particular to whether it should be permitted to override statutes, subject to a 'notwithstanding clause'. The unique solution adopted in the Human Rights Act is the subject of Chapters 3 to 4 of this book.

1.25   The incorporation of the Convention is not the end of the story. The Convention is by no means a perfect human rights treaty and there remain gaps in the protection of human rights in the United Kingdom. The Convention was drafted in the aftermath of the Second World War and, although it is a 'living instrument', the values it embodies are those of a different generation. If the Convention were to be drafted today, a number of rights might be included that are not currently found within its scope. For example, the Convention does not contain a right to freedom of information;[24] the anti-discrimination provision is 'parasitic' in that it applies only where another Convention right has been violated;[25] there is little specific

---

[23] 16 July 1994.
[24] See ch 7, para 7.366.
[25] See discussion of Art 14 and Protocol 12 in ch 8, para 8.159.

recognition of children's rights or environmental rights; and it does not contain an absolute prohibition against self-incrimination for criminal defendants.[26] In addition, the types of Convention rights are limited in range compared with the nature of rights more broadly, and offer little protection to social and economic rights. In contrast, the Charter of Fundamental Rights of the European Union contains more wide-ranging rights, including employment, equality, and children's rights.[27] The Convention's deficiencies are replicated in the Human Rights Act, which simply incorporated the Convention in English law.

D. THE HUMAN RIGHTS ACT AS A CONSTITUTIONAL INSTRUMENT

In the lead-up to the enactment of the Human Rights Act, some commentators expressed concern about the relationship between the new statute and the existing constitutional arrangements. The flashpoint for many was the perceived tension between the English tradition of regarding the sovereignty of the democratic Parliament as being the cornerstone of its (unwritten) constitution and the fact that the Convention was to be enforceable in the courts.[28] Similar concerns have resurfaced in recent attacks on the Human Rights Act, with detractors claiming that it gives the judiciary the power to override the will of the democratically elected Parliament and draws judges into societal debates in a manner that is alien to the UK's constitutional settlement. To gauge the strength of these criticisms, each of the claims is examined below.

1. Parliamentary sovereignty and entrenchment

The idea that Parliament is the supreme legal power has been a consistent theme in English law as reflected in the writings of Coke, Blackstone, and Dicey. The doctrine has several elements. According to the theory, the sovereign legislature (the Queen, the House of Lords, and the House of Commons) can make and repeal any legislation whatsoever, so that no Parliament can bind its successors. As a result, it is impossible to 'entrench' particular legislation (for example, a Bill of Rights) by specifying that it would be repealable only under some specially safeguarded process. A corollary is that no act of the sovereign legislature can be invalid in the eyes of a court, because Parliament alone has the legal and political power to make laws. The potency of the parliamentary sovereignty theory has been diluted by the changes to the domestic legal system effected by the European Communities Act

1.26

1.27

---

[26] For further discussion, see Wadham, 'Why Incorporation of the European Convention on Human Rights is Not Enough', in Gordon and Wilmot-Smith (eds), *Human Rights in the United Kingdom* (Oxford: Oxford University Press, 1996); and Wadham and Taylor, 'Bringing More Rights Home' [2002] EHRLR 713.

[27] The Charter is discussed in ch 5.

[28] See, eg Ewing, 'The Human Rights Act and Parliamentary Democracy' [1999] MLR 79.

1972, but it still carries some force. A strict adherence to the doctrine would be problematic. It would limit the ability of courts to uphold human rights and could mean that a future Parliament could legislate such rights out of existence. To protect fundamental rights, some form of 'entrenchment' is necessary.

1.28   The solution adopted in the Human Rights Act is a complex one, reflecting a delicate political compromise between 'incorporating' Convention rights and retaining parliamentary sovereignty. The rule of construction in section 3 of the Human Rights Act places courts under a strong interpretative obligation to read and give effect to all legislation, whether primary or secondary, old or recent, in a way which is compatible with Convention rights 'so far as it is possible to do so'. Section 4 makes it clear that if a conflict between the provisions of a piece of legislation and Convention rights cannot be overcome, higher courts will have to make a declaration of incompatibility. The court cannot 'strike down' the offending Act, and so it remains operative after such a declaration. The scheme of the Human Rights Act means that the only legal effect of a declaration of incompatibility is to permit (but not oblige) a minister to amend the impugned legislation by a 'remedial order' under section 10. If the declaration of incompatibility is not accepted by the Government, and there is no overwhelming parliamentary pressure to change the law, there is no domestic legal obligation to change the law. Further, section 6(3) excludes Parliament from the definition of 'public authority' so that it is not bound by the provisions of the Human Rights Act.

1.29   This form of legislation for human rights is not as strong as the Canadian model, which gives courts the power to strike down primary legislation but allows the legislature to enact measures for a limited period 'notwithstanding' its contravention of provisions in the Charter of Fundamental Rights and Freedoms. It is, however, much stronger than the New Zealand model, which imposes only a weak obligation upon courts to 'prefer' an interpretation of legislation that is consistent with the Bill of Rights Act over an inconsistent one if possible.

1.30   Ultimately, the Human Rights Act protects the principle of parliamentary sovereignty because it does not permit the Convention to be used so as to override primary legislation: if a statute is clear in its terms, and clearly incompatible with the Convention, courts must give effect to it. Equally, if the terms of the primary legislation require subordinate legislation made under it (which will usually be in a statutory instrument) to be interpreted in a way that means that the subordinate legislation is incompatible with the Convention, it must still be given effect even though this may result in a breach of a Convention right.[29]

2. Politicizing the judiciary?

1.31   Before the Human Rights Act came into force, some legal and academic commentators[30] warned that it would infringe the basic constitutional tenet that

---

[29] For more details, see Bamforth, 'Parliamentary Sovereignty and the Human Rights Act 1998' [1998] PL 572.

[30] See n 28. See also Griffith, *The Politics of the Judiciary*, 5th edn (London: Fontana Press, 1997).

'Parliament makes the laws, the judiciary interpret them'.[31] The strong approach to statutory construction required by section 3 would lead to a politicization of the judiciary and an encroachment on Parliament's constitutional sphere. However, English courts reviewing controversial issues is not a new phenomenon. The Human Rights Act may have brought about a more intense degree of judicial scrutiny of executive and parliamentary action, but not scrutiny of a different kind. Indeed, one of the important effects of the Human Rights Act has been to focus public attention and debate on the proper nature and scope of the judicial function.

In response to criticisms of judicial activism, the former Lord Chief Justice Lord Woolf has pointed out that: 1.32

> ...judges are only doing what they have to swear to do on appointment and that is to give a judgement according to law. The law now includes the HRA. By upholding the HRA the courts are not interfering with the will of Parliament. On the contrary, when they interfere, the judges are protecting the public by ensuring that the Government complies with the laws made by Parliament. The courts are therefore acting in support of Parliament and not otherwise.[32]

The Human Rights Act itself provides a mechanism for balancing the role of the executive, Parliament, and the courts in the form of section 19. It presumes that new legislation is to be (and can be) read compatibly with the Convention. When legislation is introduced into Parliament for a second reading, the introducing minister must make a statement that, in his or her view, the legislation is compatible with the Convention, or make a statement that, although the legislation is not compatible with the Convention, the Government still wishes to proceed. It is unlikely that governments will often wish to state publicly that they are acting incompatibly with an internationally binding human rights instrument, though they have been prepared to do so on occasion. Where a 'section 19' statement is made, Parliament has the opportunity to thoroughly examine the minister's assertion before the Bill is passed. Reports of the Joint Parliamentary Committee on Human Rights (see para 1.42) demonstrate that section 19 statements have the potential to be powerful democratic tools for scrutinizing Bills, when Parliamentarians press for detailed reasoning behind statements of compatibility from the Government, rather than accepting generalized, uninformative statements that Bills are Convention compliant. A section 19 statement of compatibility also gives a strong indication to the judiciary that the Government intended its new legislation to be human rights compliant and that the judges are able to proceed with their judicial scrutiny with that intention in mind.   1.33

Despite some commentators' claims, since the Human Rights Act came into force judges have erred on the side of caution rather than judicial activism.[33] They have developed the concept of a 'discretionary area of judgment' (sometimes called 'deference') which considers when it is appropriate (and when it is not) for courts to   1.34

---

[31] Lord Diplock in *Duport Steels Ltd v Sirs* [1980] 1 WLR 142.
[32] 'The Impact of Human Rights', speech at Oxford Lyceum, 6 March 2003.
[33] See Leigh and Masterman, *Making Rights Real: The Human Rights Act in its First Decade* (London: Hart Publishing, 2009) and Brice Dickson, *Human Rights and the United Kingdom Supreme Court* (London: Oxford University Press, 2013).

defer to decisions made by other constitutional bodies such as the legislative, executive, or administrative branches. The appropriateness and breadth of the discretionary area of judgment that should be applied have been hotly debated by Law Lords, practitioners, and academics alike and are considered in more detail in Chapter 4.[34]

1.35   The notion of 'democratic dialogue' is the most helpful for evaluating the interaction between Parliament, the executive, and the judiciary under the new constitutional arrangement ushered in by the Human Rights Act.[35] This 'dialogue' takes place when a court, in reviewing legislative and executive action, scrutinizes the justification for laws or actions which limit fundamental human rights within the framework of the Convention, and seeks to make the law compatible with the Convention, by interpretation, if possible, or to declare the fact of incompatibility, if not. The final word on the content of law, however, still rests with Parliament. In the leading Canadian Supreme Court case of *Vriend v Alberta*[36] Iacobucci J concluded:

> ...a great value of judicial review and this dialogue among the branches is that each of the branches is made somewhat accountable to the other. The work of the legislature is reviewed by the courts and the work of the court in its decisions can be reacted to by the legislature in the passing of new legislation...This dialogue between and accountability of each of the branches has the effect of enhancing the democratic process, not denying it.

1.36   Despite the ongoing concerns about parliamentary sovereignty and judicial activism, both the judiciary and government have acknowledged the place of the Human Rights Act in the UK constitution. Lord Bingham has called the Human Rights Act 'an important constitutional instrument'.[37] As Lord Justice Laws has explained, this is so because the Act conditions the legal relationship between citizen and state and determines the scope of what we now regard as fundamental constitutional rights.[38]

E. THE INSTITUTIONAL FRAMEWORK—CREATING A CULTURE OF RESPECT FOR HUMAN RIGHTS

1.37   Many commentators, including the authors, hoped that as well as transforming the legal landscape, the 1998 Act would have a broad impact on our political and social culture. There are two dimensions to this new culture—ethical and institutional. The ethical dimension involves individual members of society developing an understanding that they enjoy certain rights by virtue of being human (not merely as a contingent gift of the state); *and* that with these rights comes the responsibility to

---

[34] See ch 4, paras 4.119–4.130.
[35] See, eg Clayton, 'Judicial Deference and "Democratic Dialogue": the Legitimacy of Judicial Intervention under the Human Rights Act 1998' [2004] PL 33; Hickman, 'Constitutional Dialogue, Constitutional Theories and the Human Rights Act 1998' [2005] PL 306.
[36] [1998] 1 SCR 495.
[37] *Brown v Stott* [2003] 1 AC 681, 703.
[38] See Laws LJ in *Thoburn v Sunderland City Council* [2002] 3 WLR 247.

respect the human rights of other individual citizens. Developing an institutional human rights culture involves mainstreaming fundamental principles into the design and delivery of policy, legislation, and public services so that decisions taken by public authorities such as schools and hospitals are proportionate, rational, and respectful of fundamental rights. The obligation on public authorities imposed by the Human Rights Act goes beyond non-interference with rights and requires such bodies to take active steps to protect people's rights against interference by others.[39]

The Act's aim of creating an institutional human rights culture has not been suc-   1.38
cessful. Research undertaken on the effect of the Human Rights Act has demonstrated that public bodies have not taken advantage of the benefits a human rights culture could offer for improved decision-making by using the framework of the Act to inform best practice. Instead, public bodies have confined human rights to their legal compliance departments, adopting a minimalist approach to protecting people's fundamental rights by 'Strasbourg-proofing' their policies and procedures to avoid litigation.[40]

The Human Rights Act is also widely misunderstood and mistrusted by the   1.39
public, caricatured by the popular press as a 'charter for criminals and terrorists'. As we discuss later, the future of the Act is uncertain. The failure to set up a body at the Human Rights Act's inception to promote understanding and awareness of the benefits of human rights left it vulnerable to these attacks because it was without a powerful, institutional champion to defend the benefits of human rights. This failure was belatedly and inadequately remedied by the creation of the Equality and Human Rights Commission.[41]

1. A human rights culture in Parliament?

Both the Labour Party Consultation Paper, *Bringing Rights Home*, and the White   1.40
Paper, *Rights Brought Home*, stated that 'Parliament itself should play a leading role in protecting the rights which are at the heart of parliamentary democracy'.[42] A Human Rights Committee has proved to be a fundamental part of this. The idea of a Human Rights Committee in Parliament originated in Francesca Klug's *A People's Charter: Liberty's Bill of Rights*.[43] Klug's suggestion was that the new Committee could conduct inquiries on a range of human rights issues, produce reports to assist the Government and Parliament in deciding what action to take, and range more widely, examining issues relating to the other international obligations of the United Kingdom.

---

[39] See ch 2, para 2.39.
[40] British Institute of Human Rights, 'Something for Everyone: The Impact of the Human Rights Act and the Need for a Human Rights Commission' (2002); Audit Commission, 'Human Rights: Improving Service Delivery' (2003); EHRC, 'Human Rights Inquiry' (2009).
[41] See para 1.45 below.
[42] Straw and Boateng, 'Bringing Rights Home: Labour's Plans to Incorporate the ECHR into UK Law: A Consultation Paper' (1997); White Paper, 'Rights Brought Home: The Human Rights Bill' (Cm 3782, 1997). See app 2.
[43] London: National Council for Civil Liberties, 1991.

1.41 The Joint Committee on Human Rights (JCHR) (a Select Committee consisting of members of both Houses of Parliament) was appointed in January 2001. Its terms of reference are to consider:

(a) matters relating to human rights in the United Kingdom (excluding consideration of individual cases);

(b) proposals for remedial orders, draft remedial orders, and remedial orders made under section 10 of, and laid under Schedule 2 to, the Human Rights Act; and

(c) in respect of draft remedial orders and remedial orders, whether the special attention of the House should be drawn to them on any of the grounds specified in Standing Order 73 (Joint Committee on Statutory Instruments).

1.42 The JCHR carries out important work, including prolific scrutiny of important bills, and, in the future, intends to expand its pre-legislative scrutiny work (to draw the attention of Parliament and the Government to any potential pitfalls in relation to a proposed policy course) and include a new strand of work related to post-legislative scrutiny (to assess whether the implementation of new laws has produced unwelcome human rights implications).[44] It has had an important influence on Parliament and, in particular, on controversial and human rights sensitive pieces of legislation such as the Anti-Terrorism, Crime and Security Act 2001 and the Terrorism Act 2006.[45]

2. The Equality and Human Rights Commission

1.43 One of the initial tasks the JCHR undertook was an inquiry into whether a Human Rights Commission was needed. It concluded that the case for setting up a Commission for Human Rights was compelling.[46] Without it, the development of a 'culture of understanding of rights and responsibilities' envisaged by the original proposals was stalled.

1.44 After a series of consultation papers between 2002 and 2004, the Government confirmed that it would set up a new, single Commission for Equality and Human Rights and brought forward legislation to establish that body.[47] There were good reasons for establishing an integrated body. Not only have other countries demonstrated the practical benefits of linking human rights and equality work (for example in the Australian Human Rights and Equal Opportunity Commission), but, conceptually, human rights and equality are inextricably linked. Equality is treated

---

[44] For accounts and assessments of the work of the JCHR to date, see JCHR, *The Committee's Future Working Practices* 23rd Report (2005–2006) (available at <http://www.parliament.uk>); Lester, 'Parliamentary Scrutiny of Legislation under the Human Rights Act 1998' [2002] EHRLR 432; Feldman, 'The impact of human rights on the UK legislative process' (2004) 25(2) Stat LR 91; Hiebert, 'Parliament and the Human Rights Act: can the JCHR help facilitate a culture of rights?' (2006) 4(1) IJCL 1; Leigh and Masterman, *Making Rights Real: The Human Rights Act in its First Decade* (London: Hart Publishing, 2009).
[45] For a detailed analysis, see JCHR, *The Committee's Future Working Practices* 23rd Report (2005–2006) app 5 (available at <http://www.parliament.uk>).
[46] JCHR, *The Case for a Human Rights Commission* 6th Report (2002–2003), HL 67-I, HC 489-I.
[47] Equality Act 2006 (EA 2006).

as a fundamental human right in the core international human rights treaties, and human rights and equality derive from the same fundamental principle: equal respect for the inherent dignity of all.

The Equality and Human Rights Commission[48] started work in October 2007. 1.45
The Equality Act 2006 set out specific legal duties for the Commission, including a duty to promote understanding of the importance of human rights and to encourage compliance with the Human Rights Act.[49]

In order to carry out its duties the Equality Act provided the Commission with 1.46
a range of legal powers. In particular, it can conduct formal inquiries into any matters relating to its duties,[50] intervene in litigation,[51] bring judicial review in its own name,[52] and provide legal assistance to individuals in proceedings concerning the equality enactments.[53] In June 2009 the Commission published the results of its Inquiry to assess the effectiveness and enjoyment of a culture of respect for human rights in Great Britain.[54] The Inquiry found that while the vast majority of people want to see human rights embedded in national law, there were significant misunderstandings and misconceptions about human rights. Where a human rights approach has been adopted, the Inquiry found that it led to speedy positive resolution of problems and systemic changes in service delivery by public authorities.

The Scottish Parliament has also set up the Scottish Human Rights Commission, 1.47
which set out its first strategic plan in December 2008.[55] This Commission has its own powers and duties but these are restricted to devolved matters—matters within the competence of the Scottish Parliament.[56]

The creation of these Commissions represented an important opportunity to 1.48
improve understanding of the Human Rights Act as well as the ECHR, and to promote human rights. The Equality and Human Rights Commission took some time to come to terms with its role and remit, and to resolve the issues arising from the merger of the three equality commissions.

The Equality and Human Rights Commission was criticized by the Parliamentary 1.49
Joint Human Rights Committee, in 2010:

We have sometimes been frustrated at the EHRC's lack of engagement in major human rights debates. We heard nothing from the Commission on policing and protest, for example, an issue with which we were engaged for a calendar year from June 2008 and which was the subject of considerable public debate, particularly after the G20 protests in April 2009. We were also critical of the evidence we received from the EHRC during our business and human rights inquiry,

---

[48] EA 2006, s 1 establishes the 'Commission for Equality and Human Rights' but the body has adopted the name 'Equality and Human Rights Commission'.
[49] EA 2006, ss 3, 8, 9, 10, and 11.
[50] EA 2006, s 16.
[51] EA 2006, s 30. See, eg *R (JL) v Secretary of State for Justice* [2008] UKHL 68, [2008] 3 WLR 1325.
[52] EA 2006, s 30(1).
[53] EA 2006, s 28.
[54] Equality and Human Rights Commission, 'Our Human Rights Inquiry' (June 2009), available at: <http://www.equalityhumanrights.com/human-rights/our-human-rights-inquiry/>.
[55] EA 2006, s 7; and see <http://www.scottishhumanrights.com>.
[56] Scottish Human Rights Commission Act 2006.

because it was limited to equality matters, indicating a broader failure to integrate effectively equality and human rights work.[57]

1.50   In the four years since this session, the substance of the Equality and Human Rights Commission's work on human rights has improved, notably through the publication of a review of the UK's compliance with the European Convention on Human Rights.[58] This was followed up in August 2014 by a major review of the UK's progress against the recommendations from the second cycle of the UN Universal Periodic Review.[59] The Commission has also undertaken two inquiries into key human rights issues—the Disability Harassment and Home Care Inquiries (the latter providing a substantial evidence base which contributed to the enhancement of the Human Rights Act through the Care Act 2014). The Commission has also exercised its power under section 30 of the Equality Act 2006 to make interventions in key human rights cases.[60] The Equality and Human Rights Commission also now convenes a Business and Human Rights network and has published human rights guidance for businesses.[61]

1.51   The relationship between the Equality and Human Rights Commission and parliamentary institutions has now also been strengthened. The Commission now meets bi-annually with the Parliamentary Joint Human Rights Committee to present its business plan and to hold wider discussions on human rights concerns. At the most recent session, the Commission presented a positive body of work to the Committee, and discussed again its role to promote human rights. Although the Commission regularly uses blogs and social media as well as press statements to influence the dialogue on human rights, its Chair, Baroness O'Neil, pointed out to the Committee that countering the trends in media debates on human rights is a 'Sisyphean task'.[62]

F. THE FUTURE OF HUMAN RIGHTS PROTECTION IN THE UNITED KINGDOM

1.52   Since the Human Rights Act came into force it has been the focus of intense political debate. The Act is widely blamed for administrative and judicial decisions that

---

[57] The Equality and Human Rights Commission, 2 March 2010.

[58] The Human Rights Review (EHRC 2012) <http://www.equalityhumanrights.com/about-us/our-work/human-rights/human-rights-review>.

[59] *Mid-Term Universal Periodic Review Report, EHRC, August 2014 and* see <http://www.upr-info.org/en/review/United-Kingdom/Session-13---May-2012/Follow-up>.

[60] See eg *Al-Skeini v UK* [2011] 52 EHRR 18 (in the European Court of Human Rights); *R (Smith) v Ministry of Defence* [2013] UKSC 41, [2014] 1 AC 52 (in the Supreme Court); and *Burnip v Birmingham City Council & Secretary of State for Work & Pensions* [2012] EWCA Civ 629, [2013] PTSR 117 (in the Court of Appeal, establishing the importance of other international legal instruments in determining ambit of the European Convention on Human Rights).

[61] A Guide to Business and Human Rights <http://www.equalityhumanrights.com/sites/default/files/publication_pdf/A%20guide%20to%20business%20and%20human%20rights_1.pdf>.

[62] The Work of the Equality and Human Rights Commission, Wednesday 14 May 2014, Uncorrected Transcript of Proceedings to the JCHR, HC1294.

have been caricatured as privileging the rights of criminals and terrorists over their victims. In particular, the Convention prohibition on deporting individuals to countries where there is a real risk that they will be tortured has attracted the scorn of the press and, more recently, decisions by the courts which have prevented the deportation of non-British citizens who have committed serious criminal offences—based on the fact that they (or more likely their children) have established family ties in the UK (and deporting them would breach their right to family life). The Act also received ferocious criticism from media organizations for enabling the judiciary to create a law of privacy unsanctioned by Parliament, but this criticism has lost some of its fervour in the wake of the evidence of newspapers hacking into mobile telephones of celebrities and others and the Leveson Report. Amongst human rights advocates, there is a consensus that the Government 'failed to explain the basic philosophy of the Human Rights Act to the people'.[63] As the Equality and Human Rights Commission found in its Human Rights Inquiry, there is a general lack of public awareness of the positive role that human rights can play in individual lives.

Reform of the Human Rights Act has been under consideration almost since its inception. It was as far back as 2007 that former Prime Minister Gordon Brown published a Green Paper[64] and a statement[65] exploring the possibility of a British Bill of Rights as part of a wider programme of constitutional reform. The JCHR contributed to the debate by undertaking a formal inquiry into a Bill of Rights, which reported in August 2008.[66] It found that the case for a Bill of Rights had been made out, but emphasized that the Bill could not be a vehicle for diluting the protections of the Human Rights Act; rather, it should add to those rights already protected.   1.53

In March 2009, the Labour Government formally launched the consultation process into a Bill of Rights in the publication by the Ministry of Justice of its long-awaited Green Paper, *Rights and Responsibilities: Developing our Constitutional Framework*.[67] The Green Paper set out preliminary proposals for a 'Bill of Rights and Responsibilities', but the 2010 general election intervened before the consultation was completed.   1.54

In the Coalition Agreement between the Conservatives and Liberal Democrats following the election it was stated: 1.55

We will establish a Commission to investigate the creation of a Bill of Rights that incorporates and builds on all our obligations under the European Convention on Human Rights, ensures that these rights continue to be enshrined in British law, and protects and extends British liberties. We will seek to promote a better understanding of the true scope of these obligations and liberties.[68]

---

[63] JCHR, *A Bill of Rights for the UK?* 29th Report (2007–2008), HL 165-I, HC 150-I, vol II, Klug Ev 1.
[64] *The Governance of Britain* (Cm 7170, 2007).
[65] Prime Minister's statement on constitutional reform, HC, col 819 (3 July 2007).
[66] JCHR, *A Bill of Rights for the UK?* 29th Report (2007–2008), HL 165-I, HC 150-I.
[67] Cm 7577, 2009.
[68] Cabinet Office, 'The Coalition: our programme for government' (May 2010), available at: <http://www.cabinetoffice.gov.uk/sites/default/files/resources/coalition_programme_for_government.pdf>, 11.

1.56   The inclusion of this issue in the Coalition's founding document recognizes both its importance as well as its controversial nature. The Commission on a Bill of Rights was established in March 2011, earlier than planned, after a political frenzy over prisoners' voting rights during which Parliament refused to sanction giving certain categories of prisoners the right to vote as required by the decision of the European Court judgment in *Hirst v UK*.[69]

1.57   As a result of negotiations between the Coalition parties, the Commission's terms of reference limited it to proposing a Bill of Rights that 'incorporates and builds on all our obligations' under the Convention. It therefore favoured using the Convention rights as an explicit starting point

1.58   The Commission reported at the end of 2012. There was, however, no consensus on what, if anything, needed to change.[70] However, there was concern by some members of the Commission that the debate in the Commission was moving towards a discussion of removing rights, and particularly towards withdrawing from the ECtHR.

1.59   In October 2014 the Conservative Party announced new and radical proposals that it intends to pursue if it is elected in May 2015. The announcement stated:

> At the heart of the reform will be a new British Bill of Rights and Responsibilities that will restore common sense to the application of human rights in the UK. A draft of the Bill will be published for consultation before Christmas. Among other things the Bill will stop terrorists and other serious foreign criminals who pose a threat to our society from using human rights to prevent deportation. It will make it clear that people have clear responsibilities to society, and that there is a proper balance between rights and responsibilities in British law.

> The Bill will remain faithful to the basic principles of human rights which the United Kingdom signed up to in the original European Human Rights Convention, but it will reverse the mission creep that has meant human rights law being used for more and more purposes, and often with little regard for the rights of society as a whole.[71]

1.60   The document suggested that the Party would publish a consultation and draft Bill before the end of 2014 but that appears to have been delayed. The Conservative proposals in summary suggest the following.

(a) For domestic law:
- the repeal of the Human Rights Act;
- the enactment instead of a 'British Bill of Rights and Responsibilities';
- the Bill will not include the requirement (currently in section 2 of the HRA) to have regard to decisions of the Strasbourg court;
- instead the Bill will require the UK courts only to take account of the substantive text of the ECHR (not the jurisprudence of the ECtHR), so that Convention rights 'are applied in accordance with the original intentions';

---

[69] *Hirst v UK (No 2)* (2005) 19 BHRC 546.
[70] The Commission on a Bill of Rights' report Ministry of Justice, 'A UK Bill of Rights?—The Choice Before Us', 18 December 2012.
[71] 'Protecting Human Rights in the UK: The Conservatives' Proposals for Changing Britain's Human Rights Law', 3 October 2014.

- it is also suggested that the new Bill will set out some specific limitations and exemptions to the rights currently enjoyed under the HRA. In particular:
  - to limit the 'use of rights to the most serious cases',
  - to prevent rights applying to the 'British Armed forces overseas',
  - terrorists and serious criminals 'who pose a significant threat to the security and safety of UK citizens' would lose their right to stay in the UK, and
  - 'no one will be able to claim human rights to step outside the law'; the example used here is of travellers using the right to a home to challenge planning decisions;

(b) In relation to the ECtHR:
  - '[e]very judgement [sic] that UK law is incompatible with the Convention will be treated as advisory' and a new parliamentary procedure will be introduced to consider such judgments, which 'will only be binding in law if Parliament agrees that it should be enacted as such';
  - during the passage of the Bill the Government will try to negotiate with the other Member States in the Council of Europe 'to seek recognition that our approach is a legitimate way of applying the Convention. In the event we are unable to reach that agreement, the UK would be left with no alternative but to withdraw from the European Convention on Human Rights';
  - in addition, the Government would ensure that the current discussions over the accession of the European Union and its constituent bodies to the ECHR took account of and respected the UK's new approach;
  - in its proposed wider negotiations with the EU pending the 'in or out' referendum, a new Conservative Government would address anything in the relationship between the EU and the UK 'which encroaches upon our new human rights framework'. This must refer to the EU's Charter of Fundamental Rights and the extent of its jurisdiction and impact.

The proposals have been condemned as unworkable by many lawyers in the UK, human rights NGOs and others, including Dominic Grieve QC MP (Conservative Attorney General from May 2010 to July 2014),[72] Kenneth Clarke QC MP (Conservative Secretary of State for Justice from May 2010 to September 2012),[73] Tim Owen QC and Alex Bailin QC,[74] and Professor Conor Gearty.[75] The Council of Europe itself responded to the proposals by stating: **1.61**

1. We take note of these proposals by the Conservative Party.
2. We also take note they are not draft legislation.
3. As they stand, the proposals are not consistent with the ECHR.[76]

---

[72] *Independent*, 4 October 2014.
[73] *The Guardian*, 3 October 2014.
[74] <https://www.scribd.com/doc/241813468/Opinion-on-HRA-repeal>.
[75] <http://www.theguardian.com/commentisfree/2014/oct/03/tories-proposal-british-bill-of-rights-incoherent-human-rights-act-strasbourg>.
[76] 3 October 2014.

1.62   We make the following observations on the Bill of Rights proposals:

- They are based on some factual mis-statements of law: for example wrongly stating that the Strasbourg court has banned whole life sentences,[77] and suggesting that the Strasbourg court's judgments are currently binding in national law.
- It is inaccurate to suggest that British courts are bound by interpretations of Convention rights by the Strasbourg courts: section 2 is only a duty to have regard to them and, indeed, section 3(2) prevents courts from interpreting law compatibly with Convention rights as interpreted by the ECtHR if legislation expressly requires this.
- The suggestion that the living instrument doctrine will be abolished—as a matter of domestic law—would have the odd and perverse effect that interpretation of the ECHR would be stuck in the 1950s when the Convention was drafted, so that situations which were not in contemplation at that time (such as legal recognition of same-sex relationships; or consideration of the legality of retaining DNA) could not be tested by reference to how the core values of the Convention apply to twenty-first-century problems.
- The suggestion that protection of rights would be limited to 'the most serious cases' begs the question of who decides what are 'the most serious cases': it is implicit that the legislature would seek to bind the hands of the courts on what is regarded as sufficiently 'serious' to enjoy protection, in contrast to the present position, whereby the courts decide whether infringement of a qualified right is proportionate in the circumstances, which include the extent of interference with the underlying right.
- The proposal to prevent rights applying to British Armed Forces overseas would overturn the *Smith* judgment of the Supreme Court and the *Al-Skeini* judgment of the Grand Chamber of the ECtHR, so domestic law on the extent of the UK's 'jurisdiction' would be at odds with the concept in international law. It would also mean that a victim of a breach of human rights abroad (whether a British soldier *qua* victim or victim of a British state agent) would have a direct remedy only in the ECtHR in Strasbourg.
- The suggestion that some criminals would lose their Article 2 and 3 rights in respect of safety on return would again put domestic law on a collision course with well-established Strasbourg case law in cases like *Soering v UK* (1989) 11 EHRR 439 and *Chahal v UK* (1997) 23 EHRR 413. It also seems incompatible with the fundamental principle of equality before the law, and the absolute nature of the rights to life and freedom from torture. Irrespective of the position of the UK in relation to the ECHR, it would be a breach of the European Convention for the Prevention of Torture, the UN Convention Against Torture, and the ICCPR to allow a person to be sent out of the UK to another country if they are likely to be tortured in that other country. Therefore the idea that the proposals can create a situation where 'those who pose a national security risk to

---

[77] See ch 6, para 6.88.

this country or have entered it illegally cannot rely on questionable human rights claims to prevent their deportation' is highly questionable.

- If 'no-one will be able to claim human rights to step outside the law', there would be no mechanism in which a domestic court can test the compatibility of statutory provisions with human rights standards (in contrast to the present system where a court which considers that a statutory provision is incompatible with human rights standards can make a declaration to that effect). For example, a statutory prohibition of gay sex (such as existed in Northern Ireland until the judgment in *Dudgeon v UK* (1981) 4 EHRR 149) would be unassailable in domestic law.

- Resiling from the HRA would mean renegotiating the devolution settlements with Wales and Scotland and could breach the Good Friday agreement which settled the Northern Ireland conflict and which specifically requires the incorporation of the (full) Convention into Northern Irish law.

- A law which rendered Strasbourg judgments 'advisory' only would breach Article 46 ECHR, which requires signatory states—as a matter of international law—to abide by judgments against them. It is inconceivable that the Council of Europe could agree to this. If—as the Secretary of State for Justice suggests—Britain would then withdraw from the Council of Europe, it would be the only country in Europe not to be a member other than Belarus, and the only country ever to withdraw from a human rights instrument which it had signed, apart from Venezuela and North Korea.

- The suggestion that the Government would 'ensure' that the current discussions over the accession of the European Union and its constituent bodies to the ECHR took account of and respected the UK's new approach could only mean a veto.

- It is also inconceivable that the EU would allow the UK to 'withdraw' from the Charter of Fundamental Rights.

Many of the proposals could place the UK in breach of its other international law commitments. They fail to address how the proposals might interact with the parallel treaties and mechanisms of the Council of Europe, including, for instance, the European Committee for the Prevention of Torture (ECPT) which imposes the same standards on the UK as the ECtHR and whose processes develop as the Court elaborates the provisions in Article 3. There is also no mention of the treaties and mechanisms of the United Nations, particularly those which the UK has ratified and which are binding on it as a matter of international law, including the International Covenant on Civil and Political Rights (ICCPT) (which largely mirrors the rights in the Convention) or the Convention Against Torture (CAT) (which largely mirrors the jurisprudence and principles of the ECtHR on Article 3 of the ECHR).   1.63

In short, the October 2014 proposals could—if pursued—create a international law crisis and threaten the principles of equality under the law and protection of fundamental human rights in the United Kingdom.   1.64

2

THE FRAMEWORK OF THE
EUROPEAN CONVENTION ON
HUMAN RIGHTS

A. INTRODUCTION

The European Convention for the Protection of Human Rights and Fundamental **2.01** Freedoms (Convention) is an international human rights treaty agreed by states that are members of the Council of Europe. The Council of Europe was established in 1949 as part of the Allies' programme to 'reconstruct durable civilization on the mainland of Europe'.[1] Today it has 47 members with a wide variety of political traditions, including many former Communist states from Eastern Europe. The Convention came into force on 3 September 1953.

---

[1] *Rights Brought Home: The Human Rights Bill* (Cm 3782, 1997) para 1.1.

2.02   The rights guaranteed by the Convention are modelled on those contained in the UN Universal Declaration of Human Rights (1948), but the content of the rights and qualifications to them are more specific, reflecting the states' intention that the rights be legally enforceable. The Convention's provisions are mostly civil and political in nature (with the notable exceptions of the right to property and the right to education in Protocol 1). However, the interpretation of Convention rights may extend into the sphere of social and economic rights[2] in order to 'safeguard the individual in a real and practical way'.[3] As well as allowing states to bring proceedings against one another, individuals are able to enforce their Convention rights against states that have accepted the right of 'individual petition'.

2.03   The United Kingdom ratified the Convention in 1951 but, unlike many of the other signatories, did not set about incorporating the Convention rights into domestic law. Incorporation was thought to be unnecessary, as it was believed that the rights safeguarded by the Convention already flowed from English common law.

2.04   In 1966, the United Kingdom accepted the right of individual petition. This has meant that, even before its incorporation into domestic law, the Convention offered individual litigants in Britain the possibility of redress in international law where their civil liberties had been infringed by the state, and where no adequate remedy could be provided by the domestic courts. (It is important to appreciate that, as a matter of international law, the Convention creates rights against states, not against private individuals.)

2.05   The Convention originally established three bodies to monitor human rights within the countries that had ratified it: the European Commission of Human Rights (ECmHR),[4] the European Court of Human Rights (ECtHR),[5] and the Committee of Ministers. All three were based in Strasbourg. Until November 1998, the ECmHR and the ECtHR heard complaints from individuals about violations of their rights. The ECmHR exercised a 'screening' function, and could refer cases to the ECtHR for a final determination. However, Protocol 11 to the Convention brought major changes to the Strasbourg system. From November 1998, the ECmHR ceased to exist. Instead, a one-tier system was introduced in which all cases are dealt with by different chambers of the ECtHR. Decisions of the ECtHR are binding on the country concerned.[6]

2.06   The Convention is unlike a UK statute. Its broad provisions cannot be interpreted according to the traditional English 'black-letter' approach that closely defines the

---

[2] See, eg *Sidabras v Lithuania* [2004] ECHR 55480/00; *R (Limbuela) v Secretary of State for the Home Department* [2005] UKHL 66, [2006] 1 AC 396.

[3] *Airey v Ireland* (1979) 2 EHRR 305, para 26.

[4] Established in 1954.

[5] Established in 1959.

[6] Note that Protocol 14 to the Convention, which came into force on 1 June 2010, empowers the Committee of Ministers to ask the ECtHR to interpret a final judgment if it encounters difficulties in doing so when supervising its execution. In order to further the aim of rapid execution of judgments, Protocol 14 also allows the Committee of Ministers to decide, in exceptional circumstances and with a two-thirds majority, to initiate proceedings of non-compliance in the Grand Chamber of the ECtHR in order to make the state concerned execute the Court's initial judgment.

scope and content of a power. The ECtHR, and latterly the UK courts under the Human Rights Act 1998, have developed a sophisticated jurisprudence built upon underlying principles and interpretative techniques which 'flesh out' the scope of the rights to give them meaning in the context of individual cases. The domestic approach to the principles discussed below is considered in Chapter 4.

B. INTERPRETING THE CONVENTION

The interpretative principles set out below should not be treated in isolation, with one given more importance than another—they are part of a single, complex jurisprudential exercise to ensure that the 'object and purpose' of the Convention are fulfilled.   **2.07**

1. 'Object and purpose'

The Convention is an international treaty and as such should be interpreted in accordance with Articles 31–33 of the Vienna Convention on the Law of Treaties 1969 (the Vienna Convention). Article 31(1) states: **2.08**

A treaty shall be interpreted in good faith in accordance with the ordinary meaning to be given to the terms of the treaty in their context and in light of its object and purpose.[7]

The Convention is intended to be interpreted purposively, that is, to give effect to its central purposes. The text, Preamble, annexes, and related agreements and instruments of the contracting states are relevant to determining what these are.[8] The ECtHR has held that the 'objects and purpose' of the Convention include: **2.09**

(a) the 'maintenance and further realization of human rights and fundamental freedoms'[9] and the 'protection of individual human rights'.[10] The effective protection of the rights of the individual has been described by the ECtHR as the 'overriding function of this Convention';[11]

(b) the promotion of the ideals and values of a democratic society,[12] which supposes 'pluralism, tolerance and broadmindedness'[13] so as to achieve a balance between individual and group interests which 'ensures the fair and proper treatment of minorities and avoids any abuse of a dominant position';[14]

(c) the rule of law.[15]

---

[7] See also Vienna Convention, Art 33(4).
[8] Vienna Convention, Art 31(2).
[9] Preamble to the Convention.
[10] *Soering v UK* (1989) 11 EHRR 439.
[11] *Austria v Italy* (1961) 4 YB 116, para 138.
[12] *Kjeldsen, Busk Madsen and Pedersen v Denmark* (1979) 1 EHRR 711.
[13] *Handyside v UK* (1976) 1 EHRR 737.
[14] *Young, James and Webster v UK* (1982) 4 EHRR 38.
[15] Preamble to the Convention; *Golder v UK* (1979) 1 EHRR 524, para 35; *Klass v Germany* (1978) 2 EHRR 379, para 55; *Salabiaku v France* (1988) 13 EHRR 379, para 28; *Gorraiz Lizarraga v Spain* App No 62543/00, 10 November 2004, para 64.

2.10   As the essence of the Convention is to protect the fundamental rights of persons from violation by contracting parties, limitations or qualifications of the rights set out in the Convention are to be narrowly construed.[16] The ECtHR will try to:

> ...seek the interpretation that is most appropriate in order to realize the aim and achieve the object of the treaty; not that which would restrict to the greatest possible degree the obligations undertaken by the parties.[17]

2. Effectiveness principle

2.11   The Convention is intended to guarantee rights that are not merely 'theoretical and illusory' but 'practical and effective'.[18] The ECtHR is concerned with the reality of the individual's position and will 'look behind appearances and examine the realities of the procedure in question'.[19]

2.12   In order for some rights to provide 'effective' protection in accordance with the 'object and purpose' of the Convention, it may be necessary to read an element into a right that is not expressly provided for. An example of reading in these 'implied rights' can be found in the ECtHR's interpretation of Article 6 in *Golder v UK*.[20] In that case a prisoner complained that he could not get to court at all—a right not expressly contained in the text of Article 6. The ECtHR considered that to interpret Article 6 as merely providing procedural guarantees in the course of existing proceedings would enable contracting parties to remove the jurisdiction of the courts in relation to certain claims and thus undermine the protection of the right. To correct this, the ECtHR held that the right of access to the courts constituted 'an element which is inherent in the right stated by Article 6(1)'.[21]

2.13   The ECtHR has also recognized that in order to secure truly effective protection, certain rights must be read as imposing obligations on the state to take action to ensure that they are protected. This doctrine of positive obligations is considered more fully at paras 2.32 to 2.39.

3. Autonomous concepts

2.14   Some specific Convention terms are 'autonomous', in the sense of having a particular meaning defined by the ECtHR, and the concepts they contain may go beyond their ordinary or domestic meaning. This is necessary both so that there is uniformity of meaning and understanding across the different national legal systems of the parties to the Convention, and to protect human rights from

---

[16] *Sunday Times v UK (No 1)* (1979) 2 EHRR 245, para 65.
[17] *Wemhoff v Germany* (1968) 1 EHRR 55, para 8.
[18] *Marckx v Belgium* (1979) 2 EHRR 330, para 31; *Artico v Italy* (1981) 3 EHRR 1, para 33.
[19] *Deweer v Belgium* (1980) 2 EHRR 439.
[20] (1979) 1 EHRR 524.
[21] Ibid, para 35.

the possibility of being undermined by manipulation of terms by contracting states.

Examples of these autonomous concepts include the free-standing definitions of 'criminal charge' and 'civil rights and obligations' under Article 6. The ECtHR has created its own classification criteria for these concepts. These criteria are not solely dependent on the classification determined by the domestic law of the respondent country. Without this 'autonomous concepts' doctrine a state could, without breaching Article 6, exercise arbitrary power and act in a manner repugnant to the rule of law: it could 'do away with its courts, or take away their jurisdiction to determine certain classes of civil actions and entrust to it organs dependent on the Government'.[22] Other concepts, such as 'private life' and 'family life', have developed incrementally since 1950 to ensure that the protection offered by the Convention is 'effective'. Further consideration of these terms is found in Chapter 6.

2.15

The 'autonomous concepts' doctrine has become important in English law, sometimes in stopping domestic courts from artificially cutting down the scope of a Convention article.[23] However, the 'autonomous concepts' doctrine has also been used to prevent the Human Rights Act from becoming a mechanism for a more expansive interpretation of the scope of Convention rights than that afforded by the Strasbourg organs.[24]

2.16

4. Dynamic interpretation

The Convention is not to be interpreted as it would have been by those who drafted it 60 years ago. It is a 'living instrument which must be interpreted in the light of present-day conditions'.[25] As such its meaning will develop over time and new case law will develop in an organic way without old case law being specifically overruled. Thus, when an English court is considering the meaning and effect of a decision of the ECmHR or the ECtHR, it must nevertheless interpret the Convention by the standards of society today, and not those when the Convention was drafted or when older cases were decided.

2.17

The case law surrounding the Article 8 rights of transsexuals provides a good example of the 'growth' of the Convention to accommodate changing social attitudes. In *Rees v UK*[26] the ECtHR considered that the rule that a transsexual could

2.18

---

[22] *Golder v UK* (1979) 1 EHRR 524, para 35; cited by Lord Hoffmann in *Runa Begum v Tower Hamlets* [2003] UKHL 5, [2003] 2 AC 430 at [29].

[23] See, eg *Han v Commissioners of Customs and Excise; Martins v Commissioners of Customs and Excise* [2001] EWCA Civ 1040, [2001] 4 All ER 687.

[24] *Secretary of State for Work and Pensions v M* [2006] UKHL 11, [2006] 2 AC 91 (though note that the ECtHR subsequently disagreed with the House of Lords on what the ambit of Art 1 of Protocol 1 and Art 8 were in *JM v UK* App No 37060/06, 28 September 2010); *R v Briggs-Price* [2009] UKHL 19, [2009] 1 WLR 1101. See, to the same effect, *R (A) v London Borough of Croydon* [2009] UKSC 8, [2009] 1 WLR 2557 at [64].

[25] *Tyrer v UK* (1978) 2 EHRR 1, para 31; *Johnson v Ireland* (1986) 9 EHRR 203, para 53.

[26] (1987) 9 EHRR 56.

not alter her birth certificate to reflect her gender reassignment did not, by the standards of the mid-1980s, contravene Article 8. But it was conscious of the seriousness of the problems and distress faced by people in that situation and stated:

> The Convention has always to be interpreted and applied in the light of the current circumstances. The need for appropriate legal measures should therefore be kept under review having regard particularly to the scientific and societal developments.[27]

2.19 Having followed its decision in *Rees* in a number of cases,[28] the ECtHR changed tack in *Goodwin v UK*[29] and held that in present conditions, the lack of legal recognition of the applicant's new gender did result in a violation of Article 8. The ECtHR stated that:

> It is of crucial importance that the Convention is interpreted and applied in a manner which renders its rights practical and effective, not theoretical and illusory. A failure by the Court to maintain a dynamic and evolutive approach would indeed risk rendering it a bar to reform or improvement.[30]

There are, however, limits to the extent to which the ECtHR is willing to interpret the Convention in the light of changing social attitudes. In *Schalk and Kopf v Austria*,[31] for instance, the ECtHR refused to accept that Article 12 protected the right to same-sex marriage.

5. Recourse to other human rights instruments

2.20 In interpreting the Convention, the ECtHR is required by the Vienna Convention on the Interpretation of Treaties to take account of 'any relevant rules of international law applicable in the relations between the parties'.[32] The ECtHR has regularly cited the Vienna Convention, holding that the Convention 'cannot be interpreted in a vacuum' and 'should, so far as possible be interpreted in harmony with other rules of international law of which it forms part'.[33] Council of Europe instruments such as Conventions and Resolutions of the Parliamentary Assembly, the European Social Charter, and separate European Union materials may be relevant.[34] In addition, UN human rights instruments such as the International Covenant on Civil and Political Rights, the Convention on the Elimination of all

---

[27] Ibid, para 47.

[28] See *Cossey v UK* (1990) 13 EHRR 622; *Sheffield and Horsham v UK* (1999) 27 EHRR 163.

[29] (2002) 35 EHRR 18.

[30] Ibid, para 74. For a more sceptical view of the Convention as a 'living instrument', see Baroness Hale, 'The Limits of the Evolutive Interpretation of the Convention', speech given at the opening of the ECtHR's judicial year, 28 January 2011: <http://www.echr.coe.int/NR/rdonlyres/D4E2008C-FBAE-4 32A-AF4D-BF862D69035A/0/20110128_SEMINAIRE_Discours_Baroness_Hale_EN.pdf>.

[31] App No 30141/04, 24 June 2010.

[32] Vienna Convention, Art 31(3)(c).

[33] *Al-Adsani v UK* (2001) 34 EHRR 273, para 55; *Al-Saadoon and Mufdhi v UK* App No 61498/08, 2 March 2010, para 126.

[34] For a detailed examination of the interrelationship between EU law and the Convention, see ch 5.

Forms of Racial Discrimination, and other standards and 'general comments' from the human rights bodies of the UN have been used to help determine the scope of fundamental human rights.[35]

Indeed, the ECtHR now regards recourse to other international law as a manda- **2.21** tory interpretative tool for the proper construction of the ECHR—in particular when considering the definition and scope of discrimination. In *Demir & Baykara v Turkey*[36] the Grand Chamber held that:

in defining the meaning of terms and notions in the text of the Convention, [it] *can and must* take into account elements of international law other than the Convention, the interpretation of such elements by competent organs, and the practice of European States reflecting their common values.

Likewise, in *Opuz v Turkey*,[37] the Court concluded that that 'when considering the definition and scope of discrimination against women, in addition to the more general meaning of discrimination as determined in its case-law...the Court *has to have regard to* the provisions of more specialised legal instruments and the decisions of international legal bodies on the question of violence against women' (emphasis added).

Thus, there are now proliferating examples of use by the ECtHR of relevant **2.22** international law rules when interpreting the Convention. For example, in *Demir*, the Court took into account the jurisprudence arising under International Labour Organization Conventions and the European Social Charter to determine the scope of freedom of association under Article 11 of the Convention, overruling its previous holdings that the right to bargain collectively and to enter into collective agreements did not constitute an inherent element of Article 11. In *Opuz*, it cited the UN Convention on the Elimination of Discrimination Against Women (CEDAW), among other instruments, to create a positive obligation to protect women against foreseeable violence. In *T and V v UK*,[38] the ECtHR relied in part on the UN Convention on the Rights of the Child (UNCRC) and the Standard Minimum Rules for the Administration of Juvenile Justice ('Beijing Rules') to find that the UK's procedures for trying children charged with serious crimes did not enable the defendants to participate fully and effectively in the trial process and so violated their Article 6 rights to a fair trial. Similarly, in *S and Marper v UK*, the ECtHR drew on the UNCRC in condemning the indefinite retention of children's DNA on the UK police database.[39]

---

[35] See, eg *Sejdic and Finci v Bosnia and Herzegovina* App Nos 27996/06 and 34836/06 28 BHRC 201, paras 19 and 43.

[36] (2009) 48 EHRR 54 at [85],

[37] (2010) 50 EHRR 28 at [185]; see too *Eremia v Moldova* [2014] 58 EHRR 2.

[38] (2000) 30 EHRR 121.

[39] (2008) 25 BHRC 557, para 124. For an example of the domestic courts referring to the UNCRC, see *R (Williamson) v Secretary of State for Education and Employment* [2005] UKHL 15, [2005] 2 AC 246 at [80] per Baroness Hale.

The ECtHR also regularly cites the EU Charter of Fundamental Rights,[40] and took the United Nations Convention on the Rights of Persons with Disabilities into account when considering local authority social care provision in *Macdonald v UK*.[41]

6. Jurisdiction

2.23 The basis for the jurisdictional scope of the Convention is found in Article 1, which provides that states 'shall secure to everyone within their jurisdiction the rights and freedoms defined in Section 1 of this Convention'. The meaning of the phrase 'within their jurisdiction' has been considered by the Grand Chamber of the ECtHR in the leading cases of *Bankovic v Belgium and ors*,[42] and *Al-Skeini v UK*.[43] The Court considered that jurisdiction should be interpreted in accordance with the principles of public international law, which holds that states are ordinarily only responsible for acts and omissions in their national territory. However, it accepted that there were certain, limited situations in which a state may be responsible for acts or omissions occurring outside its territory. The first is where a contracting state, through its agents, exercises control and authority over an individual.[44] The second situation is where one contracting state is occupied by the armed forces of another: the occupying state should be held accountable for breaches of human rights within the occupied territory, for otherwise there would be a 'vacuum' of protection within the 'Convention legal space'. This does not mean, however, that jurisdiction under Article 1 can never exist outside the territory covered by the Council of Europe Member States.[45] The third situation, confirmed to exist in *Al-Skeini*, concerns acts carried out in the territory of a non-contracting state which is under the 'effective control' of a contracting state as a consequence of military action. In *Al-Skeini*, the Court held that the Convention was engaged in relation to the killing of Iraqi citizens by UK army personnel in security operations near Basra, which was part of Iraq over which the UK had assumed responsibility for the maintenance of security following the removal from power of the Ba'ath regime.[46]

2.24 Notably, Article 1 is not incorporated into English law under the Human Rights Act. The domestic approach to extraterritoriality, which was revised in light of *Al-Skeini v UK*, is considered in Chapter 4[47] and Chapter 6.[48]

---

[40] See, eg *Schalk and Kopf v Austria* App No 30141/04, 24 June 2010.
[41] App No 4241/12, 20 May 2014. See also use of the UNCRDP in *Kiyutin v Russia* [2011] 53 EHRR 26; *Seal v UK* [2012] 54 EHRR 6; and *Kiss v Hungary* [2013] 56 EHRR 38.
[42] (2007) 44 EHRR SE5.
[43] (2011) 30 BHRC 561.
[44] See, eg *Soering v UK* (1989) 11 EHRR 439.
[45] *Al-Skeini v UK* (2011) 30 BHRC 561, para 142.
[46] Ibid, para 149.
[47] See ch 4, paras 4.101–4.103.
[48] See ch 6, paras 6.04–6.08.

C. THE SCOPE OF CONVENTION RIGHTS

1. Absolute, limited, and qualified rights

In broad terms, Convention rights may be placed into three categories: 'absolute' 2.25 rights capable of no derogation; rights which are expressly or impliedly limited; and rights which are expressly qualified. This is not a precise taxonomy but a way of understanding the nature and structure of the Convention rights.

(a) *Absolute rights*

Absolute rights under the Convention include the right to life under Article 2 (except 2.26 in respect of deaths resulting from lawful acts of war), the prohibition on torture under Article 3, the prohibition on slavery and servitude under Article 4(1), and the right not to be subjected to retrospective criminal offences under Article 7(1).[49] No derogations from these articles are permitted under Article 15 and there are no circumstances in which infringements of these rights can be justified in the public interest.

The power of absolute rights was illustrated in *Chahal v UK* in which the 2.27 ECtHR was asked to consider the UK's attempt to expel a suspected Sikh terrorist despite the real risk of his being subjected to torture in the receiving country.[50] The ECtHR held that, despite the national security threat posed by the applicant, 'the Convention prohibits in absolute terms torture or inhuman or degrading treatment or punishment irrespective of the victim's conduct'.[51] If a claimant can prove on the balance of probabilities that the state has acted in violation of an absolute right, the state is not entitled to mount a justification of its conduct. This principle has come under sustained attack from the British Government (and the tabloid press). The Government intervened in *Saadi v Italy* to attempt to change the ECtHR's view of absolute rights, but the ECtHR reiterated the traditional principles in forceful terms.[52]

(b) *Limited rights*

Limited rights include Article 5 (right to liberty and security of the person), 2.28 Article 6 (fair trial rights), Article 12 (right to marry and found a family), Protocol 1, Article 2 (right to an education), and Protocol 1, Article 3 (right to free elections).

---

[49] The right to hold a religion or belief under Art 9(1) is sometimes considered absolute, but Art 9 can be derogated from under Art 15. See ch 7, para 7.547.

[50] (1997) 23 EHRR 413.

[51] Ibid, para 78.

[52] (2008) 24 BHRC 123. The Government's response to the ECtHR's case law has been to seek assurances concerning deportees from states where torture is known to be endemic. These assurances have been challenged before the domestic courts: see in particular *RB (Algeria) v Secretary of State for the Home Department* [2009] UKHL 10, [2009] 2 WLR 512.

These rights can be restricted in explicit and finite circumstances as set out in the article itself, or may be subject to restrictions implied by the ECtHR.[53]

2.29   Restrictions have been implied into the right to education under Article 2 of Protocol 1[54] and into fair trial rights (in addition to the express limitations set out in Article 6).[55] However, any limitations are to be construed narrowly, as a wide interpretation 'would entail consequences incompatible with the notion of the rule of law from which the whole Convention draws its inspiration'.[56] In *Ashingdane v UK* the ECtHR held that the right of access to the Court may be subject to restrictions, but that any limitation 'will not be compatible with Article 6(1) if it does not pursue a legitimate aim and if there is not a reasonable relationship of proportionality between the means employed and the aim sought to be achieved'.[57] Thus, implied restrictions will be subject to the general principles applicable to the qualified rights (discussed at para 2.41).

(c) *Qualified rights*

2.30   The 'qualified rights' are those that include a general qualification provision in the second paragraph of the article. They are the rights that most obviously raise the conflicts with the overall interests of society or the rights of others—for example, the right to respect for private life (Article 8), freedom of thought, conscience, and religion (Article 9), freedom of expression (Article 10), freedom of assembly and association (Article 11), and the right to the enjoyment of possessions (Protocol 1, Article 1).

2.31   'Qualified rights' are usually set out in two parts in the text of the Convention. The first paragraph of the article sets out the substantive right, and it is then qualified in the second paragraph. The precise terms of the limitations vary (contrast, for example, Article 10(2) with Article 8(2)), but a restriction will be compatible with the Convention only if it meets the general principles applicable to all restrictions on rights, namely it is 'in accordance with the law'; the interference is directed towards an identified legitimate aim; and the aim is 'necessary in a democratic society' (which encompasses the test of 'pressing social need' and proportionality). These general principles are considered in detail at paras 2.40–2.68.

2. Positive obligations

2.32   The principal purpose of the Convention is to protect individual rights from infringement by states, and this is achieved by the imposition of so-called 'negative' obligations on the states, which require them to refrain from interference with the rights in question. However, the wording of certain articles also imposes positive

---

[53] See the discussion of the controversial 'inherent limitations' doctrine in Clayton and Tomlinson, *The Law of Human Rights*, 2nd edn (Oxford: Oxford University Press, 2009) 377–81.

[54] See, eg *Sahin v Turkey* (2007) 44 EHRR 5, para 154.

[55] See, eg *Golder v UK* (1975) 1 EHRR 524.

[56] *Engel v Netherlands* (1976) 1 EHRR 647, para 69.

[57] (1985) 7 EHRR 528.

duties on the state, such as the obligation under Protocol 1, Article 3 to hold free elections. In addition to these express positive obligations, the ECtHR has recognized that there is a broader need for positive steps to be taken by the state to provide the legal or institutional structures or resources to protect human rights—for example, to provide laws which prevent private parties from infringing individual rights, to provide proper institutional protection from domestic violence, or to provide free legal assistance in criminal cases under Article 6(3)(c), or to enable access to institutions to provide education under Protocol 1, Article 2.

The ECtHR has expressly declined to develop any 'general theory' of positive obligations, and thus attempts to extract key principles from the jurisprudence of the ECtHR in order to locate positive obligations in a coherent legal framework have been subject to some controversy.[58] It is, however, accepted that the legal basis for reading the Convention in a way which imposes positive obligations is found in a combination of: the overarching duty on states in Article 1 'to secure to everyone within their jurisdiction' the rights and freedoms set out in the Convention; express wording in some articles (for example, the right to life 'shall' be protected by law); the principle set out in Convention case law that protection of rights is intended to be 'practical and effective' not merely theoretical; and the right to an adequate remedy for arguable breaches of Convention rights under Article 13.   2.33

Starmer has argued that there are five main positive duties under the Convention: 2.34

(a) a duty to have in place a legal framework which provides effective protection for Convention rights;

(b) a duty to prevent breaches of Convention rights;

(c) a duty to provide information and advice relevant to a breach of Convention rights;

(d) a duty to respond to breaches of Convention rights; and

(e) a duty to provide resources to individuals to prevent breaches of their Convention rights.[59]

The types of legal and administrative measures that the ECtHR has held are necessary to fulfil these duties vary according to the article in issue. For example, Article 2 provides that the right to life 'shall be protected by law', and this has been interpreted as an obligation on the state to: 2.35

...secure the right to life by putting in place effective criminal law provisions to deter the commission of offences against the person, backed up by law enforcement machinery for the prevention, suppression and sanctioning of breaches of such provisions.[60]

Although the ECtHR varies in the extent of the measures it will hold necessary to comply with its positive protective obligations, it is still accurate to say

---

[58] See Mowbray, *The Development of Positive Obligations under the European Convention on Human Rights by the European Court of Human Rights* (London: Hart Publishing, 2004).

[59] Starmer, 'Positive Obligations under the Convention', in Jowell and Cooper (eds), *Understanding Human Rights Principles* (London: Hart Publishing/JUSTICE, 2001).

[60] *Osman v UK* (2000) 29 EHRR 245.

that not only is the state required to adopt an adequate system of law to deter and punish individuals guilty of violating the Convention rights of others, but it is also recognized that the police[61] and other relevant public bodies[62] can be under a positive obligation to take reasonable operational measures to prevent a violation of individuals' rights under Articles 2 and 3. The Court has also, more recently, started to use other Articles of the Convention to hold that states are under a duty to protect vulnerable individuals from foreseeable third-party mistreatment. For example, in *CN v United Kingdom*,[63] the Court held that Article 4 required a positive obligation to have in place and enforce an adequate criminal law and investigative framework to protect people from being subjected to forced labour; and in *Eremia v Moldova*,[64] it held that failure properly to investigate or to support a complainant of domestic violence amounted to condoning the discriminatory attitudes which underlay it, contrary to Articles 3 and 14. In *KU v Finland*,[65] it reached a similar conclusion under Article 8, and more recently in *S v Sweden*,[66] the Court forcefully emphasized the need for a state to have a criminal law framework in place to protect individuals from violations of Convention standards by third parties.

2.36 In cases under Article 8, the ECtHR recognizes that access to relevant information can help individuals to protect their Convention rights. In *Guerra v Italy*[67] the ECtHR established that, on the specific facts of the case, the respondent state was under a positive obligation to provide information to the applicants who lived near a 'high risk' chemical factory and were very likely to be adversely affected by environmental pollution. In *McGinley and Egan v UK*[68] the ECtHR held that when a government engages in hazardous activities, such as nuclear testing, which might have hidden adverse effects on the health of those involved, 'Article 8 requires that an effective and accessible procedure be established which enables persons to seek all relevant and appropriate information'.[69]

2.37 When determining whether or not a positive obligation exists, the ECtHR will have regard to 'the fair balance that has to be struck between the general interest of the community and the interests of the individual, the search for which balance is inherent in the whole of the Convention'.[70]

2.38 A number of factors may have a bearing on the extent of any positive obligation, including whether the right in question is broadly or narrowly defined; whether essential aspects of a right are at issue; the extent of any burden that may

---

[61] Ibid.

[62] See, eg local authorities in *Z v UK* (2002) 34 EHRR 3.

[63] [2013] 56 EHRR 24.

[64] [2013] ECHR 3564/11.

[65] [2009] 48 EHRR 52.

[66] [2014] 58 EHRR 36.

[67] (1998) 26 EHRR 357.

[68] (1999) 27 EHRR 1.

[69] Ibid, para 101. See also *Taskin v Turkey* (2006) 42 EHRR 50; *Fadeyeva v Russia* [2005] ECHR 55723/00; *Öneryildiz v Turkey* (2004) 18 BHRC 145.

[70] *Goodwin v UK* (2002) 35 EHRR 18.

be imposed on the state; and the uniformity of views or practices in other contracting states.[71] However, one of the most important factors taken into consideration by the ECtHR is the severity of the effect of the omission on the applicants' rights (particularly their fundamental rights such as those protected by Articles 2 and 3, or their intimate rights such as those of 'private and family life' protected under Article 8).[72] The more serious the effect, the more likely it is that the state will be obliged to prevent or remedy it.

In a series of recent cases, the ECtHR has developed a duty under Article 8 in 2.39 certain circumstances not to deprive a person of the home he or she already has, even where in domestic law no duty to supply him/her with one exists.[73] In *Mosley v UK*, however, the ECtHR found that the United Kingdom was not under a positive obligation to put in place a system requiring the pre-notification of articles to the subject of them.[74] Much therefore depends on the facts and on the margin of appreciation given to the state in any particular case.[75]

D. RESTRICTING CONVENTION RIGHTS

The Convention seeks to balance the rights of the individual against other public 2.40 interests, but the object of human rights jurisprudence in democratic systems is not simple majoritarian rule. The rule of law is also required to ensure that democracy does not mean that the tyranny of the majority causes disproportionate interference with the rights of minorities. Once a complaint has been shown to infringe a limited or qualified right, the Strasbourg institutions consider the justification advanced by the state in order to determine whether there has been a violation.

The Convention seeks to ensure that the limitations placed upon an individual's 2.41 protected rights, in the name of the common or competing interests, are imposed only if they are:

(a) prescribed by law; and

(b) intended to achieve a legitimate objective; and

(c) 'necessary in a democratic society' (which incorporates the vital requirement of proportionality).

These general principles govern all restrictions on rights, regardless of precise terms of the article and whether it is limited or qualified.

---

[71] See the discussion in Clayton and Tomlinson, *The Law of Human Rights*, 2nd edn (Oxford: Oxford University Press, 2009), 364–9.

[72] *Mosley v United Kingdom* [2012] 1 FCR 99 [109]; see also *Swift v Secretary of State for Justice* [2012] EWHC 2000 (QB), [27].

[73] *Connors v UK* (2005) 40 EHRR 9; *McCann v UK* (2008) EHRR 47; *Kay v UK* App No 37341/06, 21 September 2010.

[74] *Mosley v UK* [2012] 1 FCR 99.

[75] See chs 6, 7, and 8 for a more detailed discussion of positive obligations arising under particular articles of the Convention.

1. Legality

2.42 The rule of law is at the heart of the Convention. It is described in the Preamble as part of the 'common heritage' that the signatories share, and is one of the 'fundamental principles of a democratic society'.[76] No interference with a right protected under the Convention is permissible unless the citizen is able to ascertain the legal basis for the interference. In the absence of such detailed authorization by the law, any interference, however justified, will violate the Convention. In Strasbourg jurisprudence, a derogation must also have an ascertainable legal basis.

2.43 The legal basis for a measure naturally includes statute law, but the ECtHR has ruled that secondary legislation,[77] applicable rules of EU law,[78] the common law,[79] and even rules of a professional body[80] may be sufficient if validly made and available to those bound by them.

2.44 In addition to being formally prescribed by law, the law itself must fulfil the substantive requirement that it have the appropriate 'qualities' to make it compatible with the rule of law.[81] The ECtHR explained this concept in *Sunday Times v UK (No 1)*:

> Firstly, the law must be adequately accessible: the citizens must be able to have an indication that is adequate in the circumstances of the legal rules applicable to a given case. Secondly, a norm cannot be regarded as a 'law' unless it is formulated with sufficient precision to enable the citizen to regulate his conduct.[82]

2.45 The accessibility rule is intended to counter arbitrary power by providing that a restriction cannot be justified, even if it is authorized in domestic law, unless the applicable law is published in a form accessible to those likely to be affected by it. Internal guidelines from government departments or agencies probably do not fulfil the accessibility requirement unless they are published or their content made known.[83]

2.46 The certainty rule is intended to enable individuals likely to be affected by a restriction on their rights to understand the circumstances in which any such restriction may be imposed, and to enable such individuals to foresee with a reasonable degree of accuracy the consequences of their actions.[84] Where the state covertly monitors its citizens it is still required to adhere to minimum safeguards to ensure that it does not wield its power arbitrarily.[85]

2.47 For instance, in *Liberty v UK* the Court found that the law regulating the system of interception of telephone calls between the United Kingdom and Ireland did not

---

[76] *Iatridis v Greece* App No 31107/96, 25 March 1999, para 62. See also *R (Gillan) v Commissioner of the Police for the Metropolis* [2006] UKHL 12, [2006] 2 AC 307 at [34].

[77] *Barthold v Germany* (1985) 7 EHRR 383.

[78] See *Groppera Radio AG v Switzerland* (1990) 12 EHRR 321.

[79] *Sunday Times v UK (No 1)* (1979) 2 EHRR 245.

[80] *Barthold v Germany* (1985) 7 EHRR 383.

[81] See *Kopp v Sweden* (1999) 27 EHRR 91, paras 55 and 64.

[82] (1979) 2 EHRR 245, para 49.

[83] *Govell v UK* [1999] EHRLR 121.

[84] *Silver v UK* (1983) 5 EHRR 347.

[85] *Weber and Saravia v Germany* [2006] ECHR 54934/00.

'indicate with reasonable clarity the scope and manner of exercise of the relevant discretion conferred on the public authorities'.[86] And in *Gillan and Quinton v UK*, the Court found that the 'stop and search' powers under the Terrorism Act 2000, which gave the police extremely broad discretion both to authorize searches and to decide to carry them out, were neither sufficiently circumscribed nor subject to adequate legal safeguards against abuse; they were therefore not 'in accordance with the law'.[87]

The degree of certainty required will depend on the facts of the case, but it is   2.48
clear that the ECtHR does not require absolute certainty. In *Sunday Times v UK (No 1)* the ECtHR said that:

Whilst certainty is highly desirable, it may bring in its train excessive rigidity and the law must be able to keep pace with changing circumstances. Accordingly, many laws are inevitably couched in terms which, to a greater or lesser extent, are vague and whose interpretation and application are questions of practice.[88]

Applying this principle, the ECtHR accepted that the common law relating to contempt of court was formulated with sufficient precision to satisfy the requirements of the Convention.[89]

In *Wingrove v UK*[90] and *Müller v Switzerland*,[91] cases involving freedom of   2.49
expression, the ECtHR accepted that the concepts of blasphemy and obscenity were not capable of precise definition, emphasizing 'the impossibility of attaining absolute precision in the framing of laws... in fields in which the situation changes according to the prevailing views of society'.[92] The requirement of legal certainty is thus more flexible in relation to laws whose subject matter touches 'areas of sensitive judgment where public opinion may shift'.[93]

2. Legitimate aim

Any interference by a public authority with a Convention right capable of limita-   2.50
tion must be directed towards an identified legitimate aim. Without such a legitimate aim there can be no justification for the interference.

To establish that an aim exists, the state must show that it was genuinely seeking   2.51
to advance one or more of the objectives identified in the qualifying paragraphs to the qualified articles, or, in relation to other limited rights, that it was pursuing an

---

[86] (2009) 48 EHRR 1, para 69; see also *Kennedy v UK* (2010) 52 EHRR 207, paras 155–170.
[87] (2010) 28 BHRC 420.
[88] (1979) 2 EHRR 245, para 49.
[89] See also *Steel v UK* (1998) 26 EHRR 603. Cf *Hashman and Harrup v UK* (2000) 30 EHRR 241.
[90] (1997) 24 EHRR 1.
[91] (1991) 13 EHRR 212.
[92] Ibid, para 29.
[93] Per Laws LJ in *R (ProLife Alliance) v BBC* [2002] EWCA Civ 297, [2002] 3 WLR 1080 at [24] (the Court of Appeal's decision was reversed by the House of Lords, their Lordships finding that Art 10(1) was not engaged and therefore expressing no opinion on the Court of Appeal's approach to Art 10(2): [2003] UKHL 23, [2004] 1 AC 185).

acceptable policy goal with regard to the context of the case. In general, the ECtHR and domestic courts accept the aim put forward by the state without a great deal of scrutiny, and it has been suggested that the question of whether there is a 'legitimate aim' for an interference with rights has been dealt with too cursorily.[94]

2.52　In Articles 8, 9, 10, and 11 the legitimate aims are set out in the second part of each article. Examples of aims which are considered 'legitimate' under the Convention are the interests of public safety, national security, the protection of health and morals, and the economic well-being of the country, or the protection of the rights and freedoms of others. The notion of the 'rights and freedoms of others' (in Articles 8, 9, and 11) and the 'reputation and rights of others' (Article 10) is not limited to the rights contained under the Convention. These phrases are capable of including other 'rights' and 'freedoms', including rights enshrined only in national law and rights which are not even known to national law.[95] However, the nature of the right that the state is aiming to protect may go to the separate question of the proportionality of the interference.

2.53　The legitimate aims set out under the qualified rights should be read with Article 18 of the Convention, which provides that 'The restrictions permitted under this Convention to the said rights and freedoms shall not be applied for any purpose other than those for which they have been prescribed'.[96] This is effectively a good faith provision. It is very difficult for applicants to establish that an interference was not in reality pursued for the reason claimed by the state. For example, in *Campbell v UK*[97] a prisoner complained about the authorities opening his correspondence with his lawyer. He argued that the real reason was to assess the contents. The Government claimed that the interference was for the purposes of the prevention of disorder or crime. While finding that there had been an interference of Article 8, the ECtHR saw no reason to doubt that there had been a legitimate aim for the interference.

3. 'Necessary in a democratic society'

2.54　Where the Convention allows restrictions on rights it not only requires them to be in accordance with law and justified by a legitimate aim, it also requires the interference to be 'necessary in a democratic society'. This phrase incorporates the proportionality standard that determines all permissible restrictions on rights.

2.55　The ECtHR has made clear that the term 'necessary' is not synonymous with 'indispensable', and it is certainly a less stringent test than those that appear elsewhere in the Convention: in Article 2(2) ('absolutely necessary'); Article 6(1)

---

[94] Gordon, 'Legitimate Aim: A Dimly Lit Road' [2002] EHRLR 421.

[95] *VgT Verein Gegen Tierfabriken v Switzerland* (2001) 34 EHRR 159, paras 59–62; *Chapman v UK* (2001) 33 EHRR 399, paras 80–82; see *also R (Craven) v Secretary of State for the Home Department* [2001] 2 Cr App R 181.

[96] See, eg *Refah Partisi (The Welfare Party) v Turkey* (2003) 37 EHRR 1.

[97] (1992) 15 EHRR 137.

('strictly necessary'); and Article 15(1) ('to the extent strictly required by the exigencies of the situation').[98]

Nevertheless, 'necessary in a democratic society' is a rigorous test. In *Handyside* 2.56 *v UK* and *Sunday Times v UK (No 1)* the ECtHR established that the term 'necessary' does not have the 'flexibility of such expressions as "admissible", "ordinary", "useful", "reasonable" or "desirable" [and] it implies the existence of a "pressing social need"'.[99]

The ECtHR has not developed a consistent set of principles that it uses to assess 2.57 necessity in every case. However, it set out a three-fold test in *Sunday Times v UK (No 1)* that is now generally applied in relation to the qualified rights:

(a) whether the interference complained of corresponded to a 'pressing social need'; and

(b) whether it was 'proportionate to the legitimate aim pursued'; and

(c) whether the reasons given by the national authority to justify it were 'relevant and sufficient'.[100]

When addressing limited rights, the Court may apply this test in full or simply ask whether the measures taken by the state were proportionate. Each aspect of the *Sunday Times* test is considered in turn below.

(a) *Pressing social need*

A 'pressing social need' must accord with the requirements of a democratic society, 2.58 which supposes 'pluralism, tolerance and broadmindedness'.[101] In assessing whether there is a 'pressing social need' in play, the ECtHR pays close regard to the importance of the relevant right. A very powerful need will be required if there is an interference with a right—or an aspect of a right—the ECtHR considers to be particularly important. The 'pressing social need' that the state must show in order to justify an interference with an intimate aspect of private life, for example, will be particularly strong.[102]

A 'pressing social need' is distinct from a legitimate aim. Thus, in *Dudgeon v UK* 2.59 the ECtHR recognized that one of the purposes of the legislation criminalizing homosexual behaviour was 'to afford safeguards for vulnerable members of society, such as the young, against the consequences of homosexual practices' and accepted that this was then a legitimate aim. However, it went on to say that:

It cannot be maintained in these circumstances that there is a 'pressing social need' to make such acts criminal offences, there being no sufficient justification provided by the risk of harm to vulnerable sections of society requiring protection or by the effects on the public.[103]

---

[98] *Handyside v UK* (1976) 1 EHRR 737, para 48.
[99] Ibid; *Sunday Times v UK* (1979) 2 EHRR 245, para 59.
[100] *Sunday Times v UK* (1979) 2 EHRR 245, para 59.
[101] *Handyside v UK* (1976) 1 EHRR 737.
[102] *Dudgeon v UK* (1981) 4 EHRR 149.
[103] Ibid, para 60.

2.60   In contrast, the ECtHR will generally accept the existence of a pressing social need where the state asserts national security considerations[104] or threats to the stability of its democratic institutions.[105]

(b) *Proportionality*

2.61   Proportionality is at the heart of the necessity test. Indeed, it has been called the 'dominant theme underlying the whole of the Convention'.[106] As the ECtHR put it in *Soering v UK*:

> Inherent in the whole of the Convention is a search for the fair balance between the demands of the general interest of the community and the requirements of the protection of the individual's human rights.[107]

2.62   Proportionality is a principle that helps strike that 'fair balance'. It requires a reasonable relationship between the goal pursued and the means the state has chosen to achieve that goal.[108] This means that even if a policy which interferes with a Convention right might be aimed at securing a legitimate aim of social policy, for example the prevention of crime, this will not in itself justify the violation if the means adopted to secure the aim are excessive in the circumstances. In other words, the state must not use a sledgehammer to crack a nut.

2.63   Proportionality arises in a number of different contexts. It is most commonly associated with the balancing exercise the ECtHR adopts in determining claims under Articles 8, 9, 10, and 11—as one element of the 'necessary in a democratic society' test. However, it also arises in other discrete ways in the Convention. It is the yardstick by which the scope of restrictions on implied rights are measured;[109] it is used when determining whether a positive obligation should be imposed on a contracting state;[110] it is the central mechanism for determining whether interferences with property are justified under Protocol 1, Article 1;[111] and it is relevant to the prohibition of discrimination under Article 14.[112]

2.64   Proportionality is not an exact science, and different writers have produced varying formulations of the test.[113] However, it is clear from the case law of the ECtHR

---

[104] See, eg *Leander v Sweden* (1987) 9 EHRR 433.

[105] See, eg *Refah Partisi (The Welfare Party) v Turkey* (2003) 37 EHRR 1.

[106] Reid, *A Practitioner's Guide to the European Convention on Human Rights*, 4th edn (London: Sweet & Maxwell, 2012), para I-073.

[107] (1989) 11 EHRR 439, para 89.

[108] *Fayed v UK* (1994) 18 EHRR 393, para 71.

[109] See para 2.29.

[110] See para 2.38.

[111] See ch 8, paras 8.02–8.61.

[112] See ch 7, paras 7.556–7.582.

[113] See the comparison of different approaches in Rivers, 'Proportionality and Variable Intensity of Review' (2006) CLJ 174. See also Hickman, 'The Substance and Structure of Proportionality' (2008) PL 694.

that certain general factors are relevant to the ECtHR's proportionality exercise. These include:

(a) the extent to which the interference impairs the 'very essence' of a right, which effectively means a very serious interference.[114] The ECtHR will distinguish between different types of rights arising under the same Convention article. For example, the state will need to adduce particularly weighty reasons to justify an interference with political speech. In contrast, the ECtHR gives greater latitude to the state when assessing interference with commercial speech;[115]

(b) whether the state has adopted a blanket policy that does not permit examination of the merits of individual cases. Thus, in *S and Marper* the ECtHR was particularly concerned by the 'blanket and indiscriminate nature of the power of retention' of the DNA of all those arrested for criminal offences, no matter how minor and regardless of whether the individual was ever charged.[116] A policy that only permits assessment of individual circumstances in 'exceptional' cases may also prove disproportionate;[117]

(c) whether a less-restrictive alternative, yet equally effective, measure is available to the state to achieve the legitimate aim pursued. For example, in *Campbell v UK* the ECtHR held that the blanket opening of all prisoners' mail was disproportionate because the less intrusive measure of opening only those letters reasonably considered to contain prohibited material would have achieved the same aim;[118]

(d) whether there are any effective safeguards or legal controls over the measures in question. This includes the adequacy of compensation or legal remedies for those affected by the measures.[119] In Article 10 cases, the ECtHR will also examine the opposite question: whether an award of damages for defamation is excessive taking into account all of the circumstances.[120]

The intensity of the proportionality inquiry will vary according to the right at stake. For example, where property rights are in issue the ECtHR will apply less exacting scrutiny than where there is an interference with the right to privacy or freedom of expression.[121]   2.65

Proportionality also incorporates a concept of procedural fairness. An infringement of a qualified right is less likely to be a proportionate response to a legitimate   2.66

---

[114] See, eg *Dudgeon v UK* (1981) 4 EHRR 149.

[115] See ch 7, para 7.400.

[116] App Nos 30562/04 and 30566/04, 4 December 2008. See also *O'Donoghue and ors v UK* (2010) 30 BHRC 85 (successful challenge to the scheme designed to prevent 'sham' marriages).

[117] *Dickson v UK* (2008) 24 BHRC 19.

[118] (1992) 15 EHRR 137. See also *Hirst v UK (No 2)* 19 BHRC 546, (2006) 42 EHRR 41.

[119] See, eg *Motais de Narbonne v France* App No 48161/99, 2 July 2002; *Akkus v Turkey* [1997] ECHR 19263/92.

[120] *Steel and Morris v UK* (2005) 41 EHRR 22.

[121] See, eg *Pye v UK* (2008) 46 EHRR 34.

aim if the person affected by the action was not consulted, or not given the right to a hearing, than if he or she was given such opportunities. The ECtHR has stated that, 'whilst Article 8 contains no explicit procedural requirements, the decision-making process leading to measures of interference must be fair and such as to afford due respect to the interests safeguarded by Article 8'.[122] However, in some cases this guarantee may be redundant as the stronger procedural protections of Article 6 will apply.

(c) *Relevant and sufficient reasons*

2.67 The final element of the 'necessary in a democratic society' test involves the ECtHR's assessment of whether the state's reasons for interfering with the right are 'relevant and sufficient'.[123] This is an objective test. It is not enough that the respondent state has acted 'reasonably, carefully and in good faith'.[124] The ECtHR will examine the reasons for the state's actions and determine whether they are adequate. In *Smith and Grady v UK*[125] and *Lustig-Prean and Beckett v UK*,[126] for example—cases involving a ban on homosexuals serving in the army—it was not enough for the respondent state simply to assert that the reason for the ban was 'operational effectiveness' or 'threat to morale'. Cogent evidence was needed, and the state could not provide it. Where no evidence is adduced in support of the reasons given for a restriction, a breach of the Convention is almost inevitable.[127]

2.68 The ECtHR adopted a particularly strong approach to reason-giving in *Hirst v UK*, in which it held that the state's reasons for banning convicted prisoners from voting were inadequate.[128] This was despite the lack of consensus in other Member States on this issue, and the fact that Parliament had voted for an express ban in a piece of primary legislation. The Grand Chamber stated:

> There is no evidence that Parliament has ever sought to weigh the competing interests or to assess the proportionality of a blanket ban on the right of a convicted prisoner to vote...[It] cannot be said that there was any substantive debate by members of the legislature on the continued justification in light of modern day penal policy and of current human rights standards for maintaining such a general restriction on the right of prisoners to vote.[129]

By contrast in *Animal Defenders International v UK*,[130] the Grand Chamber relied upon the extensive degree of parliamentary and judicial scrutiny to hold that a complete ban on political television advertising fell within the state's margin of

---

[122] *McMichael v UK* (1995) 20 EHRR 205, para 87.
[123] *Jersild v Denmark* (1995) 19 EHRR 1.
[124] *Olsson (No 1)* (1988) 11 EHRR 259, para 58; *Vogt v Germany* (1995) 21 EHRR 205, para 52.
[125] (1999) 29 EHRR 493, paras 71–112.
[126] (1999) 29 EHRR 548, paras 64–105.
[127] *Autronic AG v Switzerland* (1990) 12 EHRR 485.
[128] (2006) 42 EHRR 41.
[129] Ibid, para 79.
[130] [2013] 57 EHRR 21.

appreciation and so did not violate Article 10, notwithstanding that this apparently contradicted a recent Grand Chamber judgment on a similar issue.[131]

4. Restrictions specifically provided for by reservations and derogations

(a) *Reservations*

Article 57 entitles states to make reservations in respect of rights contained in the Convention. A reservation to an international treaty is a device used by a signatory state to reserve particular policies or law in order to exempt them from challenge under the instrument. They are often used as a temporary measure, which gives states time to bring their laws into line with the requirements of the Convention. Reservations can be made only at the time of signing or ratification and must comply with Article 31(1) of the Vienna Convention on the Law of Treaties, which states:

2.69

A treaty shall be interpreted in good faith in accordance with the ordinary meaning to be given to the terms of the treaty in their context and in the light of its objects and purpose.

A reservation is likely to be invalid if it seeks to circumvent key terms or underlying principles contained within the treaty in question.

2.70

There is currently one reservation by the United Kingdom to the Convention, which pertains to the second sentence of Protocol 1, Article 2 (which requires education to be provided in conformity with parents' religious and philosophical convictions). The United Kingdom has accepted this provision only so far as it is compatible with the provision of efficient instruction and training and the avoidance of unreasonable public expenditure.[132]

2.71

Any reservation must meet the requirements of Article 57(2) of the Convention and not be couched in terms that are too vague or broad for it to be possible to determine their exact scope and meaning.[133]

2.72

(b) *Derogations*

Article 15(1) of the Convention states:

2.73

In time of war or other public emergency threatening the life of the nation any High Contracting Party may take measures derogating from its obligations under this Convention to the extent strictly required by the exigencies of the situation, provided that such measures are not inconsistent with its obligations under international law.

This enables states to restrict the exercise of some of the rights and freedoms without violating the Convention. Any derogation must be proportionate to the threat and must be necessary to deal with the emergency. As a matter of international law,

2.74

---

[131] *Verein gegen Tierfabriken Schweiz v Switzerland* [2011] 52 EHRR 8.
[132] The full text of the reservation is set out in Part II of Sch 3 to the Human Rights Act 1998; see App 1.
[133] *Belilos v Switzerland* (1988) 10 EHRR 466. It has been suggested that the reservation might not withstand challenge, given the language used by the United Kingdom: Emmerson and Simor, *Human Rights Practice* (London: Sweet & Maxwell, 2000) para 1.024.

a state, by lodging a derogation in Strasbourg, can, to the extent that the derogation is lawful under Article 15, avoid a particular obligation in particular circumstances. Article 15 does not allow derogations from Article 2 (the right to life), Article 3 (freedom from torture), Article 4(1) (slavery and servitude), and Article 7 (retrospective criminal penalties).

2.75   At the time of writing the United Kingdom has no derogations in place.[134]

5. Restrictions under Articles 16, 17, and 18

2.76   The rights contained in the Convention are subject to express restrictions in three specific areas:

(a) Article 16 (restrictions on the political activities of aliens);

(b) Article 17 (restrictions on activities aimed at the destruction of Convention rights); and

(c) Article 18 (prohibition on using Convention restrictions for an improper purpose).

The exact scope of these articles is considered in detail in Chapter 7.

E. THE MARGIN OF APPRECIATION

2.77   The meaning of the term 'margin of appreciation' is not immediately apparent, originating as it does from French administrative law. It was described by Lord Hoffmann as an 'unfortunate Gallicism'.[135] In essence, it refers to the freedom that a state is permitted in the manner in which it observes Convention rights.

2.78   As Clayton and Tomlinson point out, it fulfils two functions in Convention jurisprudence.[136] First, it establishes 'an interpretative obligation' to respect the varying cultural traditions of the contracting states. As the Convention is an international human rights instrument, policed by an international court, the Strasbourg institutions have to be sensitive to the need for 'subsidiarity', that is, to ensuring that the Member States' own political and cultural traditions are respected. For example, actions that may offend religious sensibilities in one country may be a recognized act of free speech in another. Secondly, the margin of appreciation functions as a standard of review that enables the ECtHR to take a 'hands-off' approach to certain issues where national authorities are better placed to make an assessment of proportionality.

2.79   The doctrine was developed by the ECtHR in *Handyside v UK*, which concerned the publication in England in 1971 of the *Little Red School Book*, which was intended

---

[134] See the discussion of previous derogations in ch 7, paras 7.567 –7.578.

[135] 'The Universality of Human Rights', Judicial Studies Board Annual Lecture 2009, available at <http://www.judiciary.gov.uk/training-support/judicial-college/Annual+Lectures>.

[136] *The Law of Human Rights*, 2nd edn (Oxford: Oxford University Press, 2009) 315.

for children and included a section on sex.[137] The police seized the books and a forfeiture order was obtained on the grounds that the books contravened the Obscene Publications Act 1959. The applicant claimed a violation of the right to freedom of expression and the Government argued that the restriction was necessary for the purpose of the 'protection of morals'. The Court accepted that the limitation was 'prescribed by law' and thus had to decide whether the limitation in question was proportionate and 'necessary in a democratic society'. The Court stated:

By reason of their direct and continuous contact with the vital forces of their countries, state authorities are in principle in a better position than the international judge to give an opinion on the extent of these requirements as well as on the 'necessity' of a 'restriction' or 'penalty' intended to meet them.

Nevertheless, this power of appreciation is not unlimited. Over the years, the   **2.80** Court has developed its case law in this area such that it can be said that the margin of appreciation has become a central element of the ECtHR's method of reasoning. The case law was summarized in *S and Marper v UK*[138] as follows:

A margin of appreciation must be left to the competent national authorities... The breadth of this margin varies and depends on a number of factors including the nature of the Convention right in issue, its importance for the individual, the nature of the interference and the object pursued by the interference. The margin will tend to be narrower where the right at stake is crucial to the individual's effective enjoyment of intimate or key rights... Where a particularly important facet of an individual's existence or identity is at stake, the margin allowed to the State will be restricted... Where, however, there is no consensus within the Member States of the Council of Europe, either as to the relative importance of the interest at stake or as to how best to protect it, the margin will be wider.

In recent cases, however, this final factor appears to have held less sway. In *Hirst*   **2.81** *v UK* the ECtHR made clear that the lack of a common European approach to the problem was not in itself determinative of the issue[139] and indicated that certain forms of blanket interference with rights could fall outside the margin of appreciation altogether:

such a general, automatic and indiscriminate restriction on a vitally important Convention right must be seen as falling outside any acceptable margin of appreciation, however wide that margin might be... While the Court reiterates that the margin of appreciation is wide, it is not all-embracing.[140]

It might be said that the Court often uses the 'margin of appreciation' concept   **2.82** to avoid ruling on acutely sensitive issues which involve an element of political controversy. In *Lautsi v Italy*, for instance, the Grand Chamber (overturning an earlier Chamber decision) held that the decision whether crucifixes should be present in state-school classrooms was, in principle, a matter falling within the margin

---

[137] (1976) 1 EHRR 737 (following the ECmHR in *Lawless v Ireland (No 3)* (1979–1980) 1 EHRR 15).

[138] (2008) 25 BHRC 557, para 102; for a fuller exposition, see *Mosley v UK* App No 48009/08, 10 May 2011, paras 108–111.

[139] *Hirst v UK (No 2)* (2005) 19 BHRC 546, (2006) 42 EHRR 41, para 81.

[140] Ibid, para 82. See also *Dickson v UK* (2008) 24 BHRC 19.

of appreciation of the respondent state, and that in light of this, the decision did not lead to a form of indoctrination such as to violate Article 2 of Protocol 1 to the Convention.[141] And in *Mosley v UK*, the Court found that whether or not a pre-notification requirement should be imposed on the press to protect a person's privacy fell within the state's margin of appreciation.[142]

2.83   In its use as a standard of review, the margin of appreciation is controversial. Many commentators consider that the doctrine is applied carelessly and without clear guiding principles, and suggest that it may be a means of avoiding the proportionality analysis in difficult cases.[143] A former judge of the Court trenchantly criticized the doctrine for allowing the Court to evade its responsibility to articulate the reasons why its intervention in particular cases may or may not be appropriate.[144] Lord Hoffmann suggested that while the ECtHR has failed to enunciate the principles on which the margin of appreciation is based, it has not taken it 'nearly far enough'.[145] According to Lord Hoffmann, it is 'constitutionally inappropriate' for an international court to determine domestic questions such as the proportionality of landing regulations at Heathrow,[146] and the margin of appreciation should be enthusiastically employed to delegate proportionality decisions to national authorities.

2.84   As discussed in Chapter 4, the margin of appreciation should not be employed by the domestic courts.[147]

---

[141] (2011) 54 EHRR 60.

[142] (2011) 31 BHRC 409. See also *Animal Defenders International v UK* [2013] 57 EHRR 21.

[143] See, eg Lord Lester of Herne Hill QC, 'Universality Versus Subsidiarity: A Reply' [1998] EHRLR 73; Clayton and Tomlinson, *The Law of Human Rights*, 2nd edn (Oxford: Oxford University Press, 2009) 319–20.

[144] See Macdonald, 'The Margin of Appreciation', in Macdonald, Matscher, and Petzold (eds), *The European System for the Protection of Human Rights*, 3rd edn (The Hague: Kluwer Law International, 1993).

[145] 'The Universality of Human Rights', Judicial Studies Board Annual Lecture 2009, available at <http://www.judiciary.gov.uk/training-support/judicial-college/Annual+Lectures>. See also Lord Sumption, 'The Limits of the Law', Sultan Azlan Shah Lecture, Kuala Lumpur, 20 November 2013, available at <http://www.supremecourt.uk/docs/speech-131120.pdf>.

[146] *Hatton v UK* (2003) 37 EHRR 28.

[147] See ch 4, paras 4.119–4.130.

3

THE FRAMEWORK OF THE
HUMAN RIGHTS ACT

A. INTRODUCTION

3.01 The Human Rights Act is a special statute imbued with constitutional significance. It is described in its long title as an Act to give 'further effect' to the rights and freedoms guaranteed under the European Convention for the Protection of Human Rights and Fundamental Freedoms (Convention). The special status of the Human Rights Act has been recognized judicially,[1] academically,[2] and by parliamentarians.[3]

3.02 Since the Human Rights Act came into force it has altered the interpretation and use of the common law and all other legislation in cases involving human rights issues. The overriding objective of the Act is to weave the Convention into the existing legal system, so that all courts will consider Convention arguments, and rights which could have been obtained in Strasbourg can be secured in national courts, while minimizing disruption to the existing legal system. The method adopted, however, is a complex one, reflecting a delicate political compromise between 'incorporating' Convention rights and retaining parliamentary sovereignty.

3.03 The Human Rights Act created a general statutory requirement that all legislation, primary or secondary, whenever enacted, must be read and given effect in a way which is compatible with Convention rights *whenever possible*. This principle of construction, contained in section 3 of the Human Rights Act, requires generous and progressive interpretation to give effect to the purpose of this constitutional statute. If it is not possible to interpret legislation in a compliant way then the higher courts may declare the legislation to be incompatible with the Convention.

3.04 This principle of construction applies to all litigation, whether or not a public authority is involved. It can, therefore, affect the rights of private persons between themselves. But the Human Rights Act does not directly create a new cause of action for 'breach of the Convention' against private bodies.

3.05 However, by virtue of section 6, the Human Rights Act requires public authorities—including courts—to act compatibly with the Convention unless they are prevented from doing so by statute. This means that the courts have their own primary statutory duty to give effect to the Convention unless positively prevented from doing so. Section 7 gives the 'victim' of any act of a public authority which is incompatible with the Convention power to challenge the authority in court using the Convention to found a cause of action or a defence.

3.06 This chapter explains the mechanism of the Human Rights Act, and the effect it has had in proceedings involving public and private authorities. It starts with a very brief summary of the Human Rights Act mechanism, followed by an overview of the key provisions of the Act and its relationship with the common law. The next part contains a more detailed analysis of the main operative provisions of the

---

[1] See, eg *R v Offen* [2001] 1 WLR 253, 275 per Lord Woolf; *Thoburn v Sunderland City Council* [2002] EWHC 195 (Admin), [2002] 3 WLR 247 per Laws LJ.

[2] See Jowell and Cooper (eds), *Delivering Rights: How the Human Rights Act is Working* (London: Hart Publishing, 2003) 2.

[3] Constitution Committee, Sixth Report, Session 2006–2007, para 8.

Act and how they interact. No further explanation of the Act can proceed without the discussion in the following section of what the Act means by the terms 'public authority' and 'functions of a public nature'. The chapter then examines some of the ways in which the Act has been applied in litigation involving private parties. The final section concerns statutory 'special cases'. Procedural issues concerning bringing a claim under the Human Rights Act, key Convention concepts in domestic law, and the remedies available under the Act are discussed in Chapter 4.

B. SUMMARY OF THE EFFECTS OF THE HUMAN RIGHTS ACT

In summary, the wide-reaching effects of the Human Rights Act are as follows.   3.07

(a) In *all* cases in which Convention rights are in question, the Human Rights Act gives 'further effect' to the Convention, whether the litigants are private persons or public authorities. It does this in three ways:
  (i)   by obliging courts to decide all cases before them (whether brought under statute or the common law) compatibly with Convention rights unless prevented from doing so either by primary legislation or by provisions made under primary legislation which cannot be read compatibly with the Convention;[4]
  (ii) by placing an obligation upon courts to interpret existing and future legislation in conformity with the Convention wherever possible;[5]
  (iii) by requiring courts to take Strasbourg case law into account in all cases, in so far as they consider it is relevant to proceedings before them.[6]

(b) The Human Rights Act does not make Convention rights *directly* enforceable against a private litigant, nor against a functional public authority (that is, a body which is not obviously public in form but which has some functions of a public nature) if it is acting in a private capacity.[7] But in cases against a private litigant, or functional public authority acting in exercise of its private law functions, the Human Rights Act may still have an effect on the outcome, because the court:
  (i)   is obliged to interpret legislation in conformity with the Convention wherever possible;
  (ii) must exercise any judicial discretions compatibly with the Convention; and
  (iii) must ensure that its application of common law or equitable rules is compatible with the Convention.

(c) Section 7 of the Human Rights Act creates directly enforceable rights against public bodies. First, it has introduced a new ground of illegality into

---

[4] Section 6(1)–(3).
[5] Section 3.
[6] Section 2(1).
[7] See paras 3.61–3.73.

proceedings brought by way of judicial review, namely, a failure to comply with the Convention rights protected by the Human Rights Act, subject to a defence that there is a clear statutory obligation to act incompatibly with the Convention. Secondly, it has created a stand-alone cause of action against public bodies that fail to act compatibly with the Convention. Thirdly, Convention rights are available via the Human Rights Act as a ground of defence or appeal in cases brought by public bodies against private persons (in both criminal and civil cases). However, the scope and meaning of 'public authority' remains in doubt following the decision of the House of Lords in *YL v Birmingham City Council*.[8]

(d) Section 7 can be used only by 'victims' of violations of the Convention, the term 'victim' being defined in section 7(7). However, even a litigant who is not defined as a 'victim', and so cannot challenge a public authority's decision directly using the provisions of the Human Rights Act, is able to rely on the court's obligation under section 3 of the Human Rights Act to interpret legislation compatibly with the Convention where possible, and to use Convention arguments in the circumstances in which this was possible before the Human Rights Act was brought into force.[9]

(e) The Human Rights Act does not permit the Convention to be used so as to override primary legislation: if a statute is clear in its terms, and clearly incompatible with the Convention, courts must give effect to it. Equally, if the terms of the primary legislation require subordinate legislation made under it (which will usually be in a statutory instrument) to be interpreted in a way which means that the subordinate legislation is incompatible with the Convention, it must still be given effect even though this may result in a breach of a Convention right. To that extent, parliamentary sovereignty is preserved.[10] But if legislation cannot be read so as to comply with the Convention, the higher courts have the power to issue 'declarations of incompatibility', and a fast-track procedure exists whereby the Government can legislate to remedy such incompatibility.[11]

C. OVERVIEW OF THE KEY PROVISIONS OF THE HUMAN RIGHTS ACT

3.08 The Human Rights Act is a short and elegantly drafted piece of legislation. It is nonetheless helpful to approach it schematically rather than simply reading the sections in the order in which they appear.

---

[8] [2007] UKHL 27, [2008] 1 AC 95.
[9] Section 11.
[10] Section 3(2)(b) and (c).
[11] Sections 4, 10, and Sch 2.

1. Section 1 and Schedule 1—definition of Convention rights

After the long title, which states that the Act gives 'further effect' to the rights
and freedoms guaranteed under the Convention, section 1 and Schedule 1 define
the 'Convention rights', which have been incorporated, subject to any designated
derogations or reservations.[12] Article 1 (the obligation on contracting states to the
Convention to 'secure' Convention rights to 'everyone within their jurisdiction')
and Article 13 (the right to an effective remedy in a national court) are not specifically designated as 'Convention rights' within this definition.

3.09

'The Convention' in this context means 'the Convention...as it has effect for
the time being in relation to the United Kingdom'.[13] The House of Lords has held
that this means that the Convention does not have effect if it is limited or extinguished by some other, overriding provision of international law, such as a UN
Security Council Resolution.[14] The effect of the Convention is usually, but not
always, territorially limited. The Supreme Court has held, following the decision
of the European Court of Human Rights in *Al-Skeini v UK*, that it covers British
armed forces serving outsider the territory of the UK.[15]

3.10

2. Section 2—interpretation of Convention rights

Section 2 requires any court or tribunal determining a question that has arisen
in connection with a Convention right to 'take into account' the jurisprudence of
the Strasbourg organs (the European Court of Human Rights, the Commission
of Human Rights, and the Committee of Ministers). This jurisprudence must be
considered 'so far as, in the opinion of the court or tribunal, it is relevant to the
proceedings in which that question has arisen', whenever the judgment, decision,
or opinion to be taken into account was handed down.[16] Section 2 is considered in
detail at para 3.50.

3.11

3. Section 3—interpretation of legislation

Section 3 is the lynchpin of the Act, 'pivotal to [its] operation'.[17] It requires primary
and subordinate legislation to be read and given effect in a way which is compatible with Convention rights, 'so far as it is possible to do so', whether the legislation in question was enacted before or after the Human Rights Act. Section 3 is
a general requirement, addressed to any person reading the legislation, not just to

3.12

---

[12] Section 1(2).

[13] Section 21(1).

[14] *R (Al-Jedda) v Secretary of State for Defence* [2007] UKHL 58, [2008] 1 AC 332 (although see now
Al-Jedda v UK (2011) 30 BHRC 637). See also *R (Quark Fishing Ltd) v Foreign Secretary* [2005] UKHL 57,
[2006] 1 AC 529 at [25], [32], [87], and [97]; and *Al-Skeini v UK* (2011) 53 EHRR 589.

[15] *R (Smith) v Ministry of Defence* [2013] UKSC 41, [2014] 1 AC 52.

[16] Section 2(1).

[17] Bradley, 'The Sovereignty of Parliament—Form or Substance?', in Jowell and Oliver (eds), *The
Changing Constitution* (Oxford: Oxford University Press, 2007) 37.

the courts. This strong interpretative obligation is one of the key provisions in the Human Rights Act. It has had an impact on all types of cases, civil or criminal, public or private, where a Convention right is at stake, because all domestic courts and tribunals are defined as 'public authorities' (under section 6(3)(a)) and must interpret statutory provisions and the common law compatibly with Convention rights wherever possible regardless of other, perhaps more literal, interpretations or precedents to the contrary. Section 3 is dealt with in more detail at para 3.33.

4. Section 19—statements of compatibility

3.13   Section 19 requires the minister with conduct of any Bill,[18] before its second reading, to either make and publish a 'statement of compatibility',[19] or openly make a statement that although he or she is unable to state that the legislation is compatible with the Convention rights, the Government nevertheless wishes to proceed with the Bill.[20] Section 19 is dealt with in more detail at para 3.45.

5. Sections 4, 5, 10, and Schedule 2—incompatibility of legislation

3.14   If it is *not* possible to read legislation so as to give effect to the Convention, then that legislation remains in force. The courts cannot, as in some constitutional structures, 'strike it down' as being incompatible with Convention principles. Section 3(2)(b) and (c) of the Act expressly provide that if legislation cannot be read compatibly, this does not affect its validity, continuing operation, or enforcement. Instead, in such circumstances, section 4 empowers the higher courts to express their view that the legislation is not compatible with the Convention by making a 'declaration of incompatibility'. If such a declaration is to be sought, the Crown has a right to be notified, and to intervene, under section 5 of the Act. In circumstances where a court has made a declaration of incompatibility, the Act provides a 'fast track' legislative procedure, by which the executive can act to cure the incompatibility, which is contained in section 10 of, and Schedule 2 to, the Act. These provisions are described in more detail in Chapter 4, para 4.93. However, it is important to note that a declaration of incompatibility—as with any declaration—is a discretionary remedy, and the Supreme Court has indicated that it will not be institutionally appropriate for it to grant a declaration of incompatibility if a similar declaration has already been made on a particular issue.[21] Thus, the ultimate decision as to whether or not to comply with international law obligations under the Convention falls—as a matter of statute—to the Crown, and not to the courts.

---

[18] There is no such requirement for Private Members' Bills.
[19] Section 19(1)(a).
[20] Section 19(1)(b).
[21] *R (Chester) v Secretary of State for Justice* [2013] UKSC 63, [2014] AC 271.

6. Section 6—acts of public authorities

Section 6 makes it unlawful in most circumstances for a public authority to act in a way which is incompatible with a Convention right. A public authority may only do so if it is required to by primary legislation, or by secondary legislation made under it, which cannot be interpreted compatibly with the Convention. 'Act' in section 6 includes failure to act.[22] This general obligation is very wide, and means that in the exercise of any power or duty, any public body must act in such a way as to give effect to the Convention. **3.15**

'Giving effect to the Convention' means more than simply requiring the public authority to avoid violating Convention rights itself. Where a public authority has positive obligations under the Convention, that is, a duty to act in such a way as to protect people from having their Convention rights violated by third parties, then section 6 will also require the public authority to give effect to these.[23] For example, a public authority could violate the right to freedom of association under Article 11 of the Convention, not only by prohibiting a demonstration, but also by failing to police it so as to ensure that demonstrators are not assaulted by violent counter-demonstrators.[24] **3.16**

Section 6(1) is limited only in so far as is necessary to preserve the concept of parliamentary sovereignty. First, section 6(2)(a) provides that the duty under section 6(1) to give effect to Convention rights does not apply if the public authority *could not* have acted differently as a result of one or more provisions of primary legislation. Section 6(2)(b) provides that section 6(1) does not apply if the authority was acting to give effect to or to enforce one or more provisions made under primary legislation which cannot be read or given effect in a way which is compatible with the Convention rights. Plainly there is some overlap between section 6(2)(a) and (2)(b), both in effect amounting to a 'primary legislation defence', and the House of Lords has recognized this.[25] In practice, section 6(2) is rarely applied.[26] Most powers or duties *can* be read in a way which is compatible with the Convention: and if public authorities do not themselves comply with section 6(1) by reading their powers and duties in a Convention-compliant way, the courts (as public authorities themselves) are under their own duties to find a reading of the legislation which permits the public authority to comply with the Convention if at all possible. **3.17**

The second limit on the effect of section 6(1) is that Parliament in its legislative capacity is not a 'public authority'[27] and so is not bound by section 6(1).[28] Thus, **3.18**

---

[22] Section 6(6).
[23] See ch 2.
[24] *Plattform Artze für das Leben v Austria* (1988) 13 EHRR 204.
[25] *R (Hooper) v Secretary of State for Work and Pensions* [2005] UKHL 29, [2005] 1 WLR 1681, where Lord Hoffmann and Lord Hope held that the appropriate defence was s 6(2)(b) and Lord Scott and Lord Brown held that it was s 6(2)(a).
[26] As to the extent and effect of s 6(2), see *Ghaidan v Godin-Mendoza* [2004] UKHL 30, [2004] 2 AC 557; see also *R (GC and C) v Commissioner of Police of the Metropolis* [2011] UKSC 21, [2011] 1 WLR 1230 at [19]–[44]; *R (Chester) v Secretary of State for Justice* [2013] UKSC 63, [2014] AC 271.
[27] Section 6(3).
[28] Ibid.

even if Parliament has failed to enact legislation which is arguably required in order to give effect to Convention principles, that is not a matter which can be challenged in domestic courts. Though the 'act' of a public authority which can be challenged includes an omission, it does not include a failure to legislate.[29]

3.19 Section 6(3)(a) makes courts and tribunals (including the House of Lords in its judicial capacity)[30] public authorities, and so subject to their own primary duty to act compatibly with the Convention. This is important when considering the effect of the Convention in private litigation, because the courts are themselves subject to a duty to 'give effect' to the Convention in reaching their decisions, if they can.

3.20 Public authorities are in a special position under the Human Rights Act, because the Convention rights scheduled to the Act can be directly enforced against them. The Convention has also been relevant in determining some cases between private individuals, as well as those between an individual and the state, because as a 'public authority' a court is obliged to act in a way which is compatible with the Convention. This 'horizontal' impact of the Human Rights Act is considered at paras 3.74–3.76.

7. Section 7—proceedings against public authorities

3.21 Section 7 deals with proceedings under the Human Rights Act, both free-standing and other proceedings in which the Act is relevant. It may be used only by a person who is or would be a 'victim' of the unlawful act,[31] a term which is analysed in Chapter 4. A 'victim' may rely on Convention rights in two ways in legal proceedings. First, under section 7(1)(a) he or she may bring free-standing proceedings against a public authority which infringes a Convention right 'in the appropriate court or tribunal'. The appropriate forum is determined by the subject matter of the claim and rules made by the Secretary of State concerned or the Lord Chancellor (which also deal with other jurisdictional matters, such as remedies).[32] Section 7(5) imposes a limitation period for bringing free-standing proceedings. Secondly, section 7(1)(b) permits a person to rely on the Convention right or rights concerned in 'any legal proceedings'. Section 22(4) provides that section 7(1)(b) can be used as a defence whenever the act in question took place, but proceedings may be instigated under section 7(1)(a) only in relation to acts committed after the Human Rights Act came into force on 2 October 2000.

---

[29] Section 6(6)(a).

[30] Section 6(4).

[31] Section 7(3) and (7).

[32] Section 7(2) and (9)–(14); Civil Procedure (Amendment No 4) Rules 2000, SI 2000/2092, concerning human rights issues in the Administrative Court; Family Procedure Rules 2011, Practice Direction 29B (the Human Rights Act 1998); CPR Pt 33 and Practice Direction 30 concerning transfer between courts; Criminal Procedure Rules 2014, rr 17.28, 65.12; and, in the Supreme Court, Supreme Court Rules 2009, r 40 and Practice Direction 9 (the Human Rights Act 1998); CPR 7.11 says that a direct claim under s 7(1)(a) in respect of a judicial act may only be brought in the High Court: see *A v B (Investigative Powers Tribunal: Jurisdiction)* [2009] UKSC 12, [2010] 2 AC 1. However, a county court is an appropriate court or tribunal to read down a statute: see *Manchester City Council v Pinnock* [2010] UKSC 45, [2011] 2 AC 104.

The Human Rights Act creates three ways in which Convention rights can be directly enforced against public authorities: **3.22**

(a) as a statutory cause of action for breach of human rights where a public authority has not acted compatibly with the Convention. For example, Scottish prisoners were awarded damages after enduring the practice of slopping out in prison.[33] A claim for damages under the Human Rights Act is not a claim for breach of statutory duty, but a free-standing statutory remedy;[34]

(b) as a head of illegality in judicial review proceedings. For example, it could be argued that a decision to refuse to allow a journalist access to a prisoner was ultra vires because rules contravened Article 10 of the Convention and the primary legislation did not require them to be read or given effect in that form, so founding a judicial review;[35]

(c) as a defence in any proceedings that a public authority might itself bring against an individual which are themselves contrary to the Convention or founded on a breach of the Convention. For example, a defendant in criminal proceedings might raise a violation of the Convention by the prosecution in his or her defence.[36]

8. Section 8—judicial remedies

Section 8(1) gives a court a wide power to grant such relief, remedies, or orders as it considers just and appropriate, provided they are within its existing powers.[37] The different remedies that may be granted by courts are discussed in Chapter 4. Briefly, damages may be awarded, but only if necessary to afford 'just satisfaction' to the claimant.[38] If another remedy or exercise of the court's power could achieve this effect, damages should not be awarded.   **3.23**

9. Section 9—judicial acts

Section 9 focuses on how the 'public body' provisions operate against courts which have allegedly acted contrary to the Convention. Although courts are public authorities, proceedings may not be brought directly against them for failure to comply with section 6(1) during the course of their determinations. Proceedings in respect of judicial acts under section 7(1)(a) may be brought only by exercising a right of appeal or as prescribed by rules. However, awards of damages may be   **3.24**

---

[33] *Somerville v Scottish Ministers* [2007] UKHL 44, [2007] 1 WLR 2734.

[34] *R (Greenfield) v Secretary of State for the Home Department* [2005] UKHL 14, [2005] 1 WLR 673, at para 19.

[35] *R v Secretary of State for the Home Department, ex p Simms* [2000] 2 AC 115.

[36] *R (Kebilene) v DPP* [2002] 2 AC 326. See also, in a civil law context, *Manchester City Council v Pinnock* [2010] UKSC 45, [2011] 2 AC 104.

[37] The powers of existing courts or tribunals may be enlarged by order: s 7(11).

[38] Section 8(3).

made against the Crown if they are necessary to compensate a person as required by Article 5(5) of the Convention.

10. Section 11—safeguard for existing human rights

3.25　Section 11 of the Act provides, for the avoidance of doubt, that reliance on Convention rights does not restrict reliance on other legal rights, or procedural methods of enforcing them. This has two important effects. First, it cannot be argued that any pre-existing right (for example under an existing discrimination statute) is impliedly limited by reference to Strasbourg jurisprudence: the Convention rights are a floor, not a ceiling. Secondly, litigants are not required to pursue alternative remedies before relying on the Convention. A Human Rights Act argument can be run at the same time as any other arguments a litigant may have, without any requirement first to exhaust alternative remedies.

11. Sections 12 and 13—respect for freedoms

3.26　Sections 12 and 13 provide specific assurances as to the respect that will be afforded to freedom of expression and freedom of thought, conscience, and religion: these are 'comfort clauses' for sections of the press and certain religious organizations.[39]

12. Designated derogations and reservations

3.27　The Human Rights Act provides for limited 'designated derogations and reservations' from the effect of the Convention under sections 1(2), 14–17, and Schedules 2 and 3. The provisions in the Convention which allow the protection of human rights to be limited are considered in Chapter 2, paras 2.40–2.76.

13. Relationship with the common law

3.28　Although the common law previously recognized some fundamental rights and the Convention could be used in some circumstances to give clarity to English law, there were clear lacunae in the protection offered to human rights in the UK. The protection of privacy, for example, has been significantly developed and extended by the application of Convention principles.[40] This has led some commentators to argue that the Human Rights Act has 'reinvigorated' the common law.[41]

3.29　　However, there is a growing judicial tendency to emphasize the power of the common law to protect rights. The relationship between the common law and the Human Rights Act was recently analysed by the Supreme Court in *Kennedy v Charity Commission*, a case concerning the scope of the right to receive information

---

[39] See the discussion at paras 3.80–3.83.
[40] See ch 7, paras 7.287–7.299.
[41] Lord Irvine, 'The Impact of the Human Rights Act' [2003] PL 308; and English and Havers (eds), *An Introduction to Human Rights and the Common Law* (Oxford: Hart Publishing, 2000).

under Article 10.[42] Lord Mance forcefully asserted the primacy of the common law as a starting point for the protection of human rights:

Since the passing of the Human Rights Act 1998, there has too often been a tendency to see the law in areas touched on by the Convention solely in terms of the Convention rights. But the Convention rights represent a threshold protection; and, especially in view of the contribution which common lawyers made to the Convention's inception, they may be expected, at least generally even if not always, to reflect and to find their homologue in the common or domestic statute law... In some areas, the common law may go further than the Convention, and in some contexts it may also be inspired by the Convention rights and jurisprudence (the protection of privacy being a notable example). And in time, of course, a synthesis may emerge. But the natural starting point in any dispute is to start with domestic law, and it is certainly not to focus exclusively on the Convention rights, without surveying the wider common law scene... Greater focus in domestic litigation on the domestic legal position might also have the incidental benefit that less time was taken in domestic courts seeking to interpret and reconcile different judgments (often only given by individual sections of the European Court of Human Rights) in a way which that court itself, not being bound by any doctrine of precedent, would not itself undertake.[43]

This new-found focus on the common law may prefigure the Supreme Court's response should the Human Rights Act be repealed. In some areas at least, common law rights could potentially provide similar protection to the Convention rights.

D. THE HUMAN RIGHTS ACT MECHANISM IN DETAIL

The key Human Rights Act mechanism is the interplay between sections 6, 3, 4, and 2, which—though they preserve parliamentary sovereignty—have fundamentally altered both the manner in which courts can scrutinize legislation and the ways in which judges must interpret common law.[44]   **3.30**

1. Section 6

As outlined earlier, section 6(1) provides that it is unlawful for a 'public authority' to act in a way which is incompatible with a Convention right. As courts and tribunals are defined as public authorities they have their own primary duty to act compatibly with the Convention.[45] Parliamentary sovereignty is preserved by section 6(2), which limits the section 6(1) duty in circumstances where the court or tribunal could not have acted differently as a result of a statutory obligation which *cannot* be read to give effect to it in a way which is compatible with the Convention rights, notwithstanding the obligation in section 3 to do so if possible. This clever device   **3.31**

---

[42] [2014] UKSC 20, [2014] 2 WLR 808.

[43] Ibid, para 46. As Lord Toulson stated at para 133: 'it was not the purpose of the Human Rights Act that the common law should become an ossuary'.

[44] *R (Kebilene) v DPP* [2002] 2 AC 326 per Lord Hope. See also *Nasseri v Secretary of State for the Home Department* [2009] UKHL 23, [2010] 1 AC 1 at [19] per Lord Hoffmann.

[45] Section 6(3)(a).

places courts and tribunals themselves under a primary obligation to give effect to Convention rights except where they are prevented from doing so by statute.

3.32   The obligation upon courts to give effect to the Convention wherever possible applies to all cases. The consequence is that Convention questions are pivotal in cases where courts or tribunals are deciding the scope of a statutory provision (even one which regulates the behaviour of one private individual to another); where they are determining what the common law is (in so far as this is within their jurisdiction); or when they are exercising a judicial discretion—for example, the exercise of judicial discretion as to whether to grant an injunction to give effect to Articles 8 and 10.[46]

2. Section 3[47]

3.33   The interpretative obligation in section 3(1) of the Human Rights Act is a strong one. The requirement that courts and tribunals *must* read primary and subordinate legislation and give it effect in a way which is compatible with Convention rights 'so far as it is possible to do so' has been held to mean 'unless it is plainly impossible'.[48] The Government rejected amendments proposed during the passage of the Human Rights Bill to reduce this to 'so far as it is *reasonable* to do so' precisely because it wished to preserve the strong obligation to find all 'possible' interpretations of a provision which were compatible with the Convention. Section 3 has been characterized as a 'strong interpretative obligation',[49] not an 'optional canon of construction'.[50]

3.34   The interpretative obligation applies to both primary and secondary legislation whenever it was enacted, that is, whether before or after the enactment of the Human Rights Act so 'it is as though legislation which predates [the Human Rights Act] and conflicts with the Convention has to be treated as being subsequently amended to incorporate the language of section 3'.[51]

3.35   The interpretative obligation in section 3(1) is a general one: a claimant seeking a declaration as to the meaning of legislation under section 3(1) need not be a 'victim'—it is sufficient that he or she has an interest and standing.[52]

3.36   The purposive approach to statutory construction is similar to that adopted by the Court of Justice of the European Union in giving effect to EU law,[53] and to

---

[46] *Re S (a child) (identification: restrictions on publication)* [2004] UKHL 47, [2005] 1 AC 593.

[47] See further Gearty, 'Reconciling Parliamentary Democracy and Human Rights' (2002) 118 LQR 248; Gearty, 'Revisiting s 3(1) of the Human Rights Act' (2003) 119 LQR 551; Sales, 'A comparison of the principle of legality and section 3 of the Human Rights Act 1998' (2009) 125 LQR 598.

[48] *R v A (No 2)* [2001] UKHL 25, [2002] 1 AC 45.

[49] See Lord Steyn and Lord Cooke in *R (Kebilene) v DPP* [2002] 2 AC 326; see also Lord Bingham in *A-G's Reference (No 4 of 2002)* [2004] UKHL 43, [2005] 1 AC 264 ('the interpretative obligation under section 3 is a very strong and far reaching one').

[50] Lord Nicholls in *Re S (care order: implementation of a care plan)* [2002] UKHL 10, [2002] 2 AC 291 at [37].

[51] Lord Woolf in *Donoghue v Poplar Housing* [2001] EWCA Civ 595, [2002] QB 48.

[52] *R (Rusbridger) v Attorney General* [2003] UKHL 38, [2004] 2 AC 357 per Lord Steyn.

[53] eg *Litster v Forth Dry Dock and Engineering Co Ltd* [1990] 1 AC 546.

those adopted by Strasbourg bodies to provide for effective, not merely theoretical, guarantees of protection for human rights.[54]

When applying section 3 in practice the courts first, using ordinary principles of statutory construction, decide whether the primary legislation is compatible with a Convention right. If there is an incompatibility they will then go on to consider the application of section 3. In doing this, courts try to isolate and identify the precise word or phrase in the legislation which is incompatible. Claimants must identify 'with precision' the particular statutory provision which is said to contravene Convention rights.[55]

The House of Lords has confirmed that section 3 may require legislation to be given a Convention-compliant meaning even where there is no ambiguity in the statute which would lead to doubt about its alternative 'natural' meaning.[56] Additionally, the obligation under section 3 may sometimes require the courts to adopt a linguistically strained interpretation of legislation.[57] As well as potentially modifying both the meaning and effect of primary and secondary legislation, it has been accepted that this exercise may also require the court to depart from the parliamentary intention behind the Act.[58]

Courts may comply with the interpretative obligation by 'reading in' additional words so as to give effect to the presumed intended effect of the Convention, or by 'reading down' so as to apply a narrow interpretation of the legislation and enable the court to render it compatible with Convention rights. For example, in *R (GC) v Commissioner of Police of the Metropolis*, section 3 was applied so as to read down section 64(1A) of the Police and Criminal Evidence Act 1984 (which provides that fingerprints and DNA samples 'may be retained after they have fulfilled the purposes for which they were taken'); it did not give the police the power to retain such data from all suspects indefinitely.[59] In this way, the domestic provision was consistent with Article 8 of the Convention.[60] Another technique the courts may use involves clarifying what the effect of the provision is without altering the ordinary meaning of the words used.[61]

In *Ghaidan v Godin-Mendoza*[62] the House of Lords stressed that the strong interpretative obligation in section 3 is crucial to the working of the Human Rights Act, that it should provide the main remedy, and that 'in practical effect there is a strong rebuttable presumption in favour of an interpretation consistent with Convention rights'. A broad approach to interpretation is necessary to fulfil the 'core remedial

3.37

3.38

3.39

3.40

---

[54] See ch 2, paras 2.07–2.19.

[55] *R v A (No 2)* [2001] UKHL 25, [2001] 1 AC 45 at [110] per Lord Hope.

[56] Lord Nicholls in *Ghaidan v Godin-Mendoza* [2004] UKHL 30, [2004] 2 AC 557 at [29].

[57] *R v A (No 2)* [2001] UKHL 25, [2001] 1 AC 45 at [4]–[45] and [67]–[68] per Lord Steyn.

[58] Lord Nicholls in *Ghaidan v Godin-Mendoza* [2004] UKHL 30, [2004] 2 AC 557 at [30].

[59] [2011] UKSC 21, [2011] 1 WLR 1230.

[60] In this way, the Supreme Court gave effect to the ECtHR judgment in *S and Marper v UK* (2008) 48 EHRR 1169 and departed from its earlier decision in *R (S) v Chief Constable of the South Yorkshire Police* [2004] UKHL 39, [2004] 1 WLR 2196.

[61] Lord Hope in *R v Lambert* [2001] UKHL 37, [2002] 2 AC 545.

[62] [2004] UKHL 30, [2004] 2 AC 557 at [50].

purpose' of section 3. Arguments based on parliamentary sovereignty, though a significant consideration, should not be used to limit the interpretative obligation in section 3 or the constitutional purpose of the Human Rights Act to protect Convention rights.[63] During the passage of the Human Rights Bill, the Lord Chancellor said that 'in 99% of all cases that will arise, there will be no need for judicial declarations of incompatibility because of the intended impact of s 3'.[64] Despite occasional reminders by the House of Lords that parliamentary sovereignty is a judge-made doctrine, potentially capable of judicial limitation, the supremacy of Parliament 'is still the *general* principle of our constitution'.[65] Ultimately, the structure of the Human Rights Act preserves parliamentary sovereignty. If Parliament disagrees with the courts' interpretation of a statute in line with the Convention it is free to override their decision by amending the legislation and expressly reinstating the provision that conflicts with fundamental rights[66]—although 'the courts will of course decline to hold that Parliament has interfered with fundamental rights unless it has made its intentions crystal clear'.[67]

3.41   However, though stronger than any previous rule of interpretation, section 3 is still:

only a rule of interpretation. It does not entitle the judges to act as legislators... The compatibility is to be achieved only so far as this is possible. Plainly this will not be possible if the legislation contains provisions which expressly contradict the meaning which the enactment would have to be given to make it compatible.[68]

Similarly, when reading words into legislation, the courts have stressed that these words must be consistent with the scheme and essential principles of the legislation.[69]

3.42   The leading case on the limits of section 3 is *Re S (care order: implementation of care plan)*.[70] The House of Lords held the Court of Appeal's attempt to construe the Children Act 1989 as compatible with the Convention departed too far from the scheme of the legislation and key principles of the Children Act: 'a meaning which departs substantially from a fundamental feature of an Act of Parliament is likely to have crossed the boundary between interpretation and amendment'.[71] Similarly, in *R (Wright) v Secretary of State for Health*, the statute could not properly be read in a compatible manner. Baroness Hale declined to set out how she would 'right'

---

[63] Ibid at [106] per Lord Rodger.

[64] *Hansard*, HL, col 840 (5 February 1998).

[65] See Lord Steyn in *R (Jackson) v Attorney-General* [2005] UKHL 56, [2006] 1 AC 262 at [102]; also Lord Hope at [107] and Baroness Hale at [159].

[66] Cf Gearty, 'Reconciling Parliamentary Democracy and Human Rights' (2002) 118 LQR 248.

[67] *R (Jackson) v Attorney-General* [2005] UKHL 56, [2006] 1 AC 262 at [159] per Baroness Hale.

[68] *R v A (No 2)* [2001] UKHL 25, [2001] 1 AC 45 at [108]. See also *R v Lambert* [2001] UKHL 37, [2002] 2 AC 545 at [79] per Lord Hope; *R v Secretary of State for the Home Department, ex p Anderson and Taylor* [2002] UKHL 46, [2003] 1 AC 837.

[69] Lord Bingham in *R v Secretary of State for the Home Department, ex p Anderson and Taylor* [2002] UKHL 46, [2003] 1 AC 837 at [70].

[70] [2002] UKHL 10, [2002] 2 AC 291.

[71] Ibid at [40].

the problem, emphasizing that it was not for their Lordships 'to attempt to rewrite the legislation'.[72]

Compatible interpretation through section 3(1) is also impossible where the leg- 3.43 islation in question has wide-ranging implications and raises policy issues which it would be inappropriate or impossible for courts to determine, or would require the construction of a wide-ranging new extra-statutory scheme.[73]

When examining the rationale which underlies legislation and determining the 3.44 policy objective of particular provisions, courts can refer to sources outside the statute such as white papers, *Hansard*, and explanatory notes. However, resort to materials such as *Hansard* should be rare and the court should be careful to use them only as background material, not treat the ministerial or other statement as indicative of the objective intention of Parliament, and assess the proportionality of any statutory measure by reference to the facts of the case before the court alone.[74]

3. Interplay of sections 3 and 19

Section 19 requires the minister introducing a piece of legislation to express 3.45 an opinion as to the compatibility of the legislation with the Convention. It is intended to encourage the executive to address the issue of whether proposed legislation is compatible with the Convention at a formative stage. A statement of compatibility under section 19(1)(a) is also intended to act as evidence that a Convention-compliant interpretation of the legislation is intended by Parliament, and to be 'a strong spur to the courts to find means of construing statutes compatibly with the Convention'.[75] Cabinet Office guidance says that if, after further debate or amendment, a minister considered that the provisions of a Bill no longer met the standards required for a section 19(1)(a) statement, 'it would be a breach of the Ministerial Code to proceed towards Royal Assent without either amending the provisions or informing Parliament of the issue'.[76] It is only in very rare circumstances that a minister has made a statement under section 19(1)(b) that, although he cannot be sure that legislation may be incompatible with the Convention, the Government wishes to pass it anyway.[77]

---

[72] [2009] UKHL 3, [2009] 1 AC 739 at [39].

[73] *Re S (care order: implementation of a care plan)* [2002] UKHL 10, [2002] 2 AC 291; *Bellinger v Bellinger* [2003] UKHL 11, [2003] 2 AC 467; *R (Wright) v Secretary of State for Health* [2009] UKHL 3, [2009] 1 AC 739 at [39]; *AS (Somalia) v Secretary of State for the Home Department* [2009] UKHL 32, [2009] 1 WLR 1385.

[74] See Lord Nicholls in *Wilson v Secretary of State for Trade and Industry* [2003] UKHL 40, [2004] 1 AC 816 at [61]–[67].

[75] Lord Irvine of Lairg, Tom Sargant Memorial Lecture, 16 December 1997.

[76] Cabinet Office, *Guide to Making Legislation: ECHR*, 6 May 2009, available at <http://www.cabinetoffice.gov.uk>.

[77] See the s 19(1)(b) statement made in respect of the ban on the broadcasting of political advertising in ss 319 and 321 of the Communications Act 2003, made in the light of *Vgt Verein gegen Tierfabriken v Switzerland* (2001) 34 EHRR 159. The House of Lords—and later the Grand Chamber of the EctHR—in fact held the ban to be compatible with Art 10 in *R (Animal Defenders International) v Secretary of State for Culture, Media and Sport* [2008] UKHL 15, [2008] 1 AC 1312 and *Animal Defenders International v United Kingdom* [2013] 57 EHRR 21.

3.46   In practice, a statement under section 19 has not had a significant effect upon courts.[78] Lord Hope described it as 'no more than expressions of opinion by the minister...they are not binding on the court, nor do they have any persuasive authority'.[79] When Whitehall assesses whether a particular provision complies with the Convention, it applies the traditional 'Strasbourg-proofing' test, which existed before the Human Rights Act—that is, whether, on the balance of probabilities, the provisions of the Bill would be found compatible with Convention rights if challenged in court.[80] In addition, ministers seem to assume that all those public authorities that have to implement the provision will act in compliance with the Convention if they have the power to do so. So, for instance, a Bill that gave wide discretion to the police to act in ways which would clearly violate the Convention would still be assessed as complying with the Convention because the discretion would be constrained by the Human Rights Act.[81]

4. Interplay of sections 3 and 4[82]

3.47   The dividing line between interpreting and legislating under section 3 of the Human Rights Act has an important impact upon the power conferred on higher courts to make 'statements of incompatibility' under section 4. Section 4 states that, where legislation cannot be read compatibly with the Convention, courts are empowered to make a declaration of incompatibility. Logically, if courts find it impossible to construe primary legislation compatibly with the Convention under section 3 then, as 'a measure of last resort',[83] they should declare it incompatible under section 4.

3.48   In *Secretary of State for the Home Department v MB*[84] the Court of Appeal applied section 3 to achieve a Human Rights Act-compatible construction of the 'control order' provisions in the Prevention of Terrorism Act 2005, and reversed the declaration of incompatibility made by the High Court.[85] However, in *R (Hooper) v Secretary of State for Work and Pensions*[86] the provisions of the Social Security (Contributions and Benefits) Act 1992 relating to 'widows' could not be read under section 3 to include 'widowers'. As a result, the court held that the discriminatory provisions (on the grounds of sex within Article 14 read with Article 8) were incompatible with the Convention, and the court made a declaration of incompatibility under section 4 of the Human Rights Act.

---

[78] Though see Lord Bingham in *Animal Defenders* at [33] explaining why the s 19(1)(b) statement in fact gave Parliament's judgment on the importance of the legislation particular weight.

[79] *R v A (No 2)* [2001] UKHL 25, [2002] 1 AC 45 at [69] per Lord Hope.

[80] Home Office evidence to the Joint Committee on Human Rights (as set out in para 15 of JCHR Report 2000–2001, HL 66, HC 332).

[81] *R v A (No 2)* [2001] UKHL 25, [2002] 1 AC 45.

[82] See Sales, 'Rights—consistent interpretation and the Human Rights Act 1998' (2011) 127 LQR 217.

[83] Lord Steyn in *Ghaidan v Godon-Mendoza* [2004] UKHL 30, [2004] 2 AC 557.

[84] [2006] EWCA Civ 1140, [2007] QB 415.

[85] See also the appeal to the House of Lords: [2007] UKHL 46, [2008] 1 AC 440.

[86] [2003] EWCA Civ 813; and upheld by the House of Lords at [2005] UKHL 29, [2005] 1 WLR 1681.

When the whole scheme of the legislation is inconsistent with Convention rights 3.49 (or where it contains several incompatibilities) it is unlikely that section 3 can be used to remedy the defect in the statute. Therefore, the courts will need to turn to section 4 and consider making a declaration of incompatibility. For example, in *R (Wright and ors) v Secretary of State for Health* the House of Lords considered it impossible to use section 3 to interpret the 'provisional blacklisting' provisions for care workers in the Care Standards Act 2000 in a Human Rights Act-compliant manner, and therefore declared the relevant provisions incompatible.[87] And in *R (F) v Secretary of State for the Home Department* the Supreme Court likewise held that the indefinite requirements imposed on those convicted of sexual offences to notify the authorities of their travel plans by virtue of the Sexual Offences Act 2003 were incompatible with Article 8 of the Convention; a declaration of incompatibility was therefore made.[88]

5. Section 2[89]

Section 2 is the provision by which Convention rights have been 'brought much 3.50 more fully into the jurisprudence of the courts throughout the United Kingdom and their interpretation... far more subtly and powerfully woven into our law'.[90] It provides that a court or tribunal determining a question which has arisen under any statute in connection with a Convention right *must* take account of any judgment, decision, declaration, or advisory opinion of the ECtHR, opinion or decision of the Commission, or decision of the Committee of Ministers, whenever made or given, so far as, in the opinion of the court or tribunal, it is relevant to the proceedings in which that question has arisen. The decisions of the different Strasbourg organs carry different weights, and decisions of the Court sitting as a Grand Chamber take precedence.[91]

In the view of the Grand Chamber, our courts are obliged to apply Strasbourg 3.51 decisions.[92] However, section 2 of the Human Rights Act requires a court only to take a Strasbourg judgment into account, and not to follow it.[93] In the first decade of the Human Rights Act, the domestic courts took the view that the purpose of section 2 was to ensure that the same Convention rights are enforced under the Human Rights Act as would be enforced by the Strasbourg Court and section 2

---

[87] [2009] UKHL 3, [2009] 1 AC 739.

[88] [2010] UKSC 17, [2011] 1 AC 331.

[89] Klug and Wildbore, 'Follow or Lead? The Human Rights Act and the European Court of Human Rights' [2010] EHRLR 621.

[90] See *Rights Brought Home: The Human Rights Bill* (Cm 3782, 1997) para 1.14.

[91] See ch 8.

[92] *Home Secretary v AF (No 3)* [2009] UKHL 28, [2010] 2 AC 269. See also *R (Anderson) v Secretary of State for the Home Department* [2002] UKHL 46, [2003] 1 AC 837 at [18] and *Cadder v HM Advocate* [2010] UKSC 43, [20101] 1 WLR 2601 at [46].

[93] *R v Horncastle* [2009] UKSC 14, [2010] 2 AC 373 (a seven-judge court).

did not enable courts to adopt an autonomous domestic meaning of Convention rights.[94] As Lord Bingham said in *R (Ullah) v Special Adjudicator*:[95]

It is of course open to member states to provide for rights more generous than those guaranteed by the Convention, but such provision should not be the product of interpretation of the Convention by national courts, since the meaning of the Convention should be uniform throughout the states party to it. The duty of national courts is to keep pace with the Strasbourg jurisprudence as it evolves over time: no more, but certainly no less.[96]

Occasionally, the Supreme Court went further than strictly required by Strasbourg, generally when ECtHR jurisprudence was not well developed,[97] but in general *Ullah* was interpreted to require a strict adherence to Strasbourg decisions. As Lord Rodger famously stated in *AF (No 3)*: 'Strasbourg has spoken, the case is closed.'[98]

3.52   In the last few years, the willingness of the domestic courts to depart from Strasbourg case law has increased. It was established early in the life of the Human Rights Act that one circumstance in which domestic courts may decline to follow Strasbourg case law is when the decision is based on a clear misunderstanding of domestic law or procedure.[99] The principle was stretched in *R v Horncastle* in which the Supreme Court actively entered into a dialogue with the Strasbourg court over the admission of hearsay evidence in criminal trials.[100] The Supreme Court declined to follow the decision in *Al-Khawaja and Tahery v UK* and effectively invited the UK to appeal to the Grand Chambers to reconsider its decision in *Al-Khawaja*.[101] The Grand Chamber accepted the Supreme Court's analysis of the hearsay rules and found that hearsay could be admitted in certain circumstances without violating Article 6.[102]

3.53   Many senior judges have now questioned the wisdom of the *Ullah* principle. Baroness Hale argued in 2011 that the 'mirror principle...can suggest a position of deference [to the Strasbourg court] from which it is difficult to have an effective dialogue'.[103] In *Ambrose v Harris*, Lord Kerr attacked the '*Ullah*-type reticence'

---

[94] *N v Secretary of State for the Home Department* [2005] UKHL 31, [2005] 2 AC 296; *R (Ullah) v Special Adjudicator* [2004] UKHL 26, [2004] 2 AC 323; *R (Al Jedda) v Secretary of State for Defence* [2007] UKHL 58, [2008] 1 AC 332.

[95] [2004] UKHL 26, [2004] 2 AC 323.

[96] See also Lord Hope in *N v Secretary of State for the Home Department* [2005] UKHL 31, [2005] 2 AC 296 at [25]. This case has been consistently followed on numerous occasions by the House of Lords and Supreme Court.

[97] See, eg *Re G* [2008] UKHL 38, [2009] 1 AC 173; *EM (Lebanon) v Secretary of State for the Home Department* [2008] UKHL 64, [2009] 1 AC 1198.

[98] *Secretary of State for the Home Department v AF (No 3)* [2009] UKHL 28, [2010] 2 AC 269 at [98]. See also *Manchester City Council v Pinnock* [2010] UKSC 45, [2011] 2 AC 104 at [48].

[99] *R v Spear* [2002] UKHL 31, [2003] 1 AC 734 at [12]–[13], declining to follow *Morris v UK* (2002) 34 EHRR 1253; see *R v Horncastle* [2009] UKSC 14, [2010] 2 AC 373, declining to follow *Al Khawaja and Tahery v UK* (2009) 49 EHRR 1 (the latter case is currently pending before the Grand Chamber), and *Tomlinson and ors v Birmingham City Council* [2010] UKSC 8, [2010] 2 WLR 471.

[100] *R v Horncastle* [2009] UKSC 14, [2010] 2 AC 373.

[101] *Al Khawaja and Tahery v UK* (2009) 49 EHRR 1.

[102] *Al Khawaja and Tahery v UK* (2011) 32 BHRC 1.

[103] 'Argentoratum Locutum: Is the Supreme Court supreme?', Nottingham Human Rights Lecture, 2011.

under which 'it is…considered wrong to attempt to anticipate developments at the supra-national level of the Strasbourg court' and which dictates that domestic courts 'should not go where Strasbourg has not yet gone'.[104] The Supreme Court has not yet revised the principle, but recent decisions reveal that it is straining at the boundaries. In *R (Nicklinson) v Ministry of Justice* the Supreme Court found that Strasbourg had given states a wide margin of appreciation to determine the compatibility with Article 8 of domestic laws prohibiting assisted suicide. It was, therefore, for the national courts to 'decide the issue for themselves, with relatively unconstraining guidance from the Strasbourg court, albeit bearing in mind the constitutional proprieties and such guidance from the Strasbourg jurisprudence, and indeed our own jurisprudence, as seems appropriate'.[105]

Section 2 does not displace the doctrine of precedent in English law. In *Kay v Lambeth London Borough Council*, the House of Lords held that lower courts remained bound to follow higher domestic authority in preference to Strasbourg case law, save in wholly exceptional cases where the previous domestic decision was reached without reference to the Convention, before the Human Rights Act was in force and led to a finding against the United Kingdom in the European Court of Human Rights.[106]

3.54

6. Interplay of sections 2 and 3

Strasbourg case law requires *effective* protection of the Convention rights, ensuring rights that are not 'theoretical or illusory but…practical and effective'.[107] Accordingly, to comply with their obligation under section 3(1) of the Human Rights Act, UK courts have to interpret statutory provisions so as to give real and effective protection to the rights that the Convention was intended to safeguard.

3.55

Under sections 2 and 3 of the Human Rights Act, the Convention must be given effect wherever possible. Because Strasbourg case law must be taken into account, the Strasbourg method of judicial reasoning has gradually entered UK legal practice over the past decade. Where there is potentially a Convention question in play, the domestic court or tribunal first has to identify the right in question, including the positive aspects of the right (that is, the obligations of the court, as a public body, to take positive steps to protect the right). Then it must identify the alleged interference with the right and look to see whether it is prescribed by law. It must then decide what objectives are said to be served by the interference, and whether the interference is necessary in a democratic society for

3.56

---

[104] *Ambrose v Harris* [2011] UKSC 43, [2011] 1 WLR 2435 at [126]. See also *Children's Rights Alliance for England (CRAE) v Secretary of State for Justice and ors* [2013] EWCA Civ 34, [2013] 1 WLR 3667, per Lord Justice Laws at [64]. See also Lord Justice Laws, 'The Common Law and Europe', The Hamlyn Lectures, 27 November 2013. He described *Ullah* as a 'wrong turning in our law', para 26.

[105] [2014] UKSC 38, [2014] 3 All ER 843 at [70].

[106] [2006] UKHL 10, [2006] 2 AC 465. Where a Court of Appeal decision is inconsistent with a later decision of the ECtHR, the Court of Appeal may, but is not obliged to, depart from its previous decision: *R (RJM)(FC) v Secretary of State for Work and Pensions* [2008] UKHL 63, [2008] 3 WLR 1023.

[107] *Artico v Italy* (1980) 3 EHRR 1, para 33; *Airey v Ireland* (1979) 2 EHRR 305.

the purposes of achieving those objectives. This involves a careful application of the principles of proportionality, and in certain circumstances an explicit balancing of the rights of individuals against the rights and freedoms of others and the general public interest.

3.57 Section 2 limits the effect of section 3 to the extent required to give effect to the doctrine of precedent. However, in the criminal context, the courts have shown themselves willing to depart from the strict principles of *stare decisis* when faced with a conflict between a binding House of Lords' decision and a more recent decision of the Privy Council.[108] Should the courts fail to follow an ECtHR decision by application of the principle of *stare decisis*, this leaves the United Kingdom open to an adverse judgment in Strasbourg. The effects of sections 2 and 11, the common law power of the courts to develop free-standing human rights principles, and the right of individual petition to Strasbourg, ought to mean that the Strasbourg jurisprudence is a long-stop or bottom line for human rights protection, but not a barrier to the development of free-standing domestic law human rights principles. It should be treated as a floor, not a ceiling.[109]

E. PUBLIC AUTHORITIES AND THE HUMAN RIGHTS ACT: MEANING OF 'PUBLIC AUTHORITY' AND 'FUNCTIONS OF A PUBLIC NATURE'

3.58 Section 6 of the Human Rights Act imposed a new statutory duty upon all public authorities to act compatibly with the Convention, and section 7 created new causes of action through which these 'vertically effective' obligations can be enforced. In other words, if a body is a public authority, then individuals have *direct* statutory remedies against them for breach of section 6(1), either by way of judicial review or for breach of statutory duty. As a result, the question of which types of bodies come within the definition of a 'public authority' for the purposes of the Act is a very important one, not only for individual litigants seeking to ascertain whether they have a cause of action, but for the overall ambit of the Act.

3.59 'Public authorities' that are subject to the direct 'vertical' effect of the Human Rights Act include core public authorities, which are 'obviously' public in nature, in respect of all their functions, whether the nature of those functions is public or private.[110] However, section 6(3)(b) and (5) also deem to be a public authority any person certain of whose functions are functions of a public nature *in respect of the performance of those public functions*, but not in respect of acts *the nature of which is private*. The concepts of 'functions of a public nature' and acts 'the nature of which is private' are therefore critical to understanding the ambit of the Act. The case law on this subject is complex and controversial.

---

[108] *R v James and Karimi* [2006] EWCA Crim 14, [2006] 1 All ER 759.

[109] For an example of the common law providing protection in circumstances where the HRA did not do so, see *HM Treasury v Ahmed (Nos 1 and 2)* [2010] UKSC 2, [2010] 2 AC 534.

[110] Section 6(3)(a).

1. 'Core' public authorities

'Core' public authorities include all bodies that are obviously public in nature, such **3.60** as government departments and ministers, local authorities, NHS Trusts, coroners, police, prisons, bodies such as the Parole Board, Legal Services Commission, and the General Medical Council. The House of Lords has favoured a relatively narrow test for core public authority status.[111] Core public authorities must act in conformity with the Convention whether exercising functions governed by public law (for example, assessment to tax) or private law (for example, employment).

2. 'Functional' public authorities

'Functional' or 'hybrid' public authorities in section 6(3)(b) include any person 'certain **3.61** of whose functions are functions of a public nature', but only in relation to public functions. Section 6(5) provides that 'In relation to a particular act, a person is not a public authority by virtue only of subsection (3)(b) if the nature of the act is private'.

The Human Rights Act was intended to apply to 'a wide rather than a narrow **3.62** range of public authorities'[112] and to encompass:

...a realistic and modern definition of the state so as to provide a correspondingly wide protection against the abuse of human rights.[113]

The Lord Chancellor said that: **3.63**

[section 6(3)(b)] is there to include bodies which are not manifestly public authorities, but some of whose functions are only of a public nature...Railtrack would fall into that category because it exercises public functions in its role as a safety regulator, but it is acting privately as a property developer. A private security company would be exercising public functions in relation to the management of a contracted out prison but would be acting privately when, for example, guarding commercial premises. Doctors in general practice would be public authorities in relation to their National Health Service functions, but not in relation to their private patients.[114]

The intention was to reflect the line of Strasbourg case law which holds that a **3.64** state cannot escape liability under the Convention by delegating essentially public functions to private bodies.[115] The effect is that a direct cause of action is available against functional public authorities for acting in breach of the Convention, and hence unlawfully, when the act under challenge is of a public nature, and in contexts where its functions would be amenable to judicial review; but not when they are acting within the scope of their *private* law activities. For example, in general, employment law questions are questions of private law.[116] However, they may be questions of public law if they relate to policy questions.[117]

---

[111] *Aston Cantlow and Wilmcote with Billesley Parochial Church Council v Wallbank* [2003] UKHL 37, [2004] 1 AC 546.
[112] *Hansard*, HL, col 1232 (3 November 1997).
[113] Jack Straw, *Hansard*, HC, cols 405–408 (17 June 1998).
[114] *Hansard*, HL, vol 583, col 811 (24 November 1997).
[115] *Costello-Roberts v United Kingdom* (1995) 19 EHRR 112.
[116] *R v East Berkshire Health Authority, ex p Walsh* [1985] QB 152.
[117] *R v Crown Prosecution Service, ex p Hogg* [1994] COD 237.

3.65 The extent to which private organizations performing delegated public functions should be regarded as functional public authorities has proved controversial.[118] In *Aston Cantlow Parochial Church Council v Wallbank*[119] the determining factor was said to be whether the nature of the function performed was public.[120] It was held that there should be a 'generously wide' interpretation of public function but that there was 'no single test of universal application ... given the diverse nature of governmental functions and the variety of means by which these functions are discharged today'.[121]

3.66 However, although the House of Lords in *Aston Cantlow* appeared to lay down a broad functional approach, it did not expressly overrule the decisions in earlier cases in which courts had taken rather narrower approaches to what factors were relevant to deciding whether a body was a 'functional' public authority. Those cases focused more narrowly on the institutional features of the situation, rather than the nature of the functions being performed, and their place in public service provision.[122] Relevant features, in rendering a function which would otherwise be private, public, had been held to include, for example, whether the body was exercising statutory authority not available to private persons,[123] and the proximity of the relationship between the private body and the delegating public authority.

3.67 The Joint Committee on Human Rights (JCHR) expressed concern about the 'deficit' in protection resulting from the *Leonard Cheshire* decision[124] for those who received public services on a contracted-out basis.[125]

3.68 Since then, a number of cases in the lower courts examined the issue of which bodies are 'functional public authorities' for the purposes of the Human Rights Act.[126] They sometimes appeared to focus closely on the legal nature of the *body* in question, and inadequately on the reality of the functions that particular bodies

---

[118] See JCHR Report, 'The Meaning of Public Authority under the Human Rights Act', 7th Report (2003–04), HL 39, HC 382, February 2004); Sunkin, 'Pushing Forward the Frontiers of Human Rights Protection: The Meaning of Public Authority under the Human Rights Act' [2004] PL 643; Oliver, 'Functions of a Public Nature under the Human Rights Act' [2004] PL 329; Craig, 'Contracting Out, the Human Rights Act, and the Scope of Judicial Review' (2002) 118 LQR 551.

[119] [2003] UKHL 37, [2004] 1 AC 546.

[120] Ibid at [41] per Lord Hope.

[121] Ibid at [12] per Lord Nicholls.

[122] Eg *Donoghue v Poplar Housing Association* [2001] EWCA Civ 595, [2002] QB 48 at [58]; *R (Heather) v Leonard Cheshire Foundation* [2002] EWCA Civ 366, [2002] 2 All ER 936.

[123] See *R (A) v Partnerships in Care Ltd* [2002] EWHC 529 (Admin), [2002] 1 WLR 2610, where the decision of managers of a private psychiatric hospital to alter the care and treatment of a patient was an act of a public nature, susceptible to judicial review, and the hospital managers were, by virtue of the statutory regime and regulations under the Registered Homes Act 1984 and the Mental Health Act 1983, a public authority for the purposes of the Human Rights Act.

[124] *R (Heather) v Leonard Cheshire Foundation* [2002] EWCA Civ 366, [2002] 2 All ER 936.

[125] JCHR, 'The Meaning of Public Authority under the Human Rights Act', 7th Report (2003–2004), HL 39, HC 382, February 2004.

[126] See, eg *Cameron v Network Rail Infrastructure Ltd* [2006] EWHC 1133 (QBD); *R (Mullin) v Jockey Club Appeal Board (No 1)* [2005] EWHC 2197 (Admin), [2006] ACD 2; *R (Beer) v Hampshire County Council* [2003] EWCA Civ 1056, [2004] 1 WLR 233; *R (West) v Lloyds of London* [2004] EWCA Civ 506, [2004] 3 All ER 251, supply of electricity; *James v London Electricity plc* [2004] EWHC 3226 (QB).

are performing, notwithstanding that Jack Straw (then Home Secretary) had said, when introducing the Bill:

...as we are dealing with public functions and with an evolving situation, we believe that the test must relate to the substance and nature of the act, not to the form and legal personality.[127]

The law therefore took a serious, and, in our view, wrong turn when, in 2007, **3.69** the House of Lords considered the point of principle in *Leonard Cheshire* and, by a bare majority of 3–2, endorsed it in what is now the leading case on the meaning of 'functions of a public nature', *YL v Birmingham City Council*.[128] In that case, the House of Lords held that a privately owned care home which provided accommodation and care for an elderly and vulnerable resident which was both arranged and paid for by the local authority nonetheless did not perform a 'function of a public nature' in doing so. Although the House of Lords endorsed the list of factors it had earlier set out in *Aston Cantlow*, the judges in the majority and the minority afforded significantly different weight to the various factors in that balance.

The majority of the House of Lords in *YL* (Lord Scott, Lord Mance, and Lord **3.70** Neuberger) held that there was a distinction between the council's function in arranging and paying for the care and accommodation pursuant to its statutory duty, and that of the private company in providing the care and accommodation under contract, on a commercial basis (albeit paid for by public money), rather than on the basis of a direct subsidy from public funds. They focused heavily on the company's commercial purposes:

It is neither a charity nor a philanthropist...It receives no public funding, enjoys no special statutory powers, and...charge[s] whatever fees in its commercial judgment it thinks suitable.[129]

In a strongly worded dissent, Lord Bingham and Baroness Hale disagreed. Lord **3.71** Bingham said:

When the 1998 Act was passed, it was very well known that a number of functions formerly carried out by public authorities were now carried out by private bodies. Section 6(3)(b) of the 1998 Act was clearly drafted with this well-known fact in mind. The performance by private body A by arrangement with public body B, and perhaps at the expense of B, of what would undoubtedly be a public function if carried out by B, is in my opinion, precisely the case which section 6(3)(b) was intended to embrace. It is, in my opinion, this case.[130]

Baroness Hale attached importance to the public interest in the provision of such care, the fact that there was public funding for such care, and the coercive powers of the state,[131] and concluded:

Taken together, these factors lead inexorably to the conclusion that the company, in providing accommodation, health and social care for [YL], was performing a function of a public nature.

---

[127] *Hansard*, HC, cols 409–410 (17 June 1998).
[128] [2007] UKHL 27, [2008] 1 AC 95.
[129] Ibid at [26] per Lord Scott.
[130] Ibid at [20].
[131] Ibid at [67]–[69].

This was a function performed for [YL] pursuant to statutory arrangements, at public expense and in the public interest.[132]

3.72   With respect, we agree with the minority in that case that the decision of the majority does not reflect the clear intention of Parliament in adopting a 'functional' approach to the concept of a 'public authority', but, rather, places an erroneous focus on the nature of the provider and its commercial motivation.[133]

3.73   The consequence of *YL* has been considerable uncertainty as to the ambit of the Human Rights Act. For example, the Court of Appeal has held that housing management functions performed by a registered social landlord were 'public functions'.[134] It has also led to a serious protection gap for vulnerable individuals in relation to public services procured from the private sector. As the JCHR pointed out following its inquiry into this issue, the consequence is that 'a central provision of the Human Rights Act has been compromised in a way which reduces the protection it was intended to give to people at some of the most vulnerable moments in their lives'.[135]

F. PRIVATE PARTIES AND THE HUMAN RIGHTS ACT

3.74   The Convention is not 'directly effective' against private litigants. In litigation concerning purely private bodies, or 'functional public authorities' in pursuit of their 'functions of a private nature', there is no stand-alone cause of action for 'breach of the Convention' under section 7 of the Act.[136] It is not therefore possible for one private individual to sue another private legal person for a tort of 'breach of the Convention'.

3.75   The Convention is, however, indirectly enforceable against a private legal person in the following ways:

(a)   Where the effect of a statutory provision is in question in a dispute between private individuals, the courts—as 'public authorities' for the purposes of the Act—are under an obligation to interpret the legislation so as to accord with the Convention (under section 3 in conjunction with section 6(3) of the Human Rights Act). For example, in *Wilson v First County Trust (No 2)*[137] both parties were 'private' individuals. This did not prevent the Court of Appeal deciding that the bar against enforcing a credit agreement breached the pawnbroker's

---

[132] Ibid at [73].

[133] See also the criticisms of Baroness Hale (one of the minority) in her speech to the Salford Human Rights Conference, 4 June 2010: <http://www.supremecourt.gov.uk/docs/speech_100604.pdf>.

[134] *London Quadrant Housing Trust v Weaver* [2009] EWCA Civ 58, [2010] 1 WLR 363.

[135] JCHR, 'The Meaning of Public Authority under the Human Rights Act', 7th Report (2003–2004), HL 39, HC 382, February 2004.

[136] *Campbell v MGN Ltd* [2004] UKHL 22, [2004] 2 AC 457; and the Court of Appeal in *X v Y* [2004] EWCA Civ 662 at [58]. See also the rationale advanced by Murray Hunt in 'The "Horizontal Effect" of the Human Rights Act' [1998] PL 423 and Lord Steyn in '2000–2005: Laying the Foundations of Human Rights Law in the United Kingdom' [2005] EHRLR 349.

[137] [2001] EWCA Civ 633, [2002] QB 74.

right of access to a court under Article 6 of the Convention and the right to property under Article 1 of Protocol 1.[138]

(b) Similarly, where there is a judicial discretion to be exercised, section 6 requires it to be exercised so as to give effect to a Convention right (for example, in civil proceedings between private parties when the court has a discretion regarding the admission of evidence obtained in breach of a Convention right).

(c) Where the rights in question touch upon positive obligations (especially under Articles 2, 3, 4, 8, 10, 11, or 14) the court is itself under a positive obligation to protect individuals from the violation of their rights by other private individuals. For example, in *Venables and Thompson v Newsgroup Newspapers and Associated Newspapers Ltd*[139] the two children who had been convicted of the murder of James Bulger were granted permanent injunctions preventing publication of further information about them on the basis that the Court of Appeal was under a positive obligation to secure their right to life (Article 2) and right to respect for private life (Article 8). The Strasbourg jurisprudence on such positive obligations is a developing field. See paras 2.32–2.39.

(d) Where the courts are dealing with cases involving the common law they are under an obligation to develop the common law to be compatible with Convention rights (by virtue of section 6(3)). The 'horizontal' effects of the Human Rights Act in private litigation have been most marked in this area.

The effects of the Convention on evolving the common law torts have most clearly been seen in a series of cases concerning the privacy of public figures, in which the boundaries of common law torts have been transformed, analysed further in Chapter 7. It has now become clear that a litigant, A, who wishes to use a Convention argument in a case brought against a private opponent, B, will certainly be able to do so if A finds an existing private law argument on which to 'hang' the Convention argument (for example, breach of confidence in tort in relation to an infringement of the right to respect for private life). A could also focus the action on a public body, C, which has failed to protect A's rights from being violated by B. In this way Convention standards have infiltrated, influenced, and even created new common law rights, and will continue to do so.   3.76

G. EXCEPTIONS AND SPECIAL CASES

The Human Rights Act is principally a constitutional instrument of general application. However, one important omission from the Schedule to the Act (Article 13) and two specific provisions (sections 12 and 13) about particular interest groups (the press and religious organizations) require brief explanation.[140]   3.77

---

[138] See also the House of Lords' decision at [2003] UKHL 40, [2004] 1 AC 816 (reversed on other grounds).

[139] [2001] 2 WLR 1038; and *Campbell v MGN Ltd* [2004] UKHL 22, [2004] 2 AC 457.

[140] For a full discussion of the scope and content of Arts 8, 9, 10, and 13 of the Convention, see ch 7.

1. Article 13

3.78   Article 13 imposes a duty on the state to provide the opportunity to test at a national level whether a Convention right has been violated. It guarantees in general terms that there is a suitable national avenue of redress capable of providing a remedy in an appropriate case. However, it does not mean that states have to ensure that a *particular* result is secured. So, for example, the right will be breached where the victim has no right of recourse in the domestic courts[141] or where primary legislation excludes any such challenge. Article 13 is not a free-standing right (that is, a claim cannot be founded on the article alone and must be brought in connection with an alleged breach of another Convention right), but it is not necessary to show a breach of another Convention right before the court can consider its application—it is enough to show that the complaint in relation to the other right is 'arguable' but cannot be argued because there is no means for this to be done before a national court.[142]

3.79   Although Article 13 is not one of the rights included in the Schedule to the Human Rights Act, it was intended that the Act itself would give effect to Articles 1 and 13 by securing the rights and freedoms of the Convention. In other words, Article 13 is given effect by establishing a scheme under which Convention rights can be raised and remedied before UK courts. In *Re S (FC) and ors* Lord Nicholls said:

> Article 13 guarantees the availability at the national level of an effective remedy to enforce the substance of Convention rights. Sections 7 and 8 seek to provide that remedy in this country. The object of these sections is to provide in English law the very remedy article 13 declares is the entitlement of everyone whose rights are violated.[143]

2. Section 12

3.80   The object of section 12 is to emphasize that the courts must pay due regard to Article 10 and the right to freedom of expression contained in that article. It was a response to lobbying by some sections of the press during the passage of the Human Rights Bill which argued that the judiciary might interpret Article 8 of the Convention (right to respect for private and family life) in a way which unacceptably limited the freedom of the press. In practice, those concerns are not justified[144] and section 12 has had little effect.

3.81   Section 12 has a number of components. First, it prevents 'gagging injunctions' being granted *ex parte* except in the rarest of circumstances. It provides that if a court is considering whether to grant any relief that might affect the exercise of the Convention right to freedom of expression *ex parte*, there is a presumption

---

[141] *Halford v United Kingdom* (1997) 24 EHRR 523.

[142] *Boyle and Rice v United Kingdom* (1988) 10 EHRR 425.

[143] [2002] UKHL 10, [2002] 2 AC 291 at [61].

[144] See *Re S (A child) (identification) restrictions on publication* [2004] UKHL 47, [2005] 1 AC 593, in which Lord Steyn explained the 'balancing exercise' that needs to take place in order to balance the competing demands of respect for private life and freedom of expression.

against the grant of such relief.[145] 'No such relief is to be granted' unless the court is satisfied that the person seeking the relief has taken all practicable steps to notify the defendant, or there are compelling reasons why the defendant should not be notified.[146] Secondly, the merits of the claimant's case must be tested before any such restraint is made. Section 12(3) provides that no relief is to be granted so as to restrain publication before trial unless the court is satisfied that the applicant is likely to establish that publication should not be allowed.[147] Thirdly, section 12(4) provides that the court must have 'particular regard' to the right to freedom of expression, and that where the proceedings relate to material which the respondent claims is, or which appears to the court to be, journalistic, literary, or artistic material, the court must have regard to the extent to which the material has, or is about to, become available to the public, or it is, or would be, in the public interest for the material to be published.[148] It must also have regard to any relevant privacy code such as the code issued by the Press Complaints Commission.

Perhaps because Article 10 itself requires 'particular regard' to be given to the right to freedom of expression, in practice, domestic courts have made clear that section 12 adds little to existing domestic or Strasbourg jurisprudence[149] and the court will need to form its own view on the balance between Articles 8 and 10 on the facts of a particular case. This topic has been one of acute public controversy (and considerable public misunderstanding), fuelled by the granting of the first 'super-injunction' in the *Trafigura* case[150] and a number of anonymized injunctions.[151] Whilst it is fairly clear that super-injunctions have been applied for only rarely, and have normally been granted (if at all) only for a limited period, it has been stressed that 'such injunctions [should] only be granted following intense scrutiny by the court in the individual case, and only when it is strictly necessary as a means to ensure that justice is done'.[152]

3.82

---

[145] For a discussion of the scope of the term 'relief', see *A v British Broadcasting Corporation (Scotland)* [2014] UKSC 25, [2014] 2 All ER 1037.

[146] Section 12(1) and (2). Note that in *X & Y v Persons Unknown* [2007] EMLR 290 Eady J concluded that its ambit covered not only the parties to the proceedings but also non-parties who in practice are likely to have their Art 10 right constrained by an injunction. The Report of the Committee on Super-Injunctions, chaired by Lord Neuberger, emphasized that a failure to provide advance notice is only justifiable in exceptional circumstances: para 3.22.

[147] See *Cream Holdings v Banerjee* [2004] UKHL 44, [2005] 1 AC 253 where the House of Lords considered the test under s 12(3) and accorded it a relatively limited effect. See also *Campbell v MGN Limited* [2004] UKHL 22, [2004] 2 AC 457 at [55] per Lord Hoffmann and at [141] per Baroness Hale; and, recently, *ETK v News Group Newspapers* [2011] EWCA Civ 439 at [10(6)].

[148] See *Green Corns Ltd v Clavery Group* [2005] EWHC 958 (QB), where the fact that the information in question was available to the public did not justify withholding an injunction under s 12 because the information was not so widely in the public domain, and re-publication could have an effect and was likely to impact on Art 8 rights.

[149] For the courts' general approach, see *Ashdown v Telegraph Group* [2001] EWCA Civ 1142, [2001] 3 WLR 1368; *Clayton v Clayton* [2006] EWCA Civ 878; and *Re Ward; BBC v CAFCASS Legal* [2007] EWHC 616 (Fam).

[150] *RJW & SJW v The Guardian News and Media Ltd*, Order of Maddison J of 11 September 2009.

[151] See, in particular, *CTB v News Group Newspapers and Imogen Thomas* [2011] EWHC 1232 (QB) (injunction granted) and *Terry v Persons Unknown* [2010] EWHC 119 (QB) (injunction refused).

[152] Report of the Committee on Super-Injunctions, para 2.37; see also para 2.28.

3. Section 13

3.83   During the passage of the Human Rights Bill, fears were expressed on behalf of the Church of England, for example, that the Human Rights Act might lead to questions about whether they could refuse to marry gay couples,[153] or dismiss church schoolteachers who had lost their faith. To address these fears, section 13 provides that if the court's determination of any question under the Act might affect the exercise by a religious organization, whether as an organization or by its members collectively, of the Convention right to freedom of thought, conscience, and religion, it must have particular regard to the importance of that right. This is something that is inherent in the structure of Article 9 of the Convention, which is where that guarantee is to be found. Since the whole scheme of the Convention is to give particular regard to a prima facie right, permitting derogations from it only if they are necessary, proportionate, and so on, the effect of this section is really to add political comfort to religious interests rather than to add anything in terms of practical effect.[154] In most cases where a dispute about the meaning of section 13 might arise, the question is now one governed by the provisions protecting people from discrimination on the grounds of religion or belief,[155] or on the grounds of sexual orientation.[156]

---

[153]   The Marriage (Same Sex Couples) Act 2013 provides that no person can be compelled to perform a marriage of same-sex couples, thus enabling the church to opt out of solemnizing same-sex unions.

[154]   See per Richards J (as he then was) in *R (Amicus) v Secretary of State for Trade and Industry* [2004] EWHC 860 (Admin), [2004] ELR 31 at [41]: 'section 13 of the 1998 Act does not give greater weight to [Art 9] rights than they would otherwise enjoy under the Convention'; see too *R (Williamson) v Secretary of State for Education and Employment* [2002] EWCA Civ 1926 (for s 13 discussion, not overruled by House of Lords); and *R (Surayanda) v Welsh Ministers* [2007] EWCA Civ 893. Ordinarily, the courts do not refer to s 13 when applying Art 9 of the Convention: see, eg *Ladele v London Borough of Islington* [2009] ICR 387 (EAT) and [2009] EWCA Civ 1357, [2010] IRLR 211.

[155]   Equality Act 2010, s 10.

[156]   Equality Act 2010, s 12.

4

ENFORCING THE HUMAN RIGHTS ACT

A. INTRODUCTION

4.01 The Human Rights Act was intended to 'bring rights home', so that any remedy which can be secured in Strasbourg is available in national courts and tribunals. This chapter deals with the practicalities of how the Human Rights Act seeks to achieve this objective and addresses the domestic application of the European Convention for the Protection of Human Rights and Fundamental Freedoms (Convention) concepts discussed in Chapter 2.

4.02 In recognition of the espoused aim of the Act, section 7 is constructed so that litigants can raise Convention arguments in existing causes of action, claims, and proceedings; or, if no such domestic law causes of action are available, to bring stand-alone proceedings to allege breach of a Convention right against a public authority as a statutory tort.

4.03 Section 7 provides that a person who claims that a 'public authority'[1] has acted, or proposes to act, in a way that is incompatible with Convention rights[2] can either bring proceedings against the authority in an appropriate court or tribunal or can raise the Convention arguments concerned in any legal proceedings, but only if he or she can show he or she is, or would be, a 'victim' of the unlawful act.[3]

4.04 The creation of new causes of action against public authorities has brought with it new procedural issues, many of which remain unresolved over a decade after the Act came into force. One such issue is the way in which limitation periods for bringing proceedings directly under section 7(1)(a)[4] interact with other relevant limitation periods. The questions of standing and third-party interventions are important, in particular to the evolution of 'public interest' litigation, because section 7(7) requires English courts to *apply* Strasbourg case law on who is a victim, not simply to 'have regard' to it. This means that the limitations which the European Court of Human Rights (ECtHR) cases impose could restrict the circumstances in which important public interest questions are raised. There are also jurisdictional questions as to where proceedings involving section 6(1) should be brought.

4.05 To 'bring rights home' effectively, the Human Rights Act was drafted to ensure that victims of violations of Convention rights could seek remedies in domestic courts which would afford them 'just satisfaction' for any breaches of Convention rights they had suffered. Reflecting this intention, the Act creates both a cause of action, including a right to damages, under section 8, *and* gives higher courts the power to grant 'declarations of incompatibility' under section 4. The courts also retain existing remedies that fall within the jurisdiction of the relevant court, so other remedies which can be and are awarded under section 8(1) are familiar, such as (in a civil law context): damages; declarations; injunctions; and a mandatory quashing or prohibiting order in judicial review proceedings governed by Part 54 of the Civil Procedure Rules

---

[1] The definition of this term is discussed in ch 3.
[2] Section 6(1).
[3] Section 7(1).
[4] Section 7(5).

(CPR). In criminal proceedings, the remedies available to a defendant who establishes a violation of his or her Convention rights include: an order withdrawing the issue of a summons; a motion to quash an indictment; a stay of the criminal proceedings as abuse of process; the dismissal of the prosecution; the exclusion of evidence (or an order requiring the inclusion of evidence); or even (to reflect the breach) a reduction in sentence. The Court of Appeal has the power to quash a conviction where there has been a breach of Article 6 in the course of the trial.

However, the case law on damages for violations of the Act is increasing but   4.06
remains relatively underdeveloped, and despite the broad phrasing of section 8 permitting courts to grant any relief or remedy within their powers as they consider 'just and appropriate', imaginative remedies remain relatively rare.

B. THE APPROPRIATE FORUM FOR AN ARGUMENT UNDER THE HUMAN RIGHTS ACT

The Human Rights Act was designed to ensure that the Convention becomes an   4.07
intrinsic part of all aspects of the UK legal system and that all courts and tribunals are able to consider arguments brought under the Convention. It does not provide any sort of reference procedure whereby an argument about a Convention point must be sent to a special court for adjudication. Convention arguments are available in every public forum in which legal rights are determined, from the magistrates' court to the Supreme Court (even though only the higher courts have the power to make a declaration of incompatibility and the power to award damages is restricted—see Chapter 3). Section 7 refers to bringing proceedings against a public authority 'in the appropriate court or tribunal'[5] and to relying on Convention rights 'in any legal proceedings',[6] including as a defence.

The ambit of the phrase 'legal proceedings' is not clear, and there may be litiga-   4.08
tion in future about what constitutes a 'legal proceeding'. For example, is a complaint to a statutory ombudsman a legal proceeding? In most cases, the debate is not important because the body conducting the proceeding is itself a public authority and so under a duty to interpret the law in line with the Convention. But questions may arise in relation to non-statutory self-regulatory organizations, especially those apparently subject to contract rather than judicial review, such as the insurance ombudsman or the Jockey Club.[7]

The 'appropriate court or tribunal' is determined by rules issued under the   4.09
Human Rights Act[8] but, broadly, claims go to the court or tribunal most accustomed to dealing with claims analogous to the subject matter in question. For example, the Civil Procedure (Amendment No 4) Rules 2000[9] set out the procedure

---

[5] Section 7(1)(a).
[6] Section 7(1)(b).
[7] See *R v Disciplinary Committee of the Jockey Club, ex p Aga Khan* [1993] 1 WLR 909.
[8] Section 7(2) and (9).
[9] SI 2000/2092.

to be adopted in the Administrative Court; and the Family Procedure Rules 2010[10] give details of the treatment of human rights issues in the family courts. Practice Direction 9 of the Supreme Court Rules 2009[11] makes provision for the treatment of human rights points in the Supreme Court.

4.10 Some illustrative examples of an appropriate forum are as follows. In a false imprisonment claim, a person who wishes to claim damages for breach of Article 3 (freedom from torture or inhuman or degrading treatment) or Article 5 (the right to liberty and security of the person) could bring a claim for breach of statutory duty under section 6(1) of the Human Rights Act in the High Court. Alternatively, the breach could be the basis for a habeas corpus or judicial review application. A demonstrator who is prosecuted for obstruction of the highway or obstruction of a police officer may be able to invoke the right to peaceful assembly in Article 11 as a defence in the Crown Court or magistrates' court. Article 5 arguments can also be used, for example, to argue for the release of a person before the Mental Health Review Tribunal. A taxpayer who wishes to contend that a tax demand based on the withdrawal of an extra-statutory concession is insufficiently precise and hence contrary to Protocol 1, Article 1, might be heard before the Special Commissioners of the Inland Revenue.

4.11 It should be remembered, however, that the lower courts and tribunals do not have the power under section 4(5) of the Human Rights Act to issue a declaration of incompatibility. Where proceedings are brought in the county court and a question of making a declaration of incompatibility has arisen, Part 30 of the CPR requires the court to consider transferring the proceedings to the High Court. However, it is not necessary to transfer the proceedings to the High Court merely because a breach of a Convention right is alleged.[12]

4.12 This cumbersome (and potentially time-consuming) solution to the problem of jurisdiction might have been avoided if the Government had adopted a 'residual reference' procedure akin to a reference to the Court of Justice of the European Union, for cases where an inferior court or tribunal dealing with a Human Rights Act point considered that there might be a case for a declaration of incompatibility that would be beyond its jurisdiction to award. Under such a procedure the declaration could have been made by the High Court but as part of the main proceedings.

4.13 In civil proceedings generally, where a party is seeking to rely on any provision of, or right arising under, the Human Rights Act, or seeks a remedy available under the Act, he or she must, in the statement of case:

(a) give precise details of the Convention right which it is alleged has been infringed and details of the alleged infringement;

(b) specify the relief sought;

(c) state whether the relief sought includes a declaration of incompatibility pursuant to section 4 of the Human Rights Act and, if so, give precise details of

---

[10] SI 2010/2995. Practice Direction 29B (the Human Rights Act 1998).
[11] SI 2009/1603.
[12] See *V (a child) (care proceedings: human rights claims)* [2004] EWCA Civ 54 at [8].

the legislative provision which is alleged to be incompatible and details of the alleged incompatibility;

(d) state whether the relief sought includes damages in respect of a judicial act (to which section 9(3) applies) and, if so, the judicial act complained of and the court or tribunal which is alleged to have made it; and

(e) give details of any finding of unlawfulness by another court or tribunal upon which the claim is based.[13]

Where a declaration of incompatibility is sought, the Court may at any time consider whether notice should be given to the Crown so that it can be joined as a party to the proceedings.[14] Unless the Crown has been given 21 days' formal notice (or other such period as the court directs) the court may not make a declaration of incompatibility.[15] **4.14**

This is a complex area and reference to the detailed procedures to be followed should be sought out from comprehensive practitioner works such as the *White Book*[16] and *Archbold*.[17] **4.15**

C. STANDING: WHO MAY BRING PROCEEDINGS UNDER THE HUMAN RIGHTS ACT?

Any private, natural, or legal person can use the Human Rights Act. This includes companies, since to restrict the benefit of the Act to natural persons would probably infringe the provisions of Articles 6 and 14 (right to a fair trial in respect of civil rights and obligations, and right not to be discriminated against in application of the Convention rights).[18] By virtue of section 7(1) and (3), however, the Act cannot be used to bring proceedings only by a person who is not, or would not be, a 'victim' of the violation (under Article 34 of the Convention), even if he or she would otherwise have standing to be a party to judicial review proceedings on the broader test of 'standing' employed under Part 54 of the CPR. **4.16**

The 'victim' provision means that it is necessary to determine whether a particular litigant is a 'victim' in order to decide whether the litigant can use the Human Rights Act; and if the litigant is *not* a victim, but still has standing, the court has to decide on the extent to which the litigant can nevertheless raise Convention arguments under the pre-Act conditions. **4.17**

Prior to the Human Rights Act coming into force it was widely anticipated that the 'victim' test would severely hamper its impact and development. However, from the early days of the Human Rights Act this anticipated problem was mitigated by **4.18**

---

[13] CPR Practice Direction 16, para 15.
[14] See CPR Pt 19 and the accompanying Practice Direction.
[15] CPR 19.4A(1).
[16] (London: Sweet & Maxwell, 2014).
[17] (London: Sweet & Maxwell, 2013).
[18] For the position of public bodies, see para 4.22 below.

the relaxed rule on third-party interventions and '*amicus*' briefs which had already evolved before the Act came into force.[19] The powers of the new Equality and Human Rights Commission (discussed below) also go some way to addressing this problem.

1. Victims

4.19   The concept of a victim in section 7(7) of the Human Rights Act is taken from Article 34 of the Convention as amended by Protocol 11.[20] This provides that the Court 'may receive applications from any person, non-governmental organization or group of individuals claiming to be the victim of a violation'. Pursuant to section 7(7), only an applicant who would have standing as a victim to bring proceedings in the ECtHR is a victim for the purposes of section 7. According to the ECtHR, a person has standing as a victim only if directly affected by the act or the omission that is the subject of the complaint. However, in *JM v UK* the Court held that an applicant is not required to show that he or she has suffered (financial) prejudice: that is relevant only in the context of just satisfaction.[21] There is, however, no role for individual 'public defenders' of human rights to be recognized.[22]

4.20   However, in Strasbourg case law it is not necessary for standing that the applicant has actually suffered the consequences of the alleged breach, provided there is a risk of the applicant being directly affected by it in the future.[23] For example, a gay man living in Northern Ireland was allowed to complain (successfully) about the criminalization of all homosexual conduct in private between consenting males, even though he had not yet been prosecuted under the law.[24] The risk of being affected must be a real threat, not a theoretical possibility.[25] Examples include cases in which challenges were made to legislation discriminating against children born out of wedlock, who were held to be victims of that legislation,[26] and a case where a litigant successfully persuaded the Court that she was a victim of the ban on divorce in Ireland because of the consequences for certain family relationships.[27] The ECtHR approach has been reflected in English decisions such as *R (Hooper) v Secretary of State for Work and Pensions* where the House of Lords considered that the applicants were 'victims' for the purposes of the Article 34 test because they

---

[19] See, eg *R v Bow Street Magistrate, ex p Pinochet (No 2)* [2000] 1 AC 119, in which Amnesty International was granted leave to intervene; and *R v Department of Health, ex p Source Informatics* [2000] 2 WLR 940, in which there were four interveners raising human rights arguments.

[20] Before the amendment the provision was in Art 25, to which the earlier case law refers.

[21] (2010) 30 BHRC 60, at [27].

[22] See *Klass v Germany* (1978) 2 EHRR 214. See, similarly, *JR1, Re Judicial Review* [2011] NIQB 5 (finding that an eight-year-old child did not have standing to challenge on Art 2 grounds the decision by police to introduce tasers in Northern Ireland).

[23] *Klass v Germany*, ibid; and *Marckx v Belgium* (1979) 2 EHRR 330.

[24] *Dudgeon v United Kingdom* (1981) 4 EHRR 149; and *Norris v Ireland* (1988) 13 EHRR 186.

[25] *Campbell and Cosans v United Kingdom* (1982) 4 EHRR 293. See also *R (Burke) v The General Medical Council* [2005] EWCA Civ 1003, [2005] 3 WLR 1132 for a discussion of this issue in a domestic context.

[26] *Marckx v Belgium* (1979) 2 EHRR 330.

[27] *Johnston v Ireland* (1986) 9 EHRR 203.

could establish that they would have claimed the benefits alleged to have breached Article 14 had it been open to them to do so.[28] Further, at least in Article 2 cases, close family members of the deceased are entitled to be treated as 'victims'.[29]

A very liberal interpretation of 'victim' by the ECtHR was seen in *Open Door and*   4.21
Dublin Well Woman v Ireland where it was held that two abortion advice centres and two counsellors who *offered* abortion advice, and women of childbearing age wishing to *receive* it, all had standing to challenge an injunction which was held to breach Article 10.[30] In contrast, in *Ahmed v United Kingdom* four local government officers and their trade union (UNISON) complained about the effect of statutory regulations which restricted the political activities of civil servants.[31] The European Commission on Human Rights (ECmHR) declared the application admissible in relation to the four individuals, but inadmissible in relation to UNISON, as it was not directly affected by restrictions on free speech. Similarly, in *Re Medicaments and Related Classes of Goods (No 4)* the Court of Appeal held that a trade association was not a victim as its rights were not directly affected.[32]

Applying the Article 34 test of who is a 'victim',[33] the House of Lords in *Aston*   4.22
Cantlow and Wilmcote with Billesley Parochial Church Council v Wallbank confirmed that local authorities are not able to use the Human Rights Act.[34] In *R (Westminster City Council) v Mayor of London* the High Court held that a local authority could also not be considered a 'non-governmental organization' for the purposes of Article 34 and so could not bring proceedings under the Act.[35]

2. Standing of public interest groups

While the victim requirement will not generally pose a problem to a potential liti-   4.23
gant, in the context of judicial review proceedings it could shut out public interest groups, which have traditionally been permitted to bring judicial review proceedings in appropriate cases, from initiating proceedings on the basis that they do not 'suffer' from the unlawful action.

However, as the Human Rights Act is not intended to remove existing rights,   4.24
Administrative Court judges have not generally used the section 7(3) definition of

---

[28] [2005] UKHL 29, [2005] 1 WLR 1681 at [59] per Lord Hoffmann *obiter*.

[29] *Rabone v Pennine Care NHS Trust* [2010] EWCA Civ 698 at [92]. See also *R (Holub) v Secretary of State for the Home Department* [2001] 1 WLR 1359 in which the Court of Appeal at [14] considered *obiter* that the parents of a minor whose Convention rights have been breached have standing to complain under s 7.

[30] (1992) 15 EHRR 244.

[31] (1995) 20 EHRR CD 72, 77–8.

[32] [2001] EWCA Civ 1217, [2002] 1 WLR 269.

[33] *Austria Municipalities v Austria* (1974) 17 YB 338.

[34] [2003] UKHL 37, [2004] 1 AC 546. See in particular Lord Hope at [43]–[47]. In *Olympic Delivery Authority v Persons Unknown* [2012] EWHC 1012 (Ch), the High Court took the right to property of the Olympic Delivery Agency into account in granting an injunction against protestors. The correctness of this judgment is questionable in view of *Aston Cantlow*.

[35] [2002] EWHC (Admin) 2440. See also Davis, 'Public authorities as "victims" under the Human Rights Act' (2005) 64(2) CLJ 315.

'victim' to draw back from the liberal approach they have adopted to standing in general.[36]

4.25 The stringency of the 'victim' test in the context of judicial review is mitigated in two ways:

(a) In exceptional cases, the courts will permit a declaration to be sought that a proposed course of conduct is unlawful if it is incompatible with Convention rights. These cases can be brought on the basis of 'sufficient interest' alone rather than the applicant having to establish victim status under the strict provisions of the Human Rights Act. This opens up the possibility of the court making use of the interpretative power in section 3, as well as making a declaration of incompatibility under section 4.[37] In *Rusbridger and Toynbee v Attorney-General*[38] the House of Lords warned that the courts will exercise this jurisdiction rarely and that it should not be used to 'spring-clean' the statute book by application of section 3 in cases where there is no practical question of a breach of Convention rights occurring.[39]

(b) Since the coming into force of the Equality Act 2006 and the creation of the Equality and Human Rights Commission (the Commission) there is another potential way for this gap to be filled. The Commission may not only intervene in existing proceedings, but may also take 'own name' proceedings, including judicial review, to prevent breaches of the Human Rights Act.[40]

3. Standing of the Equality and Human Rights Commission

4.26 The issue of the Commission's standing is dealt with in the Equality Act 2006. The Commission may either institute or intervene in litigation 'if it appears to the Commission that the proceedings are relevant to a matter in connection with which the Commission has a function'.[41] To facilitate this power section 30(3) provides:

The Commission may, in the course of legal proceedings for judicial review which it institutes (or in which it intervenes), rely on section 7(1)(b) of the Human Rights Act 1998 (breach of Convention rights); and for that purpose—

(a) the Commission need not be a victim or potential victim of the unlawful act to which the proceedings relate,

---

[36] A rare example of a restrictive approach is found in *Re Medicaments and Related Classes of Goods (No 4)* [2001] EWCA Civ 1217, [2002] 1 WLR 269 (distinguishing between the positions of two different trade associations).

[37] See also *Taylor v Lancashire County Council and Secretary of State for the Environment, Food and Rural Affairs* [2005] EWCA Civ 284 where it was held *obiter* that it would not be appropriate to grant a s 4 declaration where the applicant had not been and could not be personally affected by the legislation at issue.

[38] [2003] UKHL 38, [2004] 1 AC 357.

[39] Ibid at [36] per Lord Hutton and [61] per Lord Walker. See also the Court of Appeal's comments in *R (Burke) v The General Medical Council* [2005] EWCA Civ 1003, [2005] 3 WLR 1132.

[40] Equality Act 2006, s 30.

[41] Section 30(1).

(b) the Commission may act only if there is or would be one or more victims of the unlawful act,

(c) section 7(3) and (4) of that Act shall not apply . . .

Section 30(2) is of similar effect in relation to Scottish proceedings.

This gives the Commission the power to take 'test and illustrative cases'[42] directly, **4.27** and intervene in cases brought by others (interventions are dealt with separately below at para 4.35). The Commission has repeatedly stated its commitment to using strategic litigation to achieve improvements to legal protection of human rights and against discrimination, and to bolster its policy initiatives and monitoring duties.

In practice, the Commission's exercise of its litigation powers in relation to the **4.28** Human Rights Act to date has largely been through interventions; the first use of the Commission's power to bring a claim for judicial review in relation to human rights concerned the lawfulness of the guidance given to the security services on interviewing overseas detainees and the use of intelligence obtained as a result.[43]

D. LIMITATION PERIODS: ARE THERE TIME LIMITS FOR BRINGING A CLAIM UNDER THE HUMAN RIGHTS ACT?

Section 7(5) of the Human Rights Act creates a primary limitation period of **4.29** one year for cases against public bodies alleging a breach of a Convention right, beginning with the date on which the act complained of took place. This can be extended where the court considers it 'equitable having regard to all the circumstances'. Although in some cases the High Court has listed the factors to be taken into account under section 7(5),[44] it is clear that such a 'prescriptive approach' is not appropriate, and it is for the court to examine in the circumstances of each individual case all the relevant factors, 'look at the matter broadly and attach such weight as is appropriate'.[45]

Under section 7(5)(b) the usual one-year limitation period is also subject to any **4.30** more restrictive rule which imposes a stricter time limit in relation to the proceeding in question (for example, the three-month time limit for bringing proceedings by way of judicial review contained in Part 54 of the CPR). The one-year time limit applies only to claims that directly allege breach of the Convention by a public authority, that is, only where there is a cause of action created by section 7(1)(a). There is no time limit to the interpretative obligation in section 7(1)(b).

---

[42] See *EHRC Legal Strategy 2008/09*, available at <http://www.equalityhumanrights.com>.

[43] *R (Equality and Human Rights Commission) v the Prime Minister and others* [2011] EWHC 2401 (Admin), [2012] 1 WLR 1389. The Commission has also occasionally exercised its power to bring proceedings in relation to equality matters: see, eg *R (EHRC) v Secretary of State for Justice* [2010] EWHC 147 (Admin) and *Commission for Equality and Human Rights v Griffin and ors* [2010] EWHC 3343 (Admin) (the latter proceedings brought in relation to discriminatory provisions in the British National Party's constitution).

[44] *Weir v Secretary of State for Transport* [2004] EWHC 2772 (Ch), [2005] UKHRR 154; *Cameron v Network Rail* [2006] EWHC 1133 (QB), [2007] 1 WLR 163; *Dobson v Thames Utilities* [2007] EWHC (QB) 2021.

[45] *Dunn v Parole Board* [2008] EWCA Civ 374, [2009] 1 WLR 728.

4.31   Since the Human Rights Act came into force, the time limits imposed on personal injury claims have been challenged unsuccessfully by claimants who argued that the Limitation Act 1980 should be interpreted in line with Convention rights and asked the courts to apply section 3 of the Human Rights Act retrospectively.[46] In *Dunn v Parole Board* the claimant prisoner had been recalled to prison while on licence four years before instituting proceedings.[47] He argued unsuccessfully that an extension of time should be granted as he had brought his claim within one year of the House of Lords' decision in *R (Smith) v Parole Board*, which established that Article 5(4) was engaged when a prisoner was recalled.[48] The Court of Appeal rejected this argument, but importantly noted that, on the evidence, the decision in *Smith* had played no part in the prisoner's delay; if it could have been shown that he had been waiting for this decision, the court's exercise of discretion may have differed. In claims for damages for personal injury brought under the Human Rights Act, the courts have been reluctant to extend time beyond the one-year limitation date in section 7(5).[49]

4.32   A critical issue that remains to be decided concerns when time begins to run in the case of a continuing act such as unlawful segregation or detention. Section 7(5)(a) of the Human Rights Act refers to 'the date on which the act complained of took place'; the question in such cases is whether time runs from the date the act ceased, or when it began. To a potential claimant this makes all the difference. If time runs from the beginning of the act, it would not be open to a person who was subjected to a continuing unlawful act or failure to act to take proceedings to bring it to an end while it was still continuing after the expiry of one year after its commencement, without appealing to the discretion of the court to extend this period. There are also practical ramifications regarding the remedies available, as the court would have to consider whether to award 'just satisfaction' for the entirety of the period, or only for a one-year period prior to the date on which proceedings were issued. In cases involving unlawful detention the quantum differential could be very large depending on the answer to this question. In *A v Essex County Council* Baroness Hale expressed the view (*obiter*) that time begins to run from the date the breach ended.[50] The European Court of Human Rights has accepted a complaint in *A* and judgment is awaited.

---

[46] *Rowe v Kingston upon Hull City Council* [2003] EWCA Civ 1281 on whether a dyslexic's claim for negligence against his former school was within the time limit for bringing a personal injury claim under s 14 of the Limitation Act; and *A v Hoare* [2008] UKHL 6, [2008] 1 AC 844 in which a victim of an intentional sexual assault argued that the cut-off imposed by s 2 of the Limitation Act should be extended in light of the Human Rights Act.

[47] [2008] EWCA Civ 374, [2009] 1 WLR 728.

[48] [2005] UKHL 1, [2005] 1 WLR 350.

[49] See, eg, *Bedford v Bedfordshire County Council* [2013] EWHC 1717 (QB), [2014] LGR 44.

[50] [2010] UKSC 33, [2011] 1 AC 280 at [113], referring to *Somerville v Scottish Ministers* [2007] UKHL 44, [2007] 1 WLR 2734.

E. RETROSPECTIVITY

Following some initial, rather confusing decisions it is now clear that, apart from **4.33** the exception created by section 22(4) case law, the Human Rights Act does not apply retrospectively to the acts of courts, tribunals, or public authorities which took place prior to 2 October 2000. This encompasses criminal proceedings and appeals[51] and civil law cases.[52] The House of Lords has held that the interpretative obligation in section 3 does not, in general, apply to acts, agreements, or transactions made before the Human Rights Act came into force,[53] but their Lordships have left open the possibility that in some circumstances the presumption against the retrospective application of section 3 might be rebutted where this would not give rise to unfairness.[54] As time goes on, the retrospectivity provisions become of diminishing practical importance.

Section 6(1) created new positive causes of action for acts or omissions that took **4.34** place on or after 2 October 2000, when the Human Rights Act came into force. However, it can provide a defence to proceedings brought by the public authority whenever the act or omission complained of took place—whether before or after the Act was in force. For example, a prosecution that relies on evidence gathered in violation of Article 8 in 1999 could be challenged by a defendant on that basis at a trial taking place now (after 2 October 2000—although in practice this is of course now unlikely). But a decision taken on 1 October 2000 by a public authority cannot be challenged by way of judicial review, or on the basis that it was a breach of statutory duty under section 6(1). The reason for this curious feature is that section 22(4) of the Human Rights Act (which came into force before 2 October 2000) provides that section 7(1)(b) (reliance on the Convention in legal proceedings) applies to proceedings *brought by or at the instigation of a public authority* whenever the act in question took place, but otherwise only to acts taking place after the coming into force of that section.

F. INTERVENTIONS IN HUMAN RIGHTS ACT CASES

The Commission's power to litigate directly has the potential to mitigate the restric- **4.35** tive provisions of section 7 of the Human Rights Act. To date, the tight terms of

---

[51] *R v Lambert* [2001] UKHL 37, [2002] 2 AC 545; although cf *R v Kansal (No 2)* [2001] 3 WLR 1562; see also *R v Lyons* [2002] UKHL 44, [2002] 3 WLR 1562.

[52] See *In re McCaughey* [2011] UKSC 20 at [58] per Lord Phillips. In that case, the Supreme Court held that an inquest into a death resulting from acts of agents of the state which took place before the entry into force of the Act had to comply with the procedural obligations imposed by Art 2 of the Convention. In so holding, the court reversed its previous decision in *In re McKerr* [2004] UKHL 12, [2004] 1 WLR 807, which was unsustainable in the light of the intervening judgment of the ECtHR in *Šilih v Slovenia* (2009) 49 EHRR 996.

[53] See, eg *Wilson v First County Trust* [2003] UKHL 40, [2004] 1 AC 816.

[54] Ibid at [21] per Lord Nicholls and at [101]–[102] per Lord Hope.

section 7 have been offset by public interest groups supporting individuals who can establish their claim to be victims, and also by such groups acting as third-party interveners in relevant cases; the Commission itself frequently intervenes in proceedings commenced by others.

1. Interventions by public interest groups

4.36   The Human Rights Act does not give an express right to intervene, except to the Crown, and, as detailed below (para. 4.41), the Commission also has a statutory power to intervene. However, the Supreme Court and the Court of Appeal have shown themselves increasingly willing to allow third-party interventions under the normal rules of court.[55] In 2000, there were five petitions for leave to intervene in House of Lords' cases (with one granted leave to make full written and oral submissions, and four written submissions alone), rising to 14 petitions only two years later in 2002 (with eight being granted full oral and written submissions, and four written submissions alone).[56] The increase has been exponential since then; indeed, in public law cases raising human rights issues in the Supreme Court, interveners are now the norm rather than the exception.

4.37   The reason for this rapid growth of interventions is clear: they can provide considerable benefits to courts and litigants, particularly in the context of the Human Rights Act where experience from other countries and details of other international human rights standards may be of great use. They can draw to the court's attention the wider significance of a point in a way that an individual litigant may be unable to do. They may provide supporting statistical or other evidence. They can help the court to determine whether an interference with a Convention right is 'necessary in a democratic society' or 'proportionate' by drawing to the court's attention the wider social significance or effects of a particular outcome.[57] For example, in *YL v Birmingham City Council* detailed witness statements and submissions were presented to the courts by the British Institute of Human Rights, Help the Aged, and the National Council on Ageing, adding important contextual evidence as to the practical ramifications of the narrow definition of 'public authority' under section 6.[58]

4.38   The courts are also increasingly willing to allow multiple interventions, and 'joint' interventions are also becoming more commonplace. For example, in *A and ors v Secretary of State for the Home Department*[59] a consortium of 14 international human rights organizations (including Human Rights Watch and Amnesty International) intervened in the House of Lords' case, which held that evidence obtained under torture from third parties by foreign state agents is not admissible

---

[55] See CPR Pt 54; Practice Direction 37 of the House of Lords' *Practice Directions Applicable to Civil Appeals*, 2007–2008 edn; and Practice Direction 34 of the House of Lords' *Practice Directions Applicable to Criminal Appeals*, 2007–2008 edn.

[56] See Hannett, 'Third Party Intervention: In the Public Interest?' [2003] PL 128.

[57] See Arshi and O'Cinneide, 'Third-party Interventions: The Public Interest Reaffirmed' [2004] PL 69.

[58] [2007] UKHL 27, [2008] 1 AC 95. The case is analysed in ch 3.

[59] [2005] UKHL 71, [2006] 2 AC 221.

in UK domestic courts. In *Re E*[60] the House of Lords recognized the specialist expertise that statutory bodies and NGOs can and have offered in public interest cases, Lord Hoffmann noting that:

In recent years the House has frequently been assisted by the submissions of statutory bodies and non-governmental organisations on questions of general public importance. Leave is given to such bodies to intervene and make submissions, usually in writing but sometimes orally from the bar, in the expectation that their fund of knowledge or particular point of view will enable them to provide the House with a more rounded picture than it would otherwise obtain. The House is grateful to such bodies for their help.[61]

However, judges have on occasion expressed irritation at the increased workload caused by intervening parties; it is clear that any intervention must add value and not merely repeat points made by one of the main parties to the proceedings.[62]   4.39

The future of public interest interventions is currently in some doubt after the Government introduced measures in the Criminal Justice and Courts Bill to prevent third-party interveners from seeking their costs against other parties, and to require the court to order that an intervener must pay other parties' costs arising from the intervention. The court will only have discretion to depart from this rule in exceptional circumstances. The measures would have the undesirable effect of deterring organizations with specialist expertise, and which often represent disadvantaged and marginalized people, from intervening for fear that they will incur considerable costs. The Bill is currently before Parliament.   4.40

2. Interventions by the Equality and Human Rights Commission

The Commission, with the permission of the court, can intervene in cases, including judicial review, where the Commission is not a party.[63] The Commission made 29 interventions in its first year of existence, including one in the Grand Chamber of the European Court of Human Rights.[64] It is understood that, to date, no court or tribunal has refused an application by the Commission to intervene.   4.41

The Commission's role in an intervention is not to support one side or the other; it is to provide independent arguments to the court to promote the objectives set out for it in the Equality Act 2006 (discussed more fully below at para 4.45).[65]   4.42

The Commission has intervened in a number of cases concerning human rights, and at a range of levels. Examples include: 4.43

- *R (GC & C) v The Commissioner of Police of the Metropolitan Police*: implementation of the *S and Marper* decision of the ECtHR regarding DNA retention in the UK;[66]

---

[60] [2008] UKHL 66, [2008] 3 WLR 1208 at [2], [6], and [69].
[61] Ibid at [2].
[62] Ibid at [2]–[3] per Lord Hoffmann and [69] per Lord Brown.
[63] Equality Act 2006, s 30.
[64] *RP v United Kingdom* App No 38245/08.
[65] See Equality Act 2006, ss 3, 8–11.
[66] [2011] UKSC 21, [2011] 3 All ER 859.

- *R (Smith) v Secretary of State for Defence*: jurisdictional application of human rights protection for British military personnel; right to an Article 2 investigation;[67]

- *R (JL) v Secretary of State for the Home Department* (House of Lords): the Article 2 investigative duty arising from near-death incidents in custody;[68]

- *R (RJM) v Secretary of State for Work and Pensions* (House of Lords): the scope of Article 14 and whether 'other status' includes homelessness;[69]

- *R (G) v The Governors of X School* (Supreme Court): extent to which legal representation is required under Article 6 in employment tribunal proceedings (where the consequences go beyond the employment context);[70]

- *JM v United Kingdom* (ECtHR): whether same-sex couples are a 'family' for the purposes of Article 8;[71]

- *R (T) v Secretary of State for the Home Department*: whether the disclosure of warnings and cautions by the police violates Article 8.[72]

G. OTHER MEANS OF ENFORCEMENT BY THE EQUALITY AND HUMAN RIGHTS COMMISSION[73]

4.44 The Equality and Human Rights Commission has extensive legal powers, including the power to take judicial review proceedings in its own name to prevent breaches of the Human Rights Act, and the power to intervene in proceedings taken by others which raise human rights issues.[74] The Commission also has a range of other enforcement tools at its disposal, including the power to conduct formal inquiries and to fund organizations providing legal assistance in human rights. This allows the Commission to enforce the Human Rights Act without necessarily engaging in litigation. The Commission also undertakes legal policy work, including briefing ministers and parliamentarians on human rights issues in draft legislation, and contributing to international treaty monitoring bodies. These non-litigation legal powers are dealt with below. The Commission also has wide-ranging research, communication, and education functions which are not dealt with in this text, but which also allow it to promote human rights and ensure compliance with the Human Rights Act. In 2011, the Government proposed significant reform of the Commission's powers, but after public consultation and resistance in the House of

---

[67] [2010] UKSC 29, [2011] 1 AC 1.
[68] [2008] UKHL 68, [2009] 1 AC 588.
[69] [2008] UKHL 63, [2009] 1 AC 311.
[70] [2011] UKSC 30, 1 AC 167, 3 WLR 237.
[71] (2010) 30 BHRC 60.
[72] [2014] UKSC 35.
[73] See, generally, O'Cinneide, 'The Commission For Equality And Human Rights: A New Institution For New And Uncertain Times' (2007) 36(2) Industrial Law Journal 141.
[74] See para 4.40 above.

Lords, only limited reforms were made in the Enterprise and Regulatory Reform Act 2013.[75]

1. The duties of the Commission

The Equality Act 2006 sets out the Commission's legal duties. Section 3 contains a general duty:

4.45

The Commission shall exercise its functions under this Part with a view to encouraging and supporting the development of a society in which—
  (a) people's ability to achieve their potential is not limited by prejudice or discrimination,
  (b) there is respect for and protection of each individual's human rights,
  (c) there is respect for the dignity and worth of each individual,
  (d) each individual has an equal opportunity to participate in society, and
  (e) there is mutual respect between groups based on understanding and valuing of diversity and on shared respect for equality and human rights.

Section 8 of the 2006 Act sets out the Commission's specific legal duties in relation to equality and diversity, including the duties to promote understanding and encourage good practice in relation to equality and diversity, and to 'work towards the elimination of unlawful discrimination'. Section 10 requires the Commission to promote understanding of the importance of good relations and encourage good practice in relations between members of different groups and others.

The Commission's specific legal duties concerning human rights are set out in section 9. 'Human rights' in this context includes the Convention rights, but also 'other human rights' not set out in the Convention.[76] Section 9(1) provides that:

4.46

The Commission shall, by exercising the powers conferred by this Part—
  (a) promote understanding of the importance of human rights,
  (b) encourage good practice in relation to human rights,
  (c) promote awareness, understanding and protection of human rights, and
  (d) encourage public authorities to comply with section 6 of the Human Rights Act 1998 (compliance with Convention rights).

In fulfilling a duty under section 8 or 10 the Commission must also take account of any relevant human rights.

Section 11(1) requires the Commission to 'monitor the effectiveness of the equality and human rights enactments' and provides that it may advise central government on its findings, make recommendations to it regarding whether to amend, repeal, or consolidate any of the equality and human rights enactments, and advise central or devolved government (in Scotland, Wales, or Northern Ireland) about the effect of an enactment, or the likely effect of a proposed change of law.[77] This

4.47

---

[75] For instance, the Commission's powers and duties under ss 10 and 19 of the Equality Act 2006, to promote good relations between and within groups were repealed by the 2013 Act.

[76] Equality Act 2006, s 9(2)(b). The Commission must, however, have particular regard to the importance of exercising its powers in relation to the Convention rights: s 9(3).

[77] Ibid, s 11(2). Recently, the Commission has published briefings (available on its website) on the following Bills, among others: Terrorism Prevention and Investigation Measures Bill; Health and Social Care Bill;

'pre-emptive' role—preventing breaches of the Human Rights Act before they occur—is not unfamiliar: the Parliamentary Joint Committee on Human Rights (JCHR) scrutinizes all government Bills and picks out those with significant human rights implications for further examination.

2. Legal assistance

4.48 The Commission's powers in relation to human rights issues with no equality dimension are limited. Unless there is an equality dimension to the case, the Commission does not have the power to give legal assistance to individuals on human rights grounds alone.

3. Legal policy

4.49 In addition to monitoring the effectiveness of equality and human rights laws, the Commission seeks through its legal work to influence the development of future legislation and policies likely to have an impact on equality and human rights. This includes: cooperating with the Scottish Commission for Human Rights, the Northern Ireland Human Rights Commission, and the Equality Commission for Northern Ireland; making submissions to international treaty monitoring bodies; and drafting statutory and non-statutory guidance.

4. Inquiries, investigations, and assessments

4.50 The Commission has a range of investigation and assessment powers. It may conduct an inquiry, or undertake an investigation or assessment (sections 16, 20, and 31). It has power to require any person to provide written or oral evidence or relevant documents, which gives teeth to its inquiry powers.

(a) *Inquiries*

4.51 The Commission may conduct 'an inquiry into a matter' relating to any of its duties under sections 8 (equality), 9 (human rights), or 10 (groups).[78] Schedule 2 to the Equality Act deals with the logistics of such inquiries: terms of reference, representations, evidence, reports, recommendations, and the effects of reports. Inquiries can be general or specific; they could be thematic (for example, related to one particular Convention right), sectoral (looking at, for example, the treatment of children in custodial establishments that are managed by private companies), or relate to one or more named parties.

4.52 Inquiries have included examinations into home care of older people, non-natural deaths in detention of adults with mental health conditions,

Protection of Freedoms Bill; Localism Bill; Public Bodies Bill; Terrorist Asset-Freezing etc Bill; Identity Documents Bill—Commons Second Reading; Borders, Citizenship and Immigration Bill; Coroners and Justice Bill; Crime, Security, Policing and Counter-Terrorism Bill.

[78] Equality Act 2006, s 16(1).

disability related harassment, and human trafficking in Scotland.[79] In June 2009 the Commission published its *Human Rights Inquiry* which assessed progress towards the effectiveness and enjoyment of a culture of respect for human rights in Britain and made a number of recommendations as to how the current human rights framework might be better integrated into public service provision and explained to the public.[80]

(b) *Investigations and assessments*

An investigation is a tool that enables the Commission to investigate whether or not a particular person (natural or legal) has committed an unlawful act, or failed to comply with a notice given to that person by the Commission, or an agreement that person has made with the Commission following an earlier finding that the person has behaved unlawfully.[81] The Commission may also conduct an assessment of a public authority's compliance with the public sector duties regarding gender, race, and disability. The power to initiate investigations and assessments is restricted to the Commission's equality remit.

4.53

H. REMEDIES

1. Damages

(a) *Jurisdiction and procedure*

Section 8(1) of the Human Rights Act authorizes a court which has found that an act or proposed act of a public authority is unlawful, to grant 'such relief or remedy, or make such order, within its powers as it considers just and appropriate'. This can be used to found a claim for relief, including damages, against a public authority. Courts and tribunals of limited jurisdiction cannot award a remedy if it is outside their statutory power to do so. For example, an employment tribunal is not able to order an injunction to prevent a discriminatory dismissal going ahead (because it has no statutory power to do so), even if it were to consider this necessary to afford just satisfaction of a Convention right.

4.54

Section 8(2) permits a court to make an award of damages under the Act where it has the power to award compensation (even if it is not otherwise called 'damages'). This, in principle, includes statutory tribunals such as employment tribunals. Criminal courts cannot award damages under section 8(2).[82]

4.55

The Court of Appeal laid down procedural guidelines for courts considering claims for damages in respect of maladministration leading to a breach of

4.56

---

[79] For a full list, see <http://www.equalityhumanrights.com/legal-and-policy/our-legal-work/inquiries-and-assessments>.

[80] See <http://www.equalityhumanrights.com/human-rights/our-human-rights-inquiry/inquiry-report/>.

[81] Equality Act 2006, s 20(1).

[82] *R v Galfetti* [2002] EWCA Civ 1916, [2002] MHLR 418.

Convention rights in *Anufrijeva v Southwark London Borough Council*.[83] The guidelines, which are of general importance, included the following:

(a) A claim for damages alone cannot be brought by judicial review but it should still be brought in the Administrative Court by an ordinary claim. Courts should look critically at any attempt to recover damages under the Human Rights Act for maladministration by any procedure other than judicial review.

(b) Claimants should first exhaust (or explain why it would not be more appropriate to use) any available internal complaint procedure, or proceed by making a claim to the parliamentary or local government ombudsman.

(c) If there is a legitimate claim for other relief, permission should, if appropriate, be limited to that relief, and consideration given to deferring permission for the damages claim, adjourning or staying that claim until use has been made of alternative dispute-resolution procedures.

(d) In determining quantum of damages, citations should in general be limited to three authorities, and, except in exceptional circumstances, the hearing should be limited to half a day.

(b) *Principles of assessment*

4.57 There is no automatic entitlement to damages under the Human Rights Act—courts may exercise their power to award damages to victims whose Convention rights have been breached but they are not bound to do so in all cases. Section 8(3) provides that damages are to be awarded only where they are necessary to afford 'just satisfaction' to the victim. When courts are deciding whether a monetary award is necessary they will take account of all the circumstances of the case, including any other remedy granted by the court or any other court, and the consequences of any decision (of that or any other court) in respect of the breach.[84]

4.58 Section 8(4) provides that a court or tribunal deciding whether to award damages and how much to award must take into account the principles applied by the ECtHR in relation to the award of compensation under Article 41 of the Convention. As Silber J pointed out in *R (N) v Secretary of State for the Home Department*,[85] section 8(4) requires the court to take into account the *principles*, whereas section 2(1) requires it to take into account the *decisions*, suggesting that it is open to the court, having identified any relevant principles from the Strasbourg

---

[83] [2003] EWCA Civ 1406, [2004] QB 1124. For a more detailed discussion of the practical ramifications of the guidelines laid down in *Anufrijeva*, see Clayton, 'Damage Limitation: The Courts and the Human Rights Act Damages' [2005] PL 429; and for analysis as to when the guidelines apply, see Whitfield/Public Law Project, 'Between a Rock and a Hard Place: ADR after Anufrijeva' (Winter 2003/4), available at <http://www.publiclawproject.org.uk>.

[84] See, eg *Dobson v Thames Water Utilities* [2009] EWCA Civ 28, [2009] 3 All ER 319 (where damages were available in nuisance against a sewerage undertaker, such damages themselves constituted just satisfaction and no further damages were awarded).

[85] [2003] EWHC 207 (Admin) at [180].

case law, to then seek assistance on quantum from other sources.[86] However, it is difficult to identify a concrete set of principles from the ECtHR case law on Article 41 to which domestic courts can refer when considering awarding damages under the Human Rights Act. As the Law Commission put it, the 'most striking feature' of the Strasbourg case law on damages is 'the lack of clear principles as to when damages should be awarded and how they should be measured'.[87] Despite this practical problem, it is possible to identify the following broad themes that have been used by the ECtHR:[88]

(a) Compensation is discretionary and will be awarded only if 'necessary', bearing in mind the circumstances of the case as a whole. It is not uncommon for the Strasbourg Court to decline to award compensation on the basis that a declaration of unlawful conduct is sufficient remedy for an applicant. Equally, the ECtHR refuses to award just satisfaction to applicants, such as terrorist suspects, that it considers 'undeserving'.[89]

(b) There must be a 'causal link' between the breach of the applicant's Convention rights, any alleged resulting harm, and the compensation sought.

(c) The principle of compensation is *restitutio in integrum*, that is, that the applicant is, so far as possible, put back into the situation in which he or she would have been but for the violation of his or her Convention rights.[90] Exemplary or punitive damages are not recoverable. The ECtHR does not expressly award aggravated damages, but the conduct of both the applicant and/or the respondent state and the gravity of the violation may either lessen or enhance the amount of damages awarded.[91]

The ECtHR measures 'just satisfaction' under three heads: pecuniary loss, non-pecuniary loss, and costs and expenses: 4.59

(a) *Pecuniary loss* Where applicants have claimed for things such as loss of earnings and career prospects under Article 6(1), the ECtHR has rarely held that a procedural failing has caused pecuniary loss and refuses to speculate on what the outcome of proceedings would have been had the violation not occurred.[92] However, in *Barberà v Spain* the ECtHR held that there had been a loss of opportunity (to prove innocence) as a result of a procedural failing.[93]

---

[86] See Clayton, 'Damages under the Human Rights Act', paper presented to the Human Rights Lawyers' Association, 1 December 2003; available at <http://www.hrla.org.uk>.

[87] Law Commission, *Damages under the Human Rights Act* (Law Com No 266, 2000) (Cm 4853) para 3.4.

[88] Ibid, s III. See also the analysis of Lord Woolf in *Anufrijeva v Southwark London Borough Council* [2003] EWCA Civ 1406, [2004] QB 1124.

[89] See *McCann v United Kingdom* (1995) 21 EHRR 97.

[90] *Kingsley v United Kingdom* (2002) 35 EHRR 10.

[91] For further analysis of the ECtHR's approach to exemplary, punitive, and aggravated damages, see Shelton, *Remedies in International Human Rights Law* (Oxford: Oxford University Press, 2005) 360.

[92] *Saunders v United Kingdom* (1997) 23 EHRR 313.

[93] (1988) 11 EHRR 360.

(b) *Non-pecuniary loss* The ECtHR has awarded non-pecuniary damages in respect of pain, suffering, and physical or psychological injury,[94] including distress and anxiety.[95]

(c) *Costs and expenses* The test applied by the ECtHR is whether the costs were actually and necessarily incurred in order to prevent, or obtain redress for, the breach of the Convention, and were reasonable as to quantum.

4.60 The approach of the English courts to damages under the Human Rights Act to date has reflected, and attempted to develop, the broad themes discernible in the ECtHR jurisprudence.[96] In *R (Faulkner) v Secretary of State for Justice*, the Supreme Court considered how English courts should take Strasbourg judgments into account when determining 'just satisfaction'.[97] Lord Reed drew three conclusions that will guide lower courts when they determine the quantum of damages to award in a human rights claim:

> First, at the present stage of the development of the remedy of damages under section 8 of the 1998 Act, courts should be guided, following *Greenfield*, primarily by any clear and consistent practice of the European court. Secondly, it should be borne in mind that awards by the European court reflect the real value of money in the country in question. The most reliable guidance as to the quantum of awards under section 8 will therefore be awards made by the European court in comparable cases brought by applicants from the UK or other countries with a similar cost of living. Thirdly, courts should resolve disputed issues of fact in the usual way even if the European court, in similar circumstances, would not do so.[98]

The High Court recently applied *Faulkner* in a claim for damages for the failure by the police to effectively investigate rapes and sexual assaults committed by serial rapist, John Worboys.[99] The court examined awards made by the Strasbourg Court for claims from other signatory states and made adjustments for higher cost of living in the UK and for inflation since the date of the awards.

(c) *Quantum*

4.61 The quantum of awards granted by the Strasbourg Court is generally cautious, particularly for 'non-pecuniary' damage such as in cases of unlawful detention. For example, in *Johnson v United Kingdom* the Strasbourg Court awarded damages of £10,000 for a wrongful detention in a maximum security psychiatric hospital lasting three-and-a-half years.[100]

4.62 Finally, it should be noted that the level of awards under section 8 of the Human Rights Act should not affect the proper level of damages an applicant is entitled to

---

[94] See, eg *Aydin v Turkey* (1998) 25 EHRR 251.
[95] *Doustaly v France*, 70 Rep Judg & Dec 1998 II 850.
[96] See *Anufrijeva v Southwark London Borough Council* [2003] EWCA Civ 1406, [2004] QB 1124; and *R (Greenfield) v Secretary of State for the Home Department* [2005] UKHL 14, [2005] 1 WLR 673.
[97] [2013] UKSC 23, [2013] 2 AC 254.
[98] Ibid, at [39].
[99] *DSD and NBV v Commissioner of the Police for the Metropolis* [2014] EWHC 2493 (Admin).
[100] (1999) 27 EHRR 296.

receive for breach of any other tort, such as false imprisonment. Section 11 of the Act provides that a person may rely on a Convention right without prejudice to any other right or freedom conferred on him or her by or under any (other) law having effect in the United Kingdom.

At the time the Human Rights Act came into force there was considerable debate   4.63
over the nature of the remedy contained in the statute and the impact this would then have on the assessment of quantum.[101] The most authoritative examination of the topic was contained in the report by the Law Commission, *Damages under the Human Rights Act*,[102] which described sections 6 and 7 as 'creat[ing] a new cause of action, which is in effect a form of action for breach of statutory duty, but with the difference that the remedy is discretionary rather than of right'.

The Law Commission also expressed the view that damages for tort were the   4.64
most relevant domestic analogy to damages under section 8 of the Human Rights Act, and suggested that courts could treat the quantum rules in tort as the prima facie measure to be applied—unless the results were inconsistent with Strasbourg case law under Article 41.[103]

However, in *R (Greenfield) v Secretary of State for the Home Department*,[104] Lord   4.65
Bingham rejected the submissions that damages under the Human Rights Act should not be on the low side compared to tortious awards; that English courts should be free to depart from the scale of damages awarded by the ECtHR; and that English awards (whether tortious or public law remedies) should provide the appropriate comparator. He pointed out that: the objectives of the Human Rights Act were different and broader than those of a tort statute; a finding of a violation is an important part of a claimant's remedy and an important vindication of the right asserted; and the purpose of incorporating the Convention was to give claimants the same remedies they would recover in Strasbourg. He also pointed out that section 8(4) requires the courts to take into account the principles of the ECtHR in determining the amount of damages. He suggested that the courts under the Human Rights Act 'should not aim to be significantly more or less generous than the ECtHR might be expected to be, in a case where it was willing to make an award at all'.

The approach taken by the English courts to date has been disappointing, and   4.66
the general principles formulated by the House of Lords in *Greenfield* and *Faulkner* are more restrictive than the terms of the Human Rights Act itself would mandate. The effect of their Lordships' approach has been that damages for breaches

---

[101] Lester and Pannick, 'Law Com No 266 (2000): The Impact of the Human Rights Act on Private Law: The Knight's Move' (2000) 116 LQR 380 (referring to the creation of a 'constitutional tort' of infringing Convention rights); Clayton and Tomlinson, *The Law of Human Rights* (Oxford: Oxford University Press, 2000) para 21.21 (referring to the creation of a public law remedy).

[102] Law Commission, *Damages under the Human Rights Act* (Law Com No 266, 2000) (Cm 4853) para 4.20.

[103] See *R (Bernard) v London Borough of Enfield* [2001] EWCA Civ 1831, [2002] HLR 860 in support of this approach; likewise *Anufrijeva v Southwark London Borough Council* [2003] EWCA Civ 1406, [2004] QB 1124.

[104] [2005] UKHL 14, [2005] 1 WLR 673 at [19].

of Convention rights are considered and awarded rarely, with successful claimants often receiving no damages.[105] Even where they are available, they are generally much lower than the comparable awards for race or sex discrimination. There is a powerful argument that this approach not only has the effect of downgrading human rights but also frustrates the intention of the Human Rights Act, which envisaged domestic courts being able to provide an effective remedy for breaches of Convention rights. This restrictive approach also causes difficulty in obtaining public funding for cases because of the relatively low monetary value assigned to human rights cases—although many should still pass the criteria for funding under the 'public interest' test.[106]

4.67   That said, the courts have made sizeable damages awards in a few recent cases. For example, in *R (B) v Director of Public Prosecutions*[107] the Divisional Court found that the Director of Public Prosecutions (DPP) had breached the claimant's Article 3 rights in deciding to terminate a prosecution on the eve of the trial on the irrational basis that the victim could be put before the jury as a credible witness because he suffered from mental illness. It awarded damages in the amount of £8,000. In *OOO v Commissioner of Police of the Metropolis*[108] the court made awards of £5,000 to each claimant for breaches of the police's positive obligation to investigate (well-founded) allegations of inhuman and degrading treatment. In *DSD and NBV v Commissioner of the Police for the Metropolis* the High Court awarded £22,250 and £19,000 to the claimants respectively for the failure by the police to investigate and apprehend a serial rapist which led to assaults on the claimants.[109]

4.68   It should be borne in mind that, in judicial review proceedings in particular, where separate damages hearings are ordered after the substantive hearing, settlement on quantum will often be reached. This means that the reported case law does not necessarily reflect the reality of Human Rights Act awards.

(d) *Claims against judicial bodies and Parliament*

4.69   In general, it is not possible to make a claim for damages against a court which has breached the Convention, even though it is a public authority. Where a first instance court acts unlawfully, section 9 of the Human Rights Act requires proceedings in respect of its decision to be brought on appeal from the decision, by way of judicial review or in such other forum as may be prescribed by rules. However, there is provision in section 9(3) and (4) for awards of damages against the Crown where any judicial body has been guilty of a breach of Article 5 in, for example, cases of false imprisonment following a bail application. To claim this remedy, the 'appropriate person', if not already a party to the proceedings, must be joined.[110] The appropriate person (defined in section 9(5)) is the minister responsible for the

---

[105] See, eg *R (SL) v Commissioner of Police for the Metropolis* [2008] EWHC 1442 (Admin).
[106] This is a particular problem in Art 5 'false imprisonment' cases taken in the county courts.
[107] [2009] EWHC 106 (Admin).
[108] [2011] EWHC 1246 (QB).
[109] [2014] EWHC 2493 (Admin).
[110] See also CPR 19.4A.

court concerned, or a person or government department nominated by him or her. In *R (KB) v Mental Health Review Tribunal* the claimants were awarded 'modest' damages after they had established breaches of Article 5(4) rights arising from the failure of the MHRT to deal speedily with their applications for a review of their detention.[111]

There is *no* right in damages where the breach of the Convention is caused by an Act of Parliament. It is still not clear how the Human Rights Act intends 'just satisfaction' to be afforded in cases where the breach of the Convention is a consequence of a statutory provision, and where a court has made a declaration of incompatibility under section 4, given the failure to incorporate Article 13. It is possible that *ex gratia* payments of compensation under section 10 are intended to be the appropriate remedy.[112]   **4.70**

This is an area of law which changes rapidly, and reference should be made to up-to-date discussions and analysis in practitioner texts, such as the *White Book*, the European Human Rights Law Review, and the UK Human Rights Reports (see Chapter 10 for further details).   **4.71**

2. Section 4—declarations of incompatibility

One of the remedies provided by the Human Rights Act that has been used relatively regularly is the 'declaration of incompatibility'. Under section 4(2), higher courts have the option of declaring that primary legislation is incompatible with the Convention if it is impossible for them to interpret the legislation in such a way as to render it compatible. However, the making of a declaration of incompatibility does not result in the proceedings being resolved in favour of the litigant whose rights were violated. As the courts must give primacy to the statute, this declaration does not affect the validity, continuing operation, or enforcement of the legislation, and 'is not binding on the parties to the proceedings in which it is made'.[113]   **4.72**

Section 4 is a central part of the carefully crafted mechanism in the Human Rights Act which allows for a balance between the constitutional principles of parliamentary sovereignty and judicial protection of human rights (see Chapter 1). A declaration of incompatibility does not 'strike down' legislation but brings any tension between Convention rights and a particular statutory scheme to the attention of Parliament. It also triggers the power to take remedial action in response under section 10, which provides a 'fast-track' procedure for the amendment of legislation to bring it into line with human rights principles. However, unlike for judgments of the ECtHR, there is no legal obligation on the Government to take remedial action following a declaration of incompatibility, nor upon Parliament to accept any remedial measures the Government may propose.   **4.73**

---

[111] [2003] EWHC 193 (Admin), [2004] QB 936.

[112] See, eg *R (H) v Mental Health Review Tribunal* [2001] EWCA Civ 415, [2001] 3 WLR 512 and the payment scheme established by the Government following a declaration of incompatibility.

[113] Section 4(6)(b). It is understood that this provision is designed to allow the Government to take a different position from that of the court should the case be argued in the ECtHR.

4.74   A declaration of incompatibility is intended to be 'a measure of last resort...[which]...must be avoided unless it is plainly impossible to do so'.[114] The courts try to avoid making such declarations by striving to find meanings for statutory provisions that conform with the Convention under the strong interpretative obligation in section 3 of the Human Rights Act, which allows the courts to construe legislation compatibly with Convention rights.

4.75   The Supreme Court has declined to make a declaration of incompatibility where it was possible for guidance to be disapplied and legislation interpreted in a Convention-compatible manner.[115]

4.76   Even where it is not possible to interpret a provision compatibly with Convention rights, courts retain their discretion whether to grant a declaration (which is exercised according to the normal principles governing the grant of declarations). The circumstances in which a declaration might be made were set out in *Wilson v First County Trust Ltd (No 2)*.[116]

4.77   Finally, where a complaint relates to the absence of legislation it is important to note that any lacuna in a statutory scheme cannot result in a declaration of incompatibility under the Human Rights Act.[117]

(a) *Jurisdiction, procedure, and notice provisions*

4.78   The power to make declarations of incompatibility is available only in the higher courts. These include the High Court, the Court of Appeal, and the Supreme Court, but not the various tribunals that sit in place of the High Court and from which appeals lie to the Court of Appeal (for example, the Employment Appeal Tribunal and the Immigration Appeal Tribunal).[118]

4.79   There is no strict requirement that a person who seeks a declaration of incompatibility is a 'victim' within the definition of section 7, provided he or she has sufficient interest and standing.[119] However, the court will normally only grant a declaration of incompatibility to a person who is a victim of an actual or proposed breach of a Convention right, and in any event a person cannot apply for a declaration of incompatibility on the basis of a hypothetical argument, or if he or she is not adversely affected by the measure in question.[120] But a declaration of incompatibility may serve a useful purpose even if the Government has already indicated an intention to change the law.[121]

---

[114] See Lord Steyn in *R v A (No 2)* [2001] UKHL 25, [2002] 1 AC 45 at [44].

[115] *R (GC and C) v Commissioner of Police of the Metropolis* [2011] UKSC 21, [2011] 1 WLR 1230.

[116] [2001] EWCA Civ 633, [2002] QB 74 at [46]; overruled on other grounds by the House of Lords at [2003] UKHL 40, [2003] 3 WLR 568.

[117] See *Re S (minors) (care order: implementation of care plan)* [2002] 2 UKHL 10, [2002] 2 AC 291.

[118] See ch 3 for further detail as to the duties of the lower courts when confronted with compatibility arguments.

[119] *R (Rusbridger) v Attorney General* [2003] UKHL 38, [2003] 3 WLR 232 at [21] per Lord Steyn.

[120] *Taylor v Lancashire County Council and Secretary of State for the Environment, Food and Rural Affairs* [2005] EWCA Civ 284, [2005] HRLR 17.

[121] *Bellinger v Bellinger* [2003] UKHL 21, [2003] 2 AC 467.

(b) *Examples of declarations of incompatibility in specific cases*

Although there have been many challenges to legislation since the Human Rights Act came into force, declarations of incompatibility have been made and upheld by the courts in a relatively small number of cases.[122]   4.80

In most instances the Government has responded to the declarations issued by the courts by amending, repealing, or introducing new legislation. Examples include the following: 4.81

(a) *R v Secretary of State for the Home Department, ex p Anderson* involved a challenge to the Home Secretary's power under the Crime (Sentences) Act 1997 to set the minimum period that must be served by a mandatory life sentence prisoner before he was considered for release on licence.[123] Following the Strasbourg ruling in *Stafford v United Kingdom*[124] the House of Lords found that the involvement of the Home Secretary, as a member of the executive, in fixing the tariff term of imprisonment for those convicted of murder was incompatible with Article 6(1). The impugned law was repealed by the Criminal Justice Act 2003 and new sentencing provisions were introduced in Chapter 7 of, and Schedules 21 and 22 to, that Act.

(b) In *Blood and Tarbuck v Secretary of State for Health* section 28(6)(b) of the Human Fertilisation and Embryology Act 1990 was declared incompatible with Article 8, and/or Article 14 taken together with Article 8, to the extent that it did not allow a deceased father's name to be given on the birth certificate of his child.[125] The law was amended by the Human Fertilisation and Embryology (Deceased Fathers) Act 2003.

(c) In *Bellinger v Bellinger* a post-operative male-to-female transsexual appealed against a decision that she was not validly married to her husband because the law still regarded her as a man.[126] The House of Lords held that section 11(c) of the Matrimonial Causes Act 1973 was incompatible with Articles 8 and 12 of the Convention as it denied a post-operative transsexual wishing to have her marriage legally recognized her right to respect for family and private life. The declaration of incompatibility was made following the Strasbourg Court's decision in *Goodwin v United Kingdom*[127] and Parliament enacted the Gender Recognition Act 2004 to remedy the breach.

(d) *R (Morris) v Westminster City Council and First Secretary of State*[128] concerned an application for local authority accommodation by a single mother (a British

---

[122] The government database that listed declarations of incompatibility is no longer available. A list of declarations can be found in the government's annual 'Report to the Joint Committee on Human Rights on the Government response to human rights judgments'. The most recent report for 2012–13 listed 28 declarations of incompatibility.

[123] [2002] UKHL 46, [2003] 1 AC 837.

[124] (2002) 35 EHRR 32.

[125] Sullivan J, 28 February 2003.

[126] [2003] UKHL 21, [2003] 2 AC 467.

[127] (2002) 35 EHRR 18.

[128] [2005] EWCA Civ 1184, [2006] 1 WLR 505.

citizen) whose child was subject to immigration control. It was held that section 185(4) of the Housing Act 1996 was incompatible with Article 14 to the extent that it required a dependent child who was not a British citizen to be disregarded when determining whether the parent (who is a British citizen) has priority need for housing. A similar declaration was granted in *R (Gabaj) v First Secretary of State*,[129] except that in this case it was the claimant's pregnant wife (rather than the claimant's child) who was subject to immigration control. The law was amended by Schedule 15 to the Housing and Regeneration Act 2008 (not yet in force), although the JCHR has doubted whether these provisions are sufficient to address the incompatibility.[130]

(e) *R (Clift) v Secretary of State for the Home Department; Secretary of State for the Home Department v Hindawi*[131] was a conjoined appeal in which the appellants were all former or serving prisoners. The issue on appeal was whether the early release provisions, to which each of the appellants was subject, were discriminatory. Sections 46(1) and 50(2) of the Criminal Justice Act 1991 were declared incompatible with Article 14 taken together with Article 5 on the basis that they discriminated on grounds of national origin. The provisions had already been repealed and replaced by the Criminal Justice Act 2003, but continued to apply on a transitional basis to offences committed before 4 April 2005. Section 27 of the Criminal Justice and Immigration Act 2008 therefore amended the Criminal Justice Act 1991 to remove the incompatibility in the transitional cases.

(f) In *R (Wright and ors) v Secretary of State for Health* the House of Lords found the 'provisional blacklisting' provisions for care workers in the Care Standards Act 2000 incompatible with Articles 6 and 8.[132] By the date of the House of Lords' judgment, the transition to a new scheme under the Safeguarding Vulnerable Groups Act 2006 was already underway. The new scheme did not include the feature of provisional listing which was the subject of challenge in the *Wright* case.

(g) *R (F and Thompson) v Secretary of State for the Home Department* concerned the indefinite requirements imposed on those convicted of sexual offences to notify the authorities of their travel plans by virtue of the Sexual Offences Act 2003. The Supreme Court held that these requirements were incompatible with Article 8 of the Convention; a declaration of incompatibility was therefore made.[133]

---

[129] CO/7458/2005, 28 March 2006.

[130] JCHR, *Monitoring the Government's Response to Human Rights Judgments: Annual Report 2008*, 31st Report (2007–2008), HL 173, HC 1078, para 95.

[131] [2006] UKHL 54, [2007] 1 AC 484.

[132] [2009] UKHL 3, [2009] 2 WLR 267.

[133] [2010] UKSC 17, [2011] 1 AC 331, 2 WLR 992. For details of other cases, see *R (H) v Mental Health Review Tribunal* [2001] EWCA Civ 415, [2001] 3 WLR 512; *R (Wilkinson) v Inland Revenue Commissioners* [2003] EWCA Civ 814, [2003] 1 WLR 2683; and *International Transport Roth GmbH v Secretary of State for the Home Department* [2002] EWCA Civ 158, [2002] 3 WLR 344.

In June 2011 the Government published the draft Sexual Offences Act 2003 (Remedial) Order 2011 in response to the judgment.[134]

(h) *R (T) v Chief Constable of Greater Manchester and ors* concerned the blanket disclosure of convictions and cautions under the provisions of the Police Act 1997 and Rehabilitation of Offenders Act 1974 (Exceptions) Order 1975. The claimants argued that they were incompatible with the Article 8 right to private life. The Court of Appeal found the provisions incompatible with Article 8 and made a declaration of incompatibility. Parliament amended the legislation to reflect the judgment.[135]

(c) *Difficulties with the declaration of incompatibility procedure*

Unfortunately the declaration of incompatibility procedure does not tend to have speedy results. For example, the amendments to the Criminal Justice Act 1991 made as a result of *Clift* (above) only came into force in July 2008, although the judgment was handed down in December 2006—and this has been one of the speediest responses.[136] In one case, the High Court made a declaration of incompatibility in November 2006,[137] the Court of Appeal overturned it in October 2007,[138] and the House of Lords then reinstated the declaration on 21 January 2009.[139] The legislation was repealed with effect from 12 October 2009.   **4.82**

Even when attempts are made to rectify the incompatibility identified in a declaration, they may not succeed in doing so. For example, it has been doubted whether the measures introduced in the Housing and Regeneration Act 2008, intended to respond to the declarations in the *Morris* and *Gabaj* cases[140] (concerning discrimination in access to social housing), remove the risk that Strasbourg or the domestic courts will find a further violation of Articles 8 and/or 14.[141]   **4.83**

In the anti-terrorism context, the Government struggled to find a human rights compatible means of detaining suspected terrorists. As set out in Chapter 6, Article 3 (the right not to be subject to torture, inhuman, or degrading treatment or punishment) prevents the return of foreign nationals to countries where they would face a real risk of torture regardless of whether those nationals present a national security threat to the United Kingdom.[142] The Government first attempted to deal with this   **4.84**

---

[134] See <http://www.homeoffice.gov.uk/publications/about-us/legislation/sexual-offences-remedial-order>.

[135] The Government appealed the Court of Appeal decision to the Supreme Court after amending the legislation. The Supreme Court upheld the Court of Appeal decision: *R (T) v Chief Constable of Greater Manchester* [2014] UKSC 35.

[136] See JCHR, *Monitoring the Government's Response to Human Rights Judgments: Annual Report 2008*, 31st Report (2007–2008), HL 173, HC 1078, para 107.

[137] *R (Wright and ors) v Secretary of State for Health and Secretary of State for Education and Skills* [2006] EWHC 2886 (Admin).

[138] [2007] EWCA Civ 999, [2008] 2 WLR 536.

[139] [2009] UKHL 3, [2009] 2 WLR 267.

[140] See para 4.81(d).

[141] See JCHR, *Monitoring the Government's Response to Human Rights Judgments: Annual Report 2008*, 31st Report (2007–2008), HL 173, HC 1078, para 95.

[142] *Chahal v UK* (1997) 23 EHRR 413.

problem in 2001 by derogating from Article 5 (the right to liberty)[143] and introducing a form of detention without trial for foreign terror suspects.[144] In a landmark judgment in *A and ors v Secretary of State for the Home Department* ('the *Belmarsh* case')[145] the House of Lords held the derogation order to be in breach of the Convention, and the detention provisions to be incompatible with Articles 5 and 14 of the Convention, as the order was disproportionate and permitted detention in a way that discriminated on the grounds of nationality or immigration status. In response, the Government withdrew the derogation and repealed the provisions relating to detention without trial, instead putting in place a new regime of 'control orders' (a form of house arrest) under the Prevention of Terrorism Act 2005. Control orders were tested in the House of Lords and also found, in certain circumstances, to infringe the right to liberty.[146] The Coalition Government abolished control orders and introduced Terrorism, Prevention and Investigation Measures, which cease automatically after two years (with the possibility of renewal), but continue to subject individuals to restrictive civil measures on the basis of suspicion of involvement in terrorist activity.[147]

4.85   In response to criticism from the JCHR of its failure to speedily and effectively respond to declarations of incompatibility, the Government's rather feeble response has simply been that:

> The Government has to date never refused to present remedial measures to Parliament following a final declaration of incompatibility.[148]

4.86   In our view, while the Government may never have refused to respond as such, periods of years (or even months when dealing with urgent issues or vulnerable groups) throughout which it claims to be 'considering how to remedy the incompatibility' are unacceptable, and undermine the Government's claim that the regime is compliant with Article 13 (the right to an effective remedy). It might be noted that the ECtHR has held that the declaration of incompatibility is not (yet) an effective remedy for breach of a Convention right, given the various other restrictions on its availability (the facts that it does not assist the individual litigant, that it is not binding, and that ministers can exercise the power to amend under section 10 only where there are 'compelling reasons' for doing so—see below),[149] although it has indicated that, in time, the United Kingdom could potentially persuade the Court otherwise:

> It is possible that at some future date evidence of a long-standing and established practice of ministers giving effect to the courts' declarations of incompatibility might be sufficient to persuade the Court of the effectiveness of the procedure.[150]

---

[143] Human Rights Act (Designated Derogation) Order 2001, SI 2001/3644.

[144] Anti-Terrorism, Crime and Security Act 2001, s 23.

[145] [2004] UKHL 56, [2005] 2 AC 68.

[146] *Secretary of State for the Home Department v JJ* [2007] UKHL 45, [2008] 1 AC 385.

[147] Terrorism, Investigation and Prevention Act 2011.

[148] Ministry of Justice, *Responding to Human Rights Judgments: Government Response to the Joint Committee on Human Rights' Thirty-first Report of Session 2008* (Cm 7524), 5.

[149] Second Monitoring Report, paras 110–121. See *Burden and Burden v UK* (2008) 24 BHRC 709.

[150] *Burden and Burden v UK* (2007) 44 EHRR 709.

Regrettably, the Government appears to have taken this judgment as 'an endorsement of its current approach',[151] rather than a heavy hint from Strasbourg to adopt a clear and consistent policy. As matters stand, the declaration of incompatibility is not an effective remedy for Convention purposes, which means that a litigant need not, at present, pursue such a remedy before going to Strasbourg if it is the only one realistically available in order to exhaust domestic remedies.

A further worrying lacuna in the Act relates to the position where the Government 4.87 ignores a judgment of the ECtHR condemning the United Kingdom for violating Convention rights. The domestic courts have thus far taken the general view that once a declaration of incompatibility has been made, no further relief will be granted. This issue has been particularly acute following the refusal of successive Governments to implement the judgment of the ECtHR in *Hirst v UK (No 2)*[152] in relation to the prohibition on serving prisoners being able to vote.[153]

Given the continued existence of legislation which cannot be read compatibly 4.88 with Convention rights, there can be no question of a statutory tort being committed under section 6 of the Human Rights Act. Consequently, there is no right to damages under section 8 of the Act or any other remedy for the ongoing violation of Convention rights. One can therefore readily appreciate why the ECtHR has held that the declaration of incompatibility mechanism does not amount to an effective remedy for the purposes of Article 13 of the Convention.

The number of declarations will undoubtedly continue to grow as the courts 4.89 grapple with the issues raised by the Convention and the Human Rights Act. To keep up to date, students and practitioners should refer to Chapter 8 for details of sources of current information.

(d) Costs

One serious issue is the question of how costs are awarded in cases where declara- 4.90 tions of incompatibility are sought. In previous editions of this book, we argued that where a declaration of incompatibility is made by the court, costs should not be awarded against the unsuccessful litigant. During the passage of the Human Rights Bill, at committee stage in the House of Lords, an amendment to ensure that the Crown at least bore its own expenses was debated. The Government rejected the proposal, preferring to allow the courts to use their current discretion as to how costs are dealt with. It was suggested that factors for the court to consider included whether the case put forward by the person seeking the declaration had merit and whether there was any wider public interest in the matter. Also relevant were the means of the parties and, of course, the outcome of the application for a declaration.

---

[151] Ministry of Justice, *Responding to Human Rights Judgments: Government Response to the Joint Committee on Human Rights' Thirty-first Report of Session 2008* (Cm 7524), 39.

[152] (2006) 42 EHRR 41.

[153] See *R (Chester) v Secretary of State for Justice* [2013] UKSC 63. The European Court of Human Rights has recently ruled that prisoners are not entitled to compensation for unlawful disenfranchisement: *Firth and ors v UK*, App No 47784/09, 12 August 2014.

4.91   The Privy Council has recognized that an award of costs against an unsuccessful applicant may not always be appropriate in litigation involving important questions of fundamental rights as '*bona fide* resort to rights under the constitution ought not to be discouraged'.[154]

4.92   In fact, the evidence suggests that where a claimant obtains a declaration of incompatibility, the courts are likely to regard him or her as having 'won' and award costs against the relevant Secretary of State. However, this unresolved issue has a potentially 'chilling' effect on the protection of Convention rights, as litigants may be reluctant to take test cases under the Human Rights Act if they may obtain a declaration of incompatibility but still face a substantial adverse costs order.[155]

3. Section 10—'fast-track' procedure

4.93   A declaration of incompatibility under section 4 should prompt legislative change—either directly by amendment of primary legislation, or under the Human Rights Act's fast-track procedure. Indeed, in practice declarations of incompatibility do usually prompt such change, although this change may be slow to come about. As of 1 June 2011 19 declarations of incompatibility have become final. Of these:

- 11 have been remedied by later primary legislation;
- two have been remedied by a remedial order under section 10 of the Human Rights Act;
- three relate to provisions that had already been remedied by primary legislation at the time of the declaration;
- three have not yet been remedied.

As these statistics show, such changes are usually made through amendments to primary legislation or the introduction of new legislation, and the fast-track procedure is very rarely used. The JCHR, which has been highly critical of the Government's failure to speedily and effectively respond to both declarations of incompatibility in the domestic courts and adverse judgments from Strasbourg, has recommended that greater use should be made of remedial orders.[156]

4.94   The fast-track procedure is contained in section 10 of, and Schedule 2 to, the Human Rights Act. It is a power to take remedial action (in respect of both declarations of incompatibility and ECtHR judgments) through the making of a remedial order in certain circumstances. Under section 10 this power can be triggered:

---

[154] *Abnee v DPP* [1999] 2 AC 294; and *New Zealand Maori Council v Attorney General of New Zealand* [1994] 1 AC 466.

[155] See Liberty, *Litigating the Public Interest: Report of the Working Group on Facilitating Public Interest Litigation* (July 2006), available at <http://www.adminlaw.org.uk/docs/Litigating%20the%20Public%20Interest.pdf>.

[156] JCHR, *Monitoring the Government's Response to Human Rights Judgments: Annual Report 2008*, 31st Report (2007–2008), HL 173, HC 1078, para 6.

(a) following a declaration of incompatibility made under section 4 where all parties have exercised or abandoned any rights of appeal or the time limit for appealing has expired;

(b) where the Government decides, following a decision of the ECtHR, that a provision of legislation is incompatible with a Convention right. It is not necessary that the judgment of the Court is in favour of the applicant; or

(c) in relation to incompatible subordinate legislation, where a minister considers that it is necessary to amend the parent legislation.

If there are 'compelling reasons' for doing so, section 10 empowers a minister to make a 'remedial order' embodied in a statutory instrument that amends legislation so far as necessary to remove its incompatibility with the Convention. The Human Rights Act provides two procedures for making a remedial order: a standard procedure in Schedule 2, paragraph 2(a), and an emergency procedure in Schedule 2, paragraph 2(b). **4.95**

A remedial order can be fairly wide in scope, have retrospective effect, and can 'make different provision for different cases'. This retrospective effect is limited by Schedule 2, paragraph 1(3), which states that, 'no person is to be guilty of an offence solely as a result of the retrospective effect of a remedial order'. The power to change the law retrospectively could be used to backdate a change to the date of the domestic court's decision on incompatibility or the judgment of the ECtHR. **4.96**

The standard procedure[157] is a 'positive resolution procedure'. The minister must first[158] lay before Parliament a document containing a draft of the proposed order together with what is called the 'required information', which is: **4.97**

(a) an explanation of the incompatibility that the proposed order seeks to remove, including particulars of the court declaration, finding, or order that caused the minister to propose a remedial order; and

(b) a statement of the reasons for proceeding under section 10 and for making an order in the terms proposed.[159]

This document must be before Parliament for at least 60 days, during which time representations about the draft order may be made to the minister, either by Parliament in the form of a report or resolution, or by any other person. The minister can amend the draft in the light of these representations. Whether or not the draft is amended it must be laid before Parliament again, this time accompanied by a summary of any representations that have been made and details of any changes made as a result. The order does not come into effect unless it is approved by a resolution of each House within 60 days after it is laid for the second time. **4.98**

Under the emergency procedure[160] the minister may make the order before laying it before Parliament, but must state in the order that it appears to him or her that, **4.99**

---

[157] Schedule 2, para 2(a).
[158] Schedule 2, para 3.
[159] Schedule 2, para 5.
[160] Schedule 2, para 2(b).

because of the urgency of the matter, it is necessary to make it without prior parliamentary approval. However, after making an order under this emergency procedure the minister must[161] lay the order before Parliament, with the required information, for 60 days, during which time representations may be made, as under the standard procedure. The minister can amend the order in the light of the representations, but, whether or not it is amended, the order must be laid before Parliament again, with a summary of representations and details of amendments, and it will cease to have effect 120 days after it was made unless it is approved by a resolution of each House. In the only example to date of the fast-track procedure being used, this was the method adopted. Following the Court of Appeal's decision in *R (H) v Mental Health Review Tribunal*[162] the Secretary of State introduced the Mental Health Act 1983 (Remedial) Order 2001[163] using this urgent procedure. This route was probably used because the problem involved fundamental rights to personal liberty and, if not rectified quickly, would have created confusion as the tribunal system would have been unsure what burden of proof it should be applying.

4.100   The power given by section 10 to amend legislation applies to both primary and secondary legislation. This provision allows campaigners, lobbyists, and lawyers to make representations to government to amend primary legislation following any case in the ECtHR that raises questions about legislation. The Government is not, of course, bound to act by way of either primary or secondary legislation, even following a declaration of incompatibility. However, if it does not do so, it would be a virtual certainty that the victim could then seek just satisfaction in the ECtHR. This would then impose an obligation on the Government as a matter of international law to remedy its violation. However, the Strasbourg Court has held on a number of occasions that the discretionary nature of the power under section 10, and the statutory limitations on the circumstances in which it can be used, prevent it from constituting an 'effective remedy' in Convention terms.

I. KEY CONVENTION CONCEPTS IN THE DOMESTIC COURTS

4.101   As discussed in Chapter 2, there are particular interpretative concepts that the ECtHR has developed in order to give meaning and effect to the Convention. The domestic courts have adopted these concepts when interpreting Convention rights under the Human Rights Act. As revealed by the number of successful applications to Strasbourg made after the Human Rights Act came into force, the domestic courts do not always apply Convention principles in the same manner as the ECtHR. The following discussion of some of the key concepts highlights points of similarity and divergence.

---

[161] Schedule 2, para 4.
[162] [2001] EWCA Civ 415, [2001] 3 WLR 512.
[163] SI 2001/3712.

1. Territoriality[164]

We discuss the approach of the ECtHR to extraterritoriality of the Convention   **4.102**
in Chapter 2.[165] The UK courts have struggled with extra-territoriality in a number of cases which we discuss in greater detail in Chapter 6.[166] After some to and
fro between the UK courts and the ECtHR, the approach of the domestic and
European courts is now consistent and it is agreed that the Convention will apply
extra-territorially in exceptional circumstances. These circumstances include the
important category of 'state agent authority and control'. Whenever the state
through its agents exercises control and authority over an individual, the state will
be under an obligation to secure to that individual the rights and freedoms under
the Convention that were relevant to the situation of that individual. The Supreme
Court has now accepted that the UK has jurisdiction over its armed forces abroad
and is obliged to respect the rights of its soldiers when they serve abroad.[167]

2. Positive obligations

As discussed in Chapter 2,[168] positive obligations provide a critical interpretative   **4.103**
tool for the ECtHR to expand the protection of the Convention beyond the bare
minimum authorized by the text of the articles. Domestic courts have proved cautious in imposing positive obligations on public authorities, aware that political and
economic considerations are often at stake. The nature of positive obligations was
considered by the House of Lords in *R (Pretty) v DPP*, a case questioning whether
the applicant, who suffered from terminal motor neurone disease, could claim a
right to die under Articles 2 and 8 of the Convention.[169] Following Strasbourg
authority, Lord Bingham emphasized that the question of whether a positive obligation exists depends on striking a fair balance between the general interests of the
community and the interests of the individual. Diane Pretty's application was not
upheld by either the House of Lords or the Strasbourg Court.[170]

  Domestic cases on the scope of positive obligations have largely concerned Article   **4.104**
2, Article 3, and Article 8.[171] The first two sets of cases have met with the most success in domestic courts. In a trio of cases—*Amin*,[172] *Middleton*,[173] and *JL*[174]—the
House of Lords found violations of the positive obligation under Article 2 to conduct an investigation into deaths or near-deaths in custody. In *Savage v South Essex
Partnership NHS Foundation Trust* the House of Lords found that the obligation

---

[164] See ch 2, para 2.23.

[165] See ch 2, paras 2.23–2.24.

[166] See paras 6.04 –6.08.

[167] *R (Smith) v Ministry of Defence* [2013] UKSC 41, [2014] AC 52.

[168] See ch 2, paras 2.32–2.39.

[169] [2001] UKHL 61, [2002] 1 AC 800.

[170] (2002) 35 EHRR 1.

[171] For further detail, see ch 7.

[172] *R (Amin) v Secretary of State for the Home Department* [2003] UKHL 51, [2004] 1 AC 653.

[173] *R v Coroner for Western District of Somerset, ex p Middleton* [2004] UKHL 10, [2004] 2 AC 182.

[174] *R (JL) v Secretary of State for Justice* [2008] UKHL 68, [2008] 3 WLR 1325.

to protect life extends to providing a proper system for the supervision of mental patients.[175] In *R (B) v Director of Public Prosecutions*[176] and *OOO v Commissioner of Police of the Metropolis*,[177] discussed at para 4.67 above, the High Court found breaches of the state's positive obligations under Article 3.

4.105   Positive obligations under Article 8 are harder to establish. In *Re S (a care plan)* the House of Lords rejected the Court of Appeal's development of a positive obligation to secure a child in care with 'a family for life'.[178] In *Secretary of State for Work and Pensions v M* the House of Lords said that Strasbourg was 'well aware' of the dangers of any 'unrestrained and unprincipled' extension of Article 8, and stated that many social welfare measures with only an indirect effect on private or family life were not even within the ambit of the duty to respect it.[179] In *R (Mcdonald) v Royal Borough of Kensington and Chelsea*, the Supreme Court held that while in principle there could be a positive obligation on local authorities to provide social care support, there was no such obligation to the claimant to provide nursing staff overnight to avoid the indignity of wearing incontinence pads.[180] That said, the courts have occasionally recognized the potential role for positive obligations under Article 8: in *Bryant and ors v Commissioner of Police for the Metropolis* the High Court held that it is arguable that the police are under a positive obligation to inform citizens of information that indicates that respect for their private life is potentially threatened.[181]

4.106   Where an omission by a public authority can be said to amount to inhuman or degrading treatment, the court may be more willing to impose a positive obligation. In *R (Limbuela) v Secretary of State for the Home Department*, for example, the House of Lords held that Article 3 required basic subsistence to be given to asylum-seekers.[182] In *DSD and NBV v Commissioner of Police for the Metropolis*, the High Court found that there was a positive duty imposed upon the police to conduct investigations into particularly severe violent acts perpetrated by private parties in a timely and efficient manner.[183] The police failure to investigate serious claims of sexual assault violated the claimants' Article 3 rights.

3. Legality

4.107   As discussed in Chapter 2,[184] the requirement of legality is a critical first step to determining whether any limitation on rights can be justified. It has been considered in the

---

[175] [2008] UKHL 74, [2009] 2 WLR 115.

[176] [2009] EWHC 106 (Admin).

[177] [2011] EWHC 1246 (QB).

[178] See *W and B (children: care plan)* [2001] EWCA Civ 757, [2001] 2 FLR 582.

[179] [2006] UKHL 11, [2006] 2 AC 91, [2006] 2 WLR 637.

[180] [2011] UKSC 33, [2011] 4 All ER 881. The ECtHR held that the case did not need to be analysed in terms of positive obligations but by reference to the negative obligation, as the claimant had experienced a reduction in care support: *Mcdonald v UK* App No 4241/12, 20 May 2014.

[181] [2011] EWHC 1314 (Admin) at [54].

[182] [2005] UKHL 66, [2006] 1 AC 396.

[183] [2014] EWHC 436 (QB).

[184] See ch 2, paras 2.42–2.49.

domestic context on a number of occasions since the Human Rights Act came into force. The House of Lords adopted the approach of the ECtHR in *R v Shayler*.[185] Lord Hope explained that the court had to address itself to three questions: whether there was a legal basis in domestic law for the restriction; whether the law was sufficiently accessible and precise; and, finally, whether the law had been arbitrarily applied.[186]

The Lords strayed from this strict approach in *R (Gillan) v Commissioner of Police for the Metropolis*, a case concerning the use by the Metropolitan Police of random stop-and-search powers under the Terrorism Act 2000.[187] The basis on which the police decided to stop and search individuals had never been published; nor had members of the public been informed that random stop-and-search powers were being deployed in the London area. However, their Lordships found that the bare fact that the Act authorized the powers was sufficient guarantee of legality. Lord Bingham accepted that powers were broadly drawn, but stated that 'a measure of vagueness was inevitable if excessive rigidity was to be avoided' and, in any event, there were 'strong reasons' for not publishing details of the authorizations and confirmations.[188] This approach was not in keeping with the Strasbourg jurisprudence, as the ECtHR subsequently found.[189]   **4.108**

Recent domestic decisions have more satisfactorily upheld the principle of legality. In *R (Laporte) v Chief Constable of Gloucestershire* the House of Lords found that action taken to prevent demonstrators from reaching a demonstration was not prescribed by domestic law as there had been no imminent breach of the peace to justify intercepting the demonstrators.[190] Likewise, in the case of *R (Moos and McClure) v Commissioner of Police of the Metropolis*[191] the Divisional Court held that there had been no imminent breach of the peace such as to justify 'kettling' on the facts of the case. In *R (T) v Secretary of State for the Home Department* the Supreme Court found that the statutory procedure for disclosure of convictions and cautions fell foul of the principle of legality.[192] Lord Wilson disagreed, arguing that it was necessary to preserve a distinction between legality and necessity, and that the legislation was disproportionate but not inadequately precise.[193]   **4.109**

4. Proportionality

(a) *Introduction and overview*

As discussed in Chapter 2,[194] proportionality is the standard of review applied by the ECtHR in its assessment of justifications for infringing limited and qualified   **4.110**

---

[185] [2002] UKHL 11, [2003] 1 AC 247.
[186] Ibid at [56].
[187] [2006] UKHL 12, [2006] 2 WLR 537.
[188] Ibid at [33].
[189] *Gillan and Quinton v UK* Application 4158/05, 12 January 2010.
[190] [2006] UKHL 55, [2007] 2 AC 105.
[191] [2011] EWHC 957 (Admin).
[192] [2014] UKSC 35.
[193] Ibid, at [38].
[194] See ch 2, paras 2.61–2.66.

Convention rights. This is the standard now adopted under the Human Rights Act, which has heralded a far closer level of scrutiny of public decision-making than was previously the case in ordinary domestic judicial review proceedings. In relation to all qualified rights, the question is whether any intrusion into the right is lawful, in the sense of having a lawful basis, being intended to meet a legitimate aim, and being a means of achieving that aim which is 'necessary in a democratic society'. The standard of scrutiny, in most judicial review proceedings, is therefore now that of 'proportionality' rather than the previous standard, which permitted judicial interference only in cases of 'irrationality'. However, the precise parameters of the concept of proportionality have not yet been fully defined. Moreover, the debate has sometimes turned on whether, why, and to what extent, courts ought to 'defer' to the decisions reached by other arms of government or expert decision-makers. This section considers the current law on the test for determining whether there is a departure from or exception to a Convention principle. The next section addresses the concepts of deference and the 'discretionary area of judgment'.

(b) *The development and application of the proportionality principle in domestic law*

4.111   Before the Human Rights Act came into force, the test for challenging the actions of public authorities by way of judicial review was that they must be unlawful or 'irrational'; in Lord Diplock's oft-quoted explanation of *Wednesbury*[195] unreasonableness, 'a decision which is so outrageous in its defiance of logic or accepted moral standards that no sensible person who had applied his mind to the question to be decided could have arrived at it'.[196] It was very hard to challenge a decision on this basis; and although in later cases, where fundamental rights were at stake, the test was redefined so that the greater the interference with fundamental rights, the greater the level of scrutiny required,[197] the ECtHR held that even this reformulated level of scrutiny was insufficient to meet the requirements of Article 13 of the Convention.[198]

4.112   Despite judicial reluctance to adopt the proportionality standard in administrative law, the concept was not alien to the English judiciary.[199] Before the Human Rights Act came into force, judges in English courts commonly encountered it in the context of EU law.[200] The language used in Convention case law differs from the more formal EU test, but the concept of proportionality—and the Continental legal traditions from which it has derived—are very similar in both systems,[201] and in practice, proportionality principles derived from Convention case law are applied equally in cases governed by EU law (and vice versa).[202]

---

[195] *Associated Provincial Picture Houses Ltd v Wednesbury Corp* [1948] 1 KB 223.

[196] *Council of Civil Service Unions v Minister for the Civil Service* [1985] AC 375, 410.

[197] See the formulation in *R v Ministry of Defence, ex p Smith* [1996] QB 517.

[198] See *Smith and Grady v UK* (1999) 29 EHRR 493; *Hatton v UK* (2003) 37 EHRR 28.

[199] See Olley, 'Proportionality at Common Law' [2004] JR 197; Walker, 'Unreasonableness and Proportionality', in Supperstone, Goudie, and Walker (eds), *Judicial Review*, 3rd edn (London: Butterworths, 2005).

[200] See, eg *R v Secretary of State for Employment, ex p Equal Opportunities Commission* [1995] 1 AC 1.

[201] See *R (Countryside Alliance and ors) v Attorney General* [2007] UKHL 52, [2008] 1 AC 719.

[202] See *Secretary of State for Defence v Elias* [2006] EWCA Civ 1293, [2006] IRLR 934.

The classic domestic formulation of proportionality was made by the Privy   4.113
Council in *De Freitas v Permanent Secretary of Ministry of Agriculture, Fisheries,
Lands and Housing*.[203] Drawing on Canadian and South African jurisprudence,
Lord Clyde set out a three-stage test, asking whether: the policy in question pursues
a sufficiently important objective; the rule or decision under review is rationally
connected with that objective; and the means adopted are no more than necessary
to achieve that objective.

That approach to proportionality was expressly endorsed, in the context of the   4.114
Human Rights Act, by the House of Lords in *R (Daly) v Secretary of State for
the Home Department* in which Lord Steyn underlined the 'material difference'
between the Convention principle of proportionality and *Wednesbury* unreasonableness.[204] He said that proportionality was a more sophisticated test than mere
reasonableness or rationality as it permitted the court to assess the balance struck
by the decision-maker. He emphasized, however, that proportionality did not mean
a shift to a merits review, and that the intensity of the review would depend on the
subject matter in hand, even in cases involving Convention rights.

Following the further decision of the House of Lords in *Huang v Secretary of*   4.115
State for the Home Department,[205] a fourth limb must be added to the *De Freitas*
test for assessing whether a measure constitutes a proportionate means of achieving a legitimate aim, namely whether the measure achieves a fair balance between
the interests of the individuals affected and the wider community. The *Huang* test
has since been widely used.[206] Properly applied, it offers a structured and rigorous
approach. So, for example, in *R (Laporte) v Chief Constable of Gloucestershire*, the
House of Lords rejected an argument that it should be deferential to 'on the spot'
police decisions.[207] The police had failed to discharge the burden of establishing
that all the actions they took were proportionate and constituted the least restriction necessary to the rights of freedom of speech and freedom of peaceful assembly.
Similarly, in *Huang* itself the House of Lords held that an immigration adjudicator had to decide for him or herself whether an impugned decision to remove an
asylum seeker was proportionate, and, if not, reverse it. The adjudicator must not
simply check the rationality of the primary decision-maker's decision; he or she
must decide proportionality on the merits.[208] And in *Manchester City Council v
Pinnock*, the Supreme Court held that a court which was asked by a local authority to make an order for possession of a person's home had to have, when assessing

---

[203] [1999] 1 AC 69.

[204] [2001] 2 WLR 1622.

[205] [2007] UKHL 11, [2007] 2 AC 167. For a different set of questions to be asked, at least in an Art
8 context, see *R (F) v Secretary of State for Justice* [2010] UKSC 17, [2010] 2 WLR 992 at [41] per Lord
Phillips: '(i) What is the extent of the interference with article 8 rights? (ii) How valuable are the notification requirements [regarding a sex offender's foreign travel plans] in achieving the legitimate aims [of the
legislation in question]? and (iii) to what extent would that value be eroded if the notification requirements
were made subject to review?'

[206] See, eg *Re E* [2008] UKHL 66, [2008] 3 WLR 1208.

[207] [2006] UKHL 55, [2007] 2 AC 105.

[208] [2007] UKHL 11, [2007] 1 AC 167.

the proportionality of making the order, the power to resolve any relevant dispute of fact; limitation of the court's power to one based on traditional judicial review principles was inadequate.[209]

4.116 The Supreme Court re-stated the principle of proportionality in *Bank Mellat v Her Majesty's Treasury* as follows:

the question depends on an exacting analysis of the factual case advanced in defence of the measure, in order to determine (i) whether its objective is sufficiently important to justify the limitation of a fundamental right; (ii) whether it is rationally connected to the objective; (iii) whether a less intrusive measure could have been used; and (iv) whether, having regard to these matters and to the severity of the consequences, a fair balance has been struck between the rights of the individual and the interests of the community. These four requirements are logically separate, but in practice they inevitably overlap.[210]

Lord Justice Laws has questioned the utility of the fourth question, suggesting that there is 'is real difficulty in distinguishing this from a political question to be decided by the elected arm of government'.[211] He has subsequently argued that 'the law owes to the public a clearer boundary between what is for the judges and what is for Government and Parliament'.[212] His point is a forceful one. The vexed notions of deference, 'discretionary area of judgment', justiciability, and proportionality have frequently intermingled in human rights jurisprudence. This confusion was evident in *R (Countryside Alliance and ors) v Attorney General*, a case concerning hunting bans.[213] The House of Lords afforded a wide 'margin of discretionary judgment' to the legislature in this matter of social policy and found that any interference with the claimants' proprietary rights under Article 1 of Protocol 1 was justifiable. However, the approaches adopted by their Lordships to the questions of proportionality and deference differed sharply. Lord Bingham suggested that a 'degree of respect' should be accorded to the decision of a majority of the country's democratically elected representatives, and stated:

The democratic process is liable to be subverted if, on a question of moral and political judgment, opponents of the Act achieve through the courts what they could not achieve in Parliament.[214]

4.117 Lord Brown disagreed:

The democratic process is a necessary but not a sufficient condition for the protection and vindication of human rights. Sometimes the majority misuses its powers. Not least this may occur when what are perceived as moral issues are involved... I simply cannot regard the ethical objection of the majority as a sufficient basis for holding the ban to be 'necessary'.... How then can the ban be reconciled with the values of 'pluralism, tolerance and broadmindedness', these 'hallmarks of a democratic society'? Most would regard adultery (assuredly a pursuit engaging article

---

[209] [2010] UKSC 45, [2010] 3 WLR 1441, especially at [45] and [74].
[210] [2013] UKSC 39, [2014] AC 700 at [20].
[211] *Miranda v Secretary of State* [2014] EWHC (Admin) 255, [2014] 3 All ER 447 at [40].
[212] *R (Tigere) v Secretary of State for Business, Innovation and Skills* [2014] EWCA Civ 1216 at [31].
[213] [2007] UKHL 52, [2008] 1 AC 719.
[214] Ibid at [45].

8) as unethical (and often causing suffering too). But could an intolerant majority therefore ban it and then argue that this was 'necessary in a democratic society'? Surely not.[215]

As this disagreement indicates, and as commentators have noted,[216] despite the fact that the proper ambit of the proportionality test has reached the higher courts on a number of occasions, there has not yet emerged a principled approach to its application.   **4.118**

(c) *Deference and the 'discretionary area of judgment'*

The role of courts, in the Convention system of rights protections, is to scrutinize the 'necessity' of infringements to human rights. However, the ECtHR is conscious of the limits of the social judgments it can make as a supranational court, lacking sensitivity to nuances of the particular societies of the Council of Europe states. Thus, as explained in Chapter 2,[217] the European Court frequently invokes what it calls the 'margin of appreciation' to afford Member States a reasonable sphere within which it will not interfere with their power to evaluate their public policy decisions, though they are subject to review.   **4.119**

This doctrine is an international one, based on the limitations of the international court. It has no place in domestic arrangements for protecting human rights and should not be used when the Convention is applied by national courts. It was created to allow national judicial bodies a degree of flexibility; to enable an international judicial review system to give due weight to local political and cultural traditions; and to take into account the geographical, cultural, philosophical, historical, and intellectual distance between the judges in Strasbourg and local institutions. The domestic courts do not need the doctrine because this gap does not exist. As the Grand Chamber stated in *A v UK*:   **4.120**

The doctrine of the margin of appreciation has always been meant as a tool to define relations between the domestic authorities and the Court. It cannot have the same application to the relations between the organs of State at the domestic level...the question of proportionality is ultimately a judicial decision...[218]

In the first case on the Human Rights Act to reach the House of Lords, *R (Kebilene) v DPP*, this position was confirmed.[219] Lord Hope stated that the doctrine of margin of appreciation: **4.121**

...is an integral part of the supervisory jurisdiction which is exercised over state conduct by the international court. By conceding a margin of appreciation to each national system, the court has recognised that the Convention, as a living system, does not need to be applied uniformly by all states but may vary in its application according to local needs and conditions. This technique is not available to the national courts when they are considering Convention issues arising within their own countries. But in the hands of the national courts also the Convention

---

[215] Ibid at [157]–[159].
[216] See, eg Hickman, 'The Substance and Structure of Proportionality' [2008] PL 694.
[217] See ch 2, paras 2.77–2.84.
[218] (2009) 26 BHRC 1.
[219] [2000] 2 AC 326.

should be seen as an expression of fundamental principles rather than as a set of mere rules. The questions which the courts will have to decide in the application of these principles will involve questions of balance between competing interests and issues of proportionality.[220]

4.122   However, the concept of 'deference' or a 'discretionary area of judgment' has been embraced by domestic courts as a means of respecting democratic decision-making and avoiding judicial determination of sensitive matters of social policy. In early Human Rights Act jurisprudence, a concept of 'deference' to the legislature was developed, which, in essence, involved the domestic courts attempting to translate the international law concept of 'margin of appreciation' into domestic law. In *International Transport Roth GmbH v Secretary of State for the Home Department*, for example, Laws LJ made plain that, for him, deference was one of the ways of resolving what he viewed as a tension between parliamentary sovereignty and fundamental rights, given the Human Right Act's halfway house between legislative supremacy and constitutional supremacy. He went so far as to say that, in some contexts, 'the deference is nearly absolute'.[221]

4.123   Commentators were highly critical of this approach, as it resulted in the scope of section 3 being inappropriately constrained, and determined by the courts' construction of the boundaries of deference.[222] Klug argued that it was fundamentally misguided, and misunderstood the scheme of the Human Rights Act:

> Concluding that there cannot be 'no-go' areas for judges under the HRA does not, however, necessarily require them to intrude on the rightful role of elected and accountable politicians. The Act was specifically structured to allow the courts to uphold rights while also retaining parliamentary authority. Behind the construction of ss 3 and 4 was a carefully thought-out constitutional arrangement that sought to inject principles of parliamentary accountability and transparency into judicial proceedings without removing whole policy areas to judicial determination. In other words it sought to create a new dynamic between the two branches of the State.[223]

4.124   As the courts looked to the concept of deference to shape their interpretative function, they began to list factors that determined how and when the courts should 'defer'. They included vague, nebulous concepts such as 'the culture and conditions of the British State',[224] but also concrete issues, such as whether the right in question in the case was absolute or qualified, and the subject matter of the case. The concept of 'deference' is not one that appears on the face of the Human Rights Act. However, two possible theoretical bases have been advanced by commentators: (i) constitutional legitimacy, and (ii) institutional competence.

---

[220] Ibid, 380.

[221] [2002] EWCA Civ 158, [2003] QB 78 at [75].

[222] Klug, 'Judicial Deference under the Human Rights Act 1998' (2003) 2 EHRLR 125.

[223] Ibid. See also Feldman, 'Article 14 ECHR and Deference', paper delivered to the Administrative Law Bar Association, 6 December 2005 (arguing that the suggestion that certain questions are *incapable of decision* by a court, because they raise no questions of legality, in turn suggests that in certain cases there is no authority in the United Kingdom capable of authoritatively saying that a decision is unlawful and granting a remedy).

[224] *International Transport Roth GmbH and ors v Secretary of State for the Home Department* [2002] EWCA Civ 158, [2003] QB 78 at [81] per Laws LJ.

(i) *Constitutional legitimacy* This is the suggestion that, as a matter of constitu- 4.125
tional law and constitutional principle, the courts are less democratically accountable, and therefore less legitimate, than the elected branches of government, in
particular when dealing with issues of acute social sensitivity, such as terrorism.[225]

This approach was powerfully advanced by Lord Hoffmann in *R (Prolife* 4.126
Alliance) v BBC.[226] He held that a social judgement as to the 'offensiveness' or otherwise of material contained in a proposed party election broadcast was one which
Parliament had decided was apt to be reached by the broadcasters themselves, and
that it would be contrary to the principle of the separation of powers for the courts
to abrogate that role. Similarly, in *R (Nicklinson) v Ministry of Justice* the Supreme
Court held that decisions about whether to decriminalize assisted suicide raised
controversial questions of social policy that should be decided by Parliament.[227]
Speaking extra-judicially, Lord Sumption has issued a strong critique of 'judicial
law-making' and suggested that rights should be developed via political processes,
rather than the courts.[228]

(ii) *Institutional competence* Another, more nuanced argument for a form of defer- 4.127
ence is based on 'institutional competence'—the idea that the courts and the legislature have differing expertise, and also differing access to the relevant information.

This approach has been proposed by, among others, Lord Steyn. He wrote an 4.128
influential article in Public Law which was highly critical of Lord Hoffmann's
approach in the *ProLife Alliance* case, instead commending the 'balanced approach'
to deference based on institutional competence. 'At the risk of over-simplification',
he said:

The rule of law requires that courts do not surrender their responsibilities. So far as the courts
desist from making decisions in a particular case it should not be on grounds of separation of
powers, or other constitutional principle. Deference may lead the courts not to make their own
decisions on an issue. The degree of deference which the courts should show will, of course,
depend on and vary with the context. The true justification for a court exceptionally declining
to decide an issue, which is within its jurisdiction, is the relative institutional competence or
capacity of the branches of government.[229]

This approach to deference, based on relative institutional competence, has been 4.129
applied in a number of cases, the courts indicating that there is an area of judgment
within which the judiciary will defer, on democratic grounds, to the considered
opinion of the legislature or the executive. The Lord Chancellor summarized this
approach in 2006:

Whether and to what extent the courts will recognise a 'discretionary area of judgment'
depends upon the subject matter of the decision being challenged, but policy decisions made

---

[225] See, eg *(RB) Algeria v Secretary of State for the Home Department* [2009] UKHL 10, [2009] 2 WLR 512.
[226] [2003] UKHL 23, [2004] 1 AC 185.
[227] [2014] UKSC 38.
[228] Lord Sumption, 'The Limits of the Law', 27th Sultan Azlan Shah Lecture, 20 November 2013, available at: <http://www.supremecourt.gov.uk/docs/speech-131120.pdf>.
[229] Steyn, 'Deference: A Tangled Story' [2005] PL 346, 352.

by Parliament on matters of national security, criminal justice and economic policy are accorded particular respect.[230]

4.130 A third approach is to say that the language of deference is inappropriate and unhelpful, within a structured approach to proportionality analysis. Given the requirement for courts to 'give effect' to human rights principles, under section 6(1) and (3) of the Human Rights Act, the mechanism for avoiding courts overstepping the mark and becoming legislators is for Parliament to pass legislation which cannot be interpreted compatibly with the Convention (and so which renders it impossible for courts to act compatibility with the Convention, under section 6(2)). The domestic courts must themselves apply the doctrine of proportionality, and consider the limits of their 'institutional competence' only in order to determine what is proportionate in particular circumstances, having regard to the subject matter of the issue in play, and the subject matter of the particular complaint before them.[231]

J. ENFORCEMENT OF THE HUMAN RIGHTS ACT IN SUMMARY

4.131 Regardless of the rhetoric as to the constitutional significance of the Human Rights Act, its key purpose was to give citizens a practical right to use the Convention in our national courts—to 'bring rights home'. The Human Rights Act seeks to achieve this through the various mechanisms described in this chapter, bolstered by the Equality and Human Rights Commission's powers to bring cases in its own right and to inquire into human rights issues. Human rights arguments can now be made and relied upon in any court or tribunal in the United Kingdom. There remain, however, a number of logistical and conceptual difficulties with the Human Rights Act which undermine its ability to ensure that rights are 'practical and effective' rather than 'theoretical and illusory'. In particular, the courts' restrictive approach to Human Rights Act remedies has been disappointing, especially given the broad statutory leeway in section 8; and the repeated and lengthy delays by government in responding to declarations of incompatibility from the courts frustrate the Act's central purpose.

4.132 Pre-emptive measures to protect and promote human rights are, of course, preferable to 'after-the-fact' remedies. Ideally, there should be less litigation under the Human Rights Act, not because of restrictions on access to justice, but because fewer statutes, rules, or practices that violate human rights remain in force. The importance of pre-emptive measures has long been recognized by many jurisdictions throughout Europe, which have processes of 'abstract review' whereby the judiciary is able to evaluate the general compliance of Bills or recently enacted statutes

[230] *Review of the Implementation of the Human Rights Act*, Executive Summary (25 July 2006), 4, available at <http://www.justice.gov.uk>.
[231] See, in particular, the speech of Lord Nicholls in *Ghaidan v Godin-Mendoza* [2004] UKHL 30, [2004] 2 AC 557 at [19].

for their compatibility with Convention rights.[232] While no such process exists under the Human Rights Act (apart from the limited and exceptional approach adopted in *R (Rusbridger) v Attorney General*),[233] there are now a number of forms of pre-legislative scrutiny, including the Commission's power to advise government on the likely effect of a proposed change of law or existing enactment.[234] The Joint Committee on Human Rights also plays a crucial role, highlighting concerns at an early stage. Indeed, this is recognized by the Cabinet Office guidance to ministers, which reminds them that, in preparing a compatibility statement for a Bill pursuant to section 19 of the Human Rights Act, they should bear in mind that the Joint Committee 'will report on the ECHR issues raised by a Bill and is likely to examine closely the arguments put forward by the department justifying interference with a Convention right'.[235]

---

[232] See also the discussion of the Select Committee on the Constitution on 'advisory declarations' (in which the courts would be called upon to give guidance to the Government on Convention rights): Sixth Report (2006–2007), HL 151, para 11.

[233] [2003] UKHL 38, [2004] 1 AC 357.

[234] Equality Act 2006, s 11(2).

[235] Cabinet Office, *Guide to Making Legislation: ECHR*, 9 July 2014, available at <https://www.gov.uk/government/publications/guide-to-making-legislation>.

5

THE INTERACTION BETWEEN CONVENTION PRINCIPLES AND EUROPEAN UNION LAW

A. INTRODUCTION

This chapter concerns the ways in which Convention arguments are considered in   **5.01**
cases within the scope of European Union (EU) law.[1] This is not the place for a
wide discussion of the history or present state of development of human rights in
the law of the EU. Nor is it the source of a detailed discussion of the emerging case
law on the European Charter of Fundamental Rights. Sources of more detailed
analysis of these subjects are given in Chapter 10. However, no lawyer dealing with
an argument of EU law (or of application of the law of the EU by UK authorities)
can afford to ignore Convention arguments. This is because:

(a) EU law is informed by Convention principles;

(b) EU law is part of the law of the United Kingdom. In the EU's fields of compe-
    tence, Article 4(3) TEU requires Member States to give effect to EU law, and
    section 2 of the European Communities Act 1972 requires UK courts to give
    EU law rights effect in the United Kingdom. The doctrines of supremacy and

---

[1] Pursuant to the Lisbon Treaty, discussed in more detail at para 5.17. The distinction between the
European Community and the European Union (EU) was abolished; henceforth there was to be just one
body, the EU, which would have its own legal personality: see Arts 1 and 47 of the Treaty on European
Union (TEU).

direct effect, together with the interpretative *Marleasing*[2] principle, are relevant in this regard;

(c) sections 3 and 6 of the Human Rights Act require UK courts to give effect to Convention principles wherever possible, and this includes cases where they are relevant to interpreting questions of EU law;

(d) the European Court of Human Rights (ECtHR) has been prepared to consider the compatibility with the Convention of actions of Member States which have been taken in order to comply with obligations under EU law;

(e) there may be circumstances in which there are tactical or procedural advantages in using the Convention through EU law, or in using Convention arguments in determining the scope of EU obligations;

(f) lawyers need to be able to assess whether there is an advantage in arguing a case on the basis of the EU Charter of Fundamental Rights rather than (or as well as) on the basis of the Convention;

(g) if, as the Conservative party says will be in its manifesto for the May 2015 general election,[3] a post-2015 government abolishes the Human Rights Act, the Convention may still remain part of UK law in fields of EU competence by virtue of the TEU and the European Communities Act 1972.

5.02   This chapter outlines the developing doctrine of fundamental rights in EU case law, and then examines how EU and Convention principles will overlap in practice.

B. THE DEVELOPING DOCTRINE OF FUNDAMENTAL RIGHTS IN EU LAW

5.03   Pursuant to Article 6(2) TEU, the EU 'shall accede' to the European Convention for the Protection of Human Rights and Fundamental Freedoms (Convention). In April 2013, a Draft Agreement on Accession of the European Union to the European Convention of Human Rights was reached between the Council of Europe and the European Commission. This development is considered later (see paras 5.17–5.18). For present purposes it should be noted that the EU has not, at the time of writing, acceded to the Convention. Indeed, in Opinion 2/13, published on 18 December 2014, shortly before this book went to press, the Court of Justice of the European Union (CJEU[4]) cast doubt on whether it is yet possible for it to do so. However, that does not mean that the EU courts have not recognized the importance of fundamental rights protection as a matter of EU law and the 'special significance' of the Convention, to which all Member States are party, as a source of such protection.[5] The CJEU has

---

[2] Case C–106/89 *Marleasing SA v La Comercial Internacional de Alimentacion* [1990] ECR I–4135.

[3] *Protecting Human Rights in the United Kingdom*, 3 October 2014.

[4] Referred to here throughout for consistency as the CJEU. Note that before the three constituent courts of the EU were brought together under Article 19 TFEU (for these purposes), relevant decisions were generally taken by the European Court of Justice (ECJ), one of the three constituent courts of the CJEU.

[5] *Opinion 2/94 on Accession by the Community to the ECHR* [1996] ECR I–1759 at [33]. The 'Copenhagen criteria' for accession require candidate countries to protect human and minority rights, which in practice means ratification of the Convention prior to accession to the Union.

undoubtedly developed a doctrine of 'fundamental rights' in EU law, which the other institutions have reinforced through documents such as the Charter of Fundamental Rights. Article 2 TEU reinforces the importance of such rights in the EU legal order. It reads:

The Union is founded on the principles of human dignity, freedom, democracy, equality, the rule of law and respect for human rights, including the rights of persons belonging to minorities. These values are common to the Member States in a society in which pluralism, non-discrimination, tolerance, justice, solidarity and equality between men and women prevail.

Echoing almost word-for-word the CJEU's jurisprudence, Article 6(3) TEU provides:

Fundamental rights, as guaranteed by [the Convention] and as they result from the constitutional traditions common to the Member States, shall constitute general principles of Union law.

The growing importance of that fundamental rights jurisprudence is explained both by the expanding scope of EU competence and by increased awareness of the importance of human and other fundamental rights across the EU. 5.04

The EU—then known as the European Economic Community—began its life as a largely economic body, but its competence has gradually expanded over many areas—for example, free movement of persons, asylum, extradition, and certain aspects of foreign and security policy—which raise human rights issues that are particularly sensitive. Talk of human rights within the EU was amplified by the adoption in 1997 at the Treaty of Amsterdam of what is now Article 19 of the Treaty on the Functioning of the European Union (TFEU) and the measures which have used it as a legislative base,[6] and by the adoption in December 2000 of the Charter of Fundamental Rights (see paras 5.11–5.16). 5.05

The protection of fundamental rights was, however, not found in the Treaty but was 'discovered' by the CJEU as a 'general principle' of EU law. By common consent this development occurred as a reaction to the concern expressed by the German Constitutional Court in the 1970s about the CJEU's similar 'discovery' of the principles of supremacy and direct effect of EU law, which the German court saw as a potential threat to rights protected by the German Constitution.[7] There is now a considerable body of CJEU case law, much of which has stressed the importance of the Convention as a source for the EU's law of fundamental rights. In Advisory Opinion 2/94,[8] the CJEU held that the EU did not, then, have competence to accede to the Convention. However, the CJEU was at pains to assert (para 33) that: 5.06

...it is well settled that fundamental rights form an integral part of the general principles of law whose observance the Court ensures. For that purpose, the Court draws inspiration from the constitutional traditions common to the Member States and from the guidelines supplied

---

[6] Directive (EC) 2000/43 implementing the principle of equal treatment between persons irrespective of racial or ethnic origins [2000] OJ L180/22; and Directive (EC) 2000/78 [2000] OJ L303/16 ('the Framework Employment Directive').

[7] See, generally, Craig and De Burca, *EU Law: Text, Cases and Materials*, 5th edn (Oxford: Oxford University Press, 2011) ch 11.

[8] [1996] ECR I–1759.

by international treaties for the protection of human rights on which the Member States have collaborated or of which they are signatories.[9]

5.07   The CJEU has applied its fundamental rights jurisprudence to Member States when they apply EU law as well as to the EU's own institutions. It has held that Member States implementing, or derogating from, EU rules must do so in a way that is compatible with fundamental rights that derive in particular from the Convention.[10] For example, in *Elliniki Radiophonia Tileorassi AE (ERT) v Dimotiki Etairia Pliroforissis (DEP)*,[11] restrictions on television licences (which constituted a derogation from free movement rights) were considered by reference to Article 10 of the Convention. In his opinion in *Konstantinidis v Stadt Altensteig-Standesamt*,[12] Advocate-General Jacobs said that an EU national could 'oppose any violation of his fundamental rights' when exercising EU free movement rights in another Member State. This was reflected by the judgment of the CJEU in *Carpenter v Secretary of State for the Home Department*.[13] In the *Carpenter* case it was held that the decision to deport the applicant interfered with her husband's free movement rights and that the United Kingdom could invoke reasons of public interest to justify the national measure which did this only if it was compatible with fundamental rights. Having regard to the case law of the ECtHR, the decision to deport the applicant did not strike a fair balance between the right of Mr Carpenter to respect for his family life and the maintenance of public order.

5.08   That does not mean that the CJEU and ECtHR always interpret Convention rights harmoniously. For example, the two courts have interpreted the principle of protection against self-incrimination in divergent ways.[14] In addition, there is sometimes a direct conflict between Convention rights and a freedom considered by EU law to be 'fundamental', such as the free movement of goods. It may be that the CJEU weighs the competing interests differently from the ECtHR.[15] Nonetheless, divergences have in practice been rare. However, Opinion 2/13 underscores the CJEU's perception that in EU constitutional terms, it should have the last word on all matters of EU law.

5.09   It has been unclear how far the CJEU regards the standards in the Convention as a minimum below which the EU may not fall, or merely as 'inspiration' or 'guidelines',[16]

---

[9] This is a doctrine which has frequently been reiterated in the case law of the CJEU: see, inter alia, Case C–20/00 *Booker Acquaculture Ltd (t/a Marine Harvest McConnell) v Scottish Ministers* [2003] ECR I–7411 and Case C–105/03 *Criminal Proceedings Against Pupino* [2005] ECR I-5285, paras 58–60. The CJEU has gone further, and recognized the 'special significance' of the Convention as a source of principles of EU law: see, eg Case 36/75 *Rutili v Ministre de l'Interieur* [1975] ECR 1219 and Case C–112/00 *Schmidberger v Austria* [2003] ECR I–5659, para 71.

[10] See, eg Case C–20/00 *Booker Acquaculture v Secretary of State for Scotland* [2003] ECR I–7411.

[11] Case C–260/89 [1991] ECR I–2925, paras 41–45.

[12] Case C–168/91 [1993] ECR I–1191.

[13] Case C–60/00 [2002] ECR I–6279.

[14] Compare Case 374/87 *Orkem v Commission* [1989] ECR 3283 with *Funke v France* (1993) EHRR 297.

[15] For an example of such conflict, namely a conflict between freedom of expression and assembly, in the form of an environmental demonstration, and the free movement of goods, see Case C–112/00 *Schmidberger v Austria* [2003] ECR I–5659, paras 71–77.

[16] Case 136/79 *National Panasonic (UK) Ltd v Commission* [1980] ECR 2033; Case C–427/85 *Commission v Germany* [1989] ECR I–1263; Case C–299/95 *Kremzow v Austria* [1997] ECR I–2629; Case C–85/96 *Martinez Sala v Freistaat Bayern* [1998] ECR I–2691; Case C–274/96 *Criminal Proceedings*

although it frequently refers to the jurisprudence of the ECtHR, particularly in cases where there is a directly engaged Convention right, such as Article 6 or 8.[17] That is particularly so where the right in question is also one found in the Charter of Fundamental Rights. In other cases where human rights arguments are relevant, again, the CJEU makes extensive reference to the ECtHR's decisions, and this is a developing trend.[18] In *J McB v LE*,[19] the CJEU appeared to go further, ruling that where Charter rights parallel ECtHR rights, the CJEU should follow any clear and consistent case law of the ECtHR, (so that in that case, the rights in Article 7 of the Charter, which contained rights corresponding to those guaranteed by Article 8(1) ECHR, 'must therefore be given the same meaning and scope as Article 1(1) of the ECHR as interpreted by the caselaw of the European Court of Human Rights'). However, whatever the theoretical principles, and whatever the tendency to convergence in the case law, there have been some cases in which the CJEU has decided issues that plainly do engage matters within the ambit of Convention rights in a way that appears to differ from the ECtHR's decisions, without making reference to them. This arises particularly where the issue in the case is the content of a Convention right and its application to the EU legal order and its prerogatives. In *Emesa Sugar (Free Zone) NV v Aruba*,[20] for example, the CJEU reviewed its own procedures by reference to Article 6 of the Convention, distinguished the case law of the ECtHR in ways which have surprised some commentators, and held that there was no violation of the right to a fair trial.

5.10 In sum, although Convention standards are not, formally speaking, part of EU law, they are undoubtedly the most important source for establishing the 'common traditions' of the EU Member States. Whether or not the CJEU always applies Convention principles correctly, it is clear that it affords special significance to the decisions of the ECtHR, and considers them at least as persuasive as the UK courts do when considering them under section 2 of the Human Rights Act.[21] In effect, the CJEU applies the Convention directly, by requiring EU secondary law, acts of the institutions, and rules of national law within the scope of EU law to be reviewed for conformity with Convention principles. This suggests that the Convention standards are (already) regarded as a requisite minimum standard of human rights protection in the EU.

C. THE EU CHARTER OF FUNDAMENTAL RIGHTS

5.11 The Charter is an EU instrument—it is wholly distinct from the Convention, though clearly informed by it. The Charter is addressed to the EU and its institutions, and

---

Against Bickel [1998] ECR I–7637; Case C–105/03 *Criminal Proceedings against Pupino* [2005] ECR I-5285; Case T–315/01 *Kadi v Council and Commission* (Case T-315/01) [2005] ECR II-3649.

[17] See, eg Case C-450/06 *Varec SA v Belgium* [2008] ECR I–581 (on Art 8).
[18] See, eg *Ocalan v Council of the European Union* [2007] ECR I–439, paras 71, 81.
[19] Case C–400/10, [2010] ECR I–08965, paras 48, 53.
[20] Case C–17/98 [2000] ECR I–665.
[21] See Case C–465/07 *Elgafaji v Saatssecretaris an Justitie* [2009] ECR I-921, [2009] 1 WLR 2100, para 28.

Member States when they are implementing Union law, and requires states to promote the rights contained in it. Originally 'solemnly proclaimed' in 2000, the Charter was seen by some as simply an attempt to 'codify' the fundamental rights which were protected under EU law and by others as a highly symbolic 'constitutional' moment in the EU's history. Whilst originally not legally binding,[22] that changed with the adoption of the Lisbon Treaty: now, by virtue of Article 6(1) TEU, it has the same legal status as the TEU and TFEU; in other words, it is part of EU primary law. It is apparent from the growing body of case law that the Charter is treated by the CJEU as 'hard law', and it soon may be that consideration of Charter principles in effect takes over as the primary source of human rights protection in the EU and within the scope of EU law, rather than consideration of 'fundamental rights' more loosely defined by reference to Convention standards. In the light of Opinion 2/13, it may be that Charter standards become more important than Convention standards as a guarantee of human rights in the EU legal order.

5.12   The Preamble to the Charter refers to the values set out in Article 2 TEU and 'reaffirms' the Convention, the Social Charters adopted by the EU and the Council of Europe, and the case law of both the CJEU and ECtHR. The substance of the Charter is divided into six chapters: I Dignity; II Freedoms; III Equality; IV Solidarity; V Citizens' Rights; and VI Justice. The final chapter, VII, contains general clauses which relate to the interpretation and scope of application of the Charter, including the bodies to which it is addressed.

5.13   It will immediately be seen that the rights and principles set out in the Charter go beyond the rights found in the Convention and include various specific equality rights,[23] a host of socio-economic rights,[24] and various political rights.[25] That said, a distinction should be drawn between 'rights' and 'principles' set out in the Charter: according to Article 51(1) thereof, the rights must be 'respected'; the principles merely 'observed'.[26] The extent to which the CJEU will recognize the significance of this distinction is one of the various interesting issues which will doubtless arise for consideration.

5.14   Articles 51 to 54 of the Charter set out general provisions on its interpretation and scope of application. Article 51 provides, importantly, that the Charter applies to the EU institutions and to the Member States only when they are implementing EU law. Whilst this may have been an attempt to restrict the Charter's scope of application, it has not stopped the CJEU from applying it to acts of Member States in situations

---

[22] This did not stop the CJEU and even the ECtHR from regarding it as a reference point for fundamental rights protection: see, respectively, Case C–540/03 *European Parliament v Council* [2006] ECR I–5769, para 38 and *Goodwin v UK* (2002) 35 EHRR 18, para 100.

[23] See, eg Arts 24 and 25 on the rights of the child and the elderly respectively.

[24] See, eg Art 35 on the right of access to preventive healthcare and to benefit from medical treatment.

[25] See, eg Art 39 on the right to vote and to stand as a candidate at elections to the European Parliament.

[26] See also Art 52(5) of the Charter: '[t]he provisions of this Charter which contain principles may be implemented by legislative and executive acts taken by institutions, bodies, offices and agencies of the Union, and by acts of Member States when they are implementing Union law, in the exercise of their respective powers. They shall be judicially cognisable only in the interpretation of such acts and in the ruling on their legality.' See also the Explanations Relating to the Charter of Fundamental Rights [2007] OJ C303/17 (the relevance of which is explained by Art 52(7) of the Charter) on this point.

where they were not implementing EU law.[27] Moreover, the scope of EU law has been interpreted very widely indeed. So in *Aklagaven v Fransson*,[28] the CJEU applied Charter standards to Swedish trial procedures which were solely a matter of domestic law because the criminal proceedings in question concerned VAT fraud, and VAT law has an EU underpinning.

The relationship between the Charter and the Convention is set out in Article 52(3), which provides: 5.15

> Insofar as this Charter contains rights which correspond to rights guaranteed by the Convention for the Protection of Human Rights and Fundamental Freedoms, the meaning and scope of those rights shall be the same as those laid down by the said Convention.

This provision shall not prevent Union law providing more extensive protection. In other words, Convention rights represent a minimum standard for EU law.[29] However, in the light of Strasbourg cases concerning return of asylum seekers to EU countries where their rights are not fully protected and respected, and Opinion 2/13, in which the CJEU sought to assert its legal primacy in the EU, it is now open to doubt as to what a Member State is intended to do if the CJEU and ECtHR interpret Convention standards in different ways. Article 53 provides that the Charter does not restrict or adversely affect fundamental rights as recognized more generally by EU law, by general international law, by international agreements to which the EU or all its Member States are party, or by the Member States' constitutions. Finally, Article 54 prohibits the abuse of the rights safeguarded by the Charter.

In *Zagorski v Secretary of State for Business, Innovation and Skills* the High Court   5.16
held that the jurisdictional reach of the Charter was no wider than that of the Convention. Whilst there was no provision in the Charter akin to Article 1 of the Convention, Article 52(3) of the Charter had a 'vital bearing' on the issue: in the court's view, not only the material but also the personal scope of the Charter was to be the same as that of the Convention.[30]

D. ACCESSION TO THE CONVENTION

The ECtHR is not, at present, prepared to consider the conformity of the actions   5.17
of EU bodies themselves with Convention standards, even if creatively addressed

---

[27] See, eg Joined Cases C–570 and 571/07 *Perez and Gomez* [2010] ECR I–04626, 1 June 2010 and Case C–34/09 *Zambrano* [2011] ECR I–01177, 8 March 2011. See also Case C–555/07 *Kücükdeveci v Swedex GmbH* [2010] 2 CMLR 33, 19 January 2010 and Case C–176/12 *Association de Mediation Sociale v Union Locale des syndicats CGT* [2014] 2 CMLR 41 (allowing for the Charter to be given horizontal direct effect, ie to be relied upon in proceedings between private parties).

[28] Case C–617/10, [2013] 2 CMLR 46.

[29] For an example of a case in which the CJEU has gone further than the ECtHR in terms of fundamental rights protection, see Case C–465/07 *Elgafaji v Staatssecretaris van Justitie* [2009] ECR I–921 (requirements for refugee status under Art 3 of the Convention).

[30] [2010] EWHC 3110 (Admin), [2011] HRLR 6 at [73].

as an application against all EU Member States.[31] As already explained, however, the TEU mandates the EU to accede to the Convention, though, in the light of Opinion 2/13, how this will occur is open to serious doubt. Protocol 8 to the Lisbon Treaty on the EU's accession to the Convention provides than any such agreement shall make provision for preserving the specific characteristics of the Union and Union law. Thus, there will be many matters that require resolution. One such matter is whether responsibility for complying with the Convention rests with the Member States, collectively or individually, or with the Union institutions. Another concerns the relationship between the CJEU and ECtHR: it is clear that the CJEU wishes to ensure that it is always in a position to assess the validity of EU acts for Convention compliance before the ECtHR itself does so (upon application by an aggrieved party), and so a mechanism will need to be devised to ensure that this will be possible. The particular scenario in which, absent a specific mechanism, there would be a risk of the CJEU not having such a review function is where a claimant indirectly challenges an EU act on Convention grounds by attacking an implementing measure of the competent national authority. If the national court considers there to be no serious grounds on which to impugn the EU act and therefore dismisses the claim, and assuming appellate courts dismiss any appeals, the claimant will have exhausted domestic remedies and so will be entitled to apply to the ECtHR.[32]

5.18   The Council of Europe and the European Commission reached a Draft Agreement on Accession of the European Union to the European Convention on Human Rights on 5 April 2013. Article 4(1) of this Draft Agreement provided for the EU to be co-respondent in cases before the ECtHR in which a Member State is alleged to have breached the Convention in implementing EU law. In such a case, if the CJEU had not yet assessed the compatibility with Convention rights at issue of the provision of EU law at stake, it would be given the opportunity to make such an assessment. The parties in the case before the ECtHR were to have been allowed to make observations about this assessment. Under the Draft Agreement, if the ECtHR had found a violation in a case in which a Member State and the EU were co-respondents, both would be responsible for the violation unless the ECtHR had decided that only one of them would be held responsible (Article 3(7)).

5.19   The Draft Agreement would not, by itself, have meant that accession of the EU to the ECHR was imminent. Before a final agreement could have been reached under EU law, Article 218(1) TFEU required an opinion from the CJEU on the compatibility of the agreement with the EU Treaties. Had that opinion been positive, the Agreement would still have required the unanimous agreement of the Council of the EU and the approval of all EU Member States (Article 218(8) TFEU). From the

---

[31] See *Guérin Automobiles v 15 Members of the EU* App No 5157/99, which was declared inadmissible on 4 July 2000; and *Segi and ors v 15 Members of the EU* App No 6422/02.

[32] In January 2011 the Presidents of the CJEU and ECtHR issued a joint communication in which they called for the creation of a procedure which would allow for an 'internal' review, possibly under an accelerated procedure, prior to the ECtHR conducting its 'external review': see <http://www.echr.coe.int/NR/rdonlyres/02164A4C-0B63-44C3-80C7-FC594EE16297/0/2011Communication_CEDHCJUE_EN.pdf>.

Council of Europe side, it would also have required ratification by all ECHR states. However, on 18 December 2014, just before this book went to press, the CJEU issued Opinion 2/13,[33] in which it concluded that the Draft Agreement providing for the EU's accession to the ECHR is incompatible with EU law.

Opinion 2/13 has led to considerable comment and criticism.[33A] The ramifica- 5.19A
tions are still unknown. In particular, there has been discussion as to whether the ECtHR will continue to regard there as being a rebuttable presumption that a Member State of the EU acting in compliance with EU law also complies with the ECHR. There is a high degree of uncertainty as to what may follow. But it is clear that it is now very unlikely that the EU will accede to the ECHR any time soon.

E. THE INTERACTION OF EU LAW AND CONVENTION PRINCIPLES IN UK COURTS

Opinion 2/13 concluded (at paragraph 258) that the Draft Agreement was not 5.20
compatible with Article 6(2) TEU or with Protocol 8 EU in that it was liable to affect the specific characteristics and autonomy of EU law. The particular problems which were identified in the Opinion were that Article 53 of the ECHR treats the Convention as a floor not a ceiling (it provides that the Convention does not limit or derogate from any of the human rights and fundamental freedoms which may be ensured under the laws of any Member State or under any other agreement to which it is a party); but Article 53 of the Charter requires Member States to abide by EU law, and in the *Melloni* decision C399/11, 26 February 2013, it was held that Member States may not set standards of human rights protection higher than Charter standards in order to avoid obligations under EU law in respect of cross-border aspects of the European Arrest Warrant. The CJEU considered that the Draft Agreement might undermine mutual trust between Member States under EU law. The CJEU also said that the Draft Agreement was contrary to Article 344 TFEU because it did not preclude the possibility of disputes as between Member States or between the Member States and the EU concerning the application of the ECHR within the scope of EU law being brought before the ECtHR, which would undermine the fundamental constitutional character of the CJEU.

First, many cases that involve EU law rights concern the balance to be struck 5.21
between a right contained in EU law and the state's power to protect a competing public interest (for example, public order or public safety). In such cases, a public authority might argue that the public interest exception to the underlying EU law right is engaged. Whether this is in fact the case involves a decision as to whether

---

[33] http://curia.europa.eu/juris/document/document.jsf?text=&docid=160882.
[33A] see http://eutopialaw.com.

the proposed restriction on the underlying right can be justified in the public interest. The scope of the state's power to restrict the underlying EU law right may be limited by having regard to case law of the ECtHR. For example, in the *Carpenter* case described at para 5.07, the scope of the exception to free movement rights contained in Article 56 TFEU was limited by the CJEU 'in the light of the fundamental right to respect for family life' as it had been interpreted by the ECtHR. More recently, in *J McB v LE*,[34] the CJEU ruled that where Charter rights are equivalent to ECHR rights, the CJEU must follow any clear and consistent jurisprudence of the ECtHR.

5.22 Secondly, the ECtHR has been clear that the fact that a Member State may be acting so as to give effect to an obligation imposed upon it by EU law will not justify a breach of the Convention, if one exists. So, in *Cantoni v France*,[35] the ECtHR held that a national legislative provision based on a Community directive did not remove the provision from the scope of the Convention or the Member State from its responsibility to ensure that offences imposed by implementing measures complied with Article 7 of the Convention. And in *Matthews v UK*,[36] the applicant, a resident of Gibraltar, successfully challenged the failure to afford her a vote in EU elections, even though she did not reside in a territory which was defined as part of the United Kingdom for the purposes of European parliamentary elections. The ECtHR nonetheless found a breach of Article 3 of Protocol 1 by the United Kingdom. It has usually been considered that this scenario would arise only rarely, in cases where the CJEU had offered an opinion on the human rights compatibility of the measure in question,[37] however, some commentators have questioned whether the Strasbourg Court will continue to operate a rebuttable presumption that a state acting compatibly with EU law will comply with Convention principles, following the publication of Opinion 2/13.

5.23 Thirdly, we have seen that the Charter is broader, in terms of the rights enumerated, than the Convention and that the CJEU is prepared to give it a liberal

---

[34] [2010] ECR I–08965 at [53].

[35] Reports of Judgments and Decisions 1996-V, 1614.

[36] (1999) 28 EHRR 361.

[37] Note *Bosphorus Hava Yollari Turizm Ve Ticaret AS v Ireland* (2006) 42 EHRR 1, in which the Grand Chamber of the ECtHR said that there was a rebuttable presumption that a state would not depart from Convention standards in acting so as to comply with its obligations as a member of another international organization (such as the EU). This presumption held only *if* the relevant international organization offered protection of fundamental rights which was *at least equivalent* to that provided by the Convention. The ECtHR found that the EU did offer such protection; however, if in any individual case the Court considered that the protection of Convention rights within the structure of the international organization was 'manifestly deficient', the presumption could be rebutted. The rebuttable presumption that the EU offered equivalent protection to human rights was called into question, however, in *Michaud v France* [2014] 59 EHRR 9. In that case, the ECtHR declined to presume that EU law contained equivalent protection to the Convention when considering whether an obligation on lawyers to report reasonable suspicion of money laundering or terrorist financing, pursuant to the EU Money Laundering Directive, was compatible with Article 8 ECHR. Firstly, a Directive granted a Member State a 'margin of manoeuvre' as to how an obligation was to be achieved. Secondly (and 'above all') it distinguished the *Bosphorus* case because the French *Conseil d'état* had not referred the question to the CJEU, and so there was no preliminary ruling of the CJEU on this subject in the *Michaud* case.

interpretation in terms of its scope of application. Where EU law is in play, therefore, it may go further than the Convention. Conversely, however, Article 53 of the Charter and the *Melloni* principle, which was affirmed by the CJEU in Opinion 2/13, may sometimes mean that EU law acts as a ceiling on permissible UK human rights protection.

Fourthly, even after the incorporation of the Convention into domestic law, there may be cases in areas covered by EU law rights in which the Convention will be more effective if it is used in conjunction with EU law than on its own through the Human Rights Act. The most obvious is where the provision complained of is contained in a statute that falls within the sphere of EU competence. Pursuant to section 2 of the European Communities Act 1972 and the case law of the CJEU, EU law has supremacy over conflicting provisions of domestic law—it can override even Acts of Parliament where it is directly effective—and domestic law must be interpreted, so far as possible, in light of any relevant EU law, whether directly effective or not (the so-called *Marleasing* principle[38]). This means that EU law can be used to 'strike down' inconsistent domestic legislation.[39] This makes EU law in some respects more powerful than the Human Rights Act, which explicitly prevents the courts from using the Convention to 'strike down' incompatible primary legislation.[40]

In spheres of EU competence, it may therefore be more beneficial to use the Convention through EU law rather than through the Human Rights Act alone where the challenge is to primary legislation. Whereas the Act alone would permit the court only to declare the domestic legislation incompatible with the Convention (see section 4), if primary domestic legislation contravenes directly effective EU legislation, the national court is required to disapply the primary domestic legislation. Therefore, if a court or tribunal could be persuaded that a provision of EU law must be interpreted in accordance with the Convention, and where EU law is directly effective, the Convention standard will become part of domestic law even to the extent of overriding inconsistent domestic provisions.[41]

Fifthly, if an argument falls within both Convention and EU law, more beneficial remedies might be available under EU law than could be obtained under the Human Rights Act alone. The Human Rights Act expressly excludes the possibility of obtaining damages against the state for a failure to legislate (see Chapter 3, para 3.18). However, under EU law damages must in principle be available if the state has committed a 'sufficiently serious' breach of EU law (including where the

5.24

5.25

5.26

---

[38] Case C–106/89 *Marleasing SA v La Comercial Internacional de Alimentacion* [1990] ECR I–4135. The *Marleasing* principle is that when a national court interprets domestic law in a field governed by a directive, or other non-directly effective provision of EU law, it must do so in the light of the wording and purpose of EU legislation. See also Case C–92/92 *Collins v Imtrat Handelsgesellschaft mbH* [1993] ECR I–5145.

[39] See Case 152/84 *Marshall v Southampton and South West Hampshire Area Health Authority (Teaching)* [1986] QB 401 and Case C–213/89 *Factortame* [1990] ECR I–2433.

[40] See s 3(2)(b) and (c).

[41] For example Case C–271/91 *Marshall v Southampton and South West Hampshire Area Health Authority (Teaching) (No 2)* [1993] ICR 893.

Government has failed to transpose a directive into domestic law on time), as a result of which loss is suffered.[42] There is some debate as to whether concepts such as that of proportionality are identical under Convention and EU law.[43]

5.27   Finally, there are other tactical areas in which the interaction of EU and Convention law may be considered. For example, section 7 of the Human Rights Act gives only 'victims' of acts standing to sue. The English courts have arguably adopted a more generous attitude to representative standing in some cases involving EU law.[44] Therefore, in cases engaging EU law, it is arguable that this restrictive approach to standing would not apply, and so a 'representative' applicant may be able to argue Convention points that would not be available under the Human Rights Act alone.

5.28   Another example is that there may be a difference between an 'emanation of the state' as defined in EU law and a 'public authority' for Convention purposes. It is not yet completely settled whether there is a distinction between:

(a) the test used in judicial review proceedings,[45] in which questions as to the *sources* of power as well as the functions are potentially relevant;

(b) the test used in EU law, in which a body is held to be an emanation of the state, regardless of its legal form, if it has been made responsible pursuant to a measure adopted by the state for providing a public service, or where it has been given special powers,[46] and the definition of 'public authority' in the Human Rights Act, section 6 (see Chapter 3, paras 3.58 to 3.73).

F. CONCLUSION

5.29   It will be appreciated from this brief overview of the protection of fundamental rights under EU law that EU law, the Convention, and domestic law cannot be 'compartmentalized': the interaction between them, and the tactical benefits of pleading rights under one rather than (or in addition to) the other, must be considered carefully in any relevant case.

---

[42] See Case C–6/90 *Francovich v Italy* [1991] ECR I–5357 and Joined Cases C–46 and 48/93 *Brasserie du Pêcheur SA v Germany* [1996] ECR I–1029.

[43] See *R (Elias) v Secretary of State for Defence* [2006] EWCA Civ 1293, [2006] 1 WLR 3213 at [174]; cf *R (Countryside Alliance) v Attorney General* [2007] UKHL 52, [2008] 1 AC 719 at [132] and [162]–[166].

[44] See, eg *R v Secretary of State for the Environment, ex p Friends of the Earth* [1996] Env LR 198, compared with the rejection of standing for Consumer Associations by the CJEU in Case T–224/10 *Association belge des consommateurs test-achats ASBL v Commission supported by Électricité de France* [2011] ECR II, nyr, at paras 65–7, though cf Case C–229/05 *Ocalan v Council of the European Union* [2007] ECR I–439, para 80.

[45] See, eg *R v Panel on Take-overs and Mergers, ex p Datafin plc* [1987] QB 815.

[46] See Case C–188/89 *Foster v British Gas plc* [1990] ECR I–3313.

6

THE CONVENTION
RIGHTS: ABSOLUTE RIGHTS

A. INTRODUCTION

This chapter summarizes the content of Articles 1–4 of the European Convention **6.01** for the Protection of Human Rights and Fundamental Freedoms (Convention). These rights are generally considered absolute, in the sense that no restriction may be placed upon them and no derogation from them may be made under Article 15. Further discussion of the nature of absolute rights can be found in Chapter 2.[1]

For each article, an overview is given of the jurisprudence of the European **6.02** Court of Human Rights (ECtHR) and any remaining important cases from the European Commission on Human Rights (ECmHR). Where the domestic

---

[1] See ch 2, paras 2.25–2.27.

courts have considered an article in claims brought under the Human Rights Act, their approach is discussed alongside the European case law, and any divergences are noted.

6.03   When inviting a court to consider Convention jurisprudence under section 2 of the Human Rights Act it is important to be aware that the decisions are context-specific and often fact-sensitive. The Strasbourg organs confine themselves to an examination of the particular case before them. They are not required to review an entire system or practice, but only to determine whether the manner in which this system or practice was applied to or affected the individual applicants gave rise to any violations of the Convention. Nevertheless, the Court often sets out new principles in cases (more often in Grand Chamber cases), and those principles will then be regularly repeated in all subsequent judgments.

B. ARTICLE 1: JURISDICTION

6.04   Article 1 binds contracting parties to the Convention to secure the other Convention rights to everyone, regardless of their nationality, 'within their jurisdiction'. This effectively establishes a jurisdictional limitation on the application of the Convention. Contracting parties are responsible under the Convention for their actions within their own territory even if the effects of their actions are felt abroad, as in cases of deportation to countries where there is a real risk of torture.[2]

6.05   It is less clear when 'jurisdiction' covers extraterritorial acts. The ECtHR set out its interpretation of extraterritorial jurisdiction in *Bankovic v UK and ors*, which concerned the question of whether the bombing of Serbia, which was not party to the Convention, by contracting parties entailed responsibility under the Convention.[3] The Court took a restrictive view of jurisdiction under Article 1, finding that the jurisdictional competence of a state was primarily territorial but recognized some limited exceptions to this principle including where a state party was in 'effective control' of a foreign territory through military occupation, invitation, or acquiescence. In those circumstances, the territory in question could fall within the jurisdiction of the contracting party.

6.06   The ECtHR has considered extra-territorial jurisdiction as a result of the presence of UK forces in Iraq. In *R (Al-Saadoon and anor) v Secretary of State for Defence* the Court of Appeal addressed the plight of two Iraqi nationals who were in UK custody in Iraq, having been accused of the murder of two British servicemen.[4] They were about to be handed over to the Iraqi High Tribunal prior to the expiration of the United Nations Mandate for the presence of UK forces in Iraq in order to face war crimes charges, the sentence for which was death by hanging. In a remarkable narrowing of the principle of jurisdiction, the Court of Appeal held that in order for jurisdiction to be established under Article 1, the appellants had to show that the

---

[2] See, eg *Chahal v UK* (1997) 23 EHRR 413.
[3] (2001) 11 BHRC 435.
[4] [2009] EWCA Civ 7.

United Kingdom had the 'legal power to fulfill substantial governmental functions as a sovereign state'. The European Court rejected the Court of Appeal's reasoning. It found that respecting the applicants' Convention rights did not involve any breach of Iraqi sovereignty and the applicants' transfer violated Article 3.[5]

The European Court modified its approach to extraterritoriality in the recent decision of *Al-Skeini v UK*.[6] In the domestic decision, *R (Al-Skeini and ors) v Secretary of State for Defence*, the House of Lords had followed the ECtHR's reasoning in *Bankovic*, and found that the claims under Article 2 resulting from the death of five Iraqi citizens who had been killed during the course of military operations conducted by British forces did not fall within the jurisdiction of the Convention.[7] The Grand Chamber disagreed. Conflating the categories of exceptional extraterritorial jurisdiction in *Bankovic* it held:

> following the removal from power of the Ba'ath regime and until the accession of the Interim Government, the United Kingdom...assumed in Iraq the exercise of some of the public powers normally to be exercised by a sovereign government. In particular, the United Kingdom assumed authority and responsibility for the maintenance of security in South East Iraq. In these exceptional circumstances, the Court considers that the United Kingdom, through its soldiers engaged in security operations in Basrah during the period in question, exercised authority and control over individuals killed in the course of such security operations, so as to establish a jurisdictional link between the deceased and the United Kingdom for the purposes of Article 1.[8]

In his concurring opinion, Judge Bonello commented that 'A considerable number of different approaches to extra-territorial jurisdiction have so far been experimented with by the Court on a case-by-case basis'.[9] It remains to be seen whether *Al-Skeini* is another experiment or the last word on jurisdiction.

Following the decision of the House of Lords in *Al-Skeini*, a jurisdictional issue arose in a series of claims concerning the deaths of UK servicemen in Iraq. Their families argued that the Convention rights applied to them while they were on active service abroad. The Supreme Court first considered the claims in *R (Smith) v Secretary of State for Defence*.[10] The Court applied the House of Lords' decision in *Al-Skeini* and held that deaths outside British military bases were not within the jurisdiction of the Convention. Following the decision of the Grand Chamber in *Al-Skeini v UK*, the Supreme Court reconsidered its position in *R (Smith) v Ministry of Defence*.[11] It concluded that jurisdiction could arise from the control and authority exercised by a contracting state over its soldiers and the package of rights in the Convention could be divided and tailored to the particular circumstances of the extra-territorial act in question.

6.07

6.08

---

[5] *Al-Saadoon and Mufdhi v UK* (2010) 51 EHRR 212. See also ch 9, para 9.14.
[6] (2011) 53 EHRR 589.
[7] [2007] UKHL 26, [2008] 1 AC 153.
[8] (2011) 53 EHRR 589, at para 149.
[9] Concurring opinion of Judge Bonello, at para 7.
[10] [2010] UKSC 29, [2011] AC 1.
[11] [2013] UKSC 41, [2014] 1 AC 52.

C. ARTICLE 2: RIGHT TO LIFE

6.09   Article 2 has, not surprisingly, been described by the ECtHR as 'one of the most fundamental provisions in the Convention'.[12] With very limited exceptions, it cannot be subject to derogation under Article 15, and those exceptions are now irrelevant given the ratification and incorporation by the United Kingdom of Protocol 13. Article 2 is comprehensive, imposing a substantive obligation to protect the right to life, a substantive prohibition on the taking of life, and a procedural obligation to investigate the taking of life. The ECtHR and the domestic courts must, when called upon to make their assessment in an Article 2 case, apply 'most anxious' or 'particularly thorough' scrutiny.[13]

6.10   Although Article 2 does not explicitly prohibit the use of a death penalty that has been properly authorized, this sentence is now 'redundant' in light of Protocols 6 (which abolishes the death penalty in peacetime) and 13 (which extends the abolition to wartime).[14] The ECtHR confirmed in *Al-Saadoon and Mufdhi v UK* that the scope of Article 2 of the Convention has evolved as a result of state practice so as to prohibit the death penalty in all circumstances and that its use will also violate Article 3.[15]

1. 'Everyone'

6.11   The precise starting point of the right to life under Article 2 is controversial. Early case law suggested it applied post-natally only.[16] However, more recent ECtHR cases have indicated that this is not a hard-and-fast line. In *Boso v Italy*, the ECtHR accepted, without deciding the issue, that a foetus could potentially be a 'victim' under Article 34.[17] In *Vo v France* the Grand Chamber specifically noted that:

> The Court has yet to determine the issue of the 'beginning' of 'everyone's right to life' within the meaning of this provision and whether the unborn child has such a right.[18]

6.12   In the United Kingdom, the courts have held that, prior to birth, a foetus has no legal rights or interests.[19]

6.13   In *Evans v UK* the Grand Chamber of the ECtHR stated that in the absence of any European consensus on the scientific and legal definition of the beginning of

---

[12] *McCann v UK* (1995) 21 EHRR 97, para 197.

[13] *Sergey Shevchenko v Ukraine* App No 32478/02, 4 April 2006, para 42; *Aktas, v Turkey* [2003] ECHR 24351/94, para 271; *McCann v UK* (1995) 21 EHRR 97, para 150.

[14] Per Hammarberg, Commissioner for Human Rights, *Viewpoint* (Strasbourg: Office of the Commissioner for Human Rights, 21 August 2006). At the time of writing, all 47 members of the Council of Europe have signed Protocol 6, but Russia has yet to ratify it. Forty-five members have signed Protocol 13 and 40 have ratified it.

[15] App No 61498/08, 2 March 2010.

[16] *Paton v UK* (1980) 19 DR 244.

[17] App No 50490/99, 5 September 2002. The case was held inadmissible on other grounds.

[18] [2004] 2 FCR 577, para 82.

[19] *Evans v Amicus Healthcare Ltd* [2004] EWCA Civ 727, [2005] Fam 93.

life, 'the issue of when the right to life begins comes within the margin of appreciation which the Court generally considers that States should enjoy in this sphere'.[20]

In *Vo v France* (see para 6.11) the Grand Chamber sidestepped the issue of   6.14
whether Article 2 applies to the foetus, taking a 'decision not to decide', which
has been criticized.[21] The applicant suffered a miscarriage after she was mistakenly
given a procedure for removal of a coil while five months pregnant, and brought
a criminal complaint of unintentional homicide against the doctor. The French
courts held that the foetus was not a human person for the purposes of the French
Criminal Code.[22]

The Grand Chamber did not decide whether Article 2 applied to the foetus,   6.15
instead holding that, even if it did apply, France had not violated its provisions
because its administrative remedies were sufficient. The majority considered it
'neither desirable, nor even possible... to answer in the abstract' the question of
whether a foetus is a person.[23]

However, a minority of three judges did examine the word 'everyone' and consid   6.16
ered that Article 2 was applicable in light of scientific advances that enable a foetus
to reach viability earlier.[24] In their view, this would not necessarily render abortion
illegal under the Convention; a non-absolute right to life for the foetus could be
recognized, thus balancing the interests of the foetus and the mother.[25]

In *Tysiac v Poland* the ECtHR did not engage directly with the question of foetal   6.17
rights under Article 2 in the case of a woman denied a therapeutic abortion despite
significant risks to her eyesight as a consequence of her pregnancy.[26] Determining
the case under Article 8, the ECtHR held that the failure of the Polish authorities
to provide effective mechanisms for determining whether she met the conditions
for obtaining a lawful abortion violated her right to a private life. In an emotive dissent, Judge Borrego Borrego held that the majority favoured 'abortion on demand'
and their reasoning implied that the child's 'right to be born' contradicted the
Convention.[27]

In *A, B and C v Ireland* the Court again refused to determine whether the foetus   6.18
had a right to life under Article 2, reiterating that the question of when the right to
life begins falls within the state's margin of appreciation.[28] Most recently, in *Senturk
v Turkey*, the European Court considered a complaint of breach of Article 2 arising
out of the death of a mother and her unborn child following grossly negligent medical
treatment. The Court found that the life of the foetus was intimately connected with
that of the mother such that the Article 2 complaint in respect of the foetus did not

---

[20] (2007) 22 BHRC 190, para 46.
[21] See also Goldberg, 'Vo v France and Fetal Rights: The Decision Not to Decide' [2005] 18 Harvard Human Rights Journal.
[22] [2004] 2 FCR 577, para 19.
[23] Ibid, para 85.
[24] Ibid, concurring opinion of Judge Costa; see also the dissenting opinion of Judges Rees and Mularoni.
[25] Ibid, annex (b), para 12.
[26] (2007) 22 BHRC 155.
[27] Ibid, paras 13–15, dissent of Judge Borrego Borrego.
[28] App No 25579/05, para 237.

require separate examination. In these circumstances, it found no reason to depart from the approach in *Vo* and *A, B and C*.[29] The Court's reluctance to determine this issue is understandable in light of the divergence of European opinion on abortion, but it is legally unsatisfactory. To apply a margin of appreciation to the scope of a concept, rather than the extent of obligation to protect a particular right, sits oddly with the 'autonomous concepts' doctrine used elsewhere in the Convention.

2. Obligation to protect the right to life

6.19   The first sentence of Article 2 imposes a positive obligation on states to protect the right to life. This obliges states to 'take appropriate steps to safeguard the lives of those within [their] jurisdiction'.[30] The principal specific duty arising from this positive obligation is to provide effective criminal legislation supported by law enforcement machinery.[31] However, this also requires the state to have in place a legislative and administrative framework to effectively deter threats to life more broadly.[32] For example, in the health care context, this entails having effective administrative and regulatory systems in place designed to protect patients from professional incompetence resulting in death.[33] And, in the context of danger-ous activities, it may require state regulation to ensure the effective protection of citizens whose lives might be endangered by the inherent risks of the activities in question.[34]

6.20   In addition to the general positive duty, the ECtHR has affirmed that, in certain circumstances, the state will be obliged 'to take preventive operational measures to protect an individual whose life is at risk from the criminal acts of another indi-vidual'[35] or from suicide.[36] This obligation is enhanced in respect of individuals in a particularly vulnerable position, such as persons in state custody,[37] persons detained under mental health legislation,[38] or persons conscripted into the armed services.[39]

6.21   One situation in which this positive obligation arises concerns the duty of the police to protect members of the public. In the famous case of *Osman v UK*, the applicant argued that the police had violated Article 2 by failing to protect him and his father from a schoolteacher known to have been obsessed with the applicant. The teacher shot and wounded the applicant and killed his father. The ECtHR held that in order for the positive obligation to be engaged, the state authorities must

---

[29]   (2013) 35 BHRC 685 at [107]–[109].

[30]   *Osman v UK* (2000) 29 EHRR 245, para 115.

[31]   *Keenan v UK* (2001) 3 EHRR 913, para 88.

[32]   *Öneryildiz v Turkey* (2004) 18 BHRC 145.

[33]   *Powell v UK* (2000) 30 EHRR CD 362; *Rabone v Pennine Care NHS Trust* [2012] UKSC 2, [2012] 2 AC 72 at [19] and [93].

[34]   *Öneryildiz v Turkey* ibid at [90], considered further at para 6.22.

[35]   *Osman v UK* (2000) 29 EHRR 245.

[36]   *Keenan v UK* (2001) 3 EHRR 913.

[37]   Ibid, para 90; *Edwards v UK* (2002) 12 BHRC 190; *R (JL) v Secretary of State for Justice* [2008] UKHL 68, [2008] 3 WLR 1325 at [38].

[38]   *Savage v South Essex Partnership NHS Foundation Trust* [2008] UKHL 74, [2009] 2 WLR 115.

[39]   *Kylynç v Turkey* App No 40145/98, 7 June 2005, para 41.

have known or ought to have known that th...
yet failed to take measures within the scope of t...
might have been expected to avoid that risk.[40] The ...
reasonably could and there was therefore no violatio...
Officer L, the House of Lords focused on whether there w...
in determining the existence and extent of a positive obligatio...
life.[41] It is now clear that the real and immediate risk to life need...
or identifiable person or persons for an operational duty to arise.[42]

The broad scope of the Article 2 positive obligation is demonstra...
of *Öneryildiz v Turkey*.[43] The Grand Chamber unanimously held that ...
violated Article 2 by failing to take appropriate steps to prevent the accide...
of the applicant's relatives, slum dwellers at a rubbish tip, due to a landslide...
either by implementing appropriate measures for waste storage or providing infor...
tion to people living on slum land regarding the dangers they faced. The ECtHR ha...
extended the *Öneryildiz* principle to natural disasters. In *Budayeva and ors v Russia* the
ECtHR ruled that the Russian authorities had not taken all possible steps to mitigate
the impact of mudslides on the applicants' lives.[44]

The ECtHR has also extended the scope of the positive obligation to encompass   6.23
failure by the state to take action to prevent domestic violence. In *Opuz v Turkey* the
state failed to prosecute a husband who had repeatedly attacked his wife and daughter,
eventually killing his wife.[45] The ECtHR held that prosecutions should have been
pursued despite the withdrawal of the victim's complaints.

Although Article 2 has the potential to touch a broad range of state activities, the   6.24
requirement of a 'real and immediate' risk to life has been said to set a high threshold
for engagement of the operational duty.[46] In *Van Colle v Chief Constable of Hertfordshire
Police*, a man intending to give evidence in a Crown Court trial for theft was murdered
by the defendant.[47] The House of Lords held that the high threshold for state liability
imposed by the *Osman* test had not been met on the facts. The fact that the victim had
been an intended witness for the prosecution (the state) did not increase the nature of
the duty on the police. The ECtHR unanimously reached the same conclusion holding
that, while the relevant officer ought to have been aware of an escalating situation of
intimidation of a number of prosecution witnesses (including Mr Van Colle), there was
no decisive stage when the officer knew or ought to have known of a real and immediate risk to the life of Mr Van Colle.[48] Two judges appended concurring opinions
expressing concern at the restrictive nature of the *Osman* test.[49]

---

[40] *Osman v UK* (2000) 29 EHRR 245, para 116.
[41] *Re Officer L* [2007] UKHL 36, [2007] 1 WLR 312 at [22] *et seq*.
[42] *Sarjantson and another v Chief Constable of Humberside Police* [2014] QB 411.
[43] (2004) 18 BHRC 145.
[44] App Nos 15339/02, 21166/02, 20058/02, 11673/02 and 15343/02, 20 March 2008.
[45] (2009) BHRC 159.
[46] See, eg *Younger v UK* (2003) 33 EHRR CD 252; *Mastromatteo v Italy* [2002] ECHR 37703/97.
[47] [2008] UKHL 50, [2008] All ER 977.
[48] App No 7678/09, 13 November 2012.
[49] Judges Garlicki and Vucinic.

the defendant did not violate
om a neighbour the defendant

1ust provide appropriate medi-
ot extend to cases of mere med-
ct of detention by the state.[52]
tion Trust, the House of Lords
iped from detention in a hospi-
hat Article 2 could be engaged
was that set out by the ECtHR
immediate risk of a detained
must do all that can be reason-

me Court considered the case
tted to hospital as an informal
ot; she subsequently committed
ie leave. It held that an opera-
icide arose because the hospital

had assumed responsibility for the patient's safety, she was under the hospital's control, and the hospital had the statutory means to prevent her leaving. The duty was breached because, at the time that she went on home leave, there was a real and immediate risk of suicide and no reasonable psychiatrist would have allowed her to leave.

6.29   Assisted suicide was considered by the House of Lords in *R (Pretty) v Director of Public Prosecutions*[56] and the ECtHR in *Pretty v UK*.[57] It was argued that Article 2 extends beyond the right to life and protects the more comprehensive right to self-determination in relation to issues of life and death. However, both the House of Lords and the ECtHR rejected this, holding that Article 2 does not confer a right to die.[58] Despite this approach to assisted suicide, Article 2 does not impose a continuing obligation to provide treatment to patients in a permanent vegetative state.[59]

---

[50] [2009] UKHL 11, [2009] AC 874.

[51] *Tarariyeva v Russia* App No 4353/03, 13 December 2006; *Renolde v France* App No 5608/05, 16 October 2008.

[52] *Powell v UK* (2000) 30 EHRR CD 362; *Dodov v Bulgaria* App No 59548/00, 17 January 2008; *Savage v South Essex Partnership NHS Foundation Trust* [2008] UKHL 74, [2009] 2 WLR 115; *R (Humberstone) v Legal Services Commission* [2010] EWCA 1479, (2010) 118 BMLR 79.

[53] [2008] UKHL 74, [2009] 2 WLR 115.

[54] (2001) 33 EHRR 913.

[55] [2012] UKSC 2, [2012] 2 AC 72.

[56] [2001] UKHL 61, [2002] 1 AC 800. See also *R (Purdy) v Director of Public Prosecutions* [2009] UKHL 45, [2010] 1 AC 345.

[57] (2002) 35 EHRR 1.

[58] Cf *Savage v South Essex Partnership NHS Foundation Trust* [2008] UKHL 74, [2009] 2 WLR 115 at [11] per Lord Scott.

[59] *NHS Trust v M* [2001] Fam 348. Cf *R (Burke) v General Medical Council* [2005] EWCA Civ 1003, [2006] QB 273.

In the context of armed conflict, the House of Lords has held in *R (Gentle) v Prime Minister* that Article 2 does not apply to the process of deciding on the legality of sending British troops into combat overseas.[60] In that case, the mothers of two British soldiers who died in the Iraq conflict argued that the failure to take proper steps to ascertain whether the participation in the invasion of Iraq would comply with international law violated Article 2. The Lords held unanimously that it was impossible to infer a duty to comply with international law from the Government's positive obligation to protect life within its jurisdiction. In *R (Smith) v Secretary of State for Defence* it was accepted by the Government that the failure to protect a soldier from heatstroke could violate Article 2 where the soldier died within the UK's jurisdiction, as understood under the Convention.[61] The Justices expressed differing views of the applicability of Article 2 in combat situations and the question whether poor equipment or training may violate Article 2 remains live.[62]   **6.30**

The Supreme Court returned to the question of the applicability of Article 2 in combat situations in *R (Smith) and another v Ministry of Defence*,[63] concerning Article 2 claims brought by widows of British soldiers killed in Iraq on the basis of alleged shortcomings in the provision of vehicles and equipment. The Court again divided on the correct approach. The majority held that decisions were likely to fall beyond the reach of Article 2 where they concerned either, on the one hand, (i) training, procurement, or the conduct of operations taken at a high level of command and closely linked to the exercise of political judgment or policy, or, on the other, (ii) decisions closely linked to avoiding death or injury of persons actively engaged in direct contact with the enemy. But it was not prepared to exclude the possibility of a breach of Article 2 in respect of decisions falling in between and declined to strike out the claims on the facts as they stood.[64] The minority considered this approach to be unclear and unprincipled and would have held that Article 2 had no application to this type of decision at all.[65] The overriding difficulty for the Supreme Court was the limited guidance from the ECtHR on the application of Article 2 in this context. Notwithstanding the majority's pragmatic approach, the underlying issues of principle remain live and will no doubt arise in future cases both domestically and before the ECtHR.   **6.31**

3. Prohibition on taking life

In addition to the protective obligation, Article 2 expressly prohibits the state from intentionally taking life. Unintentional taking of life is implicitly prohibited in a situation where the use of force is permitted under Article 2(2), but the force used is more than absolutely necessary and results in death.[66]   **6.32**

---

[60] [2008] UKHL 20, [2008] 1 AC 1356.

[61] [2010] UKSC 29, [2011] AC 1.

[62] Ibid at [127] per Lord Rodger and at [195] per Lord Mance.

[63] [2013] UKSC 41, [2014] AC 52.

[64] per Lord Hope at [76].

[65] Per Lord Mance at [148]–[151].

[66] *McShane v UK* (2002) 35 EHRR 23, para 93.

6.33   It has been held by the domestic courts that an operation to separate conjoined twins, which would inevitably result in the death of one of them, would not violate the prohibition on intentional killing since the intention of the doctors performing the operation was to save the life of one twin rather than take the life of the other.[67]

6.34   Killing arising through state negligence may amount to a violation of Article 2, for example if a warning shot kills someone.[68]

6.35   Intentional killing and unintentional killing through the use of force which exceeds the Article 2(2) exceptions must be subject to criminal sanctions.[69]

4. Procedural obligation

6.36   The protection of the substantive rights under Article 2 requires that there should be an effective official investigation into deaths resulting from the use of force.[70] This investigative obligation is known as the 'procedural aspect' of Article 2. The case law under Article 2 is equally applicable to the investigative obligation under Article 3.[71]

6.37   As the ECtHR has held, the rationale for inferring an obligation to investigate is based on the positive obligation to protect life: the state is required to maintain a system of law that values and protects life.[72] The obligation is engaged both where death has resulted from state use of force, and where death has resulted from a state's failure to protect the right to life.[73] It is not necessary that a state agent is directly involved in the death.[74] In *Opuz v Turkey* the ECtHR considered that a case of prolonged domestic abuse of a mother and daughter, which had led to the mother's death, engaged the procedural obligation under Article 2.[75]

6.38   The essential purpose of the investigation has been described by the Grand Chamber of the ECtHR, as follows:

> to secure the effective implementation of the domestic laws safeguarding the right to life and, in those cases involving state agents or bodies, to ensure their accountability for deaths occurring under their responsibility...However, the investigation should also be broad enough to permit the investigating authorities to take into consideration not only the actions of the state agents who directly used lethal force but also all the surrounding circumstances, including such matters as the planning and control of the operations in question, where this is necessary in order to determine whether the state complied with its obligation under art 2 to protect life.[76]

---

[67] *Re A (children) (conjoined twins: surgical separation)* [2001] Fam 147.

[68] *Ogur v Turkey* (2001) 31 EHRR 40, para 83. See also *McShane v UK* (2002) 35 EHRR 23, para 102.

[69] *Osman v UK* (2000) 29 EHRR 245 (intentional killing); *McShane v UK* (2002) 35 EHRR 23, para 93 (unintentional killing resulting from the use of force).

[70] *McCann v UK* (1995) 21 EHRR 97, para 161; *R v Coroner for Western District of Somerset, ex p Middleton* [2004] UKHL 10, [2004] 2 AC 182.

[71] See, eg *Opuz v Turkey* (2009) 27 BHRC 159, para 168.

[72] See, eg *Gül v Turkey* (2002) 34 EHRR 28, para 88; *Brecknell v UK* (2008) 46 EHRR 957, para 65. See also *R (Sacker) v West Yorkshire Coroner* [2004] UKHL 11, [2004] 1 WLR 796 at [11].

[73] *R (Smith) v Secretary of State for Defence* [2010] UKSC 29, [2011] AC 1 at [87] per Lord Phillips.

[74] *Menson v UK* [2003] ECHR 47916/00; *R (JL) v Secretary of State for Justice* [2008] UKHL 68, [2008] 3 WLR 1325 at [26].

[75] (2009) 27 BHRC 159.

[76] *Al Skeini v UK* (2011) 30 BHRC 561 at [163].

A 'separate and autonomous' procedural obligation can arise in respect of deaths **6.39** which have occurred prior to the date of the state's ratification of the Convention (meaning that no breach of the state's substantive obligations could arise) where steps in the investigation have occurred, or should have occurred, post-ratification. In *Silih v Solvenia* the majority of the Grand Chamber stated:

The procedural obligation to carry out an effective investigation under Article 2 has evolved into a separate and autonomous duty [which] . . . can be considered to be a detachable obligation arising out of Article 2 capable of binding the state even when the death took place before the critical date [the date of the entry into force of the Convention with respect to that state party].[77]

The Supreme Court applied *Silih* in *Re McCaughey*.[78] Revisiting (in part) the **6.40** earlier House of Lords' decision in *Re McKerr*,[79] the court was at pains to stress that there was no continuing obligation to investigate deaths that occurred before the introduction of the Human Rights Act, but where the state had decided to hold an inquest into such a death, it had to be Article 2 compliant. The Supreme Court, however, regarded aspects of the ECtHR's reasoning in *Silih* as 'far from clear'.[80]

In *Janowiec v Russia*,[81] the Grand Chamber sought to clarify the applicable prin- **6.41** ciples. It confirmed that a renewed procedural duty could be triggered by credible new material emerging after the coming into force of the Convention concerning events pre-dating this otherwise critical date. However, in all but certain exceptional cases, a procedural duty would only be triggered where the period of time between the underlying events and the critical date was reasonably short (in any case not exceeding ten years) and a major part of the investigation had, or should have been, carried out after the entry into force of the Convention.

In *Keyu v Secretary of State for Foreign and Commonwealth Affairs*,[82] the Court **6.42** of Appeal found that the *Janowiec* principles would have required an investigation to be instigated in respect of the notorious Batang Kali massacre by a patrol of the Scots Guards in a British Protected State within the former Federation of Malaya in 1948, five years before the UK's ratification of the Convention. However, it held that the Article 2 claim was barred by the House of Lords' decision in *Re McKerr*, which remained binding authority that the Human Rights Act did not apply with retrospective effect to breaches of Convention rights occurring before 2 October 2000. The Supreme Court's decision in *Re McCaughey* only applied where the state had itself decided to instigate further investigations after the coming into force of the Human Rights Act on 2 October 2000, in contrast to the present case where all previous investigations had ended long before 2000. It was therefore a matter for the Supreme Court whether *Re McKerr* should be re-visited more broadly.

---

[77] [2009] ECHR 571, para 69.
[78] [2011] UKSC 20.
[79] [2004] UKHL 12, [2004] 2 All ER 409.
[80] eg Lord Philip at [49]. Lord Rodger, dissenting, would have declined to re-visit *Re McKerr* and to apply *Silah* in domestic law.
[81] App nos 55508/07 and 29520/09, 21 October 2013, GC.
[82] [2014] EWCA Civ 312, [2014] 4 All ER 99.

6.43   The precise form of the Article 2 investigation is flexible, but, in all cases, the authorities must engage the investigative mechanism on their own initiative.[83] In order to guarantee its effectiveness, the investigation must be independent,[84] prompt,[85] and open to an element of public scrutiny.[86] The ECtHR has confirmed that the procedural obligation continues to apply even in difficult security conditions, including in a context of armed conflict, and that all reasonable steps must be taken to ensure that an effective, independent investigation is conducted into alleged breaches of the right to life.[87]

6.44   The requirement of independence means that it is necessary for the persons responsible for carrying out the investigation to be independent from those implicated in the events. This requires a lack of hierarchical or institutional connection, such as where the investigator belongs to the same police force as those under investigation.[88] The ECtHR has held that an investigation into the actions of British soldiers in Iraq by the Special Investigation Branch was not sufficiently independent from the military chain of command because Special Branch was not free to decide for itself when to start and cease an investigation, and the commanding officer had the final say whether the matter should be referred for prosecution.[89] The procedural duty also requires practical independence. For example, where the issue to be investigated is whether national policy is adequate to meet the state's Article 2 obligations, the fact that the investigator had spent his working life applying that policy may deprive him of the practical independence necessary to perform his work effectively.[90]

6.45   In *McShane v UK*, the applicant's husband was killed when a security forces' vehicle struck a hoarding under which he had fallen during a disturbance in Belfast.[91] The applicant complained that there was no effective investigation into her husband's death. Although there was a police investigation and inquest proceedings were scheduled to commence, the ECtHR held that a number of deficiencies rendered both inconsistent with the investigative obligation. In particular, the involvement of police officers indirectly connected with the security operation in the police investigation was held to cast doubts on its independence. A series of delays in both the investigation and inquest proceedings, including a delay of over five months in questioning the driver of the vehicle, demonstrated a lack of the requisite promptness.

---

[83] *Nachova and ors v Bulgaria* [2005] ECHR 43577/98, para 111.

[84] *Brecknell v UK* (2008) 46 EHRR 957.

[85] See, eg *Angelova v Bulgaria* (2007) 23 BHRC 61; *Brecknell v UK* (2008) 46 EHRR 957.

[86] *Edwards v UK* (2002) 12 BHRC 190, paras 69–73; *Ramsahai and ors v Netherlands* [2007] ECHR 52391/99, para 353. See also *R (D) v Secretary of State for the Home Department* [2006] EWCA Civ 143, [2006] 3 All ER 946.

[87] See, eg *Al Skeini v UK* (2011) 30 BHRC 561 at [164].

[88] See, eg *Shanaghan v UK* [2001] ECHR 37715/97 at [104].

[89] *Al Skeini v UK* (2011) 30 BHRC 561.

[90] *SP v Secretary of State for Justice* [2009] EWHC 13 (Admin) at [81].

[91] [2002] ECHR 43290/98.

Although the degree of public scrutiny may vary from case to case, it is neces- **6.46** sary in all cases for the victim's next of kin to be involved to the extent required to safeguard their legitimate interests.[92] However, in *Hackett v UK*, concerning a sectarian murder in Northern Ireland, the ECtHR said that in the early stages of an investigation, particularly when there is an indeterminate possibility of other persons being criminally charged, Article 2 may require fairly minimal family involvement.[93] As the investigation progresses, the public and family should be informed of its findings and recommendations. The family does not have an automatic right to be given access to police reports or investigative materials.[94]

In *Ramsahai v Netherlands*, the Grand Chamber emphasized that the primary **6.47** characteristic of an effective investigation is that it is 'adequate', and adequacy may be compromised by the possibility of collusion between police officers involved in the incident.[95] Adequacy requires that the investigation is capable of leading to the identification and punishment of those responsible. Accordingly, civil proceedings will not constitute an effective investigation.[96]

The domestic courts have hewed close to the ECtHR's approach to the proce- **6.48** dural duty under Article 2. In the cases of *R (Amin) v Secretary of State for the Home Department*,[97] *R v Coroner for Western District of Somerset, ex p Middleton*,[98] and *R (JL) v Secretary of State for Justice*,[99] the House of Lords found violations of the investigative obligation in the context of deaths or near-deaths in custody. *Amin* concerned a death in a young offenders' institution. The deceased, an Asian man, was battered to death with a wooden table leg by his white cellmate who had a history of violent and racist behaviour. A number of investigations were commenced, but the Secretary of State refused the family's request for a public inquiry into the death on the grounds that such an inquiry would add nothing of substance and would not be in the public interest.

The House of Lords held that the investigations conducted were neither singly **6.49** nor cumulatively adequate for the purposes of Article 2. While the ECtHR had not prescribed a particular model of investigation suitable for all cases, it had laid down minimum standards that had to be adhered to whatever the form of the investigation. A properly conducted inquest could have discharged the state's obligation under Article 2 but, in its absence, it was necessary for the death to be publicly investigated before an independent judicial tribunal with an opportunity for the relatives to participate.

---

[92] *Edwards v UK* (2002) 12 BHRC 190, para 73.
[93] (2005) 5 EHRLR 543.
[94] *R (Green) v Police Complaints Authority* [2004] UKHL 6, [2004] 1 WLR 725.
[95] [2007] ECHR 52391/99. See also *R (Saunders) v Independent Police Complaints Commission* [2008] EWHC 2372 (Admin).
[96] *McShane v UK* [2002] ECHR 43290/98, para 125. See generally Thomas, Straw, Machover and Friedmann, *Inquests: A Practitioner's Guide* (London: LAG, 2014).
[97] [2003] UKHL 51, [2004] 1 AC 653.
[98] [2004] UKHL 10, [2004] 2 AC 182.
[99] [2008] UKHL 68, [2008] 3 WLR 1325.

6.50   In *Middleton* an inquest had taken place in relation to a prisoner who hanged himself in his prison cell. The coroner directed the jury by reference to section 11(5) of the Coroners Act 1988, and the Coroners Rules, that their findings were confined to the identity of the deceased and to 'how', when, and where he came by his death, and that they could express no opinion on any other matter. 'How' was narrowly interpreted in section 11(5) and the Rules to connote 'by what means', and they could not return a verdict of neglect, since this might appear to determine criminal or civil liability.

6.51   The House of Lords, however, held that the inquest was the means by which the state sought to discharge the obligation under Article 2 to investigate the accountability of state agents for deaths which occurred when the deceased was their responsibility, and it should culminate in 'an expression of the jury's conclusion on the central, factual issues in the case'.[100] The narrow interpretation of 'how' the deceased came by his death, coupled with the jury's inability to refer to neglect previously accepted by the domestic courts, meant that in many cases the central issue could not be determined and, accordingly, the current coronial regime did not meet the requirements of Article 2.[101] The court held that the word 'how' in section 11(5) should be interpreted to connote 'by what means and in what circumstances'.[102] The *Middleton* case led to those inquests that were held to discharge the state's Article 2 obligations becoming known as *Middleton* inquests.

6.52   The scope of the investigative duty was clarified again in *R (JL) v Secretary of State for Justice* in which the House of Lords considered the requirements of Article 2 in the context of near-suicides in prison.[103] Lord Phillips stated that 'death requires a spectrum of different types of investigation, depending upon the circumstances of the particular case'.[104] In some cases where death has resulted, a coroner's inquest will satisfy Article 2, while in others it may be necessary to hold a full-blown public inquiry (referred to as a 'D-type' inquiry).[105] In the case of a near-suicide in custody that leaves the prisoner with the possibility of a serious long-term injury, it would automatically be necessary to hold an 'enhanced investigation'. Their Lordships considered that a D-type inquiry might be required in a variety of circumstances that it was not appropriate to prescribe.[106] The Coroners and Justice Act 2009 now makes provision for suspending an inquest where the death is likely to be adequately investigated by an inquiry under the Inquiries Act 2005.[107]

6.53   Despite the wealth of authority that has developed in this area, there remains some uncertainty about the application of Article 2 to inquests in certain contexts. In medical negligence cases, for example, there has been confusion about the

---

[100] [2004] UKHL 10, [2004] 2 AC 182 at [13], [16]–[20].
[101] Ibid at [30]–[32].
[102] This is now enshrined in s 5(2) of the Coroners and Justice Act 2009.
[103] See n 98 above.
[104] Ibid at [31].
[105] See *R (D) v Secretary of State for the Home Department* [2006] EWCA Civ 143, [2006] 3 All ER 946.
[106] Cf Lord Brown at [104].
[107] Coroners and Justice Act 2009, Sch 1.

proper form of an inquest.[108] The position appears to have been clarified by the decision in *R (Humberstone) v Legal Services Commission* in which the Court of Appeal stated that a *Middleton* inquest would be necessary only in limited circumstances which did not include allegations of ordinary medical negligence where the person was not in state custody.[109] The court accepted, however, that there might be a fine line between ordinary negligence and systemic failings. In *R (Smith) v Ministry of Defence*[110] the Supreme Court examined the necessity for a *Middleton* inquest into the deaths of soldiers on active service. The majority of the court rejected the argument that all military deaths on active service required a *Middleton* inquest on the grounds that death of a soldier did not raise any presumption of a breach of the substantive obligation under Article 2.

Compliance with the procedural obligation is closely related to the Article 13   6.54
right to an effective remedy. The very purpose of an investigation is to secure the effective implementation of domestic laws which protect the right to life and, in those cases involving state agents or bodies, to ensure their accountability for deaths occurring under their responsibility. However, violation of Article 2 stemming from non-compliance with the procedural obligation will not necessarily constitute a violation of Article 13.[111]

5. Use of force

Article 2(2) details the circumstances in which it is permissible to use lethal   6.55
force. All these situations involve curbing violence or the control of prisoners or criminals—generally, maintaining law and order. The crucial test for these exceptions is that 'no more force than is absolutely necessary' is used. The ECmHR examined this phrase in *Stewart v UK*, and held that force is 'absolutely necessary' if, having regard to the nature of the aim pursued, the dangers and risks inherent in the situation, and all relevant circumstances, it is 'strictly proportionate to the achievement of the permitted purpose'.[112] In this way, it is a stricter test than that found under paragraphs 2 of Articles 8–11. The ECmHR found that the exceptions included in Article 2(2) indicate that this provision extends to, but is not concerned exclusively with, intentional killing.

The leading case on the use of lethal force is still *McCann v UK*, in which three   6.56
Provisional IRA members were shot and killed by British soldiers in Gibraltar in 1988. The ECtHR held, by a slim 10–9 vote, that there had been a violation of Article 2.[113] In making its decision, the ECtHR took into consideration 'not only

---

[108] See *R (Goodson) v HM Coroner for Bedfordshire and Luton* [2004] EWHC 2931 (Admin); *Takoushis v HM Coroner for Inner London* [2005] EWCA Civ 1440; *Moss v HM Coroner for North and South Districts of Durham and Darlington* [2008] EWHC 2940 (Admin). See, further, Millar, 'Human Rights Considerations for the Clinical Negligence Practitioner'. (2005) 11(6) AvMA Medical and Legal Journal 243.

[109] [2010] EWCA Civ 1479, (2010) 118 BMLR 79.

[110] [2013] UKSC 41, [2014] 1 AC 52.

[111] *McShane v UK* [2002] ECHR 43290/98.

[112] (1984) 38 DR 162.

[113] (1995) 21 EHRR 97.

the actions of the organs of the state who actually administer the force but also the surrounding circumstances including such matters as the planning and control of the actions under examination'. The concept of 'planning and control' is critical. The ECtHR held that the state must give appropriate training, instructions, and briefing to its agents who are faced with a situation where the use of lethal force is possible.[114] The state must also exercise 'strict control' over any operations that may involve use of lethal force.

6.57   Since the decision in *McCann*, the ECtHR has sometimes appeared to take a more lenient line on absolute necessity. In *Andronicou v Cyprus*, for example, police shot a gunman and his hostage, mistakenly believing that the gunman had more ammunition and weapons than he actually possessed.[115] The ECtHR held that the police actions were adequately designed and controlled to minimize the risk to the lives of the gunman and his hostage. Even though the police were mistaken about the gunman's weapons, they had good reason to believe as they did, and were pursuing the legitimate aims of Article 2(2).

6.58   Similarly, in *Bubbins v UK*, the ECtHR found no violation of Article 2 where an individual was mistakenly shot dead by a police officer after he pulled a replica gun which the officer believed to be real.[116] The ECtHR held that it could not substitute its own assessment for that of the officer in the situation and that his actions were proportionate.

6.59   However, the Grand Chamber echoed *McCann* in *Nachova v Bulgaria*, reiterating both the strictness of the applicable test and the importance of operational planning.[117] The ECtHR condemned the 'deplorable disregard for the preeminence of the right to life' displayed by the manner in which the operation was planned and controlled.[118] In contrast, in *Giuliani and Gaggio v Italy*, the Grand Chamber found no breach in respect of the fatal shooting of a violent demonstrator by an Italian police officer during the G8 summit in Genoa, finding no failings in the organization and planning of the event in so far as they could be linked directly to the death.[119]

6.60   According to the ECtHR, Article 2 requires an appropriate administrative and legal framework to be put in place defining the limited circumstances in which officers can use arms and force in line with international standards, and with regard to the fundamental value of life.[120] Applying these principles, the Court has, for example, found to be deficient the legal framework in Bulgaria which permitted the police to fire on any fugitive member of the armed forces who did not immediately surrender following an oral warning and the firing of a warning shot in the air, and did not contain clear safeguards to prevent the arbitrary deprivation of life.[121]

---

[114] See also *Gül v Turkey* (2002) 34 EHRR 28.
[115] (1997) 25 EHRR 491.
[116] App No 50916/99, 17 March 2005.
[117] [2005] ECHR 43577/98.
[118] Ibid, para 105.
[119] App No 23458/02, 24 March 2011.
[120] Ibid, para 97.
[121] Ibid, paras 99–102.

6. Standing

Relatives of the deceased are considered 'victims' of breaches of Article 2, within   6.61
the meaning of Article 34.[122] The ECtHR has also held that an individual whose
life is put at serious risk may be a victim for Article 2 purposes.[123] In *Savage v
South Essex Partnership NHS Foundation Trust*, Lord Scott suggested (the point
was not in fact in issue in the case) that complaints concerning breaches of the
substantive obligations under Article 2 could not be brought by victims' relatives on the grounds that private causes of action were open to the relatives to
pursue.[124] This is inconsistent with the case law of the ECtHR, which domestic
courts are obliged to apply under section 2 of the Human Rights Act.[125] In
Rabone v Pennine Care NHS Trust,[126] the Supreme Court firmly disapproved
these *obiter* comments and confirmed that family members can be 'victims' of
both a substantive and a procedural breach of Article 2 arising out of the death
of their family member.[127]

It is not necessary for a person to have died in order for a claim under Article 2   6.62
to be brought. A living applicant may bring a claim for state conduct that put his
or her life at grave risk.[128]

D. ARTICLE 3: PROHIBITION OF TORTURE

Article 3 concerns freedom from torture and inhuman and degrading treat-   6.63
ment. Like Article 2, it is one of the most fundamental provisions of the
Convention.[129] Its importance is reflected in its absolute and non-derogable
status.[130]

It places a negative duty on the state not to inflict the proscribed suffering on   6.64
human beings, as well as a positive duty to ensure that these forms of suffering are
not endured. In common with Article 2, it also includes a procedural obligation to
conduct an effective investigation in certain circumstances.[131]

Article 3 applies irrespective of the conduct of an applicant.[132]   6.65

---

[122] *Brecknell v UK* App No 32457/04, 27 November 2007; *Yasa v Turkey* (1999) 28 EHRR 408; *McShane v UK* (2002) 35 EHRR 23, para 93.

[123] *Osman v UK* (2000) 29 EHRR 245.

[124] [2008] UKHL 74, [2009] 2 WLR 115 at [2]–[3].

[125] See ch 4.

[126] [2012] UKSC 2, [2012] 2 AC 72.

[127] At [44]–[48] per Lord Dyson, and see also Lady Hale at [92].

[128] See, eg *Acar v Turkey* [2005] ECHR 36088/97, para 79; *R (JL) v Secretary of State for Justice* [2008] UKHL 68, [2008] 3 WLR 1325.

[129] *Pretty v UK* (2002) 35 EHRR 1.

[130] *Saadi v UK* (2008) 24 BHRC 123.

[131] *Assenov v Bulgaria* (1998) 28 EHRR 652; *Šečić v Croatia* (2007) 23 BHRC 24; *R (Green) v Police Complaints Authority* [2004] UKHL 6, [2004] 1 WLR 725.

[132] *Chahal v UK* (1997) 23 EHRR 413; *Gäfgen v Germany* App No 22978/05, 3 June 2010; *Hassan-Daniel v HMRC* [2010] EWCA Civ 1443.

1. Scope of Article 3

6.66 In *Ireland v UK* the ECtHR considered the types of treatment that are prohibited by Article 3.[133] It characterized the prohibited activities as follows:

(a) *torture*: deliberate inhuman treatment that causes very serious and cruel suffering;

(b) *inhuman treatment*: treatment that causes intense physical and mental suffering; and

(c) *degrading treatment*: treatment that arouses in the victim a feeling of fear, anguish, and inferiority capable of humiliating and debasing the victim and possibly breaking his or her physical or moral resistance.

6.67 As a threshold standard, treatment must attain 'a minimum level of severity' to fall within Article 3.[134] In *Ireland v UK* the ECtHR described the determination of this minimum level as 'relative' and set out some criteria, such as the duration of the treatment, its physical or mental effects, and, in some circumstances, the sex, age, and state of health of the victim.[135] These factors are relevant in two contexts: when determining whether the suffering caused is sufficient to amount to inhuman or degrading treatment or punishment; and when distinguishing between these lesser kinds of ill-treatment and torture.

6.68 As the Convention is a living instrument, acts that have previously been classed as inhuman treatment, for example, could well be classed differently in the future.[136] In keeping with the Strasbourg approach, the domestic courts accept that the concept of 'torture' is not immutable and may shift over time. Lord Bingham indicated in *A and ors v Secretary of State for the Home Department (No 2)* that the conduct complained of in *Ireland v UK* may well be considered to now fall within the definition of 'torture'.[137]

6.69 Further, treatment which does not violate Article 3 may nevertheless violate the right to autonomy and dignity now recognized under the rubric of Article 8.[138] Conversely, treatment may constitute such a gross breach of another article of the Convention as to amount to inhuman or degrading treatment under Article 3.[139]

(a) *Torture*

6.70 Torture is an aggravated form of inhuman or degrading treatment or punishment. Classification of treatment as torture implies suffering of a particular intensity and cruelty.[140] Such treatment will usually have a purpose such as

---

[133] (1978) 2 EHRR 25.

[134] Ibid.

[135] Ibid, para 162.

[136] *Selmouni v France* (2000) 29 EHRR 403.

[137] [2005] UKHL 71, [2006] 2 AC 221 at [53].

[138] *Wainwright v UK* [2006] ECHR 807.

[139] See, eg *East African Asians v UK* (1981) 3 EHRR 76.

[140] *Ireland v UK* (1978) 2 EHRR 25.

obtaining information or a confession, or inflicting punishment.[141] The ECtHR has found that the distinction between 'torture' and 'inhuman or degrading treatment' was intended to 'attach a special stigma to deliberate inhuman treatment causing very serious and cruel suffering'.[142] The Court attaches significant importance to drawing the distinction between the different forms of ill-treatment, and will do so even where the state has accepted that its conduct broadly violated Article 3.[143]

In *Aydin v Turkey* the complainant had been raped, blindfolded, beaten, stripped, and sprayed with high-pressure water while in the custody of the Turkish security forces. This treatment was held to amount to torture. The ECtHR commented that a finding of torture would have been made even in the absence of rape.[144] The accumulation of similarly violent and humiliating treatment was classified as torture in *Selmouni v France*, where the complainant had been urinated on, threatened with a blowtorch, and severely beaten by the police.[145] In *Husayn (Abu Zubaydah) v Poland* the Court had no difficulty in concluding that the techniques deployed by the CIA, including water boarding and stress position, in interrogating terrorist suspects on Polish territory constituted torture.[146]

6.71

Mental anguish alone may constitute torture if it reaches a certain level of severity.[147] The ECtHR has found that the threat of torture can violate the prohibition on inhuman and degrading treatment provided it is sufficiently real and immediate.[148]

6.72

The Strasbourg Court has developed a strong principle that a state may not extradite an individual to a country where there are substantial grounds for believing that there is a real risk that he or she would be subjected to torture or ill-treatment.[149] This principle has been the subject of extensive case law before both the ECtHR and domestic courts.[150]

6.73

The House of Lords considered its duties relating to the prohibition of torture under international law in *Jones v Saudi Arabia*.[151] The court upheld the principle of sovereign state immunity and unanimously denied jurisdiction in a claim brought by four UK citizens to seek redress against acts of torture committed against them by a foreign state and its officials. The ECtHR agreed with the House of Lords.[152] Although not of direct relevance to Article 3, the decision is indicative of a cautious approach to torture-related issues in the absence of a settled consensus at international level.

6.74

---

[141] *Greek Case* (1969) 12 YB 1.
[142] See, eg *Ciorap v Moldova* [2007] ECHR 12066/02, para 62.
[143] *Gäfgen v Germany* App No 22978/05, 3 June 2010.
[144] (1997) 25 EHRR 251.
[145] (2000) 29 EHRR 403.
[146] App No 755/13, 24 July 2014.
[147] *Denmark v Greece* (1969) 12 YB 1.
[148] *Campbell and Cosans v UK* (1982) 4 EHRR 293, para 26; *Gäfgen v Germany* App No 22978/05, 3 June 2010.
[149] *Soering v UK* (1989) 11 EHRR 439.
[150] See paras 6.99–6.108.
[151] [2006] UKHL 26, [2007] 1 AC 270.
[152] *Jones and ors v UK* (2014) 59 EHRR 1.

(b) *Inhuman and degrading treatment or punishment*

6.75   The terms 'inhuman' and 'degrading' bear different meanings under the Convention, though one is rarely found to exist without the other.

6.76   Treatment or punishment is considered 'inhuman' where it is premeditated, applied over a period of hours at a stretch, and causes either actual bodily injury or intense physical or mental suffering.[153] Whether treatment or punishment is degrading depends on all the circumstances: the nature and context of the treatment or punishment and the method and manner of its execution.[154] As judicial punishment inevitably entails a degree of humiliation, degrading punishment must involve a degree of humiliation or debasement that exceeds that which is usual in punishment.[155] Unlike torture, it is not necessary that there be any specific intention or purpose such as intent to debase, although an aim to humiliate or debase will be highly relevant.[156]

6.77   In *Ireland v UK* the ECtHR examined five techniques used by the British Government to interrogate prisoners allegedly involved in terrorism, which included forcing them to stand against a wall in an uncomfortable position, hooding, subjecting them to loud, continuous noise, and depriving them of food, drink, and sleep. Although not rising to the level of torture, the ECtHR determined that these practices constituted degrading treatment and, therefore, violated Article 3.[157]

6.78   Race discrimination may constitute degrading treatment. In *East African Asians v UK* the applicants were British passport holders but had been refused permission to take up residence in the United Kingdom. The ECmHR considered that the discriminatory immigration legislation constituted an interference with their human dignity which amounted to degrading treatment in the sense of Article 3 of the Convention.[158]

6.79   In *Soering v UK* the European Court concluded that 'death row phenomenon' experienced by many prisoners awaiting execution in the United States constituted inhuman and degrading treatment.[159] States cannot extradite suspected criminals to countries where there is a real risk of exposure to such treatment.

2. State responsibility

6.80   The state is responsible for the actions of its agents under Article 3. In *Cyprus v Turkey* the ECmHR found the state responsible for rapes committed by its soldiers as satisfactory action had not been taken to prevent these attacks and disciplinary measures after the conduct were insufficient.[160] The ECtHR held in *Ireland v UK* that the higher authorities of a state are 'under a duty to impose their

---

[153] See, eg *Kudla v Poland* (2002) 35 EHRR 11, para 92.
[154] *Tyrer v UK* (1978) 2 EHRR 1.
[155] Ibid.
[156] *Peers v Greece* (2001) 33 EHRR 51.
[157] (1978) 2 EHRR 25.
[158] (1981) 3 EHRR 76.
[159] (1989) 11 EHRR 439; *Al-Saadoon and Mufdhi v UK* App No 61498/08, 2 March 2010.
[160] (1976) 4 EHRR 482.

will on subordinates and cannot shelter behind their inability to ensure that it is respected'.[161]

3. Negative obligation

Article 3 is generally characterized as containing both a negative obligation to refrain from inflicting harm and a positive obligation to protect people from a real and immediate risk of harm. The utility of this analysis has been questioned by Lord Brown, who suggested that 'the real issue in all these cases is whether the state is properly to be regarded as responsible for the harm inflicted (or threatened) upon the victim'.[162] The ECtHR has itself blurred the boundaries between the positive and negative duties on occasion.[163] Nevertheless, there is a critical distinction to be drawn between the two: the obligation not to do harm is absolute, while the positive obligation requires the state to do all that it reasonably can to prevent harm from occurring.[164] **6.81**

(a) *Counter-terrorism*
The House of Lords considered the negative obligation in the leading counter-terrorism decision *A v Secretary of State for the Home Department (No 2)*,[165] the second key case concerning the Government's legislative response to the terrorist attacks in the United States on 11 September 2001. The applicants were detained under Part IV of the Anti-Terrorism, Crime and Security Act 2001 on the Home Secretary's suspicion of involvement in or links to international terrorism. They appealed against their detention to the Special Immigration Appeals Commission (SIAC). The SIAC was entitled to receive evidence that would not be admissible in court. At issue before the House of Lords was whether evidence which may have been obtained through torture abroad could be admissible in UK proceedings. **6.82**

Their Lordships held unanimously that evidence of a suspect or witness which had been obtained through torture had long been regarded as inherently unreliable, unfair, offensive to ordinary standards of humanity and decency, and incompatible with the principles on which courts should administer justice. The opinions drew not only on Article 3 jurisprudence and international law, but also on the common law, Lord Bingham referring to the unacceptability of torture as a 'constitutional principle',[166] Lord Nicholls as 'a bedrock moral principle in this country'.[167] **6.83**

Although unanimous on the central issue, the House divided in relation to the application of the exclusionary rule. A majority determined that the SIAC should admit evidence unless it was established on the balance of probabilities that it had been obtained by torture. **6.84**

---

[161] (1978) 2 EHRR 25, para 159.
[162] *R (Limbuela) v Secretary of State for the Home Department* [2005] UKHL 66, [2006] 1 AC 396 at [92].
[163] *Mubilanzila Mayeka v Belgium* [2006] 3 FCR 637.
[164] See *Re E* [2008] UKHL 66, [2008] 3 WLR 1208 at [10] per Baroness Hale.
[165] [2005] UKHL 71, [2006] 2 AC 221.
[166] Ibid at [51].
[167] Ibid at [64].

6.85   In *Ahmed and anor v R* the Court of Appeal applied *A (No 2)* in considering whether a prosecution should be stayed because the defendant claimed that UK authorities had been complicit in his torture in Pakistan after he was alleged to have committed the offences.[168] The Court of Appeal dismissed the appeal on the basis that the torture must have had an impact on the trial, which in this case it had not.

6.86   In joined cases *RB (Algeria) v Secretary of State for the Home Department* the House of Lords adopted a different approach to the admission of torture evidence in a foreign trial.[169] RB and OO were terrorist suspects whom the Government wished to deport to states with a reputation for ill-treatment. They claimed that if they were deported, they would face trials at which evidence obtained by torture would be admitted. The House of Lords held that the use of evidence obtained by torture in a foreign trial would not necessarily amount to a 'flagrant denial of justice' sufficient to prevent the deportation of the suspect.[170] The ECtHR considered the applications of RB and OO in *Othman v UK*.[171] It disagreed with the House of Lords and found that there was a real risk that evidence obtained by the torture of third parties would be used in the trial and would therefore violate Article 6.

(b) *Sentencing*

6.87   Criminal sentences have been an active field of Article 3 complaints. In *Kafkaris v Cyprus* the applicant was found guilty of premeditated murder which carried a mandatory sentence of life imprisonment without any possibility for a judicial body to consider the applicant's detention thereafter.[172] The majority of the Grand Chamber suggested that a sentence of life imprisonment, if irreducible, might raise an issue under Article 3. However, the provisions of the Cypriot Constitution which conferred on the President a discretion to remit, suspend, or commute a life sentence were sufficient to render the sentence reducible despite the fact that they had been exercised very infrequently.

6.88   Whole life tariffs have recently led to a stand-off between the ECtHR and the UK Government. While the Court of Appeal accepted in 2001 that the imposition of an automatic life sentence could constitute inhuman and degrading treatment,[173] the question whether whole life tariffs imposed at the discretion of the judge are compatible with the Convention has proved more controversial.[174] The Grand Chamber considered the question in *Vinter and ors v UK*. It held that in order for whole life sentences under section 269 of the Criminal Justice Act

---

[168] [2011] EWCA Crim 184.

[169] [2009] UKHL 10, [2009] 2 WLR 512.

[170] See ch 7, para 7.80.

[171] *Othman Abu Qatada* (2012) 55 EHRR 1, 32 BHRC 62.

[172] [2008] ECHR 21906/04, para 98. See also the separate opinion of Sir Nicholas Bratza who considered that whole life sentences were intrinsically inhuman. See also *De Boucherville v Mauritius* [2008] UKPC 37, (2008) 25 BHRC 433, at [8].

[173] [2001] 1 WLR 253 at [95]. See also *R (Wellington) v Secretary of State for the Home Department* [2008] UKHL 72, [2009] 2 WLR 48, discussed at para 6.103.

[174] *R v Lichniak and Pyrah* [2002] UKHL 47, [2003] 1 AC 903. See also *R v Bieber* [2008] EWCA Crim 1601.

2003 to remain compatible with Article 3, there had to be a possibility of review and release.[175] It found that the operation of the provision in section 30 of the Crime (Sentences) Act 1997 that allows the Secretary of State to release a prisoner on licence where there are exceptional circumstances amounting to compassionate grounds was not sufficiently clear to constitute an adequate review mechanism. The decision inflamed the British popular press and the Government announced that it would refuse to implement the judgment. A solution may have been found by the Court of Appeal in *R v McLoughlin*.[176] The specially constituted five-judge panel held that the Grand Chamber had not outlawed whole life tariffs per se and that it had been wrong to conclude that UK law did not provide for release. Section 30 provided for possible exceptional release and the Secretary of State was bound to exercise the power in compliance with principles of public law and Article 3. Despite the best endeavours of the Court of Appeal, it is unlikely that this will be the last word on the issue.

(c) *Detention*

Prison conditions have been held to constitute degrading treatment.[177] For example, in *Price v UK* the ECtHR held that the detention of a severely disabled person in conditions where she was dangerously cold, risked developing sores because her bed was too hard, and was unable to go to the toilet or keep clean without the greatest of difficulty, constituted degrading treatment contrary to Article 3, despite the absence of any intention to subject her to degrading treatment.[178]   6.89

In a separate concurring opinion in *Price*, Judges Bratza and Costa suggested that Article 3 may be breached through a lack of adequate sentence planning, a view which could have wider ramifications in relation to systemic failings by the state to provide adequate mental health or palliative care in prison.   6.90

The effect of prison conditions on relatives can also lead to a violation of Article 3. In *Salakhov and Islyamova v Ukraine* the European Court held that a mother's mental suffering caused by the failure to treat her dying son while he was imprisoned constituted inhuman and degrading treatment.[179]   6.91

There have so far been relatively few challenges to domestic prison conditions on the basis of Article 3. In *Napier v Scottish Ministers* compensation was awarded to a prisoner who had had to endure the practice of slopping-out common in Scottish prisons at the time.[180] The ECtHR has ruled in a number of cases that overcrowding can violate Article 3[181] and in light of the ever-increasing UK prison population, it is likely that the issue will eventually be raised before the domestic courts.   6.92

---

[175] (2013) 34 BHRC 605.
[176] [2014] EWCA Crim 188, [2014] 3 All ER 73.
[177] See, eg *Kalashnikov v Russia* (2002) 36 EHRR 34; *Peers v Greece* (2001) 33 EHRR 51; *Napier v Scottish Ministers* [2002] UKHR 308; *R v Governor of Frankland Prison, ex p Russell* [2000] 1 WLR 2027.
[178] (2002) 34 EHRR 53.
[179] App no 28005/08, 14 March 2013.
[180] [2002] UKHR 308.
[181] See, eg *Kalashnikov v Russia* (2002) 36 EHRR 34.

6.93   Detention for the purposes of immigration control may also violate Article 3. In *Popov v France* the detention for 15 days of two young children and their parents in a holding centre for illegal immigration violated Article 3.[182]

6.94   Detention in the mental health context could give rise to a breach of Article 3. In *R (Munjaz) v Mersey Care NHS Trust* the House of Lords found by a majority that a hospital's policy on seclusion of mentally ill patients contained sufficient safeguards to prevent ill-treatment.[183] The ECtHR agreed with the House of Lords.[184]

6.95   In *R (Bary) v Secretary of State for Justice* two immigrants with pre-existing mental health conditions, who were detained indefinitely in a secure unit Category A prison separated from the general prison population, challenged the conditions in which they were detained.[185] The High Court found that they had not satisfied the high threshold imposed by Article 3: the intention of the restrictive prison regime was not to debase the men, their mental conditions were closely monitored, and other factors were responsible for the limited deterioration in their mental health.

(d) *Mental health*

6.96   In the context of compulsory treatment for mental health disorders, the ECtHR has held that 'as a general rule, a measure which is a therapeutic necessity cannot be regarded as inhuman or degrading'.[186] The court must satisfy itself that the medical necessity has convincingly been shown to exist.[187]

4. Positive obligations

(a) *Investigative duty*

6.97   The ECtHR has held that the combined effect of Articles 1 and 3 is to require an effective official investigation into credible allegations of serious ill-treatment, whether by state agents or private actors.[188] The investigation, as with that under Article 2, should be capable of leading to the identification and punishment of those responsible for the violation. In *Boiceno v Moldova* the ECtHR emphasized that the investigation must be thorough:

That means that the authorities must always make a serious attempt to find out what happened and should not rely on hasty or ill-founded conclusions to close their investigation or as the basis of their decisions.[189]

---

[182] App No 39472/07, 19 January 2012.

[183] [2005] UKHL 58, [2006] 2 AC 148.

[184] *Munjaz v UK* App No 2913/06, 9 October 2012.

[185] [2010] EWHC 587 (Admin). See also *R (Reetha Suppiah and ors) v Secretary of State for the Home Department* [2011] EWHC 2 (Admin).

[186] *Herczegfalvy v Austria* (1992) 15 EHRR 437, para 82.

[187] Ibid. See *R (B) v Ashworth Hospital Authority* [2005] UKHL 20, [2005] 2 AC 278.

[188] *Assenov v Bulgaria* (1998) 28 EHRR 652; *Šečić v Croatia* (2007) 23 BHRC 24; *Opuz v Turkey* (2009) 27 BHRC 159.

[189] [2006] ECHR 41088/05, para 123.

In *Husayn (Abu Zubaydah) v Poland* the Court considered that the Polish Government had failed to conduct an appropriate investigation into '*prima facie* credible allegations' that terrorist suspects were detained and tortured on its territory.[190] The Polish parliamentary inquiry that took place was clearly inadequate as it was conducted in private and produced no findings.

In *R (AM) v Secretary of State for the Home Department* a majority of the Court   6.98
of Appeal held that the Government had failed to satisfy its obligation to investigate ill-treatment during a disturbance at an immigration detention centre where detainees were kept confined while water leaked into their cells and then ordered into the exercise yard while still wet.[191] The Court of Appeal rejected the proposition that because the victim in an Article 3 claim was still alive and therefore had recourse to law, the investigation was not governed by the same principles as those under Article 2. The court held that the primary question was whether the victim could secure adequate investigation without an ad hoc inquiry instituted by the state. The purpose of the investigation was, as under Article 2, to maximize future compliance with Article 3.[192] The case law on the obligation under Article 2 should therefore be considered equally applicable to Article 3.

As a result of allegations of ill-treatment of Iraqi detainees by UK forces, the   6.99
Government has been forced to establish two public inquiries. The Baha Mousa Inquiry reported its findings in 2011. The report concluded British soldiers had subjected detainees to 'serious, gratuitous violence' and made 73 recommendations to improve the treatment of detainees in British custody. The Al Sweady Inquiry into the abuse and unlawful killing of Iraqi detainees at a British military camp finished hearing oral evidence in 2014 and the report is awaited. The Ministry of Defence established the Iraq Historic Allegations Team (IHAT) in 2010 to investigate further claims of mistreatment. The High Court has found that the IHAT is sufficiently independent to satisfy the procedural requirements of Article 3 but ordered the Secretary of State to provide additional safeguards, including the appointment of a judge to oversee the investigations.[193]

The Detainee Inquiry, established in 2010 to look into claims that UK agents   6.100
were complicit in torture of terrorist suspects abroad, was concluded before it could report after the Metropolitan Police began investigations into the allegations.

(b) *Prevention*

As well as refraining from inflicting treatment violating Article 3, states also have a   6.101
positive obligation to prevent it. This obligation means that states must take certain steps to ensure that individuals within their jurisdiction are not subjected to torture or other forms of ill-treatment, including that administered by private individuals or agents of other states.[194] Furthermore, the positive obligation to prevent harm

---

[190] App No 755/13, 24 July 2014.
[191] [2009] EWCA Civ 219.
[192] Ibid at [57].
[193] *R (Mousa) v Secretary of State for Defence (No 2)* [2013] EWHC 1412 (Admin).
[194] *Mahmut Kaya v Turkey* (1999) 28 EHRR 1; *Z and ors v UK* (2002) 34 EHRR 3; *Husayn (Abu Zubaydah) v Poland* App No 755/13, 24 July 2014.

must be interpreted in a way which is not incompatible with other Convention rights. For example, social workers cannot take such extreme steps to protect a child from the potential risk of harm in a family that they disproportionately infringe the child's right to respect for his family life under Article 8.[195]

6.102　In *A v UK* the child applicant had been hit by his stepfather with a stick.[196] The stepfather was charged with assault occasioning actual bodily harm. The stepfather contended that the assault amounted to reasonable punishment, which was a defence to a charge of assault of a child by a parent, and he was acquitted. The ECtHR decided that there was a violation of Article 3 because the law failed adequately to protect the child by insufficiently defining what constituted 'reasonable punishment'.[197]

6.103　As a result of the decision, Parliament introduced section 58 of the Children Act 2004 to remove the defence of reasonable punishment to charges of assault occasioning actual bodily harm. However, it is still possible to raise the defence in cases of common assault. It remains to be seen whether section 58 will satisfy the ECtHR.[198]

6.104　In both *Z v UK*[199] and *E v UK*[200] the ECtHR found that the United Kingdom had breached Article 3 in failing to protect children from prolonged abuse and neglect which the authorities knew about. In *E*, they had failed to monitor the family after a stepfather had been convicted of sexual abuse. The ECtHR held that 'a failure to take reasonably available measures which could have had a real prospect of altering the outcome or mitigating the harm is sufficient to engage the responsibility of the state'.[201] In *O'Keeffe v Ireland* the Grand Chamber held that the Irish authorities had failed to protect primary school children from sexual abuse.[202]

6.105　The ECtHR has recently considered state obligations in relation to domestic violence. It held in *Eremia v Moldova*[203] that failure properly to investigate or to support a complainant of domestic violence amounted to condoning the discriminatory attitudes which underlay it, contrary to Articles 3 and 14.

6.106　The House of Lords considered the extent of the obligation to prevent harm in *Re E*.[204] Catholic schoolgirls on their way to school in Northern Ireland were subjected to a barrage of abuse over a number of months by protestors lining their

---

[195] *Re B* [2008] UKHL 35, [2009] 1 AC 11.

[196] (1998) 5 BHRC 137.

[197] (1999) 27 EHRR 611. See also *Tyrer v UK* (1978) 2 EHRR 1; *Campbell v UK* (1982) 4 EHRR 293; and *Costello-Roberts v UK* (1993) 19 EHRR 112.

[198] In *Northern Ireland Commissioner for Children and Young Peoples' Application* [2007] NIQB 115, the Northern Ireland High Court considered that the law satisfied Art 3. The Court of Appeal held that the Commissioner was not a victim under the Human Rights Act and did not consider the substantive issue: [2009] NICA 10. See also Hamilton, 'Smacking children: has the Government implemented the judgment of the European Court of Human Rights in *A v UK*?' (2007) 238 Childright 10–13.

[199] (2002) 34 EHRR 97.

[200] (2003) 36 EHRR 519.

[201] Ibid, para 99.

[202] [2014] 35 BHRC 601.

[203] 28 May 2013, App No 3564/11.

[204] [2008] UKHL 66, [2008] 3 WLR 1208.

route to school. The House was in no doubt that the children had been subjected to inhuman and degrading treatment, but found that the police had done all they reasonably could to protect the children from harm.[205] By contrast, in *DSD and NBV v Commissioner of Police for the Metropolis* the High Court found that there was a positive duty imposed upon the police to conduct investigations into particularly severe violent acts perpetrated by private parties in a timely and efficient manner. The police failure to investigate a series of sexual assaults by a serial rapist violated the claimants' Article 3 rights.[206]

As the ECtHR made clear in the case of *Pretty v UK*, the positive obligation to   6.107
prevent ill-treatment does not extend to the provision of a lawful opportunity for assisted suicide in circumstances of significant physical and mental suffering.[207]

(c) *Deportation and removal*

The positive obligation also manifests itself in the principle established in the   6.108
Soering case that a state may not extradite an individual to a country where there are substantial grounds for believing that there is a real risk that he or she would be subjected to torture or ill-treatment.[208]

In *Chahal v UK* the ECtHR made it plain that the question of whether Article 3   6.109
prevented deportation was not influenced by the fact that the individual under threat of deportation posed a threat to national security.[209]

This issue was revisited in *Saadi v Italy*, in which the United Kingdom intervened   6.110
to argue that the *Chahal* principle should be modified to allow a degree of risk of torture to be balanced against the threat posed to the public or the state.[210] The Grand Chamber unanimously rejected these arguments and robustly reasserted the absolute character of Article 3. It was not possible to distinguish between torture by a Convention state and torture by another state to which the Convention state has removed the victim.[211]

Domestic courts have grappled with the implications of these decisions on a   6.111
number of occasions. *R (Bagdanavicius) v Secretary of State for the Home Department* concerned a Lithuanian family who claimed that they were at risk, due to their Roma origins, of inhuman or degrading treatment from non-state actors if returned to Lithuania.[212] The House of Lords held that on any claim against removal on Article 3 grounds the court had to make an assessment of conditions in the receiving country so that it could determine whether there was a real risk of ill-treatment when returned, which would violate Article 3. As any harm inflicted by non-state agents would not violate Article 3 unless the state had failed to provide reasonable

---

[205] The claim failed in the ECtHR, see *PF and EF v UK* App No 28326/09, 23 November 2010.
[206] [2014] EWHC 2493 (Admin).
[207] (2002) 35 EHRR 1. See also *R (Nicklinson) v Ministry of Justice* [2014] UKSC 38.
[208] *Soering v UK* (1989) 11 EHRR 439.
[209] (1997) 23 EHRR 413.
[210] (2008) 24 BHRC 123.
[211] Ibid, para 138.
[212] [2005] UKHL 38, [2005] 2 AC 668.

protection, to avoid expulsion on Article 3 grounds an individual must establish, first, a real risk of suffering serious harm from non-state agents, and secondly, that the receiving country did not provide a reasonable level of protection against such harm for those within its territory. The test was not satisfied in this case.

6.112   In *R (Wellington) v Secretary of State for the Home Department* the House of Lords considered the application of Article 3 to the extradition of a murder suspect to Missouri.[213] If found guilty, the appellant would automatically receive a sentence of life imprisonment without parole. The sentence could only be reduced by the governor, who had almost never exercised his right to commute such sentences. Relying on a passage in the ECtHR's decision in *Soering*, Lord Hoffmann held that 'the desirability of extradition is a factor to be taken into account in deciding whether the punishment likely to be imposed in the receiving state attains the "minimum level of severity" which would make it inhuman and degrading'.[214] As he accepted, this creates a 'relativist' approach to the scope of inhuman and degrading treatment.[215] Applying this reasoning, the majority of the House held that an irreducible sentence might breach Article 3 domestically, but if imposed by a foreign country it would only contravene Article 3 if it were disproportionate to the crime committed.[216] The European Court gave detailed consideration to the reasoning of the House of Lords in *Harkins and Edwards v UK*.[217] It disapproved of Lord Hoffman's view, stating that an assessment of the minimum level of severity under Article 3 should not be informed by the reasons for extradition.[218]

6.113   The House of Lords considered the adequacy of diplomatic assurances to prevent a violation of Article 3 in *RB (Algeria) v Secretary of State for the Home Department*.[219] Their Lordships held that the two terrorist suspects could be deported because the Government could properly rely on the assurances made by Algeria and Jordan that they would not be mistreated. This was so despite the fact that the assurances did not entirely eliminate the risk of mistreatment.[220] In *Othman v UK* the European Court considered the Jordanian assurances and accepted that they were adequate.[221]

6.114   In *R (Klimas) v Prosecutors General Office of Lithuania* the High Court found that extradition to a Convention state in which prison conditions were said to be inhuman could not breach Article 3 because the requesting state was itself subject to human rights obligations under the Convention and the individual could challenge his conditions on arrival.[222] The decision is at odds with ECtHR case law which has

---

[213] [2008] UKHL 72, [2009] 2 WLR 48.

[214] Ibid at [24].

[215] Ibid at [27].

[216] Baroness Hale and Lord Carswell agreed with Lord Hoffmann. Lord Brown and Lord Scott preferred to interpret Art 3 as imposing absolute standards.

[217] App Nos 9146/07 and 32650/07, 13 February 2012.

[218] Ibid at [124].

[219] [2009] UKHL 10, [2009] 2 WLR 512, applied in *Inzunza v USA* [2011] EWHC 920 (Admin).

[220] [2009] UKHL 10, [2009] 2 WLR 512 at [114] per Lord Phillips.

[221] *Othman Abu Qatada* (2012) 55 EHRR 1, 32 BHRC 62.

[222] [2010] EWHC 2076 (Admin).

held that the fact a person is removed to a contracting state does not relieve the state of its obligations under Article 3.[223]

In a dramatic extension of the *Soering* principle, the ECtHR held in *D v UK* that deportation of the applicant who suffered from HIV/AIDS to his home country where he would not receive adequate medical treatment would violate Article 3.[224] The applicant was near death and the ECtHR referred to the 'very exceptional circumstances' of the case and the 'compelling humanitarian considerations at stake'.[225]   6.115

However, in *N v Secretary of State for the Home Department* the House of Lords unanimously held that returning a seriously ill, HIV-positive woman to Uganda would not constitute inhuman or degrading treatment.[226] It was accepted that her condition had stabilized after lengthy medical treatment in the United Kingdom, and that she would remain well for 'decades' if this continued; in Uganda, this treatment would not be accessible to her and the inevitable outcome of this would be an early death 'after a period of acute physical and mental suffering'.[227] Their Lordships distinguished *D v UK* as N's present medical condition was not critical and she remained fit to travel.   6.116

N confirms that the domestic courts consider the *D* case to be wholly exceptional, and that the obligation not to remove on health grounds will be triggered only in very extreme factual circumstances. The ECtHR has affirmed the correctness of the House of Lords' approach, emphasizing that expulsion of an alien who is suffering from a serious mental or physical illness to a country where the facilities for the treatment of that illness are inferior to those available in the deporting state will only raise an issue under Article 3 in a very exceptional case.[228] However, the courts have shown some willingness to consider health claims under Article 8, which does not impose the high threshold of Article 3.[229]   6.117

(d) *State support*

The application of Article 3 to welfare provision has not frequently been considered by the ECtHR. In *O'Rourke v UK* the applicant was evicted from temporary accommodation provided for him when he came out of prison.[230] He lived on the streets, to the detriment of his various medical conditions. In an admissibility decision, the Strasbourg Court held that this experience did not attain the requisite level of severity to engage Article 3.   6.118

The Court of Appeal and House of Lords have found that denying state support to individuals lacking other means of subsistence or shelter may amount to   6.119

---

[223] *KRS v UK* App No 32733/08, 2 December 2008.
[224] (1997) 24 EHRR 423. Cf *Bensaid v UK* (2001) 33 EHRR 205.
[225] (1997) 24 EHRR 423, para 54.
[226] [2005] UKHL 31, [2005] 2 AC 296.
[227] Ibid at [20] per Lord Hope.
[228] *Nnyanzi v UK* App No 21878/06, 8 April 2008. See also *KH (Afghanistan) v Secretary of State for the Home Department* [2009] EWCA Civ 1354.
[229] See *R (SQ) v Upper Tribunal Immigration and Asylum Chamber* [2013] EWCA 1251.
[230] App No 39022/97, 26 June 2001.

inhuman or degrading treatment.[231] Distinguishing the decision in *O'Rourke*, the House of Lords held in *R (Limbuela) v Secretary of State for the Home Department* that a decision to withdraw support to an asylum-seeker under section 55 of the Nationality, Immigration and Asylum Act 2002 violated Article 3.[232] In determining whether treatment in a particular case had reached the minimum level of severity required by Article 3, the court was not to apply a more exacting test where the treatment or punishment which would otherwise be found to be inhuman or degrading was the result of legitimate government policy. The correct test was for the court to look at the context and facts of the particular case, including factors such as the age, sex, and health of the claimant, and the length of time spent or likely to be spent without the required means of support, and ask whether the 'entire package' of work restrictions and deprivations that surrounded the claimant was so severe that it could properly be described as inhuman or degrading treatment. The threshold of severity will be crossed where a person deprived of support under section 55 is obliged to sleep in the street, or is seriously hungry or unable to satisfy the most basic requirements of hygiene. This approach arguably goes further than the ECtHR has yet and offers a rare example of domestic courts interpreting rights more generously than Strasbourg.[233]

(e) Self-inflicted conditions

6.120 In cases concerning political prisoners the ECtHR has been faced with the question of whether the fact that harm is self-inflicted negates or dilutes a state's positive obligation under Article 3.[234] Following periods on hunger strike a number of Turkish prisoners suffered physical and mental effects of malnutrition, which in some cases took an extreme form (irreversible brain damage). The ECtHR held that, while the Convention could not be interpreted as laying down a 'general obligation' to release a detainee on health grounds, the prisoner's clinical picture was now one of the factors which a state must take into account under Article 3 in assessing a person's fitness for detention.

6.121 The ECtHR found that their imprisonment violated Article 3, and that the self-inflicted nature of their conditions did not release Turkey from its Article 3 obligations.[235]

6.122 In *Hassan-Daniel v HMRC* the Court of Appeal, considering the state's obligations to a drug smuggler who died from ingestion of drugs while in detention, found that the criminality defence, which holds that it is offensive to public notions of fairness to compensate someone for their own criminal conduct in civil claims, did not apply to claims brought under the Human Rights Act 1998.[236]

---

[231] *R (Limbuela) v Secretary of State for the Home Department* [2005] UKHL 66, [2006] 1 AC 396. See also *R (Q and ors) v Secretary of State for the Home Department* [2003] EWCA Civ 364, [2004] QB 36.

[232] [2005] UKHL 66, [2006] 1 AC 396.

[233] Cf *R (EW) v Secretary of State for the Home Department* [2009] EWHC 2957 (Admin). See Leigh and Masterman, *Making Rights Real: The Human Rights Act in its First Decade* (London: Hart Publishing, 2009) 79–80.

[234] See, eg *Tekin Yildiz v Turkey* App No 22913/04, 10 November 2005.

[235] Ibid.

[236] [2010] EWCA Civ 1443.

5. 'Warning' decisions

The ECtHR will on occasion specifically indicate to a state that a particular course 6.123
of conduct could violate Article 3, effectively sending a warning to the state about
its future conduct.[237]

E. ARTICLE 4: PROHIBITION OF SLAVERY AND FORCED LABOUR

Article 4 concerns the twin issues of slavery or servitude (Article 4(1)) and forced 6.124
or compulsory labour (Article 4(2)). Article 4(1) is another of the rights from which
no derogation is allowed under Article 15. However, the Article 4(2) prohibition is
both derogable under Article 15 and subject to the exceptions listed in Article 4(3).

Relatively few Article 4 complaints have been heard by the ECtHR or ECmHR, 6.125
and only one has been upheld.[238] There have been only a handful of domestic cases
raising Article 4 issues.

1. Slavery and servitude

'Slavery' was eventually defined by the ECtHR in 2005. In *Siliadin v France* the 6.126
ECtHR drew on historical notions, citing the Slavery Convention of 1926: 'slavery
is the status or condition of a person over whom any or all of the powers attaching
to the right of ownership are exercised.'[239] For four years the applicant, a minor
at the time, whose passport was confiscated and who had no immigration status, worked for private individuals against her will and without pay, although no
physical force was used. The ECtHR held that this constituted servitude and forced
labour, but not slavery.

'Servitude' differs from slavery in that no ownership of the person is claimed. The 6.127
ECmHR has suggested that:

In addition to the obligation to provide another with certain services the concept of servitude
includes the obligation on the part of the 'serf' to live on another's property and the impossibility
of changing his condition.[240]

The ECtHR's judgment in *Van Droogenbroeck v Belgium* provides further guid- 6.128
ance as to the meaning of servitude. A sentence of two years in prison followed by
ten years 'at the Government's disposal' did not amount to 'that particularly serious
form of deprivation of liberty' that constitutes servitude; nor did it 'go beyond what
is "ordinary" in this context since it was calculated to assist him in reintegrating
himself into society'.[241] In *CN and V v France* the ECtHR clarified the distinction

---

[237] See, eg *Gürbüz v Turkey* App No 26050/04; *Kuruçay v Turkey* App No 24040/04; *Uyan v Turkey* App
No 7454/04 (all 10 November 2005); *Balyemez v Turkey* App No 32495/03, 12 December 2005.
[238] *Siliadin v France* (2005) 20 BHRC 654.
[239] Ibid, para 122.
[240] *Van Droogenbroeck v Belgium*, Case B44 (1980) Com Rep, para 79.
[241] (1982) 4 EHRR 443, paras 58–60.

between servitude and forced labour, stating that servitude was an aggravated form of forced labour that depended on the victim's belief, based on objective evidence, that their situation was immutable.[242]

2. Forced or compulsory labour

6.129   The Strasbourg approach to the concept of 'labour' is a generous one. It is not limited to physical labour and encompasses all forms of work.[243]

6.130   In order for labour to be forced or compulsory, the work or service must be 'extracted from the person under the menace of any penalty' and performed involuntarily.[244] There is clear scope for overlap between the concepts of forced labour and servitude.

6.131   The complaints deemed admissible under Article 4(2) have usually fallen into two categories: treatment of prisoners, and professionals compelled to provide their services free to the community. In *Van der Mussele v Belgium* a barrister tried to extend the boundaries of Article 4 when he claimed that being made to do *pro bono* legal work for indigent defendants violated the prohibition on forced labour.[245] The ECtHR asked whether the labour imposed 'a burden which was so excessive or disproportionate to the advantages attached to the future exercise of the profession that the service could not be treated as having been voluntarily accepted'.[246] Ruling against the barrister, the ECtHR relied on the fact that he had entered the profession of his own will, knowing that *pro bono* work was expected of him.[247]

6.132   Article 4 has rarely been raised in the domestic courts.[248] The House of Lords in *Sepet v Secretary of State for the Home Department* rejected an argument that Article 4 recognized a fundamental right to refuse to undertake military service on grounds of conscience.[249] The Supreme Court applied *Van de Mussele* in *R (Reilly) v Secretary of State for Work and Pensions*.[250] It found that the requirement that a person undertake unpaid work as a condition of receiving job seeker's allowance did not fulfill the characteristics of forced labour.

6.133   In *R (Ullah) v Special Adjudicator* the House of Lords held that a claim under Article 4, if strong enough, would succeed under Article 3, but it would be inconsistent with the humanitarian principles underpinning the Convention to accept that, if the facts were strong enough, a claim would be rejected even if it were based on Article 4 alone.[251]

---

[242] App No 67724/09, 11 October 2012.

[243] *Van der Mussele v Belgium* (1983) 6 EHRR 163.

[244] *Siliadin v France* (2005) 20 BHRC 654, clarifying earlier case law of the ECmHR; *X v Germany* (1974) 17 YB 148, drawing on the International Labour Organization Convention of 1930.

[245] (1983) 6 EHRR 163. See also *Steindel v Germany* App No 29878/07, 14 September 2010.

[246] (1983) 6 EHRR 163, para 37.

[247] Cf *Zarb Adami v Malta* (2006) 20 BHRC 703.

[248] In addition to the two House of Lords' decisions discussed here, Art 4 was raised in the planning context in *MacLeod v Secretary of State for Communities and Local Government* [2008] EWHC 384 (Admin). The challenge was rejected as plainly unarguable.

[249] [2003] UKHL 15, [2003] 3 All ER 304.

[250] [2013] UKSC 68, [2014] AC 453.

[251] [2004] UKHL 26, [2004] 2 AC 323.

3. Positive obligations

The ECtHR established in *Siliadin v France* that Article 4 entailed a specific pos-   6.134
itive obligation on Member States to penalize and prosecute effectively any act
aimed at maintaining a person in a situation of slavery, servitude, or forced or compulsory labour.[252] In order to comply with this obligation the Court held that states
are required to put in place a legislative and administrative framework, capable of
realistic enforcement, to prohibit and punish individuals who violate Article 4. The
scope of the obligation is identical to that under Article 3.[253]

Until the Coroners and Justice Act was passed in 2009, there was no offence   6.135
in English law of subjecting another to servitude.[254] That failure was challenged
in *CN v United Kingdom*.[255] The Court held that there had been an ineffective
investigation into complaints of domestic servitude as a result of the absence of
legislation. The Coroners and Justice Act 2009 remedied that failure.

In *Rantsev v Cyprus and Russia* the Court reiterated the positive obligations on   6.136
states to prevent trafficking in human beings, which included a procedural obligation akin to that under Articles 2 and 3 to investigate trafficking once it had come
to the state's attention.[256] *Rantsev* was applied in *OOO and ors v Commissioner of the
Police for the Metropolis* in which a number of young Nigerian women alleged that
the police had failed to investigate their complaints that they had been trafficked
to the United Kingdom and held in slavery or servitude.[257] The High Court found
that the police were under a duty to investigate a violation of Article 4 once a credible account of an alleged infringement had been brought to their attention. The
trigger for the duty would not depend upon an actual complaint from a victim or
near relative of a victim. The investigation, once triggered, would have to be undertaken promptly. The police had taken no steps to investigate the women's situation
and had thus violated Article 4. The High Court awarded the women damages for
distress and frustration.[258]

---

[252] (2005) 20 BHRC 654.
[253] Ibid, para 89.
[254] Section 71. See general discussion in Joint Committee on Human Rights, Twenty-Sixth Report, October 2006.
[255] (2013) 56 EHRR 24
[256] (2010) 51 EHRR 1.
[257] [2011] EWHC 1246 (QB).
[258] See Ch 4, para 4.53.

7

THE CONVENTION RIGHTS: LIMITED AND QUALIFIED RIGHTS

A. INTRODUCTION

7.01 This chaptfer summarizes the content of the limited and qualified rights under Articles 5–14 of the European Convention for the Protection of Human Rights and Fundamental Freedoms (Convention) and the general restrictions on rights found in Articles 15–18. Discussion of the nature of limited and qualified rights can be found in Chapter 2.[1]

As in Chapter 6, an overview is given of the jurisprudence of the European Court 7.02 of Human Rights (ECtHR) and any remaining important cases from the European Commission on Human Rights (ECmHR). Where the domestic courts have considered an article in claims brought under the Human Rights Act, their approach is discussed alongside the European case law and any divergences are noted.

B. ARTICLE 5: RIGHT TO LIBERTY AND SECURITY

Article 5 protects the 'right to liberty and security of person'. This is a combined 7.03 right, so the phrase 'right to liberty and security of person' should be read as a whole and not as two distinct, watertight rights. 'Security of the person' must be read in the context of personal liberty, not personal safety.[2] Article 5 ensures protection from deprivations of liberty and not from other interferences with the physical liberty of the person, such as the prevention of attack or the adequacy of welfare benefits.[3]

The specific concern of the right is to ensure that no one is deprived of liberty in 7.04 an 'arbitrary fashion'.[4] In *Saadi v UK* the Grand Chamber of the ECtHR reiterated the primacy of the notion of arbitrariness under Article 5.[5] The Court emphasized that compliance with national law is not sufficient to render a detention lawful; it may still be arbitrary under the Convention. The standard of arbitrariness will vary to an extent depending on the type of detention involved, but the ECtHR indicated that where there has been an element of bad faith or deception the standard is likely to be met. Arbitrariness, however, extends beyond such circumstances, as considered below.

Article 5 does not specifically apply to the conditions in which a person is 7.05 detained.[6] However, if the place and conditions of detention do not 'genuinely conform', or rationally link, with the reason for it advanced by the state under Article 5(1)(a)–(f), Article 5 will be violated.[7]

In addition to protecting the basic right to liberty, Article 5 provides persons 7.06 who are deprived of their liberty with a number of procedural rights, detailed in paragraphs (2)–(5).

---

[1] See ch 2, paras 2.28–2.31.

[2] *East African Asians v UK* (1981) 3 EHRR 76.

[3] *Bozano v France* (1986) 9 EHRR 297.

[4] *Engel v Netherlands* (1976) 1 EHRR 647; *Brogan v UK* (1988) 11 EHRR 117; *Kurt v Turkey* (1998) 27 EHRR 373.

[5] (2008) 24 BHRC 123, paras 67–69.

[6] *Ashingdane v UK* (1985) 7 EHRR 528; *S v Airedale NHS Trust* [2003] EWCA Civ 1036, [2004] QB 395.

[7] *Mayeka v Belgium* App No 13178/03, para 102; *R (Suppiah) v Secretary of State for the Home Department* [2011] EWHC 2 (Admin).

7.07   Article 5 also applies to deprivations of liberty by a contracting state acting out-side its territory.[8] In *R (Al-Jedda) v Secretary of State for Defence* the House of Lords considered the plight of an individual detained in Iraq for over three years without charge by UK forces acting under United Nations authority.[9] A majority of the Lords concluded that the United Kingdom might lawfully, where it was neces-sary for imperative reasons of security, exercise the power to detain individuals as authorized by the Security Council, but it had to ensure that the detainee's rights under Article 5 were not infringed to any greater extent than was inherent in such detention. However, the Grand Chamber of the ECtHR disagreed, finding that the relevant Security Council resolution did not unambiguously indicate an intention to displace Article 5. Since none of the grounds in Articles 5(1)(a)–(f) authorized preventative detention, the applicant's detention violated Article 5(1).[10]

7.08   The Grand Chamber returned to the question of the extra-territorial applica-tion of Article 5 during armed interventions in *Hassan v United Kingdom*.[11] It was faced with a situation of apparent 'norm conflict' between the provision permit-ting preventative detention under international humanitarian law (IHL) and the exhaustive grounds for detention in Article 5(1), which do not include preventative detention. In a highly pragmatic decision, the Grand Chamber voted by a major-ity to 'read down' Article 5 to allow preventative detention where this is permitted under IHL. It stipulated, however, that detention must also remain in keeping with the fundamental purpose of Article 5(1) to protect the individual from arbitrariness.[12] Detention must also be subject to review pursuant to Article 5(4). It recognizes that the full guarantees of review of the lawfulness of detention by a court may not be practicable within the course of an international armed conflict, but held that the reviewing body must provide 'sufficient guarantees of impartiality and fair proce-dure' to protect against arbitrariness.[13]

7.09   The minority pointed to the drastic ramifications of the majority's decision, which permits states to intern prisoners of war, as well as civilians considered to pose a threat to security, for the duration of hostilities without the strict limita-tions that would be imposed by a requirement to derogate from Article 5 pursuant to Article 15.[14] It considered that the majority's novel reading of Article 5(1) did not 'conform with the text, object or purpose of Article 5(1) of the Convention, as this provision has been consistently interpreted by [the] Court for decades, and the structural mechanism of derogation in times of war provided by Article 15'.[15]

7.10   Article 5 rights are not absolute in the sense that they can be derogated from under Article 15. However, as these guarantees are of such fundamental importance

---

[8] *Cyprus v Turkey* (First and Second Application) (1976) 4 EHRR 482; *Freda v Italy* (1980) 21 DR 250.
[9] [2007] UKHL 58, [2008] 1 AC 332.
[10] *Al-Jedda v United Kingdom* App No 27021/08, 7 July 2011, GC at paras 100–110.
[11] App No 29750/09, 18 September 2014, GC.
[12] Ibid at [104].
[13] Ibid at [106].
[14] See further in ch 7.
[15] Ibid, dissenting opinion of Judge Spano, joined by Judges Nicolaou, Bianku, and Kalaydjieva at paras 5–6.

in a democratic society and 'executive detention is the antithesis of the right to liberty and security of person',[16] any UK Government attempt to derogate from Article 5 will be closely scrutinized by the courts.[17]

The United Kingdom lodged a derogation from Article 5(1)(f) with the Council   7.11 of Europe following the terrorist attacks in the United States on 11 September 2001, the purpose of which was to enable the detention without trial of foreign nationals suspected of links to international terrorism under the provisions of the Anti-Terrorism, Crime and Security Act 2001. In the famous case of *A and ors*, the House of Lords held that the derogation was incompatible with Articles 5 and 14 of the Convention and therefore unlawful.[18] The Grand Chamber upheld the reasoning of the House of Lords.[19]

1. Deprivation of liberty

Article 5 is concerned with actual deprivation of liberty rather than with mere   7.12 restrictions on freedom of movement.[20] As the ECtHR noted in *HM v Switzerland*, restrictions on freedom of movement are the concern of Article 2 of Protocol 4 (which is not a Convention right for the purposes of the Human Rights Act).[21]

However, it will not always be easy to distinguish between a 'deprivation of' and   7.13 a 'restriction on' liberty, since the difference is one of degree rather than nature or substance.[22] Furthermore, the case law is expressly stated to be fact-specific. In *Guzzardi v Italy* the ECtHR made clear that in determining whether there has been a deprivation:

the starting point must be the concrete situation of the individual concerned and account must be taken of a whole range of factors arising in a particular case such as the type, duration, effects and manner of implementation of the measure in question.[23]

This guidance has been repeatedly cited by the ECtHR in later cases.[24]

Examples of circumstances which the Strasbourg organs have held to amount to   7.14 deprivations of liberty include long-term measures such as house arrest;[25] short-term measures such as detention in order to carry out a compulsory blood test;[26]

---

[16] *A and ors v Secretary of State for the Home Department* [2004] UKHL 56, [2005] 2 AC 68 at [222] per Baroness Hale.
[17] See, eg *A and ors*, ibid.
[18] Ibid.
[19] (2009) 26 BHRC 1.
[20] *Engel v Netherlands* (1976) 1 EHRR 647, para 58.
[21] [2002] ECHR 39187/98. See also *Austin v Commissioner of Police for the Metropolis* [2009] UKHL 5, [2009] 2 WLR 372 at [42].
[22] *Ashingdane v UK* (1985) 7 EHRR 528, para 41.
[23] *Guzzardi v Italy* (1980) 3 EHRR 333, para 92.
[24] See, eg *HL v UK* (2004) 40 EHRR 761, para 89; *Austin and ors v United Kingdom* App Nos 39692/09, 40713/09, 41008/09, 15 March 2012, GC at [57]; *Stanev v Bulgaria* App No 36760/06, 17 January 2012, GC at para 11.
[25] *Greek Case* (1969) 12 YB 1.
[26] *X v Austria* (1979) 18 DR 154.

detention of foreign nationals for an hour prior to their being put on a chartered aircraft in order to be expelled from the country;[27] and detention of a five-year-old in an immigration detention centre without her parents.[28] An 'informal' patient in a mental hospital has also been held to be deprived of liberty,[29] as has the involuntary placement of a person lacking capacity in a care home.[30] However, the ECtHR has held that a change in a prisoner's security categorization does not engage Article 5, even though it has an effect on his likely release date,[31] and some curfews may not constitute deprivations of liberty.[32]

7.15   The ECtHR has further held that a person is not deprived of their liberty if they have validly consented to the confinement in question. However, merely giving oneself up to be taken into detention will not suffice, especially when it is not disputed that a person is legally incapable of consenting, or disagreeing, with the proposed action.[33]

7.16   In domestic law, the notion of a deprivation of liberty has on occasion been restrictively interpreted. The House of Lords has considered its meaning in relation to the Government's anti-terrorism measures on a number of occasions. In the case of *R (Gillan) v Commissioner of Police for the Metropolis* concerning random stop-and-search powers under the Terrorism Act 2000 (TA 2000) the House of Lords adopted a narrow approach to the issue of 'deprivation', holding that Article 5(1) did not bite.[34] This was despite the fact that an individual who has been stopped has no choice but to comply with the search as there is a statutory power to detain, reasonable force may be used to enforce compliance, and non-compliance is criminally punishable.

7.17   The court sounded a warning note concerning Strasbourg and comparative precedent on this issue as the jurisprudence 'is closely focused on the facts of particular cases, and this makes it perilous to transpose the outcome of one case to another where the facts are different'.[35] In *Gillan v UK* the ECtHR did not determine the application of Article 5, but noted that the coercive element of stop-and-search procedures were indicative of a deprivation of liberty.[36] The judgment suggests that the House of Lords may have adopted too limited an approach. Nevertheless in *Roberts v Chief Constable for the Metropolis*, the Court of Appeal did not consider that the ECtHR's reasoning in *Gillan v UK* required a departure from the House of Lord's approach in *R (Gillan)* and found that a stop and search under the analogous power in s 60 of the Criminal Justice and Public Order Act 1994 did not result in a deprivation of liberty.[37]

---

[27] *X and Y v Sweden* (1977–1978) 7 DR 123.
[28] *Mubilanzila Mayeka v Belgium* [2006] 3 FCR 637.
[29] *HL v UK (Bournewood)* (2004) 40 EHRR 761.
[30] *Stanev v Bulgaria* App No 36760/06, 17 Januray 2012 GC.
[31] *Ashingdane v UK* (1985) 7 EHRR 528.
[32] *Cyprus v Turkey* (1976) 4 EHRR 482, para 235; *Raimondo v Italy* (1994) 18 EHRR 237, para 39.
[33] *Stanev v Bulgaria* App No 36760/06, 17 January 2012, GC at paras 118–119.
[34] [2006] UKHL 12, [2006] 2 AC 307.
[35] Ibid at [23].
[36] (2010) 28 BHRC 420.
[37] *Roberts v Chief Constable for the Metropolis* [2014] EWCA Civ 69 at [12]–[13].

The fact-sensitive approach to Article 5 is also illustrated by the House of Lords'   7.18
determination of three cases concerning the lawfulness of 'control orders' under
the Prevention of Terrorism Act 2005. Control orders were imposed on suspected
terrorists in place of indefinite detention, which the House of Lords had ruled
unlawful in *A and ors* (para 7.11). In *Secretary of State for the Home Department v JJ*
the House of Lords considered the terms of a control order which confined the suspected terrorist to a one-bedroom flat for 18 hours every day, required visitors to be
approved in advance, and prevented him from leaving a defined urban area.[38] By a
majority of three to two it was held that the control orders constituted a deprivation
of liberty. The majority emphasized that the factual scenarios in such cases may differ and it was therefore inappropriate to specify a formula by which the legality of a
control order could be tested. In dissent, Lord Hoffmann argued that:

In order to preserve the key distinction between the unqualified right to liberty and the qualified
rights of freedom of movement, communication, association and so forth, it is essential not to
give an over-expansive interpretation to the concept of deprivation of liberty.[39]

In the cases of *E* and *MB*, the House of Lords unanimously held that various   7.19
lesser restrictions did not amount to deprivations of liberty.[40] The control order cases
are considered further in relation to Article 6 below.[41] The Terrorism Prevention
and Investigation Measures Act 2011 abolished control orders and established a
system for imposing less restrictive terrorism investigation and prevention measures
(so-called TPIMs) on terrorist suspects in part in order to avert the legal difficulties that had arisen with ensuring the compatibility of control orders with Article
5. However, there have been recent calls from a number of quarters for the reintro-
duction of control orders, which would revive the significance of the case law just
discussed.

In *Austin v Metropolitan Police Commissioner* the House of Lords continued to   7.20
adopt a restrictive approach to Article 5, finding that the detention of thousands
of protestors for several hours inside a police cordon in central London did not
constitute a deprivation of liberty.[42] Noting that detention for public safety or public order was not a permissible ground for detention under Article 5(1), the Lords
held that a pragmatic approach to the substance of the right needed to be adopted
which took account of the purpose of the detention. Where, as here, the police had
a legitimate purpose and had not acted disproportionately in their pursuit of it the
court would not consider that a deprivation of liberty had occurred. It might be
thought that this effectively sanctions preventive detention, which the ECtHR has
explicitly ruled unlawful under Article 5(1)(c).[43] This approach to deprivation of

---

[38] [2007] UKHL 45, [2008] 1 AC 385.
[39] Ibid at [44].
[40] *Secretary of State for the Home Department v E and anor* [2007] UKHL 47, [2008] 1 AC 499; *Secretary of State for the Home Department v MB* [2007] UKHL 46, [2008] 1 AC 440. See also *Secretary of State for the Home Department v AH* [2008] EWHC 1018 (Admin).
[41] See para 7.156.
[42] [2009] UKHL 5, [2009] 2 WLR 372.
[43] *Lawless v Ireland (No 3)* (1979–1980) 1 EHRR 15. See para 7.38.

liberty mirrors that adopted in relation to Article 3.[44] Faced with absolute rights, the courts apply a proportionality analysis normally reserved for justifying a breach of a qualified right to determine the scope and content of the article.

7.21   By a majority judgment, the Grand Chamber of the ECtHR agreed with the conclusion of the House of Lords regarding the engagement of Article 5. The majority was at pains to underline that this conclusion turned on the 'specific and exceptional' facts of the case where the police had had no alternative but to impose the cordon to avert a real risk of serious injury or damage. It further emphasized that the underlying public interest motive has no bearing on whether a person is deprived of their liberty, which only becomes relevant at the second stage of considering whether the deprivation was justified by one of the sub-paragraphs of Article 5(1). However, drawing a somewhat subtle distinction, the ECtHR held that the requirement to take account of the 'type' and 'manner of implementation' allowed regard to the exceptional public order context.[45]

7.22   The minority questioned how exceptional the facts of the case truly were and suggested that the majority's reasoning could be interpreted as establishing a novel and dangerous proposition that, where it is necessary to impose a coercive and restrictive measure for a legitimate public-interest purpose, the measure does not amount to a deprivation of liberty. In their view, this would undermine the unqualified nature of the right and give *carte blanche* to police authorities.[46]

7.23   The domestic courts were called on to analyse the meaning of deprivation of liberty in a context not previously considered by the ECtHR in *P and anor v Cheshire West and Chester Council*.[47] The courts were asked to determine whether living arrangements made for mentally incapacitated persons by local authorities in an ordinary domestic setting, in their best interests, constituted a deprivation of liberty. In finding that the claimants had not been deprived of their liberty, the Court of Appeal in the *P & Q* appeal took account of the 'relative normality' of the arrangements for disabled persons in the claimants' position. However, the majority of the Supreme Court found that this approach ran contrary to the fundamental principle that disabled persons have the same rights as non-disabled persons, and rejected relative normality, compliance or lack of objection, and the reason or purpose behind the placement as irrelevant factors.[48] The court instead identified a universal 'acid test' for the deprivation of liberty in this context from the ECtHR's case law founded on the dual elements that a person is (i) 'under continuous supervision and control'; and (ii) 'not free to leave'.[49]

7.24   The minority were troubled by the divergence between the majority's approach and what an ordinary person would understand by the concept of deprivation of

---

[44] See *R (Wellington) v Secretary of State for the Home Department* [2008] UKHL 72, [2009] 2 WLR 48, discussed in ch 6, para 6.107.

[45] *Austin and ors v United Kingdom* App Nos 39692/09, 40713/09, 41008/09, 15 March 2012, GC at paras 52–69.

[46] Ibid, Judges Tulkens, Spielmann and Garlicki at [3] and [8].

[47] *P and anor v Cheshire West and Chester Council* [2014] UKSC 19.

[48] Ibid, per Lady Hale, giving the leading judgment at [45]–[47] and [50].

[49] Ibid at [49].

liberty, as well as the procedural strictures that Article 5 would impose on public authorities. They would have upheld the lower Court's approach in the absence of binding ECtHR case law requiring a contrary approach.[50] The expansive approach of the majority may well be thought to be consistent with ensuring practical and effective protection against arbitrary deprivation of liberty of a very vulnerable category of persons in circumstances where, unlike in *Austin*, any deprivation of liberty can lawfully be sanctioned under one of the exhaustive grounds of detention under Article 5(1), namely Article 5(1)(e).

These cases vividly illustrate the challenges of applying the unqualified protec-   7.25
tion of Article 5(1) flexibility and creatively to the plethora of functions of the modern state whilst ensuring both that it remains a practical and effective safeguard and that it does not unacceptably compromise other individual and public interests.

2. Exceptions to the right to liberty

Article 5(1) sets out an exhaustive list of exceptions to the prohibition on depriva-   7.26
tion of liberty in paragraphs (a)–(f). This list is to be given a narrow interpretation, and the excepted forms of detention must be both lawful and in accordance with a procedure prescribed by law.[51]

The United Kingdom fell foul of these principles in *HL v UK*. The ECtHR found   7.27
that the system for detaining mental patients without capacity breached Article 5 because there were no fixed procedural rules governing the admission and continued detention of the patients.[52]

(a) *Article 5 (1)(a)*

Article 5(1)(a) permits 'the lawful detention of a person after conviction by a com-   7.28
petent court'. A competent court under this article is one with jurisdiction to try the case.[53] It is not necessary that the proceedings before the court have fully complied with all the requirements of Article 6. Only if a conviction occurs as a result of proceedings which were a 'flagrant denial of justice' will Article 5(1)(a) be violated by the failure to conform with Article 6 standards.[54] A real risk of a 'flagrant breach' of Article 5 can be relied on to resist expulsion to another state. This would arise, for example, where there was a real risk of the receiving state arbitrarily detained the individual for many years without the intention of bringing him to trial, or imprisoning him for a substantial period on the basis of a previous conviction following a flagrantly unfair trial.[55]

In order for a detention to be 'lawful' there must be a court judgment that justi-   7.29
fies the confinement, as well as lawful procedures followed to effect the detention.

---

[50] Ibid at [98]–[100], and [105] per Lords Carnwath and Hodge, with whom Lord Clarke agreed.
[51] *Winterwerp v Netherlands* (1979) 2 EHRR 387; *Amuur v France* (1996) 22 EHRR 533; *A and ors* (2009) 26 BHRC 1; *Medvedyev v France* App No 3394/03, 29 March 2010.
[52] (2004) 40 EHRR 761. See discussion in *G v E* [2010] EWCA Civ 822, [2011] 1 FLR 239.
[53] *X v Austria* (1987) 11 EHRR 112.
[54] *Stoichkov v Bulgaria* (2007) 44 EHRR 14.
[55] *Othman Abu Qatada* (2012) 55 EHRR 1, 32 BHRC 62.

Strasbourg has held that Article 5(1)(a) does not permit the ECtHR to review convictions or sentences imposed by a domestic court, though any such decision would have to comply with Articles 3 and 6.[56]

7.30 Strasbourg considered the relationship between detention and conviction under Article 5(1)(a) in *Weeks v UK*.[57] A prisoner who had received an indeterminate life sentence was recalled to prison after his release. The ECtHR held that it was necessary for there to be a causal connection between the original conviction and detention. In this case the causal connection had not been broken because the prisoner remained a danger to the public. The Court reached a different conclusion in *Stafford v UK*.[58] The continued detention of a prisoner after he had served a prison sentence for forgery on the basis of an earlier mandatory life sentence from which he had been released on licence was not sufficiently causally connected to his original conviction to satisfy the requirements of Article 5(1)(a).

7.31 The House of Lords addressed the application of Article 5(1)(a) in *Secretary of State for Justice v James and ors*.[59] The claimants were convicted of specified violent and sexual offences, which deemed them to pose a significant risk of serious harm to members of the public, and were sentenced to an indeterminate sentence for public protection (IPP). Their only hope for release was to prove to the Parole Board that they no longer proved a threat to the public. However, the Secretary of State had systemically failed to provide sufficient places on the behaviour programmes that the claimants needed to undertake to prove to the Parole Board that they no longer posed a threat. As a result, the Parole Board was unable to recommend their release. The court found that the failure to provide behaviour programmes did not itself breach Article 5(1)(a). It was only when a matter of years had passed without the Parole Board being able to conduct an effective review of the case that the causal connection between the conviction and detention would arguably be broken.

7.32 When the case was considered by the ECtHR,[60] it disagreed with the House of Lords, finding a breach of Article 5(1). The ECtHR accepted that a causal link between the original sentence and the detention remained, but held that the absence of an opportunity to embark on rehabilitative courses, the successful completion of which was indispensable to establishing suitability for release, rendered continued detention arbitrary and contrary to Article 5(1). The ECtHR recognized that it would be unrealistic to expect rehabilitative work to be immediately available to prisoners and appears to have founded the breach on the substantial periods of delay in the applicants' cases.[61]

7.33 The precise scope and implications of the important decision in *Lee, James and Wells v United Kingdom* will fall to be worked out in subsequent decisions. In *obiter* comments in *Re Corey's Judicial Review*,[62] Lord Mance noted that if the decision

---

[56] *Krzycki v Germany* (1978) 13 DR 57; *Weeks v UK* (1987) 10 EHRR 293.

[57] (1987) 10 EHRR 293. See also *Van Droogenbroeck v Belgium* (1982) 4 EHRR 443, para 40.

[58] (2002) 35 EHRR 32. Cf *Waite v UK* (2003) 36 EHRR 54; *R (Hirst) v Secretary of State for the Home Department* [2006] EWCA Civ 945, [2006] 1 WLR 3083.

[59] [2009] UKHL 22, [2010] 1 AC 553.

[60] *Lee, James and Wells v United Kingdom* App Nos 25119/09, 57715/09, and 57877/09, 18 September 2012.

[61] Ibid at [194] and [220].

[62] [2014] AC 516.

meant that IPP prisoners had to be released in such circumstances, this would obviously be problematic. However, he considered that there were indications in the ECtHR's judgment that this was not the case.[63] In *R (Haney and anor) v Secretary of State for Justice*, the Secretary of State sought to contend that *Lee, James and Wells* was wrongly decided and should not be followed domestically.[64] The Court of Appeal held that the decision whether to follow the ECtHR's decision in preference to the House of Lords' judgment was preeminently a matter for the Supreme Court and granted permission to appeal without offering a view on the question. The appeal was heard in May 2014 and judgment is awaited.

(b) *Article 5(1)(b)*

Article 5(1)(b) sanctions the detention of a person who has failed to observe a court   7.34
order or fulfil a legal obligation. In the latter case, the arrest and detention must be for the purpose of securing the fulfilment of the legal obligation and not punitive in character. Court orders can include failure to pay a court fine,[65] submit to a court-ordered medical examination,[66] and breach of a bind-over to keep the peace.[67] Legal obligations found to justify detention have included the obligation to undertake military service,[68] to keep an identity card,[69] and to comply with a police officer's instruction under public order legislation not to engage in a brawl at a football match.[70] In domestic law, failure by a bankrupt to cooperate with a trustee in bankruptcy has also been found to fall within Article 5(1)(b).[71] The controversial domestic anti-terrorism power to detain individuals for questioning at airports without the need for reasonable grounds for suspicion of an offence in Schedule 7 of the Terrorism Act 2000 has been found to fall within Article 5(1)(b).[72]

The ECtHR has held that the order or obligation must be clear, the person   7.35
detained must usually be given an opportunity to comply, and detention must be the only reasonable way to secure the fulfilment of the order or obligation. This test was applied in *Beet v UK*, the ECtHR finding that the magistrates acted outside their jurisdiction in jailing a pensioner who had not paid her council tax.[73] In *Gatt v Malta* the ECtHR examined for the first time the system of detention

---

[63] Ibid at [64]. A majority of the Court agreed with these observations.
[64] [2013] EWCA Civ 1587 at [8] and [10].
[65] *Airey v Ireland* (1977) 8 DR 42 (ECommHR).
[66] *X v Germany* (1975) 3 DR 92.
[67] *Steel v UK* (1998) 28 EHRR 603.
[68] *Johansen v Norway* (1985) 44 DR 155.
[69] *Freda v Italy* (1980) 21 DR 250.
[70] *Ostendorf v Germany* App No 15598/08, 17 March 2013. Taking a different approach to the Divisional Court in *Hicks v Chief Commissioner of the Metropolis*: see the judgment of the Court of Appeal at [93] [2014] EWCA Civ 3.
[71] *Hickling v Baker* [2007] EWCA 287, [2007] 1 WLR 2386.
[72] *Beghal v Director of Public Prosecutions* [2014] 1 All ER 529 (an appeal against the Divisional Court's judgment will be heard by the Supreme Court); *Elosta v Commissioner of Police for the Metropolis* [2013] EWHC 3397 (Admin), [2014] 1 WLR 239; *R (Miranda) v Secretary of State for the Home Department* [2014] 3 All ER 447.
[73] [2006] RA 384. Cf *Benham v UK* (1996) 22 EHRR 293.

for non-compliance with the lawful order of a court that occurs commonly across Europe.[74] The Court emphasized the importance of the proportionality of the measure, stating that the authorities must take account of circumstances such as the purpose of the order, the practical possibility of complying with it, and the length of the detention.

(c) *Article 5(1)(c)*

7.36   Article 5(1)(c) concerns the arrest or detention of suspects in the course of the administration of criminal justice. In essence, it contemplates arrest and detention on remand. Arrest or detention is lawful only if it is based on a reasonable suspicion that a person has committed a crime, or when it is reasonably considered necessary to prevent a person from committing a crime or from fleeing after committing one. Detention must be a proportionate measure in the circumstances.[75]

7.37   The test of reasonable suspicion is an objective one; an honestly held suspicion is insufficient. The applicants in *Fox v UK* had been arrested under the Northern Ireland (Emergency Provisions) Act 1978, which required only that the arresting official 'genuinely and honestly' suspected the person arrested to be a terrorist.[76] The ECtHR found a violation of Article 5(1)(c) on the basis that this was a lower standard than reasonable suspicion, as 'reasonable suspicion supposes the existence of facts or information which would satisfy an objective observer that the person concerned may have committed the offence'.[77]

7.38   Article 5(1)(c) does not authorize preventive detention. In *Lawless v Ireland (No 3)* the state argued that the second limb of Article 5(1)(c), permitting detention where it is reasonably necessary to prevent a crime, allowed preventive detention of terrorist suspects.[78] The ECtHR held that this would 'lead to conclusions repugnant to the fundamental principles of the Convention'.[79] An arrest is lawful under Article 5(1)(c) only if the purpose is to bring the detainee before a competent legal authority, though the fact that the suspect may not ultimately be brought before a court or charged with a crime does not undermine the arrest since 'the existence of such a purpose must be considered independently of its achievement'.[80] Thus it has been held by the Court of Appeal that it suffices that an arresting officer is aware that his power of detention is time-limited and that an extension beyond this time limit requires the authorization by a Court, even if the individual is in fact released before this point.[81]

7.39   In *R (Hicks) v Commissioner of Police of the Metropolis*, the Court of Appeal declined to follow a suggestion in the ECtHR decisions of *Ostendorf v Germany*[82]

---

[74] App No 28221/08, 27 July 2010.
[75] *Ladent v Poland* App No 11036/03, 18 March 2008.
[76] (1990) 13 EHRR 157.
[77] Ibid, para 32. Cf *Murray v UK* (1994) 19 EHRR 193; *O'Hara v UK* (2002) 34 EHRR 32.
[78] (1979–1980) 1 EHRR 15.
[79] Ibid, para 14. See also *M v Germany* (2009) 28 BHRC 521.
[80] *Brogan v UK* (1988) 11 EHRR 117.
[81] *Hicks v Chief Commissioner of the Metropolis* [2014] EWCA Civ 3, at [85].
[82] App No 15598/08, 17 March 2013.

and *Jecius v Lithuania*[83] that Article 5(1)(c) only permits arrest and detention where there is an intention to bring the detainee before a court *on suspicion of his having committed a criminal offence*. It found this reading to be manifestly inconsistent with both earlier ECtHR cases and with the provision in Article 5(1)(c) for arrest and detention where 'it is reasonably considered necessary to prevent his committing an offence'.[84]

In *R (Laporte) v Chief Constable of Gloucestershire* the House of Lords considered   7.40 the detention of a group of anti-war protestors who had been detained on their coach on the way to a demonstration.[85] The police believed that some protesters were likely to cause a breach of peace, and so the coaches were prevented from proceeding to the demonstration and forcibly returned. The Court of Appeal had held that whether a breach of the peace was sufficiently imminent to justify taking action was dependent on all the circumstances. Article 5-compliant action required to prevent an apprehended breach of the peace might, in certain situations, involve action affecting a wholly innocent individual. This approach was clearly out of step with Strasbourg jurisprudence and was rejected by the House of Lords. Though the case was determined under Articles 10 and 11, their Lordships held, in line with ECtHR jurisprudence, that no power or duty arose to take any preventive action whatsoever unless and until the police reasonably believed that an actual breach of the peace was imminent.

(d) *Article 5(1)(d)*

Article 5(1)(d) covers the detention of minors for the purposes of educational super-   7.41 vision or for the purpose of bringing a minor before a competent legal authority. The accepted European classification of a 'minor' is a person under the age of 18. This exception is designed primarily to cover education and the detention of children for purposes such as placement in care or secure accommodation. The ECtHR will consider whether the purpose of the detention genuinely conforms to that of Article 5(1)(d). The words 'educational supervision' are not equated rigidly with notions of classroom teaching, and in the context of a young person in local authority care, educational supervision can embrace wider aspects of the parental rights for the benefit and protection of the person concerned.[86] However, in *P and anor v Poland*,[87] the ECtHR unsurprisingly held that detention of a 14-year-old, who had been the victim of rape and was seeking an abortion, with the purpose of separating her from her parents (who supported her obtaining an abortion) and in order to prevent the abortion taking place could under 'no stretch of the imagination' be considered to have been ordered for educational supervision within the meaning of Article 5(1)(d).

(e) *Article 5(1)(e)*

Article 5(1)(e) is drafted in language which now appears very dated. It permits the   7.42 detention of those with infectious diseases, persons of unsound mind, alcoholics,

---

[83] (2002) 35 EHRR 16.
[84] *Hicks v Chief Commissioner of the Metropolis* [2014] EWCA Civ 3 at [68]–[81].
[85] [2006] UKHL 55, [2007] 2 AC 105.
[86] *Koniarska v United Kingdom* App No 33670/96, 12 October 2000.
[87] [2013] 1 FCR 476.

drug addicts, and vagrants. According to early Strasbourg authorities, these people are specified because 'they have to be considered as occasionally dangerous for public safety' and 'their own interests may necessitate their detention'.[88]

7.43 The ECtHR has emphasized that in applying Article 5(1)(e), it is essential that there be legal certainty and an absence of arbitrariness. The detention must be 'necessary' in the circumstances and in accordance with the principle of proportionality.[89] In our view, an extremely high standard of justification would be necessary to render such detention proportionate. The mere fact of being, for example, a drug addict will be unlikely to justify detention under Article 5(1)(e) without some other factor (such as an objective reason to believe that the person in question would harm himself or herself or others).

7.44 The combination of the requirement of 'lawfulness' under Article 5(1)(e) and the obligation on the state to allow judicial review of detention under Article 5(4) has led to a number of decisions against measures in states, including the United Kingdom, relating to the detention of psychiatric patients and residential care for those who lack capacity. There have been very few cases relating to the other categories of person covered by Article 5(1)(e).

7.45 The ECtHR has held that three elements will be necessary to justify the detention of persons of unsound mind:

(a) the individual must be reliably shown to be of unsound mind;

(b) the mental disorder must be of a kind or degree warranting compulsory confinement;

(c) the validity of continuing detention depends upon the persistence of the mental disorder.[90]

7.46 Subsequent cases have confirmed that the burden of proof in establishing these criteria when both detaining and continuing to detain mental patients falls on the authorities.[91] A measure taken without the prior consultation of the interested person will attract especially careful scrutiny.[92]

7.47 Article 5(1)(e) imposes no requirement that the mental condition be amenable to treatment.[93] In *Reid v UK* the ECtHR held, agreeing with the decision of the Privy Council, that:

confinement may be necessary not only where a person needs therapy, medication or other clinical treatment to cure or alleviate his condition, but also where the person needs control and supervision to prevent him, for example, causing harm to himself or other persons.[94]

---

[88] *Guzzardi v Italy* (1980) 3 EHRR 333.
[89] *Enhorn v Sweden* App No 56529/00, 25 January 2005, para 36.
[90] *Winterwerp v Netherlands* (1979) 2 EHRR 387; *Johnson v UK* (1997) 27 EHRR 296; *Stanev v Bulgaria* App No 36760/06, 17 January 2012, GC at [145].
[91] See, eg *Reid v UK* [2003] ECHR 94, paras 69–74.
[92] *Stanev v Bulgaria* App No 36760/06, 17 January 2012, GC at [157].
[93] *Reid v UK* [2003] ECHR 94.
[94] Ibid, para 52.

Article 5(1)(e) is frequently addressed by domestic courts dealing with mental   7.48
health claims.[95] The important decision of the European Court in *HL v United
Kingdom* identified what became known as the 'Bournewood gap'.[96] The Court
held, contrary to the approach of the House of Lords, that the use by HL's doctors of the common law doctrine of necessity did not meet the requirement in
Article 5 of the European Convention that such a detention must be carried out 'in
accordance with a procedure prescribed by law'. There was therefore a gap in the
protection afforded to mental health patients who had been admitted to hospital
or residential care without due process. In response to *HL*, a complex procedure
for authorizing a deprivation of liberty for individuals who lack capacity was introduced under the Mental Capacity Act 2005. It was found by the Court of Appeal
to 'plug the Bournewood gap'.[97]

In *Enhorn v Sweden*, one of the rare cases to address the other grounds for   7.49
detention under Article 5(1)(e), the ECtHR emphasized the 'last resort' nature of
the power to detain in order to prevent the spreading of infectious diseases.[98] In
assessing the lawfulness of such detention the 'essential criteria' which the ECtHR
requires are that the spreading would be dangerous for public health and safety;
detention of the person is necessary in order to prevent spreading; and less severe
measures have been considered and found to be insufficient to safeguard the public
interest. The ECtHR took a stricter view in relation to delay in release than that in
Johnson, stating simply, 'when these criteria are no longer fulfilled, the basis for the
deprivation of liberty will cease to exist'.[99]

(f) *Article 5(1)(f)*

Article 5(1)(f) provides wide grounds for deprivation of liberty. In *Zamir v UK* it   7.50
was held that, in a deportation context, the lawfulness of the detention depends
only on whether the intention behind the detention was the deportation of the
detainee; detention can only be justified if the intended deportation was the genuine reason for the detention.[100] The ECtHR will not examine the proportionality of the decision to deport.[101] The scope of its review is limited to examining
whether there is a legal basis for the detention and whether the decision of the
courts on the question of lawfulness could be described as arbitrary in light of
the facts of the case. As the domestic courts have put it, Article 5(1)(f) requires

---

[95] See, eg *R (Munjaz) v Mersey NHS Trust* [2005] UKHL 58, [2006] 2 AC 148; *R (H) v Secretary of State for Health* [2005] UKHL 60, [2006] 1 AC 441; *R (B) v Ashworth Hospital Authority* [2005] UKHL 20, [2005] 2 AC 278; *R v Grant* [2001] EWCA Crim 2611, [2002] QB 1030.

[96] (2004) 40 EHRR 761.

[97] *G v E* [2010] EWCA Civ 822, [2011] 1 FLR 239.

[98] (2005) 41 EHRR 633.

[99] Ibid, para 44.

[100] (1983) 40 DR 42. See also *R (Vovk) v Secretary of State for the Home Department* [2006] EWHC 3386 (Admin).

[101] *Saadi v UK* (2008) 47 EHRR 427; *SK (Zimbabwe) v Secretary of State for the Home Department* [2011] UKSC 23 at [76].

that 'the power to detain be exercised reasonably and for the prescribed purpose of facilitating deportation'.[102]

7.51   The ECmHR expanded the scope of Strasbourg review in *Lynas v Switzerland*, holding that detention can cease to be lawful if the extradition or deportation proceedings are not carried out diligently or amount to an abuse of power.[103]

7.52   The case of *Chahal v UK* introduced a further limit on state power under Article 5(1)(f) by finding that detention is justified only if actual deportation proceedings are in progress.[104] While proceedings must be brought with requisite diligence, the majority of the ECtHR did not consider that the applicant's detention for over four years while proceedings were conducted violated Article 5(1)(f). The Grand Chamber reiterated the requirement that deportation proceedings be in progress in *A and ors v UK*.[105]

7.53   In a controversial judgment on the application of Article 5(1)(f) to asylum seekers who had surrendered to immigration authorities and then been detained by the United Kingdom in 'reception centres', a majority of the Grand Chamber in *Saadi v UK* agreed with the domestic courts[106] and found that:

until a state has 'authorised' entry to the country, any entry is 'unauthorised' and the detention of a person who wishes to effect entry and who needs but does not yet have authorisation to do so, can be, without any distortion of language, to 'prevent his effecting an unauthorised entry'.[107]

A minority of six judges held that Article 5(1)(f) did not justify the detention of those who had not sought to evade the authorities.

7.54   By contrast, in *R (Nadarajah) v Secretary of State for the Home Department* the Court of Appeal found that the appellants' confinement in an immigration detention centre violated Article 5(1)(f).[108] The policy under which they were held was not accessible and therefore their detention failed to meet the standard of lawfulness imposed by the Convention. Domestic decisions on the lawfulness of immigration detention are based on principles enshrined in English law prior to the Human Rights Act 1998, known as the *Hardial Singh* principles, which guarantee the same, if not greater, protection as Article 5(1)(f).[109]

7.55   The UK derogation from Article 5(1)(f) and its consideration in the case of *A and ors* is discussed in detail under Article 15.[110]

---

[102]   *R (Lumba and Mighty) v Secretary of State for the Home Department* [2011] UKSC 12, [2011] 2 WLR 671 at [30].

[103]   (1976) 6 DR 141.

[104]   (1997) 23 EHRR 413, para 113.

[105]   (2009) 26 BHRC 1.

[106]   See *R (Saadi and ors) v Secretary of State for the Home Department* [2002] UKHL 41, [2002] 1 WLR 3131.

[107]   *Saadi v UK* (2008) 24 BHRC 123, para 65. Cf *Riad and Idiab v Belgium* App Nos 29787/03 and 29810/03, 24 January 2008.

[108]   [2003] EWCA Civ 1768. See also *R (Lumba and Mighty) v Secretary of State for the Home Department* [2011] UKSC 12, [2011] 2 WLR 671.

[109]   *R v Governor of Durham Prison, ex p Hardial Singh* [1984] 1 WLR 704; *SK (Zimbabwe) v Secretary of State for the Home Department* [2011] UKSC 23 at [12].

[110]   See para 7.608.

3. Procedural safeguards

(a) *Article 5(2)*

Under Article 5(2), everyone arrested has the right to be informed promptly in a 7.56
language he or she understands of the reasons for the arrest and of any charge. The
ECtHR has held that the purpose of this obligation is to enable the arrested person
to challenge the lawfulness of the detention.[111]

The European Court has held that the terms 'arrest' and 'charge' under 7.57
Article 5(2) are not intended to limit the duty to give reasons to the criminal
context.[112] The duty applies equally to all detention, including that of mental health
patients. Reasons need not be in writing, and formal notification may not be necessary if the reasons are made clear during the arrest. It will generally be insufficient
only to make reference to the relevant statutory provisions authorizing the arrest.[113]

In *Saadi v UK* the ECtHR found that the Government had violated Article 5(2).[114] 7.58
The applicant was arrested and detained in an immigration reception centre without explanation until his representative was informed of the basis for his detention
some 76 hours after his arrest. The Grand Chamber held that reasons had not been
supplied promptly.

(b) *Article 5(3)*

There are two limbs to Article 5(3). First, it requires that anyone arrested shall be 7.59
brought promptly before a judge or other officer authorized by law to exercise judicial power. The aim of this requirement is to impose a limit on the length of detention authorized by Article 5(1)(c) and thereby ensure that provisional detention is
not unreasonably prolonged.[115] Secondly, the trial should occur within a reasonable
time and bail should be granted unless there are sufficient reasons not to release the
detainee. Article 5(3) applies solely to criminal offences.[116] The Grand Chamber has
held that these two requirements are not 'logically or temporally linked'.[117]

The reasonableness of a period of detention under the first limb of Article 5(3) 7.60
(being brought promptly before a judge) is a matter of fact and degree.[118] In *Wemhoff
v Germany* the ECtHR developed a two-part test: are the reasons advanced for the
detention relevant and sufficient, that is, does the public interest outweigh the right
to liberty in an individual case; and if so, have the proceedings been unduly prolonged by avoidable delay?[119] Periods of detention that have been held to contravene
Article 5(3) include detention without charge for four days and six hours,[120] and

---

[111] *X v UK* (1982) 4 EHRR 188.
[112] *Van der Leer v Netherlands* (1990) 12 EHRR 567, para 27.
[113] *Ireland v UK* (1978) 2 EHRR 25.
[114] (2008) 24 BHRC 123.
[115] *Wemhoff v Germany* (1968) 1 EHRR 55; *Neumeister v Austria* (1968) 1 EHRR 91.
[116] *De Wilde, Ooms and Versyp v Belgium* (1971) 1 EHRR 373.
[117] *McKay v UK* (2006) 24 BHRC 471.
[118] *Punzelt v Czech Republic* (2000) 33 EHRR 1159.
[119] (1968) 1 EHRR 55.
[120] *Brogan v UK* (1988) 11 EHRR 117.

detention in police custody for 14 days.[121] Furthermore, the ECtHR has repeatedly highlighted that the official reviewing detention must be independent in order to satisfy Article 5(3).[122]

7.61   In response to the terrorist threat posed by Al-Qaeda, the UK Government repeatedly extended the pre-charge detention period permitted for individuals suspected of terrorist offences from the standard 36 hours allowed under the Police and Criminal Evidence Act 1984. Under the Terrorism Act 2000 the maximum period of detention without charge in such cases was seven days. This was amended to extend detention to 14 days by the Criminal Justice Act 2003, and to 28 days by the Terrorism Act 2006. The 28-day period was subject to yearly renewal by affirmative order, and the Coalition Government allowed the period to revert to 14 days.

7.62   In relation to the second limb of Article 5(3) the presumption is that bail should be granted, and denial of bail must be justified by relevant and sufficient reasons. In *Gault v UK* the ECtHR held that the fact that the applicant's third retrial would be held promptly was not sufficient reason for denial of bail.[123] As the Court emphasized, Article 5(3) does not permit a choice for the authorities between a speedy trial and granting bail. It is legitimate for the courts to adjust the recognizance required by way of bail to reflect the gravity of the offence or the extent of financial liability.[124]

7.63   Reasons for refusing bail that are justified include:

(a) a risk that the accused will fail to appear at the trial;[125]

(b) a risk that the accused may interfere with the course of justice;[126]

(c) a risk of further offences;[127] and

(d) the preservation of public order.[128]

In any of these situations, the reason advanced must be justified by the facts in the particular case. It is not permissible to place decisive reliance on the gravity of the charges to justify lengthy periods of pre-trial detention.[129] In *Caballero v UK* the automatic denial of bail under section 25 of the Criminal Justice and Public Order Act 1994 in the case of persons charged with or convicted of homicide or rape after a previous conviction of such an offence was held to be a breach of Article 5(3).[130]

---

[121] *Aksoy v Turkey* (1996) 23 EHRR 553. See also *Sakik and ors v Turkey* (1998) 26 EHRR 662; *Öcalan v Turkey* (2003) 37 EHRR 10.

[122] See, eg *Klamecki v Poland* (2003) 39 EHRR 7.

[123] (2008) 46 EHRR 1202; *Allen v UK* [2011] Crim LR 147.

[124] *Mangouras v Spain* App No 12050/04, 28 September 2010.

[125] *Stögmüller v Austria* (1979–1980) 1 EHRR 155.

[126] *Wemhoff v Germany* (1968) 1 EHRR 55.

[127] *Toth v Austria* (1991) 14 EHRR 551.

[128] *Letellier v France* (1991) 14 EHRR 83.

[129] *Kislitsa v Russia* App No 29985/05, 19 June 2012, GC at [36].

[130] (2000) 30 EHRR 643.

Parliament amended this section in order to comply with the judgment making provision for the grant of bail only in exceptional circumstances.

The House of Lords considered the amended section 25 in *R (O) v Crown Court at Harrow*.[131] The appellant, accused of various sexual offences, remained in detention after the judge refused to extend the limit as the prosecution had not acted with due diligence in bringing the case to trial. The Lords held that there was no breach of Article 5(3) in such circumstances so long as the refusal of bail remained justified under section 25.   **7.64**

(c) *Article 5(4)*

Under Article 5(4), any detainee must be able to challenge the lawfulness of his detention. Review must be by a court and must be speedy. The 'court' does not necessarily have to be a classic court of law, which is formally part of the state's judicial machinery. However, the body must 'exhibit the necessary judicial procedures and safeguards appropriate to the kind of deprivation of liberty in question, including most importantly independence of the executive and of the parties'.[132] In addition, the body must have the ability to decide the lawfulness of the detention and to order release if detention is found to be unlawful.[133] The right of review does not extend to a review of any underlying decision on which the detention is based, such as a deportation or extradition order.[134]   **7.65**

In *Weeks v UK* the ECtHR found that the Parole Board could be considered a court for the purposes of Article 5(4) but for the inadequate procedures for involving the detainee in the review of his detention.[135] These deficiencies were corrected and the Parole Board now fulfils the function of a court under Article 5(4).   **7.66**

The ECtHR has deliberately refrained from stating timeframes that will or will not be considered speedy; this issue cannot be assessed in the abstract. It has explicitly noted that Article 5(4)'s expedition requirement is more exacting than that of Article 6(1): 'while one year per instance may be a rough rule of thumb in Article 6(1) cases, Article 5(4), concerning issues of liberty, requires particular expedition'.[136]   **7.67**

Accordingly, the approach of the ECtHR is to examine the particular facts of the case before it and to consider whether, in those specific circumstances, there was a failure to proceed with reasonable speed. Domestic law will not be determinative of this issue.[137]   **7.68**

However, in *Zamir v UK* the ECmHR held that seven weeks between applying for habeas corpus and the actual hearing violated Article 5(4).[138]   **7.69**

---

[131] [2006] UKHL 42, [2007] 1 AC 249.

[132] *Benjamin and Wilson v UK* (2003) 36 EHRR 1, para 33. See also *Chahal v UK* (1997) 23 EHRR 413.

[133] *Benjamin and Wilson v UK*, ibid.

[134] *RB (Algeria) v Secretary of State for the Home Department* [2009] UKHL 10; *R (Halligen) v Secretary of State for the Home Department* [2012] UKSC 20.

[135] (1987) 10 EHRR 293.

[136] *Reid v UK* [2003] ECHR 94, para 79.

[137] See, eg *Yaman v Turkey* App No 32446/96, 2 November 2004.

[138] (1983) 40 DR 42.

7.70   In cases of prolonged detention, this right has ongoing effect and the article requires the availability of a process to enable the lawfulness of the detention to be reviewed at reasonable intervals.[139]

7.71   There has been a series of key cases where the ECtHR has held that Article 5(4) requires a regular review of the lawfulness of continuing detention, particularly where the circumstances of the detention change over time affecting justification for detention. Thus, there have been successful challenges to the lawfulness of detention: in psychiatric hospitals;[140] during post-tariff mandatory life imprisonment, where the Home Secretary has a veto power over Parole Board decisions;[141] during the discretionary period of discretionary life sentences;[142] and of young people convicted of murder and detained.[143]

7.72   In the decision of *Winterwerp v Netherlands* the ECtHR held that the judicial proceedings referred to in Article 5(4) need not always be attended by the same guarantees as those required by Article 6(1) for civil or criminal litigation.[144] In *Reinprecht v Austria* the Court found that a public hearing, which is a specific right under Article 6, does not extend to proceedings concerning the review of the lawfulness of detention.[145] Noting the differing purposes of the guarantees of Articles 5 and 6, the Court held that this 'difference of aims explains why Article 5(4) contains more flexible procedural requirements than Article 6 while being much more stringent as regards speediness'.[146] However, certain guarantees will apply equally to Article 5. Adversarial proceedings, the exchange of evidence, and equality of arms, for instance, are essential features of the protections in Article 5(4).[147] In *Allen v UK* the European Court held that Article 5(4) guaranteed the right for those charged with criminal offences to appear at the prosecution's appeal against bail.[148]

7.73   In *A and ors v UK*, concerning the indefinite detention of foreign terrorist suspects under the Anti-Terrorism Crime and Security Act 2001, the Grand Chamber considered the extent of disclosure required by the guarantee of procedural fairness in Article 5(4).[149] In the proceedings before the Special Immigration Appeals Commission, the applicants had been denied access to 'closed material', deemed too sensitive to reveal on the grounds of national security. The 'special advocate' procedure designed by the Government was intended to remedy any unfairness in the lack of disclosure by permitting the special advocate to see the closed material and make submissions on the detainee's behalf. The Grand Chamber concluded that there was no difficulty in principle with such a procedure so long as the allegations

---

[139] *Bezicheri v Italy* (1989) 12 EHRR 210.
[140] *X v UK* (1980) Series B 41.
[141] *Stafford v UK* (2002) 35 EHRR 32.
[142] *Weeks v UK* (1987) 10 EHRR 293; *Thynne v UK* (1990) 13 EHRR 666.
[143] *Hussain v UK* (1996) 22 EHRR 1; *T and V v UK* (1999) 30 EHRR 121.
[144] (1979) 2 EHRR 387.
[145] [2005] ECHR 67175/01.
[146] Ibid, para 40.
[147] *Sanchez-Reisse v Switzerland* (1986) 9 EHRR 71; *Weeks v UK* (1987) 10 EHRR 293; *Klamecki v Poland* (2003) 39 EHRR 7.
[148] App No 18837/06, 30 March 2010.
[149] (2009) 26 BHRC 1.

in the open material were 'sufficiently specific' for the detainee to provide information to his representatives with which to refute them. This was the case in respect of five of the applicants. In two cases, however, the open material consisted of general assertions that the detainee would have been unable to refute. In these cases Article 5(4) was breached.[150]

Appellants before the domestic courts have frequently raised arguments founded on Article 5(4). In the mental health context, the High Court has stated that: 7.74

regular reviews by the court are not merely desirable, not merely a matter of good practice; they go, as both the Strasbourg jurisprudence and the domestic case-law make clear, to the very legality of what is being done.[151]

The ECtHR has held that, in the mental health context, special procedural safeguards may be called for in order to protect the interests of persons who, on account of their mental disabilities, are not fully capable of acting for themselves.[152] Thus in *MH v UK*,[153] the ECtHR held (disagreeing with certain reasoning of the House of Lords[154]) that it would be wholly unreasonable to expect the applicant, who lacked capacity, or her mother, to issue a complicated *habeas corpus* petition to test the lawfulness of her detention. Additional compensatory safeguards were required. The ECtHR found a breach in respect of an initial period under domestic procedure during which no such safeguards were in place, but not thereafter when the Secretary of State was under a duty under the Human Rights Act to refer the applicant's case to the Mental Health Tribunal of his or her own motion.   7.75

The most common Article 5(4) challenges arise in the context of Parole Board proceedings.[155] Article 5(4) deeply divided their Lordships in the case of *Roberts v Parole Board*.[156] At issue was the creation of a special advocate procedure in order to prevent Roberts from discovering the source of information concerning him. The majority held that the procedure was either covered by an express authorization stemming from the Parole Board Rules, or could be implied from the duty of the Board to conduct hearings which reconciled the interests of the prisoner, the public, and the informant. Such a procedure, they held, may or may not comply with Article 5(4), but this can only be judged after the case by determining whether the process as a whole has resulted in a procedure and decision which involves 'significant injustice to the prisoner'.[157] The minority disagreed, finding that the lack of specific authorization for the procedure rendered it unlawful.   7.76

---

[150] The effect of this was felt in relation to Art 6 in *Secretary of State for the Home Department v AF (No 3)* [2009] UKHL 28. See also *R (Rex Cart and ors) v Upper Tribunal and anor* [2009] EWHC 3052 (Admin).

[151] *Re BJ (Incapacitated Adult)* [2009] EWHC 3310 (Fam), [2010] 1 FLR 1373 at [10].

[152] *Stanev v Bulgaria* App No 36760/06, 17 January 2012, GC at [170].

[153] App No 11577/06, 22 October 2013.

[154] *R (H) v Secretary of State for Health* [2006] 1 AC 441.

[155] For a full discussion, see Livingstone, Owen, and Macdonald, *Prison Law*, 4th edn (Oxford: Oxford University Press, 2008).

[156] [2005] UKHL 45, [2005] 2 AC 738.

[157] Ibid at [83] per Lord Woolf.

7.77   As in many of the cases before the ECtHR, a central focus of the domestic courts has been on the period of detention after a prisoner has served the determinate part of the sentence (known as the tariff period in life sentences) when he remains detained on the grounds of continuing dangerousness. The courts have established that once a prisoner has been lawfully detained within the meaning of Article 5(1)(a), the review required by Article 5(4) is incorporated within the sentence of the original court and the prisoner is entitled to no further review beyond the normal appeal process.[158] However, the position becomes more complex after the determinate or tariff element of the sentence has been served.

7.78   In *R (Noorkoiv) v Home Secretary and Parole Board*, the Court of Appeal considered the delay between the expiry of the tariff period of the appellant's automatic life sentence and the decision of the Parole Board to release him.[159] The court held that the delay of two months was incompatible with Article 5(4). The fact that the delay occurred as a result of resource constraints was no justification in light of the 'imperative need to release from prison any post-tariff prisoner who no longer remains a danger'.[160]

7.79   The House of Lords considered the application of Article 5(4) to prisoners serving determinate sentences who had reached a point in their sentence when legislation governing early release meant that they could be considered for release by the executive, and held that, in contrast to indeterminate sentence prisoners, those entitled to early release did not have any right to speedy review of their detention.[161]

7.80   The Supreme Court recently considered the right to a speedy review of determinate sentence prisoners upon recall from release on licence. Faced with a conflict between its previous case law[162] and case law of the ECtHR,[163] the Court followed the ECtHR case law and held that Article 5(4) had no application to the recall of a determinative sentence prisoner released on licence pursuant to early release powers. Lady Hale, concurring in the result, sounded a note of caution regarding the Court's reasoning, observing that there was a further principled distinction to be drawn between those determinate sentence prisoners released pursuant to mandatory release powers (where there is a right for the case to be heard by the Parole Board on recall) and those released pursuant to discretionary release powers such as the appellant (where there is not). The majority thought that Lady Hale's reasoning may give the ECtHR cause to reconsider its case law but was not prepared to draw this distinction. It may well have been preferable had the majority done so to ensure the coherence of the law. However, it is to be hoped that the ECtHR will now take up the majority's invitation to do so in a suitable case.

---

[158]   *R (Giles) v Parole Board* [2003] UKHL 42, [2004] 1 AC 1.
[159]   [2002] HRLR 36.
[160]   Ibid, para 58.
[161]   *R (Black) v Secretary of State for Justice* [2009] UKHL 1, [2009] 2 WLR 282; *R (Whiston) v Secretary of State for Justice* [2014] UKSC 39.
[162]   In particular, *R (Smith) v Parole Board* [2005] UKHL 1, [2005] 1 WLR 350.
[163]   In particular the case of *Brown v United Kingdom* App No 986/04, 26 October 2004.

A narrow approach to Article 5(4) was adopted by Lord Hope in *Secretary of State* 7.81
for Justice v James, who suggested that it would only be in a case where the Parole
Board had been repeatedly denied the reports necessary to complete its review that
Article 5(4) would be violated.[164] However, Lord Brown (with whom a majority
agreed) took a broader approach.[165] The Court of Appeal subsequently followed
Lord Brown's approach, finding that 'routine delays' in referring prisoners' cases to
the Parole Board may breach Article 5(4).[166]

4. Positive obligations

The positive obligations recognized under Article 5 have historically been relatively 7.82
limited. It has been accepted that Article 5 imposes an obligation to protect vulnerable individuals from deprivation of liberty by private actors. In *Storck v Germany*
the applicant alleged a violation of Article 5 because of her forced confinement in a
private psychiatric institution.[167] The ECtHR held that the authorities were obliged
'to take measures providing effective protection of vulnerable persons, including
reasonable steps to prevent a deprivation of liberty of which the authorities have or
ought to have knowledge'.[168]

In *Re A and C* the High Court considered the extent of local authority obliga- 7.83
tions where the authority is aware of restrictions on the liberty of vulnerable individuals.[169] The court set out in detail the measures that should be taken in such
circumstances, including investigation, monitoring, and taking reasonable steps to
bring the situation to an end.[170]

The ECtHR and domestic courts have held that Article 5(4) is not concerned 7.84
with detention conditions or the treatment of those detained.[171]

In *El-Masri v the Former Yugoslav Republic of Macedonia*,[172] the Grand Chamber 7.85
considered a case where the Macedonian authorities had unlawfully detained the
applicant in a hotel and then handed him over to the United States authorities in
the knowledge that he would be subject to extraordinary rendition. It held that
Article 5 lays down an obligation not only to refrain from active infringements
of Article 5, but also to take appropriate steps to provide protection against an
unlawful interference of Article 5 to everyone within its jurisdiction. This included

---

[164] [2009] UKHL 22, [2010] 1 AC 553, where Lord Hope held at [21]: 'As in the case of Article 5(1), it
will only be if the system breaks down entirely because the Parole Board is denied the information that it
needs for such a long period that continued detention has become arbitrary that the Article 5(4) guarantee
would be violated and the prisoner will be entitled to a remedy in damages.'

[165] At [60], where he said: 'I accept that article 5(4) requires the basic rule 6 dossier to be made available: without this the Board simply cannot function.'

[166] *R (Faulkner) v Secretary of State for Justice and anor* [2010] EWCA Civ 1434 at [45]–[46].

[167] (2006) 43 EHRR 6.

[168] Ibid, para 102.

[169] *Re A and C* [2010] EWHC 978 (Fam), [2010] 2 FLR 1363.

[170] Ibid, paras 80–96.

[171] *Ashingdane v UK* (1985) 7 EHRR 528, paras 44, 52; *R (Cawser) v Secretary of State for the Home
Department* [2003] EWCA Civ 1522; though see *Mayeka v Belgium* [2006] 3 FCR 637.

[172] App No 39630/09, 13 December 2012, GC.

a procedural obligation to conduct a prompt effective investigation into an arguable claim that a person has been taken into custody and has not been seen since. The Court found that Macedonia had inter alia breached the procedural aspect of Article 5 by failing to undertake any meaningful investigation into the applicant's credible allegations that he was detained arbitrarily.[173] Since the applicant had been handed over to the United States authorities in circumstances where it was clear that there would be a 'flagrant breach' of his Article 5 rights, the Macedonian authorities were also held responsible for his subsequent detention by the United States authorities.

5. Right to compensation

7.86 Article 5(5) guarantees a right to compensation if a person has been detained in violation of Article 5. This provision requires a binding award of compensation that can be enforced by the courts.[174] It is reflected in section 9(3)–(5) of the Human Rights Act for detentions occurring after the Act came into force.[175] Only compensatory—not exemplary—damages can be awarded.[176] In determining damages under Article 5, regard must be had to the ECtHR's case law on the award of damages under Article 41 of the Convention and to the fact that a finding of breach may be sufficient compensation.[177] In *R (Faulkner and Sturnham) v Secretary of State for Justice and anor*,[178] the Supreme Court reiterated that the applicable principles for the award of damages and quantum of awards in domestic law were to be drawn primarily from any clear and consistent practice of the ECtHR.

C. ARTICLE 6: RIGHT TO A FAIR TRIAL

7.87 The right to a fair trial is a paradigm human right. It is central to the existence of the rule of law, because the guarantee of all other rights depends upon the proper administration of justice.[179] As the House of Lords held in *Secretary of State for the Home Department v AF (No 3)* the right to a genuinely fair trial is a 'core principle' which cannot give way to competing concerns.[180] It has 'a position of pre-eminence in the Convention'[181] and is explicitly referred to in the Preamble. Given the

---

[173] Ibid at [230]–[243].

[174] See, eg *Brogan v UK* (1988) 11 EHRR 117; *Fox v UK* (1990) 13 EHRR 157; *Caballero v UK* (2000) 30 EHRR 643; *Curley v UK* (2001) 31 EHRR 14.

[175] *R (Wright) v Secretary of State for the Home Department* [2006] EWCA Civ 67.

[176] Human Rights Act, s 9; *R (KB) v Mental Health Review Tribunal (Damages)* [2003] EWHC 193 (Admin), [2004] QB 936.

[177] *R (Greenfield) v Secretary of State for the Home Department* [2005] 1 WLR 673; *R (Degainis) v Secretary of State for Justice* [2010] EWHC 137 (Admin).

[178] [2013] 2 AC 254.

[179] *Golder v UK* (1975) 1 EHRR 524, para 35; Jayawickrama, *The Judicial Application of Human Rights Law* (Cambridge: Cambridge University Press, 2002) 480.

[180] [2009] UKHL 28, [2009] 3 WLR 74.

[181] Harris, O'Boyle, Bates, and Buckley, *Harris, O'Boyle and Warbrick: Law of the European Convention on Human Rights*, 2nd edn (Oxford: Oxford University Press, 2009) 202.

importance of the rule of law to a democratic society, the courts have repeatedly emphasized that Article 6 should be given a broad and purposive interpretation, and its exceptions narrowly construed. In *Delcourt v Belgium*, for example, the ECtHR stated that:

In a democratic society within the meaning of the Convention, the right to a fair administration of justice holds such a prominent place that a restrictive interpretation of Article 6 (1) would not correspond to the aim and the purpose of that provision.[182]

In keeping with this broad interpretive approach, Article 6 offers protection which goes beyond the trial itself, extending to any part of the criminal or civil process which may impact on the outcome of a case. For example, considering whether or not a trial is fair can include making sure that proper procedures have been followed by the police at the investigation and charging stages. 7.88

Article 6 does not apply to all proceedings which one might consider to be 'legal', and the nature of proceedings must therefore be carefully considered together with a number of other significant limitations set out in Article 6. Article 6(1) applies to determinative legal proceedings generally, whether criminal or civil. Although the specific guarantees in Article 6(2) and (3) relate to criminal cases only, the overarching requirements of Article 6(1) may under certain circumstances require similar guarantees even in civil proceedings. Criminal practitioners should also bear in mind that the Article 6(1) case law may be of relevance to them, even when it concerns civil matters. 7.89

The courts have repeatedly held that the right to a fair trial protected by Article 6(1) is absolute in the sense that a conviction obtained in breach of it cannot stand, but the constituent elements of Article 6 are not unlimited. 'The only balancing permitted is in respect of what the concept of a fair trial entails.'[183] The central consideration in any limitation of the constituent rights is whether the essence of the overarching right to a fair hearing is preserved.[184] In determining whether this is the case, the ECtHR will have regard to the proceedings as a whole, including appellate proceedings, and may consider whether or not the appellate proceedings have rectified any defect which arose at the first instance hearing.[185] For example, in *Gäfgen v Germany*, an important case on Article 3, the ECtHR held that in the context of the use of evidence obtained by inhuman and degrading treatment, the fairness of a criminal trial was only compromised where breach had been shown to have had a bearing on the outcome of the proceedings against the defendant.[186] The 7.90

---

[182] (1970) 1 EHRR 335, para 25. See also *Moreira de Azevedo v Portugal* (1990) 13 EHRR 721, para 66; *R (Morgan Grenfell and Co Ltd) v Special Commissioner of Income Tax* [2002] UKHL 21, [2003] 1 AC 563; *Multiplex v Croatia* App No 58112/00, 10 July 2003, para 44.

[183] See, eg *Heaney and McGuinness v Ireland* (2001) 33 EHRR 12; *R v A (No 2)* [2001] UKHL 25 at [38] per Lord Steyn who confirmed *Brown v Stott* [2001] 2 WLR 817.

[184] See, eg *Heaney and McGuinness v Ireland* (2001) 33 EHRR 12; *R v Sellick (Santino)* [2005] EWCA Crim 651, [2005] 1 WLR 3257.

[185] *Edwards v UK* (1993) 15 EHRR 417.

[186] (2011) 52 EHRR 1 at [178]. See Greer, 'Should police threats to torture suspects always be severely punished? Reflections on the Gafgen case' (2011) 11(1) HRLR 67–89.

judgment of fairness is fact-sensitive and dependent on the issues of the particular case.[187] It must also be noted that fairness is a constantly evolving concept so procedures once deemed to be fair may occasionally merit reassessment.[188]

7.91 Although derogation from Article 6 is permitted in theory, any such derogation would be extremely difficult to justify.

1. Scope of Article 6

7.92 The ECtHR has repeatedly confirmed that the definitions of the core elements of Article 6(1)—'determination', 'civil rights and obligations', and 'criminal charge'— are to be given an *autonomous* (or independent) Convention meaning. This ensures that the application of the fair trial guarantee is consistently and fairly applied, and is not dependent on the varying meanings of such terms in the national laws of Member States.[189] The ECtHR concerns itself with what fairness demands in particular circumstances.[190] Thus, although an examination of the claimant's rights as a matter of domestic law is the proper starting point, it is also necessary to look behind appearances and investigate the realities of the procedure.[191]

7.93 As with Articles 2 or 3, a Member State may be responsible for violation of Article 6 by exposing an individual within its jurisdiction to an unfair trial by deporting or extraditing him or her to a third country.[192] However, there is no breach of Article 6 unless there is a real risk of a 'flagrant violation' of the fundamental rights protected by Article 6, meaning a breach so fundamental as to amount to a nullification or destruction of the very essence, of the guaranteed rights.[193] Examples include use of torture evidence; conviction *in absentia* with no possibility subsequently to obtain a fresh determination of the merits of the charge; a trial which is summary in nature and conducted with a total disregard for the rights of the defence; detention without any access to an independent and impartial tribunal to have the legality of the detention reviewed; and deliberate and systematic refusal of access to a lawyer, especially for an individual detained in a foreign country.[194] The principle was found to be breached by the ECtHR for the first time in the *Abu Qatada* case on the basis of a real risk of use of torture evidence by the Jordanian authorities.[195]

7.94 The evidential threshold for a 'flagrant denial of justice' was considered by the House of Lords in *RB (Algeria) and ors v Secretary of State for the Home Department* (part of the *Abu Qatada* litigation). It held that a high degree of assurance that

---

[187] *R v S* [2010] EWCA Crim 1579.

[188] *R v H* [2004] UKHL 3 [2004] 2 AC 134.

[189] *Engel v Netherlands* (1976) 1 EHRR 647; *Adolf v Austria* (1982) 4 EHRR 313.

[190] *König v Federal Republic of Germany* (1978) 2 EHRR 170.

[191] *Crosbie v Secretary of State for Defence* [2011] EWHC 879 (Admin) at [80].

[192] *Soering v United Kingdom* (1989) 11 EHRR 439.

[193] *R (Ullah) v Secretary of State for the Home Department* [2004] UKHL 26; *Othman Abu Qatada* (2012) 55 EHRR 1, 32 BHRC 62.

[194] *Othman Abu Qatada*, ibid at paras 259 and 267.

[195] Ibid. This decision was applied domestically by the Special Immigration Appeals Commission, and upheld by the Court of Appeal in *Othman v Secretary of State for the Home Department* [2013] EWCA Civ 277.

evidence obtained from torture of third parties would be relied on was required to engage the principle.[196] However, when the case reached the ECtHR, it held that the familiar 'real risk' test from the Article 2 and 3 expulsion cases was applicable and found this to be satisfied on the evidence before it, distinguishing this case from the general and unspecific alleged breach found to be insufficient by the Grand Chamber in the *Mamatkulov and Askarov* case.[197]

That is not to say, however, that a more pervasive defect in a receiving state's judicial system cannot be relied upon: thus in *Kapri v Lord Advocate*,[198] a case concerning alleged systemic judicial corruption in Albania, the Supreme Court found that it was not obvious that the only way that the 'flagrant denial of justice' test could be met was by pointing to particular facts or circumstances affecting the case of the particular individual. It considered that the allegations made in the case before it were sufficiently serious to require the case be remitted.

7.95

(a) *Determination*

Article 6 applies only to the 'determination' of civil rights or obligations, or criminal charges. 'Determination' essentially requires that there be a dispute or 'contestation',[199] and a resolution procedure. It encompasses all proceedings (including those between private parties), the result of which is 'decisive' for civil rights and obligations[200] or which involves the individual being 'substantially affected' in relation to a criminal charge.[201] Article 6, therefore, requires the following criteria to be met:

7.96

(i) there must be a genuine and serious dispute ('contestation') of a legal nature which is related to a recognized right or to the scope or the manner in which it is exercised;[202]

(ii) the outcome of the proceedings is directly decisive for these rights and obligations (this requires something more than a 'tenuous connection or remote consequences');[203] and

(iii) these rights are 'civil' in the autonomous sense of the Convention.

The Strasbourg and domestic case law contain many examples of quasi-legal proceedings that were held to fall outside the scope of Article 6 because there was no 'determination'—most notably, inquiries or investigations. For example, in *Fayed v UK* the ECtHR held that Article 6 was not engaged in relation to a Department of Trade and Industry inspector's highly critical report on a takeover by the applicant that was essentially investigative, and did not itself determine any dispute.[204]

7.97

---

[196] [2009] UKHL 10 [2009] 2 WLR 512.

[197] Ibid at [281]–[287].

[198] [2013] UKSC 48.

[199] See, eg *König v Germany* (1978) 2 EHRR 170, para 87.

[200] *Ringeisen v Austria* (1971) 1 EHRR 466, para 94.

[201] *Deweer v Belgium* (1980) 2 EHRR 439, para 46; *Heaney and McGuinness v Ireland* (2001) 33 EHRR 12; *Quinn v Ireland* [2000] ECHR 36887/97.

[202] *Pudas v Sweden* (1988) 10 EHRR 380.

[203] See *Le Compte, Van Leuven and De Meyere v Belgium* (1981) 4 EHRR 1, para 47.

[204] (1994) 18 EHRR 393.

7.98   Although the courts usually consider only final decisions to be 'determinations', in certain circumstances pre-trial proceedings and interim decisions will also fall within the term's remit. In *Micallef v Malta*,[205] departing from its historic approach, the Grand Chamber held that where interim proceedings (such as an injunction application) can be regarded as determining the issue in the proceedings, they would fall within the scope of Article 6.[206]

7.99   The House of Lords in *R (Wright and ors) v Secretary of State for Health and Secretary of State for Education and Skills* held that the interim 'listing' of care workers, which prevented them working with vulnerable adults, had so great an effect on the rights of the persons affected as to amount to a determination, even though in theory the measures were only provisional.[207]

7.100   In *R (G) v Governing Body of X School*,[208] the Supreme Court considered whether disciplinary proceedings against a teacher by a school attracted the protection of Article 6 due to their potential impact on the subsequent determination by the Independent Safeguarding Authority (ISA) as to whether the teacher would be barred from teaching. The Supreme Court approved a pragmatic and context-sensitive test, derived by the Court of Appeal from the ECtHR case law, whether the initial proceedings would have a 'substantial influence or effect' on the latter proceedings. It found that this test was not satisfied due to the fact that the ISA was required to form its own independent view on a different question to that considered by the school's disciplinary panel.[209]

7.101   Costs proceedings have usually been regarded as part of a 'determination' of civil rights and obligations.[210]

(b) *Civil rights and obligations*

7.102   The autonomous Convention meaning of 'civil rights and obligations'[211] requires the arguable existence of a legal right recognized under domestic law.[212] In order to amount to a 'right' it must be more than a mere expectation or hope,[213] or a mere privilege.[214] It was essentially on the latter basis that the Court of Appeal held that Article 6 was not engaged by the prison disciplinary process associated with segregation of young offenders in *R (King and Bourgass) v Secretary of State for Justice*. The majority held that there was no right to associate under domestic

---

[205] App No 17056/06, 15 October 2009.
[206] App No 17056/06, 15 October 2009, at [83]–[86].
[207] [2009] UKHL 3, [2009] 2 WLR 267 at [21] per Baroness Hale.
[208] [2011] UKSC 30, 1 AC 167, 3 WLR 237.
[209] Ibid. In particular, see [69]–[84] per Lord Dyson.
[210] See, eg *Robins v UK* (1998) 26 EHRR 527; *Ziegler v Switzerland* [2002] ECHR 33499/96.
[211] See, eg *Benthem v Netherlands* (1986) 8 EHRR 1, para 34; *Ferrazzini v Italy* (2002) 34 EHRR 1068. See, generally, Dutertre, *Key Case-Law Extracts: European Court of Human Rights* (Strasbourg: Council of Europe, 2004) 171–9.
[212] *Roche v United Kingdom* (2006) 42 EHRR 30; See also *Acquaviva v France* App No 19248/91, 21 November 1995, para 46; *Le Compte, Van Leuven and De Meyere v Belgium* (1981) 4 EHRR 1, para 47; *Powell & Rayner v United Kingdom* (1990) 12 EHRR 355.
[213] Ibid.
[214] *Bolois v Luxembourg* App No 37575/04, 2 April 2012, GC, at paras 96–99.

law—association was merely a normal privilege. The fact that the decision engaged Article 8 of the Convention did not suffice to render the claimants' rights under the Human Rights Act in dispute within the prison's disciplinary process (as opposed to in any later judicial review proceedings directly invoking rights protected by the Human Rights Act).[215]

The autonomous meaning of a 'civil' right or obligation was explained by the ECtHR in *König v Germany* as follows:　　　　　　　　　　　　　　　　　7.103

> Whether or not a right is to be regarded as civil within the meaning of this expression in the Convention must be determined by reference to the substantive content and effects of the right—and not its legal classification—under the domestic law of the state concerned... Only the character of the right (at issue) is relevant.[216]

Accordingly, the mere fact that the right or obligation is governed by administrative law, as defined by the domestic legal order, does not prevent it from having a civil character for the purposes of Article 6.

As an example, in *Pudas v Sweden* the ECtHR held that grant of a taxi licence　7.104 entailed certain consequential civil rights under Swedish law to continue the business under the licence, which was found to fall within the scope of Article 6.[217]

The ECtHR's case law makes clear that in many respects, 'civil rights and obli-　7.105 gations' is a wide phrase, whatever may have been the original intention of the drafters of the Convention. It has been held to cover areas as diverse as property rights,[218] family rights,[219] the right to engage in commercial activities, the right to compensation, the right to practise a profession,[220] and certain welfare benefits. The House of Lords indicated that a 'without notice' local authority application to close a care home on health and safety grounds would constitute a determination of civil rights and obligations).[221] So would antisocial behaviour orders,[222] control orders,[223] a domestic terrorist asset freezing order,[224] and confiscation proceedings following conviction.[225]

---

[215] [2012] EWCA Civ 376, per Maurice Kay and Lloyd LJJ, Elias LJ dissenting. The Supreme Court granted permission to appeal on 17 March 2014.

[216] (1978) 2 EHRR 170, paras 89, 90.

[217] (1988) 10 EHRR 380.

[218] *Sporrong & Lonnroth v Sweden* (1983) 5 EHRR 35.

[219] See, eg *W v United Kingdom* (1987) 10 EHRR 29.

[220] See, eg *König v Germany* (1978) 2 EHRR 170; *Wickramsinghe v UK* App No 31503/96, 9 December 1997 (ECmHR), analysed in [1998] EHRLR 338. Cf *R (Puri) v Bradford Teaching Hospitals NHS Foundation Trust* [2011] EWHC 970 (Admin).

[221] *Jain v Trent Strategic Health Authority* [2009] UKHL 4, [2009] 2 WLR 248.

[222] *R (McCann) v Crown Court at Manchester* [2002] UKHL 39, [2003] 1 AC 787.

[223] *Secretary of State v F (No 3)* [2009] UKHL 28; cf *R v Twomey and ors (No 2)* [2011] EWCA Crim 8.

[224] *Mastafa v HM Treasury* [2013] 1 WLR 1621, per Collins J, finding such designation to be indistinguishable from the imposition of a control order, and distinguishing the Court of Appeal's judgment in *Secretary of State for the Foreign Office and Commonwealth Affairs v Maftah* [2011] EWCA Civ 350 on the basis of the international context and focus of the challenge to designation on a UN asset freezing list in that case.

[225] *R v Briggs-Price* [2009] UKHL 19; see also *Serious Organised Crime Agency v Gale* [2010] EWCA Civ 759, [2010] 1 WLR 2881.

7.106   However, matters of pure administrative discretion are not covered. These include decisions as to tax obligations,[226] categorization of prisoners,[227] 'age assessments' of individuals claiming to be children (although disputed decisions are determined by an independent and impartial tribunal thus engaging Article 6),[228] the right to stand for public office,[229] immigration decisions relating to the entry, stay, and removal or extradition of foreign nationals,[230] actions and inactions in the international sphere regarding the listing of persons for asset freezing,[231] and the right to freedom of movement within the EU.[232]

7.107   The distinction between 'civil' or 'private' rights, and 'pure public rights' is also an autonomous concept which does not exactly chime with the distinction between these concepts in domestic law. In *Ringeisen v Austria* the ECtHR noted that Article 6 may be triggered in situations where the public law decisions of public authorities have clear consequences for the private law rights of individuals, but is not engaged unless the intrinsic nature of the right or obligation determined is 'private'.[233] In general terms, the ECtHR considers the substance of the right and balances the public law features against the private law features. If private law features are predominant, Article 6 will apply.[234]

7.108   The balance struck by the ECtHR does not necessarily follow traditional domestic characterization. For example, in *R (Alconbury Developments Ltd) v Secretary of State for Environment, Transport and the Regions*,[235] the House of Lords followed ECtHR case law in finding that planning determinations involved the determination of civil rights within the meaning of Article 6, notwithstanding that such determinations might traditionally be considered by English lawyers to involve 'public law rights' only. Lord Hoffmann was driven to observe:

> Apart from authority, I would have said that a decision as to what the public interest requires is not a 'determination' of civil rights and obligations. It may affect civil rights and obligations but it is not, and ought not to be, a judicial act such as article 6 has in contemplation.[236]

7.109   As a result of the ECtHR's dynamic interpretation, the phrase has continued to expand.[237] The concept of 'pure public rights' has been significantly reduced in

---

[226] *Ferrazzini v Italy* (2002) 34 EHRR 1068 in relation to direct taxation; see also *King v United Kingdom* [2004] STC 911.

[227] *Brady v UK* (1979) 3 EHRR 297.

[228] *R (A) v Croydon London Borough Council; R (M) v Lambeth London Borough Council* [2008] EWCA Civ 1445. This was overturned on appeal: [2009] UKSC 8.

[229] *Pierre-Bloch v France* (1998) 26 EHRR 202.

[230] *Maaouia v France* (2001) 33 EHRR 42; *R (BB) v SIAC* [2012] EWCA Civ 1499; *Lukaszewski v District Court in Torun* [2012] UKSC 20.

[231] *Secretary of State for the Foreign Office and Commonwealth Affairs v Maftah* [2011] EWCA Civ 350, as interpreted in *Mastafa v HM Treasury* [2013] 1 WLR 1621.

[232] *Adams and Benn v UK* (1997) 23 EHRR CD 160.

[233] See, eg *Pudas v Sweden* (1988) 10 EHRR 380.

[234] *Feldbrugge v Netherlands* (1986) 8 EHRR 425; *Deumeland v Germany* (1986) 8 EHRR 448 (Series A-100); *Ali v Birmingham City Council* [2010] UKSC 8.

[235] [2001] UKHL 23, [2003] 2 AC 295.

[236] [2001] UKHL 23, [2003] 2 AC 295 at [74] per Lord Hoffmann. See also *Secretary of State for the Foreign Office and Commonwealth Affairs v Maftah* [2011] EWCA Civ 350.

[237] *Salesi v Italy* (1998) 26 EHRR 187.

recent years, with the ECtHR increasingly willing to find a 'civil right' within, or alongside, a public law right.

For example, the ECtHR originally held that only claims regarding welfare benefits   7.110 which formed part of contributory schemes could constitute the subject matter of disputes for 'the determination of civil rights'. This was on the basis of their similarity to private insurance schemes.[238] However, Article 6 was subsequently held to also apply to disputes over entitlements to certain non-contributory welfare benefits, where it could be said that the applicant had an assertable right of an individual and economic nature.[239] In *Stec v UK* the Grand Chamber confirmed this development and further held that it was in the interests of the coherence of the Convention as a whole that the autonomous concept of 'possessions' in Article 1 of Protocol 1 should be interpreted in a way which is consistent with the concept of pecuniary rights under Article 6.[240]

The application of Article 6 to social security benefit entitlements has raised a   7.111 concern regarding the judicialization of public decision making, with the associated cost and delay to decision making. As the ECtHR observed in *Feldbrugge v The Netherlands*:

The judicialisation of dispute procedures, as guaranteed by article 6(1), is eminently appropriate in the realm of relations between individuals but not necessarily so in the administrative sphere, where organisational, social and economic considerations may legitimately warrant dispute procedures of a less judicial and formal kind.[241]

Due to the fast developing character of the ECtHR's case law, the domestic   7.112 courts for a number of years declined to rule on the limits of the application of Article 6 in this context where it considered it unnecessary to do so. Thus, for example, in *Begum (Runa) v Tower Hamlets*, the House of Lords considered the adequacy of the procedure in respect of the provision of housing under the Housing Act 1996 on the assumption that this involved a 'civil right' without deciding the question.[242] However, in *Ali v Birmingham City Council*, the Supreme Court held that the time had come to seek to bring greater clarity to this area and definitively held that housing benefit did not fall within the scope of Article 6.[243] Lord Hope drew a fundamental distinction based on the extent of the evaluative judgment involved in determining entitlement:

cases where the award of services or benefits in kind is not an individual right of which the applicant can consider himself the holder, but is dependent upon a series of evaluative judgments by the provider as to whether the statutory criteria are satisfied and how the need for it ought to be met, do not engage article 6(1). In my opinion they do not give rise to 'civil rights' within the autonomous meaning that is given to that expression for the purposes of that article.[244]

---

[238] *Feldbrugge v the Netherlands* (1986) 8 EHRR 425.

[239] *Salesi v Italy* App No 13023/87, 26 February 1993.

[240] See the decision on admissibility in (2005) 41 EHRR SE18 at [48].

[241] (1986) 8 EHRR 425, 443, para 15.

[242] [2003] UKHL 5, [2003] 2 AC 430. See also *R (A) v Croydon London Borough Council; R (M) v Lambeth London Borough Council* [2009] UKSC 8; 'age assessments' of asylum seekers, regarding whether or not they are 'children' and so are protected under the Children Act 1989.

[243] [2010] UKSC 8, [2010] 2 AC 39.

[244] Ibid, para 49.

7.113   One area where the distinction between public and 'civil rights' has historically caused particular difficulties is in relation to employment issues. The traditional view was that matters concerning public employment did not concern 'civil rights' as defined by Strasbourg.[245] However, in *Pellegrin v France* the Grand Chamber held that only decisions concerning those with functions relating to the 'specific activities' of the public service and direct or indirect participation in the powers conferred by public law would be outside the protection provided by Article 6.[246] In *Eskelinen v Finland*[247] the Grand Chamber repeated that Article 6 was not excluded from determinations of employment disputes on the basis of the special relationship between the civil servant and the state. It was presumed to apply, unless the dispute in issue clearly related to the exercise of state power.[248]

7.114   An important area in which the concept of a pure public right remains relatively un-eroded is the state's power to control its borders by determining the conditions of entry, stay, and removal of foreign nationals.[249] However, as considered elsewhere in this text, these matters are subject to the protections of other Convention rights, in particular Articles 2 and 3 (concerning the prohibition on removal where there is a real risk of Article 2 or 3 treatment), and Article 8 (concerning the negative and positive aspects of the right to respect for family and private life).

(c) Criminal charge

7.115   Article 6 protects an individual who is 'charged with a criminal offence' when he or she is subject to a procedure for the 'determination' of that criminal charge. The term 'charge' should be given a substantive rather than a formal meaning, in the sense that the court should consider the scope of what is at stake and not the mere classification in domestic law.[250]

7.116   (i) *What is 'criminal'?* When deciding whether proceedings are 'criminal' for the purposes of the Convention, the courts are not bound by the label given by the state. In *Engel v Netherlands*.[251] the Court held that a determination that an individual faced a criminal charge rested on three criteria:

(a) the classification of the offence under the domestic legal system which should be the initial starting point;

(b) the nature of the offence; and/or

(c) the nature and degree of severity of the penalty 'liable to be imposed'.

---

[245] See, eg *Kosieck v Germany* (1987) 9 EHRR 328; *Neigel v France* (2000) 30 EHRR 310; *Balfour v UK* (1997) EHRLR 665; *Huber v France* (1998) 26 EHRR 457.

[246] (2001) 31 EHRR 651, para 66.

[247] (2007) 45 EHRR 43.

[248] Ibid, para 62. *Eskelinen* was also applied in *R (MK (Iran)) v Secretary of State for the Home Department* [2009] EWHC 3452 (Admin).

[249] *Maaouia v France* (2001) 33 EHRR 42; *R (BB) v SIAC* [2012] EWCA Civ 1499.

[250] *Deweer v Belgium* (1979–80) 2 EHRR 439, paras 42, 44, and 46.

[251] (1976) 1 EHRR 647.

In practice the last two criteria have carried the greatest significance. The *Engel* criteria have been regularly applied by the Strasbourg and domestic courts.[252] The courts have emphasized that the first criterion, the domestic classification, must be seen as 'no more than a starting point'.[253] One important consideration is whether the intention of a provision is punitive or preventative: preventative measures are generally not considered to be 'criminal'.[254]

The second and third of the *Engel* criteria are usually considered as alternatives.[255] For the criminal protections of Article 6 to apply it is enough either that the offence in question is of a 'criminal' nature, or that the offence makes the person liable to what amounts to a 'criminal' sanction given its nature or degree of severity.[256] However, a cumulative approach may be adopted where separate analysis of each individual criterion does not make it possible to reach a clear conclusion as to the existence of a criminal charge.[257]   **7.117**

In relation to the second criterion, the criminal limb of Article 6 may be engaged by the nature of the matter determined, notwithstanding its relatively minor nature. For example, tax and surcharge proceedings have been held to constitute criminal charges where they have a deterrent and punitive purpose despite having a relatively light penalty;[258] and committal proceedings for contempt are also considered criminal given that liberty is at stake and that the acts in question must be proved to the criminal standard of proof.[259]   **7.118**

The third *Engel* criterion is often the key issue. The Court held in *Engel* that 'in a society subscribing to the rule of law, there belong to the "criminal" sphere deprivation of liberty liable to be imposed as a punishment, except those which by their nature, duration or manner of execution cannot be appreciably detrimental' so the courts must take into account 'the seriousness of what is at stake, the traditions of the Contracting States and the importance attached by the Convention to respect   **7.119**

---

[252] See, eg *Campbell and Fell v UK* (1985) 7 EHRR 165; *Ezeh and Connors v UK* (2004) 39 EHRR 1 (Grand Chamber); see, eg *Tangney v Governor of Elmley Prison and Secretary of State for the Home Department* [2005] EWCA Civ 1009; *MB v Secretary of State for the Home Department* [2007] UKHL 46, [2008] 1 AC 440.

[253] *Engel v Netherlands* (1976) 1 EHRR 647, para 82; *R (LG) Board of Governors of Tom Hood School* [2010] EWCA Civ 142 (Admin), [2009] EWHC 369.

[254] *MB v Secretary of State for the Home Department* [2007] UKHL 46, [2008] 1 AC 440; *R (McCann) v Crown Court at Manchester* [2002] UKHL 39, [2003] 1 AC 787; *R (G) v Governing Body of X School* [2010] EWCA Civ 1 (this issue was not subject to appeal to the Supreme Court).

[255] *Öztürk v Germany* (1984) 6 EHRR 409; *Lutz v Germany* (1988) 10 EHRR 182; [1987] ECHR 9912/82.

[256] See, eg *Öztürk v Germany* (1984) 6 EHRR 409, para 54; *Lutz v Germany* (1988) 10 EHRR 182, para 55.

[257] See, eg *Bendenoun v France* (1994) 18 EHRR 54, para 47; *Benham v UK* (1996) 22 EHRR 293, para 56; *Garyfallou AEBE v Greece* (1999) 28 EHRR 344, para 33; *Lauko v Slovakia* (2001) 33 EHRR 40, para 57; *Ezeh and Connors v UK* (2004) 39 EHRR 1 (Grand Chamber), para 86; *Tangney v Governor of Elmley Prison and Secretary of State for the Home Department* [2005] EWCA Civ 1009 at [24].

[258] See, eg *Jussila v Finland* (2007) 45 EHRR 39 (Grand Chamber).

[259] *Daltel Europe Ltd (in liquidation) and 5 ors v Hassan Ali Makki and ors* [2006] EWCA Civ 94; *Raja v Van Hoogstraten* [2004] EWCA Civ 968, [2004] 4 All ER 793; *Hammerton v Hammerton* [2007] EWCA Civ 248, [2007] 2 FLR 1133.

for the physical liberty of the person'.[260] It is the nature and severity of the penalty 'liable to be imposed' which is determinative, rather than the penalty actually incurred.[261] The ECtHR has also held that 'where deprivation of liberty is at stake, the interests of justice in principle call for legal representation'.[262]

7.120   Thus, although classification of prisoners, for example, falls outside the criminal sphere,[263] prison discipline may engage the criminal limb of Article 6,[264] even in respect of proceedings which are not classified as 'criminal' in domestic law.[265]

7.121   However, since a prisoner serving a life sentence is not vulnerable to a punishment imposing additional days of imprisonment, the Court of Appeal has held that internal disciplinary charges against such a prisoner do not amount to 'criminal charges'.[266] Parole Board decisions are not criminal because the decisions to release depend upon assessment of risk to the public rather than punishment.[267]

7.122   The domestic courts have adopted a narrow definition of 'criminal charge' in the context of suspected terrorists, focusing on the intention of the measures rather than their effects. For example, the House of Lords has found that non-derogating control orders are not 'criminal' since they are preventive in purpose, even though they impose very severe restrictions on the controlee's private life and freedom of movement.[268] However, the civil limb of Article 6(1) applied and entitled those subject to such orders to 'such measure of procedural protection as was commensurate with the gravity of the potential consequences'.[269] The domestic courts have also held that registration on the Sex Offenders' Register is not criminal determination as, inter alia, it does not involve a punishment and is not a public announcement of guilt.[270] Nor does exclusion from school involve the determination of a criminal charge.[271]

7.123   (ii) *What is a charge?* In addition to satisfying the 'criminal' criteria, the allegation must also constitute a 'charge'. These two features are often considered coterminously but the ECtHR has confirmed that for a person to be charged, his or her situation must be 'substantially affected'.[272] This may take place at arrest, charge, or when the person becomes aware that 'immediate consideration' is being given to

---

[260] *Engel v Netherlands* (1976) 1 EHRR 647, para 82.

[261] See *Campbell and Fell v UK* (1985) 7 EHRR 165, para 72; *Weber v Switzerland* (1990) 12 EHRR 508, para 34; *Demicoli v Malta* Series A No 210, 27 August 1991, para 34; *Benham v UK* (1996) 22 EHRR 296, para 56; *Garyfallou AEBE v Greece* (1999) 28 EHRR 344, paras 33–34; *Ezeh and Connors v UK* (2004) 39 EHRR 1 (Grand Chamber), para 120.

[262] *Benham v UK*, (1996) 22 EHRR 296, para 61.

[263] *R (Sunder) v Secretary of State for the Home Department* [2001] EWHC Admin 252, [2001] All ER (D) 55 (Apr).

[264] *Campbell and Fell v UK* (1985) 7 EHRR 165, para 69.

[265] *Ezeh and Connors v UK* (2004) 39 EHRR 1 (Grand Chamber); *Jussila v Finland* (2007) 45 EHRR 39.

[266] *Tangney v Governor of Elmley Prison* [2005] EWCA Civ 1009.

[267] *R (Smith) v Parole Board* [2005] UKHL 1.

[268] *MB v Secretary of State for the Home Department* [2007] UKHL 46, [2008] 1 AC 440.

[269] Ibid at [24].

[270] *R (R) v Durham Constabulary* [2005] UKHL 21, [2005] 2 All ER 369.

[271] *R (V) v Independent Appeal Panel for Tom Hood School* [2010] EWCA Civ 142.

[272] *DeWeer v Belgium* (1980) 2 EHRR 439, para 46.

a possible prosecution, depending on the facts of the case.[273] However, car owners being required to identify the driver of a speeding vehicle at the time it was caught on a speed camera or radar-trap are not 'substantially affected' so as to be 'charged' within the autonomous meaning of Article 6(1).[274] The courts have confirmed that giving warnings or cautions to offenders does not amount to the determination of a criminal 'charge',[275] but there has been a suggestion that this position may change in light of the scheme of 'conditional cautions' under the Police and Justice Act 2006, as they include a power for prosecutors to attach punitive measures as conditions of cautions.[276] This has not yet been tested in the courts.

2. Rights protected by Article 6(1)

Article 6(1) sets the overall standard of what a fair trial requires, whether the context is civil or criminal. The more extensive detailed provisions in Article 6(2) and (3) apply only to criminal charges, though equivalent guarantees may be required in particular civil circumstances. Courts have frequently held that common law and Article 6(1) standards of fairness march 'hand in hand', and that the result ought to be the same whichever is applied.[277]   7.124

The court will imply into Article 6(1) such safeguards as are necessary to guarantee a 'real and effective' fair trial. For example, Article 6 implicitly guarantees the right of access to a court.[278] This may necessitate that the grant of legal aid even in civil cases will be required if the case is particularly complex and the principle of 'equality of arms' requires.[279] The provision of legal aid will depend on the facts and circumstances of each case.[280]   7.125

Article 6(1) does not compel states to provide appeal courts, but, where they exist, they must comply with Article 6 and effective access must therefore be ensured.[281]   7.126

Although the elements of the right to a fair trial under Article 6(1) which apply to both civil and criminal proceedings may be limited in the public interest, this does not mean that they are qualified rights. It is essential that any attempt to limit the constituent elements of Article 6 is seen as a different exercise to the approach taken to qualify rights guaranteed under Articles 8, 9, 10, and 11. Article 6 limitations   7.127

---

[273] *X v UK* (1978) 14 DR 26 (1998) 25 EHRR CD88.

[274] *Rieg v Austria* App No 63207/00, [2005] ECHR 184, para 54; *O'Halloran and Francis v UK* (2008) 46 EHRR 21.

[275] *R v UK* (2007) 44 EHRR SE17; *R (R) v Durham Constabulary* [2005] UKHL 21, [2005] 2 All ER 369.

[276] Discussed by Brownlee, 'Conditional cautions and fair trial rights in England and Wales: form versus substance in the diversionary agenda?' (2007) Crim LR 129.

[277] *R (Smith) v Parole Board* [2005] UKHL 1, [2005] 1 WLR 350; *Kulkarni v Milton Keynes NHS Hospital Trust* [2009] EWCA Civ 789, [2009] IRLR 829; *Secretary of State for the Home Department v AF (No 3)* [2009] UKHL 28 at [96] per Lord Scott, [2010] 2 AC 269.

[278] *Golder v UK* (1975) 1 EHRR 524; *Moldovan and ors v Romania* (2007) 44 EHRR 16.

[279] *Airey v Ireland* (1979) 2 EHRR 305.

[280] *Steel and Morris v UK* (2005) 41 EHRR 22.

[281] *Sommerfeld v Germany* (2003) 36 EHRR 33, although this was not considered further in the Grand Chamber's decision: *Sommerfeld v Germany* (2004) 38 EHRR 35.

are subject to a particularly strict test of necessity and proportionality.[282] In no case may they restrict or reduce the access left to the individual in such a way or to such an extent that the very essence of the right is impaired.[283]

(a) *General entitlements in criminal and civil proceedings under Article 6(1)*

7.128   A litigant, or potential litigant, has the following rights to:

(i)   real and effective access to a court. Under certain circumstances a lack of state legal assistance can interfere with the right of access to court depending upon the nature and complexity of the case;[284]

(ii)   a hearing before an independent and impartial tribunal established by law;

(iii) a hearing in public;

(iv) a hearing within a reasonable time;

(v)   a real opportunity to present their case. This is premised on the concept of the need for 'equality of arms' between the parties and may include the provision of legal assistance or an oral hearing if the circumstances require this; and

(vi) a reasoned decision.

7.129   (i) *Access to a court* The right of access to a court is one of the checks on the danger of arbitrary power.[285] Although the right of access to a court is not explicitly set out under Article 6(1), in the early decision of *Golder v UK* the ECtHR recognized the right as a prerequisite of the exercise of the right to have a claim heard at all.[286] Thus, in that case, a prisoner's lack of access to a lawyer was held to violate his right of (effective) access to a court. A right of access to a court may be violated by, for example, a substantive provision,[287] a procedural rule (such as an immunity),[288] or an administrative practice.[289] When deciding whether the right of access is barred by a practice or provision, the domestic courts have said that the 'crucial question' is whether, as a matter of substance rather than procedure, the relevant provision of national law has the effect of preventing an issue that ought to be decided by a court from being so decided.[290]

7.130   The nature of the right of access to the court calls for regulation by the state and may vary in time and place according to the needs and resources of the community and of individuals.[291] However, these restrictions must not be such as to limit the

---

[282] *Van Mechelen v Netherlands* (1998) 25 EHRR 647.

[283] See *Golder v UK* (1975) 1 EHRR 524; *Belgian Linguistic Case No 2* (1968) 1 EHRR 252; and *Secretary of State for the Home Department v AF (No 3)* [2009] UKHL 28 at [106] per Baroness Hale, [2010] 2 AC 269.

[284] *Airey v Ireland* (1979) 2 EHRR 305.

[285] *Wilson v First County Trust Ltd (No 2)* [2003] UKHL 40, [2004] 1 AC 816 at [35].

[286] (1975) 1 EHRR 524.

[287] *Ashingdane v UK* (1985) 7 EHRR 528, para 57.

[288] *Osman v UK* (2000) 29 EHRR 245.

[289] *Golder v UK* (1975) 1 EHRR 524.

[290] *Wilson v First County Trust Ltd (No 2)* [2003] UKHL 40, [2004] 1 AC 816 at [35].

[291] *Golder v UK* (1975) 1 EHRR 524.

effectiveness of the right; restrictions imposed must be legally certain,[292] pursue a legitimate aim,[293] and be proportionate to the aim pursued.[294]

A number of categories of restriction on the access right have emerged. They include restrictions linked to types of actions (eg immunities, limitation periods, strike-out provisions), or to classes of litigant (minors, vexatious litigants, bankrupts, and prisoners).[295] 'Special advocate' procedures will not necessarily violate Article 6, provided the essence of the right to a fair trial is not impaired. A procedural bar, such as requiring a mental patient to obtain leave of the court before issuing a claim, or a restriction of the types of claims which can be brought (eg on the basis of state immunity) must be properly scrutinized for compatibility with Article 6. However, they will not necessarily violate the right of access to a court.[296] Similarly, to deny access to a court or on grounds of an immunity will only be compatible with Article 6 (1) if it satisfies the tests of necessity and proportionality. In two recent cases, the Grand Chamber has found restrictions on access to court to determine employment claims relating to the dismissal of employees at embassies, based on state immunity, not to be justified where the employees' role and the employment claims in question in no way engaged relevant sovereign interests. In so finding, it has remarked on a discernable trend in international and comparative law towards limiting state immunity in respect of employment-related disputes.[297]

7.131

However, the ECtHR has to date held that international law has not similarly developed so as to restrict state immunity for civil claims against another state or its officials for compensation for acts of torture. In *Al-Adsani v United Kingdom*,[298] the Grand Chamber held by a bare majority that the application of an immunity for a civil claim against Kuwait under the State Immunity Act 1978 was not a disproportionate interference with the right of access to Court since it gave effect to principles of international law, but left open a different outcome if customary international law were subsequently to develop. Recently, in *Jones v United Kingdom*,[299] the ECtHR held by a majority that, while there had been considerable debate about an exception to state immunity for acts of torture, international law had not yet developed sufficiently to warrant departing from *Al-Adsani*. It therefore upheld the House of Lords' conclusion that the immunity was proportionate. In a dissenting

7.132

---

[292] *Société Levage Prestations v France* (1996) 24 EHRR 351, paras 40–50.
[293] *Ashingdane v UK* (1985) 7 EHRR 528.
[294] *Canea Catholic Church v Greece* (1999) 27 EHRR 521, paras 34–42.
[295] *M v United Kingdom* (1987) 52 DR 269.
[296] See, eg *Seal v Chief Constable of South Wales* [2007] UKHL 31, [2007] 1 WLR 1910 (case pending before the ECtHR); *Seal v UK* (2010) ECHR 1976; *Markcovic v Italy* (2007) 44 EHRR 52 (Grand Chamber); *Jones v Kingdom of Saudi Arabia* [2006] UKHL 26, [2007] 1 AC 270; following *Al-Adsani v UK* (2001) 34 EHRR 273. See also *Matthews v Ministry of Defence* [2003] UKHL 4, [2003] 1 AC 1163 (Art 6(1) not engaged by legislation preventing an ex-serviceman from bringing a personal injury claim against the Ministry of Defence); *Fogarty v UK* (2002) 34 EHRR 302; *Tinnelly & Sons Ltd and ors and McElduff and ors v UK* (1999) 27 EHRR 249.
[297] *Sabeh el Leil v France* App No 34869/05, 29 June 2011, GC and *Cudak v Lithuania* App No 15869/02, 23 March 2010, GC.
[298] (2001) 34 EHRR 273.
[299] App Nos 34356/06 and 40528/06, 14 January 2014.

opinion, Judge Kalaydjieva remarked on the surprising divergence between the restrictive application of immunity to employment disputes and the retention of a broad immunity for acts of torture.

7.133 The ECtHR has sometimes rejected the UK's approach to immunities within its substantive law. For example, in *Osman v UK* it held that, what it interpreted as a blanket ban on bringing a negligence action against the police for failure to prevent a crime against a foreseeable target, on public policy grounds, violated the claimant's right of access to a court under Article 6(1). It prevented a court considering the competing public interests in a case before it, and so constituted a disproportionate interference with a person's right to a determination on the merits. This decision was criticized, academically[300] and judicially.[301] The House of Lords in *Barrett v Enfield LBC* stated that there was no 'blanket immunity' and that English law had been misunderstood by the ECtHR.[302] Rather, the test applied was whether the imposition of a duty of care was 'fair, just and reasonable' in all the circumstances.

7.134 The ECtHR in *Z and ors v UK* (an Article 3 case) accepted the House of Lords' clarification in *Barrett*.[303] *Z v UK* retained the principle that any automatic exclusionary rule based on public policy will still violate Article 6, but endorsed the flexible 'fair, just and reasonable approach'. The House of Lords has since affirmed that there is no automatic 'knock-out' immunity from suit for the police, and instead a flexible, context-specific, test applies.[304]

7.135 (ii) *A hearing before an independent and impartial tribunal established by law* Article 6(1) requires an 'independent and impartial tribunal established by law'. The courts have held that it is 'of fundamental importance in a democratic society that the courts should inspire confidence in the public and above all, as far as criminal proceedings were concerned, in the accused'.[305] If a defendant raises the issue of impartiality, it must be investigated unless it is 'manifestly devoid of merit'.[306]

7.136 When deciding whether a tribunal is independent, the following factors are to be considered:

(i)   the way its members are appointed;

(ii)   their term of office;

(iii) the existence of safeguards against outside pressures; and

(iv)   whether the body appears independent.[307]

---

[300] See, eg Gearty, ' *Osman* Unravels' (2002) 65 MLR 87, (1998) 29 EHRR 245.

[301] *Barrett v Enfield London Borough Council* [2001] 2 AC 550.

[302] Ibid.

[303] (2002) 34 EHRR 97. See also *Al-Adsani v UK* (2001) 34 EHRR 273; *McElhinney v Ireland* (2002) 34 EHRR 13; *Fogarty v UK* (2002) 34 EHRR 302.

[304] *Brooks v Commissioner for Police for the Metropolis* [2005] UKHL 2, [2005] 2 AC 176.

[305] *Padovani v Italy* App No 13396/87, 26 February 1993, para 27.

[306] *Remli v France* (1996) 22 EHRR 253.

[307] *Ringeisen v Austria* (1979–80) 1 EHRR 455; *Campbell and Fell v the United Kingdom* (1985) 7 EHRR 165; *Le Compte, Van Leuven and De Meyere v Belgium* (1981) 4 EHRR 1; *Belilos v Switzerland* (1988) 10 EHRR 466.

This final point is important as the courts are not only concerned with actual impartiality, but also require the appearance of impartiality. The ECtHR has ruled that any doubts entertained by an accused as to lack of impartiality of a court have to be both subjectively and objectively justified in order to raise an issue under Article 6.[308]

The ECtHR found a breach of Article 6(1) in *McGonnell v UK* where the bailiff, who presided over the Royal Court of Guernsey in legal proceedings concerning the applicant's planning appeal, had also been sitting as the deputy bailiff over the States of Deliberation when the earlier, detailed development plan had been adopted.[309] However, there is no absolute requirement for complete separation of powers. For example, in *Kleyn v Netherlands* it was held that a body that both advised on the drafting of legislation and then determined appeals against planning decisions did not violate Article 6.[310] In *Jorgic v Germany* the ECtHR examined the concept of a tribunal 'established by law', and found that a prosecution for genocide in a German court did not breach the principle of legality, as genocide was a *jus cogens* and domestic law reasonably permitted extraterritorial jurisdiction in such cases.[311]

The ECtHR has found a number of violations in respect of military tribunals.[312] The Court has ruled that some court martials have violated the impartiality requirement.[313] The Court has also ruled that the trial of a civilian by military court martial, in the absence of special circumstances, will always be contrary to Article 6.[314]

The United Kingdom amended its procedures, introducing the Armed Forces Act 1996, but the ECtHR found in *Morris v UK* that, while these changes went 'a long way' to addressing the problems identified in the earlier decisions, the court martial procedure still did not comply with Article 6(1).[315] The House of Lords subsequently distinguished the ECtHR's conclusion, finding in *R v Spear* that the 'European Court did not receive all the help that was needed to form a conclusion' as it did not have all the relevant information about safeguards against impartiality or lack of independence.[316]

In *Re Twaite* the Court of Appeal held that majority verdicts given by a board of lay members in a court martial did not inherently contravene Article 6.[317]

7.137

7.138

7.139

7.140

---

[308] *Remli v France* (1996) 22 EHRR 253; *Findlay v United Kingdom* (1997) 24 EHRR 221; *Incal v Turkey* (2000) 29 EHRR 449; and *Grieves v United Kingdom* (2004) 39 EHRR 2.

[309] (2000) 30 EHRR 289. See also *Langborger v Sweden* (1989) 12 EHRR 416; *Pabla Ky v Finland* (2006) 42 EHRR 34; *Olujic v Croatia* (2011) 52 EHRR 26; *R (Barclay) v Secretary of State for Justice* [2008] EWCA Civ 1319.

[310] (2004) 38 EHRR.

[311] (2008) 47 EHRR 207. See also *Lavents v Latvia* App No 58442/00, 28 November 2002; *Zand v Austria* [1981] ECC 50.

[312] See, eg *Incal v Turkey* (2000) 29 EHRR 449.

[313] See, eg *Findlay v UK* (1997) 24 EHRR 221; *Hood v UK* (2000) 29 EHRR 365.

[314] *Martin v United Kingdom* (2007) 44 EHRR 31.

[315] (2002) 34 EHRR 52. See also *Grieves v UK* (2004) 39 EHRR 2.

[316] [2002] UKHL 31, [2003] 1 AC 734 at [12] per Lord Bingham.

[317] [2010] EWCA Crim 2973, [2011] 1 Cr App R 249.

7.141 The majority of UK cases relating to impartiality under this head involve criminal proceedings and, more particularly, allegations of jury bias. The specific facts of the cases are important in determining whether evidence of possible bias or preference on the part of a juror will undermine the presumption of impartiality. In a surprising decision, the Court of Appeal in *R v Alexander* held that there was no reason to rebut the presumption that the jury was impartial despite the fact that the foreman of the jury had subsequently written, following the verdict, to proposition prosecuting counsel, referring to his performance in the trial and the achievement of convictions in a congratulatory fashion.[318] The court held that the test was whether a fair-minded and informed observer would not have concluded that there was a real possibility, or real danger, that the jury was biased. A crucial issue is whether the allegation of bias is investigated. In *Farhri v France*, there was an allegation of improper communication between the prosecutor and members of the jury which was not investigated and this was found to violate the complainant's right to a hearing by an independent and impartial tribunal.[319]

7.142 The ECtHR has also considered the question of possible juror bias in a number of other cases. In *Pullar v UK*, the ECtHR found no violation of Article 6 when the applicant was convicted by a jury that included an employee of a key prosecution witness.[320] By contrast, a violation was found in *Sander v UK*.[321] During the applicant's trial, a letter was received by the judge from a jury member complaining that two fellow jurors were making racist remarks and jokes. The ECtHR held that the judge, having been informed of a serious allegation and in possession of a partial admission, should have discharged the jury. Redirection of the jury to stress the importance of avoiding racial prejudice was inadequate.[322] However, it should be noted that a judge is under no obligation to discharge jurors simply because there is an allegation by a defendant of a juror making a racist comment. In *R v Bajwa*, the alleged racist comment had not been admitted and the judge had applied himself with 'great care and sensitivity' in investigating the issue.[323] It should be noted that the House of Lords has ruled that evidence emerging *after* the verdict has been delivered of things said by jurors is inadmissible and cannot be used as evidence of an article violation.[324] The importance of jury deliberations remaining secret has been acknowledged by the ECtHR as a legitimate feature of English trial law.[325]

7.143 In *Hanif and Khan v United Kingdom*,[326] the ECtHR considered whether there were sufficient safeguards against bias arising from a police officer serving on a jury (following the removal of automatic ineligibility for jury service of police officers by the Criminal Justice Act 2003). The Court found a violation of Article 6 on the

---

[318] [2004] EWCA Crim 2341.

[319] (2009) 48 EHRR 34; *Gregory v United Kingdom* (1998) 25 EHRR 577.

[320] (1996) 22 EHRR 391. In similar vein, see *R v Thoron (Francois Pierre)* [2001] EWCA Crim 1797.

[321] (2001) 31 EHRR 44.

[322] Cf the domestic consideration of *Sander* in *R v Qureshi* [2001] EWCA Crim 1807, [2002] 1 WLR 518.

[323] [2007] EWCA Crim 1618. Cf *R v OKZ* [2010] EWCA Crim 2272.

[324] *R v Mirza (Shabbir Ali)* [2004] UKHL 2.

[325] *Gregory v United Kingdom* (1998) 25 EHRR 577.

[326] App Nos 52999/08 and 61779/08, 20 December 2011.

facts of the case, emphasizing that the case turned to a significant extent on a challenge to the evidence of police officer witnesses and that one of the police witnesses was in fact personally acquainted with the jury member. In these circumstances, directions and warnings from the trial judge were insufficient to guard against the risk that the juror might, albeit subconsciously, favour the evidence of the police.

In principle, a jury trial may be rendered unfair by adverse media publicity particularly when 'publicity is unremitting and sensational'.[327] However, the ECtHR has held that the fact that high profile criminal cases will inevitably attract comment by the media does not mean that any media comment will inevitably prejudice a defendant's right to a fair trial. Cogent evidence of concerns about jurors' impartiality will be required to convince the court that the trial was unfair.[328]   7.144

(iii) *Public hearing* A public hearing is an essential feature of the right to a fair trial.[329] Article 6(1) explicitly provides a right to a public hearing, in order to protect litigants 'from the administration of justice in secret with no public scrutiny'[330] and to maintain public confidence in the judicial system.[331] This right applies to traditional courts as well as to any other hearings that come under Article 6, including disciplinary hearings of professionals.[332] This usually, but not universally, requires an oral hearing attended by the parties (in criminal cases the prosecutor and the accused, and in civil cases by the civil parties) which is open to the public.[333] An oral hearing is not necessarily required at appellate level.[334] If a public hearing is not held in a lower court, the defect may be cured by a public hearing at a higher level but only if the appeal court is able to consider the merits of the case and is competent to deal with the entirety of the matter.[335]   7.145

It is possible for an individual to voluntarily waive the right to a public hearing, for example where the claimant has entered into a contractual agreement providing for arbitration.[336] A waiver must be made in an unequivocal manner and must not run counter to any important public interest.[337] In the criminal context, the Court of Appeal Criminal Division has held that the right to a public hearing under Article 6 will not be violated where national security concerns or the need to protect witnesses lead to a criminal trial being held wholly or partly in private.[338] Any restriction imposed must be 'strictly required' in the particular factual circumstances of the case.[339] The principle was recently affirmed in *Guardian News and*   7.146

---

[327] *Abu-Hamza No 1 v UK* App No 31411/07, 18 January 2011, para 39.
[328] Ibid.
[329] *Axen v Germany* (1984) 6 EHRR 195.
[330] *Pretto v Italy* (1984) 6 EHRR 182, para 21.
[331] *Diennet v France* (1996) 21 EHRR 554, para 33.
[332] Ibid.
[333] *Fischer v Austria* (1995) 20 EHRR 349.
[334] *Axen v Germany* (1984) 6 EHRR 195; *Monnell and Morris v UK* (1988) 10 EHRR 205.
[335] *Diennet v France* (1996) 21 EHRR 554.
[336] *Stretford v Football Association* [2007] EWCA Civ 238, [2007] All ER (Comm) 1.
[337] *Håkansson and Sturesson v Sweden* (1991) 13 EHRR 1; cf *Deweer v Belgium* (1979–80) 2 EHRR 439.
[338] *R v Yam* [2008] EWCA Crim 269.
[339] Ibid at [34].

Media v AB and ors where the Court of Appeal overturned a trial judge who had ordered that a terrorism trial be held entirely in private.[340]

7.147   On occasion the ECtHR will accept general presumptions in favour of private hearings, for example as in *B v UK* concerning the presumption of privacy in hearings under the Children Act 1989.[341] However, where a case concerned the transfer of custody of a child to a public institution rather than a dispute between parents over a child's residence, then the reasons for excluding a case from public scrutiny had to be subjected to careful examination.[342]

7.148   The requirement for a public hearing includes an obligation that judgment is also to be pronounced publicly. Unlike the limitations that apply to a public trial, the right to public pronouncement of the judgment is unqualified. This does not necessarily require that the judgment be read in open court, provided the outcome is publicly available.[343]

7.149   (iv) *Reasonable time* Article 6(1) calls for the hearing to be held within a 'reasonable time'. Unlike Article 5(3), which applies only to individuals under arrest, this provision applies to civil and criminal cases and whether an accused is being held or is on bail. The guarantee 'underlines the importance of rendering justice without delays which might jeopardise its effectiveness and credibility'.[344] This issue accounts for more judgments at the ECtHR than any other and frequently reflects systemic problems with patterns of systemic violations in some countries.[345]

7.150   The 'time' that must be 'reasonable' is the period between the laying of the 'charge' and the imposition of the sentence or final determination in civil matters. What constitutes a reasonable time will depend on the circumstances. However, particularly relevant factors include the complexity of the case, the applicant's conduct and that of the competent authorities, and the importance of what was at stake for the applicant.[346] The advanced age of the applicant may also be relevant.[347] Complexity concerns questions of fact as well as law.[348] Another key factor is the length of time since the events occurred, before the institution of proceedings.[349]

7.151   Delay by an applicant weakens a complaint that a dispute has not been resolved within a reasonable time, but a litigant must not be penalized for making use of all available procedures to pursue their defence, nor can they be expected to expedite proceedings against them.[350] In relation to the conduct of the authorities, the state is under a duty to ensure those who play a role in proceedings avoid unnecessary

---

[340] [2014] All ER (D) 88 (Jun).

[341] (2002) 34 EHRR 19.

[342] *Moser v Austria* [2007] 1 FLR 702.

[343] *Pretto v Italy* (1984) 6 EHRR 182.

[344] *Stögmüller v Austria* (1979–80) 1 EHRR 155.

[345] See Greer, *The European Convention on Human Rights: Achievements, Problems and Prospects* (Cambridge: Cambridge University Press, 2006).

[346] *Gast and Popp v Germany* (2001) 33 EHRR 37; *Pélissier and Sassi v France* (2000) 30 EHRR 715; *Georgiev v Bulgaria* App No 4551/05, 24 February 2011.

[347] *GOC v Poland* App No 48001/99, 23 October 2001.

[348] *Triggiani v Italy* [1991] ECHR 20.

[349] *Korbely v Hungary* (2008) 25 BHRC 382. Cf *McFarlane v Ireland* [2010] ECHR 1272.

[350] *Eckle v Federal Republic of Germany* (1983) 5 EHRR 1.

delay and only delays that are attributable to the state are relevant.[351] A more rigorous standard applies if the accused is in custody and a delay in proceedings may cause pre-trial detention to be unlawful under Article 5(3).[352] Certain types of civil cases will need to be dealt with more expeditiously than others, such as those concerning children or a life-threatening illness.[353] The ECtHR will include all the time taken to resolve the matter, including appeals and the resolution of who pays the costs in the proceedings.[354]

The House of Lords took a robust approach to the right to a hearing within a 'reasonable time' in *Magill v Porter*. It was held that this right is an independent element of Article 6(1), which should not be subsumed by general considerations of the right to a fair trial and which does not require the complainant to show himself prejudiced by the delay.[355] Furthermore, breach of the right is not dependent upon evidence of prejudice having been caused by the delay.[356]   7.152

A breach of the 'reasonable time' requirement in the criminal context does not require a criminal trial to be discontinued or a conviction quashed unless the fairness of the trial itself has been compromised. Thus an appropriate remedy for delay falling short of this is a public acknowledgement of the breach and an order for expedition to cure the breach.[357] In civil matters, the Court of Appeal held in *Bangs v Connex South Eastern* that unreasonable delay by the tribunal in promulgating its decision may amount to a serious procedural error or material irregularity giving rise to a question of law in the 'proceedings before' the tribunal where the delay means that there is a real risk that a litigant has been deprived of the substance of his or her right to a fair trial under Article 6(1).[358]   7.153

(v) *The opportunity to present one's case* To be real and effective, this aspect of Article 6(1) must include the principle of equality of arms, which means that a fair balance must be struck between the parties. What that means varies with the circumstances. What is required is 'a reasonable opportunity' to present one's case and evidence 'under conditions that do not place [one] at a substantial disadvantage vis-à-vis [one's] opponent'.[359] This will sometimes, but not always, require disclosure of evidence relied on by the other party[360] and an entitlement to be present at the   7.154

---

[351] *Zimmerman and Steiner v Switzerland* (1984) 6 EHRR 17; *Boddaert v Belgium* (1993) 16 EHRR 242; *Ewing v UK* (1988) 10 EHRR 141.

[352] *Jablonski v Poland* (2003) 36 EHRR 27.

[353] *Hokkanen v Finland* [1996] 1 FLR 289; *Damnjanovic v Serbia* [2009] 1 FLR 339; *H v France* (1990) 12 EHRR 74.

[354] See, eg *Somjee v UK* (2003) 36 EHRR 16; *Darnell v UK* (1993) 18 EHRR 205; *Darnell v UK* (1993) 18 EHRR 205.

[355] [2001] UKHL 67, [2002] 2 AC 357. See also *Attorney General's Reference (No 2 of 2001)* [2001] 1 WLR 1869; *R v HM Advocate* [2002] UKPC D3, [2004] 1 AC 462.

[356] [2001] UKHL 67, [2002] 2 AC 357. See also *Attorney General's Reference (No 2 of 2001)* [2001] 1 WLR 1869; *R v HM Advocate* [2002] UKPC D3, [2004] 1 AC 462.

[357] Eg *Spiers v Ruddy and HM Advocate General* [2007] UKPC D2, [2008] AC 873. See also *Attorney General's Reference (No 2 of 2001)* [2001] 1 WLR 1869; *R v HM Advocate* [2002] UKPC D3, [2004] 1 AC 462.

[358] [2005] EWCA Civ 14, [2005] 2 All ER 316.

[359] Ibid.

[360] See *Ruiz-Mateos v Spain* (1993) 16 EHRR 505; *Ruiz Torija v Spain* (1995) 19 EHRR 55.

hearing. This requirement can be breached merely by procedural inequality, without the need for quantifiable unfairness.[361]

7.155 The extent to which Article 6(1) requires disclosure is a fact-sensitive issue. The ECtHR has held that generally all evidence must be produced in the presence of the accused at a public hearing with a view to adversarial argument.[362] But, Article 6 does not automatically mean 'an absolute or unqualified right to see every document'.[363] There may be competing interests, such as protecting witnesses or keeping secret police methods of investigation of crime. However, measures that restrict defence rights have to be strictly necessary to be permissible under Article 6, and must leave the essence of the right unimpaired.[364]

7.156 In *AF (No 3)* the House of Lords applied the decision of the Grand Chamber in *A and ors v UK*[365] and held that non-disclosure to a person subject to a control order on grounds of national security could not go so far as to deny a party knowledge of the essence of the case against him.[366] If the open material used against a controlee consisted purely of general assertions, and the case against him was based solely or to a decisive degree on closed materials, the requirements of a fair trial would not be satisfied, regardless of how cogent the case based on the closed materials might be. Where the interests of national security were concerned in the context of combating terrorism, however, it might be acceptable not to disclose the source of evidence that founded the grounds of suspecting that a person had been involved in terrorism-related activities.

7.157 In an interesting application of the equality of arms principle, the Court of Appeal has held the right of the Attorney General to veto an order of the domestic information tribunal ordering disclosure of information under freedom of information legislation to infringe the equality of arms principle because it permitted 'one party (and particularly a public authority) to override a decision of a court merely because he disagrees with it'.[367]

7.158 The domestic courts have considered whether Article 6(1) guarantees a right to legal representation in disciplinary proceedings which may be determinative of a person's civil right to practise his or her profession. In *R (G) v Governors of X School* the Court of Appeal held that the level of procedural protection afforded by Article 6 will depend on what is at stake for the individual in question, but legal representation was required to give effect to Article 6(1) in the circumstances of the case.[368] However, as we have seen, the Supreme Court overruled the Court of Appeal's finding that Article 6 was engaged.[369]

---

[361] *Bulut v Austria* (1997) 24 EHRR 84; *Fischer v Austria* [2002] ECHR 3382/96.

[362] See, eg *Edwards v UK* (1992) 15 EHRR 417; *Lamy v Belgium* (1989) 11 EHRR 529.

[363] *Roberts v Nottinghamshire Healthcare NHS Trust* [2008] EWHC 1934 (QB) at [25].

[364] *Rowe and Davis v UK* (2000) 30 EHRR 1.

[365] (2009) 26 BHRC 1.

[366] *Secretary of State for the Home Department v AF (No 3)* [2009] UKHL 28, [2010] 2 AC 269.

[367] *R (Evans) v Her Majesty's Attorney General* [2014] EWCA Civ 254.

[368] [2011] UKSC 30, 1 AC 167, 3 WLR 237; Supreme Court judgment awaited at time of writing. See also *Kulkarni v Milton Keynes Hospital NHS Trust* [2009] EWCA Civ 789, [2009] IRLR 829.

[369] [2012] 1 AC 167.

Following the Government's restrictions on the availability of legal aid in the   7.159
Legal Aid and Sentencing and Punishment of Offenders Act 2013, the circumstances in which Article 6 (and other Convention rights) require the grant of legal
aid to ensure the right of access to Court has become a much more acute issue. In *R*
(Gudanaviciene) v Director of Legal Aid Casework, the High Court found that a test
in government guidance requiring that it was 'practically impossible' for a litigant
to effectively present their case without legal aid (which had been derived from an
old ECmHR case of *X v UK*[370]) set the bar too high: the question was whether there
was effective access to the Court so as to ensure overall fairness.[371]

(vi) *A reasoned decision* Article 6(1) requires a court to give reasons for its judg-   7.160
ment. The extent of this duty varies according to the nature of the decision and
the circumstances of the case.[372] 'Sparse' reasoning will not violate Article 6(1) per
se, and a detailed answer is not required to every argument,[373] but the court must
address the essential issues submitted to its jurisdiction.[374] This right is particularly
important in cases where the applicant wishes to exercise a right of appeal.[375] In
relation to lay juries, the court has upheld the validity of their use, provided there
are safeguards in the proceedings for the applicant to be able to understand why
he or she had been found guilty.[376] This case was applied, domestically, in *R v
Lawless*.[377]

The common law duty to give reasons has been held to be sufficient to satisfy   7.161
Article 6 requirements.[378]

(b) *Specific safeguards in respect of determination of criminal charges*
The overarching protection offered by Article 6(1) is further supplemented by the   7.162
specific guarantees in Article 6(2) and (3). The courts have, under Article 6(1) alone
or in association with the specific protections of Article 6(2) and (3), considered
matters as diverse as evidence from anonymous witnesses;[379] entrapment;[380] witnesses giving evidence behind screens;[381] accomplices;[382] undercover agents;[383]
undercover police officers; and pleas of guilt from co-defendants.[384] Article 6(1)

---

[370] (1984) 6 EHRR 136.
[371] [2014] EWHC 1840 Admin at [28].
[372] See, eg *McGinley and Egan v UK* (1999) 27 EHRR 1.
[373] *Van de Hurk v Netherlands* (1994) 18 EHRR 481.
[374] *Helle v Finland* (1997) 26 EHRR 159, paras 55–60; *Hiro Balani v Spain* (1995) 19 EHRR 566.
[375] *Hadjianastassiou v Greece* (1993) 16 EHRR 219.
[376] *Taxquet v Belgium* App No 926/05, 16 November 2010. See Roberts, 'Does Article 6 of the European
Convention on Human Rights Require Reasoned Verdicts in Criminal Trials?' (2011) 11 HRLR 2.
[377] [2011] EWCA Crim 59.
[378] *English v Emery Reimbold & Strick* [2002] EWCA Civ 605.
[379] *Kostovski v Netherlands* (1989) 12 EHRR 434; *Windisch v Austria* (1990) 13 EHRR 281; *Doorson v
Netherlands* (1996) 22 EHRR 330; *Van Mechelen v Netherlands* (1997) 25 EHRR 647.
[380] *Teixeira de Castro v Portugal* (1999) 28 EHRR 101.
[381] *X v UK* (1992) 15 EHRR CD 113.
[382] *X v UK* (1976) 74 DR 115.
[383] *X v Germany* (1989) 11 EHRR 84.
[384] *MH v UK* [1997] EHRLR 279.

also affords criminal defendants specific protections which are implied into its text in addition to those in Article 6(2) and (3). They include:

(i)   a limited right to silence;

(ii) the right to effective participation in their trials;

(iii) the right to equality of arms.

7.163   (i) *Right to silence* The right to silence and the privilege against self-incrimination are core, albeit implicit, elements of the right to a fair trial.[385] They are regarded by the ECtHR as 'generally recognised international standards which lie at the heart of the notion of a fair procedure under article 6'.[386] They support the presumption of innocence and protect against 'improper compulsion' by the police and judicial authorities.[387] They mean that an accused may not be compelled to answer questions during the investigation or to testify in court.[388] Thus, the use of improperly obtained evidence would violate Article 6(1).[389]

7.164   However, these notions are not absolute.[390] The ECtHR has confirmed that it may be permissible for a trial judge to leave a jury with the option of drawing an adverse inference from an accused's silence as occurs under the Criminal Justice and Public Order Act 1994. The jury must be properly directed as to a defendant's silence.[391] However, in *Adetoro v UK* the ECtHR found that a judge's failure to direct a jury properly in relation to the defendant's silence in a police interview did not violate Article 6(1) because he had not been convicted on the strength of his silence alone and there had been no unfairness in the trial as a whole.[392] Thus, adverse inferences cannot be the primary ground for conviction and a violation of Article 6 is to be determined in the light of all the circumstances of the case, having particular regard to the situations where inferences may be drawn, the weight to be attached to them, and the degree of compulsion inherent in the situation.[393]

7.165   A test of general fairness alone is not a sufficient safeguard to ensure that a person's Convention rights are protected. Some actions will violate Article 6 protection in principle irrespective of the fairness of later proceedings. In *Salduz v Turkey* the ECtHR held that the absence of a lawyer while in police custody had irretrievably affected a defendant's rights and this could not be remedied by his opportunity to challenge the evidence against him at trial or subsequently on appeal.[394] This

---

[385] *Murray v United Kingdom* (1996) 22 EHRR 29; *Funke v France* [1993] 1 CMLR 897.

[386] Ibid.

[387] *Saunders v UK* (1997) 23 EHRR 313.

[388] *R v Kearns* [2002] EWCA Crim 748, [2002] 1 WLR 2815.

[389] *Jalloh v Germany* (2007) 44 EHRR 32. See also *G v UK* (1983) 35 DR 75; *Gafgen v Germany* (2011) 52 EHRR 1; Greer, 'Should police threats to torture suspects always be severely punished? Reflections on the Gafgen case' (2011) 11(1) HRLR 67.

[390] *Condron and Condron v UK* (2001) 31 EHRR 1.

[391] Ibid. See also *Beckles v UK* (2003) 36 EHRR 13; *Heaney and McGuinness v Ireland* (2001) 33 EHRR 12.

[392] [2010] All ER (D) 109 (Apr).

[393] *John Murray v UK* (1996) 22 EHRR 29. Cf *Heaney and McGuinness v Ireland* (2001) 33 EHRR 12.

[394] (2009) 49 EHRR 19 at [54].

was a violation of Article 6(3)(c) in conjunction with Article 6(1).[395] This was applied domestically by the Supreme Court in *Cadder v HM Advocate*.[396] 'Admirable' as they were, later safeguards to the right to a fair trial could not rectify the unfairness which arose from a detained person having answered questions in the absence of a lawyer in his first interview.[397]

The privilege against self-incrimination does not generally apply to the production of blood, hair, or other physical or objective specimens used in forensic analysis, or voice samples.[398] Car owners can be required to disclose the driver of a vehicle in relation to a speeding offence as this was part and parcel of a regulatory regime relating to the use of motor cars and did not limit the privilege against self-incrimination sufficiently to constitute a breach of Article 6(1).[399] However, the production of drugs, which a street drug dealer had swallowed by the forcible administration of emetics, was found to nevertheless violate the prohibition on self-incrimination due to the nature and degree of compulsion used.[400]

7.166

(ii) *Right to effective participation* One of the 'essential requirements' of Article 6(1) read with Article 6(3)(d) is that a person 'charged with a criminal offence' is entitled to take part in the hearing and to be present when tried,[401] subject only to very tightly defined exceptions.[402] This is because a defendant has to be given a proper opportunity to question witnesses giving evidence against him or her.[403] Thus, the entitlement is not only to be physically present, but to be present in a meaningful sense: to be able to hear, follow, and understand proceedings, and to effectively participate through giving evidence and through a lawyer. For example, if the defendant is a child, the proceedings should take account of his or her age, level of maturity, and intellectual and emotional capabilities. This may involve special treatment.[404] Effective participation requires that the defendant has a broad understanding of the nature of the trial process and of what is at stake, including the significance of any possible penalty.[405]

7.167

(iii) *Equality of arms* The comments made in the preceding section on equality of arms also relate to criminal cases. In criminal cases, equality of arms means that a defendant and prosecution should enjoy a relatively level playing field at trial. This protection under Article 6(1) overlaps with some of the specific guarantees of Article 6(3) and the requirement for adversarial proceedings.[406] In practice, the requirement of equality of arms includes each party being afforded the opportunity to cross-examine the other's evidence and findings.[407] This can include, when

7.168

---

[395] Ibid.
[396] [2010] UKSC 43 (SC) at [70] per Lord Rodgers.
[397] Ibid.
[398] *PG and JH v UK* [2001] ECHR 44787/98.
[399] *O'Halloran and Francis v UK* (2008) 46 EHRR 21.
[400] *Jalloh v Germany* (2006) 20 BHRC 575.
[401] *Hulki Gunes v Turkey* (2006) 43 EHRR 15.
[402] *Hermi v Italy* (2008) 46 EHRR 46. Cf *Ekbatani v Sweden* (1991) 13 EHRR 504.
[403] *Hermi v Italy* (2008) 46 EHRR 46.
[404] *SC v UK* (2004) 40 EHRR 226.
[405] Ibid. Applied domestically in *R (C) v Sevenoaks Youth Court* [2009] EWHC 3088 (Admin).
[406] *Ruiz-Mateos v Spain* (1993) 16 EHRR 505; *Krcmar v Czech Republic* (2001) 31 EHRR 41.
[407] *X v Austria* (1972) 42 CD 145.

read with Article 6(3), an obligation on the prosecution to disclose any material in their possession, or to which they could gain access, which may assist the accused in exonerating him or herself or in obtaining a reduction in sentence.[408] It also means that defence and prosecution witnesses should be examined under the same conditions.[409] Both parties should certainly have the right to be represented by counsel, as well as the right to appear in person. In some cases equality of arms will require one party to be legally aided.[410]

7.169   In *Secretary of State for the Home Department v MB* Lord Bingham said that the ability of an individual to meet the case against him or her is integral to the notion of equality of arms which in turn is inherent in the concept of a fair trial.[411] However, mechanisms such as special advocates[412] and public interest immunity (PII) certificates,[413] which prevent the defendant directly knowing the evidence against him or her, will not necessarily violate Article 6(1) provided they do not undermine the very essence of the right (see above). The ECtHR jurisprudence, however, illustrates that evidence may only be withheld from the defendant if strictly necessary, a standard substantially higher than ordinary proportionality, and that evidence *must* be disclosed where it is necessary for an accused person to meet the case against him or her.[414]

7.170   The equality of arms guarantee is frequently read with Article 5(4) of the Convention, which allows the defendant to see the case against him or her so that he or she may challenge detention.

(c) *Composite approach*

7.171   The court assesses the fairness of a trial by reference to the process as a whole. It is the overall process which must reach the required standard.

7.172   A first instance decision determinative of civil rights and obligations need not necessarily meet Article 6(1) standards on its own, provided it is subject to supervision on an appeal or susceptible to judicial review, which is compliant.[415] However, the converse is not true: it cannot be said that there can never be an

---

[408] *Jespers v Belgium* (1983) 5 EHRR CD305; *Foucher v France* (1998) 25 EHRR 234. Cf *Mckeown v UK* App No 6684/05, 11 January 2011; *Allison v Her Majesty's Advocate* [2010] UKSC 6; *McInnes v Her Majesty's Advocate* [2010] UKSC 7.

[409] *Bönisch v Austria* (1987) 9 EHRR 191.

[410] *Steel and Morris v UK* (2005) 41 EHRR 22.

[411] *Secretary of State for the Home Department v MB; Secretary of State for the Home Department v AF* [2007] UKHL 46, [2008] 1 AC 440.

[412] *A and ors v UK* (2009) 26 BHRC 1; *Al-Rawi v Security Service* [2010] EWCA Civ 482 (Supreme Court decision pending); *Tariq v Home Office* [2010] EWCA Civ 462 (Supreme Court decision pending); *Secretary of State for the Home Department v MB; Secretary of State for the Home Department v AF* [2007] UKHL 46, [2008] 1 AC 440. See also *Secretary of State for the Home Department v AF (No 3)* [2009] UKHL 28, [2010] 2 AC 269.

[413] *Rowe and Davis v UK* (2000) 30 EHRR 1.

[414] See, eg *Fitt v UK* (2000) 30 EHRR 480; *Garcia Alva v Germany* (2001) 37 EHRR 335; *R v H* [2004] UKHL 3, [2004] 2 AC 134; *Secretary of State for the Home Department v MB; Secretary of State for the Home Department v AF* [2007] UKHL 46, [2008] 1 AC 440.

[415] See, eg *Edwards v UK* (1992) 15 EHRR 417, paras 51–54.

Article 6 breach if there is a fair appeal. Some breaches cannot be cured by appeal.[416]

In the case of *Tsfayo v UK* the ECtHR held that a housing benefit review board 7.173 staffed by councillors was not 'independent' because the members of the board were members of the local authority which stood to gain from the decision, and it was not one where the decision-maker 'required a measure of professional knowledge of experience'; the issue was simply one of fact. Judicial review could not adequately correct errors of fact because the Administrative Court 'did not have jurisdiction to rehear the evidence or substitute its own views as to the applicant's credibility'.[417]

In the event of unfairness, the ECtHR does not necessarily require a 'full judicial 7.174 rehearing' of all matters of fact and discretion when dealing with administrative decision-making in specialized areas. Where the decision-maker has examined the facts, a review of the lawfulness of the decision may suffice.[418] Guidance on when a full merits review would be required was given in a Northern Irish case, *Re Brown's Application*.[419] The court suggested that the 'bare judicial review' approach might be appropriate where the fact-finding process undertaken by the administrative body is tangential or incidental—the implication being that a more robust form of judicial review could be required when the fact-finding is central.

3. Article 6(2): presumption of innocence

Article 6(2) provides that everyone charged with a criminal offence shall be pre- 7.175 sumed innocent until proven guilty according to law. However, an equivalent protection is implied into certain civil cases which the Convention regards as 'criminal', such as professional disciplinary proceedings. This presumption is violated if a judicial decision or, in some circumstances, a statement by a public official concerning a person charged with a criminal offence, reflects an opinion that he or she is guilty before his or her guilt has been proved according to law.[420] The presumption requires, inter alia, that when carrying out their duties, the members of a court should not start with the preconceived idea that the accused has committed the offence charged; the burden of proof is on the prosecution, and any doubt should benefit the accused. For the presumption to be meaningful the prosecution will need to produce evidence of guilt in the trial[421] and the defendant has a right to be heard in his or her own defence.[422]

---

[416] *Findlay v UK* (1997) 24 EHRR 221; *Rowe and Davies v UK* (2000) 30 EHRR 1; *Condron and Condron v UK* (2001) 31 EHRR 1; *De Cubber v Belgium* (1985) 7 EHRR 236; and *R (G) v Governing Body of X School* [2011] UKSC 30, 1 AC 167, 3 WLR 237.

[417] (2009) 48 EHRR 18, para 47. See also *Begum v Tower Hamlets LBC* [2003] UKHL 5, [2003] 2 AC 430; *R (Wright) v Secretary of State for Health* [2009] UKHL 3, [2009] 1 AC 739.

[418] *Bryan v UK* (1995) 21 EHRR 342.

[419] [2003] NIJB 168. See also *Re Brolly (Anne)* [2004] NIQB 69.

[420] *Allenet de Ribemont v France* (1995) 20 EHRR 557; *Fatullayev v Azerbaijan* (2011) 52 EHRR 2.

[421] *Barberà v Spain* (1988) 11 EHRR 360.

[422] *Minelli v Switzerland* (1983) 5 EHRR 554.

7.176   Article 6(2) governs criminal proceedings in their entirety 'irrespective of the outcome of the prosecution'—so an acquittal or the lack of any conviction will not negate the state's responsibility for violating the presumption of innocence by prejudging the accused's guilt.[423] However, it applies only to the offence with which the accused is charged and does not extend to the sentencing process when decisions are being made regarding the length of sentence, quantum of a fine, or the amount of property to be confiscated,[424] although the House of Lords has held that the presumption of innocence does apply to confiscation proceedings via Article 6(1) so that if the prosecution rely on criminal offending to prove the existence of benefit, they must have proved that offending (albeit only to the civil standard).[425]

7.177   The ECtHR has held that the presumption of innocence may be violated in particular circumstances where, following an acquittal, a court or other authority expresses an opinion of continuing suspicion which amounts in substance to a determination of guilt of the person concerned.[426] In *R (Adams) v Secretary of State for Justice* the Supreme Court held that these cases did not lead Article 6(2) to have any bearing on the question whether a person should be entitled to compensation for a miscarriage of justice,[427] and this was upheld by the Grand Chamber of the ECtHR in *Allen v United Kingdom*.[428]

(a) *Reverse onus provisions*

7.178   'Reverse onus' provisions that require the defendant to prove certain elements of his or her defence do not violate the presumption of innocence per se as long as the overall burden of establishing guilt remains with the prosecution.[429] Equally, the provision does not necessarily prevent presumptions of law or fact from being in favour of the prosecution and against the defendant. These presumptions must be 'within reasonable limits'.[430]

7.179   In *R (Kebilene) v DPP* certain members of the House of Lords indicated, in *obiter* comments, that reverse onus provisions may not violate Article 6(2).[431] However, the use of section 3 of the Human Rights Act to translate an apparently legal burden into an evidential burden in *R v Lambert* indicated that at least in certain circumstances, the domestic courts would hold that the placement of a legal burden on an accused contravenes Article 6(2).[432] The leading decision is now *Sheldrake v DPP*, which confirms that reverse onus provisions may on occasion breach Article 6(2).[433] However,

---

[423] See, eg *Kazmierczak v Poland* App No 4317/04, 10 March 2009, para 55.
[424] See, eg *Phillips v UK* (2001) 11 BHRC 280; *R v Rezvi* [2002] UKHL 1; *R v Benjafield* [2002] UKHL 2, [2003] 1 AC 1099.
[425] *R v Briggs-Price* [2009] UKHL 19.
[426] See, eg *Sekanina v Austria* (1994) 17 EHRR 221; *Orr v Norway* App No 31283/04, 15 May 2008.
[427] [2011] UKSC 18.
[428] App No 25424/09, 12 January 2013.
[429] *Lingens v Austria* (1982) 4 EHRR 373.
[430] *Salabiaku v France* (1988) 13 EHRR 379; *R v G* [2008] UKHL 37, [2009] 1 AC 92.
[431] [2000] 2 AC 326. See also *Barnfather v Islington Education Authority* [2003] EWHC 418 (Admin), [2003] 1 WLR 238.
[432] [2001] UKHL 37, [2002] 2 AC 545. See also *Lynch v DPP* [2001] EWHC Admin 882, [2003] QB 137.
[433] [2004] UKHL 43, [2005] 1 AC 264.

the House of Lords rejected as 'inappropriate' the guidance set out by a five-judge Court of Appeal in that case, and did not provide clear principles for courts to apply in future cases.

(b) Right to silence

The right to silence and 'adverse inferences' have been considered by the ECtHR   7.180
under Article 6(1) in conjunction with Article 6(2).[434] It has been held that 'there can be no doubt that the right to remain silent under police questioning and the privilege against self-incrimination are generally recognized international standards which lie at the heart of the notion of a fair procedure under Article 6'.[435] Cases in relation to the right to silence are set out at 7.163–7.166.

4. Article 6(3): specific rights in criminal cases

In addition to the safeguards set out in Article 6(1), an individual facing a crimi-   7.181
nal charge benefits from the additional rights set out in Article 6(3). Article 6(3) is described as containing 'an enumeration of specific applications of the general principle stated in paragraph 1 of the Article'.[436] It establishes five specific safeguards which constitute a non-exhaustive list of the minimum rights to be afforded a defendant.

(a) Article 6(3)(a)

Article 6(3)(a) guarantees the defendant the right 'to be informed promptly, in a   7.182
language which he understands and in detail, of the nature and cause of the accusation against him'. It relates to the information required to be given to the accused at the time of the charge or the commencement of the proceedings, and requires the prompt, intelligible notification of charges. Vague and informal knowledge is insufficient.[437] Thus, it goes further than the requirement of notification of reasons for detention under Article 5(2). The right to know the case against the accused is essential to preparing an informed defence. It also ensures that the offence of which a person is convicted is the one with which he or she was charged.[438] Article 6(3)(a) also requires that a defendant be notified in a language that he or she understands,[439] and that the charges be formulated with adequate precision.[440] However, although oral explanations of the content and import of written charges may be sufficient, if the defendant is not conversant with the court's language, he or she

---

[434] *Murray v UK* (1996) 22 EHRR 29; *Saunders v UK* (1997) 23 EHRR 313 (violation of Art 6(1) by the use at the applicant's criminal trial of statements obtained from him by DTI Inspectors in exercise of their statutory powers under the Companies Act 1985 to compel him to answer questions and provide information). For domestic discussion of *Saunders*, see *R v Dimsey* [2001] UKHL 46, [2002] 1 AC 509.

[435] *Murray v UK* (1996) 22 EHRR 29; *Funke v France* [1993] 1 CMLR 897.

[436] *Artico v Italy* (1981) 3 EHRR 1, para 32; *Edwards v UK* (1992) 15 EHRR 417.

[437] *T v Italy* [1992] ECHR 14104/88.

[438] *Pélissier and Sassi v France* (2000) 30 EHRR 715.

[439] *Brozicek v Italy* (1989) 12 EHRR 371.

[440] *Mattoccia v Italy* (2003) 36 EHRR 47.

may be put at a disadvantage if he or she is not provided with a written translation of the indictment in a language he or she understands.[441] The protection is context-specific, so where, for example, the charge is serious and the person charged has mental problems and difficulties understanding the charge, states must do more than simply inform him or her of the bare charge.[442]

(b) Article 6(3)(b)

7.183   Article 6(3)(b) requires that the accused be given adequate time and facilities to mount a defence. This is linked to Article 6(3)(c) and the right to legal assistance. The principle is relative and will depend on all the circumstances of the case, including the complexity and the stage of the proceedings.[443] A balance has to be achieved between allowing adequate time and ensuring proceedings are conducted within a reasonable time. However, the courts have held that sufficient time to allow proper preparation is essential.[444] The ECtHR's approach is pragmatic, but the Court has confirmed that Article 6(3)(b) recognizes 'the right of the accused to have at his disposal, for the purpose of exonerating himself or to obtain a reduction in his sentence, all relevant elements that have been or could be collected by the competent authorities'.[445] Complaints have been declared inadmissible because the defect has been cured on appeal, but this does not discharge the judge of the duty to confirm that this right is being protected in proceedings. If it is not, the judge must also consider whether the trial can proceed.[446] Any restrictions on the right must be no more than strictly necessary and must be proportionate to identified risks.[447]

7.184   The right under Article 6(3)(b) is fact-specific, and does not extend to a free-standing positive duty on those bringing disciplinary proceedings to gather exculpatory evidence in favour of those accused of misconduct. In *R (Johnson and Maggs) v Professional Conduct Committee of the Nursing and Midwifery Council* (a disciplinary case which fell to be decided as a 'criminal' case in accordance with Article 6) it was held that the professionals accused of misconduct had not been at a disadvantage in obtaining the documents themselves. Beatson J held that a two-stage test was to be applied: first, whether the challenges in the circumstances of the case provided sufficient information to enable those charged to know, with reasonable clarity, the case they had to meet, and whether they knew enough about the charges to enable them to prepare their defences; secondly, and if the first stage was not satisfied, whether the only remedy was a stay of proceedings.[448]

---

[441] *Kamasinski v Austria* (1991) 13 EHRR 36.
[442] *Vaudelle v France* (2003) 37 EHRR 16.
[443] *Albert and Le Compte v Belgium* (1983) 5 EHRR 533.
[444] *Öcalan v Turkey* (2005) 41 EHRR 45.
[445] *Jespers v Belgium* (1983) 5 EHRR CD 305. See also *Can v Austria* (1985) 8 EHRR 121 and *Hadjinastassiou v Greece* (1992) 16 EHRR 219.
[446] *UK Campbell and Fell v UK* (1985) 7 EHRR 165.
[447] *Kurup v Denmark* (1986) 8 EHRR CD 93; *Kröcher and Möller v Switzerland* (1984) 6 EHRR 345.
[448] [2008] EWHC 885 (Admin).

(c) *Article 6(3)(c)*

Article 6(3)(c) provides that everyone charged with a criminal offence has: **7.185**

(i)   the right to defend him or herself;

(ii) the right to legal assistance of his or her choosing; and

(iii) the right to free legal assistance if the interests of justice so require and he or she lacks sufficient means.

The provision aims to guarantee the right to an effective defence. Thus, it is not **7.186** necessary to prove that the absence of legal assistance had caused actual prejudice in order to establish a violation. These principles apply to the pre-trial stages as well as to the trial itself.[449] In *Imbrioscia v Switzerland*, the ECtHR was asked to consider whether the defendant was entitled to have a lawyer present at pre-trial questioning. It held that Article 6(3) may be relevant to the pre-trial stages if and so far as the fairness of the trial is likely to be seriously prejudiced by an initial failure to comply with its provisions.[450] The ECtHR went further in *Salduz v Turkey*, confirming that:

as a rule, access to a lawyer should be provided as from the first interrogation of a suspect by the police, unless it is demonstrated in the light of the particular circumstances of the case that there are compelling reasons to restrict this right. Even where compelling reasons may exceptionally justify denial of access to a lawyer, such restriction...must not unduly prejudice the rights of the accused under Article 6. The rights of the defence will in principle be irretrievably prejudiced when incriminating statements made during police interrogation without access to a lawyer are used for a conviction.[451]

The provision also gives the right for a detained person charged with a criminal **7.187** offence to communicate with his or her lawyer out of hearing of other persons. In *S v Switzerland* the ECtHR confirmed that '[f]ree communication between a lawyer and his detained client is a fundamental right which is essential in a democratic society, above all in the most serious of cases'.[452] Consequently, it rejected an argument that intrusive acts such as surveillance of a lawyer, the presence of a police officer at consultation, or the interception of communication were necessary because of fears of collusion.

Article 6(3)(c) also covers the right to free legal assistance on the grounds of **7.188** (1) insufficient means, and (2) the interests of justice. In *Benham v UK* the ECtHR considered whether the lack of availability of full legal aid for a committal hearing in a poll tax case constituted a violation of Article 6. In answering this question, the ECtHR stated that regard must be had to the severity of the penalty at stake and the complexity of the case. In general, the ECtHR held that where 'deprivation of liberty is at stake, the interests of justice in principle call for legal representation'.[453]

---

[449] *Imbrioscia v Switzerland* (1993) 17 EHRR 441.
[450] Ibid; *Magee v UK* (2001) 31 EHRR 822.
[451] (2008) 26 BHRC 223 at [55].
[452] (1991) 14 EHRR 670. See also *Brennan v UK* (2002) 34 EHRR 18.
[453] (1996) 22 EHRR 293. See also *Perks and others v United Kingdom* (2000) 30 EHRR 33.

In the particular case the ECtHR found a violation of Article 6(1) and (3)(c) of the Convention taken together. Legal aid may also be required 'in the interests of justice' for an appeal against conviction or sentence.[454] This is particularly relevant when an appellant appears for him or herself against a QC and a junior counsel for the Crown, as occurred in *Granger v UK*. The ECtHR in that case found a violation of Article 6(3)(c), citing the defendant's obvious lack of understanding regarding the intricacies of the law in the face of the professional prosecution.[455] The Court of Appeal has also held that this right extends to committal proceedings for contempt of court as, in the absence of unreasonable behaviour, a litigant in person, a person who is liable to be sent to prison, is entitled to legal representation.[456]

7.189   The right to be provided with legal representation means the right to be provided with genuine and effective representation, not the mere presence of a lawyer.[457] Assigning a legal representative does not in itself ensure the effectiveness of assistance afforded to an accused.[458] Thus, failures on the part of the lawyer can effectively deprive the accused of his right to legal assistance.[459] However, the state cannot be held responsible for every shortcoming of the accused's lawyer.[460] The duty on the court is to 'intervene only if a failure by legal aid counsel to provide effective representation is manifest or sufficiently brought to their attention in some other way'.[461] It should also be noted that although the right is formulated as a choice between acting in person or being legally represented, the ECtHR has confirmed that the right to represent oneself in person is not an absolute one.[462]

(d)   *Article 6(3)(d)*

7.190   Article 6(3)(d) ensures the accused's right 'to examine or have examined witnesses against him and to obtain the attendance and examination of witnesses on his behalf under the same conditions as witnesses against him'. This is in keeping with the 'equality of arms' principle outlined in Article 6(1). Although it refers to 'witnesses', it has been held to cover physical evidence. For example, the ECtHR found that the right had been violated in *Papageorgiou v Greece* where the court in a fraud trial had failed, despite repeated requests, to produce originals of cheques.[463]

7.191   This provision does not guarantee an absolute right to call witnesses or a right to force the domestic courts to hear a particular witness. The requirement imposes an overall requirement of fairness, including equality of arms, so an applicant will have to establish that the failure to hear a particular witness prejudiced his or her case.[464]

---

[454] *Granger v UK* (1990) 12 EHRR 469. See also *Hoang v France* (1993) 16 EHRR 53.
[455] (1990) 12 EHRR 469.
[456] *Hammerton v Hammerton* [2007] EWCA Civ 248.
[457] *Artico v Italy* (1980) 3 EHRR 1.
[458] *Imbrioscia v Switzerland* (1994) 17 EHRR 441.
[459] *Czekalla v Portugal* [2002] ECHR 657.
[460] *Sannino v Italy* (2009) 48 EHRR 25.
[461] *Kamasinski v Austria* (1991) 13 EHRR 36, para 65.
[462] *Croissant v Germany* (1993) 16 EHRR 135.
[463] (2004) 38 EHRR 30.
[464] *X v Switzerland* (1982) 28 DR 127.

The ECtHR has held that this question falls within a wide margin of appreciation on the part of judicial authorities.[465] Limitations on the right are possible, and the ECtHR has approved them on a variety of grounds, such as vulnerable witnesses giving evidence anonymously, behind screens, or via pre-recorded video interviews.[466] The ECtHR has held that a genuine fear of reprisals may justify reliance on hearsay evidence but this should be counter-balanced with procedures which preserve the rights of the defence and that these procedures may vary from case to case.[467] However the permissible justifications for anonymous witnesses are strictly limited.[468] The obligation to permit challenges to the witness in person may have to be balanced against the state's obligation to protect life under Article 2. The courts have held that to compel police or military witnesses to give evidence without anonymity may constitute a breach of their Article 2 right to life.[469]

The House of Lords concluded in *R v Davis* that the domestic law in this area had intruded too far upon the right. Their Lordships found that the law had developed incrementally in such a way that while no single step towards trials with anonymous witnesses was obviously wrong, the cumulative effect of these individual steps had eroded the essence of the right under Article 6(3)(d).[470] The effect of the judgment was to prevent witnesses from giving evidence anonymously if concealing their identity from the defendant and their lawyers hindered cross-examination or other challenges to their credibility. In response, Parliament rushed to legislate to overturn the ruling, and the Criminal Evidence (Witness Anonymity) Act 2008 was passed within days. This has abolished the existing common law rules on anonymity of witnesses and replaced them with a framework in which witness anonymity orders could be granted by the court on the application of the prosecutor or defendant. The Act has since been replaced by sections 86 to 97 of the Coroners and Justice Act 2009.[471]   7.192

In a line of cases, the ECtHR has held that a conviction cannot be based either solely or to a decisive extent on evidence from anonymous witnesses.[472] In *Al-Khawaja v UK* the ECtHR propounded a rule whereby the introduction in evidence of a hearsay statement which constituted the sole or decisive evidence against the defendant would breach Article 6(3)(d) and the general right to a fair trial under Article 6, unless the defendant had had an opportunity at some stage to cross-examine the maker of the statement, or unless the maker of the statement   7.193

---

[465] Ibid.

[466] See, eg *SN v Sweden* (2004) 39 EHRR 13; *PS v Germany* (2003) 36 EHRR 61; see also *R v Camberwell Green Youth Court, ex p D* [2005] UKHL 4, [2005] 1 WLR 393. Cf *PS v Germany* (2003) 36 EHRR 61.

[467] *Saïdi v France* (1994) 17 EHRR 251; *Van Mechelen and ors v Netherlands* (1998) 25 EHRR 647; *R v Davis* [2008] UKHL 36; *Al-Rawi v Security Service* [2010] EWCA Civ 482 (appeal pending); *Doorson v Netherlands* (1996) 22 EHRR 330, para 67.

[468] *Van Mechelen and ors v Netherlands* (1998) 25 EHRR 647.

[469] *Re Officer L* [2007] UKHL 36, [2007] 1 WLR 312.

[470] [2008] UKHL 36.

[471] See Ormerod, Choo, and Easter, 'The "Witness Anonymity" and "Investigative Anonymity" Provisions' [2010] Crim LR 368. For a discussion of relevant case law, see Ormerod, 'Evidence: hearsay evidence—anonymous witness' [2011] 6 Crim LR, 475–479.

[472] *Doorson v Netherlands* (1996) 22 EHRR 330; *Kostovski v Netherlands* (1990) 12 EHRR 434.

was kept from giving evidence through fear induced by the defendant.[473] This rule conflicted with the decision of the Court of Appeal in *R v Horncastle*.[474] The Court of Appeal held that, provided the provisions of the Criminal Justice Act 2003 were observed, there was no breach of Article 6 and in particular Article 6(3)(d), if the conviction was based solely or to a decisive degree on hearsay evidence. In a striking departure from normal practice, the Supreme Court declined to follow the ECtHR on the basis that it was a rare occasion 'where this court has concerns as to whether a decision of the Strasbourg Court sufficiently appreciates or accommodates particular aspects of our domestic process'.[475] Amongst the reasons given for this conclusion, the court found that in almost all the ECtHR cases in which violations of Article 6(3)(d) had been found it was clear that if the law of England and Wales had been applied, the relevant evidence would have been declared inadmissible, and the defendant would not have been convicted.

7.194   The Grand Chamber of the ECtHR subsequently revisited the sole or decisive rule following the Supreme Court's decision in *Horncastle*. Whilst not prepared to accept the Supreme Court's criticisms of the rule, the Grand Chamber was prepared to accept that the rule should not be applied inflexibly and that, where a hearsay statement is the sole or decisive evidence against a defendant, admission of this evidence would not automatically result in a breach of Article 6. Admission of such evidence must be subject to the most searching scrutiny, but the question was always whether there were sufficient counterbalancing factors to ensure the overall fairness of the trial.[476] In *R v Ibrahim*,[477] the Court of Appeal found the Grand Chamber's approach to be reconcilable, in substance, with that of the Court of Appeal and Supreme Court in *Horncastle*. The development of the law on the 'sole and decisive' rule has been cited as an example of 'constructive dialogue' between the domestic courts and the ECtHR.[478]

(e) *Article 6(3)(e)*

7.195   Article 6(3)(e) guarantees the right to the free assistance of an interpreter if the accused cannot understand or speak the language used in court. The ECtHR has held, in *Luedicke and ors v Germany*, that the provision absolutely prohibits a defendant being ordered to pay the costs of an interpreter.[479] Further, it confirmed that this principle covered 'those documents or statements in the proceedings instituted against him which is necessary for him to understand in order to have the benefit of a fair trial'.[480] However, in *Kamasinski v Austria* the Court held that this

---

[473] (2009) 49 EHRR 1.

[474] [2009] EWCA Crim 964.

[475] [2009] UKSC 14 at [11].

[476] *Al Khawaja and Tahery v UK* (2011) 32 BHRC 1 at [147].

[477] [2012] EWCA Crim 837; [2012] 4 All ER 225. See now also *R v Riat and ors* [2012] EWCA Crim 1509; [2013] 1 All ER 349, explaining the guidance in *R v Ibrahim*.

[478] *Pinnock v Manchester City Council* [2011] 2AC 104 at [48] per Lord Neuberger.

[479] (1979–80) 2 EHRR 149.

[480] Ibid, paras 40, 48.

did not necessarily mean that written translations of all documentation had to be provided. Assistance is provided so that the defendant 'should be... [able] to have knowledge of the case against him and to defend himself, notably by being able to put before the court his version of the events'.[481]

Once it has been established that interpretation is required, informal and unprofessional assistance is unlikely to be sufficient. In *Cuscani v UK* the ECtHR found a violation of Article 6(3)(e) after a judge had accepted defence counsel's suggestion that they 'make do and mend' in the absence of an interpreter and instead call on the accused's brother to assist when required. The ECtHR held that the trial judge should have guarded the defendant's interests 'with scrupulous care' and satisfied himself that the absence of an official interpreter did not prejudice the defendant's full involvement in his sentencing hearing.[482]   7.196

5. Protocol 7

Protocol 7 supplements and, in some cases, deals with gaps in Article 6 protection. For example, it supplements the protection afforded to criminal defendants by providing a right of appeal against conviction (Protocol 7, Article 2); and it provides procedural protection for aliens whom the state seeks to expel (Protocol 7, Article 1). Protocol 7 is analysed in Chapter 8, paras 8.141–8.151.   7.197

The United Kingdom has not yet signed or ratified Protocol 7.   7.198

D. ARTICLE 7: NO PUNISHMENT WITHOUT LAWFUL AUTHORITY

Article 7 guards against the retrospective application of criminal law. It provides 'effective safeguards against arbitrary prosecution, conviction and punishment'[483] and is thus a crucial element of the rule of law, the protection of which is one of the central purposes of the Convention.[484] Article 15 permits no derogation from Article 7 in time of war or other emergency.   7.199

Article 7(1) has two limbs: it forbids finding an individual guilty of a crime which was not a crime at the time it was committed (the prohibition on 'retrospective offences'), and it forbids a heavier penalty being imposed than that which was in effect at the time of the crime (the prohibition on 'heavier penalties').   7.200

The ECtHR has made clear that three interrelated principles underpin Article 7.[485] First, 'only the law can define a crime and prescribe a penalty'. Secondly, an offence must be clearly defined in law, enabling individuals to know what acts and omissions   7.201

---

[481] (1991) 13 EHRR 36.
[482] (2003) 36 EHRR 2.
[483] *Korbely v Hungary* (2009) 25 BHRC 382, para 69.
[484] See, eg *Jorgic v Germany* (2007) 25 BHRC 287, para 100.
[485] *Kokkinakis v Greece* (1994) 17 EHRR 397.

will attract criminal liability. Thirdly, 'the criminal law must not be extensively construed to an accused's detriment, for instance by analogy'.

7.202　Article 7(1) covers both legislation and the actions of the courts, subject to the narrow exception detailed in Article 7(2).[486]

7.203　Having regard to its potentially wide application, Article 7 is relatively underused both in Strasbourg and domestically. In many cases involving criminal laws with uncertain content or scope, reliance is placed only on Articles 5 and 6, together with one of the qualified rights if they are engaged (such as Articles 10 and 11 in relation to public order offences). Many of these cases also raise issues under Article 7 but claimants tend not to argue the point.

1. 'Criminal'

7.204　Article 7 is applicable only to criminal proceedings resulting in a conviction and/or the imposition of a criminal penalty. It does not bite if a prosecution is abandoned.[487]

7.205　Measures not covered by Article 7, since they do not result in a finding of guilt or the imposition of a criminal penalty, include changes to parole rules[488] and remission procedures,[489] extradition,[490] and procedures for adding a conviction to an individual's criminal record.[491] There are also a number of early Strasbourg authorities holding that Article 7 does not apply to preventive detention[492] or internment[493] (although such measures may, of course, violate Article 5).

7.206　Article 7 is not applicable to civil proceedings. However, as with Articles 5 and 6, 'criminal' is an autonomous concept and proceedings which are classified as civil domestically may nevertheless be considered criminal by Strasbourg.[494]

2. Article 7(1): retrospective offences

7.207　The first sentence of Article 7(1) prohibits convicting or punishing people for behaviour which was not criminal under national or international law at the time it was committed. It guards against both the development of the law to impose criminal liability on acts that were not previously considered criminal and the extension of existing offences to include acts which were not previously covered by the offence.[495]

---

[486] *Kafkaris v Cyprus* (2008) 25 BHRC 591, para 139.

[487] *X v UK* 3 Digest 211 (1973).

[488] *Hogben v UK* (1986) 46 DR 231.

[489] *Kafkaris v Cyprus* (2008) 25 BHRC 591.

[490] *X v Netherlands* (1976) 6 DR 184; *Marais v Governor of HMP Brixton* [2001] EWHC 1051 (Admin).

[491] *X v Germany* 3 YB 254.

[492] *De Wilde Ooms and Versyp v Belgium* (1971) 1 EHRR 373, para 87; cf *M v Germany* (2009) 28 BHRC 521.

[493] *Lawless v Ireland (No 3)* (1979–1980) 1 EHRR 15, para 19.

[494] 'Autonomous concepts' in the Convention are explained further in ch 2, paras 2.14 –2.16.

[495] *Kingston v UK* App No 27837/95, 9 April 1997.

When speaking of 'law', Article 7—as elsewhere in the Convention—is referring   7.208
to a concept that incorporates qualitative requirements, notably those of accessibility and foreseeability.[496]

Most complaints made under the first sentence of Article 7(1) raise the uncer-   7.209
tainty or lack of precision of laws already in place, rather than entirely new statutes
or laws being made which apply retrospectively. The key issue is usually whether
the development or application of the existing law in the case was 'reasonably
foreseeable'.

A paradigmatic example of such a case was *R v R*, heard before the passing of the   7.210
Human Rights Act 1998, in which the House of Lords abolished the common law
immunity for husbands who raped their wives.[497] In finding that the immunity was
anachronistic and offensive, their Lordships held that 'the common law is...capable
of evolving in the light of changing social, economic and cultural developments'.[498]

The House of Lords' decision was upheld when the case reached Strasbourg.[499]   7.211
The ECtHR held that with the benefit of legal advice, the applicant husband could
have foreseen that his actions might attract criminal liability and therefore Article 7
was not violated. The Court of Appeal has subsequently held that, even where the
marital rape occurred in 1970, a solicitor would have advised that exceptions to the
'irrevocable consent' rule were being developed and so the development in the law
did not offend Article 7.[500]

The ECtHR will ask whether a judicial development of the law is not only rea-   7.212
sonably foreseeable but also 'consistent with the essence of the offence'. Thus in
Khodorkovsky and Lebedev v Russia, even though the ECtHR found that an interpretation of an offence of tax evasion adopted by the Russian Courts was novel, it
found no violation of Article 7 as it was a reasonable interpretation of the relevant
provisions and consistent with the essence of the offence.[501]

Cantoni v France[502] and *Chauvy v France*[503] have reiterated that the reasonable   7.213
foreseeability requirement may be satisfied if the individual could have regulated
his or her behaviour following appropriate legal advice. The ECtHR considers the
legal advice caveat to be particularly relevant to individuals engaged in professional or commercial activities which are risky, such as selling alternative medicines
(*Cantoni*) or publishing (*Chauvy*).

Laws that confer a discretion are not inconsistent with the Convention pro-   7.214
vided the scope of the discretion and the manner of its exercise are indicated with
sufficient clarity. In the case of *O'Carroll v UK* the applicant was convicted of
knowingly evading the prohibition on the importation of indecent material, in

---

[496] *Cantoni v France* Reports of Judgments and Decisions 1996-V, 15 November 1996, 1627, para 29;
O'Carroll v UK App No 35557/03, 15 March 2005, 6.
[497] [1992] 1 AC 599.
[498] Ibid, 601.
[499] *SW v UK* (1995) 21 EHRR 363.
[500] *R v C* [2004] EWCA Crim 292, [2004] 1 WLR 2098.
[501] App Nos 11082/06 and 13772/05, 25 July 2013 (2014) 59 EHRR 7.
[502] App No 17862/91, 15 November 1996.
[503] [2004] ECHR 64915/01.

connection with his receipt of photographs of a young naked child engaging in normal outdoor activity, such as playing on a beach.[504] He unsuccessfully argued that the law was not sufficiently precise for him to know in advance whether his behaviour was criminal. The ECtHR held that the fact that it is for a jury to decide in indecency cases whether the matter in question is indecent is not in breach of Article 7. The ECtHR will give greater leeway in areas involving imprecise concepts, such as 'indecency'.

7.215   In a series of cases, the ECtHR considered convictions based on international criminal law. In *Jorgic v Germany* it found that the conviction of a Bosnian Serb for genocide did not infringe Article 7.[505] It did not prevent the gradual clarification of the criminal law by judicial determination from case to case. Conversely, in *Kononov v Latvia* the Grand Chamber, disagreeing with the Chamber's judgment, found that the applicant could have reasonably foreseen that acts committed during the Second World War amounted to a war crime under the *jus in bello* applicable at the time. There was therefore no violation of Article 7.[506] The Grand Chamber reached a different conclusion in respect of an applicant convicted for crimes against humanity committed during the Hungarian Revolution of 1956 on the basis that it was not established by the domestic courts that his crimes were part of state policy and therefore one of the constituent elements of the crime was absent.[507]

7.216   English law has long recognized a general prohibition on retrospectivity in the criminal law.[508] In *R v Rimmington* Lord Bingham set out two common law principles on retrospectivity that are 'entirely consistent with article 7(1) of the European Convention':[509]

...no one should be punished under a law unless it is sufficiently clear and certain to enable him to know what conduct is forbidden before he does it; and no one should be punished for any act which was not clearly and ascertainably punishable when the act was done.[510]

7.217   It is clear that in the domestic courts, as in Strasbourg, the requirement of legal certainty has been flexibly interpreted. Given the relative paucity of Article 7 cases, it is as yet unclear whether the domestic courts' approach is wholly in line with that of the ECtHR.

7.218   The leading domestic case prior to the enactment of the Human Rights Act was *C v DPP*, in which Lord Lowry set out criteria for 'judicial lawmaking' in the criminal sphere.[511] These criteria are broader than those set out in the Strasbourg jurisprudence, and do not rule out a court setting aside 'fundamental legal doctrines' in an individual case (although such a course should not be taken 'lightly').

---

[504] App No 35557/03, 15 March 2005.
[505] (2008) 47 EHRR 6.
[506] (2009) 25 BHRC 317.
[507] *Korbely v Hungary* (2009) 25 BHRC 382.
[508] *R v Misra* [2004] EWCA Crim 2375, [2005] 1 Cr App R 328 at [29]–[34].
[509] [2005] UKHL 63, [2006] 1 AC 459 at [33].
[510] Ibid at [32].
[511] [1996] AC 1, 28.

Article 7 places further limits on judicial creativity beyond those set out by Lord Lowry, and the criteria he proposes should be treated with caution.

The House of Lords has indicated that, even when dealing with a precisely   7.219
drafted statute, Article 7 may allow for some interpretative leeway.[512] The Northern Ireland Court of Appeal found that defendants who belonged to the 'Real Irish Republican Army' (Real IRA) belonged to a proscribed organization within the meaning of the Terrorism Act 2000, even though that Act proscribed only the IRA and not the Real IRA, a separate organization. The House of Lords stated that the Court of Appeal had been correct to reject the defendants' Article 7 submission: 'while acknowledging, on the authority of *Kokkinakis v Greece* that a criminal offence must be clearly defined in law, the court was of opinion that the offence charged against the acquitted person had been clearly defined'.[513]

Their Lordships reached the same conclusion in *R v Rimmington* in respect of the   7.220
common law offence of public nuisance.[514] Lord Rodger stated:

While a lack of coherence in defining the scope of an offence may offend modern eyes, it does not follow that there is any violation of article 7. If the individual elements of the crime are identified clearly enough and the law is applied according to its terms, potential offenders and their advisers know where they stand: they cannot complain because the law could perhaps have been formulated more elegantly.[515]

The Article 7 compliance of strict liability offences was considered in *R v*   7.221
Muhamad.[516] The appellant argued that a strict liability offence was inconsistent with the general requirement for sufficiently clear criminal provisions. The Court of Appeal rejected this, holding that only legal uncertainty, rather than factual uncertainty, contravenes Article 7. In *R v Budimir and Rainbird* the Court of Appeal found that Article 7 had not been breached by convictions for an offence, which failed to comply with a procedural requirement imposed by EU law and was therefore technically unenforceable against them.[517]

3. Article 7(1): heavier penalties

Article 7(1) also prohibits the imposition of a heavier penalty than that applicable   7.222
at the time the offence was committed. Where the law changes between the time of the commission of an offence and final judgment in a defendant's case, the court must apply the law more leniently to the defendant. The latter principle is not stated expressly in Article 7 and was elucidated for the first time by the Grand Chamber in *Scoppola v Italy*.[518] Where later domestic sentencing laws are not expressed to have

---

[512] *R v Z* [2005] UKHL 35, [2005] 2 AC 645.
[513] Ibid at [15] per Lord Bingham; citing with approval [2005] NI 106 at [51]–[52].
[514] [2005] UKHL 63, [2006] 1 AC 459.
[515] Ibid at [45].
[516] [2002] EWCA Crim 1856, [2003] QB 1031.
[517] [2010] EWCA Crim 1486, [2010] 3 CMLR 1377.
[518] *Scoppola v Italy* [2009] ECHR 10249/03.

retrospective effect, this can create difficulties for the application of the principle in domestic law.[519]

(a) Penalty

7.223 As with the term 'criminal', 'penalty' has an autonomous meaning and the classification of a measure in domestic law will not be decisive. Relevant factors include:[520]

(a) whether the measure was imposed following a conviction for a criminal offence (the ECtHR's 'starting point' in Article 7 cases);[521]

(b) its classification in domestic law;

(c) its nature and purpose;

(d) the procedures involved in its making;

(e) the procedures involved in its implementation; and

(f) its severity.

7.224 In *Adamson v UK* the ECtHR found that the retrospective imposition on the applicant, a man who had been convicted of a sex offence but had served his sentence and been released, of an obligation to register with the police was not a 'penalty' and therefore did not violate Article 7.[522] In *M v Germany* the ECtHR found that a measure which turned a limited period of detention into an unlimited period constituted an additional penalty.[523] In subsequent cases it has made clear that the state cannot invoke its positive obligation to prevent Article 2 and 3 treatment in order to justify a retrospective increase in sentence contrary to Article 7.[524]

7.225 In *Welch v UK* the applicant was arrested on drug charges in November 1986. In January 1987 a law concerning the seizure of any proceeds gained as a result of the drug trade came into effect. The applicant argued that if this new law were applied to him, it would constitute retrospective criminal legislation in breach of Article 7. The ECtHR ruled that the retrospective application of the confiscation order was a penalty and offended Article 7. It found that Mr Welch faced more 'far-reaching detriment' as a result of the government seizure than he would have at the time he perpetrated the crimes.[525]

7.226 In *Gurguchiani v Spain* the European Court held for the first time that deportation may constitute a penalty where it virtually automatically replaced a custodial sentence imposed on the accused.[526] However, the Grand Chamber has held that deportation for the purposes of public protection following a criminal conviction does not generally constitute a penalty where it is imposed primarily as

---

[519] Eg *R v Doherty* [2014] EWCA Crim 1197.

[520] *Welch v UK* (1995) 20 EHRR 247, paras 27, 28; *Adamson v UK* App No 42293/98, 26 January 1999.

[521] *Jamil v France* (1995) 21 EHRR 65.

[522] App No 42293/98, 26 January 1999. See also *Gardel v France* App No 16428/05, 17 December 2009.

[523] (2009) 28 BHRC 521. See also *K v Germany* App No 61827/09, 7 June 2012, and *G v Germany* App No 65210/09, 7 June 2012.

[524] *K v Germany* and *G v Germany*, ibid.

[525] (1995) 20 EHRR 247, para 34.

[526] App No 16012/06, 15 December 2009.

a preventative rather than as a punitive measure.[527] Similarly, in *AT (Pakistan) v Secretary of State for the Home Department* the Court of Appeal held that automatic deportation could not be characterized as a penalty as one reason for such a measure was to prevent a person reoffending in the United Kingdom.[528]

There is a question mark over the domestic courts' approach to the meaning of 'penalty' within Article 7. They have tended to adopt a narrow approach, treating the factors identified by the ECtHR in *Welch v UK* as a checklist of requirements, each of which must be satisfied in order for a measure to be considered a 'penalty'. In *Gough v Chief Constable of Derbyshire*, for example, the Court of Appeal found that orders banning attendance at, and travel to, football matches do not constitute penalties.[529] In *R v Field; R v Young* the Court of Appeal held that an order disqualifying the appellants from working with children was not a penalty, and so could be imposed in respect of offences committed before the implementation of the statutory provisions creating the order.[530] The domestic courts in *Gough* and *Field; Young* focused almost exclusively on the aim of the measure and did not fully consider its severity or the behaviour to which it was linked. 7.227

(b) *Sentencing*

The rule against heavier penalties may also be violated by a failure to apply the relevant sentencing rules, even if the distinction between the appropriate and actual sentence is minimal.[531] This strict approach is in keeping with the importance of the rule of law under the Convention. However, in a series of cases the ECtHR has pared back its earlier approach under this limb of Article 7(1). It has imported the 'foreseeability' test from the first limb of Article 7(1) and applied it in relation to whether or not a heavier penalty has been imposed than that which the offence attracted at the time of commission. In doing so it has given a widened margin of appreciation to states than had previously been the case under Article 7. The reasoning in these cases gives cause for concern as it weakens protection from retrospective penalties. 7.228

In *Taylor v UK* the ECtHR found no breach of Article 7 where a 15-year-old boy received an 18-month custodial sentence following his conviction for theft and assault.[532] He had just passed his fourteenth birthday at the time of the offence, but owing to delays on the part of the Crown Prosecution Service and Stratford Youth Court his case did not come to trial until a year later, 11 days after his 15th birthday. Had he been convicted of these offences when aged 14 he could not have received a custodial sentence. 7.229

The ECtHR accepted the Government's argument that the relevant statutory provisions were clear and foreseeable given legal advice, as in English law the basic 7.230

---

[527] *Uner v the Netherlands* [2006] ECHR 873, para. 56.
[528] [2010] EWCA Civ 567, [2010] NLJR 806.
[529] [2002] EWCA Civ 351, [2002] QB 1213.
[530] [2002] EWCA Crim 2913, [2003] 1 WLR 882.
[531] See, eg *Gabarri Moreno v Spain* App No 68066/01, 22 July 2003. The judgment is available only in French.
[532] App No 48864/99, 3 December 2002.

rule for determining what sentencing power the court has is the defendant's age at the date of conviction, not his age at the date of commission. The ECtHR thus upheld the imposition of a penalty to which Taylor was not liable at the time he committed the offence on the basis of foreseeability.

7.231   The Grand Chamber has taken the *Taylor v UK* principle a step further. In *Achour v France* it held that the rule against heavier penalties will not be violated by a new statutory provision if the development is broadly foreseeable given previous criminal justice policies.[533] As the French courts had taken 'a clear and consistent position since the late nineteenth century' on the application of new recidivism rules, the applicant was 'manifestly capable' of regulating his conduct in light of this case law.[534]

7.232   It is also clear from *Achour v France* that the practice of taking past events into consideration should be distinguished from the notion of retrospective application of the criminal law. In that case the applicant had been found guilty of drug trafficking in 1984, and served time in prison until 1986. In 1994 new provisions came into effect which changed the law on recidivism. They stipulated that where a person who had already been convicted of a serious crime or offence punishable by ten years' imprisonment committed, within ten years of the expiry of the previous sentence, a further offence, the maximum sentence and fine imposable for any further offence should be doubled. The applicant was sentenced in 1997 for a further drug offence and had his sentence doubled on the basis of the 1997 laws. The Grand Chamber (overturning an earlier Chamber decision) found no violation of Article 7. He was not being punished for the earlier offence; rather, the new rules had been applicable when he committed the second offence in 1997, as he had been a recidivist in legal terms at that time.[535]

7.233   In the case of *Kafkaris v Cyprus* the Grand Chamber considered Article 7 in relation to a prisoner sentenced to life imprisonment for pre-meditated murder.[536] At the time of his sentence, the provisions of the Cypriot Criminal Code provided for a mandatory full-life sentence but the executive and authorities worked on the assumption that the Prison Regulations, which provided for remission of life sentences, imposed a maximum sentence of 20 years. A change to the Prison Regulations then abolished remission of life sentences and the applicant was expected to serve a full-life term.

7.234   The Grand Chamber found that there was no question of the retrospective imposition of a heavier penalty because the change in the law was not a part of the 'penalty' imposed upon him but rather related solely to the 'execution of the sentence'. Nonetheless, a majority of the Grand Chamber held that there had been a breach of Article 7. Recognizing for the first time a free-standing notion of 'quality of law' in Article 7, akin to the 'prescribed by law' criterion in relation to the qualified rights,

---

[533] (2007) 45 EHRR 2.
[534] Ibid, para 52.
[535] (2007) 45 EHRR 2.
[536] (2008) 25 BHRC 591.

the majority concluded that Cypriot law was not sufficiently clear for the applicant to discern the scope of the penalty of life imprisonment and therefore Article 7 had been breached. As the dissenting judges noted,[537] the majority's reasoning is obscure. If the nature of the sentence was unforeseeable at the time of its imposition, then a later extension in that same sentence ought logically to constitute a heavier penalty. It remains to be seen whether the ECtHR will apply the notion of the 'quality of law' in future judgments on Article 7.[538]

In *Del Rio Prada v Spain*,[539] the Grand Chamber held, by a majority, that a change in the way in which remission was calculated under Spanish law breached Article 7. There had been a prior consistent practice whereby remission accrued through employment was calculated by reference to a statutory 30-year maximum period of detention rather than the notional total period of individual sentences imposed. However, a judicial decision altered this approach so that the applicant would, contrary to her clear expectation based on prior practice, be released a significant number of years later. The Court found this novel judicial interpretation not to be reasonably foreseeable and to go beyond 'mere prison policy' so as in effect to redefine the penalty imposed. The minority would have held the change to fall within the state's margin of appreciation in respect of measures relating to the execution of the penalty identified in *Kafkaris*. **7.235**

In line with the Strasbourg jurisprudence on sentencing, the domestic courts have held that an increase in sentencing guidelines is not inconsistent with Article 7, provided the sentence does not exceed the maximum applicable at the time of commission of the offence.[540] **7.236**

In *R v Offen* the Court of Appeal rejected the argument that the imposition of an automatic life sentence after the commission of a second serious offence constituted a heavier penalty for the first offence.[541] The correctness of this approach has been confirmed by the Grand Chamber's decision in *Achour v France*.[542] **7.237**

There has been a stream of cases concerning the application of Article 7 to 'extended' sentences.[543] These sentences comprise both a custodial and a licence period, and may be imposed upon individuals convicted of certain serious offences. The domestic courts have followed the approach in *Achour v France*. In *R v Uttley* the House of Lords held that the imposition of the licence period for sentences prior to coming into effect of the relevant statute would not breach Article 7.[544] The **7.238**

---

[537] See the joint partly dissenting opinion of Judge Loucaides and Judge Jociene.

[538] See *Ismoilov and ors v Russia* [2008] ECHR 2947/06 for an example of the concept applied in relation to Art 5.

[539] App No 42750/09, 21 October 2013, GC.

[540] *R v Alden and Wright* [2001] EWCA Crim 296, [2001] 2 Cr App R 275; *R v Bao* [2007] EWCA Crim 2871.

[541] [2001] 1 WLR 253.

[542] (2007) 45 EHRR 2.

[543] *JT* [2003] EWCA Crim 111; *R v R (B)* [2003] EWCA Crim 2199, [2004] 1 WLR 490; *R (Uttley) v Secretary of State for the Home Department* [2004] UKHL 38, [2004] 1 WLR 2278.

[544] Ibid.

defendant in *Uttley* had his complaint against the UK Government declared inadmissible by the ECtHR, indicating that the position adopted by the House of Lords is Convention-compliant.[545]

7.239   In *R v Bamber* the Court of Appeal upheld a whole life tariff for murder imposed after a review of the sentence in accordance with the Criminal Justice Act 2003 on the basis that the law against retrospectivity ensured that the sentence could not be increased or extended following review.[546]

7.240   In a rare finding of a violation of Article 7, the Court of Appeal held that the enforcement of a confiscation order made against an individual under the Drug Trafficking Act 1994 would offend the prohibition on heavier penalties as the order would have been discharged under the Act in force at the time of the offence.[547] However, the appellant had not sought an appropriate remedy—a declaration of incompatibility—and thus the court could not itself discharge the order.

4. Article 7(2): general principles of law of civilized nations

7.241   Article 7(2) sets out a narrow exception to the general principles embodied in Article 7(1). It permits retrospectivity in relation to behaviour which was 'criminal according to the general principles of law recognized by civilized nations'. The original purpose behind it was to ensure that the rule against retrospectivity did not affect the laws passed in the aftermath of the Second World War in order to punish war crimes, treason, and collaboration.[548]

7.242   As Article 7(1) already provides that it will not be violated if the conduct in question was illegal under international law at the time of commission, Article 7(2) is rarely relied upon in European Court decisions. The Court has repeatedly held that where it makes a finding under Article 7(1) it will not consider Article 7(2).[549]

7.243   The scope of the conduct covered by Article 7(2) is unclear. It could cover, for example, behaviour condemned by the international community, but not yet having achieved the status of an international 'crime', such as (arguably) 'aggression'.[550]

7.244   Domestic courts have relied not only on the ECtHR's flexibility principle under Article 7(1); they have also pointed to the Article 7(2) exception. In the marital rape cases, for example, the courts have noted that Article 7(2) provides ample justification for a man's trial for the rape of his wife, according to the general principles recognized by civilized nations.[551]

7.245   In *Maktouf and Damjanovic v Bosnia and Herzegovina*, the Grand Chamber rejected an argument that if an act was criminal under 'the general principles of law recognised by civilised nations' within the meaning of Article 7(2) at the time

---

[545] App No 36946/03, 29 November 2005.
[546] [2009] EWCA Crim 962.
[547] *Togher v Revenue and Customs Prosecution Office* [2007] EWCA Civ 686, [2008] QB 476.
[548] *Papon v France* App No 54210/00, 15 November 2001, ECHR 2001-XII.
[549] See, eg *Streletz, Kessler and Krenz v Germany* (2001) 33 EHRR 751, para 108.
[550] See, further, *R v Jones and Ayliffe* [2006] UKHL 16, [2007] 1 AC 136.
[551] See, eg *R v C* [2004] EWCA Crim 292, [2004] 1 WLR 2098.

when it was committed, then the rule of non-retroactivity of crimes and punishments did not apply.[552]

E. ARTICLE 8: RIGHT TO RESPECT FOR
PRIVATE AND FAMILY LIFE

The overarching concern of Article 8 is to protect 'rights of central importance to 7.246
the individual's identity, self-determination, physical and moral integrity, maintenance of relationships with others and a settled and secure place in the community'.[553] These rights apply to 'everyone', which includes legal persons in some circumstances.[554]

Article 8 formally comprises four elements: private life; family life; home; and 7.247
correspondence; but it is a sprawling article that encompasses a growing number of diverse rights, including the right to privacy. In some cases an interference will affect more than one of the elements of Article 8, and in rare cases all four elements will be violated.[555] Given their scope, Article 8 rights are often closely connected to other rights protected under various other Convention articles, in particular Articles 9, 10, 11, and Protocol 1, Article 1.

Article 8 has provided extremely fertile ground for domestic litigation. It has 7.248
been raised in a vast number of contexts and has proved influential in many areas. The impact of Article 8 on domestic law has been more marked than that of some other articles. This is in part because of the absence of any established free-standing right to privacy in UK law prior to the Human Rights Act 1998.[556]

Since the introduction of the Human Rights Act 1998 domestic judgments 7.249
concerning Article 8 have generally been in step with Strasbourg, sometimes even going further than the ECtHR.[557] Like the ECtHR, the domestic courts' threshold for engaging Article 8(1) is generally low, as Lord Bingham acknowledged in *London Borough of Harrow v Qazi*.[558] However, there have been a number of cases in which domestic courts and Strasbourg have markedly diverged.[559] In common with their approach under other articles of the Convention, the domestic courts have on occasion adopted a narrow view of the rights protected under Article 8 and a relaxed approach to proportionality under Article 8(2).

---

[552] App Nos 2312/08 and 34179/08, 18 July 2013 at [72].

[553] *Connors v UK* (2005) 40 EHRR 9, para 82.

[554] *Wieser and Bicos Beteiligungen v Austria* (2008) 46 EHRR 54.

[555] See *Ayder and ors v Turkey* [2004] ECHR 23656/94, para 119; *Selçuk and Asker v Turkey* (1998) 26 EHRR 477, para 86; *Mentes and ors v Turkey* [1998] ECHR 23186/94, para 73.

[556] See *Wainwright v Home Office* [2003] UKHL 53, [2004] 2 AC 406; *Wainwright v UK* (2006) 42 EHRR 41. See also *Malone v Commissioner of Police* [1979] Ch 344; *Kaye v Robertson* [1991] FSR 62.

[557] In particular, in relation to non-traditional relationships, see *Ghaidan v Godin-Mendoza* [2004] UKHL 30, [2004] 2 AC 557; *Fitzpatrick v Sterling Housing* [2001] 1 AC 27.

[558] [2003] UKHL 43, [2004] 1 AC 983 at [8]–[10]. See also *R (Wood) v Commissioner of Police of the Metropolis* [2009] EWCA Civ 414 at [28].

[559] See, eg *S and Marper v UK* (2008) 48 EHRR 1169; *Kay v UK* App No 37341/06, 21 September 2010.

1. Positive obligations

7.250 The notion of 'respect' under Article 8 encompasses both a positive and a negative aspect. As the ECtHR explained in early cases:

[It] does not merely compel the state to abstain from interference: in addition to this, there may be positive obligations inherent in an effective respect for private and family life even in the sphere of the relations of individuals between themselves.[560]

This dual aspect has given the article much of its breadth in both European and domestic law. Since the early decisions under Article 8, which recognized positive obligations only where there was a serious impact on core rights, the positive aspect of Article 8 now accounts for a very significant part of the ECtHR's jurisprudence.[561]

7.251 The principles applicable to the positive and negative obligations will be similar.[562] In imposing either such obligation, regard must be had to the fair balance that has to be struck between the competing interests of the individual and of the community as a whole.[563] As the ECtHR has held, the concept of 'respect' is 'not precisely defined' and therefore the state enjoys a certain margin of appreciation in how it discharges its positive or negative obligations.[564]

7.252 Many of the positive obligations recognized under Article 8 have been procedural. It is well-established, for example, that there is an obligation on the state to allow parents sufficient involvement in decisions taken by public authorities in relation to fostering and access arrangements and taking children into care.[565] In domestic law, the High Court has held that it is arguable that the police may be under a positive obligation to inform citizens of information that indicates that respect for their private life is potentially threatened.[566] The House of Lords has held that barring individuals suspected of misconduct from work without the right to make representations violates Article 8.[567]

7.253 Article 8 may also impose substantive positive obligations on the state. The ECtHR has accepted that in some circumstances it may be necessary to provide social housing in order to fulfil Article 8 obligations.[568] In *Anufrijeva v Southwark LBC* the Court of Appeal held that Article 8 was capable of imposing a positive obligation on the state to provide an individual with welfare support in order to ensure respect for his or her private and family life, although it was unlikely that it

---

[560] *Marckx v Belgium* (1979) 2 EHRR 330, para 31; *Airey v Ireland* (1979) 2 EHRR 305, para 32; *Secretary of State for Work and Pensions v M* [2006] UKHL 11, [2006] 2 AC 91 at [62].

[561] See Mowbray, *The Development of Positive Obligations under the European Convention on Human Rights by the European Court of Human Rights* (London: Hart Publishing, 2004).

[562] See, eg *Evans v UK* (2008) 46 EHRR 34, para 75.

[563] See, eg *Von Hannover v Germany* (2006) 43 EHRR 7, para 57; *Botta v Italy* (1998) 4 BHRC 81, para 33; *Keegan v Ireland* (1994) 18 EHRR 342, para 49.

[564] *Ucar v Turkey* [2006] ECHR 52392/99, para 135.

[565] *W v UK* (1987) 10 EHRR 29; *R v UK* (1988) 10 EHRR 74; *T and KM v UK* (2002) 34 EHRR 2.

[566] *Bryant and ors v Commissioner of Police for the Metropolis* [2011] EWHC 1314 (Admin) at [54].

[567] *R (Wright) v Secretary of State for Health and anor* [2009] UKHL 3, [2009] 2 WLR 267; see also *R (Royal College of Nursing and ors) v Secretary of State for the Home Department* [2010] EWHC 2761 (Admin).

[568] *Marzari v Italy* (1999) 28 EHRR CD 175; *O'Rourke v UK* App No 39022/97, 26 June 2001; cf *Chapman v UK* (2001) 10 BHRC 48.

would require an individual to be provided with welfare support when his or her predicament was not sufficiently severe to engage Article 3.[569] The Grand Chamber has also held that a failure to have in place certain criminal laws, such as suitable laws criminalizing child pornography, will breach the state's positive obligations under Article 8.[570]

The imposition of positive obligations is not unbounded, however. Controversially, the ECtHR has at times refrained from recognizing obligations in relation to provisions for the disabled. In *Botta v Italy*, for example, it was held that respect for private life did not extend to giving a disabled person a right of access to the beach.[571] The ECtHR and the domestic courts have repeatedly held that Article 8 does not guarantee a right to medical treatment or particular level of social care.[572] It is notable, too, that both Strasbourg and the domestic courts often take a 'light touch' approach to justification in cases raising positive obligations, emphasizing the resource implications of imposing a positive obligation.[573] This is well illustrated by *R (McDonald) v Royal Kensington and Chelsea Royal LBC*,[574] in which the Supreme Court gave short shrift to the contention that withdrawal of a care package for a urinary incontinent severely mobility-impaired individual, so as to require her to resort to use of incontinence pads during the night, violated Article 8. The ECtHR upheld the Supreme Court's decision, noting the breadth of the state's margin of appreciation in respect of decisions with resource implications.[575] 7.254

2. Article 8(2)

Article 8 is a qualified right. In order to be justified, however, an interference by the state with a person's Article 8 rights must fall within one of the exceptions detailed in Article 8(2) and must meet the general requirements of justification (it must be in accordance with law and necessary in a democratic society). 7.255

Concerns about whether or not a measure is in accordance with the law previously arose relatively rarely under Article 8, but have received increasing prominence. In the case of *Liberty v UK*, for example, the ECtHR considered the system of mass interception of telephone calls between the United Kingdom and Ireland, finding that the law did not 'indicate with reasonable clarity the scope and manner of exercise of the relevant discretion conferred on the public authorities'.[576] The 7.256

---

[569] [2003] EWCA Civ 1406, [2004] QB 1124.
[570] *Soderman v Sweden*, App No 5786/08, 12 July 2013, GC.
[571] (1998) 26 EHRR 241; *R (D) v Haringey LBC* [2005] EWHC 2235 (Admin).
[572] *Sentges v Netherlands* [2003] ECHR 715; *Pentiacova v Moldova* (2005) 40 EHRR SE23; *R (T and ors) v London Borough of Haringey* [2005] EWHC 2235 (Admin); *R (AC) v Berkshire West Primary Care Trust* [2011] EWCA Civ 247; *R (Condliff) v North Staffordshire PCT* [2011] EWHC 872 (Admin); *R (Macdonald) v Royal Borough of Kensington and Chelsea* [2010] EWCA Civ 1109.
[573] *Abdulaziz, Cabales and Balkandali v UK* (1985) 7 EHRR 471, para 67; *Pentiacova v Moldova* App No 14462/03, 4 January 2005; *R (W) v Lambeth LBC* [2002] EWCA Civ 613, [2002] 2 FLR 327; *Ekinci v London Borough of Hackney* [2001] EWCA Civ 776, [2002] HLR 2.
[574] [2011] UKSC 33, [2011] 4 All ER 881.
[575] *McDonald v UK* App No 4241/12, 20 May 2014.
[576] (2009) 48 EHRR 1, para 69.

United Kingdom's secret programme of mass surveillance, which came to light following the revelations by the US whistleblower Edward Snowden, is to be considered by the ECtHR in *Big Brother Watch and anor v United Kingdom*, and in particular whether the system of authorization under the Regulation of Investigatory Powers Act 2000 suffices to render the interferences with Article 8 rights in accordance with law.[577]

7.257   In a recent decision in *Gillan v UK* the ECtHR, in disagreement with the House of Lords, held that the powers of stop and search under the Terrorism Act 2000 were overbroad and did not contain adequate safeguards against abuse.[578] The decision highlights that the requirement that an interference must be 'in accordance with the law' imposes a substantive as well as a formal burden on the state to ensure that the quality of the law accords with Convention safeguards against arbitrariness.

7.258   The bulk of cases turn on questions of proportionality under Article 8(2). A different degree of scrutiny applies depending on the nature of the right at stake. Thus, in cases concerning the 'most intimate aspects of private life' the Court adopts a more intensive standard of review.[579] The cases considered under the four elements of Article 8 below illustrate the fact-sensitive application of the proportionality standard.

3. Private life

7.259   The ECtHR takes a broad approach to the notion of 'private life'. In *Niemietz v Germany* the Court held that the concept could not be restricted to an 'inner circle' in which an individual chooses to live his or her life, but also encompassed the right to develop one's personality through relationships with others.[580] More recently, the ECtHR has referred to a 'zone of interaction of a person with others' in public or private that falls within private life.[581] In *Gillan v UK* the ECtHR affirmed this approach and found that a search of a person and his belongings conducted by a police officer in a public place constituted a 'clear interference' with Article 8.[582]

7.260   Increasingly, the ECtHR emphasizes the importance of the principle of personal autonomy manifested in the ability to conduct one's life as one chooses.[583] As it stated in *Pretty v UK*:

> Though no previous case has established as such any right to self-determination as being contained in Article 8 of the Convention, the Court considers that the notion of personal autonomy is an important principle underlying the interpretation of its guarantees.[584]

---

[577] App No 57180/2013, communicated to the UK Government on 9 January 2014.
[578] (2010) 28 BHRC 420.
[579] See, eg *Dudgeon v UK* (1981) 4 EHRR 149.
[580] (1992) 16 EHRR 97, para 29.
[581] *PG and JH v UK* [2001] ECHR 44787/98, para 56; *Peck v UK* (2003) 36 EHRR 41, para 57; *Von Hannover v Germany No 2* App Nos 40660/08 and 60641/08, 7 February 2012, GC at [95], (2012) 55 EHRR 15.
[582] (2010) 28 BHRC 420.
[583] Marshall, 'A right to personal autonomy at the European Court of Human Rights' (2008) EHRLR 337.
[584] (1998) 26 EHRR 241, para 32.

The Court found that there could be an interference with Article 8 where an individual was prevented by law from exercising his or her choice about how and when to die, but such an interference was justified by Article 8(2).[585]

'Physical and mental integrity' are also aspects of private life that the state is obliged to protect.[586] This has led to findings of violations for failure to obtain consent for medical treatment[587] and failure to protect women from domestic violence.[588] In *Tysiac v Poland* the ECtHR found that the failure to permit the applicant to have a therapeutic abortion in order to protect her sight from deterioration violated her right to a private life.[589] In *Tysiac* the Court preferred to analyse the case on the basis of physical integrity rather than personal autonomy, but it is now clear from the decision in *A, B and C v Ireland* that the right to personal autonomy will also be engaged in the abortion context.[590] In many cases the line between physical integrity and personal autonomy may not always need to be clearly drawn. — 7.261

The domestic courts have spoken in similar terms of the notion of private life. Lord Bingham held in *R (Razgar) v Secretary of State for the Home Department* that it extended 'to those features which are integral to a person's identity or ability to function socially as a person'.[591] In *R Purdy v DPP* the House of Lords accepted, that Article 8 encompassed a right to choose how to die.[592] Baroness Hale said: 'If we are serious about protecting autonomy we have to accept that autonomous individuals have different views about what makes their lives worth living.'[593] — 7.262

In *R (Countryside Alliance) v Attorney General*, the House of Lords found that Article 8(1) was not engaged by the ban on hunting with dogs under the Hunting Act 2004.[594] A majority of their Lordships considered that the public nature of fox hunting distinguished it from cases such as *Pretty* that had involved 'very personal and private concerns'.[595] Only Lord Brown lamented that Article 8(1) did not cover 'wider concepts of self-fulfilment'. In fact, the Strasbourg approach to private life is likely to encompass hunting activities. As the ECtHR has stated, Article 8 protects the 'totality of social ties' between an individual and his community.[596] — 7.263

However, the ECtHR has at times clearly indicated that certain matters fall outside the scope of even the broad reach of the concept of 'private life'. For example, in *Gilberg v Sweden*, the Grand Chamber made clear that the imposition of a criminal conviction does not in itself constitute an interference with the convict's right to respect for private life, despite the foreseeable personal, social, psychological, and economic suffering for the convicted person.[597] — 7.264

---

[585] See also *R (Purdy) v DPP* [2009] UKHL 45, [2010] 1 AC 345.
[586] See, eg *Bensaid v UK* (2001) 33 EHRR 10, para 47.
[587] *MAK and RK v UK* App Nos 45901/05 and 40146/06, 23 March 2010.
[588] See, eg *A v Croatia* App No 55164/08, 14 October 2010.
[589] (2007) 22 BHRC 155.
[590] App No 25579/05, 16 December 2010.
[591] [2004] UKHL 27, [2004] 2 AC 368.
[592] [2009] UKHL 45, [2010] 1 AC 345.
[593] Ibid at [66].
[594] [2007] UKHL 52, [2008] 1 AC 719.
[595] Ibid at [15].
[596] *Üner v Netherlands* (2007) 45 EHRR 14, para 59.
[597] App No 41723/06, 3 April 2012 at [68].

7.265   As the cases just discussed illustrate, it is impossible to identify precisely the boundaries of private life, but the following examples illustrate some of the areas in which Strasbourg and the domestic courts have found that it exists for the purposes of Article 8(1).

(a) *Sexuality and transsexuality*

7.266   It is clear that sexuality is not only an element of private life for the purposes of Article 8, but 'a most intimate aspect' of the individual's private life.[598] Homosexual activity falls within the sphere of private life.[599] The ECtHR held in *Smith and Grady v UK* that investigations conducted by the Ministry of Defence into the sexual orientation of members of the services, together with their consequent discharge from the armed forces, constituted 'especially grave' interferences with their private lives. The ECtHR rejected the Government's argument that such a policy was justified to preserve the morale of the fighting forces, saying that the Ministry of Defence could not ignore widespread and developing views in other contracting states in favour of the admission of homosexuals into the armed forces of those states.[600] Similarly, in *EB v France* the Court found a violation of Article 14 in conjunction with Article 8 in circumstances where the homosexual applicant, who was in a stable long-term relationship, was refused approval for adoption having regard, among other things, to her 'conditions of life'.[601] Similarly, in *X and Y v Austria*, the Grand Chamber held that a law excluding unmarried same-sex partners from adopting their partner's children, in circumstances where opposite-sex unmarried partners could do so, violated Article 14 in conjunction with Article 8.[602]

7.267   Article 8 has been held to protect the right of a transsexual to have his or her new gender respected by the state, though it does not impose any obligation to provide gender reassignment surgery.[603] In *B v France* the ECtHR held that the French Government violated Article 8 when it refused to allow a change to the applicant's birth certificate.[604] Though the ECtHR took a different view in a number of cases from the United Kingdom in the 1980s and 1990s,[605] in the landmark case of *Goodwin v UK* it was held that the United Kingdom had failed to comply with a positive obligation to ensure the right of the applicant, a post-operative male-to-female transsexual, to respect for her private life, in particular through the lack of legal recognition given to her gender reassignment.[606] The Court found that there was no longer a margin of appreciation on such issues as society could 'reasonably be expected to tolerate a certain inconvenience to enable individuals to live in

---

[598] *Dudgeon v UK* (1981) 4 EHRR 149.
[599] *ADT v UK* (2001) 31 EHRR 33.
[600] (2000) 29 EHRR 548.
[601] (2008) 47 EHRR 21.
[602] App No 19010/07, 19 February 2013.
[603] *R (AC) v Berkshire West Primary Care Trust* [2011] EWCA Civ 247.
[604] (1992) 16 EHRR 1.
[605] *Rees v UK* (1987) 9 EHRR 56; *Cossey v UK* (1990) 13 EHRR 622; *Sheffield and Horsham v UK* (1999) 27 EHRR 163.
[606] (2002) 35 EHRR 18.

dignity and worth in accordance with the sexual identity chosen by them at great personal cost'.[607]

Following the *Goodwin* case, the House of Lords issued a declaration of incompatibility in relation to legislation that failed to recognize the validity of a purported marriage in 1981 between a man and a male-to-female transperson.[608] The law was subsequently changed by the Gender Recognition Act 2004.[609]   7.268

In *R (AB) v Secretary of State for Justice* the High Court considered that a decision to keep a post-operative male-to-female transsexual in a women's prison violated Article 8.[610]   7.269

(b) *Parenthood*

The ECtHR has consistently held that the right to start a family is not protected by respect for family life, which depends on existing family relations.[611] However, decisions about whether or not to become a parent may fall within the scope of private life. In *Evans v UK*[612] the Grand Chamber of the ECtHR upheld the Court of Appeal's decision that the legal obligation to obtain the male partner's consent to the storage and implantation of embryos created prior to the breakdown of his relationship with the applicant did not violate Article 8.[613] The Court accepted that 'private life' encompassed the right to respect for the decision to become a parent, but that right had to be balanced with the male partner's right under Article 8 to choose not to become a parent. The domestic law struck a fair balance between the two rights.   7.270

In contrast to *Evans*, in *Dickson v UK* the ECtHR took the view that there had been a violation of Article 8 on account of the refusal to allow a request for artificial insemination treatment by a prisoner whose wife was at liberty, since a fair balance had not been struck between the conflicting public and private interests.[614] In a recent decision concerning IVF (in-vitro fertilization) the ECtHR found that there was no obligation on the state to provide IVF but if it made such provision it had to do so in a non-discriminatory manner.[615]   7.271

Recently in *S and H v Austria*, the Grand Chamber held by a majority that a prohibition on the use of donor eggs and sperm did not violate Article 8 at the relevant point in time that the domestic decisions were taken (1999), but it noted that this was an area subject to particularly dynamic development in science and law, and appeared to signal that it could well reach a different conclusion in the future.[616]   7.272

---

[607] Ibid, para 91.
[608] *Bellinger v Bellinger* [2003] UKHL 21, [2003] 2 AC 467.
[609] See also *Grant v UK* (2007) 44 EHRR 1 considering the delay in implementing the legislation.
[610] [2009] EWHC 2220 (Admin).
[611] See para 7.307.
[612] *Evans v UK* (2008) 46 EHRR 34.
[613] (2007) 22 BHRC 190. Cf *L v Human Fertilisation and Embryology Authority* [2008] EWHC 2149 (Fam), [2008] 2 FLR 1999.
[614] (2007) 24 BHRC 19.
[615] *ISH and ors v Austria* App No 57813/00, 1 April 2010.
[616] *S and H v Austria* App No 57813/00, 3 November 2011.

7.273   The ECtHR has held that Article 8 protects the right to choose where to give birth. In *Ternovszky v Hungary* the Court found that the liability of midwives to prosecution for assisting at home births violated Article 8.[617]

(c) Private information

7.274   The right to a private life under Article 8 also includes the right in certain circumstances not to have private information retained by the state or disclosed to third parties. This includes, for example, the retention of private information by the police,[618] the unnecessary disclosure of confidential medical data in legal proceedings,[619] and the unauthorized passing on of medical information from a hospital to authorities in the process of verifying a claim for social insurance and disability benefit.[620] Article 8 also imposes a positive obligation on the state to provide copies of personal information it stores unless there are compelling reasons for refusing to do so.[621]

7.275   In *R (S) v Chief Constable of South Yorkshire* the House of Lords considered the long-term retention of DNA taken in the course of criminal investigations as authorized by section 64 of the Police and Criminal Evidence Act 1984.[622] A majority of their Lordships found that while the taking and use of such information could constitute an interference under Article 8(1), the retention of the samples could not.

7.276   In a striking decision, the Grand Chamber in *S and Marper v UK* held that the majority of the House of Lords had adopted too narrow a view; DNA retention was an interference with the right to privacy.[623] Moreover, 'the blanket and indiscriminate nature of the powers of retention of the fingerprints, cellular samples and DNA profiles of persons suspected but not convicted of offences' failed to strike a fair balance between the interests of the state and individual.[624] In response to the decision the Coalition Government enacted arrangements for limited retention or deletion depending on individual circumstances in the Protection of Freedoms Act 2012. The Protection of Freedoms Bill was in its early stages when the Supreme Court decided the appeal in *R (GC) v Metropolitan Police Commissioner*,[625] a rerun of *S and Marper*. It was common ground that the existing system violated Article 8. The Supreme Court read down section 64 so that it imposed a wide discretion on the police to issue guidelines on the management of the database that ensured respect for Article 8 rights.

---

[617] App No 67545/09, 14 December 2010.
[618] *S and Marper v UK* (2008) 48 EHRR 1169; *R (Wood) v Commissioner of Police for the Metropolis* [2009] EWCA Civ 414, [2009] 4 All ER 951; *R (Catt) v ACPO* [2013] EWCA Civ 192, [2013] 3 All ER 583.
[619] *Z v Finland* (1998) 25 EHRR 371.
[620] *MS v Sweden* (1999) 28 EHRR 313.
[621] *KH v Slovakia* App No 32881/04, 28 April 2009.
[622] [2004] UKHL 39, [2004] 4 All ER 193.
[623] App Nos 30562/04 and 30566/04, 4 December 2008.
[624] Ibid, para 125.
[625] [2011] UKSC 21.

The Supreme Court has also considered the compatibility of lifelong registration 7.277
of sex offenders with Article 8. In *R (F and Thompson) v Secretary of State for the
Home Department* the Court held that the absence of a mechanism by which a sex
offender could review his or her lifelong inclusion on the register was a disproportionate interference with his or her private life.[626]

In *T and ors v Chief Constable of Greater Manchester*,[627] the Court of Appeal held 7.278
that the system for disclosure of spent convictions pursuant to enhanced criminal
record checks when applying for certain prescribed jobs was incompatible with
Article 8. The disclosure of such spent convictions interfered with affected individuals' private life rights both because it entailed disclosing sensitive personal
information from their past and because it prevented development of relations with
others by inhibiting employment prospects. The system, which required the disclosure of all spent convictions regardless of relevance to the position applied for,
was not a proportionate scheme. The Court of Appeal's decision was upheld by the
Supreme Court.[628]

The ECtHR has on occasion found that private life encompasses the right to pro- 7.279
tect one's reputation.[629] However, the ECtHR recently appeared to retreat from this
position. In *Karakó v Hungary* it distinguished personal integrity, which is protected
by Article 8, from mere reputation, which is explicitly referred to as a restriction on
the exercise of free speech under Article 10(2).[630] The judgment did not explicitly
overrule earlier decisions of the Court and it was therefore unclear whether harm to
reputation which does not have an impact on personal integrity is protected by Article
8. The Supreme Court considered this case law in *Re Guardian News Media* finding
that reputation was an aspect of private life and that the ECtHR had not intended to
remove it from the scope of Article 8.[631] Subsequent case law of the ECtHR has made
clear that Article 8 does indeed protect against harm to reputation.[632]

(d) *Surveillance*

In general, most forms of surveillance by the state will constitute an interference 7.280
with the right to private life and may also interfere with the right to respect for
correspondence.[633] However, in *Peck v UK* the ECtHR held that real-time CCTV
footage did not infringe Article 8(1) where the images were not recorded.[634]

In *PG v UK* the ECtHR found that the recording of a suspect in his police cell 7.281
interfered with his right to respect for private life.[635] In *R (Wood) v Commissioner of*

---

[626] [2010] UKSC 17, [2011] 1 AC 331, 2 WLR 992.
[627] [2013] EWCA Civ 25, [2013] 2 All ER 813.
[628] [2014] UKSC 35.
[629] See, eg *Pfeifer v Austria* (2007) 24 BHRC 167.
[630] App No 39311/05, 28 July 2009.
[631] [2010] UKSC 1. See also *Spiller and anor v Joseph and ors* [2010] UKSC 53, [2011] AC 852, at [75].
[632] Eg *Wegrzynowski and anor v Poland* (2013) 36 BHRC 573.
[633] See, eg *Halford v UK* (1997) 24 EHRR 523 (interception of telephone calls); *Khan v UK* (2001) 31
EHRR 45 (listening device in home).
[634] (2003) 36 EHRR 41.
[635] [2001] ECHR 44787/98.

Police for the Metropolis the Court of Appeal found that the retention by police of photographs of a protestor in the street for the purposes of gathering evidence about possible civil disorder violated Article 8.[636] However, Article 8 was not engaged by the mere taking of a photograph in the absence of aggravating circumstances.

7.282   In the pending application in *Big Brother Watch and anor v United Kingdom*,[637] the ECtHR will consider whether the United Kingdom's secret programme of mass surveillance, which came to light following the revelations by the US whistleblower Edward Snowden, is compatible with Article 8.[638] When the ECtHR previously considered the UK's surveillance regime in the Regulation of Investigatory Powers Act 2000 in *Kennedy v United Kingdom*,[639] it found it to be compatible with Article 8, noting the absence of evidence of any significant shortcomings in its application and operation. The ECtHR will need to grapple with whether the rapid development of state surveillance capabilities and corresponding use, as recently publicized, has altered this position.

(e) *Environmental damage*

7.283   The ECtHR has accepted that environmental damage, such as the amount of air traffic over an applicant's home, may interfere with an individual's private life even if the intrusions are 'unavoidable consequences of measures not directed against private individuals'.[640] In *Lopez Ostra v Spain* it was held that permitting a waste treatment plant to operate in breach of a licence condition may affect the right of enjoyment of people's homes and so affect their right to private and family life even if it did not adversely affect their health.[641] The Court has also consistently held that the failure of the authorities to deal with noise pollution by private individuals may violate Article 8.[642]

7.284   While the state enjoys a margin of appreciation in relation to environmental decisions, the ECtHR will carefully scrutinize the decision-making process undertaken by the state in imposing particular environmental burdens on groups of its citizens.[643] In *Fadeyeva v Russia* the ECtHR held:

> it is certainly within the Court's jurisdiction to assess whether the Government approached the problem with due diligence and gave consideration to all competing interests. In this respect, the Court reiterates that the onus is on the State to justify, using detailed and rigorous data, a situation in which certain individuals bear a heavy burden on behalf of the rest of the community.[644]

---

[636] [2009] EWCA Civ 414, [2009] 4 All ER 951.
[637] App No 57180/2013, communicated to the UK Government on 9 January 2014.
[638] Ibid.
[639] (2010) 29 BHRC 341.
[640] *Rayner v UK* (1986) 47 DR 5. See also *Hatton v UK* (2002) 34 EHRR 1. In both cases it was held that the intrusions were justified under Art 8(2).
[641] (1995) 20 EHRR 27. See also *Taskin v Turkey* (2006) 42 EHRR 50.
[642] See, eg *DEES v Hungary* App No 2345/06, 9 November 2010.
[643] *Hatton v UK* (2002) 34 EHRR 1.
[644] [2005] ECHR 55723/00, para 128.

Where the state fails to show how its analysis led to a particular policy decision, the ECtHR will draw an adverse inference that insufficient weight has been given to the interests of communities that are particularly badly affected. In certain circumstances, therefore, failure to conduct an environmental impact assessment (EIA) will violate the right to respect for private life, family life, and home under Article 8.[645] Conversely, where the state can demonstrate it has an appropriate regulatory system in place and has, in a particular case, appropriately weighed the relevant interests, the ECtHR will not find a breach of Article 8.[646]

The domestic courts have applied this line of Strasbourg jurisprudence in a num- 7.285 ber of cases.[647]

(f) *Public space*
In earlier jurisprudence, the Strasbourg Court appeared to suggest that the concept 7.286 of private life did not apply to public spaces. However, it is now clear that the key concept is not whether an activity takes place 'in private' or in public, but whether there is adequate respect for a 'reasonable expectation of privacy'.[648]

(g) *Private life and the media*
Article 8 protects individuals from unjustified press intrusion into their private 7.287 lives. Justification is generally based on the right to freedom of expression, and the case law on the right to privacy is therefore intimately connected to that under Article 10.

The ECtHR has often been willing to find that Article 8 outweighs the rights of 7.288 the media, notwithstanding that as a matter of principle Article 10 and Article 8 rights deserve equal respect. In *Lindon, Otchakovsky-Laurens and July v France* the Grand Chamber considered the publication of a novel that attacked Jean-Marie Le Pen, the leader of the French National Front.[649] It concluded that the applicants' convictions for defamation did not violate Article 10. While it was correct that the applicants were permitted to make immoderate statements, particularly with regard to extremist politicians, the claim that Le Pen was 'chief of a gang of killers' and a 'vampire who thrives on the bitterness of his electorate' overstepped permissible limits.[650]

The leading ECtHR case on the right to privacy is *Von Hannover v Germany* 7.289 (the *Princess Caroline* case), in which the ECtHR considered whether the publication of paparazzi photographs of the Princess in various public places, including at restaurants, shops, and a beach club, violated her right to privacy.[651] The Court held

---

[645] *Piera Giacomelli v Italy* [2006] ECHR 59909/00.
[646] Eg *Hardy and Maile v United Kingdom* App No 31965/07, 14 February 2012.
[647] See, eg *Dennis v Ministry of Defence* [2003] EWHC 793 (QB), [2003] Env LR 34; *Andrews v Reading Borough Council* [2005] EWHC 256 (QB). Cf *Marcic v Thames Water Utilities* [2003] UKHL 66, [2004] 2 AC 42.
[648] *Peck v UK* (2003) 36 EHRR 41.
[649] (2008) 46 EHRR 35.
[650] Ibid.
[651] (2006) 43 EHRR 7.

that although the Princess was in a public place she had a 'reasonable expectation of privacy' and Article 8 was therefore engaged. In reaching this conclusion, the Court emphasized that the Princess was not performing any public functions. It reiterated that justification under Article 10 will depend on the importance of the contribution made by photos or articles to a debate of general interest.[652]

7.290   A further application concerning publication of photos of the Prince of Monaco and Princess Caroline was subsequently considered by the Grand Chamber. It took the opportunity to distil the criteria to be considered in weighing Article 8 rights to privacy against the Article 10 rights of the press. Consideration needs to be given to (i) the contribution of the publication to a debate of general interest; (ii) how well known the person who is the subject of the report is; (iii) the prior conduct of the person concerned; (iv) the content, form, and consequences of publication; and (v) the circumstances in which the photo was taken (in particular, whether consent had been given). In the instant case, the German courts had weighed the relevant criteria and not exceeded the margin of appreciation in allowing publication of certain photographs taken without consent (but not surreptitiously) in tandem with an article about the health of the reigning Prince of Monaco, which the domestic courts had accepted was of value to a debate of general interest.

7.291   The ECtHR revisited its privacy jurisprudence in *Mosley v UK*.[653] The *News of the World* published details about the unconventional sexual practices of Max Mosley, the grandson of Oswald Mosley and the president of Formula One's ruling body. The High Court awarded Mosley substantial damages, noting that the fact that his behaviour might be viewed by some with disapproval did not deprive him of the right to privacy.[654] In his complaint to the ECtHR Mosley argued that Article 8 imposed a pre-notification requirement on newspapers intending to publish details of a person's private life. While the ECtHR accepted that the *News of World* had 'flagrantly' violated Mosley's private life, it found that a pre-notification requirement risked creating a chilling effect on freedom of speech. Whether or not such a requirement was necessary fell within the state's margin of appreciation. The Court did not retreat from its position that reports must contribute to a debate of general public interest and emphasized that a 'narrow interpretation' of Article 10 would be adopted where sensational and titillating reporting was involved.

7.292   Prior to the coming into force of the Human Rights Act, domestic law did not recognize a right to privacy in the terms developed by the ECtHR. The tortious actions of breach of confidence and intentional infliction of emotional suffering failed to provide any form of redress to an individual whose privacy had been intruded upon by the media. Article 8 has significantly altered the legal landscape and given rise to some of the most controversial decisions under the Human Rights Act.

---

[652] See also *Tammer v Estonia* (2001) 10 BHRC 543; *News Verlags GmbH and Co KG v Austria* (2000) 9 BHRC 625; *Krone Verlag GmbH and Co KG v Austria* [2002] ECHR 34315/96; *Eerikainen and ors v Finland* [2009] ECHR 3514/02. Cf *Editions Plon v France* [2004] ECHR 58148/00.

[653] App No 48009/08, 10 May 2011.

[654] *Mosley v News Group Newspapers* [2008] EWHC 1777 (QB), [2008] NLJR 1112.

In one of the first 'privacy' cases, *Douglas and ors v Hello! (No 3)*, the Court of 7.293
Appeal held that as a result of the Strasbourg decision in *Von Hannover* the courts
were required to develop the existing cause of action for breach of confidence in
such a way as to give effect to the competing rights of privacy and freedom of
expression conferred by Articles 8 and 10 of the Convention.[655] There would be no
new cause of action for breach of privacy.

The House of Lords considered these issues in *Campbell v MGN*, in which Naomi 7.294
Campbell sought damages for the publication of various details and photographs
relating to her treatment for drug addiction.[656] Lord Hoffmann stated:

the new approach takes a different view of the underlying value which the law protects. Instead
of the cause of action being based upon the duty of good faith applicable to confidential personal
information and trade secrets alike, it focuses upon the protection of human autonomy and
dignity—the right to control the dissemination of information about one's private life and the
right to the esteem and respect of other people.[657]

Similarly, Lord Nicholls explained that respect for privacy was the 'underlying
value' of the tort of breach of confidence, which was now 'better encapsulated as
misuse of private information'.[658]

Following Strasbourg authority, their Lordships held that the critical question to 7.295
be asked in such cases was whether a reasonable person of ordinary sensibilities, if
placed in the same situation as the subject of the disclosure, rather than the recipi-
ent, would find the disclosure offensive. Noting that photographs are in general
a particularly intrusive means of invading privacy, a majority of their Lordships
found that Naomi Campbell had a reasonable expectation of privacy in relation to
the details of her treatment. The publication could not be justified under Article
8(2) or by reference to freedom of expression.[659]

In *Re S (a child) (identification: restrictions on publication)*, a case concerning the 7.296
identification of children in legal proceedings, the House of Lords gave valuable
guidance on the balance to be struck between Articles 8 and 10 where they are in
conflict:

First, neither article [8 or 10] has *as such* precedence over the other. Secondly, where the values
under the two articles are in conflict, an intense focus on the comparative importance of the
specific rights being claimed in the individual case is necessary. Thirdly, the justifications for
interfering with or restricting each right must be taken into account. Finally, the proportionality
test must be applied to each.[660]

On an application of those principles, their Lordships held that the interference 7.297
with the child's Article 8 rights, albeit distressing, was indirect and not of the same

---

[655] [2005] EWCA Civ 595, [2006] QB 125 at [53].
[656] [2004] UKHL 22, [2004] 2 AC 457. The Lords' decision on this point was upheld in *MGN v UK* App
No 39401/04, 18 January 2011.
[657] Ibid at [51].
[658] Ibid at [14]. See also *McKennitt v Ash* [2006] EWCA Civ 1714, [2007] 3 WLR 194.
[659] See also *Murray v Express Newspapers plc* [2008] EWCA Civ 446, [2008] 3 WLR 1360.
[660] [2004] UKHL 47, [2005] 1 AC 593 at [17]. See also *A v B* [2002] EWCA Civ 237, [2003] QB 195; *In
re BBC* [2009] UKHL 34, [2009] 3 WLR 142.

order when compared with cases of juveniles directly involved in criminal trials. By contrast, the Article 10 rights at issue concerned the freedom of the press, subject to statutory restrictions, to report proceedings at criminal trials, which was a valuable check on the criminal process and promoted public confidence in the administration of justice. The consequence of granting the relief sought would be the inhibiting of the press to report criminal trials, at the expense of informed debate about criminal justice.

7.298   The Supreme Court considered the balance between Articles 8 and 10 in *Re Guardian News and Media* in which the press applied to the court to lift the anonymity orders in proceedings concerning the freezing of suspected terrorists assets.[661] In a detailed factual analysis of the balance between Article 8 and 10 in that case, the court found that Article 10 held sway. By anonymizing the parties, the court accepted that it would be harder for the press to interest readers in reports of the court proceedings. The fact that the individuals might be subject to negative publicity as a result of their lifting of anonymity could not be sufficient reason for curtailing freedom of the press.

7.299   The balancing act performed by judges in privacy cases became the subject of fierce media criticism in 2011 when it emerged that on a number of occasions the High Court had granted 'super-injunctions' preventing both the publication of private material and the very existence of the injunction itself.[662] As a result, Lord Neuberger was commissioned to write a report into the procedure relating to prior restraint in privacy cases. His report revealed that such injunctions were rarely granted and generally lasted for a very short period.[663] He recommended that in accordance with of the Human Rights Act 1998[664] the media be made aware when such an injunction had been applied for. This has subsequently become the established practice.

7.300   (i) *The right to decide how and when to die*   In *R (on the application of Pretty) v DPP*,[665] Mrs Pretty, who suffered from the progressive condition of motor neurone disease, complained that the prohibition on assisting suicide in section 2 of the Suicide Act 1961 violated her rights inter alia to private life under Article 8 of the Convention. The House of Lords held that her desire to end her life prematurely did not engage her Article 8 rights. However, the ECtHR disagreed, holding that:[666]

The very essence of the convention is respect for human dignity and human freedom. Without in any way negating the principle of sanctity of life protected under the convention, the court considers that it is under art 8 that notions of the quality of life take on significance...The

---

[661] [2010] UKSC 1, [2010] 2 AC 697. See also *In re BBC* [2009] UKHL 34, [2010] 1 AC 145.

[662] See, eg *John Terry v Persons Unknown* [2010] EWHC 119 (QB); *Donald v Ntuli* [2010] EWCA Civ 1276, [2011] 1 WLR 294.

[663] Report of the Committee on Super-Injunctions; available at <http://www.judiciary.gov.uk/media/media-releases/2011/committee-reports-findings-super-injunctions-20052011>.

[664] See para 7.451.

[665] [2001] UKHL 61, [2002] 1 All ER 1, [2002] 1 AC 800.

[666] *Pretty v UK* (2002) 12 BHRC 149.

applicant in this case is prevented by law from exercising her choice to avoid what she considers will be an undignified and distressing end to her life. The court is not prepared to exclude that this constitutes an interference with her right to respect for private life.

In three subsequent decisions, the ECtHR has stated in even clearer terms that Article 8(1) encompasses the right to decide how and when to die, and in particular the right to avoid a distressing and undignified end to life (provided that the decision is made freely).[667]   7.301

However, the ECtHR has to date held in these cases that a blanket prohibition on assisted suicide can be justified under Article 8(2). It has done so in circumstances where in 36 of the 43 Member States (including the United Kingdom) suicide is strictly prohibited and criminalized by law. The ECtHR has accepted that the prohibition is legitimately aimed at safeguarding life by protecting the weak and vulnerable (and especially those who are not in a condition to take informed decisions), and held that it remains primarily for Member States to assess the risk if the general prohibition on assisted suicides were relaxed or if exceptions were to be created.[668]   7.302

Domestically, in *R (Purdy) v DPP*,[669] the House of Lords accepted that, following *Pretty v UK*, the decision about when to end one's life engages Article 8(1). It found that guidance regarding when the Director of Public Prosecutions (DPP) would exercise his discretion under section 2(4) of the Suicide Act 1961 to allow a prosecution for aiding and abetting suicide was not formulated with sufficient precision to meet the 'in accordance with law' requirement under Article 8(2). The DPP was therefore under a duty to promulgate an offence-specific policy clarifying the relevant factors for and against prosecution and the facts and circumstances which he would take into account in deciding whether a prosecution should be brought.   7.303

Most recently, in *R (Nicklinson and anor) v Ministry of Justice*,[670] a nine-member panel of the Supreme Court rejected a challenge to the absolute prohibition on assisted suicide and the DPP's offence-specific guidelines issued following *Purdy*. A majority[671] of the Court considered that the criminal prohibition on assisted suicide represented a 'grave' interference with the right to private life and indicated that they found the arguments relied on in order to justify this by no means overwhelming, especially when the official attitude to assisted suicide seemed in practice to come close to tolerating it in certain situations. The majority was not, however, prepared at this time to hold the blanket ban to be disproportionate, though it did not consider that it would be constitutionally inappropriate for the Court to do so. Two Justices (Lady Hale and Lord Kerr) did find the prohibition to be disproportionate and would have made a declaration of incompatibility. The minority[672] considered   7.304

---

[667] *Haas v Switzerland* (2011) 53 EHRR 33 at [51]; *Koch v Germany* [2013] 1 FCR 595 [46] and [51]; and *Gross v Switzerland* (2013) 35 BHRC 187 at [60].
[668] Ibid.
[669] [2009] UKHL 45, [2010] 1 AC 345.
[670] [2014] UKSC 38, [2014] 3 All ER 843.
[671] Lord Neuberger, Lady Hale, Lord Mance, Lord Kerr, and Lord Wilson.
[672] Lord Clarke, Lord Sumption, Lord Reed, and Lord Hughes.

that the decision as to whether relaxing or qualifying the absolute prohibition on assisted suicide would involve unacceptable risks to vulnerable people was an issue preeminently for Parliament.

4. Family life

7.305 Article 8 jurisprudence has undergone an evolution, and the definition of 'family life' now firmly encompasses more non-traditional relationships. As Lord Bingham explained in *EM (Lebanon) v Secretary of State for the Home Department*, 'there is no pre-determined model of family or family life to which article 8 must be applied'.[673]

7.306 In assessing whether or not family life exists, it is the substance, not the form of the individual's circumstances that matters. The key question is whether there is 'real existence in practice of close family ties'[674] which is essentially a question of fact.[675] In *Secretary of State for Work and Pensions v M* the House of Lords identified 'love, trust, confidence, mutual dependence and unconstrained social intercourse' as the 'essence of family life'.[676] It was not, however, prepared to hold that a same-sex relationship constituted 'family life' for the purposes of Article 8 in light of the stage of development of the ECtHR case law (which at that time only protected such relationships under the private life aspect of Article 8), but did hold that the relationship between the same-sex couple and their children fell to be protected under the family life aspect.

7.307 The boundaries between Article 8 and Article 12, which protects the right to marry and found a family, are not always distinct. It is clear, however, that Article 8 does not itself protect the right to found a family; it is only applicable once family life is established, although the ambit of Article 8 will be wider for the purposes of Article 14.[677]

(a) *Couples*

7.308 Formal unions, such as a valid marriage between husband and wife, clearly fall within family life.[678] Engagements may also give rise to family life, if supported by evidence of the parties' intention to marry.[679]

7.309 The ECtHR has accepted that 'de facto family ties' may exist in the absence of such a formalized relationship. In *Kroon v Netherlands* the ECtHR determined that factors such as cohabitation and the stability of the relationship may serve to demonstrate that a relationship has sufficient constancy to amount to family life.[680] Polygamous unions may also constitute family life.[681]

---

[673] [2008] UKHL 64, [2009] 1 All ER 559 at [37].

[674] *K v UK* (1986) 50 DR 199; *Lebbink v Netherlands* [2004] 3 FCR 59.

[675] *Singh v Entry Clearance Officer* [2004] EWCA Civ 1075, [2005] QB 608 at [20]; *EM (Lebanon) v Secretary of State for the Home Department* [2008] UKHL 64, [2009] 1 All ER 559 at [37].

[676] [2006] UKHL 11, [2006] 2 AC 91 at [5] per Lord Bingham.

[677] See, eg *EB v France* (2008) 47 EHRR 21.

[678] See *Benes v Austria* (1992) 72 DR 271.

[679] *Wakefield v UK* (1990) 66 DR 251.

[680] (1994) 19 EHRR 263.

[681] *A and A v Netherlands* (1992) 72 DR 118.

(b) Homosexual and transsexual unions

The ECtHR's approach to homosexual unions has evolved. In early ECtHR case   7.310
law homosexual relationships were not protected as family life, although they were
protected under the right to private life.[682] The ECtHR finally recognized that a
stable relationship between cohabiting same-sex individuals was rightly classified as
family life in *Schalk and Kopf v Austria*.[683] However, the ECtHR held that Article 8
read with Article 14 did not guarantee homosexuals the right to marry. Moreover,
while the Court was prepared to accept that the right to marry in Article 12 need
not be limited to marriage between a man and a woman, the question whether or
not to allow same-sex marriage remained a matter for regulation by national law
and Article 12 could not yet be said to impose an obligation to grant a same-sex
couple access to marriage. More recently, in *Valliantos and ors v Greece*, the Grand
Chamber held that the exclusion of same-sex couples from the scope of a new
form of civil partnership in Greece breached Article 8 (both private and family life
aspects) in conjunction with Article 14.[684]

A similar evolution has occurred in relation to transsexual relationships. In   7.311
Goodwin v UK, in a departure from its earlier case law,[685] the ECtHR has held
that the failure to recognize the acquired gender of a post-operative transsexual
in order for that person to marry violated the right to private life and the right to
marry under Article 12.[686] In *X, Y and Z v UK* the ECtHR found de facto family
ties between X, a transsexual, Y, his female partner, and Z, Y's child by artificial
insemination.[687] In *Hamalainen v Finland*, the Grand Chamber confirmed that a
transsexual's relationship with her partner and child fell to be protected under the
family life aspect of Article 8, as well as the private life aspect.[688]

In this area, the domestic approach has proved more flexible than that of the   7.312
ECtHR. The narrow approach to 'family life' taken by the ECtHR in *S v UK*[689]
was not followed in *Ghaidan v Godin-Mendoza*[690] or *Fitzpatrick v Sterling Housing
Association Ltd*,[691] the House of Lords holding that the terms 'spouse' and 'family'
respectively under the Rent Act 1977 could apply to a homosexual partner.

However, in *Secretary of State for Work and Pensions v M*, the House of Lords   7.313
adopted a narrow view, holding that on the present state of Strasbourg jurisprudence homosexual relationships did not fall within the scope of the right to
respect for family life. While their Lordships anticipated the shift in the ECtHR's

---

[682] *Secretary of State for Work and Pensions v M* [2006] UKHL 11, [2006] 2 AC 91 at [30], though the
ECtHR indicated in *JM v UK* (2010) 30 BHRC 60 that a same-sex couple would nowadays be regarded
as a family.

[683] App No 30141/04, 24 June 2010. See also *Valliantos v Greece* App Nos 29381/09 and 32684/09, 7
November 2013.

[684] App Nos 29381/09 and 32684/09, 7 November 2013.

[685] See, eg *Rees v UK* (1987) 9 EHRR 56; *Cossey v UK* (1991) 13 EHRR 622.

[686] *Goodwin v UK* (2002) 35 EHRR 18.

[687] (1997) 24 EHRR 143.

[688] App No 37359/09, 18 July 2014.

[689] (1986) 47 DR 274.

[690] [2004] UKHL 30, [2004] 2 AC 557.

[691] [2001] 1 AC 27.

case law that has now occurred, it 'was not for the courts of this country to pre-empt that decision'.[692] In *Re G (a child)*, Baker J recognized that, following *Schalk and Kopf v Austria*,[693] it is 'now established beyond doubt that the relationship between a same-sex couple constitutes "family life" for the purposes of article 8'.[694]

7.314　Many of the issues relating to recognition of same-sex couples should no longer arise in domestic law as the Civil Partnership Act 2004 permits the legal union of same-sex couples in a manner analogous to marriage and the Marriage (Same Sex Couples) Act 2013 extended marriage under domestic law to same-sex couples from 13 March 2014.

(c) *Parents and children*

7.315　The biological parent/child relationship is well-recognized in Article 8 case law.[695] The ECtHR has held that 'the mutual enjoyment by parent and child of each other's company constitutes a fundamental element of family life'.[696] In *Boughanemi v France* the Court held that the tie between parent and child, regardless of whether the child is legitimate, could only be broken in 'exceptional circumstances'.[697]

7.316　Biological ties give rise to a strong presumption of family life,[698] but it is not conclusive. In *X v UK* the ECmHR held that no sufficient nexus existed between the biological father and an unborn foetus,[699] and a similar result was reached in *G v Netherlands* concerning a sperm donor.[700]

7.317　In *Ahrens v Germany*[701] and *Kautzor v Germany*,[702] fathers sought to rely on their family life rights to establish an entitlement to test for their paternity of children. The ECtHR was not convinced that the right to family life was engaged in either case. In the former case, the father had not demonstrated any interest or commitment to the child before or after birth; and in the latter, he had not spent any time or established a close relationship with the child. In both cases the Court found the private life aspect of Article 8 to be engaged.

7.318　The ECtHR has accepted that family life subsists between estranged parent and child (following a relationship break-up or period of separation) provided a genuine and close tie continues to exist.[703]

---

[692] [2006] UKHL 11, [2006] 2 AC 91 at [30] per Lord Nicholls. The ECtHR found a violation of Art 14 taken with Art 1 of Protocol 1: *JM v UK* (2010) 30 BHRC 60.

[693] App No 30141/04, 24 June 2010.

[694] [2013] EWHC 134 (Fam) at [113].

[695] *Ahmut v Netherlands* (1996) 24 EHRR 62.

[696] *B v UK* (1988) 10 EHRR 87. See also *EM (Lebanon) v Secretary of State for the Home Department* [2008] UKHL 64, [2009] 1 All ER 559 at [6].

[697] (1996) 22 EHRR 228, para 35.

[698] *Keegan v Ireland* (1994) 18 EHRR 342.

[699] (1980) 19 DR 244.

[700] (1993) 16 EHRR CD 38.

[701] App No 45071/09, 22 March 2012,

[702] App No 23338/09, 22 March 2012.

[703] *Berrehab v Netherlands* (1988) 11 EHRR 322.

The right of a child to identify his or her parents is encompassed by family **7.319**
life.[704] However, such cases may raise others' Article 8 rights that conflict with
the applicant's right to family life. In *Odievre v France*, for example, the Grand
Chamber held that there was no violation of Article 8 or 14 in circumstances
where the applicant was unable to obtain information about her natural family
owing to French rules governing 'anonymous births' that protected the mother's
interest in anonymity.[705]

Other familial relationships, such as that between grandparents and grandchil- **7.320**
dren[706] and siblings,[707] may also constitute family life, as may adoption[708] and foster
relationships,[709] depending always on the facts. The courts will examine factors
such as contact, length of the relationship, dependency, and emotional ties.

Family life also encompasses proceedings aimed at dissolving legal family ties. In **7.321**
Mizzi v Malta, for example, the ECtHR accepted that a legal presumption of the
husband's paternity of a child born during the period of the marriage, combined
with the absence of any domestic remedy by which he could have challenged it, violated his right to respect for both private and family life. The ECtHR found a violation of Article 8, as this was 'a situation in which a legal presumption is allowed to
prevail over biological reality'.[710]

The ECtHR has held on a number of occasions that the right to family life does **7.322**
not encompass a right to adoption.[711] Refusal to permit adoption may, however, fall
within the ambit of private life for the purposes of Article 14.[712]

(d) Immigration

The right for an 'alien' to enter or to reside in a particular country is not guaranteed **7.323**
by respect for family life,[713] but the ECtHR has held that the refusal of entry or the
removal of a person from a country where close members of his family are living
may amount to an infringement of the right to respect for family life.[714] If the family can go elsewhere to re-establish itself the ECtHR will hold that the immigration
procedures do not violate that right.[715] Similarly, there may be no violation if the
disruption is of the applicant's own making because he or she has breached immigration controls.[716] In many cases, however, an interference with Article 8(1) will

---

[704] *Mikuli v Croatia* [2002] 1 FCR 720; *Jevremovic v Serbia* [2007] 2 FCR 671; *S v London Borough of Lambeth* [2007] 1 FLR 152.
[705] (2003) 14 BHRC 526.
[706] *GHB v UK* [2000] EHRLR 545.
[707] *Mustafa and Armagan Akın v Turkey* App No 4694/03, 6 April 2010; *Senthuran v Secretary of State for the Home Department* [2004] EWCA Civ 950, [2004] 4 All ER 365.
[708] *Pini and ors v Romania* App Nos 78028/01 and 78030/01, 22 June 2004.
[709] *Gaskin v UK* (1989) 12 EHRR 36.
[710] [2006] 1 FCR 256 at [113]. See also *Kroon* (1994) 19 EHRR 263, para 40.
[711] See, eg *Fretté v France* [2003] 2 FCR 39.
[712] *EB v France* (2008) 47 EHRR 21.
[713] *Abdulaziz, Cabales and Balkandali v UK* (1985) 7 EHRR 471.
[714] *Moustaquim v Belgium* (1991) 13 EHRR 802.
[715] *Gul v Switzerland* (1996) 22 EHRR 93.
[716] *X v UK* (1987) 11 EHRR 48.

easily be established and the state will be required to justify its interference under Article 8(2).[717]

7.324   In *Uner v Netherlands*, the leading case on immigration and the right to family life, the ECtHR considered the withdrawal of a residence permit and deportation of a Turkish immigrant who had founded a family in the Netherlands and then committed a series of criminal offences.[718] The court accepted that the state was pursuing the legitimate aims under Article 8(2) of protecting public safety and preventing crime, and set out a variety of factors that had to be taken into account in the proportionality analysis, including the seriousness and nature of the offence, the length of the applicant's stay in the country from which he or she was to be expelled, the nationalities of the various persons concerned, whether there were children of the marriage, and the seriousness of the difficulties the spouse was likely to encounter in the applicant's country of origin. The Court also made it explicit that the best interests of the children were a relevant consideration in the analysis. Weighing up all these factors, the Court found that the state had struck a fair balance between state interests and respect for the applicant's family life, and noted that if his children followed him to Turkey they would still be able to return to the Netherlands to visit other family members by virtue of their Dutch citizenship.

7.325   A significant proportion of domestic decisions on family life under Article 8 concerns the removal of immigrants and asylum seekers from the United Kingdom. In general, it is accepted that Article 8(1) will be engaged by interference with family ties existing in the United Kingdom, but immigration control will almost always constitute a legitimate aim for removal under Article 8(2).[719] The critical issue will therefore be the proportionality of the interference. In a rare single judgment of the Appellate Committee in *Huang v Secretary of State for the Home Department*, their Lordships held:

> In an article 8 case where [the proportionality] question is reached, the ultimate question for the appellate immigration authority is whether the refusal of leave to enter or remain, in circumstances where the life of the family cannot reasonably be expected to be enjoyed elsewhere, taking full account of all considerations weighing in favour of the refusal, prejudices the family life of the applicant in a manner sufficiently serious to amount to a breach of the fundamental right protected by article 8.[720]

According to their Lordships, it was not necessary that a claim pass a further test of 'exceptionality',[721] but it would be a 'small minority' of cases that would succeed under Article 8.[722]

---

[717] See, eg *Omoregie v Norway* App No 265/07, 31 July 2008.

[718] (2007) 45 EHRR 14. In the domestic context see, eg *HM (Iraq) v Secretary of State for the Home Department* [2010] EWCA Civ 1322.

[719] See, eg *LK (Serbia) v Secretary of State for the Home Department* [2007] EWCA Civ 1554 at [8].

[720] [2007] UKHL 11, [2007] 2 AC 167 at [20].

[721] Correcting a misinterpretation of the House of Lords' decision in *R (Razgar) v Secretary of State for the Home Department* [2004] UKHL 27, [2004] 2 AC 368.

[722] *Huang v Secretary of State for the Home Department* [2007] UKHL 11, [2007] 2 AC 167 at [20].

Since the decision in *Huang*, the House of Lords has accepted that Strasbourg **7.326** authority suggests that 'it will rarely be proportionate' to order removal of a spouse to a country where the other spouse cannot reasonably be expected to reside or to sever 'a genuine and subsisting relationship between parent and child'.[723] In *ZH (Tanzania) v Secretary of State for the Home Department* the Supreme Court held that when the deportation of a parent also entailed the removal of a child, the best interests of the child were a primary consideration.[724] Lord Kerr stated: 'Where the best interests of the child clearly favour a certain course, that course should be followed unless countervailing reasons of considerable force displace them.'[725] This approach arguably goes further than the ECtHR has done, but it is undoubtedly warranted by the provisions of the United Nations Convention on the Rights of the Child (UNCRC).[726]

The Court of Appeal has held that, while the proportionality balance may be **7.327** different in the case of an entry clearance application to facilitate the reunion of a family as compared with a case of an immigration decision that breaks up a family unit, the same approach (and ultimate question), as identified by the House of Lords in *Huang*, applies. In other words, if family life cannot reasonably be enjoyed elsewhere, the family member must be admitted to the UK if refusing to do so would prejudice the life of the family in a manner sufficiently serious to amount to a breach of Article 8.[727]

In *R (Quila) v Secretary of State for the Home*, the Supreme Court struck down **7.328** as contrary to Article 8 a restriction in the Immigration Rules on leave to enter as the spouse of a person settled and present in the UK which required that both the sponsor and spouse be over 21 years of age. The measure pursued a legitimate and important aim of seeking to prevent forced marriages, but the extent to which the measure achieved its aim so as to justify the colossal interference with Article 8 rights was entirely unclear on the evidence. Lord Wilson described the measure as akin to using a sledgehammer to crack a nut when no attempt had been made to identify the size of the nut.[728]

In cases where an appellant's right to a family life may be breached in the country **7.329** to which he or she is removed, the domestic courts have held that removal will only be unlawful if it would 'so flagrantly violate [the appellant's] Article 8 rights as to completely deny or nullify those rights'.[729] In *EM (Lebanon) v Secretary of State for the Home Department*, the House of Lords found that the return of a mother and child to Lebanon where the child would be taken into the father's custody constituted such a flagrant denial.[730]

---

[723] *EB (Kosovo) v Secretary of State for the Home Department* [2008] UKHL 41, [2008] 3 WLR 178 at [12]. See also *Chikwamba v Secretary of State for the Home Department* [2008] UKHL 40, [2008] 1 WLR 1420.

[724] [2011] UKSC 4.

[725] Ibid at [46].

[726] The UK lifted its reservation to the UNCRC concerning immigration matters in 2008.

[727] *Muse v Entry Clearance Officer* [2012] EWCA Civ 10.

[728] [2011] UKSC 45 at [58].

[729] *R (Ullah) v Special Adjudicator* [2004] UKHL 26, [2004] 2 AC 323; approving *Devaseelan v Secretary of State for the Home Department* [2002] UKIAT 702.

[730] [2008] UKHL 64, [2008] 2 FLR 2067 at [37].

5. Home

7.330 In *Buckley v UK* the ECtHR highlighted that whether a habitation is a 'home' is highly fact-specific, and depends on 'the existence of sufficient and continuous links'.[731] The House of Lords has suggested that 'home' constitutes the place where a person 'lives and to which he returns and which forms the centre of his existence'.[732] 'Home' can also include premises which are unlawfully occupied.[733]

7.331 'Home' has been held to include a long-term hospital stay,[734] second homes,[735] and offices[736] in certain circumstances.

7.332 *Gillow v UK* makes clear that the notion of 'home' may extend to the place where one intends to live.[737] The applicants were absent from their house in Guernsey for 18 years because the husband's job caused him to travel. The Government refused the couple a new residence permit when they finally returned, arguing that this was not their home. The ECmHR and ECtHR held that, in this case, there was a right to 're-establish home life'.

7.333 So far, however, the Court has never found a violation of the notion of respect for home by a failure to provide a particular home, although it has accepted that a positive obligation to provide a home may arise in some circumstances.[738] This right may also be covered by the developing jurisprudence on legitimate expectations under Protocol 1, Article 1.[739]

7.334 The question of the compatibility of possession orders with the right to respect for the home has vexed Strasbourg and the domestic courts. The Commission rejected as inadmissible complaints against possession orders. In *Ure v UK* the applicant's tenancy came to an end on expiry of a notice to quit given by his wife, formerly a joint tenant with him, and possession was ordered.[740] The ECmHR held that his complaint under Article 8 was manifestly ill-founded because the alleged interference with his rights under the article was justified under Article 8(2).

7.335 Subsequently, the ECtHR has found that possession and eviction proceedings must be attended by procedural safeguards.[741] In *McCann v UK*, the Court held that, as regards those safeguards, whenever a person risked losing his or her home there must be a possibility of having the proportionality of the eviction measure determined by an independent tribunal.[742] A similar result was reached in *R v North and East Devon District Health Authority, ex p Coughlan* in which the Court of

---

[731] (1996) 23 EHRR 101.

[732] *London Borough of Harrow v Qazi* [2003] UKHL 43, [2004] 1 AC 983 at [8] per Lord Bingham.

[733] *Malik v Fassenfelt* [2013] EWCA Civ 798, [2013] EGILR 22 at [43].

[734] *Collins v UK* App No 11909/02, 15 October 2002; *R v North and East Devon District Health Authority, ex p Coughlan* [2001] QB 213.

[735] *Demades v Turkey* [2003] ECHR 16219/90.

[736] *Niemietz v Germany* (1992) 16 EHRR 97; *Peev v Bulgaria* [2007] ECHR 64209/01.

[737] (1986) 11 EHRR 335.

[738] See ch 6, para 6.109.

[739] See ch 8, para 8.05.

[740] App No 28027/95, 27 November 1996. See also *Wood v UK* (1997) 24 EHRR CD 69.

[741] *Connors v UK* (2005) 40 EHRR 9.

[742] [2008] LGR 474.

Appeal found that respect for the home obliged the health authority to act fairly in removing a disabled resident from a care home after it had promised her that she could remain there for life.[743]

The House of Lords considered the applicability of Article 8 to repossession   7.336
proceedings in a series of cases. After adopting too narrow a view of Article 8(1)
in *London Borough of Harrow v Qazi*,[744] a majority of the seven-member board
of the House of Lords concluded in *Kay v Lambeth London Borough Council*
that a possession order would infringe Article 8(1), but that the county courts
could work on the assumption that domestic law satisfied the requirements of
Article 8(2) and would not generally need to apply the proportionality test.[745]
Article 8(2) would be relevant only in cases where the legislation itself could be
impugned. A majority of the Lords reached the same conclusion in *Doherty v
Birmingham City Council*.[746]

In *Kay v UK* the ECtHR favoured the minority approach in *Doherty* finding that   7.337
an individual resisting possession should in principle be able to have the proportionality of the measure determined by an independent tribunal in the light of the
relevant principles under Article 8, notwithstanding that, under domestic law, the
right of occupation had come to an end.[747] The Supreme Court very swiftly adopted
the approach of the ECtHR in three housing cases heard soon after the ECtHR
decision. The court emphasized that it would be rare for proportionality to be seriously arguable.[748]

Recently, in *McDonald v McDonald*, the Court of Appeal held that no issue   7.338
of proportionality arises in respect of the grant of a possession order to a private
landlord.[749] The Court of Appeal reasoned that there was no 'clear and consistent' jurisprudence of the ECtHR, which required the contrary conclusion (whilst
accepting that a number of cases had proceeded on the assumption that Article 8
did apply in these circumstances).[750] While it is no doubt correct that the fact of a
private legal right to possession is likely to be regarded by the ECtHR as a strong
factor in support of the proportionality of granting a possession order with the
consequence that an arguable issue under Article 8 is less likely to arise, it seems
unlikely that the ECtHR would be prepared to accept that a possession order can
in all cases be made without any individualized assessment of proportionality of the
type identified in *Kay v UK* merely because property is privately owned.[751]

---

[743] [2001] QB 213. Cf *Collins v UK* App No 11909/02, 15 October 2002.

[744] [2003] UKHL 43, [2004] 1 AC 983.

[745] (2006) 20 BHRC 33.

[746] [2008] UKHL 57.

[747] App No 37341/06, 21 September 2010.

[748] *Manchester City Council v Pinnock* [2010] UKSC 45; *London Borough of Hounslow v Powell; Leeds City Council and Hall* [2011] UKSC 8.

[749] [2014] EWCA Civ 1049.

[750] It also held that it was bound to reach this conclusion by an earlier decision in *Poplar Housing and Regeneration Community Association Ltd v Donoghue* [2001] EWCA Civ 595, [2002] QB 48.

[751] This was the *obiter* view reached by Ward LJ in the earlier decision of *Malik v Fassenfelt* [2013] EWCA Civ 798, [2013] EGILR 22 at [28].

6. Correspondence

7.339   The right to respect for one's correspondence is a right to uninterrupted and uncensored communication with others. In a telephone-tapping case, *Malone v UK*, the ECtHR found that the British Government violated Article 8 when it intercepted the phone calls of the applicant, an antique dealer convicted of receiving stolen goods.[752] This decision has been applied to the monitoring of office correspondence including emails.[753]

7.340   The majority of cases concerning correspondence relate to interception of prisoners' phone calls and letters. The ECtHR has taken a consistently strict approach to such interference, finding that while some measure of control over prisoners' correspondence may be justified, 'indiscriminate, routine checking' will violate Article 8.[754] In *Szuluk v UK* the ECtHR considered that the monitoring of a prisoner's correspondence with a doctor by a prison medical officer violated Article 8.[755] The opening of even a single item of correspondence is sufficient to engage the protection of Article 8.[756]

7.341   One of the leading domestic cases on the standard of review under the Human Rights Act, *R (Daly) v Secretary of State for the Home Department*, concerned inspection of a prisoner's privileged legal correspondence.[757] The House of Lords held that the prison's policy interfered with the prisoner's rights to a significantly greater extent than could be justified.

F. ARTICLE 9: FREEDOM OF THOUGHT, CONSCIENCE, AND RELIGION

7.342   Article 9 protects the rights to hold religious and non-religious beliefs, to change those beliefs, and to manifest them in 'worship, teaching, practice and observance', whether alone or with others, in public or in private. In emphasizing the importance of freedom of thought, conscience, and religion, the ECtHR has stated that:

> Freedom of thought, conscience and religion is one of the foundations of a 'democratic society' within the meaning of the Convention. It is, in its religious dimension, one of the most vital elements that go to make up the identity of believers and their conception of life, but it is also a precious asset for atheists, agnostics, sceptics and the unconcerned. The pluralism indissociable from a democratic society, which has been dearly won over the centuries, depends on it.[758]

---

[752] (1984) 7 EHRR 14.

[753] See, eg *Halford v UK* (1997) 24 EHRR 523; *Copland v UK* (2007) 25 BHRC 216.

[754] See, eg *Jankauskas v Lithuania* [2005] ECHR 59304/00; *AB v Netherlands* (2003) 37 EHRR 48; *Wasilewski v Poland* (2004) 38 EHRR 10; *Petrov v Bulgaria* App No 15197/02, 22 May 2008.

[755] [2009] ECHR 845.

[756] *Idalov v Russia* App No 5826/03, 22 May 2012, GC at [197].

[757] [2001] UKHL 26, [2001] 2 AC 532.

[758] *Kokkinakis v Greece* (1994) 17 EHRR 397, para 31. See, more recently, *Bayatyan v Armenia* (2011) 54 EHRR 467, para 118.

The right to hold and change beliefs is often said to be absolute, while the right 7.343
to manifest one's religion or beliefs can be limited under Article 9(2).[759] However,
there is often no clear distinction between 'holding' and 'manifesting' beliefs, as
many religions have an inherent requirement that their followers proselytize. The
need to 'bear witness in word and deed' is bound up with the very existence of the
conviction itself.[760] Indeed, without a right to proselytize the 'freedom to change
one's religion or belief, enshrined in Article 9, would be likely to remain a dead
letter'.[761] Nonetheless, the distinction between holding and manifesting a belief
remains critical to the application of Article 9.

It is apparent that Article 9 will often overlap with other Convention protections, 7.344
most notably Articles 10, 11, and 14, and Protocol 1, Article 2. In cases raising
issues under both Articles 9 and 10 an applicant's complaints are often considered
solely under Article 10 if possible (perhaps because the reach of Article 10(1) is
clearer than that of 9(1)).[762]

Article 9 has not had equivalent impact to some of the other qualified rights, 7.345
notably Article 10, in Strasbourg or the domestic courts. Claims fail either on the
grounds that there has been no interference with a 'manifestation' of belief,[763] or,
increasingly, on the basis that such an interference is justified.[764]

In domestic law, religious rights are commonly protected by recourse to the 7.346
Equality Act 2010, which makes discrimination on the grounds of religion or belief
unlawful.[765] The relationship between Article 9 and the statutory equality provisions is in its infancy, but it appears that there will be cases where the approach
under Article 9 is different, and potentially more generous, than that under the
Equality Act. The cases are discussed below.

1. 'Everyone'

The rights protected by Article 9 are guaranteed to 'everyone' (including 'aliens', 7.347
regardless of whether they are yet resident in the state concerned).[766]

While this primarily refers to individuals, it also encompasses churches and asso- 7.348
ciations with religious or philosophical aims, both in their own capacity and as
representative of their members.[767] The Grand Chamber has held that Article 9

---

[759] See, eg *Darby v Sweden* Series A No 187, 9 May 1989, para 44; ECtHR judgment: (1991) 13
EHRR 774.

[760] *Kokkinakis v Greece* (1994) 17 EHRR 397, para 31.

[761] Ibid.

[762] See, eg *Paturel v France* App No 54968/00, 22 December 2005; *R (Singh) v Chief Constable of West
Midlands Police* [2006] EWCA Civ 1118, [2007] 2 All ER 297.

[763] See, eg *Ahmad v UK* (1981) 4 EHRR 126; *Copsey v Devon Clays Ltd* [2005] EWCA Civ 932, [2005]
IRLR 811; *R (SB) v Governors of Denbigh High School* [2006] UKHL 15, [2007] 1 AC 100.

[764] *Leyla Sahin v Turkey* (2007) 44 EHRR 5; *Surayanda v Welsh Ministers* [2007] EWCA Civ 893.

[765] Section 10 makes religion or belief a protected characteristic for the purposes of the Act.

[766] *Darby v Sweden* Series A No 187, 9 May 1989. See, further, Jayawickrama, *The Judicial Application of
Human Rights Law* (Cambridge: Cambridge University Press, 2002) 641, n 8.

[767] See, eg *X and Church of Scientology v Sweden* (1979) 16 DR 68. Such churches or associations may
be considered 'victims' within the meaning of Art 34 if they are non-governmental organizations: *Holy
Monasteries v Greece* (1995) 20 EHRR 1, para 49.

must be interpreted in light of Article 11, and that, consequently, the organization of religious communities must be protected by Article 9, as 'the believers' right to freedom of religion encompasses the expectation that the community will be allowed to function peacefully, free from arbitrary state intervention'.[768]

2. Freedom of thought, conscience, and religion

(a) Scope of the freedom

7.349　Article 9 protects a very broad range of beliefs, including both religious and non-religious. Belief systems based on personal morality, such as pacifism[769] and veganism,[770] are protected by the Convention. The ECtHR has not yet considered whether political convictions, such as republicanism, are within the ambit of Article 9, but the Supreme Court has stated that there is no difference for treating political beliefs any differently.[771] However, the courts will be more likely to consider political belief as a right to freedom of expression under Article 10.[772]

7.350　In order to attract the protection of Article 9, the thoughts or beliefs must attain a 'certain level of cogency, seriousness, cohesion and importance'.[773] In *Campbell and Cosans v UK* the ECtHR distinguished between 'beliefs' (protected by Article 9) and 'convictions' (protected by Protocol 1, Article 2) on the one hand, and 'opinions' and 'ideas' (protected by Article 10) on the other, though in particular cases these categories may overlap.[774] Whether the applicant can show that he or she holds a belief rather than a lesser conviction, opinion, or idea is sometimes difficult to predict and will turn on the facts of the particular case.

7.351　The judgment of the House of Lords in *R (Williamson) v Secretary of State for Education and Employment* provides guidance for domestic courts determining whether a particular belief falls within Article 9.[775] Lord Nicholls reiterated that Article 9 protects non-religious and non-theistic views:

The atheist, the agnostic and the sceptic are as much entitled to freedom to hold and manifest their beliefs as the theist. These beliefs are placed on an equal footing for the purpose of this guaranteed freedom. Thus, if its manifestation is to attract protection under Article 9 a non-religious belief, as much as a religious belief, must satisfy the modest threshold requirements implicit in this article. In particular, for its manifestation to be protected by article 9 a non-religious belief must relate to an aspect of human life or behaviour of comparable importance to that normally found with religious beliefs.[776]

---

[768] *Hasan and Chaush v Bulgaria* (2002) 34 EHRR 55. See also *Kimlya and ors v Russia* [2009] ECHR 76836/01.

[769] *Arrowsmith v UK* (1978) 3 EHRR 218.

[770] *H v UK* (1992) 16 EHRR CD 44, 45; *Jakóbski v Poland* (2010) 30 BHRC 417.

[771] *RT (Zimbabwe) v Secretary of State for the Home Department* [2012] UKSC 38, [2012] 4 All ER 843 at [36].

[772] See, eg *Redfearn v UK* (2012) 33 BHRC 713.

[773] *Campbell and Cosans v UK* (1982) 4 EHRR 293, para 36.

[774] Ibid.

[775] [2005] UKHL 15, [2005] 2 AC 246.

[776] Ibid at [24]. See also *R (Hodkin and another) v Registrar General of Births, Deaths and Marriages* [2013] UKSC 77, [2014] AC 610 at [57], discussing the meaning of religion in domestic law.

However, the domestic courts have also taken the view that not all opinions or 7.352
convictions, however sincerely or deeply held, constitute beliefs in the sense protected by Article 9. It does not protect pro-hunting views, for example, despite the
hunters' view that 'hunting is at the very core of mankind's psyche'.[777] Nor does it
protect beliefs that are not founded on religious or philosophical viewpoints, such
as a belief that children should not be raised by a same-sex couple.[778] The Supreme
Court held in *RT (Zimbabwe) v Secretary of State for the Home Department* that
Article 9 protects the right to political indifference.[779]

Freedom of religion has been held to include a negative aspect not to be required 7.353
to disclose one's religion. In the case of *Sinan Isik v Turkey*, the Strasbourg Court
ruled that it violated Article 9 to require a citizen to indicate his or her religion in
his or her application for an ID card or formally ask for the religion box to be left
empty.[780] The judgment has potentially broad ramifications for all official documents or registers.

(b) State activities

The existence of a state church does not, in itself, infringe Article 9, provided the 7.354
system includes specific safeguards for the individual's freedom of religion. An
individual may not be forced to be directly involved in religious activities against
his will (unless he has voluntarily joined as a minister of that religion),[781] nor can
the state compel an individual to pay taxes to a church.[782] However, in *C v UK* the
ECmHR found no violation of Article 9 where there is a duty to pay general taxes
that are not earmarked for a specific religious purpose, even if the state uses some of
the money to support religious communities or religious activities.[783]

The ECtHR shifted its position on the applicability of Article 9 to conscientious 7.355
objectors in *Bayatyan v Armenia*.[784] Historically, the Commission had held that
Article 9 did not guarantee a right to refuse to perform military service on the
grounds of belief because Article 4(3)(b) excluded military service from the scope
of forced labour.[785] In *Bayatyan*, the Grand Chamber argued that 'a failure by the
Court to maintain a dynamic and evolutive approach would risk rendering it a bar
to reform or improvement'[786] and held that a new approach was justified by developments in domestic legal systems that permitted alternative forms of national service for conscientious objectors. The Court concluded that the applicant's two-year

---

[777] *R (Countryside Alliance) v Attorney General* [2006] EWCA Civ 817 at [177] [2007] QB 305; citing
Chassagnou and ors v France (1999) 29 EHRR 615. Confirmed by the House of Lords at [2007] UKHL 52,
[2008] 1 AC 719.
[778] *McClintock v Department of Constitutional Affairs* [2008] IRLR 29.
[779] [2012] UKSC 38, [2012] 4 All ER 843 at [42].
[780] App No 21924/05, 2 February 2010.
[781] *X v Denmark* (1976) 5 DR 157.
[782] *Darby v Sweden* (1990) 13 EHRR 774.
[783] (1983) 37 DR 142.
[784] (2011) 54 EHRR 467. See also *Savda v Turkey* App No 42730/05, 12 June 2012.
[785] *Grandrath v the Federal Republic of Germany* 10 (1967) YB 625.
[786] Ibid, para 98.

prison sentence for failure to perform military service was disproportionate and violated Article 9.

7.356   The House of Lords considered the taxation of religious establishments in *Church of Jesus Christ of Latter Day Saints v Gallagher*.[787] In a narrow interpretation of the ambit of Article 9, it found no interference with freedom of religion taken with Article 14 where the Mormon church was unable to claim an exemption on local government rates because the church was not open to the public. Lord Scott dissented, arguing that levying taxation on a place of religious worship would be capable of breaching Article 9, and therefore withholding relief from the rates fell within its ambit for the purposes of Article 14. The European Court agreed with Lord Scott that Article 14 was engaged but found that the measures were justified.[788] It did not consider Article 9 in depth, but suggested there had not been an interference with the Church's Article 9 rights because the taxation had only a minor financial impact on the Church.

7.357   The ECtHR has frequently emphasized the state's role as 'the neutral and impartial organizer of the exercise of various religions, faiths and beliefs', and held that this duty of neutrality and impartiality is incompatible with any power on the state's part to assess the legitimacy of religious beliefs or the way in which those beliefs are expressed.[789] Accordingly, the state's role is to ensure mutual tolerance between opposing groups and, in case of conflict, 'not to remove the cause of the tension by eliminating pluralism, but to ensure that the competing groups tolerate each other'.[790] Any regulatory functions carried out by the state in relation to religious organizations must therefore be undertaken with complete neutrality.[791]

7.358   The domestic courts have similarly emphasized that the role of the state and the courts is a neutral one. In a dispute between a local authority and prospective Christian foster parents who opposed same-sex relationships on religious grounds, Munby LJ set out the position of the common law, which mirrors the Convention approach:

> The starting point of the common law is thus respect for an individual's religious principles coupled with an essentially neutral view of religious beliefs and benevolent tolerance of cultural and religious diversity. A secular judge must be wary of straying across the well-recognized divide between church and state. It is not for a judge to weigh one religion against another. The court recognises no religious distinctions and generally speaking passes no judgment on religious

---

[787] [2008] UKHL 56, [2008] 1 WLR 1852.

[788] *Church of Jesus Christ of Latter Day Saints v UK* App No 7552/09, 4 March 2014.

[789] *Manoussakis and ors v Greece* Reports of Judgments and Decisions 1996-IV, 26 September 1996, 1365; *Hasan and Chaush v Bulgaria* (2002) 34 EHRR 55, para 78; *Moscow Branch of the Salvation Army v Russia* (2006) 44 EHRR 912, para 58.

[790] *Serif v Greece* App No 38178/97, ECHR 1999-IX, para 53; *Supreme Holy Council of the Muslim Community v Bulgaria* [2004] ECHR 39023/97. Cf *Miroļubovs and ors v Latvia* App No 798/05, 15 September 2009.

[791] *Metropolitan Church of Bessarabia v Moldova* [2001] ECHR 45701/99. Cf the ECtHR's approach to manifestation of belief in *Leyla Sahin v Turkey* (2007) 44 EHRR 5, discussed at para 7.371.

beliefs or on the tenets, doctrines or rules of any particular section of society. All are entitled to equal respect.[792]

3. Manifestation of one's religion or beliefs

The right to manifest one's religion or beliefs complements the primary right of freedom of thought, conscience, and religion. In deciding whether an applicant's conduct constitutes a manifestation, the ECtHR first identifies the nature and scope of the belief. If the belief takes the form of a perceived obligation to act in a specific way, then, in principle, doing that act pursuant to that belief is itself a manifestation of that belief in practice. In such cases the act is 'intimately linked' to the belief.[793]   7.359

The Strasbourg organs traditionally took a narrow approach to manifestation and afforded close legal protection only where it was in the private sphere of the practice of a religion, and not where the manifestation of faith had an effect on the practices and behaviour of others in the secular world. For example, where a pacifist distributed leaflets to soldiers urging them to decline service in Northern Ireland, this was not an expression of her 'pacifist ideas' as it had a broader aim—to contest British policy in Northern Ireland;[794] and the refusal by a church minister to perform administrative duties in protest at amendments to national abortion legislation was not an expression of his anti-abortion beliefs.[795]   7.360

The Court has recently softened its approach to manifestation in recent decisions and taken a broader view of manifestation.[796] The leading judgment on manifestation of religious belief is now *Eweida and ors v UK*.[797] The Court considered four applications by Christian employees in the UK who claimed that their employers had breached their right to manifestation of their beliefs. They had each claimed religious discrimination contrary to the Employment Equality (Religion or Belief) Regulations 2003 in the Employment Tribunal. Ms Eweida was employed by British Airways and wished to wear a cross in contravention of the company's uniform policy. Ms Chaplin worked as a nurse and had been asked by her employer to remove her cross on health and safety grounds. Ms Ladele was a local authority registrar who refused to perform same-sex civil partnership ceremonies. Mr McFarlane was sacked as a counsellor at Relate for refusing to counsel same-sex couples. The   7.361

---

[792] *R (Johns) v Derby City Council* [2011] EWHC 375 (Admin) at [41]. See also *Ladele v London Borough of Islington* [2009] EWCA Civ 1357, [2010] IRLR 211; *Catholic Care v Charity Commission* [2010] EWHC 520 (Ch), [2010] 4 All ER 1041; *R (E) v The Governing Body of JFS and ors* [2009] UKSC 15, [2010] 1 All ER 319 at [157]; *Macfarlane v Relate Avon Ltd* [2010] EWCA Civ 771, [2010] IRLR 872 at [23]–[25]; *R (National Secular Society) v Bideford Town Council* [2012] EWHC 175 (Admin), [2012] 2 All ER 1175 at [29].
[793] *Application 10295/82 v UK* (1983) 6 EHRR 558; *R (Williamson) v Secretary of State for Education and Employment* [2005] UKHL 15, [2005] 2 AC 246; *R (Watkins-Singh) v Governing Body of Aberdare Girls' School* [2008] EWHC 1865 (Admin), [2008] ELR 561.
[794] *Arrowsmith v UK* (1978) 3 EHRR 218.
[795] *Knudsen v Norway* App No 11045/84, 42 DR 247.
[796] See, eg *Jakóbski v Poland* App No 18429/06, 7 December 2010.
[797] (2013) 34 BHRC 519.

domestic courts dismissed their claims under the Regulations on the basis that if indirect discrimination could be established by the actions of the employers, it was a proportionate means of achieving a legitimate aim.[798] Article 9 did not play a significant part in the domestic courts' reasoning.

7.362   The European Court applied the established test for establishing a manifestation of a belief, namely whether the act in question was intimately linked to the religion or belief, and found that all four of the applicants had been seeking to manifest their beliefs. The Court did not exclude their manifestations from the protection of Article 9(1) on the basis that they had an effect on others, but took that into account in the proportionality enquiry. The case suggests that the correct approach to manifestation is now a broad one which accepts that a person's sincerely held view about what they must do to manifest their belief will be sufficient to engage Article 9.

7.363   The domestic courts have considered what constitutes a manifestation of a religion or belief on a number of occasions. In an example of a broad interpretation of manifestation, the House of Lords in *R (Williamson) v Secretary of State for Education and Employment* found that parents of children in a private Christian school who wished teachers to impose corporal punishment upon the pupils were manifesting a religion or belief.[799] Their Lordships held that the statutory ban on corporal punishment in schools interfered with the parents' rights under Article 9(1) (although the ban was justified under Article 9(2)), because the essence of the parents' belief was that it was part of proper upbringing that children should, where necessary, be disciplined in a particular way at home and at school, and so, when they placed their children in a school that practised corporal punishment, the parents were manifesting that belief.

7.364   Like the ECtHR, the domestic courts require a causal link between the belief and the manifestation. For example, in *Campbell v South Northamptonshire District Council*, an appeal against the refusal of housing benefit, the Court of Appeal found no violation of Article 9 or 14 as there was no link between the refusal of housing benefit for members of a religious housing cooperative living on church property and the manifestation of their beliefs.[800] They could have elected to have entered into a commercial relationship with the church, or have lived communally in property let from a housing association—neither would have required any alteration or diminution of their communal living practices.

7.365   In *Ghai v Newcastle City Council* the High Court found that a desire to be cremated on an open-air funeral pyre was a manifestation of Hindu belief because it was 'sufficiently close to the core of one strand of orthodox Hinduism'.[801] The court distinguished the position of Sikhs, for whom open-air cremation was simply

---

[798] *Eweida v British Airways Plc* [2010] EWCA Civ 80, [2010] IRLR 3222; *Chaplin v Royal Devon and Exeter Foundation Trust* [2011] EqLR 548; *London Borough of Islington v Ladele* [2009] EWCA Civ 1357, [2010] IRLR 211; *McFarlane v Relate Avon Ltd* [2010] EWCA Civ 771, [2010] IRLR 872.

[799] [2005] UKHL 15, [2005] 2 AC 246.

[800] [2004] EWCA Civ 409, [2004] 3 All ER 387.

[801] [2009] EWHC 978 (Admin), [2009] NLJR 713 at [101]. The Court of Appeal ([2010] EWCA Civ 59, [2010] 3 All ER 380) allowed the appeal on a different point.

a matter of tradition rather than of belief. In *R (Imran Bashir) v The Independent Adjudicator and anor* the High Court held that disciplining a Muslim prisoner for failing to provide a urine sample while he was fasting interfered with Article 9.[802]

4. Interference with manifestation of religion or beliefs

The threshold for establishing an interference with a manifestation of belief was historically set very high. In cases pre-dating *Eweida*, Strasbourg found that no interference will arise when an individual is left with a choice whether or not to comply with his or her religious obligations. Thus, in *Karaduman v Turkey*, in which a Muslim woman challenged a refusal to let her graduate from university unless she was photographed without her headscarf, the Commission found that the fact that the applicant had chosen to pursue higher education in a secular university meant that she had submitted to its rules and no interference was established.[803]   7.366

The ECtHR made the same point in the context of restrictions on kosher slaughterhouses in *Jewish Liturgical Association Cha'are Shalom Ve Tesedek v France* stating: 7.367

> there would be interference with the freedom to manifest one's religion only if the illegality of performing ritual slaughter made it impossible for ultra-orthodox Jews to eat meat from animals slaughtered in accordance with the religious prescriptions they considered applicable.[804]

Where an individual is subject to the coercive powers of the state, the Court more readily found an interference with Article 9. Prisoners, for example, are subject to the coercive power of the state and have no choice but to abide by its rules. Failure to permit them to take part in weekly worship,[805] restricting their access to a priest,[806] or failing to provide appropriate food[807] violates their Article 9 rights.   7.368

In the employment field the European Commission traditionally took a particularly restrictive view of religious rights. In *Ahmad v UK*, it dismissed a complaint in which a teacher demanded that his employers accommodate his obligation to attend religious worship on a Friday. The Commission, finding that he remained free to resign if and when he found that his teaching obligations conflicted with his religious duties, dismissed his claim as manifestly ill-founded.[808] Similarly, in *Stedman v UK* the ECmHR rejected the complaint of a Christian applicant who had been dismissed for refusing to work on Sundays on the basis that the employee could resign.[809] In the admissibility decision, *Dahlab v Switzerland*, the ECtHR found that a prohibition on a female teacher wearing a headscarf while teaching in a primary school interfered with the manifestation of her religious beliefs despite the fact that she could in theory have taught at a private school where she could have   7.369

---

[802] [2011] EWHC 1108 (Admin).
[803] (1993) 74 DR 93.
[804] (2000) 9 BHRC 27, para 80.
[805] *Kuznetsov v Ukraine* [2003] ECHR 39042/97.
[806] *Poltoratskiy v Ukraine* [2003] ECHR 38812/97.
[807] *Jakóbski v Poland* App No 18429/06, 7 December 2010.
[808] (1981) 4 EHRR 126.
[809] (1997) 23 EHRR 168.

worn the headscarf.[810] However, the Court found that the wearing of a headscarf might have a proselytizing effect on young children that outweighed the teacher's right to manifest her beliefs. Therefore, the interference was justified under Article 9(2) and the application was manifestly ill-founded.

7.370   In *Eweida v UK* the European Court explicitly disavowed this jurisprudence.[811] It abandoned its previous stance that there was no interference with an employee's right to manifest her religion if the employee could find alternative employment. Instead, the court will take that into account in the overall proportionality assessment. The possibility of reasonable accommodation by the employer is therefore an essential part of the proportionality assessment.

7.371   Difficulties around the manifestation of religious belief have also arisen in the education context. In the controversial decision in *Leyla Sahin v Turkey* (the 'Sahin' case), the Grand Chamber found that a ban on students wearing headscarves at the University of Istanbul interfered with the applicant's right to manifest her beliefs.[812] This was so despite the fact that the applicant had been able to wear the headscarf at her former university and chose to continue her studies abroad. However, the Grand Chamber held that the ban was a proportionate response to the need to promote secularism in Turkey. The Court took a different approach in *Ahmet Arslan and ors v Turkey* in which members of a religious group toured the streets of Ankara in distinctive religious dress.[813] The Court found that their criminal convictions for wearing religious garb in public were unjustified on the basis that dressing as they did in a public place did not pose the same threat to secularism as it did in public institutions.

7.372   The leading domestic decision on manifestation under Article 9 remains *R (SB) v Governors of Denbigh High School* (the 'Shabina Begum' case).[814] Contrary to school policy, the claimant wished to wear a 'jilbab', a long coat-like garment that was considered to represent stricter adherence to the tenets of the Muslim faith. She argued that the uniform policy interfered with her right to manifest her religion under Article 9(1).

7.373   A majority of their Lordships accepted that Article 9(1) was 'engaged', as wearing the jilbab was a sincere manifestation of her religious belief, but found that the refusal to allow the claimant to attend school wearing a jilbab did not amount to an interference with her right to manifest her religious beliefs. The case was determined shortly after the decision of the Grand Chamber in the *Sahin* case, in which a ban on wearing a headscarf at university was deemed to constitute an interference. Lord Hoffmann distinguished *Sahin* on the basis that there were other schools that Shabina Begum might have attended where she could wear the jilbab, while all the universities in Turkey imposed a similar ban on headscarves. Notably, this choice-based rationale did not feature as part of the ECtHR's reasoning in *Sahin*,

---

[810] [2001] ECHR 42393/98.
[811] See n 832.
[812] (2005) 41 EHRR 8.
[813] App No 41135/98, 23 February 2010. Judgment available in French only.
[814] [2006] UKHL 15, [2007] 1 AC 100.

despite the fact that the applicant had been able to wear her headscarf at another university in Turkey and had chosen to continue her studies abroad. The dissenting judges did not eschew this choice-based analysis.[815] Following *Eweida*, it is now clear that this approach is inappropriate and the Supreme Court will undoubtedly reconsider its jurisprudence when it next hears an appeal that raises the issue.

5. Limitations under Article 9(2)

Article 9 is a qualified right, and the right to manifest one's beliefs and convictions may therefore be subject to the limitations set out in Article 9(2). It is notable that Article 9 is the only qualified right in the Convention that does not permit the state to interfere with it on the basis of 'national security'.   7.374

Any such limitation must meet the threefold test set out in *Sunday Times v UK (No 1)*:[816] it must be (i) prescribed by law; (ii) in pursuit of a 'legitimate aim' set out in Article 9(2); and (iii) 'necessary in a democratic society', which includes a requirement of proportionality.   7.375

As under the other qualified rights, the first two limbs of the test are generally easily satisfied.[817] However, in *SAS v France*, a case concerning the ban on wearing face veils in public, the Grand Chamber examined the question of legitimate aim in some detail.[818] The French Government claimed that the ban served multiple purposes, including public safety, gender equality, and 'respect for the minimum requirements of life in society'. The Court rejected all the Government's contended aims with the exception of the notion of 'living together'. It stated: 7.376

> The Court takes into account the respondent State's point that the face plays an important role in social interaction. It can understand the view that individuals who are present in places open to all may not wish to see practices or attitudes developing there which would fundamentally call into question the possibility of open interpersonal relationships, which, by virtue of an established consensus, forms an indispensable element of community life within the society in question. The Court is therefore able to accept that the barrier raised against others by a veil concealing the face is perceived by the respondent State as breaching the right of others to live in a space of socialisation which makes living together easier.

The Court concluded that the ban was a proportionate response to the Government's aim. The decision strains the boundaries of the concept of the rights of others and sits uneasily with the Court's previous decisions, such as *Eweida v UK*, in which it supported a tolerant attitude towards an individual's choices.

The central dispute under Article 9(2) usually concerns the application of the proportionality standard. Certain measures will attract particularly strict scrutiny   7.377

---

[815] The High Court has applied the approach in *Shabina Begum* to challenges to school uniform policy based on Article 9. See, eg *R (Playfoot) v Governing Body of Millais School* [2007] EWHC 1698 (Admin), [2007] ELR 484; *R (X) v The Headteacher of Y School* [2007] EWHC 298 (Admin), [2007] ELR 278.

[816] (1979) 2 EHRR 245.

[817] For an example of cases in which the ECtHR found an interference not 'in accordance with law', see *Poltoratskiy v Ukraine* [2003] ECHR 38812/97; *Perry v Latvia* [2007] ECHR 30273/03.

[818] (2014) 36 BHRC 617.

from the Court. For example, when an applicant complains of a criminal or civil penalty arising as a result of the manifestation of his or her beliefs, the Court will give careful consideration to the government's justification. In *Kokkinakis v Greece*, a criminal conviction of two Jehovah's Witnesses who engaged in door-to-door evangelism was held to have a legitimate aim, but to be a disproportionate response, because no consideration had been given to whether the couple had used improper means to evangelize; hence, there was a violation of Article 9.[819] Similarly, in the important case of *Thlimmenos v Greece* the Grand Chamber recognized that the exclusion of the applicant from the profession of chartered accountancy on account of a criminal conviction for religious objection to military service was disproportionate and in breach of Article 14 taken in conjunction with Article 9.[820]

7.378   A less-exacting approach is taken to complaints concerning failure to accommodate beliefs.[821] The ECtHR has consistently emphasized that in societies where several religions coexist it may be necessary to limit the right in order to reconcile the interests of the various groups and to ensure that all beliefs are respected.[822] For example, in *Dahlab v Switzerland*, the prohibition on a teacher wearing a headscarf at work was held not to have violated her right to freedom of religion, because it was designed to ensure the religious neutrality of the public education service in a society with diverse religious views and was therefore considered within the state's margin of appreciation.[823]

7.379   A majority of the Grand Chamber adopted the same approach in the *Sahin* case, upholding the prohibition on wearing headscarves in university on the basis that the principles of secularism and equality was fundamental to Turkish society.[824] Citing the words of the ECtHR in *Dahlab*, the majority found that the ban pursued a legitimate aim because the headscarf constituted a 'powerful external symbol... imposed on women by a religious precept' that infringed gender equality and posed a danger to the secular foundation of the Turkish state.[825] In a judgment notable for its deference to the arguments of the national authorities and courts, the Grand Chamber conducted only the briefest proportionality analysis, finding that the ban was within the margin of appreciation. In a strong dissent, Judge Tulkens stated: 'In a democratic society, I believe that it is necessary to seek to harmonise the principles of secularism, equality and liberty, not to weigh one against the other.'[826]

7.380   The Grand Chamber invoked the margin of appreciation to reach a different result in a highly controversial decision concerning the display of the crucifix in Italian public schools. The Court found that the crucifix was a 'passive symbol' that did not have an influence on pupils and held that the decision whether to display the crucifix was one which fell within the state's margin of appreciation. The

---

[819] (1994) 17 EHRR 397.
[820] (2000) 31 EHRR 411. See also discussion at para 7.577.
[821] See, eg *McGuinness v UK* App No 39511/98, 8 June 1999.
[822] *Kokkinakis v Greece* (1994) 17 EHRR 397, para 33.
[823] [2001] ECHR 42393/98.
[824] (2007) 44 EHRR 5.
[825] Ibid, para 111.
[826] Ibid, para 4.

case was determined under the right to education in Article 2 of Protocol 1 and Article 9 was not considered in any detail. The Grand Chamber received more state party interventions in this case than in any other before and the decision may be informed in part by a desire by the Court to avoid inflaming tensions about its role.

In *Eweida v UK*, the Court concluded that the domestic courts' approach to   7.381 proportionality in relation to Ms Eweida had been wrong. The Court of Appeal had accorded too much weight to British Airways' desire to project a certain corporate image. Ms Eweida's cross was discreet, the airline had previously authorized other items of religious dress, such as turbans and hijabs, and since Ms Eweida's case had been heard, it had amended its policy to allow staff to wear the cross. However, the Court found that there had not been a violation of the rights of the other applicants in the case. Revealing the factual sensitivity of the proportionality enquiry, the Court reached a different conclusion in Ms Chaplin's case. The health and safety concerns relating to Ms Chaplin's cross were of a greater magnitude than those in Ms Eweida's case and hospital managers were better placed to assess the legitimacy of the concerns than the courts. In relation to Ms Ladele and Mr McFarlane, the Court held that the state had a strong interest in prohibiting discrimination on the grounds of sexual orientation, and the state benefited from a wide margin of appreciation in determining how to strike the balance between the right to manifest religious belief and the employer's interest in securing the rights of others. Neither Ms Ladele's nor Mr McFarlane's Article 9 rights had been violated by their employers.

Article 9(2) has been the subject of consideration in a number of domestic cases.   7.382 The statutory ban on corporal punishment of children in schools was held to be proportionate given the importance of protecting children.[827] Limiting Article 9(1) rights through nuisance and harassment prohibitions was justified in the interests of public order.[828] The criminalization of cannabis interfered with a Rastafarian's right to manifest his religion, but it was a justifiable limitation under Article 9(2).[829] A ban in Northern Irish prisons on Catholic prisoners wearing Easter lilies to commemorate the Irish 1916 Rising was held to be proportionate and the 'minimum interference' possible in the circumstances.[830] The slaughter of a sacred bullock belonging to a Hindu temple and suffering from bovine tuberculosis was proportionate to meet the needs of public health.[831]

The House of Lords in the *Shabina Begum* case found no interference with the   7.383 claimant's rights under Article 9(1), but nevertheless went on to hold that, had there been an interference, it would have been justified under Article 9(2).[832] The refusal to permit the claimant to wear the jilbab was a proportionate response to the legitimate aim of protecting the rights and freedoms of others. The critical factor that appears to have influenced this conclusion was the care with which the school had

---

[827] *R (Williamson) v Secretary of State for Education and Employment* [2005] UKHL 15, [2005] 2 AC 246.
[828] *Church of Jesus Christ of Latter Day Saints v Price* [2004] EWHC 3245 (Admin).
[829] *R v Taylor* [2001] EWCA Crim 2263, [2002] 1 Cr App R 519.
[830] *R v Byers* [2004] NIQB 23.
[831] *Surayanda v Welsh Ministers* [2007] EWCA Civ 893. See also *Ghai v Newcastle City Council* [2009] EWHC 978 (Admin).
[832] [2006] UKHL 15, [2007] 1 AC 100.

designed a uniform policy that responded to the range of religious identities in the school community and permitted a wide variety of dress.[833]

6. Section 13 of the Human Rights Act

7.384 During the parliamentary debates on the Human Rights Bill, members of certain churches became concerned that the effect of Article 9 would be to prevent them from selecting employees in a manner consistent with the ethos and beliefs of their organization.[834]

7.385 The solution adopted by the Government is contained in section 13 of the Act. It provides that:

If the court's determination of any question under the Act might affect the exercise by a religious organization (itself or its members collectively) of the Convention right to freedom of thought, conscience, and religion, it must have particular regard to the importance of that right.[835]

7.386 Lord Nicholls in *R (Williamson) v Secretary of State for Education and Employment* noted that section 13 emphasizes the importance of the Article 9 right, as 'it is one of two Convention rights singled out for special mention, the other being freedom of expression'.[836]

7.387 Section 13 is really no more than an exhortation to apply the balance inherent in Article 9 properly and it has not featured prominently in the domestic cases concerning Article 9.[837]

7. Article 9 and the Equality Act 2010

7.388 Domestic cases claiming infringement of religious rights have commonly been brought under the Employment Equality (Religion or Belief) Regulations 2003, the Equality Act (Sexual Orientation) Regulations 2007 (which extended the prohibition of discrimination on grounds of religion or belief into the provision of goods, facilities, and services), and latterly the Equality Act 2010, which replaced the 2003 and 2007 Regulations in similar terms.[838] The applicants in the *Eweida* litigation in the European Court had all brought domestic claims under the 2003 Regulations. The domestic courts took the view that Article 9 did not add anything to the claims. The Court of Appeal considered in *Eweida* that the 2003 Regulations required that indirect discrimination required evidence of group disadvantage and could not be made out in relation to a single individual wishing to manifest her religion.[839]

---

[833] Ibid at [33] per Lord Bingham, and at [98] per Baroness Hale.
[834] For details see *Hansard*, HL, cols 747–801 (5 February 1998).
[835] For further discussion of s 13, see ch 3, para 3.83.
[836] [2005] UKHL 15, [2005] 2 AC 246 at [19].
[837] *R (Core Issues Trust) v Transport for London* [2014] EWCA Civ 34 at [94].
[838] Claims have also been made for race discrimination, see eg *R (Watkins-Singh) v Governing Body of Aberdare Girls' High School* [2008] EWHC 1865 (Admin), [2008] ELR 561.
[839] [2010] EWCA Civ 80, [2010] IRLR 3222.

It is clear from the judgment of the European Court in *Eweida* that the require-   7.389
ment of group disadvantage in domestic discrimination law prohibits adequate protection of Article 9 rights and subsequent domestic decisions will need to take a
more expansive view of indirect discrimination.

The Court of Appeal has recently recognized that Article 9 has an impact on the   7.390
interpretation of the statutory regime. In *MBA v Mayor and Burgesses of the London
Borough of Merton* it held that the ET was required to read the 2003 Regulations
compatibly with Article 9 and found that Article 9 rendered 'irrelevant' the question whether refusal to work on Sundays was a core component of a person's faith.[840]

In *Bull and another v Hall and another* the Supreme Court considered the role   7.391
of Article 9 in a claim brought by a homosexual couple against the Christian proprietors of a bed and breakfast who refused them a double room on the grounds
that it offended their beliefs.[841] The Court set out the potential conflict between
the statutory prohibition on discrimination on the grounds of sexual orientation
in the Equality Act (Sexual Orientation) Regulations 2007 and the protection for
manifestation of religious belief in Article 9. The proprietors complained that the
Regulations interfered with their Article 9 right to manifest their religion, but the
Court found that the interference was justified by the aim of preventing discrimination. As Lady Hale noted, homosexuals have long suffered an 'affront to their
dignity as human beings'[842] and the European Court has emphasized that 'very
weighty reasons' are required to justify discrimination on the grounds of sexual orientation. Ultimately, the courts seem likely to prioritize the right to sexual identity
over manifestation of religious views.[843]

G. ARTICLE 10: FREEDOM OF EXPRESSION

Freedom of expression has been described as 'the lifeblood of democracy'.[844] In   7.392
Handyside v UK the ECtHR described it as 'one of the essential foundations of…a
[democratic] society, one of the basic conditions for its progress and for the development of every man'.[845] Other theoretical justifications advanced for protecting freedom of expression are the advancement of truth in a 'market place of ideas',[846] and
self-expression.[847] In *McCartan Turkington Breen*, Lord Bingham observed that:

In a modern developed society, it is only a small minority of citizens who can participate directly
in the discussions and decisions which shape the public life of that society. The majority can

---

[840] [2013] EWCA Civ 1562.
[841] [2013] UKSC 73, [2014] 1 All ER 919.
[842] Ibid at [53].
[843] As the decision of the European Court in *Ladele* and *McFarlane* illustrates.
[844] *R v Secretary of State for the Home Department, ex p Simms* [2000] 2 AC 115, 126 per Lord Steyn. See
also *Handyside v UK* (1976) 1 EHRR 737, para 49; *McCartan Turkington Breen v Times Newspapers Ltd*
[2001] 2 AC 277, 297.
[845] (1976) 1 EHRR 737, para 49.
[846] See, eg *Abrams v US* 250 US 616 (1919), 630, per Justice Holmes.
[847] See, eg *Procunier v Martinez* 416 US 396 (1974), per Justice Marshall.

participate only indirectly, by exercising their rights as citizens to vote, express their opinions, make representations to the authorities, form pressure groups and so on. But the majority cannot participate in the public life of their society in these ways if they are not alerted to and informed about matters which call or may call for consideration and action. It is very largely through the media, including of course the press, that they will be so alerted and informed. The proper functioning of a modern participatory democracy requires that the media be free, active, professional and inquiring. For this reason, the courts, here and elsewhere, have recognized the cardinal importance of press freedom.[848]

The philosophical underpinning of Article 10 is thus rooted firmly in a notion of individual self-fulfilment experienced through participation in democratic debate.[849]

7.393 Article 10 commonly overlaps with other rights, such as the right to manifest one's beliefs (Article 9),[850] the right to protest (Article 11),[851] and the right to vote and stand for office (Protocol 1, Article 3).[852] Despite the close relationship between Article 10 and other democratic rights, it can on occasion clash with values considered to be vital to democracy. This conflict causes Strasbourg and domestic courts difficulty. On occasion, they have struggled to strike a balance between the importance of the right to freedom of expression to a democratic system and competing social interests protected under Article 10(2) or by other Convention rights, such as the right to a fair trial,[853] the right of access to a court,[854] the protection of the democratic process,[855] others' privacy,[856] and the right to respect for freedom of thought, conscience, and religion.[857] Thus, in the Grand Chamber's controversial decision upholding an absolute ban on a major Turkish political party, freedom of expression had to be sacrificed to the preeminent need to protect the democratic and secular foundations of the state.[858]

7.394 The domestic courts have recognized the right to freedom of expression at common law for many years.[859] As Laws LJ has evocatively put it, 'freedom

---

[848] *McCartan Turkington Breen v Times Newspapers Ltd* [2001] 2 AC 277, 290G–291A.

[849] See also *R v Secretary of State for the Home Department, ex p Simms* [2000] 2 AC 115; *R (Animal Defenders International) v Secretary of State for Culture, Media and Sport* [2008] UKHL 15, [2008] 1 AC 1312 at [28] per Lord Bingham.

[850] *Leyla Sahin v Turkey* (2005) 41 EHRR 8.

[851] See, eg *Hashman and Harrup v UK* (2000) 30 EHRR 241; *Rekvenyi v Hungary* (2000) 30 EHRR 519; *R (Laporte) v Chief Constable of Gloucestershire Constabulary* [2006] UKHL 55, [2007] 2 AC 105.

[852] See, eg *Hirst v UK (No 2)* (2006) 42 EHRR 41; *Kudeshkina v Russia* App No 29492/05, 26 February 2009.

[853] See, eg *Sunday Times v UK (No 1)* (1979) 2 EHRR 245.

[854] *MGN v UK* App No 39401/04, 18 January 2011.

[855] See, eg *Bowman v UK* (1998) 26 EHRR 1.

[856] See, eg *Lingens v Austria* (1986) 8 EHRR 407; *Mosley v UK* App No 48009/08, 10 May 2011; *Campbell v MGN Ltd* [2004] UKHL 22, [2004] 2 AC 457.

[857] See, eg *Otto-Preminger Institute v Austria* (1994) 19 EHRR 34.

[858] *Refah Partisi v Turkey* (2003) 14 BHRC 1.

[859] See, eg *Cassell and Co Ltd v Broome* [1972] AC 1027; *McCartan Turkington Breen v Times Newspapers* [2001] 2 AC 277; *R v Shayler* [2002] UKHL 11, [2003] 1 AC 247.

of expression is as much a sinew of the common law as it is of the European Convention'.[860] The House of Lords held on a number of occasions that the common law recognition of freedom of speech is consistent with Article 10.[861] In a recent case on the right to receive information, the Supreme Court suggested that the common law should be the starting point for any assertion of rights as it will generally be synonymous with the Convention and may offer greater protection.[862] Nonetheless, Article 10 has had an impact across a wide variety of areas, in particular in the field of media law,[863] but also in relation to advertising,[864] defamation,[865] contempt of court,[866] criminal law,[867] copyright,[868] prisoners,[869] public inquiries,[870] and public protest.[871]

Despite judicial assertions that freedom of expression receives the same, or even greater, protection at common law as under the Convention, it is clear from adverse results for the UK Government in Strasbourg in Article 10 cases that a gap may exist between the standards applied by Strasbourg and the domestic courts.[872] In particular, there are circumstances in which the domestic courts have not given the rigorous scrutiny to alleged justifications for restrictions on freedom of expression that one finds in some of the Strasbourg case law.[873]   7.395

---

[860] *R v Advertising Standards Authority Ltd, ex p Vernons Organization Ltd* [1992] 1 WLR 1289, 1293A.

[861] *Derbyshire County Council v Times Newspapers Ltd* [1993] AC 534, 551; *R (ProLife Alliance) v BBC* [2003] UKHL 23, [2004] 1 AC 185. See also *Spiller and anor v Joseph and ors* [2010] UKSC 53, [2011] AC 852 All ER 947, at [79].

[862] *Kennedy v Charity Commission* [2014] UKSC 20, [2014] 2 All ER 847. See also *A v British Broadcasting Corporation (Scotland)* [2014] UKSC 25, [2014] 2 All ER 1037 at [56]. See ch 3, para 3.29.

[863] See, eg *Douglas v Hello! Ltd* [2001] QB 967; *Campbell v MGN* [2004] UKHL 22, [2004] 2 AC 457; *R (Pro-Life Alliance) v BBC* [2003] UKHL 23, [2004] 1 AC 185.

[864] *Hertel v Switzerland* (1998) 28 EHRR 534; *Markt Intern Verlag v Germany* (1989) 12 EHRR 161; *R (British American Tobacco) v Secretary of State for Health* [2004] EWHC 2493 (Admin), [2005] ACD 27; *R (Animal Defenders International) v Secretary of State for Culture, Media and Sport* [2008] UKHL 15, [2008] 2 WLR 781.

[865] See, eg *Loutchansky v Times Newspapers Ltd* [2001] EWCA Civ 1805, [2002] QB 783; *O'Shea v MGN* [2001] EMLR 40.

[866] See, eg *Attorney General v Scotcher* [2005] UKHL 36, [2005] 1 WLR 1867.

[867] See, eg *R v Perrin* [2002] EWCA Crim 747; *R (Laporte) v Chief Constable of Gloucestershire Constabulary* [2006] UKHL 55, [2007] 2 AC 105; *Dehal v DPP* [2005] EWHC 2154 (Admin), (2005) 169 JP 581.

[868] See, eg *Ashdown v Telegraph Group* [2001] EWCA Civ 1142, [2002] 1 Ch 149.

[869] See, eg *R v Secretary of State for the Home Department, ex p Simms* [2000] 2 AC 115; *R (Hirst) v Secretary of State for the Home Department* [2002] EWHC 602 (Admin), [2002] UKHRR 758.

[870] See, eg *Persey and ors v Secretary of State for Environment, Food and Rural Affairs* [2002] EWHC 371 (Admin), [2003] QB 794; *R v Secretary of State for Health, ex p Wagstaff and Associated Newspapers* [2001] 1 WLR 292.

[871] *R (Laporte) v Chief Constable of Gloucestershire Constabulary* [2006] UKHL 55, [2007] 2 AC 105.

[872] See, eg *Steel and Morris v UK* (2005) 41 EHRR 22; *Bowman v UK* (1998) 26 EHRR 1; *MGN v UK* App No 39401/04, 18 January 2011.

[873] See, eg *R (Farrakhan) v Secretary of State for the Home Department* [2002] EWCA Civ 606, [2002] QB 1391.

1. 'Everyone'

7.396   Article 10 states that 'everyone has the right to freedom of expression'. This includes both natural and legal persons, such as the media and non-governmental organizations,[874] as well as a company whose activities are commercial.[875]

7.397   The Strasbourg organs recognize that freedom of expression is enjoyed by state employees, including civil servants,[876] doctors,[877] army officers,[878] police,[879] and the judiciary,[880] although the applicant's status may affect the ECtHR's view on the proportionality of an interference.[881] Potential recipients of information can be 'victims' for the purposes of Article 34.[882] However, trade unions cannot claim victim status on behalf of their members whose right to freedom of expression may have been violated.[883]

2. Scope of the right

7.398   Article 10 encompasses the freedom to hold ideas and incorporates the right to receive opinions and information, as well as the right to express them.[884]

7.399   Article 10(1) encompasses the right to communicate or to express oneself in any medium.[885] Words, pictures, images, emblems, and actions intended to express an idea or to present information (such as public protest, demonstration, film, or symbolic acts such as flag-burning) can constitute expression.[886] Expressive activities as diverse as graffiti,[887] dress,[888] and street performance[889] have been found to fall within Article 10(1).

7.400   Three broad types of expression have been held to attract the protection of Article 10:

(a) political expression;[890]

---

[874] *Társaság a Szábadsagjogokért v Hungary* [2009] ECHR 37374/05.

[875] See, eg *Autotronic AG v Switzerland* (1990) 12 EHRR 485; *Sunday Times v UK (No 1)* (1979) 2 EHRR 245; *Groppera Radio AG v Switzerland* (1990) 12 EHRR 321.

[876] *Vogt v Germany* (1995) 21 EHRR 205; *Ahmed v UK* (2000) 29 EHRR 1; *Guja v Moldova* App No 14277/04, 12 February 2008.

[877] *Frankowicz v Poland* App No 53025/99, 16 December 2008.

[878] *Grigoriades v Greece* (1997) 27 EHRR 464.

[879] *Rekvenyi v Hungary* (2000) 30 EHRR 519.

[880] *Wille v Lichtenstein* (1999) 30 EHRR 558.

[881] See, eg *Rekvenyi v Hungary* (2000) 30 EHRR 519; *Kudeshkina v Russia* App No 29492/05, 26 February 2009.

[882] *Open Door Counselling & Dublin Well Woman v Ireland* (1992) 15 EHRR 244.

[883] *Powell v Ireland* App No 15404/89, 16 April 1991; *Hodgson and Woolf v UK* (1987) 51 DR 136.

[884] *Sunday Times v UK (No 1)* (1979) 2 EHRR 245; *Groppera Radio AG v Switzerland* (1990) 12 EHRR 321; *Open Door Counselling & Dublin Well Woman v Ireland* (1992) 15 EHRR 244.

[885] *Oberschlick v Austria* (1997) 25 EHRR 357, para 57.

[886] *Stevens v UK* (1986) 46 DR 245; *Donaldson v UK* (2011) 53 EHRR 508.

[887] *N v Switzerland* (1983) 34 DR 208.

[888] *Vajnai v Hungary* App No 33629/06, 8 July 2008.

[889] *H & K v UK* (1983) 34 DR 218.

[890] See, eg *Lingens v Austria* (1986) 8 EHRR 103; *Bowman v UK* (1998) 26 EHRR 1; *R (Animal Defenders International) v Secretary of State for Culture, Media and Sport* [2008] UKHL 15, [2008] 1 AC 1312.

(b) artistic expression;[891] and

(c) commercial expression.[892]

As the ECtHR has emphasized, Article 10(1) does not apply solely to certain types of information or ideas, or forms of expression, and thus the categories of protected expression are not closed.[893]

Political expression is broadly defined to include comment on a matter of general public interest.[894] The House of Lords has held that it would be wrong in principle to distinguish between political discussion and 'other matters of serious public concern';[895] both will be equally protected by Article 10. Public interest includes legitimate, robust comment on public figures.[896] Political expression generally receives greater protection than the other forms, though there is no express theoretical basis for this distinction.[897] While the ECtHR has never gone so far as the US Supreme Court in *New York Times v Sullivan*,[898] which requires proof of malice in defamation cases brought by public figures, it affords considerable protection to those who criticize politicians and other public figures, such as judges, whether or not the views they express are facts or based on opinion, and whether or not they are politely or elegantly expressed, unless they are 'gratuitous personal attacks'.[899]   7.401

Artistic expression contributes 'to the exchange of ideas and opinions which is essential for a democratic society'.[900] In a majority opinion in the case of *Vereinigung Bildender Künstler v Austria* the ECtHR held that an injunction prohibiting the display of photographs of the heads of various well-known figures, including Mother Teresa, on bodies engaging in sexual activities was disproportionate.[901] By contrast, in *Lindon v Austria* the Court held that the conviction for defamation of a novelist who 'impugned the honour' of National Front leader, Jean Marie Le-Pen, did not violate Article 10.[902]   7.402

Commercial expression also attracts the protection of Article 10(1). In particular, commercial speech sometimes also raises matters of legitimate public debate and concern.[903] However, statements made for purely commercial reasons are frequently considered not to contribute to a debate on the public interest and fall 'outside the basic nucleus protected by the freedom of expression'.[904] Consequently, the ECtHR   7.403

---

[891] See, eg *Müller v Switzerland* (1988) 13 EHRR 212; *Wingrove v UK* (1996) 24 EHRR 1; *Vereinigung Bildender Künstler v Austria* (2008) 47 EHRR 5.
[892] See, eg *Barthold v Germany* (1985) 7 EHRR 383; *Colman v UK* (1993) 18 EHRR 119.
[893] *Thorgeirson v Iceland* (1992) 14 EHRR 843, para 64.
[894] Ibid; *Hertel v Switzerland* (1999) 28 EHRR 534.
[895] *Reynolds v Times Newspapers Ltd* [2001] 2 AC 127, 204 per Lord Nicholls.
[896] *Lingens v Austria* (1986) 8 EHRR 407; *Janovwskiv v Poland* (1999) 29 EHRR 705; *Yankov v Bulgaria* (2005) 41 EHRR 854; *Reynolds v Times Newspapers Ltd* [2001] 2 AC 127.
[897] *Thorgeirson v Iceland* (1992) 14 EHRR 843, para 64.
[898] (1964) 376 US 254.
[899] *Oberschlick v Austria* (1997) 25 EHRR 357; *De Haes v Belgium* (1997) 25 EHRR 1.
[900] *Vereinigung Bildender Künstler v Austria* (2008) 47 EHRR 5, para 26.
[901] Ibid.
[902] (2008) 46 EHRR 35.
[903] *Hertel v Switzerland* (1998) 28 EHRR 534.
[904] *Markt Intern Verlag v Germany* (1989) 12 EHRR 161, para 32.

often applies a wide margin of appreciation to any restriction upon purely commercial speech. Similarly, the domestic courts have emphasized that commercial expression has less significance than political or artistic expression.[905] In *R (British American Tobacco Ltd) v Secretary of State for Health*, for example, the High Court found that while the right to advertise tobacco fell within the protection of Article 10, the ban imposed by the Government was easily justified by the overwhelming health and economic costs of smoking.[906]

7.404　　In order to protect an environment in which free expression and debate is possible, Article 10 also affords strong protection to the elements of a free press, such as working practices and principles that facilitate the gathering of information, as well as the actual expression of views. In *Roemen and Schmit v Luxembourg* a journalist successfully claimed that his right not to reveal his sources had been violated by searches of his home and property following the publication of an article he had written accusing a politician of tax fraud, which was supported by legal documents.[907] The ECtHR held that 'the protection of journalistic sources is one of the cornerstones of freedom of the press'.[908] The House of Lords accepted this principle in *Ashworth Hospital Authority v MGN* but held that in exceptional circumstances an order to disclose sources may be justifiable.[909]

7.405　　Expression does not generally fall outside the protection of Article 10(1) on the basis of its content. Both popular and unpopular expression is protected, including speech that might 'offend, shock or disturb'[910] or insult another person.[911] In *Jersild v Denmark* the ECtHR found that the conviction of a journalist for aiding and abetting racist insults made in a television show violated his right to freedom of expression.[912] In *R (Farrakhan) v Secretary of State for the Home Department*, the Court of Appeal accepted that Louis Farrakhan's right to freedom of expression was engaged in circumstances where he intended to propagate anti-Semitic views.[913] There are, however, limits to the extent to which offensive expression must be tolerated. The ECtHR has traditionally been cautious in the extent of the protection it gives to artistic expression that is likely to offend, for example.[914] However, offensive images produced for a serious artistic purpose are likely to receive stronger

---

[905] *Belfast City Council v Miss Behavin'* [2007] UKHL 19, [2007] NI 89, at 16.

[906] [2004] EWHC 2493 (Admin), [2005] ACD 27. Cf *R (North Cyprus Tourism Centre Ltd) v Transport for London* [2005] EWHC 1698 (Admin).

[907] [2003] ECHR 102. See also *Saygili v Turkey* App No 19353/03, 8 January 2008.

[908] [2003] ECHR 102, para 46. See also *Sanoma Uitgevers BV v Netherlands* [2010] ECHR 38224/03.

[909] [2002] UKHL 29, [2002] 1 WLR 2033.

[910] *Handyside v UK* (1976) 1 EHRR 737, para 49; *Jersild v Denmark* (1995) 19 EHRR 1; *R (ProLife Alliance) v BBC* [2003] UKHL 23, [2004] 1 AC 185; *Grobbelaar v News Group Newspapers Ltd* [2002] UKHL 40, [2002] 1 WLR 3024.

[911] *De Haes and Gijsels v Belgium* (1997) 25 EHRR 1; *Livingstone v Adjudication Panel for England* [2006] EWHC 2533 (Admin), [2006] LGR 799 at [36], [39].

[912] (1994) 19 EHRR 1.

[913] [2002] EWCA Civ 606, [2002] QB 1391. See also *DPP v Collins* [2006] UKHL 40, [2006] 1 WLR 2223; *Connolly v DPP* [2007] EWHC 237 (Admin), [2008] 1 WLR 276; *R (Naik) v Secretary of State for the Home Department and anor* [2010] EWHC 2825 (Admin).

[914] *Muller v Switzerland* (1988) 13 EHRR 212; *Handyside v UK* (1976) 1 EHRR 737; *Otto Preminger Institut v Austria* (1994) 19 EHRR 34.

protection under Article 10 than obscene publications in other contexts that lack artistic merit.[915] In the recent decision in *Palomo Sánchez and Others v Spain* the Grand Chamber considered the extent of the protection to be given to expressions of employees that grossly insulted their employers.[916] The Court held that an attack on the respectability of individuals in the professional environment was, on account of its disruptive effects, particularly serious and capable of justifying severe sanctions.

The ECtHR and domestic courts may also accept restrictions on such speech under Article 10(2) or Article 17, to protect others from hate speech.[917] Expression is generally not protected if it is inimical to the concept of a society based on tolerance, pluralism, and broadmindedness. Thus, the Court will not permit Article 10 to protect Holocaust denial or expression of extremist anti-democratic ideas.[918] The law may also be used to avoid the potential expression of violent anti-Semitic opinion, as the Court of Appeal did in *Farrakhan*.[919] But the representation of extreme racist views may be protected by Article 10 if the intention is to expose and explain, rather than to promote, those views.[920]   **7.406**

In *Vejdeland v Sweden* the Court addressed homophobic speech for the first time.[921] The applicants had distributed leaflets in a secondary school claiming that homosexuality was 'deviant sexual proclivity' and had 'a morally destructive effect on the substance of society'. The Court emphasized that discrimination based on sexual orientation was as serious as discrimination based on race, origin, or colour, and held that the applicants' imprisonment for agitation was proportionate.   **7.407**

3. Positive obligations

The duty to protect the right to freedom of expression also imposes certain obligations upon states to help facilitate the exercise of that freedom. In common with Article 8, the Court has recognized strong procedural obligations under Article 10. In *Fuentes Bobo v Spain* the ECtHR held that Spain was in breach of Article 10 by having failed to provide a legal framework which provided an adequate remedy to protect a journalist who was dismissed by a state broadcaster for criticism of its management.[922] In *Özgür Gündem v Turkey* the ECtHR found that Turkey had a positive obligation to take investigative and protective measures following a violent and threatening campaign against a pro-PKK newspaper.[923]   **7.408**

---

[915] *Vereiningun blidender Kunstler v Austria* (2008) 47 EHRR 5; *Belfast City Council v Miss Behavin'* [2007] UKHL 19, [2007] NI 89 at [16]; *Connolly v DPP* [2007] EWHC 237 (Admin); *Interfact v Liverpool City Council* [2005] EWHC 995 (Admin), [2005] 1 LR 3118.

[916] [2011] ECHR 28955/06.

[917] See, eg *Le Pen v France* App No 18788/09, 20 April 2010; *Féret v Belgium* App No 15615/07, 16 July 2009. Judgments available in French only.

[918] *Glimmerveen and Hagenbeek v Netherlands* App Nos 8348/78 and 8406/78 (1979) 18 DR 187.

[919] See para 7.437.

[920] *Jersild v Denmark* (1995) 19 EHRR 1.

[921] [2012] ECHR 1813/07.

[922] (2000) 31 EHRR 1115.

[923] (2001) 31 EHRR 49.

7.409   In an important decision of the Grand Chamber in *Sanoma Uitgevers BV v Netherlands* the Court held that the right to protect journalistic sources should be safeguarded by sufficient procedural guarantees, including the guarantee of review by a judge or other independent and impartial decision-making body, before the police or the public prosecutor have access to information capable of revealing such sources.[924]

7.410   The ECtHR has generally been cautious about imposing substantive obligations on the state.[925] However, in *Manole and ors v Moldova* the ECtHR developed a strikingly broad obligation to ensure that the public had access to a balanced, informative, and pluralistic broadcasting service.[926] If the state decided to set up or maintain a public broadcasting service, it was essential for it to be structurally independent and impartial and to provide a forum for public debate.

7.411   It is not yet clear whether Article 10 guarantees a fully-fledged right of access to information. Traditionally, applicants have had to rely on the protection of other articles to obtain access to personal material.[927] The jurisprudence now appears to be shifting, but, as the Supreme Court has suggested, the case law 'is neither clear nor easy to reconcile'.[928] In *Leander v Sweden*, the Grand Chamber stated that the Convention did not confer an individual right to access personal information from state sources.[929] More recent judgments have thrown that into doubt. In *Társaság a Szászbadsagjogokért v Hungary* the Hungarian Civil Liberties Union was denied access to legal documents relating to the Government's drugs policy.[930] The Court tentatively suggested that it had advanced towards recognizing a general right of access to information under Article 10. Nonetheless, the Court decided the case on the limited basis that the state had interfered with the right of the press to access official documents in their role as a 'social watchdog'. A number of other decisions have recognized a right of access to personal information where the right is enshrined in domestic law.[931]

7.412   The domestic courts have struggled with the European precedents. The Supreme Court held *In Re Guardian News and Media* in which media organizations applied to the Supreme Court to have anonymity orders discharged, that the press do not have a right 'to be supplied with information which would otherwise not be available to them'.[932] Similarly, in *British Broadcasting Corporation v Sugar (decd) (No 2)*

---

[924] [2010] ECHR 38224/03.

[925] See, eg *Appleby v UK* (2003) 37 EHRR 38.

[926] [2009] ECHR 13936/02. See also *Centro Europa 7 Srl and Di Stefano v Italy* [2012] ECHR 38433/09.

[927] See, eg *Gaskin v UK* (1989) 12 EHRR 36; *KH v Slovakia* App No 32881/04, 28 April 2009.

[928] *Kennedy v Charity Commission* [2014] UKSC 20, [2014] 2 All ER 847 at [59].

[929] (1987) 9 EHRR 433, 34 DR 78ECtHR. See also *Gaskin v United Kingdom* (1989) 12 EHRR 36; *Guerra v Italy* (1998) 26 EHRR 357; *Roche v United Kingdom* (2005) 42 EHRR 599.

[930] [2009] ECHR 37374/05. See also *Matky v Czech Republic* App No 19101/03, 10 July 2006; *Kenedi v Hungary* (2009) 27 BHRC 335.

[931] See, eg *Youth Initiative for Human Rights v Serbia* App No 48135/06, 25 June 2013; *Österreichische Vereinigung zur Erhaltung, Stärkung und Schaffung v Austria* App No 39534/07, 28 November 2013.

[932] [2010] UKSC 1, [2010] 2 AC 697. Cf *R (Binyam Mohamed) v Secretary of State for Foreign and Commonwealth Affairs* [2010] EWCA Civ 65, [2010] 3 WLR 554 at [175].

the Supreme Court found that there was no right under Article 10 to disclosure by the BBC of a report held by it for journalistic purposes.[933]

Most recently, in *Kennedy v Charity Commission* the Supreme Court considered 7.413 a Freedom of Information request made by a journalist for information relating to inquiries by the Charity Commission into charitable funds raised by George Galloway. The journalist suspected that the funds had been inappropriately used for political campaigning. The Charity Commission had refused the request on the ground that the information was subject to an absolute exemption from disclosure in section 32(2) of the Freedom of Information Act 2000. The Supreme Court considered whether section 32(2) should be read down to comply with Article 10. By a majority, the Court concluded that Article 10 was not necessary for the determination of the appeal as the common law and the Charities Act 1993 enabled disclosure by the Charity Commission. If Article 10 had been necessary, the majority held that Strasbourg had not yet recognized a freestanding right to receive information from public authorities. Lord Mance suggested that it would be undesirable for it to do so:

Article 10 would itself become a European-wide Freedom of Information law. But it would be a law lacking the specific provisions and qualifications which are in practice debated and fashioned by national legislatures according to national conditions and are set out in national Freedom of Information statutes.[934]

Lords Wilson and Carnwath disagreed. They suggested that Strasbourg cases have established that Article 10 requires disclosure by public authorities in some circumstances. There will doubtless be further development of the law in this area in both Strasbourg and the domestic courts.

4. Interferences with the right to freedom of expression

In general, it will not be difficult to establish an interference with the right to 7.414 freedom of expression.[935] An interference can take any form. The ECtHR has held, for example, that confiscation of materials found on the applicant during a search including cassettes, paperback books, a diary, and a map interfered with her right to freedom of expression.[936]

Interferences with freedom of expression most commonly concern either 'prior 7.415 restraint' on publication or post-expression sanctions. Prior restraints, such as injunctions, are not inherently incompatible with Article 10 but they require careful scrutiny and will only be justified in exceptional circumstances.[937] News has a

---

[933] [2012] UKSC 4, [2012] 2 All ER 509.

[934] Ibid at [94].

[935] Cf *R (Rusbridger) v Attorney General* [2003] UKHL 38, [2004] 1 AC 357, an exceptional case in which Art 10(1) did not apply.

[936] *Foka v Turkey* App No 28940/95, 24 June 2008.

[937] *The Observer and The Guardian v UK* (1991) 14 EHRR 153; *Sunday Times v UK (No 2)* (1991) 14 EHRR 229; *Cumpana and Mazare v Romania* App No 33348/96, 17 December 2004. See also s 12(3) of the Human Rights Act 1998, discussed in ch 3, para 3.80-3.82.

very short shelf-life, and the courts have taken this into account in regularly reject-ing pre-publication delays or restrictions. In *Sunday Times v UK (No 1)* the ECtHR recognized that delaying the publication of news may amount in practice to it never being published, as news quickly becomes stale and delay would rob it of its interest and value.[938]

7.416   Post-expression sanctions can take the form of civil, criminal, or disciplinary penalties for publication, such as an award of damages for defamation or a sentence of imprisonment under hate speech legislation. As the ECtHR and domestic courts have held, the danger of such retrospective sanctions is that they have a chilling effect on freedom of speech that deters future public discussion of the subject.[939] Thus, in *Tolstoy Miloslavsky v UK* the ECtHR examined an award of libel damages finding that at £1.5 million, it was so high as to stifle freedom of speech.[940]

5. Exceptions to the right to freedom of expression

7.417   As a result of the relative ease of establishing an interference with Article 10(1), the majority of cases are determined in relation to the very substantial internal limits on the right to freedom of expression. Article 10(1) provides that it does not prevent states from requiring the licensing of broadcasting, television, or cinema enter-prises. The list of exceptions under Article 10(2) is more extensive and specific than in relation to other articles. Further, Article 10(2) specifically states that the exer-cise of the freedoms in Article 10(1) 'carries with it duties and responsibilities',[941] a phrase that does not appear in the other qualified rights. Article 10(1) can also be balanced against other rights in the Convention that may override the protection afforded to freedom of expression.

(a) *Licensing exception*

7.418   When the right to freedom of expression is limited pursuant to the licensing excep-tion in Article 10(1), it is not necessary that any of the objectives in Article 10(2) be pursued. However, the interference must still be compatible with the broad require-ments of the second paragraph.[942]

7.419   The ECtHR has recognized that restrictions should be minimal and there is a presumption in favour of free access to transmissions. For example, in *Groppera Radio AG v Switzerland* the ECtHR stated that rejections of licence applications should not be manifestly arbitrary or discriminatory, and the necessity for any restriction must be 'convincingly established'.[943] In *Centro Europa 7 S.r.l. and Di Stefano v Italy* a private television company had been granted a licence for nation-wide television broadcasting but was unable to broadcast because no frequencies

---

[938] (1979) 2 EHRR 245.
[939] See, eg *Jersild v Denmark* (1995) 19 EHRR 1, para 44; *Jameel and ors v Wall Street Journal Europe* [2006] UKHL 44, [2007] 1 AC 359 at [154].
[940] (1995) 20 EHRR 442.
[941] See *Lindon, Otchakovsky-Laurens and July v France* (2008) 46 EHRR 35, para 67.
[942] *Informationsverein Lentia v Austria* (1994) 17 EHRR 93.
[943] (1990) 12 EHRR 485, para 61.

had been allocated to it by the authorities.[944] The Grand Chamber found that the state had failed in its positive obligation to put in place an appropriate legislative and administrative framework to guarantee effective pluralism in the media.

The domestic courts have, in general, adopted a light-touch approach to the review of licensing and broadcast decisions. In the leading case, *R (Prolife Alliance) v BBC*, the House of Lords considered a decision by the BBC pursuant to its statutory broadcasting code to refuse to broadcast a party election broadcast that showed an abortion in graphic detail on the ground that it contained offensive material.[945] The Court of Appeal had held that it was only in very rare circumstances that a party election broadcast could properly be rejected by broadcasters on the grounds of taste and decency, and the broadcasters had failed to give sufficient weight to the pressing imperative of free political expression. By a majority (Lord Scott dissenting), the House of Lords disagreed, finding that the broadcasters had followed the statutory guidance without error and the court should not disturb their decision. **7.420**

In *R (Animal Defenders International) v Secretary of State for Culture, Media and Sport* the House of Lords held that the total prohibition on political advertising on television was proportionate to the need to ensure a level playing field for the expression of all lawful political opinions.[946] No such prohibition applied to other forms of media, including radio and cinema, but their Lordships concluded that the 'immediacy of television' explained why there was a pressing social need for such a prohibition.[947] Distinguishing the decision of the European Court in a very similar case,[948] Lord Bingham held that great weight should be accorded to the legislative decision because politicians were 'peculiarly sensitive to the measures necessary to safeguard the integrity of our democracy'.[949] The decision was upheld by the Grand Chamber on the grounds that the ban fell within the state's margin of appreciation.[950] **7.421**

(b) *General limitations under Article 10(2)*

Despite the apparently wide restrictions under Article 10(2), it is evident from the case law that the ECtHR will require a strong justification for interfering with the right to freedom of expression. It has developed a rigorous three-stage approach, first set out in the *Sunday Times* case, when examining a claimed justification under Article 10(2).[951] In order to be justified the interference must be: (i) in accordance with law; (ii) in pursuance of a legitimate aim; and (iii) 'necessary in a democratic society'. The Grand Chamber restated these principles in *Lindon, Otchakovsky-Laurens and July v France*, emphasizing that exceptions must **7.422**

---

[944] [2012] ECHR 38433/09.
[945] [2003] UKHL 23, [2004] 1 AC 185.
[946] [2008] UKHL 15, [2008] 1 AC 1312.
[947] Ibid at [30].
[948] *VGT Vereingegen Tierfabriken v Switzerland* (2001) 10 BHRC 473.
[949] [2008] UKHL 15, [2008] 1 AC 1312 at [33].
[950] *Animal Defenders International v UK* (2013) 34 BHRC 137. See para 7.449.
[951] *Sunday Times v UK (No 1)* (1979) 2 EHRR 245.

be 'strictly construed' and the need for them must be 'established convincingly'.[952] With some notable exceptions,[953] the European Court has adopted a reasonably robust approach to protecting freedom of speech.

7.423   In applying the three-stage test, the ECtHR generally resists the notion of 'balancing' freedom of expression under Article 10(1) against the purported legitimate aim under Article 10(2). As the ECtHR put it in the *Sunday Times* case, it 'is faced not with a choice between two conflicting principles, but with a principle of freedom of expression that is subject to a number of exceptions which must be narrowly interpreted'.[954] Thus, the two paragraphs are not equal; the right protected by Article 10(1) has presumptive weight.

7.424   (i) *In accordance with law*   In common with the other qualified rights, any restriction on freedom of expression must have a legal basis and be adequately accessible and sufficiently foreseeable. The ECtHR has generally found that this requirement has been fulfilled.[955] However, in *Sanoma Uitgevers BV v Netherlands* the Grand Chamber found that the procedure for protecting journalist's sources was inadequate and not 'in accordance with the law'.[956] *Sanoma* provides an example of the principle of 'quality of law' that imposes substantive legal requirements onto the notion of accordance with the law.[957]

7.425   The common law will not in principle fail to satisfy the requirement that an interference is prescribed by law.[958] However, in *Hashman and Harrup v UK* the ECtHR concluded that ordering the applicants to be bound over to keep the peace on the basis that their conduct was wrong in the judgment of fellow citizens was not sufficiently precise to satisfy Article 10(2).[959]

7.426   (ii) *Legitimate aim*   The only legitimate restrictions on freedom of expression are those outlined under Article 10 (2), namely:

(a) national security,[960] territorial integrity,[961] or public safety;[962]

(b) prevention of disorder[963] or crime;[964]

---

[952] (2008) 46 EHRR 35, para 45.

[953] See, eg *Refah Partisi v Turkey* (2003) 14 BHRC 1.

[954] *Sunday Times v UK (No 1)* (1979) 2 EHRR 245, para 65.

[955] See, eg ibid. Cf *Gaweda v Poland* (2004) 39 EHRR 4.

[956] [2010] ECHR 38224/03.

[957] See ch 2, para 2.44.

[958] *Sunday Times v UK (No 1)* (1979) 2 EHRR 245; *Tolstoy Miloslavsky v UK* (1995) 20 EHRR 442; *Steel v UK* (1998) 26 EHRR 603.

[959] (2000) 30 EHRR 241.

[960] See, eg *Observer v UK* (1991) 14 EHRR 153; *Sunday Times v UK (No 2)* (1991) 14 EHRR 229; *Brind and McLaughlin v UK* (1994) 77 ADR 42; *R v Shayler* [2002] UKHL 11, [2003] 1 AC 247.

[961] See, eg *Piermont v France* (1995) 20 EHRR 301; *Üstün v Turkey* [2007] ECHR 37685/02.

[962] See, eg *Ceylan v Turkey* (2000) 30 EHRR 73.

[963] See, eg *Engel v Netherlands* (1976) 1 EHRR 647; *Steel v UK* (1998) 28 EHRR 603; *Dehal v DPP* [2005] EWHC 2154 (Admin), (2005) 169 JP 581.

[964] See, eg *Marlow v UK* App No 42015/98, 5 December 2000.

(c) protection of health[965] or morals;[966]

(d) protection of the reputation[967] or rights of others;[968]

(e) prevention of the disclosure of information received in confidence;[969]

(f) maintaining the authority and impartiality of the judiciary.[970]

It is usually accepted that an interference with freedom of expression pursues a legitimate aim, often because the state relies on the broad notion of the 'rights of others'. The nature of the aim pursued will affect the enquiry into necessity and the application of the margin of appreciation.

(iii) *'Necessary in a democratic society'* This is usually the critical question in Article 10 cases.[971] A variety of factors will be relevant in the proportionality enquiry, including the extent of the limitation on expression, or 'chilling effect', the value of the particular form of expression, the objective of the expression, the medium employed by the speaker, the importance of the counterbalancing interest that the limitation on the expression in question intends to protect, and whether less-restrictive means of protecting that interest are available.   7.427

For example, amendments to the Public Order Act 1986 introduced by the Crime and Justice Act 2008 created new offences of acts intended or likely to incite hatred against a group of persons defined by religious belief or lack of it, or on grounds of sexual orientation. But the concerns of free-speech campaigners meant that these provisions were all explicitly limited so that discussion, criticism, or expressions of antipathy, dislike, ridicule, insult, or abuse of particular religious groups or the practices of their adherents, or sexual minorities and practices of their adherents were not offences. Moreover, prosecutions can only be brought with the consent of the Director of Public Prosecutions.[972]   7.428

Consistent with the theoretical basis for protecting freedom of expression, the ECtHR has repeatedly made clear that there is very limited scope under Article 10(2) for restrictions on debates concerning questions of public interest, regardless of whether they are polemical, aggressive, provocative, or even exaggerated.[973]   7.429

---

[965] See, eg *R (British and American Tobacco) v Secretary of State for Health* [2004] EWHC 2493 (Admin), [2005] ACD 27.

[966] See, eg *Open Door and Dublin Well Woman v Ireland* (1992) 15 EHRR 244; *Akdaş v Turkey* App No 41056/04, 16 February 2010; *Belfast City Council v Miss Behavin'* [2007] UKHL 19, [2007] NI 89.

[967] See, eg *Lindon, Otchakovsky-Laurens and July v France* (2008) 46 EHRR 35; *Mosley v News Group Newspapers Ltd* [2008] EWHC 1777 (Admin), [2008] NLJR 1112.

[968] See, eg *Otto-Preminger-Institute v Austria* (1994) 19 EHRR 34; *Norwood v DPP* [2003] EWHC 1564 (Admin), (2005) 169 JP 581.

[969] See, eg *Guja v Moldova* [2008] ECHR 14277/04.

[970] See, eg *Sunday Times v UK (No 1)* (1979) 2 EHRR 245.

[971] See the discussion of proportionality in general in ch 2, paras 2.61–2.66.

[972] See Public Order Act 2008, ss 29J and 29JA, and Part 3A.

[973] *Prager and Oberschlick v Austria* (1995) 21 EHRR 1; *Thoma v Luxembourg* (2001) 36 EHRR 359.

7.430   In *Steel and Morris v UK* the European Court considered the case of two Greenpeace protestors who had distributed leaflets critical of the fast-food chain McDonald's.[974] The ECtHR held that although the leaflets contained untrue and damaging statements, there was no reasonable relationship of proportionality between the injury to McDonald's reputation and the interference with the applicants' rights to freedom of expression. In particular, it was noted that the damages awarded were very substantial when compared to the applicants' limited resources and that McDonald's was a 'large and powerful corporate' entity.[975]

7.431   The objective of the expression will be critical to determining whether any restriction upon it is proportionate. For example, it will be harder to justify restrictions on racist speech that is intended to inform rather than offend.[976] The ECtHR will also take into account the medium of the publication when assessing whether an interference is proportionate. Television will have greater immediacy and impact than other forms of media, for example.[977] The nature of the expression may also affect the protection given to it by the ECtHR. In *Donaldson v UK* the Court considered that national authorities were best placed to determine whether certain badges worn by prisoners posed a threat to prison order because the domestic authorities were in a better position to understand their meaning.[978]

7.432   The ECtHR has repeatedly required particularly convincing justification for penal sanctions.[979] For example, in *Scharsach v Austria* it was held that by imposing criminal sanctions on a journalist and publisher who commented that a right-wing politician was a 'closet Nazi', the Austrian state had acted disproportionately.[980] However, there will be cases in which penal sanctions are deemed appropriate. In *Hoffer and Annen v Germany* the Court found no violation of pro-life activists' convictions for distributing defamatory material about a doctor who performed abortions on the basis that the relatively modest fines imposed were a proportionate response to the inflammatory statements.[981] Similarly, in *Monteiro da Costa Nogueira v Portugal* a majority of the Court accepted that Article 10 was not violated by criminal sanctions imposed on a doctor and politician for making defamatory allegations about criminal activity of public figures.[982] In *Vejdeland v Sweden* the Court upheld prison sentences for distribution of homophobic leaflets.[983]

---

[974] (2005) 41 EHRR 22.

[975] Ibid, para 96.

[976] See *Jersild v Denmark* (1995) 19 EHRR 1, para 33. See also *Lehideux v France* (1998) 5 BHRC 540, para 53.

[977] See, eg *Gunduz v Turkey* App No 35071/97, 4 December 2003; *Murphy v Ireland* (2003) 38 EHRR 212; *R (Animal Defenders International) v Secretary of State for Culture, Media and Sport* [2008] UKHL 15, [2008] 1 AC 1312.

[978] (2011) 53 EHRR 508.

[979] *Kyprianou v Cyprus* (2007) 44 EHRR 27.

[980] (2005) 40 EHRR 22. Cf *Prager and Oberschlick v Austria* (1995) 21 EHRR 1.

[981] (2011) 29 BHRC 654.

[982] App No 4035/08, 11 January 2011. Judgment available in French only.

[983] [2012] ECHR 1813/07.

The ECtHR considered the impact of the internet in libel claims in *Times*   7.433
Newspapers Ltd v UK (Nos 1 and 2).[984] In domestic law, the publication of a daily
newspaper's archives on its website expose it indefinitely to libel actions. Although
the Court found that there had been no violation in that case, it nevertheless held
that libel proceedings brought after a significant lapse of time might well, in the
absence of exceptional circumstances, give rise to a disproportionate interference
under Article 10.

In common with the European case law, domestic determinations of propor-   7.434
tionality will turn on the precise factual context. Contrast *Hammond v DPP*[985]
and *Dehal v DPP*,[986] for example. In *Hammond* the prosecution of an evangelical
Christian who bore anti-gay signs around a town centre was held to meet the pressing social need to show tolerance to all members of society, and held to be proportionate because Hammond was provoking violence.

The High Court reached the opposite conclusion in *Dehal*. The appellant had   7.435
been convicted for a public order offence after he put up a poster on a notice board
at a Sikh temple describing the temple's President in abusive and insulting language. In a model application of the three-stage *Sunday Times* test, Moses J held
that the mere fact that the words were irritating, contentious, unwelcome, or provocative was not enough to justify a criminal penalty unless they were intended to
provoke violence. The appellant's right to freedom of expression had been breached.

The High Court reached a similar conclusion in relation to a disciplinary sanc-   7.436
tion imposed on former London Mayor Ken Livingstone after he told a journalist
that he was 'just like a concentration camp guard'. The Court held that disciplinary
action was not 'shown to be necessary in a democratic society even though the
higher level of protection appropriate for the expression of political opinion was not
engaged'.[987] By contrast, in *Munim Abdul and ors v Director of Public Prosecutions*
the prosecution of protestors who shouted defamatory and inflammatory abuse at a
parade of British soldiers who had served in Afghanistan and Iraq was proportionate on the grounds that their behaviour posed a clear threat to public order.[988]

Although domestic case law generally follows the three-stage test set out in   7.437
Sunday Times v UK for assessing whether an interference with Article 10 rights is
justified, in some cases this test as applied to the facts of domestic cases is at odds
with the Strasbourg approach. In *R (Farrakhan) v Secretary of State for the Home
Department*, for example, the Court of Appeal was prepared to accept that the radical preacher's presence in the United Kingdom 'might provide a catalyst for disorder' that justified the Home Secretary's refusal to allow him to enter the country,
despite the absence of any evidence of the potential for disorder.[989]

---

[984] [2009] ECHR 3002/03.

[985] [2004] EWHC 69 (Admin), (2004) 168 JP 601. See also *Norwood v DPP* [2003] EWHC 1564
(Admin), (2005) 169 JP 581.

[986] [2005] EWHC 2154 (Admin), (2005) 169 JP 581.

[987] *Livingstone v Adjudication Panel for England* [2006] EWHC 2533 (Admin), [2006] LGR 799 at [39].

[988] [2011] EWHC 247 (Admin).

[989] [2002] EWCA Civ 606, [2002] QB 1391 at [58]. See also *R (Naik) v Secretary of State for the Home
Department and anor* [2010] EWHC 2825.

7.438   The House of Lords considered the role of Article 10(2) in *R v Shayler*, in which a former member of the security services disclosed confidential material contrary to the Official Secrets Act 1989.[990] He argued that disclosure had been in the national interest, and prosecution under the Act would infringe his right to freedom of expression. Accepting that the legislation interfered with Article 10(1), the House of Lords held that any restriction on freedom of expression should be subject to very close scrutiny. However, in concluding that the restrictions imposed by the Act were proportionate and pursued the legitimate aim of protecting national security, their Lordships did not engage in a thorough proportionality analysis, accepting that existing procedures for disclosure of concerns were adequate.

7.439   The Court of Appeal adopted a firmer approach to necessity in *R (Tabernacle) v Secretary of State for Defence*.[991] The court considered the rights under Articles 10 and 11 of a long-standing group of protesters that staged regular anti-nuclear protests on land owned by the Ministry of Defence, which wished to prevent the protesters from camping there. The court held that in order for the Secretary of State to justify measures prohibiting the protest, it was necessary to demonstrate 'a substantial objective justification...amounting to an undoubted pressing social need'.[992] The court's approach reveals an encouraging willingness to conduct a genuine and informed balancing exercise in which government assertions are not accepted at face value.

7.440   A more deferential approach was taken in *R (Miranda) v Secretary of State for the Home Department*.[993] Mr Miranda, the partner of investigative journalist Glen Greenwald, was stopped at Heathrow under paragraph 2(1) of Schedule 7 to the Terrorism Act 2000, which empowers the police to stop someone for the purpose of determining whether he appears to be 'concerned in the commission, preparation or instigation of acts of terrorism'. Miranda's hard drive was confiscated on the basis that it contained sensitive material that had been stolen by Edward Snowden from the US National Security Agency. The case attracted multiple interventions by civil liberties groups arguing that Miranda's detention had been an unlawful violation of journalistic freedom protected by Article 10.

7.441   The Divisional Court reviewed the legality of the police actions. Laws LJ held that Miranda's detention was authorized by the terms of Schedule 7. He considered that Article 10 did not need to be applied to determine the question of proportionality, stating that 'the common law is a sufficient arena for the debate'.[994] The confiscation had been justified by pressing national security concerns. The argument that Mr Miranda was assisting 'responsible journalism' was dismissed by the court on the basis that it was impossible for a journalist to make an assessment of the consequences of disclosure of the material in his possession. The court also

---

[990] [2002] UKHL 11, [2003] 1 AC 247.
[991] [2009] EWCA Civ 23.
[992] Ibid at [39].
[993] [2014] EWHC 255 (Admin)
[994] Ibid at [41].

rejected the claim that Article 10 required prior judicial scrutiny of interference with journalistic freedom.

(c) Conflicts with other Convention rights

In cases where Article 10 conflicts with another Convention right, the ECtHR will assess whether a 'fair balance' has been struck between the competing rights and interests. In such cases the ECtHR cannot give presumptive weight to either right, and must instead attempt to 'balance' the competing interests within the particular factual parameters of the case before it.   7.442

The most common conflict arises between freedom of information and the right to privacy under Article 8. The case law in this area is discussed under Article 8.[995] On occasion, rights under Article 10 can also conflict with other rights.[996]   7.443

The ECtHR recently considered the relationship between Article 10 and the Article 6 right of access to a court for civil litigants bringing defamation proceedings. In *Campbell v MGN (Costs)* the House of Lords held that conditional fee agreements (CFAs), under which an award of costs is increased by a success fee payable to legal representatives, did not breach Article 10 so long as the amount was proportionate.[997] The European Court disagreed.[998] The Court relied on the findings of the Jackson Review into Civil Litigation Costs, which recommended that success fees should not be recoverable from defendants. The ECtHR held that success fees at the rate of 100 per cent interfered with Article 10 by having a chilling effect on the press. The domestic costs regime did not strike a fair balance between Article 8 and Article 10. In response to the decision, the Government has stated that it intends to introduce primary legislation to reform the CFA regime along the lines proposed in the Jackson Review.[999]   7.444

In some cases the conflict between Article 10 and other rights under the Convention may be so profound that Article 17 applies. Denial of the Holocaust, for example, is deemed so offensive and contrary to established historical fact that it is removed from the protection of Article 10 by Article 17.[1000] In *Norwood v UK* the ECtHR held that the display of a poster stating 'Islam Out of Britain—Protect the British People', with a photo of the Twin Towers in flames, was such a vehement attack against Muslims that it was incompatible with Convention values.[1001]   7.445

---

[995] See paras 7.288–7.299.

[996] See *R (Woolas) v Parliamentary Election Court* [2010] EWHC 3169 (Admin), [2010] NLJR 1756, in which a three-judge Divisional Court considered the balance between Art 10 and the rights of electors not to be misled under Art 3 of Protocol 1.

[997] [2005] UKHL 61, [2005] 1 WLR 3394.

[998] *MGN v UK* App (2011) 29 BHRC 686.

[999] Ministry of Justice, 'Reforming Civil Litigation Funding and Costs in England and Wales—Implementation of Lord Justice Jackson's Recommendations: The Government Response' (March 2011).

[1000] See, eg *Chauvy v France* (2005) 41 EHRR 29; *Garaudy v France* App No 65831/01, 24 June 2003.

[1001] (2005) 40 EHRR SE11. In *Woolas* [2010] EWHC 3168 (Admin), [2010] NLJR 1756. also, it was held that deliberate falsehoods calculated to incite racial hatred did not attract the protection of Art 10.

6. Margin of appreciation

7.446 The ECtHR has claimed that in all cases, it exercises strict supervision of the margin of appreciation because of the crucial importance of the Article 10 right.[1002] However, given the cultural sensitivity of much expression, the ECtHR in fact has frequent recourse to this concept in order to defer to the courts of individual Member States, which are closer to the interests to be balanced in any individual Member State. In particular, in cases involving public morals[1003] or commercial speech,[1004] the breadth of the margin is wider than that pertaining in cases involving an issue that affects the general interest, even where a criminal penalty is at issue.[1005]

7.447 The ECtHR set out its reasons for applying a margin of appreciation in relation to cases raising questions of morality in the early case of *Handyside v UK*. The Court stated:

> it is not possible to find in the domestic law of the various Contracting States a uniform European conception of morals. The view taken by their respective laws of the requirements of morals varies from time to time and from place to place, especially in our era which is characterised by a rapid and far-reaching evolution of opinions on the subject. By reason of their direct and continuous contact with the vital forces of their countries, State authorities are in principle in a better position than the international judge to give an opinion on the exact content of these requirements as well as on the 'necessity' of a 'restriction' or 'penalty' intended to meet them.[1006]

7.448 This approach has subsequently been applied in a variety of contexts. In *Otto-Preminger Institute v Austria* the ECtHR decided that it was within the state's margin of appreciation to decide to seize a film that satirized God, Jesus, and Mary where the predominantly Catholic population might be offended by the film.[1007] A similar conclusion was reached in *Wingrove v UK*, in which the British Board of Film Classification refused a certificate for a video called *Visions of Ecstasy*.[1008]

7.449 The same approach has been taken in relation to religious advertising. In *Murphy v Ireland* the ECtHR held that it was within the state's margin of appreciation to impose a total ban on religious adverts in light of the population's particular religious sensitivities.[1009] By contrast in *Akdas, v Turkey* the ECtHR considered that the Turkish applicant's conviction for publishing a French erotic novel that had first been published in France in 1907 did not fall within the state's margin of appreciation because the book formed part of a 'European literary heritage' which all Europeans were entitled to access.[1010] In *Animal Defenders v UK* the Grand Chamber accepted that a total ban on television and radio advertising by an animal

---

[1002] *United Christian Broadcasters Ltd v UK* App No 44802/98, 7 November 2000.
[1003] See, eg *Handyside v UK* (1976) 1 EHRR 737.
[1004] See, eg *VGT Verein Gegen Tierfabriken v Switzerland* (2002) 34 EHRR 4.
[1005] *Hertel v Switzerland* (1999) 26 EHRR 534.
[1006] (1976) 1 EHRR 737, para 48.
[1007] (1994) 19 EHRR 34.
[1008] (1996) 24 EHRR 1.
[1009] (2003) 38 EHRR 212.
[1010] App No 41056/04, 16 February 2010. Judgment available in French only.

rights NGO fell within the state's margin of appreciation.[1011] It took account of the 'exacting and pertinent' reviews by parliamentary and judicial bodies and the fact that the NGO could access other forms of media, in particular the internet and social media.

Some commentators have criticized the application of the doctrine for reducing   7.450
the scope of the protection of Article 10. In *Mosley v UK* the Court found that whether or not a pre-notification requirement should be imposed on the press to protect a person's privacy fell within the state's margin of appreciation. The case did not concern an inherently sensitive issue such as public morals and the ECtHR may have invoked the margin of appreciation in order to avoid a political storm.[1012]

7. Section 12 of the Human Rights Act

Section 12(1) of the Human Rights Act requires courts considering the potential   7.451
grant of injunctive relief to afford 'particular regard' to the importance of freedom of expression. Section 12(2) and (3) enjoins courts not to grant ex parte orders restraining freedom of expression, or prior restraints, without strong justification for doing so. The provision is a 'comfort clause'; it was introduced during the passage of the Human Rights Act to address the media's concerns about potential conflicts between privacy and freedom of expression, and in support of the principle that news is a time-sensitive commodity.

The addition of section 12 has not had a significant impact on domestic juris-   7.452
prudence.[1013] The House of Lords has confirmed that section 12(3) has altered the applicable test for the grant of an injunction preventing publication. Their Lordships indicated that the general approach is that the courts should be very slow to grant an injunction where the applicant has not satisfied the court that he or she is more likely than not to succeed at trial.[1014] The Supreme Court recently emphasized that even if section 12(2) does not entitle the media to be heard at an application for an injunction, the common law principle of fairness may afford them the right to a hearing.[1015]

Lord Neuberger's report on 'super-injunctions' considered the procedure adopted   7.453
in applications for injunctions preventing publication of private material.[1016] The media was concerned that applications for injunctions were too often made without notice. The report emphasized that section 12(2) requires advance notification of an application for an injunction and stated that only exceptional circumstances would justify departure from this rule.

[1011] (2013) 34 BHRC 137.

[1012] [2011] ECHR 48009/08. See Clayton and Tomlinson, *The Law of Human Rights*, 2nd edn (Oxford: Oxford University Press, 2009) 1454.

[1013] See ch 3, para 3.82.

[1014] *Cream Holdings v Banerjee* [2004] UKHL 44, [2005] 1 AC 253; *Scottish National Party v BBC* [2010] SC 495 (Court of Session).

[1015] *A v British Broadcasting Corporation (Scotland)* [2014] UKSC 25, [2014] 2 All ER 1037 at [67].

[1016] Report of the Committee on Super-Injunctions (20 May 2011); available at <http://www.judiciary. gov.uk/publications/committee-reports-super-injunctions/>.

H. ARTICLE 11: FREEDOM OF ASSEMBLY AND ASSOCIATION

7.454   Article 11 protects the twin rights of freedom of peaceful assembly and freedom of association. Most international human rights instruments treat these as distinct rights—only the Convention and the Universal Declaration of Human Rights (UDHR) combine them in a single article. Both rights are of a political nature and both have a collective dimension, as they both protect 'people power'—individuals uniting and gathering to express or protect their common interests. Together with the right to freedom of expression, these rights are essential to the proper functioning of a democratic and pluralistic society.

7.455   Article 11 includes an express right to form and join trade unions. This was omitted from the original draft, but added at a later stage. The *travaux préparatoires* show that this is intended (as with the UDHR[1017]) to be 'a right distinct from the right of association in general'.[1018]

7.456   The majority of the domestic cases concerning Article 11 have been concerned with freedom of assembly or the right to protest, whereas the bulk of the Strasbourg jurisprudence concerns the 'association' limb of Article 11.

1. Overlap between Article 11 and other rights

7.457   Article 11 rights often overlap with Articles 9 (freedom of thought, conscience, and religion)[1019] and 10 (freedom of expression).[1020] This is because the protection of opinions and beliefs and the freedom to express them is one of the objectives of the freedom of assembly and association enshrined in Article 11.[1021] The importance of the interrelationship of Articles 10 and 11 in particular has repeatedly been emphasized by the ECtHR, and this line of authority was unanimously endorsed by the House of Lords in *R (Laporte) v Chief Constable of Gloucestershire*.[1022] Article 11 rights may also interlink with Article 8, for example where the authorities collate or retain information on an individual's political opinions or activities,[1023] or when police photograph or film protestors or would-be protestors.[1024] Article 5 may also

---

[1017] UDHR, Art 20 (freedom of association) and Art 23(4) (right to form and join trade unions).

[1018] *Travaux Préparatoires: Article 11*, Council of Europe, DH (56) 16 Or Fr, 9–11 (16 August 1956).

[1019] See, eg *Chassagnou and ors v France* (1999) 29 EHRR 615; *Sindicatul 'Păstorul cel Bun' v Romania* [2013] ECHR 2330/09; *R (Parminder Singh) v Chief Constable of West Midlands Police* [2006] EWCA Civ 1118, [2006] 1 WLR 3374.

[1020] See, eg *Hashman and Harrup v UK* (2000) 30 EHRR 241; *Rekvenyi v Hungary* (2000) 30 EHRR 519; *Christian Democratic People's Party v Moldova* App No 28793/02, 14 February 2006; *R (Laporte) v Chief Constable of Gloucestershire* [2006] UKHL 55, [2007] 2 AC 105.

[1021] *Christian Democratic People's Party v Moldova* App No 28793/02, 14 February 2006, para 62.

[1022] [2006] UKHL 55, [2007] 2 AC 105.

[1023] *Segerstedt-Wiberg and ors v Sweden* (2007) 44 EHRR 2.

[1024] *R (Wood) v Commissioner of Police for the Metropolis* [2008] EWHC 1105 (Admin), (2008) HRLR 34, [2009] EWCA Civ 414; analysed by Harris, 'Photo Opportunity' (2009) 153(13) SJ 6.

play a part, for example, where 'crowd control' measures such as cordons or 'kettling' are adopted at marches or demonstrations.[1025]

The ECtHR has a very structured approach when dealing with cases raising issues under both Article 11 and another article. If the case concerns the right to peaceful assembly, the ECtHR will examine the interference under Article 11, using it as the *lex specialis* (specialist law), but then refer to the other articles in assessing the effect of the interference and the question of proportionality.[1026] In contrast, the domestic courts often sideline Article 11, for example focusing on Article 10 rather than 11, even though the 'expression' in question involves a protest or demonstration. However, in *R (Laporte) v Chief Constable of Gloucestershire* both Lord Rodger and Lord Carswell expressly approved the Strasbourg approach of treating Article 11 as the *lex specialis* and Article 10 as the *lex generalis* in protest cases.[1027] Nonetheless, the Court of Appeal has considered Articles 10 and 11 alongside one another without imposing a hierarchy between the two.[1028] In cases involving the association limb of Article 11 both the ECtHR and the domestic courts may primarily focus on Article 9, 10, or 11, depending on the context and facts. 7.458

2. Limitations: the operation of Article 11(2)

As with Articles 8, 9, and 10, an interference with the freedoms of assembly or association will breach Article 11 unless it satisfies the three-part *Sunday Times* test: the limitation is 'prescribed by law', directed towards one or more of the legitimate aims set out in Article 11(2), and 'necessary in a democratic society' for the achievement of that aim.[1029] This three-part test is explained in more detail in Chapter 2. During the drafting of Article 11 the legitimate aims set out in Article 11(2) were expanded to include certain restrictions on the full freedom of association of members of the police, armed forces, and administration of the state, at the insistence of the United Kingdom.[1030] 7.459

Courts will often be required to 'balance' competing Convention rights to determine whether limitations on Article 11(1) rights are justified 'for the protection of the rights and freedoms of others'. However, the ECtHR will only conduct a balancing exercise where the competing right or freedom is also set out in the Convention. A different, more rigorous test applies where the Government relies on the 'rights and freedoms of others' in a more general sense. The ECtHR has said: 7.460

It is a different matter where restrictions are imposed on a right or freedom guaranteed by the Convention in order to protect 'rights and freedoms' not, as such, enunciated therein.

[1025] See, eg *Austin v Commissioner of Police of the Metropolis* [2009] UKHL 5, [2009] 2 WLR 372; analysed by Mackie, 'The lady doth protest' (2009) 153(16) SJ 32; *R (Laporte) v Chief Constable of Gloucestershire* [2006] UKHL 55, [2007] 2 AC 105.

[1026] *Ezelin v France* (1991) 14 EHRR 362.

[1027] [2006] UKHL 55, [2007] 2 AC 105 at [85] per Lord Rodger and at [93] per Lord Carswell.

[1028] *R (Gallastegui) v Westminster City Council* [2013] EWCA Civ 28, [2013] 2 All ER 579.

[1029] *Sunday Times v UK (No 1)* (1979) 2 EHRR 245.

[1030] *Travaux Préparatoires: Article 11*, n 1019.

In such a case only indisputable imperatives can justify interference with enjoyment of a Convention right.[1031]

3. Freedom of peaceful assembly

7.461 The internationally recognized right to hold demonstrations has English origins, beginning with the ancient right to petition the English crown. Since the eighteenth century, peaceful protests gradually replaced riots as a means of public expression in the United Kingdom.[1032] Yet, despite this 'long history',[1033] peaceful protests had little protection in the English law prior to the Human Rights Act.[1034]

7.462 In recent years a number of high-profile incidents has sparked public debate on the importance of and limitations on the right to protest, such as repeated police and Government attempts to remove the long-term protests established opposite the Houses of Parliament, climate change protests, anti-capitalist demonstrations, abusive protests from bystanders during soldiers' marches on return from Iraq, and student protests over tuition fees. These issues have often reached the courts and relevant cases are considered below.

7.463 It should be noted that, unusually, this is an area in which the Northern Irish and Scottish courts have arguably more experience than that of their English and Welsh counterparts. They have considered and applied Article 11 in a large number of appeals against authorities' decisions to prohibit or place conditions upon processions, particularly those organized by the Orange Order and Orange Lodges.

(a) Scope of the right to peaceful assembly

7.464 The right to freedom of peaceful assembly is one of the foundations of a democratic society. Given its importance, it must not be restrictively interpreted. It has been held to apply to marches and processions,[1035] private and public meetings,[1036] press conferences, static protests, 'sit-ins' or occupations of buildings or land,[1037] and counter-demonstrations.[1038] This right may be exercised by individuals, associations, and corporate groups.[1039] Because freedom of assembly protects 'the abstract possibility of holding an undisturbed peaceful assembly', its organizers may claim to be directly concerned by 'any negative decision of the authorities'.[1040] Parties (other than the organizers) who intend to, but are prevented from, participating in

---

[1031] *Chassagnou v France* (1999) 29 EHRR 615, para 113.

[1032] Harris, *The Right to Demonstrate* (Hong Kong: Rights Press, 2007).

[1033] See, eg JCHR, *Demonstrating Respect for Rights? A Human Rights Approach to Policing Protest*, Seventh Report (2008–2009), HL 47-I, HC 320-I (3 March 2009).

[1034] See *R (Laporte) v Chief Constable of Gloucestershire* [2006] UKHL 55, [2007] 2 AC 105 at [34].

[1035] See, eg *Christians Against Racism and Facism v UK* (1983) 21 DR 138.

[1036] See, eg *Rassemblement Jurassien and Unité Jurassienne v Switzerland* (1979) 17 DR 93.

[1037] See, eg *G v Germany* (1989) 60 DR 256; *R (Tabernacle) v Secretary of State for Defence* [2009] EWCA Civ 23.

[1038] See Mead, 'The Right to Peaceful Protest under the European Convention on Human Rights' (2007) 4 EHRLR 345.

[1039] See, eg *Hyde Park and ors v Moldova (No 4)* App No 18491/07, 7 April 2009, paras 34–36.

[1040] *Baczkowski and ors v Poland* App No 1543/06, 3 May 2007.

a protest will also have standing in Strasbourg and under section 7 of the Human Rights Act, but where no protest took place the courts may require evidence that the applicant did intend to take part before accepting that he or she is a 'victim'.[1041]

The ECtHR has held that, if the state stores personal information on individuals related to their political opinions, affiliations, and activities, in violation of Article 8, this will *ipso facto* constitute an interference with the right to freedom of peaceful assembly and association. There is no requirement to advance evidence indicating that the storage of such information has hindered the individuals' Article 11 rights in practice.[1042]   7.465

Article 11 applies only to peaceful gatherings; it does not encompass 'a demonstration where the organisers and participants have violent intentions which result in public disorder'.[1043] Violent assemblies are thus completely excluded from its scope.[1044] However, if the intention is to hold a peaceful assembly, the possibility or even likelihood of a violent counter-demonstration or disruption of the assembly by unwelcome violent participants cannot remove the assembly from the scope of Article 11(1).[1045] In such a case, issues regarding the risks of violence would instead fall to be determined under Article 11(2).[1046]   7.466

An Article 11 claim may still be successful even if the demonstration was not halted by the authorities' actions. For example, in *Baczkowski and ors v Poland* the organizers of an anti-discrimination march succeeded in persuading the ECtHR that Article 11 had been breached by the Warsaw authorities' various attempts to thwart what the mayor had described as 'propaganda about homosexuality', despite the fact that ultimately the march had gone ahead on the planned days. The Court accepted that the applicants had taken a risk given the official ban in force at the time, and that this *could* have discouraged the applicants and others from participation.[1047]   7.467

Surprisingly, given that the ECtHR has made it clear that the right to peaceful assembly must not be restrictively interpreted, a number of domestic judgments regarding protest have concluded that Article 11 is not even engaged. For example, the House of Lords in *R (Gillan) v Commissioner of Police of the Metropolis* found that the application of random 'stop and search' powers[1048] to peaceful protestors did not constitute a prima facie interference with Article 11.[1049] Similarly in *R (Wood) v Commissioner of Police for the Metropolis* the Court of Appeal found   7.468

[1041] *Patyi and ors v Hungary* App No 5529/05, 7 October 2008, paras 26–28.

[1042] *Segerstedt-Wiberg and ors v Sweden* (2007) 44 EHRR 2, para 107.

[1043] *G v Germany* (1989) 60 DR 256.

[1044] See also paras 7.643 et seq concerning Art 17 of the Convention.

[1045] See *Christians against Racism and Facism v UK* App No 8440/78, 16 July 1980 (admissibility decision) (ECmHR); *Anderson v UK* App No 33689/96, 27 October 1997 (admissibility decision) (ECmHR); analysed in (1998) EHRLR 218 and McLean, *Property and the Constitution* (Oxford: Hart Publishing, 1999) 24–6.

[1046] See, eg *R (Parminder Singh) v Chief Constable of West Midlands Police* [2006] EWCA Civ 1118, [2006] 1 WLR 3374.

[1047] App No 1543/06, 3 May 2007.

[1048] Terrorism Act 2000, s 44.

[1049] [2006] UKHL 12, [2006] 2 AC 307.

that taking photographs of a protester in the street did not engage his Article 11 rights.[1050]

7.469　Article 8 and 11 issues were intertwined in *Gillan*, and heavy reliance was placed on the conclusion in *R (S and Marper) v Chief Constable of South Yorkshire Police* that retention of DNA samples of acquitted and unconvicted individuals did not interfere with Article 8.[1051] Following the Strasbourg judgment in *S and Marper v UK* rejecting the Lords' narrow approach to Article 8, the Lords' restrictive conclusion on Article 11 is also open to question.[1052] The issue was not addressed in *Gillan v UK* as the ECtHR concluded that the statutory provisions were not provided by law under Article 8(2).[1053]

(b) *Limitations*

7.470　Most assembly cases turn on the question of the necessity and proportionality of the interference. In making this assessment the courts are alert to the need to protect protests that annoy or give offence:

> If every probability of tension and heated exchange between opposing groups during a demonstration was to warrant its prohibition, society would be faced with being deprived of the opportunity of hearing differing views.[1054]

Similarly, in the case of *R (Tabernacle) v Secretary of State for Defence* (regarding the compatibility of byelaws prohibiting camping in the vicinity of atomic weapons establishments with Articles 10 and 11) the Court of Appeal stated that:

> Rights worth having are unruly things. Demonstrations and protests are liable to be a nuisance. They are liable to be inconvenient and tiresome, or at least perceived as such by others who are out of sympathy with them.[1055]

7.471　As with Article 10, the courts will require particularly convincing reasons to justify an interference with an assembly involving political speech or debate on questions of public interest.[1056] And, given the importance of tolerance in a democratic society, in any case involving peaceful protest, a 'high threshold' will need to be overcome before it can be established that the protest will unreasonably infringe the rights and freedoms of others.[1057]

7.472　This was affirmed by the House of Lords in *R (Laporte) v Chief Constable of Gloucestershire*.[1058] The police stopped coaches of protesters on their way to a protest

---

[1050] [2009] EWCA Civ 414, [2009] 4 All ER 951.
[1051] [2004] UKHL 39, [2004] 1 WLR 2196.
[1052] *S and Marper v UK* (2008) 48 EHRR 1169.
[1053] (2010) 28 BHRC 420.
[1054] *Öllinger v Austria* App No 76900/01, 29 June 2006, para 36; *Stankov and the United Macedonian Organisation Illinden v Bulgaria* App Nos 29221/95 and 29225/95, ECHR 2001-IX, para 87.
[1055] [2009] EWCA Civ 23 at [43].
[1056] *Öllinger v Austria* App No 76900/01, 29 June 2006, para 38; *R (Laporte) v Chief Constable of Gloucestershire* [2006] UKHL 55, [2007] 2 AC 105.
[1057] OSCE/ODIHR, *Guidelines on Freedom of Peaceful Assembly*, 29 March 2007, paras 70–71.
[1058] [2006] UKHL 55, [2007] 2 AC 105.

demonstration at Fairford air base. The House of Lords held that, since there had been no indication of any imminent breach of the peace when the coaches were intercepted and searched, and since the defendant had not considered that such a breach was then likely to occur, the action taken in preventing the claimant from continuing to the demonstration had been an interference with her right to demonstrate at a lawful assembly, which was not prescribed by domestic law; further, that in any event the police action had been premature and indiscriminate and represented a disproportionate restriction of her rights under Articles 10 and 11. *Laporte* was applied by the High Court in *R (Moos and anor) v Commissioner of the Police of the Metropolis*.[1059] The court held that the 'kettling' of climate change protesters during the G20 Summit in London was disproportionate on the basis that the protestors did not pose an imminent threat of breach of the peace.

(i) *Blanket measures*   In early cases the Strasbourg organs occasionally upheld blanket bans on assemblies. For example, in *Christians Against Racism and Fascism* the ECmHR upheld a two-month ban on any demonstrations in London, finding it to be justified given the tense atmosphere at that time caused by National Front demonstrations;[1060] and in *Pendragon v UK* the ECmHR upheld a four-day prohibition on all large assemblies within a radius of four miles from Stonehenge, based on past disorder caused there by Druid followers.[1061]   7.473

However, in recent cases the ECtHR has been highly critical of 'sweeping measures of a preventative nature' based on vague exhortations of the need to protect national security or public order, finding that such blanket measures do 'a disservice to democracy and often endanger it'.[1062] It will scrutinize such bans especially closely. Similarly, in the carefully reasoned case of *Aberdeen Bon-Accord Loyal Orange Lodge 701 v Aberdeen City Council* the sheriff's court in Scotland held that the council's reasons for an outright ban on a procession were not made out and that, in any event, such a draconian measure as a 'complete prohibition' was disproportionate to the 'concern that the procession might promote religious intolerance and might interfere with the rights of other citizens to go about their business freely and lawfully'. The court emphasized that 'tolerance is what is required in a democratic society and that includes toleration of views or sentiments which may not coincide with one's own'.[1063]   7.474

(ii) *Regulation of assemblies*   Requiring authorization for an assembly will not necessarily constitute an interference under Article 11. As the ECtHR put it in *Aldemir v Turkey*:   7.475

Any demonstration in a public place may cause a certain level of disruption to ordinary life and encounter hostility. This being so, it is important that associations and others organising

---

[1059] [2011] EWHC 957 (Admin).
[1060] App No 8440/78, 16 July 1980.
[1061] App No 3146/96, 19 October 1998.
[1062] See, eg *Stankov v Bulgaria* App Nos 29221/95 and 29225/95, ECHR 2001-IX, para 97.
[1063] 2002 SLT (Sh Ct) 52; discussed in Sir John Orr's *Review of Marches and Parades in Scotland* (Edinburgh: Scottish Executive, 2005), para 5.15.

demonstrations, as actors in the democratic process, respect the rules governing that process by complying with the regulations in force.[1064]

The Court of Appeal has also noted that some protests 'betray a kind of arrogance...which assumes that spreading the word is always more important than the mess which, often literally, the exercise leaves behind'. In such a case, 'firm but balanced regulation may well be justified'.[1065] An authorization procedure may even be required as part of the state's positive obligation under Article 11 to ensure that a protest is peaceful and that participants are not deterred from expressing their views by a fear of violence.[1066]

7.476   However, regulation should not represent a hidden obstacle to freedom of assembly.[1067] The ECtHR has emphasized that, even when there is a notification requirement and it has not been complied with, 'to disband the ensuing, peaceful assembly solely because of the absence of the requisite prior notice, without any illegal conduct by the participants, amounts to a disproportionate restriction on freedom of assembly'.[1068]

7.477   Despite this clear statement of the law from Strasbourg, the domestic approach to the question of prior authorization is questionable. Of particular note is the ban on spontaneous or 'without notice' protest around the Houses of Parliament in Westminster contained in the Serious Organised Crime and Police Act 2005 (SOCPA). SOCPA introduced a number of new criminal offences applicable to the 'designated area' in the vicinity of Parliament, including organizing a demonstration in a public place there without prior authorization, which effectively ruled out spontaneous protests.[1069] There have been a number of controversial SOCPA prosecutions involving 'peaceful, low-key protestors' who did not provide advance notification to the police of their activities.[1070]

7.478   SOCPA was introduced in part to deal with Brian Haw's 'permanent peace protest' in Parliament Square that has been joined by various other permanent protesters. There have been repeated attempts to remove these protests. In *Hall and ors v Mayor of London*, the Mayor of London brought proceedings against the various protesters, claiming that they were trespassing on Parliament Square Gardens and breaking certain byelaws.[1071] The Court of Appeal found that the appellants were trespassers but that it was necessary to assess whether the Convention rights provided a defence to the claim. The court held that the removal of the protesters was proportionate with regard to the fact that there was no absolute prohibition on the protest.[1072] The Court of Appeal reached the same conclusion in relation to the Occupy camp erected in the churchyard of St Paul's Cathedral.[1073]

[1064] App No 32124/02, 18 December 2007, para 43.

[1065] *R (Tabernacle) v Secretary of State for Defence* [2009] EWCA Civ 23 at [43].

[1066] *Rassemblement Jurassien and Unité Jurassienne v Switzerland* (1979) 17 DR 93, 119 (ECmHR).

[1067] *Aldemir v Turkey* App No 32124/02, 18 December 2007, para 43.

[1068] *Bukta v Hungary* App No 25691/04, 17 July 2007, para 36.

[1069] Section 132(1)(a).

[1070] See, eg *Blum v Director of Public Prosecutions* [2006] EWHC 3209 (Admin).

[1071] [2010] EWCA Civ 817.

[1072] See also *The Mayor of London v Brian Haw and ors* [2011] EWHC 585 (QB).

[1073] *City of London Corporation v Samede and others* [2012] EWCA Civ 160, [2012] 2 All ER 1039.

In 2011, Parliament passed the Police Reform and Social Responsibility Act, **7.479** which empowered the police to seize tents erected by campaigners in Parliament Square. The Court of Appeal considered the compatibility of the legislative provisions with Article 11 in *R (Gallastegui) v Westminster City Council*.[1074] As it had held in *Hall*, the court found that the need to preserve the amenity of Parliament Square justified the limitation on protestors' rights.

In examining whether a refusal to authorize an assembly or the imposition of **7.480** restrictive conditions are proportionate, the domestic courts and the ECtHR will pay particular attention to any possible 'less restrictive means' the state could have taken to protect the legitimate aim in question without unduly impairing the right to assemble. For example, in *Öllinger v Austria* the ECtHR accepted that an assembly to commemorate Salzburg Jews killed by the SS during the Second World War could interfere with other cemetery-goers' rights to manifest their religion and mourn their dead, yet nevertheless found that prohibiting the assembly violated Article 11. In the circumstances, having a police presence on hand in case of disruption was a 'viable alternative' that would preserve the applicants' freedom of assembly while respecting mourners' sensitivities.[1075]

(iii) *Counter-demonstrations* Freedom of peaceful assembly includes both the **7.481** freedom to demonstrate and to counter-demonstrate. In *Plattform 'Ärzte für das Leben' v Austria* the applicant anti-abortion protestors complained that the state had failed to prevent the disruption of their protest by pro-abortion counter-protestors. Both the ECmHR and ECtHR held that there was a positive duty on the state to protect demonstrators from counter-demonstrators, but there was no violation of Article 11 in the particular factual circumstances.[1076]

(iv) *Penalties* Given the severity of criminal sanctions, the courts must examine **7.482** the proportionality of such measures closely in each individual case. Criminal penalties imposed on protestors who have been involved in violence, public disorder, or disruption of the highway have been upheld as Convention-compliant in a number of cases, but where such penalties are imposed on individuals without evidence that they *personally* behaved in a violent or disruptive manner, they are highly likely to be disproportionate.[1077] For example, in *Ezelin v France*, subjecting a lawyer who had taken part in a demonstration that had become violent to a disciplinary reprimand, even though his personal actions were lawful, was held to be a disproportionate infringement of his Article 11 rights to make his beliefs known in a peaceful way.[1078] The United Kingdom has a number of strict liability offences that have on their face no scope for exceptions where the defendant was acting peacefully and

---

[1074] *R (Gallastegui) v Westminster City Council* [2013] EWCA Civ 28, [2013] 2 All ER 579.
[1075] App No 76900/01, 29 June 2006.
[1076] (1988) 13 EHRR 204.
[1077] See *Steel v UK* Reports of Judgments and Decisions 1998-VII, No 91, 23 September 1998 (Art 10, but reasoning readily applicable in Art 11 cases).
[1078] (1991) 14 EHRR 362.

non-violently at all times.[1079] The compatibility of such offences with Article 11 has not yet been tested in Strasbourg.

7.483   (v) *Assemblies on private property*   The question of whether the state's positive obligation to protect the right to peaceful assembly requires it to permit access onto privately owned property to protest has been considered in Strasbourg on a number of occasions. In the leading case of *Appleby and ors v UK* the ECtHR found no violation of Article 10 or 11 where the applicants had been prevented from campaigning in a private shopping centre.[1080] It held that there is no 'freedom of forum'[1081] inherent in Article 10 and no requirement of automatic access to private property in order to exercise Article 10 or 11 rights. It noted that the applicants had alternative ways of making their views known to the public, such as gathering elsewhere and canvassing door-to-door. However, the ECtHR did note that a positive obligation could arise in other circumstances, for example in a corporate town.

7.484   Another exception to the *Appleby* principle might arise where the privately owned venue itself is directly connected to the very point of the protest. As in *Öllinger*, the choice of venue would then be an essential part of the point the demonstrators wished to make. However, such an argument did not succeed in *R (Brehony) v Chief Constable of Greater Manchester*.[1082] Restrictions imposed on a protest against Marks & Spencer's involvement in Israel were considered proportionate, even though the protest was moved some distance away from the store, thus defeating the object of urging customers not to shop there.

4. Freedom of association

(a) *Scope of the right*

7.485   Although recognized in all major international and regional human rights instruments, the nature and scope of freedom of association is controversial. Some courts and commentators have endorsed a narrow definition of freedom of association, concluding that collective bargaining and strike activity are not protected by freedom of association. Others have adopted broader definitions, holding that freedom of association includes the freedom to pursue common purposes and to engage in collective activities, and is not merely the freedom to form and join associations. The ECtHR and domestic case law reflects this tension. The ECtHR has held that the elements of the right of association are not finite, but 'subject to evolution depending on particular developments in labour relations'.[1083]

7.486   The contrast in approaches to freedom of association is evident in the only two association cases yet to have reached the House of Lords or Supreme Court, both

---

[1079] Such as the SOCPA offences discussed at para 7.477.
[1080] App No 44306/98, 6 May 2003.
[1081] Ibid, para 47.
[1082] (2005) EWHC 640 (Admin), *The Times*, 15 April 2005.
[1083] *Demir and Baykara v Turkey* [2009] 1 RLR 766 at para 146.

concerning hunting bans: *R (Countryside Alliance) v Attorney General*[1084] and *Whaley v Lord Advocate*.[1085] Their Lordships divided on the question of whether Article 11 was engaged. Lord Brown and Lord Rodger thought that it was not, because the hunt members were still free to meet; they were simply banned from doing certain things when they got together. Lord Bingham, Lord Hope, and Baroness Hale had more difficulty, on the basis that 'there can be no point in protecting the right to meet without protecting at least some of the things you might want to do together'.[1086] As Article 11 refers expressly to the activities of trade unions, Lord Bingham was not prepared to rule it out. Lord Hope and Baroness Hale took the view that it should be read in the context of Articles 9 and 10, as 'Article 9 says that you can believe what you like and manifest those beliefs, and Article 10 says that you can say what you like. And Article 11 says that you can get together with others to do all of this'.[1087] In *Whaley* Baroness Hale thus concluded:

These articles, then, are designed to protect the freedom to share and express opinions, and to try and persuade others to one's point of view, which are essential political freedoms in any democracy. On this view, the right of the hunt and its followers to gather together publicly to demonstrate in favour of their sport and against the ban, perhaps even by riding over the countryside to demonstrate what they do, is protected by Article 11. But the right to chase and kill the fox or the stag or the mink or the hare is not.[1088]

(i) *Right to form and join associations* The right to freedom of association 7.487
protects the right to join or form 'associations', including political parties and trade unions. But Article 11 does not create a right to membership of a particular association in all circumstances. In *Cheall v UK* the ECmHR decided that generally an individual has no right to belong to a particular trade union. The decision to expel Mr Cheall was analysed as the decision of a private body exercising its rights under Article 11 not to associate with him. However, the ECmHR made the point that the right of the trade union to choose its members is not absolute:

For the right to join a union to be effective the state must protect the individual against any abuse of a dominant position by trade unions...Such abuse might occur, for example, where exclusion or expulsion was not in accordance with union rules or where the rules were wholly unreasonable or arbitrary or where the consequences of exclusion or expulsion resulted in exceptional hardship such as job loss because of a closed shop.[1089]

An example of an exclusionary policy being upheld by the courts can be found 7.488
in *RSPCA v Attorney General and ors*, where the RSPCA sought guidance as to whether it could adopt a membership policy that excluded individuals who wished

---

[1084] [2007] UKHL 52, [2008] 1 AC 719.
[1085] [2007] UKHL 53, [2007] SLT 1209.
[1086] Lady Hale, 'Hunting in the House of Lords', Eldon Lecture 2008 (delivered at Northumbria University, 28 February 2008) 13.
[1087] Ibid, 14.
[1088] [2007] UKHL 53, [2007] SLT 1209 at [118].
[1089] (1985) 42 DR 178.

to change its policy on hunting. The court found that the freedom of association of the RSPCA itself 'embraces the freedom to exclude from the association those whose membership it honestly believes to be damaging the interests of the Society'. The exclusionary policy would not therefore violate Article 11.[1090]

7.489   The ECtHR has accepted that a refusal to register or give legal status to an association may constitute an interference under Article 11(1), where this has the effect of preventing collective action in a field of mutual interest.[1091] But a refusal to register will not always constitute an interference. In *Gorzelik v Poland*, for example, the Grand Chamber upheld a refusal to register an association as a 'national minority' rather than an 'ethnic regional group'. It found that the disputed restriction was essentially concerned with 'the label which the association could use in law' rather than its ability to act collectively in a field of mutual interest. As such, it did not go to the core or essence of freedom of association, and the restriction was not disproportionate. This finding was despite the fact that the 'label' of national minority carried with it improved election privileges.[1092]

7.490   In *Sindicatul "Păstorul cel Bun" v Romania* the Grand Chamber held that the refusal to register a trade union for priests was justified under Article 11.[1093] It accepted that a trade union would imperil the autonomy of the church, protected by Article 9, to respond within its own rules to any dissident movement.

7.491   (ii) *Right to non-association*   Although not expressly mentioned, Article 11 also protects the right to refuse to join an association. The ECtHR first recognized this in *Young, James and Webster v UK*, holding that 'the negative aspect of freedom of association is necessarily complementary to, and a correlative of and inseparable from its positive aspect'.[1094]

7.492   The 'closed shop' is not always a violation of Article 11. In *Young*, it was, because the refusal to join a union led to 'a threat of dismissal involving loss of livelihood' which was 'a most serious form of compulsion' and, as such, struck 'at the very substance of the freedom guaranteed by Article 11'.[1095] In contrast, in the unusual circumstances of *Sibson v UK*, an employer exercised his contractual right to transfer an employee to a different depot after he resigned from one union to join another and others refused to work with him. The ECtHR held that Mr Sibson's treatment did not 'strike at the very substance of the freedom of association guaranteed by Article 11' because there was no question of his losing his job.[1096] In *Sørenson and Rasmussen v Denmark* the ECtHR emphasized that the Convention is a living instrument, and account must be taken of changing perceptions of the relevance

---

[1090] [2002] 1 WLR 448.

[1091] *Sidiropolous and ors v Greece*, 10 July 1998, Reports of Judgments and Decisions 1998-IV, para 40; *Tsonev v Bulgaria* App No 45963/99, 13 July 2006; *United Macedonian Organization Ilinden and ors v Bulgaria* (1998) 26 EHRR CD 103.

[1092] App No 44158/98, 17 February 2004, paras 105–106.

[1093] [2013] ECHR 2330/09.

[1094] (1982) 4 EHRR 38, para 59; *Vörður Ólafsson v Iceland* App No 20161/06, 27 April 2010.

[1095] (1982) 4 EHRR 38, 59.

[1096] (1993) 17 EHRR 193. On unwanted transfers, see also *Ademyilmaz and ors v Turkey* App Nos 41496/98, 41499/98, 41501/98, 41502/98, 41959/98, 41602/98, 43606/98, 21 March 2006.

of closed shop agreements for securing the effective enjoyment of trade union freedoms.[1097] The Grand Chamber rejected the distinction between pre-entry and post-entry closed shops, and held the interference with the applicants' rights to be disproportionate as the Government had failed to demonstrate that closed shops are 'an indispensable tool' for protecting trade union freedoms.

(iii) *Public and professional bodies*   Professional regulatory bodies set up by a   7.493
state to regulate a profession, with compulsory membership within a profession, do not fall within this definition of an 'association'.[1098] A bar association, architects' association, and medical practitioners' association have been held to be outside the definition; but a taxi drivers' association has been held to fall within it.[1099]

Bodies that are a necessary and inevitable part of membership in a democratic   7.494
community are also excluded from the scope of Article 11. An objection to being associated with Government and its policies through the payment of taxes, for example, could not be made out under Article 11. In the words of a former judge of the US Supreme Court, the state 'is one club to which we all belong'.[1100]

(iv) *Trade union activities*   As with other Convention rights, freedom of associa-   7.495
tion must be practical and effective. The ECtHR has thus held that the state must 'both permit and make possible' freedom for individual trade unionists to protect their interests by trade union action.[1101] In *Sanchez Navajas v Spain* the ECtHR considered that it could infer from Article 11, read in the light of Article 28 of the European Social Charter, that workers' representatives should have access to appropriate facilities to enable them to perform their trade union functions rapidly and effectively.[1102]

However, despite their commitment to 'real and effective' Article 11 rights, the   7.496
ECtHR and domestic courts have traditionally been reluctant to recognize that collective bargaining,[1103] strike action,[1104] and a right to be consulted[1105] are closely connected to freedom of association. The Convention remains markedly more restrained in this area than other international instruments such as the European Social Charter.[1106] The law is developing, however. In *Demir and anor v Turkey* the ECtHR recently recognized that Article 11 protects the right to collective

---

[1097] App No 52562/99, 11 January 2006, para 58.

[1098] *Le Compte, Van Leuven and De Meyere v Belgium* (1981) 4 EHRR 1.

[1099] *Sigurdur A Sigurjónsson v Iceland* (1993) 16 EHRR 462.

[1100] Per Justice Holmes; cited by Justice Brandeis in *Duplex Printing Press Co v Deering* 254 US 443 (1921), 448.

[1101] *National Union of Belgian Police v Belgium* (1975) 1 EHRR 578, para 39.

[1102] App No 57442/00, 21 June 2001.

[1103] *Schmidt and Dahlstrom v Sweden* (1976) 1 EHRR 632; *Swedish Engine Drivers' Union v Sweden* (1979) 1 EHRR 617; *Gustaffson v Sweden* (1996) 22 EHRR 409; *R (National Union of Journalists) v Central Arbitration Committee* [2005] EWCA Civ 1309. Cf *Wilson and Palmer v UK* (2002) 35 EHRR 20.

[1104] *Schmidt and Dahlstrom* (1976) 1 EHRR 632, para 36.

[1105] *National Union of Belgian Police v Belgium* (1975) 1 EHRR 578.

[1106] See Art 6 of the Council of Europe's Social Charter 1961 and the International Labour Organization Conventions.

bargaining as an essential element of the right to form and join a trade union. As the ECtHR held, it is 'one of the principal means—even the foremost of such means—for trade unionists to protect their interests'.[1107] In *Enerji v Turkey* the Court acknowledged that Article 11 enshrined a right to strike.[1108] However, the right could be made subject to certain conditions and restrictions as provided by national law.

7.497 Domestic law generally adopts a conservative approach towards collective rights. While recent decisions suggest greater willingness on the part of the courts to interpret legislative provisions governing strike action in light of Article 6 of the European Social Charter and Article 11, the statutory limitations on the right to strike are unlikely to be deemed non-compliant with Article 11.[1109]

(b) *Limitations*

7.498 As with freedom of assembly, most association cases turn on the question of whether an interference is 'necessary in a democratic society'.[1110] The ECtHR has emphasized that the Article 11(2) exceptions are to be construed strictly: only 'convincing and compelling reasons'[1111] can justify restrictions on freedom of association, and 'all such restrictions are subject to a rigorous supervision by the Court'.[1112] This strict approach is due to the 'direct relationship between democracy, pluralism and the freedom of association'.[1113] The ECtHR's jurisprudence on Article 11(2) attaches particular importance to pluralism, tolerance, and broadmindedness. In that context, the ECtHR has held that although individual interests must on occasion be subordinated to those of a group, democracy does not simply mean that the views of the majority must always prevail: a balance must be achieved that ensures the fair and proper treatment of minorities and avoids any abuse of a dominant position.[1114]

7.499 The ECtHR has recognized the importance of certain types of associations in ensuring pluralism and democracy. It has often noted the 'essential role' played by political parties in this regard, but has also stated that:

Associations formed for other purposes, including those protecting cultural or spiritual heritage, pursuing various socio-economic aims, proclaiming or teaching religion, seeking an ethnic

---

[1107] [2009] IRLR 766 at [129].

[1108] App No 68959/01, 21 April 2009. Judgment available only in French.

[1109] See, eg *British Airways Plc v Unite the Union* [2010] EWCA Civ 669, [2010] IRLR 423; *RMT v Serco Ltd* [2011] EWCA Civ 226, [2011] IRLR 399.

[1110] For a rare example of a violation on the basis that an interference was not 'in accordance with law', see *Maestri v Italy* App No 39748/98, 17 February 2004.

[1111] *Tüm Haber Sen and Çinar v Turkey* App No 28602/95, 21 February 2006, para 35.

[1112] See, eg *United Communist Party of Turkey and ors v Turkey* Reports of Judgments and Decisions 1998-I, 30 January 1998, para 42; *Socialist Party and ors v Turkey* Reports of Judgments and Decisions 1998-III, 25 May 1998, para 41; *Refah Partisi (The Welfare Party) and ors v Turkey* (2003) 14 BHRC 1, para 86.

[1113] *Gorzelik and ors* (2005) 40 EHRR 4, para 88.

[1114] See *Young, James and Webster v UK* (1982) 4 EHRR 38, para 63; *Chassagnou and ors v France* (1999) 29 EHRR 615, para 112.

identity or asserting a minority consciousness are also important to the proper functioning of democracy.[1115]

Dissolution or banning of associations that pursue objectives contrary to the state will rarely be justified under Article 11. Two examples stand out. In *Refah Partisi v Turkey* the Grand Chamber unanimously upheld the ECtHR's majority finding that the ban was justified as a state is entitled to prevent implementation of a political programme that is inconsistent with Convention norms and which, if given effect, might jeopardize civil peace and a country's democratic regime.[1116] In *Herri Batasuna and Batasuna v Spain* a political party linked to the terrorist organization, ETA, was dissolved.[1117] The Court endorsed the position of the domestic courts in finding that a refusal to condemn violence amounted to an attitude of tacit support for terrorism, in the context of the long-term threat from Basque terrorism.   7.500

The ECtHR has stated that the power set out in *Refah Partisi* 'must be used sparingly'.[1118] In a series of cases against Turkey[1119] and Bulgaria[1120] the ECtHR has found that the mere fact that an association expresses separatist views and demands territorial changes in speeches, demonstrations, or manifestos does not per se amount to a threat to a country's territorial integrity. Views or words which may appear 'shocking and unacceptable' to the authorities and the majority of the population should not be suppressed on this basis. Further, in assessing whether an organization truly propagates violence the ECtHR will take into account that an association's declarations may include 'an element of exaggeration' and harsh, acerbic language in order to attract attention.[1121]   7.501

However, the recent judgment in *Vona v Hungary* suggests a more expansive approach to the dissolution of political associations.[1122] In *Vona* it held that the ban on the Hungarian Guard Association, established to defend Hungary 'physically, spiritually and intellectually', was justified under Article 11 on account of its anti-Roma rallies and demonstrations, even though the movement had not made any attempt to seize power and it did not pose an imminent threat to democracy. The Court stated that the state was entitled to act preventively if it was established that such a movement had started to take concrete steps in public life to implement a policy incompatible with the standards of the Convention and democracy.[1123]   7.502

Article 11(2) permits states to place limitations on the exercise of the Article 11(1) rights by members of the armed forces, police, or members of the administration of the state, although this clause appears to be of diminishing importance in the light of   7.503

[1115] *Gorzelik and ors* (2005) 40 EHRR 4, para 92.

[1116] (2003) 14 BHRC 1.

[1117] App Nos 25803/04 and 25817/04, 30 June 2009.

[1118] *Gorzelik and ors* (2005) 40 EHRR 4, para 95.

[1119] *Freedom and Democracy Party (ÖZDEP) v Turkey* App No 23885/94 ECHR 1999-VIII, para 41; *Yazar and ors v Turkey* App Nos 22723/93, 22724/93 and 22725/93 ECHR 2002-II, paras 57, 58.

[1120] *Stankov and United Macedonian Association Ilinden v Bulgaria* App Nos 29221/95 and 29225/95, ECHR 2001-IX, para 97; *United Macedonian Association Ilinden v Bulgaria* (1998) 26 EHRR CD 103, para 76.

[1121] *United Macedonian Association Ilinden v Bulgaria* (1998) 26 EHRR CD 103, para 77.

[1122] [2013] ECHR 35943/10.

[1123] Ibid, para 102.

the case of *Tüm Haber Sen and Cinar v Turkey* (analysed in the next paragraph).[1124] In *Council of Civil Service Unions v UK* (the 'GCHQ' case) the ECmHR took the view that staff at GCHQ were 'members of the administration of the State' and that therefore there was no breach of the Convention in the decision of the UK Government to prohibit them from trade union membership.[1125] By contrast, in *Vogt v Germany* the ECmHR found that German schoolteachers were not 'members of the administration of the State', and the ECtHR held that this part of Article 11(2) 'should be interpreted narrowly in the light of the post held by the official concerned'.[1126]

7.504   The case of *Tüm Haber Sen and Çinar v Turkey*, concerning the dissolution of a civil servants' trade union, indicates that even when an individual does fall within this part of Article 11(2), a strict approach to the question of justification is nevertheless required.[1127] The ECtHR held that, to justify interfering with the freedom of association of members of the armed forces, the police, or the administration of the state, 'only convincing and compelling reasons' would suffice.[1128]

5. Article 11 and positive obligations

7.505   In addition to imposing a negative obligation on the authorities not to interfere unjustifiably with the protected rights, Article 11 contains a positive obligation on states to secure the effective enjoyment of those rights.[1129] For example, in *Plattform 'Ärtze für das leben' v Austria* (a freedom of assembly case), the ECtHR ruled that the state had a duty to protect the participants in a peaceful demonstration from disruption by a violent counter-demonstration:

> Genuine, effective freedom of peaceful assembly cannot...be reduced to a mere duty on the part of the state not to interfere: a purely negative conception would not be compatible with the object and purpose of Article 11...Article 11 sometimes requires positive measures to be taken, even in the sphere of relations between individuals, if need be.[1130]

7.506   The ECtHR has also held on a number of occasions that a state's failure to act to protect association violated Article 11. For example, Article 11 was breached where domestic law did not prohibit employers offering financial disincentives to trade union membership.[1131] In *Danilenkov and ors v Russia*, the Court ruled that the state had a positive obligation to establish a judicial system that provided effective and clear protection against any discrimination based on membership of a trade union.[1132]

[1124] App No 28602/95, 21 February 2006.

[1125] (1987) 50 DR 228.

[1126] (1995) 21 EHRR 205.

[1127] App No 28602/95, 21 February 2006.

[1128] Ibid, para 35. The Court relied on provisions of the International Labour Organization (ILO) and Art 5 of the European Social Charter in reaching this conclusion (see para 39).

[1129] *Wilson and Palmer v UK* (2002) 35 EHRR 20.

[1130] (1988) 13 EHRR 204, para 32.

[1131] *Wilson and Palmer v UK* (2002) 35 EHRR 20. See also *Young, James and Webster v UK* (1981) 4 EHRR 38, para 49; *Gustaffson v Sweden* Reports of Judgments and Decisions 1996-II, 25 April 1996, para 45; *Sørensen and Rasmussen v Denmark* App Nos 52562/99 and 52620/99, 11 January 2006, para 57.

[1132] App No 67336/01, 30 July 2009.

In *Redfearn v UK* the Court considered the dismissal of a bus driver on the grounds that he had been elected a councillor for the British National Party. He had been unable to bring a claim for unfair dismissal because he had not been working for the required qualifying period and he attempted instead to bring a claim for race discrimination. The Court of Appeal found that he had not been discriminated against because he was white and the Race Relations Act 1976 did not apply. The Court also held that the Convention did not assist him because his employer was a private company. The European Court disagreed. By a majority of four to three (the British judge dissenting), the Court found that 'there is a positive obligation on the authorities to provide protection against dismissal by private employers where the dismissal is motivated solely by the fact that an employee belongs to a particular political party'.[1133] If he had been able to bring an unfair dismissal claim, the Court held that he could have vindicated his Article 11 rights, but it was incumbent on the Government to make comprehensive legislative provision to protect individuals discriminated against for their political beliefs. 7.507

The Government has not introduced specific legislation in response to the judgment. It might be possible for employees in any future case to bring claims under the Equality Act 2010 for discrimination on the grounds of belief. However, there is little guarantee that they would be successful in light of the restricted protection that has been given to discriminatory beliefs in the workplace.[1134] 7.508

I. ARTICLE 12: RIGHT TO MARRY AND FOUND A FAMILY

Article 12 has two constituent rights—the right to marry and the right to found a family. The state is expressly given considerable discretion to regulate the exercise of these rights. 7.509

While it has obvious links to the right to respect for family life in Article 8, Article 12 is a distinct provision (*lex specialis*) and is of much narrower scope, focusing on the right to marry and found a family rather than incidents flowing from it. The ECtHR affirmed the distinction between Articles 8 and 12 in *P, C and S v UK*, holding that complaints regarding interference with family life between a parent and child engage Article 8, but cannot be raised under Article 12.[1135] In general, the Strasbourg organs have taken a much narrower approach to the scope of Article 12 than that of Article 8. 7.510

In cases raising issues under both Article 8 and Article 12, the ECtHR has held that an interference with family life that is justified under Article 8(2) cannot at the same time constitute a violation of Article 12.[1136] 7.511

The rights under Article 12 apply not only to citizens, but also to aliens and stateless persons.[1137] 7.512

[1133] (2012) 33 BHRC 713 para 43.
[1134] See *Eweida v UK* (2013) 34 BHRC 519, discussed at para 7.361.
[1135] (2002) 35 EHRR 31.
[1136] *Boso v Italy* App No 50490/99, ECHR 2002-VII.
[1137] *Sanders v France* (1996) 87 B-DR 160, 163.

1. The right to marry

(a) *Regulation and formalities*

7.513　The right to marry is a right that can only be exercised in accordance with national law and it is therefore for the state to decide how it wishes to regulate marriage. Both formal rules (for example, concerning matters such as notice, publicity, and witnesses) and substantive rules (such as requirements relating to consent, capacity, prohibited degrees of consanguinity, or the prevention of bigamy) governing marriage are generally a matter for the state. The Convention leaves it to states to determine marriageable age. National laws imposing a minimum age of consent for lawful marriage do not amount to a breach of the right to marry under Article 12, even if they conflict with differing religious laws as to marriageable age.[1138]

7.514　The rules governing marriage must not be arbitrary or interfere with the essence of the right. For example, the imposition by the state of any substantial period of delay may injure the very essence of the right, whereas a shorter period will not.[1139]

7.515　In *Hamer v UK*[1140] and *Draper v UK*[1141] the ECmHR ruled that prohibiting prisoners from marrying was an arbitrary interference with their Article 12 rights because it served no legitimate state objective.

7.516　In *B v UK* a father-in-law and daughter-in-law challenged the provisions of the Marriage Act 1949 which prevented them from marrying, subject to obtaining a waiver through a private act of Parliament.[1142] The ECtHR found that the inconsistency between the Government's stated objectives and the waiver 'undermined the rationality and logic of the measure' and rendered it arbitrary.

7.517　Regulations must also be compatible with the exercise of other Convention rights, in particular Article 9, though this does not impose a positive obligation to match civil and religious marriage laws, nor preclude a requirement that a religious marriage ceremony may also need to be affirmed or registered under civil law.[1143]

(b) *Non-nationals*

7.518　The ECtHR has consistently held that conditions may be attached to the marriage of non-nationals in Member States for the purposes of ascertaining whether the marriage is genuine or one of convenience.[1144]

7.519　In *R (Baiai and ors) v Secretary of State for the Home Department* the House of Lords considered measures put in place by the Home Office to prevent 'sham marriages'

[1138]　*Khan v UK* (1986) 48 DR 253.

[1139]　*Hamer v UK* (1979) 24 DR 5; *F v Switzerland* (1987) 10 EHRR 411; cf *Shara and Rinia v Netherlands* (1985) 8 EHRR 307.

[1140]　(1979) 24 DR 5.

[1141]　(1980) 24 DR 72.

[1142]　(2004) 39 EHRR 30.

[1143]　*X v Germany* (1974) 1 DR 64; *Adams and Khan v UK* (1967) 10 YB 478. See, further, *Selim v Cyprus: Friendly Settlement* App No 47293/99, 16 July 2002.

[1144]　*Sanders v France* (1996) 87 B-DR 160, 163; *Klip and Krüger v Netherlands* (1997) 91 A-DR 66, 71; *R (Baiai and ors) v Secretary of State for the Home Department* [2008] UKHL 53, [2008] 3 All ER 1094 at [29].

among persons subject to immigration control.[1145] With some limited exceptions, all such persons were required to seek a certificate from the Home Secretary regardless of the status of their partner. In practice, almost all such applications were refused without regard to the applicants' individual circumstances. Their Lordships held that while the Government could legitimately take measures to prevent 'sham' marriages, the scheme disproportionately infringed the rights of non-nationals. Invoking Nazi race laws, Baroness Hale stated:

Denying to members of minority groups the right to establish formal, legal relationships with the partners of their choice is one way of setting them apart from society, denying that they are 'free and equal in dignity and rights'.[1146]

The Government amended the scheme in response to the judgment in *Baiai*. 7.520
The amended scheme was challenged in *O'Donoghue and ors v UK*.[1147] The ECtHR found that the scheme did not comply with Article 12 on the basis that whether or not to grant a certificate of approval was not based solely on the genuineness of the proposed marriage; it imposed a blanket prohibition on the exercise of the right to marry on all persons in a specified category; and the system of refunding fees to needy applicants was not an effective means of removing any breach of Article 12 as the very requirement to pay a fee acted as a powerful disincentive to marriage.

(c) *Gender and the right to marry*

Until recently, Article 12 provided only a right to marry a person who was biologically 7.521
of the opposite sex.[1148] According to Strasbourg, the adoption of biological criteria to determine sex for the purposes of marriage was 'a matter encompassed within the power of Contracting States to regulate by national law the exercise of the right to marry'.[1149]

However, in the striking decision of *Goodwin v UK* the ECtHR held that: 7.522

While it is for the Contracting State to determine *inter alia* the conditions under which a person claiming legal recognition as a transsexual establishes that gender reassignment has been properly effected or under which past marriages cease to be valid and the formalities applicable to future marriages...the Court finds no justification for barring the transsexual from enjoying the right to marry under any circumstances.[1150]

Domestic law is now in line with Strasbourg's position. In *Bellinger v Bellinger* 7.523
their Lordships issued a declaration of incompatibility, holding that section 11(c) of the Matrimonial Causes Act 1973 could not be construed so as to give effect to the decision of the ECtHR in *Goodwin*.[1151] Parliament then passed the Gender

---

[1145] [2008] UKHL 53, [2008] 3 All ER 1094.
[1146] Ibid at [44].
[1147] (2010) 30 BHRC 85. Considered by the Court of Appeal in *MM (Lebanon) v Secretary of State for the Home Department* [2014] EWCA Civ 985 in relation to Art 8.
[1148] *Rees v UK* (1987) 9 EHRR 56; *Cossey v UK* (1990) 13 EHRR 622; *Sheffield and Horsham v UK* (1999) 27 EHRR 163.
[1149] *Cossey v UK* (1990) 13 EHRR 622.
[1150] (2002) 35 EHRR 18, para 103.
[1151] [2003] UKHL 21, [2003] 2 AC 467.

Recognition Act 2004, which provides that the marriage of a person who has obtained a 'full gender recognition certificate' to a person of the same biological sex as their original sex will not be rendered void on the basis that the parties are not respectively male and female.

(d) *Same-sex marriage*

7.524   The European Court does not recognize the rights of same-sex couples to marry.[1152] In *Schalk and Kopf v Austria* the Court held that the absence of European consensus on the rights of same-sex couples meant that the Convention could not yet be interpreted to create such a right.[1153] Interestingly, the Court considered the Charter of Fundamental Rights of the European Union, which includes in Article 9 a right to marry without a reference to men or women, thus leaving the decision to states whether or not to recognize same-sex marriages. On the basis of this, the ECtHR concluded that it:

> would no longer consider that the right to marry enshrined in Article 12 must in all circumstances be limited to marriage between two persons of the opposite sex. Consequently, it cannot be said that Article 12 is inapplicable to the applicants' complaint. However, as matters stand, the question whether or not to allow same-sex marriage is left to regulation by the national law of the Contracting State.[1154]

Until same-sex couples are afforded more consistent protection across Europe, Article 12 will not expand to include them within its scope.

7.525   Domestic law is compatible with this approach. In *Wilkinson v Kitzinger* the High Court was asked to declare that the recognition of a Canadian marriage between two women domiciled in England, valid as a matter of the law of British Columbia, was valid as a marriage in the United Kingdom.[1155] Alternatively, that its recognition as a civil partnership under the Civil Partnership Act 2004, rather than a marriage, rendered English law incompatible with Articles 8, 12, and 14 of the Convention. The judge held that there was no such incompatibility: to afford legal recognition to same-sex relationships as civil partnerships rather than as 'marriages' met a legitimate aim of social policy and was proportionate.

(e) *Dissolution of marriage*

7.526   The right to marry does not include its corollary—the right to dissolve or formally end a marriage.[1156] The *travaux préparatoires* to the Convention indicate that the omission of 'dissolution' from the text of Article 12 was a deliberate departure from the wording of Article 16 of the Universal Declaration on Human Rights.[1157]

[1152] *Rees v UK* (1987) 9 EHRR 56; *Cossey v UK* (1990) 13 EHRR 622. See also the decision of the ECJ in *Grant v South-West Trains* [1998] ICR 449.

[1153] App No 30141/04, 24 June 2010.

[1154] Ibid, para 61.

[1155] [2006] EWHC 2022 (Fam), [2007] 1 FLR 295.

[1156] *Johnston and ors v Ireland* (1986) 9 EHRR 203.

[1157] Collected Edition of the Travaux Préparatoires, vol 1, 268.

2. Right to found a family

Article 12 also protects the right to 'found a family', again subject to 'national laws   7.527
governing the exercise of this right'. This right has so far only been considered in
the context of marriage; Article 12 does not create a free-standing right to found a
family in the absence of a marital relationship.[1158]

(a) *Adoption*

A family can be founded by the adoption of children.[1159] However, the Strasbourg   7.528
organs have affirmed the early decision in *X and Y v UK*[1160] that Article 12 does
not create a right to adopt.[1161] It might, however, form part of the right to personal
development under Article 8.[1162]

The Court of Appeal in *Briody v St Helen's and Knowsley Health Authority* ruled   7.529
that Article 12 does not require that a woman rendered infertile by the negligence
of an NHS hospital be entitled to damages that would enable her to proceed with
a surrogacy arrangement, nor does it include a right to be supplied with a child.[1163]

(b) *Artificial insemination*

The scope of Article 12 as a basis for challenges to restrictions and regulations   7.530
on artificial insemination or other reproductive technologies has yet to be fully
tested in Strasbourg. Cases raising these issues are more frequently brought under
Article 8.[1164]

The ECmHR admitted complaints under Articles 8 and/or 12 about the refusal   7.531
by the state to allow artificial insemination by donor treatment of prisoners' wives
in 1987[1165] and 1991,[1166] and the Grand Chamber considered the issue in *Dickson
v UK*.[1167]

Dickson concerned a challenge to the Secretary of State's refusal to give a hus-   7.532
band access to artificial insemination facilities in order for his wife to conceive. By
the time of his release, his wife would be too old to conceive and the refusal therefore extinguished their right to have a child together. By four to three, the ECtHR
held that there was no violation of Article 8 or 12 on the grounds that the United
Kingdom did not impose a blanket restriction on such activity and took relevant
factors, such as the gravity of the offence and the welfare of the child, into account
in striking a fair balance between the competing interests.[1168] The Grand Chamber
disagreed. Deciding the case under the right to family life in Article 8, it held that

---

[1158] *Marckx v Belgium* (1979) 2 EHRR 330.
[1159] *Van Oosterwijck v Belgium* (1979) 3 EHRR 581.
[1160] (1977) 12 DR 32.
[1161] *Fretté v France* (2004) 38 EHRR 21, para 32; *EB v France* (2008) 47 EHRR 21, para 41.
[1162] *EB v France* (2008) 47 EHRR 21, paras 42–46.
[1163] [2001] EWCA Civ 1010, [2002] QB 856.
[1164] See, eg *Evans v UK* (2008) 46 EHRR 34, discussed under Art 8 at para 7.270.
[1165] *PG and JH v UK*, App No 10822/84, 7 June 1987.
[1166] *GS and RS v UK* App No 17142/90, 10 July 1991.
[1167] (2007) 24 BHRC 19.
[1168] (2006) 46 EHRR 419.

the policy of permitting artificial insemination only in 'exceptional circumstances' did not accord due weight to the prisoner's rights and breached Article 8.

7.533   There is now a gap between the approach in domestic law and the Strasbourg jurisprudence. Prior to *Dickson* the Court of Appeal held that Article 12 would not be breached in such circumstances.[1169] This decision will need to be revisited in light of the Grand Chamber's decision.

7.534   In *R (Rose) v Thanet Clinical Commissioning Group* the High Court rejected a challenge to the refusal to grant a Crohn's sufferer access to assisted reproductive technology without considering the Convention rights in any detail on the basis that there was no positive obligation under Articles 8 or 12 on the state to fund particular medical treatments.[1170]

7.535   Whether Article 12 includes a right to avail oneself of advances in reproduction technology and, if so, whether a positive obligation arises upon the state to facilitate access to such technology, or even to provide it, are future questions that are likely to arise under Article 12.

3. Proportionality and Article 12

7.536   Article 12 is not explicitly qualified in the same way as Articles 8 to 11, and there has been some confusion over whether the right is in fact qualified by the same criterion as specified in those articles.[1171] In general, the ECtHR permits limitations as specified by national laws as long as they do not infringe 'the very essence of the right', but it does not normally apply the three-part proportionality analysis adopted under Articles 8 to 11.[1172]

7.537   Whatever the formal approach to proportionality under Article 12, recent cases suggest that the standard of review applied by the ECtHR and the domestic courts will be a rigorous one.[1173]

4. Positive obligations

7.538   Article 12 has not thus far been interpreted to impose extensive positive obligations on the state. The ECtHR has held that there is no obligation to ensure that a married couple can cohabit or consummate their marriage.[1174] Nor is there a duty to provide living accommodation or subsistence to maintain a family.[1175] Obligations

---

[1169] *R v Secretary of State for the Home Department, ex p Mellor* [2001] EWCA Civ 472, [2002] QB 13.

[1170] [2014] EWHC 1182 (Admin).

[1171] See *R (Baiai and ors) v Secretary of State for the Home Department* [2008] UKHL 53, [2008] 3 All ER 1094 at [46] per Baroness Hale.

[1172] See, eg *Goodwin v UK* (2002) 35 EHRR 18. Cf *F v Switzerland* (1987) 10 EHRR 411 where the ECtHR came closer to applying the standard proportionality analysis.

[1173] See, eg *Dickson v UK* (2007) 24 BHRC 19; *R (Baiai and ors) v Secretary of State for the Home Department* [2008] UKHL 53, [2008] 3 All ER 1094.

[1174] *Hamer v UK* (1979) 24 DR 5; *Draper v UK* (1980) 24 DR 72.

[1175] *Andersson and Kullman v Sweden* (1986) 46 DR 251.

such as these are more likely to arise as a consequence of respect for private and family life under Article 8.[1176]

In line with this approach, the Northern Ireland Court of Appeal held in *Re* 7.539 *Connor's Application for Judicial Review* that Article 12 does not confer an absolute right to cohabitation on spouses, and that such a right may be interfered with where necessary and proportionate.[1177]

Positive obligations under Article 12 have also been considered by the European 7.540 Court of Justice (ECJ). In *KB v NHS Pensions Agency*, the ECJ followed the ECtHR's decision in *Goodwin* in finding a violation of Article 12, but held that it was for the national courts to decide whether a transsexual could rely on the EC Treaty to gain benefits for his or her partner.[1178]

J. ARTICLE 13: RIGHT TO AN EFFECTIVE REMEDY

Article 13 does not provide a free-standing right to an effective remedy. A claim 7.541 under Article 13 must be brought in conjunction with an alleged breach of another Convention right. That breach need not be established in order for the ECtHR to find a violation of Article 13, but it must be 'arguable'.[1179] Article 13 will not apply where the applicant can obtain a remedy under another article that proscribes specific remedies, such as the right to review of detention under Article 5(4) or fair trial rights under Article 6(1).[1180]

Article 13 is not incorporated into UK law under the Human Rights Act. This 7.542 omission is discussed further in para 7.554 and in Chapter 3.[1181]

1. Effective remedy

The right to an effective remedy means that there must be both domestic proce- 7.543 dures for dealing with the substance of an 'arguable complaint' and for granting appropriate relief in cases of actual breach of the Convention.[1182] Accordingly, as the ECtHR stated in *Klass v Germany*, the available remedy must 'involve the determination of the claim as well as the possibility of redress'.[1183]

The scope of the Article 13 obligation varies depending on the nature of the com- 7.544 plaint. For example, in the case of a violation of Article 2, Article 13 will require, in addition to the payment of compensation where appropriate, an effective investigation capable of leading to the identification and punishment of those responsible for the deprivation of life, including effective access for the complainant to the

---

[1176] See, eg *Dickson v UK* (2007) 24 BHRC 19. See also the discussion under Art 8 at paras 7.250–7.254.
[1177] [2004] NICA 45.
[1178] (Case C–117/01) [2004] ECR I–541.
[1179] *Boyle and Rice v UK* (1988) 10 EHRR 425.
[1180] *Håkansson and Sturesson v Sweden* (1991) 13 EHRR 1.
[1181] See ch 3, para 3.78.
[1182] *Aksoy v Turkey* (1996) 23 EHRR 553.
[1183] (1978) 2 EHRR 214.

investigation procedure.[1184] By contrast, compensation alone may be a sufficient remedy for breaches of other articles. In all cases the requisite remedy must be 'effective' in both practice and law.[1185] The requirement of practical efficacy means that exercise of the remedy must not be unjustifiably hindered by the acts or omissions of state authorities.[1186]

7.545　　The question will often be whether all the procedures, in the lower tribunals and the courts, taken together, amount to an 'effective remedy'. For example, *Silver v UK* concerned a complaint by a prisoner that his correspondence had been interfered with contrary to Article 8 and that no effective remedy was available in respect of that breach. The ECtHR took the view that neither the prison board of visitors, the Parliamentary Commissioner for Administration, the Home Secretary, nor subsequent judicial review of the Home Secretary's decisions provided sufficiently effective remedies to comply with Article 13.[1187]

7.546　　The United Kingdom came under Article 13 scrutiny in relation to allegations of child abuse, triggering Article 3. In both *Z v UK*[1188] and *DP and JC v UK*[1189] the lack of any appropriate means of obtaining a determination of allegations that the local authority had failed to protect the applicants from ill-treatment during childhood was found to breach Article 13. More recently, the ECtHR has found a violation of Article 13 where parents of a child mistakenly taken into care before the Human Rights Act came into force could only bring a claim in negligence or judicially review the authorities' decisions.[1190]

7.547　　In *Reynolds v UK* the Court considered an application by the mother of a man who killed himself while he was a voluntary mental health patient. She argued that there had been no mechanism by which she could obtain a civil remedy, ie compensation, for an arguable breach of Article 2 arising from her son's death. The Court found a breach of Article 13 on the basis that domestic law did not, at that time, recognize the possibility of a breach of Article 2 in relation to those who were not formally detained by the state. Since the decision of the Supreme Court in *Rabone v Pennine Care NHS Trust*, it is now possible to bring a claim for compensation under the Human Rights Act in these circumstances and the UK ought no longer to be in breach of Article 13.[1191]

7.548　　The ECtHR has been critical of formal remedies that prevent examination of the merits of a claim. Thus, much of the Strasbourg case law concerning the United Kingdom addresses the extent to which *Wednesbury*-based judicial review (the standard before the implementation of the Human Rights Act), in which issues of fact can rarely be considered, can be treated as an effective remedy.[1192]

[1184] *Keenan v UK* (2001) 3 EHRR 913; *Edwards v UK* (2002) 35 EHRR 487.
[1185] *Aksoy v Turkey* (1996) 23 EHRR 553.
[1186] Ibid.
[1187] (1983) 5 EHRR 347.
[1188] (2002) 34 EHRR 3.
[1189] (2003) 36 EHRR 14.
[1190] *RK and AK v UK* [2009] 1 FLR 274. See also *MAK and RK v UK* [2010] 2 FLR 451.
[1191] [2012] UKSC 2, [2012] 2 AC 72.
[1192] See, eg *Peck v UK* (2003) 36 EHRR 41; *Hatton v UK* (2003) 37 EHRR 28.

Whether the ECtHR has regarded judicial review as an adequate remedy 7.549
appears to depend on the context, and, in particular, whether the ECtHR was satisfied that the domestic courts can afford a sufficient degree of review properly to
examine the legality of the executive's actions in the particular circumstances. In
the pre-Human Rights Act cases, the ECtHR's approach varied. In *Soering v UK*
the applicant was threatened with extradition to the United States to face a charge
of murder, to a state in which he risked being placed on death row (contrary to
Article 3). The fact that a UK court had jurisdiction to set aside a decision to extradite for this reason convinced the ECtHR that judicial review was an effective
remedy for the purposes of Article 13.[1193] Thus, in *Vilvarajah v UK*, the ECtHR
held that it had already decided that judicial review was an adequate remedy in
the context of extradition, even though, in that case, the applicant had already left
the United Kingdom.[1194]

However, in *Chahal v UK* the ECtHR held that there was no effective remedy 7.550
for violation of Article 3, and hence a violation of Article 13, where a suspected
terrorist was detained in custody for deportation purposes in response to the
Home Secretary's determination that he was a threat to national security. The
ECtHR found that Article 13 required independent scrutiny of the Article 3
claim, which did not take into consideration the national security threat.[1195]
The Special Immigration Appeals Commission was set up in response to this
judgment.

In *Smith and Grady v UK* the domestic courts could only review whether 7.551
the policy of excluding homosexuals from the armed forces was irrational, not
whether it met a pressing social need or was a proportionate infringement of
Article 8. Even the heightened 'anxious scrutiny' standard was held inadequate
to comply with Article 13.[1196] In *Hatton v UK* the Grand Chamber of the ECtHR
held that Article 13 had been violated because judicial review did not allow for
consideration of whether an increase in night flights was a justifiable limitation
on the right to respect for the private and family lives of those who lived near
Heathrow airport.[1197] The standard of review is an issue which, theoretically at
least, should have fallen into abeyance after the implementation of the Human
Rights Act, though it remains possible that it could yet form the ground of a
complaint in an appropriate case.

In a number of cases brought after the implementation of the Human Rights 7.552
Act, the European Court has found that declarations of incompatibility issued
under section 4 are not an effective remedy for a breach of a Convention right.
The primary failing of the section 4 mechanism is that it places no binding
legal obligation on the executive or legislature to amend the law following a
declaration of incompatibility, nor can it form the basis of a monetary award of

---

[1193] (1989) 11 EHRR 439. See also *Bensaid v UK* (2001) 33 EHRR 10.
[1194] (1991) 14 EHRR 248.
[1195] (1997) 23 EHRR 413.
[1196] (2000) 29 EHRR 548. See also *Peck v UK* (2003) 36 EHRR 41. Cf *D v UK* (1997) 24 EHRR 423.
[1197] (2003) 37 EHRR 28.

compensation.[1198] In *Burden and Burden v UK* the Grand Chamber held that as a result of these inadequacies a failure to seek a declaration did not mean that the applicant had not exhausted his domestic remedies.[1199] However, the Grand Chamber suggested that there might come a time when the ministerial practice of amending the law in response to a declaration was so certain that a declaration might in fact give rise to a binding obligation. If that point were reached it would be necessary to seek a declaration before making an application to the ECtHR.

2. National authority

7.553 The authority with the ability to provide the remedy must be independent of the body alleged to have breached the Convention obligation.[1200] If a body is sufficiently independent for Article 6 purposes it will also satisfy this requirement under Article 13.

3. Human Rights Act implications[1201]

7.554 Article 13 was omitted from the rights incorporated by the Human Rights Act because it was believed that the provisions of the Act itself provided an effective remedy as contemplated under Article 13.[1202] As the European case law on declarations of incompatibility shows, this has not proved to be the case.[1203]

7.555 Despite the fact that Article 13 is not incorporated, the English courts have had regard to the right since, by virtue of section 2 of the Act, Strasbourg case law must be taken into account when a UK court is considering a case 'in connection with' an incorporated right. In *R (Al-Skeini) v Secretary of State for Defence*, for example, Lord Brown held that Article 13 would be violated if the domestic courts were unable to consider extraterritorial complaints in line with the Strasbourg case law on the reach of Article 1.[1204] In *RB (Algeria) v Secretary of State for the Home Department* the House of Lords applied *Chahal v UK*[1205] in reaching its conclusion that the Special Immigration Appeals Commission procedure determined whether deportation would violate Article 3 to the extent required by Article 13.[1206]

[1198] See *Dodds v UK* App No 59314/00, 8 April 2003; *Walker v UK* App No 37212/02, 16 March 2004; *Pearson v UK* App No 8374/03, 27 April 2004; *B and L v UK* App No 36536/02, 29 June 2004.

[1199] (2008) 24 BHRC 709.

[1200] *Govell v UK* App No 27237/95, 14 January 1998; *Khan v UK* (2001) 31 EHRR 45; *Taylor-Sabori v UK* (2003) 36 EHRR 17.

[1201] See also ch 3.

[1202] *Brown v Stott* [2001] 1 WLR 817, 847; *In Re S (FC) and ors* [2002] UKHL 10, [2002] 2 AC 291 at [61]. See also Clayton and Tomlinson, *The Law of Human Rights*, 2nd edn (Oxford: Oxford University Press, 2009) paras 21.02–21.03.

[1203] See para 7.552.

[1204] [2007] UKHL 26, [2008] 1 AC 153 at [147]–[149].

[1205] (1997) 23 EHRR 413.

[1206] [2009] UKHL 10, [2009] 2 WLR 512.

K. ARTICLE 14: PROHIBITION ON DISCRIMINATION

1. The importance of Article 14

Affording equality of respect to all persons, treating like cases alike, and treating   7.556
unlike cases differently, are axioms of rational behaviour in a society which treats
each individual as having fundamentally equal worth. Equality in this sense is 'one
of the building blocks of democracy'.[1207] The non-discrimination guarantee contained in Article 14 is therefore a key provision of the Convention. As Lord Nicholls
explained in *Ghaidan v Godin Mendoza*:

> Discriminatory law undermines the rule of law because it is the antithesis of fairness. It brings
> the law into disrepute. It breeds resentment. It fosters an inequality of outlook which is demean-
> ing alike to those unfairly benefited and those unfairly prejudiced.[1208]

Recent decisions of the ECtHR have also explained the importance and value of a
realistic application of the equal treatment guarantee in protecting and preserving
a democratic society.[1209]

From its earliest cases, the ECtHR has recognized that it constitutes discrimina-   7.557
tion both to fail to treat like cases alike but also to fail to treat unlike cases differently,[1210] but beyond those early statements, the case law of the ECtHR on Article
14 was until recently relatively undeveloped. However, it has become more sophisticated, with recent important decisions such as those of the Grand Chamber in
Stec v UK and *DH v Czech Republic*,[1211] and the recent clear extension of the positive
obligations doctrine to the obligation to 'ensure equal enjoyment' of the underlying
Convention rights in *Eremia v Moldova*.[1212]

In earlier cases, the ECtHR declined to consider discrimination law arguments   7.558
where there was also a breach of a substantive right.[1213] In *Buckley v UK* Judge Pettiti
regretted that the ECtHR had missed 'an opportunity to produce...a critique of
national law and practice with regard to Gypsies and travellers in the UK that
would have been transposable to the rest of Europe, and thereby partly compensate
for the injustices they suffer'.[1214] However, later cases indicate an evolving interest in
protecting minority rights and a more imaginative and substantive approach to the
applicability of equality concepts to legal protection of minority groups.[1215]

[1207] Per Lord Hoffmann in *Matadeen v Pointu* [1999] AC 98 (Privy Council).
[1208] [2004] UKHL 30, [2004] 2 AC 557 at [9]. See also other speeches in *Ghaidan,* and the decision of
the House of Lords in *A v Secretary of State for the Home Department* [2004] UKHL 56, [2005] 2 AC 68.
[1209] *DH v Czech Republic* (2007) 23 BHRC 526.
[1210] *Belgian Linguisitics (No 2)* (1968) 1 EHRR 252, para 10.
[1211] *Stec v UK* (2005) 41 EHRR SE295; *DH v Czech Republic* (2007) 23 BHRC 526.
[1212] App No 3564/11, [2014] 58 EHRR 2 at paras 85–95.
[1213] Eg *Airey v Ireland* (1979) 2 EHRR 305; *Dudgeon v UK* (1981) 4 EHRR 149, para 69; *Smith and
Grady v UK* (2000) 29 EHRR 548; *Buckley v UK* [1996] 23 EHRR 101, [1997] PLR 10.
[1214] [1996] ECHR 20348/92, dissenting opinion of Judge Pettiti.
[1215] (2001) 33 EHRR 399; *Aziz v Cyprus* App No 69949/01 [2005] 41 EHRR 11; *JM v UK* [2011] FLR
491, [2011] 53 EHRR 6; *Opuz v Turkey* App 33401/02, [2010] 50 EHRR 28 at paras 200–202.

2. Scope of Article 14

7.559 Article 14 requires states to secure 'equal enjoyment' by everyone of the Convention rights and freedoms without 'discrimination' on a broad variety of grounds. The listed grounds of prohibited discrimination are non-exhaustive examples only ('any grounds *such as . . .*'), and 'other status' has been broadly defined. However, although Article 14 is 'deceptively simple',[1216] its application is not straightforward. It guarantees only *equal application* of the law of the Convention, and not a free-standing guarantee of equal treatment.

7.560 The protection afforded by Article 14 is therefore narrower than that found in other, more open-ended guarantees of equal treatment, such as that contained in Article 26 of the International Covenant on Civil and Political Rights 1966, or indeed Protocol 12 to the Convention itself (which the United Kingdom has declined to ratify). Article 14 requires only that the enjoyment of other Convention rights be secured without discrimination. This means that it can operate only within the 'ambit' or scope of another Convention right:

> Article 14 complements the other substantive provisions of the Convention and the Protocols. It has no independent existence since it has effect solely in relation to 'the enjoyment of the rights and freedoms' safeguarded by those provisions. Although the application of article 14 does not necessarily presuppose a breach of those provisions—and to this extent it is autonomous—there can be no room for its application unless the facts at issue fall within the ambit of one or more of the latter.[1217]

7.561 In *National Union of Belgian Police v Belgium* the ECtHR said, 'it is as though Article 14 formed an integral part of each of the articles laying down rights and freedoms whatever their nature'.[1218]

7.562 There can be a breach of Article 14 in connection with another Article of the Convention where it is established that there has not been equal enjoyment of the underlying protected right, even if the departure from the underlying right in the case of the adversely affected party would not, taken on its own, violate the underlying right. Thus, breach of Article 14 does not require a *breach* of another article but merely that the facts of the case come within the ambit of another article.[1219] However, whether alleged discrimination 'falls within the ambit' of another Convention right is not always a straightforward issue.[1220] In broad terms, Article 14 will come into play whenever the subject matter of the disadvantage

---

[1216] *AL (Serbia) v Secretary of State for the Home Department* [2008] UKHL 42, [2008] 1 WLR 1434 at [20] per Baroness Hale.

[1217] *Abudulaziz, Cabales and Balakandi v UK* (1985) 7 EHRR 471, para 71.

[1218] (1975) 1 EHRR 578.

[1219] *Abdulaziz, Cabales and Balkandali v UK* (1985) 7 EHRR 471; *Botta v Italy* (1998) 26 EHRR 241, para 39.

[1220] See the different views reached by the House of Lords and the ECtHR on whether criteria for assessing child support obligations which differentiated between those with same-sex and opposite partners fell within the ambit of 'family life': *Secretary of State for Work and Pensions v M* [2006] UKHL 11, [2006] 2 AC 91 at [13]–[16] per Lord Nicholls; but held to breach Art 14 by the ECtHR in *JM v UK* (2011) 53 EHRR 6, [2011] FLR 491.

'constitutes one of the modalities' of the exercise of a right guaranteed or whenever the measures complained of are 'linked' to the exercise of a right guaranteed.[1221]

This means that it is enough for a claimant to establish that the disadvantage 7.563 relates to the subject matter of another substantive Convention right, even if the state has chosen to make provision which is not itself required by the Convention.[1222] For example, in *Schmidt v Germany*, where only men were obliged to serve in a voluntary fire brigade or to pay a financial contribution in lieu, the ECtHR found that the requirements for work did not breach the prohibition on 'forced or compulsory labour' in Article 4 but nevertheless came within the ambit of Article 4 and thus engaged Article 14.[1223]

This approach was confirmed by the Grand Chamber in *Stec v UK*, which held 7.564 that the prohibition of discrimination extends to 'those additional rights, falling within the scope of any Convention article, for which the State has voluntarily decided to provide'. Therefore, although Article 1 of Protocol 1 does not create a right to acquire property, and places no restriction on a state's freedom to decide whether or not to have in place a social security scheme, 'if a State does decide to create a benefits scheme it must do so in a manner compatible with Article 14'.[1224]

However, it goes too far to claim that even a tenuous link with another Convention 7.565 provision will suffice for Article 14 to come into play.[1225] And in other cases the courts have limited the scope of Article 14 by taking a restricted view of what falls within the ambit of another right. In the widely criticized decision of *Botta v Italy*, it was held that the complaint that a disabled person could not obtain access to a public beach was not within the ambit of Article 8, and so could not even found the basis of a complaint under Article 14.[1226]

(a) *'Protected grounds' or 'status'*
The grounds upon which discrimination is prohibited by Article 14 are very wide. 7.566 The particular grounds of prohibited discrimination specified are only examples ('without discrimination on any ground *such as* . . .'). The non-exhaustive examples

---

[1221] *Petrovic v Austria* (2001) 33 EHRR 307, paras 22, 28.

[1222] See *Ghaidan v Godin-Mendoza* [2004] UKHL 30, [2004] 2 AC 557 at [6] per Lord Nicholls.

[1223] (1994) 18 EHRR 513. See also *Van der Mussele v Belgium* (1983) 6 EHRR 162; *Zarb Adami v Malta* (2007) 44 EHRR 33, para 46; *Belgian Linguistics (No 2)* (1968) 1 EHRR 252, para 9; *Petrovic v Austria* (2001) 33 EHRR 307; *Inze v Austria* (1987) 10 EHRR 394; *Abdulaziz, Cabales and Balkandali v UK* (1985) 7 EHRR 471, paras 65, 71, 72.

[1224] (2006) 43 EHRR 1017, paras 40, 55. Affirmed as a matter of domestic law in *R (RJM) (FC) v Secretary of State for Work and Pensions* [2008] UKHL 63, [2008] 3 WLR 1023, [2009] 1 AC 311; and by the Grand Chamber in *Carson v UK* App No 42184/05, 16 March 2010, paras 64–65.

[1225] See per Lord Hoffmann in *R (Carson) v Secretary of State for Work and Pensions* [2005] UKHL 37, [2006] 1 AC 173; and the House of Lords in *Secretary of State for Work and Pensions v M* [2006] UKHL 11, [2006] 2 AC 91 at [60].

[1226] (1998) 4 BHRC 81. It is unlikely that the same result would be arrived at today, given the strong adjurations in the case law of the ECtHR that its provisions be interpreted in the light of other specialist international law instruments such as the UN Convention on the Rights of Persons with Disabilities: see *Kiyutin v Russia* (2011) 53 EHRR 26, para 57; *Burnip v Birmingham City Council* [2012] EWCA Civ 629, [2013] PTSR 117 at 21.

given in Article 14 conclude with the open-ended phrase 'or other status' (*'toute autre distinction'* in the French text).

7.567　In *Kjeldsen, Busk Madsen and Pedersen v Denmark* the ECtHR equated 'other status' with 'personal characteristic'.[1227] This has been broadly interpreted by the Strasbourg bodies, which have held that marital status,[1228] ownership of a particular breed of dog,[1229] trade union membership, military status,[1230] conscientious objection,[1231] residence,[1232] immigration status,[1233] and imprisonment are prohibited grounds of discrimination. In *S and Marper v UK*[1234] the ECtHR rejected the approach of the House of Lords in *R (S and Marper) v Chief Constable of South Yorkshire Police*.[1235] The ECtHR held that a rule that those who had been charged or investigated by the police could have fingerprints or DNA samples held indefinitely amounted to discrimination on the basis of that status (ie having been charged or investigated, though not convicted). This reflected the Court's previous finding in *Sidabras v Lithuania* that historic facts that affect status (in that case, former membership of the KGB) are included within the protection of Article 14.[1236]

3. Discrimination

(a) *The concept*

7.568　Not all forms of differentiation amount to discrimination in Convention terms. Otherwise, Article 14 would have 'absurd results'.[1237] Discrimination occurs when:

(i) there is discriminatory treatment of individuals in 'relevantly similar'[1238] or analogous[1239] situations; and

(ii) there is no 'objective or reasonable justification' for the distinction in treatment.[1240]

7.569　The ECtHR has recognized that the 'right not to be discriminated against in the enjoyment of the rights guaranteed under the Convention is also violated when states without an objective and reasonable justification fail to treat differently persons whose situations are significantly different'.[1241] It has also recognized the

---

[1227] (1979) 1 EHRR 711.
[1228] *Sahin v Germany* (2003) 36 EHRR 43.
[1229] *Bullock v UK* (1996) 21 EHRR CD 85.
[1230] *Engel v Netherlands* (1976) 1 EHRR 647.
[1231] *Thlimmenos v Greece* (2000) 31 EHRR 411.
[1232] *Darby v Sweden* (1990) 13 EHRR 774; *Carson v UK* App No 42184/05, 16 March 2010, 70–1.
[1233] *Bah v UK* (2012) 54 EHRR 21, *Hode & Abdi v UK* (2013) 56 EHRR 27, at para 46.
[1234] App Nos 30562/04 and 30566/04 (2009) 48 EHRR 51.
[1235] [2004] UKHL 39, [2004] 1 WLR 2196 at [51].
[1236] (2006) 42 EHRR 6.
[1237] *Belgian Linguistics (No 2)* (1968) 1 EHRR 252, para 10.
[1238] *National and Provincial Building Society v UK* (1997) 25 EHRR 127, para 88.
[1239] *Lithgow v UK* (1986) 8 EHRR 329.
[1240] *Fredin v Sweden* (1991) 13 EHRR 784.
[1241] *Thlimmenos v Greece* (2000) 31 EHRR 411, para 44.

concept of indirect discrimination,[1242] and is beginning to develop the concept of a positive obligation to ensure equal protection of the laws.[1243]

(b) *Persons in an analogous situation*

Article 14 only affords the right to equal treatment to those who can show that their situation is genuinely 'analogous' or comparable with that of the other with whom equality is sought. The burden lies on the applicant to establish that there has been different treatment afforded to him or her and to another in a similar or analogous situation. Without evidence of differential treatment on a prohibited ground the claim will fail.[1244]   7.570

The ECtHR has often decided cases alleging discriminatory treatment by determining that no Article 14 question is raised because the comparison is not truly with a person in an analogous situation. For example, in *Van der Mussele v Belgium* the ECtHR held that trainee barristers could not legitimately be compared with trainees in other professions because the differences between their situations were too great.[1245] In *Stubbings v UK* the ECtHR rejected as 'artificial' the applicants' submission that, as victims of child sexual abuse, they were in an analogous position to victims of injuries inflicted negligently, as opposed to intentionally.[1246] In *Carson v UK*[1247] the Grand Chamber held that pensioners who retired abroad to countries with which the United Kingdom had not entered bilateral agreements were not in an analogous or comparable situation to those who had retired within the United Kingdom or to countries with which the United Kingdom did have such an agreement. Differences in entitlement to pension uprating therefore did not even require justification.   7.571

This approach has the potential to weaken the protection offered by Article 14 since examination of the core complaint may be precluded by technical points concerning the inappropriateness of comparators precisely because they are in a more favourable position. In more recent domestic cases on the concept of Article 14, courts have begun to stress that the selection of a comparator is only part of a 'framework' of useful analysis. It is not a barrier to asking the overarching question, namely whether two cases are sufficiently similar to require a court to ask itself whether the difference in treatment is nonetheless justified.[1248]   7.572

(c) *Failure to treat like cases differently*

It is important to understand that Article 14 does not prohibit, and may indeed require, different treatment of groups in order to correct 'factual inequalities'   7.573

[1242] *DH v Czech Republic* (2008) 47 EHRR 3.
[1243] *Opuz v Turkey* App No 33401/02 (2010) 50 EHRR 28.
[1244] See, eg *Kaya v Turkey* (1998) 28 EHRR 1, para 113.
[1245] (1983) 6 EHRR 163.
[1246] (1996) 23 EHRR 213, para 71.
[1247] (2010) 51 EHRR 13.
[1248] See *R (Carson) v Secretary of State for Work and Pensions* [2005] UKHL 37, [2006] AC 173 at [3] per Lord Nicholls; *AL (Serbia) v Secretary of State for the Home Department* [2008] UKHL 42, [2008] 1 WLR 1434 at [24]–[28] per Baroness Hale.

between them.[1249] In the leading case of *Thlimmenos v Greece*, the ECtHR considered the ban imposed by a professional regulatory body on anyone with a criminal record. The applicant had such a record because he had objected, on religious and conscientious grounds, to performing military service. Though the blanket ban on those with any criminal record was not intended to discriminate against those who had refused military service for reasons of conscience, it nonetheless had a particular adverse effect on persons with the applicant's belief, which was disproportionate and could not be justified, and was therefore held to be discriminatory on grounds of religion, contrary to Articles 9 and 14.[1250]

(d) *Indirect discrimination*

7.574   The idea that unlike cases may, in some circumstances, require different treatment overlaps with, but is not identical to, the developing concept of indirect discrimination.[1251]

7.575   Indirect discrimination, also known as 'disparate effect' or 'adverse effect' discrimination, may arise when apparently neutral policies or laws have a disproportionate impact upon a particular individual or group. The *Belgian Linguistics* decision[1252] implied that the Convention is capable of covering both direct and indirect discrimination since the ECtHR suggested that justification of a measure would be required where the 'aims *and effects*' were prima facie discriminatory. For a long time, the Strasbourg case law on this topic remained relatively undeveloped. For example, in *Abdulaziz v UK*[1253] the ECtHR declined to treat as indirectly discriminatory Immigration Rules that disqualified those who had not met their partners from entering the country for marriage, even though the 'practical effect' of the rule was race discrimination against South Asian groups with a tradition of arranged marriage. The ECtHR did not analyse the issue of indirect discrimination as an independent question, preferring to run it together with the question of justification.

7.576   However, the *Thlimennos* case (at para 7.573) acknowledged that it was the effects of a particular policy or rule which fell to be justified, and the ECtHR clearly endorsed this approach to indirect discrimination in *McShane v UK*.[1254]

7.577   *Thlimennos* addressed the question of whether it was justified to apply a generally acceptable rule without exceptions to allow for those particularly affected by it. The concept of indirect discrimination is a challenge to the justifiability of the very existence of such a rule, at least in its undifferentiated form. The ECtHR developed the concept of indirect discrimination only slowly. In

---

[1249] *Stec v UK* (2006) 43 EHRR 1017, para 51; *Belgian Lingusitics (No 2)* (1968) 1 EHRR 252, para 10; *Thlimmenos v Greece* (2000) 31 EHRR 411, para 44.

[1250] (2000) 31 EHRR 411.

[1251] The conceptual distinction was analysed by Elias LJ (with whom Maurice Kay LJ and Mummery LJ agreed) in *AM (Somalia) v Entry Clearance Officer* [2009] EWCA Civ 634, [2009] UKHRR 1073.

[1252] *Belgian Linguistics (No 2)* (1968) 1 EHRR 252.

[1253] (1985) 7 EHRR 471.

[1254] (2002) 35 EHRR 23, para 135. See also *Hugh Jordan v UK* (2003) 37 EHRR 2; *Nachova and ors v Bulgaria* (2006) 42 EHRR 43.

Nachova and ors v Bulgaria the Grand Chamber indicated that the burden of proof in such cases lies on the applicants, and the standard of proof is 'beyond reasonable doubt'—a high threshold that will limit the number of successful claims.[1255]

However, statistics did suffice as the basis for a finding of sex discrimination in the recent case of *Zarb Adami v Malta*.[1256] The applicant was called for jury service and fined when he failed to appear. He submitted that both the practice of excusal from jury service and the sanction were discriminatory on the basis of sex. In support of this contention he produced statistics demonstrating a large discrepancy in the number of women and men enrolled as jurors. As both men and women were in theory equally liable to serve as jurors and to be exempted, the 'only explanation' for the discrepancy could be that there had been a discriminatory administrative practice.

A more realistic approach to establishing indirect discrimination was firmly established by the landmark decision of the Grand Chamber in *DH v Czech Republic*.[1257] In that case, overturning an earlier Chamber judgment, the Grand Chamber took the major step of recognizing that de facto discrimination could be proved by analysis of the effects of a policy on a particular group, which therefore fell to be justified. The case concerned the significantly disproportionate placing of Roma children in 'special schools' with a reduced curriculum. The statistics for the over-representation of Roma children in such schools were such that the Court was prepared to find indirect discrimination that fell to be justified without analysing the precise facts of the individual cases before it. This represents a substantial broadening of the Court's protection against discriminatory policies or practices that have a disparate adverse effect on particular groups without any overt discriminatory intention.

This decision brings the law of the Convention closely in line with discrimination law in other jurisdictions, such as Canada, Australia, and South Africa, which have long recognized the objectionable nature of indirect discrimination. They have noted that not only does indirect discrimination lead to the social exclusion, political marginalization, and personal humiliation of minorities, but may lead to systemic discrimination. For example, factors (such as discrimination against part-time working) may have the effect of causing the marginalized group more profoundly affected by them to 'internalize' the barriers as being in some way natural and necessary, and fail to see them as discriminatory. The Canadian Supreme Court has said that:

Discrimination is then reinforced by the very exclusion of the disadvantaged group because the exclusion fosters the belief...that the exclusion is the result of 'natural' forces, for example, that women 'just can't do the job'.[1258]

7.578

7.579

7.580

[1255] Ibid.
[1256] (2007) 44 EHRR 33, paras 74–75, 80–84.
[1257] (2008) 47 EHRR 3.
[1258] *CNR v Canada (Human Rights Commission)* [1987] 1 SCR 1114, para 34. See also *Waters v Public Transport Corporation* (1991) 173 CLR 349, para 36.

7.581   Domestic courts have not had the same difficulty as the Strasbourg Court in recognizing that Article 14 encompasses both direct and indirect discrimination.[1259] In
R (Watkins-Singh) v Governing Body of Aberdare Girls' School[1260] the Administrative
Court held—basing itself on the important judgment of the ECtHR in *DH v Czech
Republic*[1261]—that the existence of an unexamined school uniform rule prohibiting
all jewellery (with no exception for a Sikh *kara*) was unjustified indirect discrimination, the failure to recognize and respect the needs and rights of members of minority groups was a serious matter, not only because it was of detriment to members
of those groups, but because it was damaging to the development of a democratic
society based on the values of tolerance, pluralism, and broadmindedness.

4. Justification

7.582   Where it is established that people in factually similar or analogous circumstances
are treated dissimilarly, or people in relevantly different situations are treated similarly, a case of prima facie discrimination arises. This will breach Article 14 unless
the differences (or failures to differentiate) have an objective and reasonable justification. This means more than a rational explanation. In *Belgian Linguistics* the
ECtHR said:

> The existence of such a justification must be assessed in relation to the aims and effects of the
> measure under consideration, regard being had to the principles which normally prevail in dem-
> ocratic societies. A difference of treatment in the exercise of a right laid down in the Convention
> must not only pursue a legitimate aim: Article 14 is likewise violated when it is clearly estab-
> lished that there is no reasonable relationship of proportionality between the means employed
> and the aim sought to be realised.[1262]

7.583   The burden of proof is on the respondent state to justify the differential treatment
with reference to these twin criteria (legitimate aim and proportionality). It is central
to the protection afforded by Article 14 to understand that what falls to be justified is
the discriminatory application or effect of the measure, and not the measure itself.[1263]

7.584   Early Strasbourg jurisprudence on justification was often unclear, with the
Strasbourg bodies blurring the separate questions of whether there had been different treatment of people in analogous situations, and whether this differential
treatment was justified.

(a) *Legitimate aim*

7.585   It is for the respondent state to advance a 'legitimate aim' in order to justify a prima
facie discriminatory measure, and states' defences have occasionally fallen at the
first hurdle.[1264]

[1259] *R (L and ors) v Manchester City Council* [2001] EWHC 707 (Admin) at [91].
[1260] [2008] EWHC 1865 (Admin), [2008] ELR 561.
[1261] (2008) 47 EHRR 3.
[1262] (1968) 1 EHRR 252, para 10.
[1263] *A and ors v Secretary of State for the Home Department* [2004] UKHL 56, [2005] 2 AC 68 at [68] per
Lord Bingham.
[1264] See, eg *Canea Catholic Church v Greece* (1999) 27 EHRR 521, para 47.

However, this is a relatively easy condition for states to fulfil. Article 14, unlike   7.586
Articles 8 to 11, has no inbuilt list of legitimate aims. The ECtHR has accepted,
for example, that supporting and encouraging the traditional family unit[1265] and
'promoting linguistic unity'[1266] constitute legitimate aims for Article 14 purposes.

(b) *Proportionality*

If the respondent state establishes that its differential treatment pursues a legitimate   7.587
aim, it must also establish that there is a 'reasonable relationship of proportionality'
between the aim and the means chosen to pursue it.

The ECtHR has rejected purported justifications by respondent states based on   7.588
generalizations rather than objective evidence. For example, in *Marckx v Belgium*
the ECtHR rejected the state's unsubstantiated assertion that mothers of illegiti-
mate children were more likely to abandon them.[1267] However, where a difference
in treatment is based on evidence of real differences in situation or need, then difference of treatment may be justified.[1268]

In *Carson* the House of Lords rejected an over-technical approach to the concept   7.589
of justification,[1269] recommending a 'simple and non-technical approach' to asking
whether or not there is 'enough of a relevant difference between X and Y to justify different treatment'.[1270] This non-technical approach has much to recommend
it, provided it does not result in thinly reasoned, impressionistic, hunch-based
judgments.

(c) *Margin of appreciation*

In assessing justification under Article 14, the ECtHR affords states 'a certain mar-   7.590
gin of appreciation in assessing whether or not and to what extent differences in
otherwise similar situations justify a different treatment'.[1271] The margin's breadth
depends on 'the circumstances, the subject matter and its background',[1272] but the
final decision as to observance of the Convention's requirements rests with the
Court.[1273]

Greater leeway is afforded in cases involving an absence of a common stand-   7.591
ard among the contracting states.[1274] However, the ECtHR is increasingly willing
to operate the 'living instrument' doctrine to develop protection—for example in

---

[1265] *Marckx v Belgium* (1979) 2 EHRR 330, para 32.
[1266] *Belgian Linguistics (No 2)* (1968) 1 EHRR 252, para 9.
[1267] (1979) 2 EHRR 330, para 32.
[1268] *R (Hooper) v Secretary of State for Work and Pensions* [2005] UKHL 29, [2005] 1 WLR 1681.
[1269] [2005] UKHL 37, [2006] 1 AC 173. The House of Lords invited courts to treat with caution the
suggested approach of the Court of Appeal in *Michalak v Wandsworth LBC* [2002] EWCA Civ 271, [2003]
1 WLR 617.
[1270] *R (Carson) v Secretary of State for Work and Pensions* [2005] UKHL 37, [2006] AC 173 at [2] per Lord
Nicholls, and at [31] per Lord Hoffmann.
[1271] *Barrow v UK* [2006] ECHR 42735/02, para 34. See also *Gillow v UK* (1986) 11 EHRR 335; *Inze v
Austria* (1987) 10 EHRR 394.
[1272] *Rasmussen v Denmark* (1984) 7 EHRR 371, para 40; *Zarb Adami v Malta* (2007) 44 EHRR 33,
para 74.
[1273] *Zarb Adami v Malta* (2007) 44 EHRR 33, para 74.
[1274] *Petrovic v Austria* (2001) 33 EHRR 307, paras 36–43.

relation to discrimination against transsexuals. It has explicitly stated that it will have regard to the changing conditions in Contracting States and respond, for example, to any emerging consensus as to the standards to be achieved.[1275]

7.592 Discrimination based exclusively on certain 'suspect' grounds, such as sex, will not usually be accepted by the ECtHR. 'Very weighty reasons' or 'particularly serious reasons' would have to be put forward before the ECtHR could regard a difference of treatment based on such a ground as compatible with the Convention.[1276] However, the 'very weighty reasons' approach has not been applied to provisions which have only an indirectly discriminatory effect on 'suspect grounds' by the domestic courts: see *AM (Somalia) v Entry Clearance Officer*.[1277]

7.593 Over the years the ECtHR has gradually expanded the grounds that will require particularly weighty or serious reasons if discrimination is to be justified,[1278] using the 'living instrument' doctrine, and these now include nationality, religion, sexual orientation,[1279] race,[1280] marital status, and birth.[1281]

7.594 This approach of applying heightened scrutiny to certain categories of discrimination ('suspect classes') is well developed in US Supreme Court jurisprudence. It received a subtle analysis by the House of Lords in *R (RJM) v Secretary of State for Work and Pensions*.[1282]

(d) *Cases where the test is 'manifestly without reasonable foundation'*

7.595 However, even in the context of 'suspect grounds' discrimination, in the context of major measures of social and economic policy, the Strasbourg and UK courts will not normally consider a measure which is rationally connected with the aims of that policy as unjustified unless it is 'manifestly without reasonable foundation'.[1283] The issue first arose in a series of cases concerning the UK's uneven pension provisions for men and women and the resulting inequality of various linked benefits,

---

[1275] *Zarb Adami v Malta* (2007) 44 EHRR 33, para 74; citing *Unal Tekeli* [2004] ECHR 29865/96, para 54; and *Stafford v UK* (2002) 35 EHRR 32, para 68. See also the development of the concept of suspect grounds of discrimination, to include sexual orientation: *EB v France* (2008) 47 EHRR 21; and the recent development of the concept of 'family life' to include same-sex relationships: *JM v UK* (2010) 30 BHRC 60.

[1276] *Van Raalte v Netherlands* (1997) 24 EHRR 503, para 39; *Schuler-Zgraggen v Switzerland*, Series A No 263, 24 June 1993, para 67; *Schmidt v Germany* (1994) 18 EHRR 513, para 24; *Karner v Austria* App No 40016/98, 24 July 2003; *BB v UK* App No 53760/00, 10 February 2004; *Abdulaziz, Cabales and Blakandali v UK* (1985) 7 EHRR 471, para 78; *DH v Czech Republic* (2007) 23 BHRC 526, para 196.

[1277] [2009] EWCA Civ 634 at [16] though note that in *R (E) v Governing Body of JFS* [2009] UKSC 15, [2010] 1 All ER 319, the Supreme Court applied the strongly structured *Huang* test to the justification for indirect race discrimination, albeit under the Race Relations Act 1976.

[1278] For a discussion of the development of the concept, see Van Dijk and Van Hoof, *Theory and Practice of the European Convention on Human Rights* (Kluwer: The Hague, 1998) 728.

[1279] *L and V v Austria* (2003) 36 EHRR 55; *EB v France* (2008) 47 EHRR 21, para 91.

[1280] *East Africans Asians v UK* (1981) 3 EHRR 76, para 207.

[1281] *Inze v Austria* (1987) 10 EHRR 394, para 41; *Pla v Andorra* (2004) 42 EHR 522, para 61.

[1282] [2008] UKHL 63, [2009] 1 AC 311 per Lord Walker. at para 5, and *AL (Serbia) v SSHD* [2008] UKHL 42, [2008] 1 WLR 1434, at paras 20–35 per Baroness Hale.

[1283] *Stec v United Kingdom* [2006] 43 EHRR 47; *Humphreys v Revenue & Customs Commissioners* [2008] UKSC 18, [2012] 1 WLR 1545, [2012] PTSR 1024, para 16.

the ECtHR grappled with the tension between the rationale underpinning the margin of appreciation doctrine and the 'suspect grounds' principle.

In *Stec v UK* various applicants (both female and male) complained of aspects   7.596
of a system of invalidity benefits, which had previously existed without discrimination, but were then 'cut off' at state retirement age (60 for women, 65 for men), resulting in new sex discrimination in the reduced earnings allowance (REA) scheme. The Grand Chamber noted that 'as a general rule, very weighty reasons would have to be put forward before the Court could regard a difference in treatment based exclusively on the ground of sex as compatible with the Convention'. On the facts of the case, however, it held that the differences in treatment were not 'manifestly without reasonable foundation' and so were within the state's margin of appreciation. The need to 'cut off' entitlement to REA at presumed date of retirement was based on economic and social judgments made by the UK Government; the gradual equalization of pension ages across the Council of Europe was permissible, and the discrimination caused by the link between state retirement age and receipt of REA had been held by the ECJ to be within that permitted by EC law.[1284]

Though the continued existence of unequal pension ages per se was not the issue   7.597
in *Stec*, the Court went on to consider whether they were themselves justified. It held that, in the light of the original justification for the measure as correcting financial inequality between the sexes, the slowly evolving nature of the change in women's working lives, and the absence of a common standard among the contracting states, these matters fell within the state's margin of appreciation.[1285] *Stec* has been followed in *Barrow v UK*.[1286]

The Supreme Court also applied this approach in *Humphreys v Revenue &*   7.598
Customs Commissioners[1287] to a change in child tax credit to give the benefit to the 'majority carer' parent in cases of family breakdown. The indirectly discriminatory effect upon fathers was an inevitable consequence of a social policy which was not manifestly without reasonable foundation, and so in this context the 'weighty reasons' analysis was not applied. However, the court said that this did not mean that the standard of scrutiny did not remain one of proportionality.

(e) *Positive obligations*

Recent case law has established that the state has a positive obligation to ensure that   7.599
systems of legal protection—such as the criminal justice system—operate in such a way as to guarantee equal protection of the law to specific groups, such as women or racial minorities. Where the evidence suggests inadequate domestic remedies, and a system which betrays an overall unresponsiveness to gender or racially based aggression, failure to investigate in a specific case may amount to violation of Article 14,

---

[1284] *Stec v UK* (2006) 43 EHRR 1017, para 51.
[1285] Ibid, paras 64–65.
[1286] [2006] ECHR 42735/02, para 35.
[1287] [2008] UKSC 18, [2012] 1 WLR 1545, [2012] PTSR 1024.

read with Articles 2 or 3.[1288] In *Eremia v Moldova*[1289] the state's inadequate approach to domestic violence amounted to condoning discrimination against women and was held to breach Article 14. This developing approach to positive obligations may mean more focus on the obligation upon signatory states to '*secure*' equal enjoyment of the other Convention rights.

L. ARTICLE 15: EXCEPTIONS IN TIME OF WAR

7.600 Article 15 allows a Government to derogate from certain of its Convention obligations during 'war or other public emergency threatening the life of the nation'. Such derogation is only permitted to the extent strictly required by the exigencies of the situation. Further, a state cannot under any circumstances use Article 15 to derogate from certain fundamental Convention provisions.

7.601 The central object of Article 15 is to enable the derogating state to return to normality and respect all human rights as soon as possible, premised on the notion that it is sometimes necessary to limit human rights in order to protect them. This rationale is not without its critics, and it has been stated that the question of derogations is an issue 'of the integrity of the Convention system of protection as a whole'.[1290]

7.602 There are five requirements for a valid derogation under Article 15:

(a) it must relate to a right that is derogable;

(b) there must be a 'war or public emergency threatening the life of the nation';

(c) the measures taken must be 'strictly required by the exigencies of the situation';

(d) the measures must comply with the state's international law obligations; and

(e) the procedural requirements must be satisfied.

1. Non-derogable rights

7.603 Article 15(2) specifies the Convention provisions from which no derogation is permitted: Article 2 (right to life—other than deaths resulting from lawful acts of war); Article 3 (prohibition on torture and inhuman or degrading treatment or punishment); Article 4(1) (prohibition on slavery and servitude); and Article 7 (prohibition on retrospective application of the criminal law).

7.604 It is possible that in the future the ECtHR may extend the list of non-derogable rights by accepting the notion of consequential non-derogability. For example, in *Aksoy v Turkey* the ECtHR observed that prompt judicial intervention

---

[1288] See *Petropoulou-Tsakisi v Greece* [2007] ECHR 44803/04; *Opuz v Turkey* App No 33401/02, 9 June 2009, at paras 199–202.

[1289] App No 3564/11, [2014] 58 EHRR 2, at paras 85–95.

[1290] *Brannigan and McBride v UK* (1993) 17 EHRR 297 per Judge Makarczyk (dissenting).

(Article 5(3)) can lead to detection of ill-treatment, which is a non-derogable prohibition (Article 3).[1291]

2. Time of war or public emergency threatening the life of the nation

The precondition to any derogation under Article 15 is the existence of war or a   7.605
'public emergency threatening the life of the nation'. No derogation concerning
the former has yet been made. The ECtHR has defined the latter as 'an exceptional
situation of crisis or emergency that affects the whole population and constitutes a
threat to the organised life of the community of which the state is composed'.[1292]

The strict nature of this threshold requirement, however, is arguably considerably   7.606
qualified by the fact that the ECtHR affords states 'a wide margin of appreciation' in determining whether or not they are facing such a public emergency. The
ECtHR considers that national authorities are in a better position than national
judges to assess the situation.[1293] Unsurprisingly, given this margin, the claimed
existence of a state of emergency has not yet been rejected by the ECtHR.

However, the ECmHR has rejected such a claim. In the *Greek Case* the Greek   7.607
Government failed to persuade the Commission that there had been a public emergency threatening the life of the nation such as would justify derogation.[1294] In its
opinion, the ECmHR described the features of such an emergency:

(a) it must be actual or imminent;

(b) its effects must involve the whole nation;

(c) the continuance of the organized life of the community must be threatened; and

(d) the crisis or danger must be exceptional, in that the normal measures or restrictions, permitted by the Convention for the maintenance of public safety, health,
and order, are plainly inadequate.

In *A and ors v UK* the Grand Chamber considered the UK's derogation from   7.608
Article 5(1) under the Anti-Terrorism, Crime and Security Act 2001 on the grounds
that the terrorist threat posed by Al-Qaeda was a 'public emergency threatening
the life of the nation'.[1295] The Grand Chamber noted that the Court's case law had
never incorporated any requirement that the emergency be temporary and thus
the derogation could not be invalidated on the ground that the threat posed by
Al-Qaeda and the consequent derogation were likely to be on-going. Nor did the
Grand Chamber accept the reasoning of Lord Hoffmann who, in a minority in
the House of Lords, had rejected the existence of an emergency, stating that the
threat had to imperil 'our institutions of government or our existence as a civil

---

[1291] (1996) 23 EHRR 553.
[1292] *Lawless v Ireland (No 3)* (1979–1980) 1 EHRR 15.
[1293] Ibid, para 28; *A and ors v UK* (2009) 26 BHRC 1.
[1294] (1969) 12 YB 1, para 153. See also Cavanaugh, 'Policing the Margins' (2006) 4 EHRLR 422, 436–7.
[1295] (2009) 26 BHRC 1.

community'.[1296] In the Grand Chamber's view that was too high a standard and a 'much broader' range of factors could legitimately be taken into account in determining the threat.[1297] The Grand Chamber applied a wide margin of appreciation to the Government's assessment of the threat and held that the Government was entitled to conclude that such an emergency existed.

7.609   In *Al-Jedda v United Kingdom*, Lord Bingham opined that it was hard to think of a situation in which the dual requirements of (i) a war or public emergency threatening the life of the nation, and (ii) that derogation be strictly required by the exigencies of the situation could ever be met when a state had chosen to conduct an overseas peace-keeping operation, however dangerous the conditions, from which it could withdraw.[1298]

7.610   This view was stated against the background of the House of Lords' understanding of the extra-territorial jurisdictional reach of the Convention prior to the *Al-Skeini v United Kingdom*[1299] and *Al-Jedda v United Kingdom* decisions.[1300] Recently, in *Mohammed v Ministry of Defence*,[1301] Leggatt J considered that this conventional understanding of Article 15 needed to be revisited in light of the dramatically expanded jurisdictional reach of the Convention following these decisions. He considered that this could be readily done by construing the phrase 'war or other public emergency threatening the life of the nation' as including, in the context of an international peace-keeping operation, a war or other emergency threatening the life of the nation on whose territory the relevant acts take place.

3. Strictly required by the exigencies of the situation

7.611   As stated in Article 15(1) and above, derogation is permitted only 'to the extent strictly required by the exigencies of the situation'. The ECmHR in *Ireland v UK* stated:

> There must be a link between the facts of the emergency on the one hand and the measures chosen to deal with it on the other. Moreover, the obligations under the Convention do not entirely disappear. They can only be suspended or modified 'to the extent that is strictly required' as provided in Article 15.[1302]

7.612   Again, the ECtHR will afford states a wide margin of appreciation in relation to this condition. However, the ECtHR still retains a supervisory role.[1303] Factors that are relevant to supervision of the margin include the nature of the rights affected by the derogation, the nature and duration of the emergency, and any safeguards against

---

[1296]   [2004] UKHL 56, [2005] 2 AC 68 at [96].
[1297]   (2009) 26 BHRC 1, para 179.
[1298]   *R (Al-Jedda) v Secretary of State for Defence* [2008] 1 AC 332 at [38].
[1299]   (2011) 30 BHRC 561.
[1300]   App No 27021/08, 7 July 2011.
[1301]   [2014] EWHC 1369 (QB) at [153]–[157].
[1302]   (1978) 2 EHRR 25, para 588.
[1303]   Ibid.

arbitrary state behaviour.[1304] The Court has insisted that general references to terrorism will not be sufficient evidence that a derogation is strictly required.[1305]

In *A and ors v UK* the Grand Chamber followed the decision of the majority of the   7.613
House of Lords and held that the UK's derogation from Article 5(1) did not satisfy the requirement of strict necessity.[1306] The derogating measures were disproportionate in that they drew a distinction between nationals and non-nationals contrary to Article 14 of the Convention.

The ECtHR is particularly strict in assessing the territorial scope of a derogation. In   7.614
Yaman v Turkey it held that it would undermine the 'object and purpose of Article 15' if, when assessing the scope of the derogation, it extended its effects to parts of Turkey not explicitly named in the derogation notice.[1307]

A similarly strict approach was adopted in *Sakik v Turkey*. The derogation was aimed   7.615
at fighting terrorism and was stated as applying to the state of emergency region. The applicants were arrested outside that region, although as part of a general operation linked to fighting terrorism in that region. The ECtHR held that Turkey could not rely on the derogation in relation to the arrests as they were outside the territorial scope of the derogation.[1308]

4. International law obligations

Any derogation must be consistent with the state's 'other obligations under interna-   7.616
tional law' (Article 15(1)). This includes both treaty obligations and obligations arising under customary international law.

In *Hassan v United Kingdom*,[1309] the Grand Chamber 'read down' Article 5 of the   7.617
Convention so as to avoid a potential conflict between Article 5 (which has been consistently interpreted as not permitting preventative detention) and the provision for preventative detention under international humanitarian law (IHL) during armed conflicts. It thereby averted the need for states to derogate from Article 5 under Article 15 in respect of preventative detention permissible under IHL. Four dissenting judges forcefully criticized the decision as contrary to the structure of the Convention, observing that:

The Convention applies equally in both peacetime and wartime. That is the whole point of the mechanism of derogation provided by Article 15 of the Convention. There would have been no reason to include this structural feature if, when war rages, the Convention's fundamental guarantees automatically became silent or were displaced in substance, by granting the Member States additional and unwritten grounds for limiting fundamental rights based solely on other applicable norms of international law.[1310]

[1304] *Brannigan and McBride v UK* (1993) 17 EHRR 297.
[1305] *Demir v Turkey* (2001) 33 EHRR 43.
[1306] (2009) 26 BHRC 1.
[1307] App No 32446/96, 2 November 2004.
[1308] Reports of Judgments and Decisions 1997-VII, 26 November 1997.
[1309] App No 29750/09, 18 September 2014.
[1310] Dissenting opinion of Judge Spano, joined by Judges Nicolaou, Bianku, and Kalaydjieva, at paras 6 and 8 in particular.

5. Procedural requirements

7.618   Article 15(3) sets out the procedural requirements when derogating from a Convention obligation. Although not expressly stated, notification to the Council of Europe must be without delay.[1311]

6. Derogations and the Human Rights Act

7.619   Section 1(2) of the Human Rights Act allows the Government to avoid the incorporation of the Convention to the extent that it has lodged a 'derogation' with the Council of Europe, as defined in section 14. Thus, as a matter of international law, the Government, by lodging a derogation in Strasbourg, can, to the extent that the derogation is lawful under Article 15, avoid a particular obligation in particular circumstances.[1312]

7.620   Section 14 of the Act identifies 'designated derogations', which, under section 16, are permitted to continue for up to five years. Section 14(5) allows the Secretary of State to amend Schedule 3 to the Act to enable the continuation of the current derogation and to add any future derogations.

7.621   The Act does not permit the United Kingdom to make a 'designated derogation' for the purposes of domestic law unless it reflects an actual derogation lodged with the Council of Europe.

7.622   The effect of making a designated derogation is to exclude the article in question from being a 'Convention right' for the purposes identified in that derogation.[1313] Any derogation is likely to be specific and to refer to particular statutory powers.

7.623   The United Kingdom currently has no derogations lodged. It has, in the past, invoked Article 15 in relation to Northern Ireland and, following the attacks of 11 September 2001, the entirety of the United Kingdom.

(a) Northern Ireland

7.624   Until February 2001 a derogation was in force that allowed the police to detain people in Northern Ireland under the Prevention of Terrorism (Temporary Provisions) Act 1989 for up to seven days. The derogation followed *Brogan v UK*, where the ECtHR had decided that periods of longer than four days' detention for interrogation without access to a judge violated the Article 5(3) requirement to bring the suspect before a judge 'promptly'.[1314] The lawfulness of the derogation was then subject to an unsuccessful challenge in *Brannigan and McBride v UK*.[1315] The introduction of judicial authorization for extended detentions in the Terrorism Act 2000 allowed this derogation to be withdrawn.

[1311]   *Lawless v Ireland (No 3)* (1979–1980) 1 EHRR 15.
[1312]   See Chowdhury, *Rule of Law in a State of Emergency* (London: Pinter, 1989).
[1313]   See s 1(2).
[1314]   (1988) 11 EHRR 117.
[1315]   (1993) 17 EHRR 539.

(b) *United Kingdom*

After the terrorist attacks in the United States on 11 September 2001, the UK   7.625
Government concluded that certain non-nationals present in the United Kingdom
were affiliated with Al-Qaeda and posed a national security threat. While the
Immigration Act 1971 allowed for the deportation of non-UK citizens whose presence in the United Kingdom was 'not conducive to the public good' (including on
grounds of national security), the Convention prevented the return of such individuals to countries where they faced a real risk of ill-treatment contrary to Article 3.

In order to address this problem, the Government introduced provisions in   7.626
Part IV of the Anti-Terrorism, Crime and Security Act 2001 that gave the Home
Secretary the power to detain non-nationals indefinitely based solely on whether he
or she had a reasonable belief that the person's presence in the United Kingdom was
a risk to national security and that he or she suspected that the person was a terrorist. The provisions were plainly contrary to the right to liberty under Article 5. The
Government therefore made an order derogating from Article 5(1)(f),[1316] which permits the detention of a non-national with a view to deportation only where 'action
is being taken with a view to deportation',[1317] on the grounds that the Al-Qaeda
threat constituted a public emergency threatening the life of the nation within the
meaning of Article 15.

The lawfulness of this derogation was successfully challenged before the House of   7.627
Lords in the first of the twin *A and ors v Secretary of State for the Home Department*
cases.[1318] The case was brought by nine foreign nationals who had been detained
under the 2001 Act. In perhaps the most important judgment since the Human
Rights Act came into force, an enlarged House of Lords allowed the appeal by
a majority of eight to one, quashing the derogation order and declaring that the
statutory provisions were incompatible with Articles 5 and 14.

A majority did, however, accept that the threshold requirement that there be   7.628
a 'public emergency threatening the life of the nation' was satisfied, despite the
absence of a specific threat of an immediate attack. Given the nature of the
large-scale terrorist attacks that had occurred, the executive and Parliament had not
erred in assessing that there was a risk of terrorist attack at some unspecified time.

In so finding, they noted that 'great weight' was to be accorded to the judgments   7.629
of the Home Secretary, the executive, and Parliament in this regard as, in Lord
Bingham's words:

They were called on to exercise a pre-eminently political judgment. It involved making a factual prediction of what various people around the world might or might not do, and when (if
at all) they might do it, and what the consequences might be if they did. Any prediction about
the future behaviour of human beings (as opposed to the phases of the moon or high water at
London Bridge) is necessarily problematical. Reasonable or informed minds may differ, and
a judgment is not shown to be wrong or unreasonable because that which is thought likely to

---

[1316] Human Rights Act 1998 (Designated Derogation) Order 2001, SI 2001/3644.
[1317] *Chahal v UK* (1997) 23 EHRR 413, para 112.
[1318] [2004] UKHL 56, [2005] 2 AC 68.

happen does not happen. It would have been irresponsible not to err, if at all, on the side of safety.[1319]

7.630 This approach to the question of whether the Government's assessment met the Article 15 criteria was rejected by Lord Hoffmann, who dissented on this point. He ruled that there was no public emergency threatening the life of the nation and that the Government therefore fell at the first hurdle:

> This is a nation which has been tested in adversity, which has survived physical destruction and catastrophic loss of life. I do not underestimate the ability of fanatical groups of terrorists to kill and destroy, but they do not threaten the life of the nation. Whether we would survive Hitler hung in the balance, but there is no doubt that we shall survive Al-Qaeda... Terrorist violence, serious as it is, does not threaten our institutions of government or our existence as a civil community.[1320]

7.631 Despite the non-intrusive approach adopted by the majority as to the question of the existence of a state of emergency, the measures themselves were subjected to strict scrutiny. Their Lordships held that the 'exigencies of the situation' test is 'a test of strict necessity, or, in Convention terminology, proportionality',[1321] and it must be particularly closely applied if the right infringed is personal liberty—among the most fundamental of Convention rights. Baroness Hale reiterated the centrality of the Article 5 guarantee:

> Neither the common law, from which so much of the European Convention is derived, nor international human rights law allows indefinite detention at the behest of the executive, however well-intentioned. It is not for the executive to decide who should be locked up for any length of time, let alone indefinitely. Only the courts can do that and, except as a preliminary step before trial, only after the grounds for detaining someone have been proved. Executive detention is the antithesis of the right to liberty and security of person.[1322]

7.632 The measures adopted were not strictly required, as they did not rationally address any threat to security, nor were they proportionate. They applied only to non-nationals, and not to British nationals who might pose the same threat. They were also capable of applying 'the severe penalty of indefinite detention' on individuals without any hostile intentions towards the United Kingdom, simply on the basis of their links to other individuals who may, in turn, be linked to Al-Qaeda. Further, this was unjustifiable discrimination on the basis of nationality or immigration status, which violated Article 14; and this approach was inconsistent with the UK's international human rights treaty obligations to afford equality before the law and to protect the human rights of all individuals within its territory.

7.633 *A and ors* demonstrates that the domestic courts are likely to afford greater leeway to the Government in its determination as to whether or not a derogation may be required. However, any measures implemented pursuant to that derogation will be

---

[1319] Ibid at [29].
[1320] Ibid at [96].
[1321] Ibid at [30] per Lord Bingham.
[1322] Ibid at [222].

subjected to close scrutiny, particularly if they impact upon rights considered fundamental under the common law, the Convention, or international law.

The Grand Chamber affirmed the House of Lords' reasoning in *A and ors v*   7.634
UK.[1323]

M. ARTICLE 16: RESTRICTIONS ON POLITICAL ACTIVITY OF ALIENS

On its face, Article 16 allows states considerable latitude to interfere with the politi-   7.635
cal rights of aliens. However, the provision has barely featured in the Strasbourg jurisprudence. Only one case has ever reached the ECtHR under Article 16, *Piermont v France*.[1324] In January 1977, the Parliamentary Assembly of the Council of Europe recommended the removal of Article 16. Although Article 16 remains in force, the Strasbourg authorities have emphasized that it should have little, if any, impact.

In *Piermont* the ECmHR expressly recognized that the provision was outdated.   7.636
It observed that:

> Those who drafted it were subscribing to a concept that was then prevalent in international law, under which a general, unlimited restriction of the political activities of aliens was thought legitimate...The Commission reiterates, however, that the Convention is a living instrument, which must be interpreted in the light of present day conditions, and the evolution of modern society.[1325]

Consonant with this interpretative direction, the expression 'political activities' might apply only narrowly to the setting-up and operation of political parties, expressions of opinion in connection with these parties, and voting in elections.

The ECmHR and ECtHR in *Piermont* also indicated that members of the   7.637
European Parliament cannot be regarded as aliens within any jurisdiction in the European Union.[1326]

The restrictive Strasbourg approach to Article 16 has been followed by the domes-   7.638
tic courts. In *R (Farrakhan) v Secretary of State for the Home Department* the Court of Appeal described the provision as 'something of an anachronism',[1327] indicating that it is unlikely to feature prominently, if at all, in domestic decisions.

In the authors' view, three further factors indicate that any little relevance Article   7.639
16 retains is fast diminishing.

First, the notion of European citizenship created by the Maastricht Treaty and   7.640
the powerful EU prohibition against discrimination on grounds of nationality

---

[1323] (2009) 26 BHRC 1.
[1324] (1995) 20 EHRR 301.
[1325] Ibid, Commission Report, paras 59–69.
[1326] (1995) 20 EHRR 301, para 64. Cf the jointly dissenting opinion of Judges Ryssdal, Matscher, and Jungwiert, and Sir John Freedland, para 4.
[1327] [2002] EWCA Civ 606.

means that Article 16 is likely to be trumped by Community considerations when the 'alien' is an EU national.[1328]

7.641　Secondly, Strasbourg and the domestic courts are increasingly protective of political activity, and both have recognized the preeminent importance of freedom of political expression.[1329] This trend, viewed in the context of the 'increased internationalization of politics'[1330] and the need for those 'opposed to official ideas and positions... to find a place in the political arena',[1331] suggests that the application of Article 16 to Articles 10 and 11 must be extremely limited.

7.642　Finally, the House of Lords in *A and ors v Secretary of State for the Home Department* cited with approval wide-ranging commentary, common law authority, and international instruments against the differential treatment of non-nationals in the exercise of Convention rights.[1332] Although *A* was not concerned with Article 16, or the articles to which it applies, their Lordships' opinions may nevertheless be seen as indicative of a move away from the 'anachronistic' motivations underpinning Article 16.

N. ARTICLE 17: PROHIBITION OF ABUSE OF RIGHTS

7.643　The aim of Article 17 is to safeguard the provisions of the Convention from abuse at the hands of those who wish to use the Convention's provisions to undermine the rights of others,[1333] and to make it impossible for such individuals or groups 'to derive from the Convention a right to engage in any activity or perform any act aimed at destroying any of the rights and freedoms set forth in the Convention'.[1334] The ECtHR has described its 'general purpose' as being 'to prevent individuals or groups with totalitarian aims from exploiting in their own interests the principles enunciated by the Convention'.[1335] It may be invoked by persons against a Government, or be used by a Government to defend its actions against persons who wish to undermine the protections and values of the Convention.

7.644　While Article 17 may be invoked by a state to restrict an individual's reliance on rights where he aims to destroy the rights of others, it may only be applied in relation to the rights that are being abused with this aim in mind. For instance, in *Lawless v Ireland* the ECtHR held that it could not be used to deny IRA members the right to liberty or a fair trial.[1336]

[1328] See *Farrakhan v Secretary of State for the Home Department* [2001] EWHC 781 (Admin) at [19] per Turner J.

[1329] See para 7.401.

[1330] *Piermont v France* (1995) 20 EHRR 301, para 5, per Judges Ryssdal, Matscher, and Jugwiert, and Sir John Freedland (dissenting).

[1331] Ibid, para 76.

[1332] [2004] UKHL 56, [2005] 2 AC 68.

[1333] *Zdanoka v Latvia* (2007) 45 EHRR 17, para 99.

[1334] *Paksas v Lithuania*, App No 34932/04, 6 January 2011, GC at para 83.

[1335] *Norwood v UK* (2005) 40 EHRR SE 11.

[1336] (1979–1980) 1 EHRR 15.

Much of the case law under Article 17 concerns freedom of expression and racial   **7.645**
hatred.[1337] In the admissibility decision *Norwood v UK*, for example, the ECtHR
upheld the domestic decision applying Article 17.[1338] The applicant, who worked for
the British National Party (BNP), claimed that his rights under Articles 10 and 14
had been violated by police removal of a BNP poster from the window of his flat
and his subsequent prosecution for a public order offence. The poster consisted of
a photograph of the Twin Towers of the World Trade Center in flames, the words
'Islam out of Britain—Protect the British People', and a symbol of a crescent and
star in a prohibition sign. The ECtHR held that the poster constituted such a vehement attack against Muslims that Article 17 applied and the applicant could not
rely on Article 10. This decision has been criticized:[1339] Article 17 is a powerful but
blunt tool that should be used sparingly.

In *Vona v Hungary*, applying a restrictive interpretation, the ECtHR found   **7.646**
Article 17 not to be engaged in a case where a political group, which had been banned
by the Hungarian Government because of its expressions of racial hatred against
Jewish and Roma citizens, complained of a breach of Article 11. The ECtHR found
that the engagement of Article 11, as opposed to Article 10, was a distinguishing
factor from earlier cases where it had found Article 17 to be engaged. Moreover,
the evidence did not prima facie reveal any act specifically aimed at the destruction
of the rights and freedoms set forth in the Convention or an intention publicly to
defend or disseminate propaganda in support of totalitarian views. The ECtHR
went on to find the banning of the group to be justified under Article 11(2).[1340]

Article 17 has been raised in the domestic courts on a number of occasions. In   **7.647**
Douglas v Hello! Ltd Sedley LJ noted that it would be inconsistent with Article 17
and section 3 of the Human Rights Act to read section 12 of the Act as giving
the right to freedom of expression presumptive priority over other rights.[1341] The
House of Lords in *DPP v Collins* also noted that Article 10 may not be invoked in
a manner incompatible with Article 17.[1342] The respondent in that case had been
convicted of an offence under the Communications Act 2003 following repeated
calls and messages to his MP in which he referred to 'Wogs', 'Pakis', 'black bas-
tards', and 'Niggers'. He did not argue that his conviction was inconsistent with
Article 10, and Lord Bingham stated that he was 'right not to do so' as 'effect
must be given...to Article 17 of the Convention'.[1343] In *Ladele v London Borough
of Islington* the Employment Appeal Tribunal (EAT) found 'considerable force' in

---

[1337] See, eg *WP and ors v Poland* App No 42264/98, 2 September 2004; *Garaudy v France* App No
65831/01, 24 June 2003; *Schimanek v Austria* App No 32307/96, 1 February 2000; *Glimmerveen and
Hagenbeek v Netherlands* App Nos 8348/78 and 8406/78, 11 October 1979. For a discussion of the applicability of Art 17 to hate speech, see Cooper and Marshall Williams, 'Hate Speech, Holocaust Denial and
International Human Rights Law' (1999) 6 EHRLR 593.
[1338] [2003] Crim LR 888.
[1339] Clayton and Tomlinson, *The Law of Human Rights*, 2nd edn (Oxford: Oxford University Press,
2009) para 15.245.
[1340] App No 35943/10, 9 July 2013.
[1341] [2001] QB 967.
[1342] [2006] UKHL 40, [2006] 1 WLR 2223.
[1343] Ibid at [14].

the argument advanced by an intervener, Liberty, that Article 17 applied where a registrar and committed Christian invoked Article 9 to protect her refusal to perform civil partnerships on the grounds that same-sex unions were a sin.[1344] When the case reached the ECtHR, the Court was invited by Liberty to invoke Article 17 if necessary, but it did not do so.[1345]

O. ARTICLE 18: LIMITATION ON USE OF RESTRICTIONS ON RIGHTS

7.648   Article 18 is a parasitic provision. An allegation that the state has acted for reasons other than those permitted under the qualified rights in Article 18(2) must be brought in conjunction with an allegation that another article has been breached. There may be a violation of Article 18 even if there is no violation of that article taken alone.[1346]

7.649   Article 18 is inapplicable to absolute rights, such as Article 3. It follows from the terms of Article 18 that 'a violation may only arise where the right or freedom concerned is subject to restrictions permitted under the Convention'.[1347]

7.650   Article 18 effectively requires a finding of 'bad faith' on the part of a state. It is, unsurprisingly, extremely difficult to make out a violation, and the Strasbourg organs have very rarely found a breach of Article 18.[1348] In the majority of cases the Strasbourg organs either found that it was unnecessary to examine the Article 18 complaint in light of their adverse findings against the state under substantive articles,[1349] or they held that the Article 18 complaint was unsubstantiated on the evidence.[1350]

7.651   In *Gusinskiy v Russia* the ECtHR found that the applicant's liberty had been restricted for a legitimate purpose under the Convention ('for the purpose of bringing him before a competent legal authority on reasonable suspicion of having committed an offence') but also for a purpose outside Article 5, namely to force him to sell his media business to the state on unfavourable terms.[1351] The detention was thus applied for a purpose other than that provided in the Convention, and the state had violated Article 18.

7.652   In three recent cases concerning the detention of high-profile opposition politicians, the ECtHR has found a breach of Article 18 in conjunction with Article 5 due

---

[1344] [2009] IRLR 154 at [126]. The EAT's decision was upheld on appeal: [2009] EWCA Civ 1357, [2010] IRLR 211 without comment on this issue.

[1345] *Eweida and ors v United Kingdom* App Nos 48420/10, 59842/10, 51671/10, and 36516/10, 15 January 2013.

[1346] *Kamma v Netherlands* (1974) 1 DR 4.

[1347] *Gusinskiy v Russia* (2004) 16 BHRC 427, para 73; *Oates v Poland* App No 35036/97, 11 May 2000.

[1348] See, eg *De Becker v Belgium* (1958) 2 YB 214; *Bozano v France* (1984) 39 DR 119; *Gusinskiy v Russia* (2004) 16 BHRC 427.

[1349] See, eg *Kaya and ors v Turkey* App No 33420/96, 21 November 2005.

[1350] *Nesibe Haran v Turkey* App No 28299/95, 6 October 2005.

[1351] (2004) 16 BHRC 427.

to evidence of improper ulterior motives for the detentions. In *Lutsenko v Ukraine*[1352] the reasons for the detention of a former Minister of the Interior explicitly indicated that his communication with the media about criminal charges against him was a basis for his arrest. In *Tymoshenko v Ukraine*,[1353] one of the reasons for the arrest of the leader of the main opposition party was to punish her for a perceived lack of respect towards the Court considering criminal charges against her. Finally, in *Mammadov v Azerbaijan*,[1354] the ECtHR concluded that the actual purpose behind the arrest of the chairman of an opposition political party was to silence or punish him for criticizing the Government and attempting to disseminate information that the Government were trying to hide. The ECtHR in each case emphasized the existence of specific evidence of the improper purpose, which overcame the general presumption of good faith. It has not been prepared to infer an improper purpose from surrounding circumstances alone.[1355]

Article 18 has been raised before the domestic courts on a number of occasions, but only as an aid to interpretation of other Convention articles. The courts have referred to Article 18 in passing, finding that phrases such as 'necessary... in the interests of national security' and 'lawfulness' must be read in light of the strict requirements of Article 18.[1356] We are not aware of any domestic case in which a violation of Article 18 itself has been alleged.   7.653

[1352] App No 6492/11, 3 July 2012.

[1353] App No 49872/11, 30 April 2012.

[1354] 10 January 2012 [2012] ECHR 18.

[1355] Eg *Khodorkovskiy and Lebedev v Russia* App Nos 11082/06 and 13772/05, 25 July 2013 at [902]–[905], (2014) 59 EHRR 7.

[1356] See, eg *R v Shayler* [2002] UKHL 11, [2003] 1 AC 247 at [57]; *S v Airedale NHS Trust* [2002] EWHC 1780 (Admin) at [91]; *R (Middleton) v Secretary of State for the Home Department* [2003] EWHC 315 (Admin) at [64]; *A v Scottish Ministers* 2002 SC (PC) 63 at [28].

8

THE CONVENTION PROTOCOLS

A. INTRODUCTION

8.01 This chapter summarizes the content of the significant Protocols of the European Convention. As in Chapters 6 and 7, an overview is given of the jurisprudence of the European Court of Human Rights (ECtHR) and any remaining important cases from the European Commission on Human Rights (ECmHR). Where the Protocol has been incorporated under the Human Rights Act the approach of domestic courts is discussed alongside the European case law, and any divergences are noted.

B. PROTOCOL 1, ARTICLE 1: PROTECTION OF PROPERTY

8.02 The extent to which, and the way in which, property interests should be protected by human rights instruments have always been controversial questions. The right to property is recognized in the Convention and the Universal Declaration of Human Rights, but it was omitted in both the International Covenant of Civil and Political Rights (ICCPR) and the International Covenant of Economic, Social and Cultural Rights (ICESCR). The subject was debated at length when these two documents were being drafted, and all accepted that individuals had a right to own property, but it proved impossible to reach agreement on a suitable text.[1]

8.03 Attempts to draft a Convention right to property were bedevilled by similar difficulties. Some argued that property was an economic interest rather than a civil/political right, and should not be protected in a human rights Convention. Others (including the United Kingdom) were sensitive to the possibility of a court interfering with important political choices, such as the state's power to nationalize industries, to create redistributive socio-economic programmes, to tax, and to fine.

8.04 These controversies explain why the initial Convention did not contain an article protecting property interests; why the right protected is to 'peaceful enjoyment of possessions' rather than a right actually to possess;[2] and why the ECtHR continues to afford a very wide margin of appreciation to states in reaching essentially political judgements about whether it is in the public interest for property rights to be curtailed.

8.05 This picture is very gradually changing, both quantitatively and qualitatively. There has been a steady increase in the number of applications raising Protocol 1, Article 1 issues. There has also been an increase in the proportion of successful applications under this article, either taken alone or with Article 14. Many of these

---

[1] See, further, Jayawickrama, *The Judicial Application of Human Rights Law: National, Regional and International Jurisprudence* (Cambridge: Cambridge University Press, 2002) 909–10.

[2] See, generally, Kingston, 'Rich people have rights too? The status of property as a fundamental right', in Heffernan (ed), *Human Rights: A European Perspective* (Dublin: Round Hall Press, 1994); Anderson, 'Compensation for Interference with Property' (1999) 6 EHRLR 543; Whale, 'Pawnbrokers and parishes: the protection of property under the Human Rights Act' (2002) EHRLR 67.

cases relate to the expropriation of land within new EU Member States or accession states, linked to the provision of funding for motorways and other infrastructure. Finally, the ECtHR continues to expand the meaning of 'possessions' to incorporate 'legitimate expectations' and even non-contributory statutory benefit entitlements, thus extending the scope of the right.

There has been fairly active domestic litigation involving Protocol 1, Article 1. It is broadly in line with the Strasbourg jurisprudence, but the domestic courts have too frequently adopted the 'hands-off' approach of the ECtHR, and on occasion mistakenly appropriated the margin of appreciation into domestic law.[3] As we emphasize elsewhere, the margin of appreciation should never be directly applied by domestic courts.[4]   **8.06**

1. The three rules

In *Sporrong and Lönnroth v Sweden* the ECtHR analysed Protocol 1, Article 1, and interpreted it as containing 'three distinct rules'.[5] This interpretation of Protocol 1, Article 1 was followed in subsequent cases.[6] In order to establish that there is a prima facie interference with the right to property it must be shown that: **8.07**

(a) the peaceful enjoyment of the applicant's possessions has been interfered with by the state (rule 1); or

(b) the applicant has been deprived of possessions by the state (rule 2); or

(c) the applicant's possessions have been subjected to control by the state (rule 3).

But interference, deprivation, or control will not violate Protocol 1, Article 1 if done 'in the public interest' or 'to enforce such laws [as the state] deems necessary to control the use of property in the public interest'.

Much of the earlier case law on the three rules is confusing, with the ECmHR and ECtHR often dealing with rules 2 and 3 before considering rule 1.[7] In recent cases, the ECtHR has adopted a more general approach, preferring to focus on the general principles in Protocol 1, Article 1 rather than finding it necessary to decide which of the three rules is applicable,[8] and on occasion expressly stated that a particular infringement cannot be classified as falling within a precise category.[9] First, the   **8.08**

---

[3] See, eg *R (Countryside Alliance) v Attorney General* [2007] UKHL 52, [2008] 1 AC 719 at [126]–[127] per Baroness Hale; *Belfast City Council v Miss Behavin'* [2007] UKHL 19, [2007] NI 89 at [16] per Lord Hoffmann; *Sinclair Collis Ltd v Secretary of State for Health* [2010] EWHC 3112 (Admin).

[4] See ch 4, paras 4.120–4.121.

[5] (1983) 5 EHRR 35, para 61. Note that the ECtHR made clear in later judgments that the three rules are not 'distinct' in the sense of being unconnected: *James and ors v UK* (1986) 8 EHRR 123; *Pye v UK* (2008) 46 EHRR 34.

[6] See, eg *Lithgow v UK* (1986) 8 EHRR 329, para 106.

[7] See, eg *James and ors v UK* (1986) 8 EHRR 123.

[8] See, eg *Katsaros v Greece* (2003) 36 EHRR 58; *Jokela v Finland* (2003) 37 EHRR 26; *Bulves AD v Bulgaria* App No 3991/03, 22 January 2009. Cf *Pye v UK* (2008) 46 EHRR 34, in which the ECtHR returned to the three-rule analysis.

[9] *Alisic and ors v Bosnia and Herzegovina and* ors App No 60642/08, 16 July 2014, at [99]. GC.

ECtHR examines whether there has been an interference with the applicant's possessions. This interference may be direct or indirect, and may involve an actual deprivation of control which prevents peaceful enjoyment of the property, or any other form of interference. Secondly, the ECtHR examines whether that interference is justified.

2. Possessions

8.09 The ECtHR has interpreted the concept of 'possessions' broadly. The term has an autonomous meaning and the definition in domestic law is not determinative.[10]

8.10 In addition to physical items and land, 'possessions' have been held to include contractual rights,[11] leases,[12] company shares,[13] crystallized debts,[14] the goodwill of a business,[15] liquor licences,[16] interests associated with a broadcasting licence,[17] and the benefit of such statutory pecuniary entitlements as from time to time exist.[18] Intangible claims to items of pecuniary value are also 'possessions' even before the claims have been realized: a claim for compensation in tort,[19] a right to compensation for lost land,[20] and a retired judge's claim to a social tenancy have all been held to constitute property.[21]

8.11 Future potential possessions will only come within the scope of Protocol 1, Article 1 if they have already been earned or an enforceable, or at least arguably enforceable, claim to them exists.[22]

8.12 Domestic cases on the scope of 'possessions' in Protocol 1, Article 1 are inconsistent. On the one hand, the domestic courts have applied a broad definition of 'possessions' in certain cases, accepting that legitimate expectations (even those arising from *ultra vires* acts of public authorities)[23] and non-contributory benefits[24] may be covered. On the other hand, a narrow approach has been evident in cases concerning

---

[10] See, eg *Holy Monasteries v Greece* (1995) 20 EHRR 1; *Öneryildiz v Turkey* (2004) 18 BHRC 145 (Grand Chamber).

[11] *Association of General Practitioners v Denmark* (1989) 62 DR 226. For a recent detailed discussion of when a contractual right amounts to a possession see *Breyer Group v Department of Energy and Climate Change* [2014] EWHC 2257 (QB).

[12] *Mellacher v Austria* (1989) 12 EHRR 391.

[13] *Bramelid and Malmstrom v Sweden* (1982) 29 DR 64.

[14] *Agneesens v Belgium* (1998) 58 DR 63.

[15] *Van Marle and ors v Netherlands* (1986) 8 EHRR 483. Lord Bingham considered this area of Strasbourg jurisprudence unclear in *R (Countryside Alliance) v Attorney General* [2007] UKHL 52, [2008] 1 AC 719 at [21]. See also *R (New London College) v Secretary of State for the Home Department* [2011] EWHC 856 (Admin) in which the High Court considered that a student sponsor licence was equivalent to a liquor licence.

[16] *Tre Traktörer AB v Sweden* (1989) 13 EHRR 309.

[17] *Centro Europa 7 SRL and Di Stefano v Italy* App No 38433/09, 7 June 2012, GC at [178].

[18] *Stec v UK* (2005) 41 EHRR SE 295, para 43; affirmed by the Grand Chamber at (2006) 43 EHRR 1017.

[19] *Pressos Compañia Naviera SA v Belgium* (1995) 21 EHRR 301.

[20] *Broniowski v Poland* (2004) 15 BHRC 573.

[21] *Teteriny v Russia* [2005] ECHR 11931/03.

[22] *Wendenburg v Germany* (2003) 36 EHRR CD 154.

[23] *Rowland v Environment Agency* [2003] EWCA Civ 1885, [2005] Ch 1; cf *Breyer Group v Department of Energy and Climate Change* [2014] EWHC 2257 (QB) at [102].

[24] *R (Carson) v Secretary of State for Work and Pensions* [2005] UKHL 37, [2006] 1 AC 173.

a range of interests. For example, housing benefit has been held to fall outside the right to property,[25] and in cases of benefit overpayments the overpaid money does not constitute a 'possession'.[26] However, the House of Lords has now affirmed the decision of the Grand Chamber in *Stec v UK*,[27] finding that disability premium was a possession for the purposes of Protocol 1, Article 1 taken with Article 14.[28]

The narrow scope of the domestic approach to possessions was criticized by the ECtHR in *JM v UK*.[29] The House of Lords had held in *Secretary of State for Work and Pensions v M* that the payment of child support did not fall within the ambit of Article 1 of Protocol 1 for the purposes of Article 14 because it was primarily concerned with the expropriation of assets for a public purpose and not with the enforcement of a personal obligation.[30] Drawing a parallel with its jurisprudence on social security benefits, the ECtHR rejected this distinction and held that the domestic rules on payment of child support by same-sex partners were discriminatory. **8.13**

(a) *Intellectual property rights*
Protocol 1, Article 1 encompasses intellectual property rights, such as patents,[31] trade marks,[32] and copyright.[33] **8.14**

However, in *Anheuser-Busch v Portugal* (the ' *Budweiser* ' case), the ECtHR ruled that while a registered trade mark is a 'possession', a trade mark application is not.[34] **8.15**

(b) *Public law rights*
(i) *State pensions and benefits* Early ECtHR cases suggested that non-contributory benefits gained by virtue of public law were not protected by Protocol 1, Article 1.[35] **8.16**

---

[25] *Campbell v South Northamptonshire DC* [2004] EWCA Civ 409, [2004] 3 All ER 387, though this decision was founded on the pre-*Stec v UK* (2005) 41 EHRR SE 295 distinction between contributory and non-contributory benefits, which is no longer good law: see *R (RJM) v Secretary of State for Work and Pensions* [2008] UKHL 63 at [59].

[26] *B v Secretary of State for Work and Pensions* [2005] EWCA Civ 929, [2005] 1 WLR 3796. In *B v United Kingdom* App No 36571/06, 14 February 2012, the ECtHR agreed that the overpaid benefits did not amount to a possession, but considered that the assertable right to future benefits, which was reduced by the overpayment, brought the subject matter of the application within the scope of Protocol 1, Article 1: at [40]–[41].

[27] (2006) 20 BHRC 348.

[28] *R (RJM) v Secretary of State for Work and Pensions* [2008] UKHL 63, [2008] 3 WLR 1023.

[29] App No 37060/06, 28 September 2010.

[30] [2006] UKHL 11.

[31] *Smith Kline and French Laboratories Ltd v Netherlands* (1990) 66 DR 70; *Lenzing AG v UK* [1999] EHRLR 132.

[32] *Anheuser-Busch v Portugal* (2007) 23 BHRC 307.

[33] *France 2 v France* App No 30262/96, 15 January 1997 (recognized through the 'rights of others' clause in Art 10(2)).

[34] (2007) 23 BHRC 307. See, further, Burkhart, 'Trade marks are possessions—but applications are not (yet)' (2006) 1 Journal of Intellectual Property Law and Practice 240.

[35] The evolution can be traced through the cases of *X v Netherlands* (1971) 3 CD 9; *Muller v Austria* (1975) 3 DR 25; *Carlin v UK* App No 27537/95; *Gaygusuz v Austria* (1996) 23 EHRR 364, para 41; *Poirrez v France* (2005) 40 EHRR 2, para 817; *Willis v UK* (2002) 35 EHRR 21; *Wessels-Bergevoert v Netherlands* [2002] ECHR 34462/97.

It is now clear from the decision of the Grand Chamber in *Stec v UK*[36] that, at least in so far as entitlement to statutory benefits from time to time existing, such rights are protected. In *Stec* it was held that there was no longer any valid analytical distinction between those social security entitlements derived from contributions and those non-contributory benefits funded through general taxation. While Protocol 1, Article 1 provided no right to the continuing provision of any particular social security benefit (that is, the state could remove it if it regarded it as being in the general public interest to do so), there was a defined statutory right to be paid a particular benefit in accordance with the rules of a statutory scheme for so long as it continued to exist, irrespective of whether the scheme was contributory or non-contributory. Consequently, such entitlements unequivocally fall within the ambit of Protocol 1, Article 1 for the application of Article 14.[37]

8.17 However, economic and social policy remains a matter for Member States. The fact that a social security benefit falls with the ambit of the concept of a 'possession' does not compel the Member State to continue to provide that benefit,[38] and even in cases where the Convention guarantees benefits to persons on the basis of what they have contributed into the social insurance system, the ECtHR has held that this cannot be interpreted as conferring an entitlement to a pension of a particular amount.[39] However, the reduction of a benefit to which an applicant has been entitled may amount to an interference with a possession, which will fall to be justified.[40]

8.18 (ii) *Legitimate expectations* The ECtHR has recognized that an individual may have a property right in the event of a sufficient 'legitimate expectation' of a benefit which is economic or property-like in nature.[41] The Grand Chamber in *Malhous v Czech Republic* defined 'possessions' so as to include legitimate expectations—existing possessions or assets, including claims, in respect of which an applicant can argue that he or she has a legitimate expectation of obtaining the effective enjoyment of a property right.[42]

8.19 In *Pine Valley Developments Ltd and ors v Ireland*, for example, a grant of planning permission created a legitimate expectation of benefits sufficient for it to qualify as a 'possession',[43] and a promise to provide land to displaced refugees sufficed in *Broniowski v Poland*.[44]

8.20 *Stretch v UK* demonstrates the ECtHR's expansive approach to this concept. The Court held that Mr Stretch had a legitimate expectation that a lease granted to him

---

[36] *Stec v UK* (2006) 43 EHRR 1017.
[37] The ECtHR reiterated its approach in *Stec* in *Carson v UK* (2010) 29 BHRC 22. See also *JM v UK* [2010] ECHR 1361; *R (British Gurkha Welfare Society and ors) v Ministry of Defence* [2010] EWCA Civ 1098.
[38] *Stec v UK* (2006) 43 EHRR 1017.
[39] *Muller v Austria* (1975) DR 25; *Carson v UK* (2010) 29 BHRC 22.
[40] *B v United Kingdom* App No 36571/06, 14 February 2012, at [41].
[41] See, further, Allen, *Property and the Human Rights Act 1998* (London: Hart Publishing, 2005) 40–78; Sales, 'Property and Human Rights: Protection, Expansion and Disruption' [2006] JR 141, paras 15–18.
[42] [2001] ECHR 33071/96.
[43] (1992) 14 EHRR 319.
[44] (2005) 40 EHRR 21.

by the local authority would be renewed and that the failure to renew breached his rights under Protocol 1, Article 1. This was despite the fact that the original grant had been *ultra vires*.[45]

The ECtHR has made clear that there are limits to the expectations it will recognize: if the claim is insufficiently concrete it will not constitute a 'possession'. In *Nerva v UK*, for example, the ECtHR found that waiters had no legitimate expectation that their tips would not be taken into account as part of their remuneration when calculating whether they were receiving the statutory minimum wage.[46] The distinction—repeatedly drawn by the ECtHR—is between a 'mere hope' and a 'legitimate expectation'.[47]   **8.21**

Claims that have no grounding in the domestic legal order are considered to be outside the ambit of Protocol 1, Article 1.[48] The criterion is not whether there is a 'genuine dispute' or an 'arguable claim', but an actual basis for claiming the possession in national law. Thus if the applicant's contention regarding the existence of a claim in domestic law is finally rejected by the national courts, there can be no 'legitimate expectation'.[49]   **8.22**

3. Positive obligations

The right to property includes a positive obligation on the state to take necessary and reasonable steps to protect it. In *Öneryildiz v Turkey* a landslide and explosion at a municipal refuse tip had destroyed the applicant's home and killed nine members of his family.[50] The Grand Chamber held that the state's failure to take steps to protect the applicant's property violated Protocol 1, Article 1. The ECtHR has adopted a similar approach to the state's obligation to protect property in the event of a natural disaster.[51]   **8.23**

The domestic courts have also recognized that Protocol 1, Article 1 includes a positive obligation. In *Marcic v Thames Water Utilities Ltd* the House of Lords accepted that the failure by Thames Water to prevent regular flooding of Mr Marcic's house with sewage was a prima facie breach of his right to property.[52]   **8.24**

The article also incorporates an implicit procedural obligation.[53] The state must afford a reasonable opportunity to individuals to put their case in order to challenge measures which interfere with their possessions. In *Paulet v United Kingdom*, the   **8.25**

---

[45] (2004) 38 EHRR 12. See also *Beyeler v Italy* (2001) 33 EHRR 52.

[46] (2003) 36 EHRR 4.

[47] See *MA v Finland* (2003) 37 EHRR CD 210; *Caisse Régionale de Crédit Agricole Mutuel v France* App No 58867/00, 19 October 2004; *Von Maltzan v Germany* (2006) 42 EHRR SE 11.

[48] *Kopecky v Slovakia* (2005) 41 EHRR 43, para 52; *Wilson v First County Trust* [2003] UKHL 40, [2004] 1 AC 84 (contract improperly executed, hence unenforceable consumer credit agreement not a possession).

[49] *Centro Europa 7 SRL and Di Stefano v Italy* App No 38433/09, 7 June 2012, GC at [173].

[50] App No 48939/99, 30 November 2004.

[51] *Budayeva and ors v Russia* App Nos 15339/02, 21166/02, 20058/02, 11673/02, and 15343/02, 20 March 2008.

[52] [2003] UKHL 66, [2004] 2 AC 42.

[53] See, eg *Jokelala v Finland* (2003) 37 EHRR 26; *Megadat.com Srl v Moldova* App No 21151/04, 8 April 2008.

UK procedure for imposing confiscation orders under the Proceeds of Crime Act 2002 (POCA), which did not allow for any individual review of the proportionality of the confiscation order, was found to breach the procedural obligation under Protocol 1 Article 1.[54] In *R v Waya*, the Supreme Court held that the relevant provisions of POCA had to be read down so as to allow consideration of the proportionality of confiscation orders made.[55]

8.26 In *Grainger v United Kingdom*, the ECtHR rejected any positive obligation on the state to protect private investors' investments in the distressed building society Northern Rock during the global financial crisis.[56] Similarly, in *Kotov v Russia*, the Grand Chamber rejected an application founded on alleged positive obligations owed by the state under Protocol 1 Article 1 in circumstances where a liquidator's deliberate and unlawful actions had caused loss to investors, holding Russia's general system of regulation to be adequate to discharge its positive obligations.[57]

4. Interference with the right to property

8.27 Possessions may be interfered with in many ways by the state. The most straightforward example is when there has been a deprivation of possessions. However, the state may also interfere with the right through excessive or arbitrary controls, or any other acts or omissions that have the effect of interfering with the use or enjoyment of the property.

(a) *Deprivation of possessions*

8.28 In assessing whether an individual has been deprived of property the ECtHR will look at the realities of the situation, not the label.[58] In some circumstances the formal legal title may remain with the owner of the property, but if his or her rights are rendered useless in practice this may amount to a de facto deprivation.

8.29 The House of Lords in *Aston Cantlow v Wallbank* held that when individuals were obliged to fulfil an obligation which they had voluntarily taken on, they were not being deprived of their possessions for the purposes of Protocol 1, Article 1.[59]

(b) *Controls on the use of property*

8.30 The second paragraph of Protocol 1, Article 1 provides that the state is entitled to 'control' the use of property 'in accordance with the general interest or to secure the payment of taxes or other contributions or penalties'. The ECtHR has held that this is to be construed in light of the general principle enunciated in the opening sentence of

---

[54] App No 6219/08, 13 May 2014, at [67].
[55] [2012] UKSC 51; (2012) 35 BHRC 293.
[56] App No 34940/10, 10 July 2012, at [42].
[57] App No 54522/00, 3 April 2012, GC.
[58] *Sporrong and Lönnroth v Sweden* (1982) 5 EHRR 35, para 63.
[59] [2003] UKHL 37, [2004] 1 AC 546.

Protocol 1, Article 1. Controls on use of property are therefore subject to the fair balance test in the same way as deprivations of possessions.[60]

Applicants will often argue that a measure constitutes a de facto deprivation, but **8.31** the ECtHR will instead find that it amounts only to a 'control'. In *Air Canada v UK*, for example, the applicants argued that the seizure of their aeroplane following a drugs find on board, and the requirement that they pay £50,000 to have it returned, amounted to a deprivation; the ECtHR instead held that it was 'a control on the use of property'.[61]

The ECtHR has held that planning controls,[62] inheritance laws, and taxes[63] con- **8.32** stitute systems of controls. In *Pye v UK* the Grand Chamber, disagreeing with the Chamber, found that the UK's statutory provisions, which transferred ownership from registered landowners to squatters after 12 years of adverse possession, constituted a control on the use of land rather than a deprivation of possessions.[64]

Controls on the use of property have also included laws requiring positive action **8.33** by property owners, as in *Denev v Sweden*, where environmental laws obliged a landowner to plant trees.[65]

In a number of cases the ECtHR has held that housing laws suspending or stag- **8.34** gering the enforcement of eviction orders by residential property owners against their tenants constitute 'controls on the use of property'. The ECtHR stated in *Mellacher v Austria* that the housing field is 'a central concern of social and economic policies',[66] warranting a wide margin of appreciation both with regard to its assessment of the existence of a problem of public concern warranting measures of control, and as to the choice of the detailed rules for the implementation of such policies.

The domestic approach has largely been in line with the tendency of the ECtHR **8.35** to find an interference with possessions to amount to a control rather than a deprivation. In *R (Countryside Alliance) v Attorney General* the House of Lords characterized a ban on fox hunting with dogs under the Hunting Act 2004 as a control on the use of property rather than a deprivation of possessions.[67] The Courts have held that the ban on cigarette vending machines in the Health Act 2009 was a control on, rather than a deprivation of, the rights of cigarette vendors.[68] In *Cusack v Harrow LBC* the Supreme Court rejected the contention that a restriction on access to a property pursuant to a local authority's power to erect barriers between carriageways and footways amounted to a deprivation of property rather than a control.[69]

---

[60] *Pye v UK* (2008) 46 EHRR 34; *R (Countryside Alliance) v Attorney General* [2007] UKHL 52, [2008] 1 AC 719.
[61] (1995) 20 EHRR 150.
[62] *Pine Valley Developments and ors v Ireland* (1992) 14 EHRR 319.
[63] *Gasus-Dosier and Fördertechnik v Netherlands* (1995) 20 EHRR 403.
[64] (2008) 46 EHRR 34.
[65] (1989) 59 DR 127.
[66] (1989) 12 EHRR 391.
[67] [2007] UKHL 52, [2008] 1 AC 719.
[68] *Sinclair Collis Ltd v Secretary of State for Health* [2010] EWHC 3112 (Admin).
[69] [2013] UKSC 40; [2013] 4 All ER 97.

(c) *Interference with peaceful enjoyment*

8.36 An interference with the right to property may occur where there is no deprivation or control, provided it impinges upon the applicant's ability peacefully to enjoy or use the possessions in question. In *Stran Greek Refineries v Greece*, for example, an arbitral award in favour of the applicant company was a possession, and there was an interference when the state passed legislation rendering the award unenforceable.[70]

5. Limitations

8.37 In determining the level of permissible interference with the right to property the ECtHR distinguishes between the types of interference. It will, in general, apply closer scrutiny to interferences involving deprivations or expropriation than to those involving control alone.

8.38 However, the test applied is broadly similar: the interference must be lawful and must achieve a 'fair balance' between the demands of the general interests of the community and the protection of the fundamental rights of individuals. There must be a reasonable relationship of proportionality between the means employed and the aim pursued. The availability of an effective remedy and compensation is relevant in assessing whether a fair balance has been struck.

(a) *Conditions provided by law*

8.39 The deprivation of property must be 'subject to the conditions provided for by law'. This requirement was not satisfied in *Hentrich v France*. A law creating a right of pre-emption over land to enable the Commissioner of Revenue to collect tax was held to violate Protocol 1, Article 1 because it 'operated arbitrarily and selectively and was scarcely foreseeable, and it was not attended by the basic procedural safeguards'.[71] In common with jurisprudence under the qualified rights, the ECtHR also applies the substantive notion of 'quality of law' to Protocol 1, Article 1.[72]

(b) *The public interest*

8.40 In deciding whether a deprivation is in the public interest the ECtHR also affords the state a wide margin of appreciation in deciding what public interest demands. The characterization of an objective of deprivation as being in the public interest is a question left almost exclusively to the determination of the state. The domestic courts have seized on the ECtHR's light touch in this area and applied a gentle standard of review.

8.41 The ECtHR's approach to the public interest is evident from cases such as *James and ors v UK*[73] and *Pye v UK*.[74] In *James* the ECtHR considered the

---

[70] (1994) 19 EHRR 293.
[71] (1994) 18 EHRR 440.
[72] *Sud Fondi Srl and ors v Italy* App No 75909/01, 20 January 2009.
[73] (1986) 8 EHRR 123.
[74] (2008) 46 EHRR 34.

compulsory transfer of ownership of residential properties in central London to the tenants of those properties pursuant to the Leasehold Reform Act 1967, which was designed to protect long-term tenants' moral entitlement to their properties at the end of their leases. The property owners complained that the compulsory nature of, and the calculation of, the price of the transfers violated Protocol 1, Article 1.

The ECtHR was unanimous in holding that compulsory transfer from one indi- 8.42 vidual to another may be a legitimate means of promoting the public interest and that the objective of eliminating social injustice by leasehold reform is within the state's margin of appreciation. It also emphasized that the public interest need not be equated with the general interest, or the interests of the majority. A deprivation of property effected in pursuance of legitimate social, economic, or other policies may be 'in the public interest' even if the community at large derives no direct benefit from that deprivation.[75] The compulsory transfer at issue was not dispro-portionate, nor was it unreasonable to restrict the right of enfranchisement to less valuable houses since they were perceived as cases of greatest hardship.

Similarly, in *Pye v UK* the UK's adverse possession laws which gave squatters 8.43 ownership of registered land after 12 years were found to fall within the state's margin of appreciation 'unless they give rise to results which are so anomalous as to render the legislation unacceptable'. In dissent, Judge Loucaides disputed the existence of a public interest in the measures, noting that in fact they encouraged the illegal use of land.

The domestic courts now follow the ECtHR's lead on adverse possession. 8.44 In *Beaulane Properties v Palmer*[76] the High Court had restricted the mean-ing of 'adverse possession' in order not to infringe the appellant's rights under Protocol 1, Article 1, but this approach was reversed by the Court of Appeal in *Ofulue v Bossert*.[77] The Court simply applied *Pye v UK*, finding that a margin of appreciation applied to the domestic legislation. It effectively abdicated the Court's responsibility properly to scrutinize the legislator's determination of the public interest.

The notion of the 'public interest' was addressed by the House of Lords in 8.45 *R (Countryside Alliance) v Attorney General*.[78] Under the Hunting Act 2004, Parliament banned fox hunting with dogs. The appellants, some of whom relied on fox hunting for their livelihood, complained that the ban interfered with their right under Protocol 1, Article 1. Their Lordships proved remarkably reluctant to scrutinize the precise nature of the public interest at stake. Lord Hope held simply that 'It was open to [the legislature] to form their own judgment as to whether [the hunting activities] caused a sufficient degree of suffering . . . for legislative action to be taken to deal with them'.[79]

---

[75] Ibid, para 45. See also *Allard v Sweden* (2004) 39 EHRR 14, para 52.
[76] [2005] EWHC 817 (Ch), [2006] Ch 79.
[77] [2008] EWCA Civ 7, [2008] 3 WLR 1253.
[78] [2007] UKHL 52, [2008] 1 AC 719.
[79] Ibid at [78].

(c) *'Fair balance'*

8.46   The need to strike a fair balance between the public interest and the rights of individual property owners pervades the whole of Protocol 1, Article 1, including its
second paragraph. Thus, in *Spadea v Italy* it was held that the applicants had been
treated fairly by the laws suspending a tenant eviction order,[80] whereas the applicant
in *Scollo v Italy* had not.[81] In both cases the suspensions of the eviction orders had
the reasonable aim of preventing a large number of people all becoming homeless at
the same time. The facts of each case meant that the application of the fair balance
test produced different results.

8.47   *Sporrong v Sweden* related to town planning in Stockholm.[82] The applicants
owned properties that were subject to lengthy expropriation permits and prohibitions on construction. The ECtHR held that there had been an interference with
the applicants' rights of property by rendering the substance of ownership 'precari-
ous and defeasible', which subjected them to an individual and excessive burden
and did not achieve a fair balance between the protection of the individual right to
property and wider public interest.

8.48   Again, in *Chassagnou v France* the ECtHR found that to compel small landowners, who were opposed to hunting, to transfer hunting rights over their land
enabling others to hunt on it, did not strike a fair balance.[83] Compensation, which
involved a right to hunt on others' property, did not assist in achieving a fair balance since the compensation was not valuable to the landowners who were ethically opposed to hunting such that the compulsion constituted an individual and
excessive burden. This decision was recently affirmed and applied by the Grand
Chamber in *Hermann v Germany*, a closely analogous case concerning hunting
rights in Germany.[84] However, *Chassagnou* and *Hermann* were distinguished in
Chabauty v France, where no violation was found in circumstances where the landowner in question was not ethically opposed to hunting.[85]

8.49   Such an excessive burden may also be present when a home is destroyed and the
applicant has no alternative accommodation (thus overlapping with Article 8).[86]

8.50   In a series of cases the ECtHR has accepted that bankruptcy systems pursue a
legitimate aim (protection of the rights of others) but in order to be proportionate
they must be limited to what is strictly necessary. This stringent test is in keeping
with the severe impact of bankruptcy on the individual.[87]

8.51   The Grand Chamber has emphasized the importance of striking a fair balance
in awarding compensation for expropriation of property. In *Perdigão v Portugal*
the expropriation compensation awarded to the applicant had been completely

---

[80] (1995) 21 EHRR 482.
[81] (1995) 22 EHRR 514.
[82] (1982) 5 EHRR 35.
[83] (2000) 29 EHRR 615.
[84] App No 9300/07, 26 June 2012.
[85] App No 57412/08, 4 October 2012, at [57].
[86] See also *Allard v Sweden* (2004) 39 EHRR 14, para 54.
[87] See, eg *Luordo v Italy* [2003] ECHR 32190/96; *Stockholms Försäkrings- och Skadeståndsjuridik AB v Sweden* [2004] BPIR 218.

absorbed by court costs.[88] In such circumstances, the Court found that the difference in legal character between the obligation on the state to pay compensation for expropriation and the obligation on a litigant to pay court costs did not prevent an overall examination of the proportionality of the interference complained of under Protocol 1, Article 1.

The fair balance test will be more loosely applied in relation to the state's decisions concerning conferment of welfare benefits, as this involves a question of scarce resources.[89] However, Article 14 operates as a check on discriminatory schemes.[90] The ECtHR will also closely examine the circumstances of any group whose existing benefits are to be removed. For example, in *Ásmundsson v Iceland* the ECtHR found a breach of Protocol 1, Article 1 when a disability pension was removed from a small class of disabled persons, but not others. This imposed an excessive and disproportionate burden on the applicant which was not justified by community interests.[91] In discrimination cases, the ECtHR will consider the position under Protocol 1 Article 1 'but for' the discriminatory ground relied upon.[92]   8.52

Taxation schemes are subjected to little scrutiny by the ECtHR, as the ability of the state to levy tax is specifically preserved in the second paragraph of Protocol 1, Article 1. The fair balance test generally applies to tax cases only in so far as it requires procedural guarantees to establish the applicant's liability to make payments—the state can decide for itself as to levels of tax, and the means of assessment and collection. As the ECtHR stated in one case, it 'will respect the legislature's assessment in [enforcing tax obligations] unless it is devoid of reasonable foundation'.[93] This permissive approach has even extended to retrospective taxation schemes.[94]   8.53

Forfeiture laws have been regularly upheld as proportionate by the ECtHR.[95] The ECtHR has also upheld the proportionality of confiscation orders under the Drug Trafficking Act 1994. In *Phillips v UK* the ECtHR rejected the complaint that such confiscation orders were unreasonably extensive, given the important role such penalties play in efforts to combat drug trafficking.[96]   8.54

The domestic courts apply the 'fair balance' test where they find a prima facie interference under Protocol 1, Article 1.[97] As in Strasbourg, proportionality is used as the measure for assessing a 'fair balance'. The courts have in general been prepared to accept justifications for interferences with property rights without great scrutiny.[98]   8.55

---

[88] App no 24768/06, 16 November 2010.
[89] See, eg *Carson v UK* (2010) 29 BHRC 22.
[90] Cf *Stec v UK* (2006) 43 EHRR 1017; *Barrow v UK* [2006] ECHR 42735/02; *Burden and Burden v UK* (2008) 47 EHRR 38.
[91] (2005) 41 EHRR 42.
[92] Eg *Fabris v France* App No 16574/08, 7 February 2013, GC, at [52].
[93] *Gasus Dosier- und Fördertechnik GmbH v Netherlands* (1995) 20 EHRR 403.
[94] *National and Provincial Building Society v UK* (1997) 25 EHRR 127.
[95] See, eg *Handyside v UK* (1976) 1 EHRR 737; *Allgemeine Gold und Silberscheideanstalt v UK* (1986) 9 EHRR 1; *Air Canada v UK* (1995) 20 EHRR 150.
[96] (2001) 11 BHRC 280.
[97] See, eg *R (Trailer and Marina Level Ltd) v Secretary of State for the Environment, Food and Rural Affairs* [2004] EWCA Civ 1580, [2005] 1 WLR 1267.
[98] See, eg *Rowland v Environment Agency* [2003] EWCA Civ 1885, [2005] Ch 1.

8.56 In *Marcic v Thames Water Utilities Ltd*, for example, the House of Lords adopted a hands-off approach to the fair balance test, stating that it considered the pertinent question to be whether the scheme set up by Thames Water to control the sewage system which had flooded Mr Marcic's house had 'an unreasonable impact' on Mr Marcic. As it did not, the court found the interference with his property rights to be justified.[99]

8.57 In *R (Countryside Alliance) v Attorney General* the House of Lords noted that there was no test of strict necessity under Protocol 1, Article 1, and that property rights could be 'more readily overridden' than the core rights such as Articles 8 and 9.[100]

8.58 In *Sinclair Collis v Secretary of State for Health*[101] the High Court stated that it would not interfere with a legislative judgment to ban cigarette vending machines cases unless it 'was *manifestly without foundation so as to be disproportionate*'. A similarly light touch standard of review was applied by the Court of Appeal, which affirmed the decision of the High Court on this point.[102]

(d) *Compensation*

8.59 The basic approach to compensation was set out by the ECtHR in *Holy Monasteries v Greece*:

> In this connection, the taking of property without payment of an amount reasonably related to its value will normally constitute a disproportionate interference and a total lack of compensation can be considered justifiable under Protocol 1, Article 1 only in exceptional circumstances. Article 1 does not, however, guarantee a right to full compensation in all circumstances, since legitimate objectives of 'public interest' may call for reimbursement of less than the full market value.[103]

8.60 A similar approach was taken in *Gaganus v Turkey* where the Court held that, in general, the amount of compensation in cases of expropriation in the public interest should bear a reasonable relationship to the value of the property.[104] However, the ECtHR emphasized in *Lithgow v UK* that where a state considers that objectives of public interest justify reimbursement at less than the full market value, the ECtHR will respect the national legislature's judgment unless manifestly without reasonable foundation.[105]

8.61 In *Vistins and Perepjolkins v Latvia*, notwithstanding the margin of appreciation enjoyed in this context, the Grand Chamber found a violation of Protocol 1, Article 1 in respect of the level of compensation for the expropriation of property by the Latvian authorities as part of the expansion of the Port of Riga. A number of factors led the Grand Chamber to the conclusion that a 'fair balance' had not been struck between the interests of the community and the applicants' fundamental

---

[99] [2003] UKHL 66, [2004] 2 AC 42.
[100] [2007] UKHL 52, [2008] 1 AC 719 at [163] per Lord Brown.
[101] [2011] EWCA Civ 437.
[102] By a majority: [2011] EWCA Civ 437, [2012] QB 394.
[103] (1995) 20 EHRR 1, para 71.
[104] App No 39335/98, 5 June 2001.
[105] (1986) 8 EHRR 329. See the House of Lords' decisions in *R v Rezvi; R v Benjafield* [2002] UKHL 2, [2003] 1 AC 1099 for consistent domestic findings on the issue of confiscation orders.

rights, including the disproportion between the current value of the property and the compensation awarded and the fact that the disparity was a result, in part, of retrospective legislation.[106]

C. PROTOCOL 1, ARTICLE 2: RIGHT TO EDUCATION

The existence and scope of 'a right to education' is one of the more controversial Convention questions. During the drafting of Protocol 1, many states expressed concern that the existence of such a right would impose onerous positive obligations upon governments. In an attempt to assuage these concerns, the opening sentence of Protocol 1, Article 2 was changed from its original positive form ('Every person has the right to education') to the current negative expression ('No person shall be denied the right to education').   **8.62**

Several states, including the United Kingdom, have entered reservations to Article 2 of Protocol 1. The UK reservation relates to the second sentence of the article (the requirement that education be provided in conformity with parents' religious and philosophical convictions). The United Kingdom has accepted this provision only so far as it is compatible with the provision of efficient instruction and training and the avoidance of unreasonable public expenditure. The reservation is set out in Part II of Schedule 3 to the Human Rights Act.   **8.63**

Strasbourg and domestic jurisprudence concerning Protocol 1, Article 2 is limited. This is often said to be due to the weak, negative phrasing of the article itself. However, Convention rights with even weaker phrasing—notably Protocol 1, Article 3, the implied right to vote—have developed despite this constraint.[107] The underdevelopment of Protocol 1, Article 2 is primarily due to the lack of cases that go to Strasbourg. The leading ECtHR decision remains *Belgian Linguistics (No 2)*,[108] decided in 1968, and only a handful of cases are heard each year.   **8.64**

Other rights that involve personal development, such as Article 8 and the 'audience right' (the right to receive information) under Article 10, have developed rapidly in recent years. The principles developed in these cases may also be relevant in the context of the right to education.   **8.65**

1. Scope of the right

In *Belgian Linguistics (No 2)* the ECtHR held that despite the negative formulation, the first sentence of Protocol 1, Article 2 clearly enshrines a positive right.[109] The content of that right was identified as follows: **8.66**

(a) a right to an effective education;

(b) a right of access to existing educational institutions;

---

[106] App No 71243/01, 25 March 2014, GC.
[107] See, eg *Hirst v UK (No 2)* (2005) 19 BHRC 546.
[108] (1968) 1 EHRR 252.
[109] Ibid.

(c) a right to be educated in the national language or in one of the national languages; and

(d) a right to obtain official recognition of completed studies.

8.67 The significance of the negative formulation was held to be that the article does not require states to establish at their own expense, or to subsidize, education of any particular type or at any particular level. Since all Member States at the time of signing the Protocol possessed, and continued to possess, a general and official educational system, there was no question of requiring each state to establish such a system. Rather, the article obliged states to guarantee that individuals could take advantage of the existing means of instruction.[110]

8.68 The right is that of the student, which can be exercised by the parents on his or her behalf when he or she is young and by the student personally when he or she grows older.

8.69 The state may require parents to send their children to school or to educate them adequately at home.[111] It may allow private education and schools, but is under no obligation to fund or subsidize these arrangements.

8.70 Until 2005 the extent of the article's applicability to higher education was unclear. Although the ECmHR as far back as 1965 stated that Protocol 1, Article 2 included 'entry to nursery, primary, secondary and higher education',[112] in a series of decisions over the next 30 years it observed that 'the right to education envisaged in Article 2 is concerned primarily with elementary education and not necessarily advanced studies such as technology'.[113]

8.71 The Grand Chamber in *Leyla Sahin v Turkey* finally clarified that Protocol 1, Article 2 undoubtedly does extend to higher education. Any existing institutions of higher education clearly come within its scope, 'since the right of access to such institutions is an inherent part of the right set out in that provision'.[114]

8.72 The Court applied *Leyla Sahin* in *Eren v Turkey*, in which it found a violation of the right where a university student's exam results had been arbitrarily annulled, thereby excluding the student from the whole university system.[115]

8.73 Despite the range of educational activities that Protocol 1, Article 2 touches, it has not proved a potent right for domestic litigants. The leading domestic case on the scope of the right is *Ali v Head Teacher and Governors of Lord Grey School*, in which the House of Lords considered the right in the context of a child temporarily excluded from school for alleged arson.[116] Lord Bingham, with whom the majority of their Lordships concurred, stated:

the guarantee is, in comparison with most other Convention guarantees, a weak one, and deliberately so. There is no right to education of a particular kind or quality, other than that prevailing in the

---

[110] *Simpson v UK* (1989) 64 DR 188.
[111] *Family H v UK* (1984) 37 DR 105.
[112] *Belgian Linguistics (No 2)* (1968) 1 EHRR 252, para 22.
[113] *X v UK* (1975) DR 2, para 50; *Kramelius v Sweden* App No 21062/92, 17 January 1996.
[114] (2007) 44 EHRR 5, paras 134, 141.
[115] [2006] ELR 155. See also *Timishev v Russia* [2005] ECHR 55762/00.
[116] [2006] UKHL 14, [2006] 2 AC 363.

state. There is no Convention guarantee of compliance with domestic law. There is no Convention guarantee of education at or by a particular institution. There is no Convention objection to the expulsion of a pupil from an educational institution on disciplinary grounds, unless (in the ordinary way) there is no alternative source of state education open to the pupil...The test, as always under the Convention, is a highly pragmatic one, to be applied to the specific facts of the case: have the authorities of the state acted so as to deny to a pupil effective access to such educational facilities as the state provides for such pupils?[117]

Their Lordships held that the student had not been denied effective access to education on the basis that he had been offered a place at a pupil referral unit, which his parents had refused.

In *Re JR17's Application for Judicial Review* the Supreme Court applied *Ali* and   8.74 found that a child's suspension from school for three months in the run-up to public examinations did not constitute a denial of the Convention right to education when very limited home tutoring had been provided.[118] The court noted that the Convention guarantees access only to that education provided by the state and not to education of a particular quality or degree.

In the context of the provision of special education, the Supreme Court in *A v Essex*   8.75 *County Council* considered the case of an autistic child who was not provided with schooling for 19 months.[119] The court rejected the approach of the Court of Appeal,[120] which had held that the state's failings needed to have been systemic to engage the Convention. However, the fact that there had been a breach of domestic legal provisions obliging the local authority to provide education did not lead to a breach of Protocol 1, Article 2. The court found that a triable issue arose only in very narrow circumstances, namely where it could have been shown that the defendant had either failed to make inquiries during any period that it knew the child was not receiving effective education or that such investigations as it conducted were wholly inadequate. The decision of the European Court in *A v UK* is awaited. Overall, the potential for domestic claims founded on the right to education is very limited.[121]

However, the narrow domestic approach may need to be reconsidered in light of   8.76 the ECtHR's judgment in *Ali v UK*,[122] handed down after the Supreme Court's decisions in *JR17* and *A v Essex*. While the ECtHR accepted that the student's temporary exclusion had been proportionate as adequate alternative provision had been offered to him, it observed that the situation 'might well be different if a pupil of compulsory school age were to be permanently excluded from one school and were not able to subsequently secure full-time education in line with the national curriculum at another school'.[123] The ECtHR therefore appears to have accepted that the requirement imposed by domestic law that a child access the national curriculum is a relevant

---

[117] Ibid at [24].
[118] [2010] UKSC 27, [2010] NI 105.
[119] [2010] UKSC 33, (2010) 30 BHRC 1.
[120] [2008] EWCA Civ 364, [2008] ELR 321.
[121] See also *R (Holub) v Secretary of State for the Home Department* [2001] 1 WLR 1359. See also *R (Mdlovu) v Secretary of State for the Home Department* [2008] EWHC 2089 (Admin).
[122] (2011) 30 BHRC 44.
[123] Ibid, para 60.

standard by which to judge compliance with Protocol 1, Article 2. As a result, it is possible that a student could claim a breach of the Convention if the education to which he or she is legally entitled under domestic law is not provided. The conclusions of the Supreme Court in *A v Essex* are likely to be revisited.

2. Parental right to educate children in conformity with convictions

8.77 The second sentence of Protocol 1, Article 2 seeks to prevent the state from indoctrinating children through the education system, by providing to parents the right to have their religious and philosophical convictions respected. This applies to all educational systems, public or private, and to all functions the state exercises with respect to education, be they academic or administrative.

8.78 The provision naturally overlaps very significantly with Article 9, and complaints brought under the second sentence of Protocol 1, Article 2 will generally be coupled with a complaint under Article 9. While such cases will be influenced by Article 9, the ECtHR has emphasized that they will be determined under Protocol 1, Article 2 as it is the *lex specialis* in the area of education.[124]

8.79 In *Campbell and Cosans v UK* two parents challenged the existence of corporal punishment in state schools, on the basis that it was contrary to their philosophical beliefs.[125] The ECtHR upheld their complaint, finding that the obligation to respect religious and philosophical convictions is not confined to the content of educational instruction but includes the organization and financing of public education, the supervision of the educational system in general, and questions of discipline.

8.80 The House of Lords considered the converse situation in *R (Williamson) v Secretary of State for Education and Employment*.[126] The claimant parents argued that the statutory ban on corporal punishment in schools was contrary to their belief in the necessity of physical punishment and thus in violation of Protocol 1, Article 2. The House of Lords accepted that a belief in corporal punishment constituted a conviction for the purposes of Article 9 and by implication for Protocol 1, Article 2, and further held that the notion of education under the second sentence was wide enough to include the manner in which discipline was maintained in school. However, the legislation pursued the legitimate aim of protecting children, and the total prohibition on corporal punishment was proportionate in the circumstances.

8.81 The extent to which the religious and philosophical convictions of parents can influence the provision of education is limited in a number of ways. First, the conviction itself must come within the limited definition set out in *Campbell v UK*. The parents must also show that the holding of the belief is the reason for their objection to what the state is doing, and that they have brought the reason for their objection to the attention of the authorities. Lastly, the state will not violate Protocol 1, Article 2 if the education system conveys religious or philosophical knowledge in an objective, critical, and pluralistic manner.

---

[124] *Folgerø v Norway* (2007) 23 BHRC 227, para 54.
[125] (1982) 4 EHRR 293.
[126] [2005] UKHL 15, [2005] 2 AC 246.

In *Kjeldsen, Busk Madsen and Pedersen v Denmark* parents challenged a law   8.82
which made sex education a compulsory component of the curriculum of state primary schools.[127] The ECtHR held that while the state was forbidden from pursuing
indoctrination, the instruction subject to challenge was a way of objectively convey-
ing information and did not therefore offend the parents' religious and philosophical convictions to the extent forbidden by Protocol 1, Article 2.

The ECtHR adopted a tougher approach in *Folgerø v Norway*, which concerned   8.83
the refusal to grant total exemption to pupils in primary and early secondary education from lessons in Christianity, religion, and philosophy.[128] Non-Christian parents alleged that the obligation on their children to follow these lessons had been
in breach of the parents' right to ensure that their children received an education in
conformity with their religious and philosophical convictions. The Grand Chamber
held that the state had not taken sufficient care that information and knowledge
included in the curriculum be conveyed in an objective, critical, and pluralistic
manner, and the system for partially exempting students from the lessons was not
an adequate mechanism to safeguard respect for the parents' convictions.

By contrast, in *Lautsi v Italy* the Grand Chamber found that the display of cru-   8.84
cifixes in Italian state school classrooms did not violate Protocol 1, Article 2.[129]
Unlike the lessons in *Folgerø*, the crucifix was essentially a 'passive symbol'.[130] The
Court held that in light of Italy's historical development, the decision to display a
crucifix fell with the state's margin of appreciation.

3. General limitations

Other than the limitation set out in the second sentence of the article, there are   8.85
no other specific qualifications to the right to education. The state may supply
any explanation for an interference with the right, but in order to be lawful the
measures must be foreseeable and bear a reasonable relationship of proportionality
between the means adopted and the alleged aim.[131]

In *Leyla Sahin v Turkey* the Grand Chamber considered the prohibition on the   8.86
hijab at universities in Turkey.[132] The applicant was a medical student who had
been subjected to disciplinary proceedings after refusing to remove her hijab in
classes. By a majority of 16 to 1, the ECtHR held that the purpose of the ban was
to protect the secular character of educational institutions. The action taken against
the applicant did not impair 'the very essence of her right to education'[133] and any
restriction was a proportionate means of pursuing the legitimate aim of secularism.
The case is notable for its very limited discussion of the educational consequences of
the headscarf ban for students such as Ms Sahin. Like other cases involving Turkish

---

[127] (1979) 1 EHRR 711. See also *Valsamis v Greece* (1996) 24 EHRR 294.
[128] (2007) 23 BHRC 227.
[129] [2011] ECHR 30814/06.
[130] Ibid, para 29.
[131] *Leyla Sahin v Turkey* (2007) 44 EHRR 5; *Ali v UK* (2011) 30 BHRC 44.
[132] (2007) 44 EHRR 5.
[133] Ibid, para 161.

secularism, the decision of the ECtHR can be explained in part by the extreme political sensitivity of the issues at stake.[134]

8.87   The House of Lords followed the *Leyla Sahin* case in *R (Begum) v Denbigh High School*, in which a girl was excluded from school for wearing the jilbab (a Muslim dress that covered her whole body).[135] Dealing only cursorily with the right to education, the House of Lords referred to their analysis in the *Ali* case (see paragraph 8.76), finding that the pupil's exclusion from education was a result of her unwillingness to comply with a uniform rule that pursued a legitimate aim.

4. Discrimination

8.88   In common with all articles of the Convention, Protocol 1, Article 2 is subject to the prohibition on discrimination in Article 14 of the Convention. This issue was raised in the leading case on Protocol 1, Article 2, *Belgian Linguistics (No 2)*, which concerned legislation that dictated the language of education in certain areas of Belgium.[136] A school that failed to comply with the language rules could suffer penalties, which included denial of public support and non-recognition. The ECtHR held that Article 14, read with Protocol 1, Article 2, could not be interpreted as guaranteeing children or parents a right to education in a language of their choice. The measures adopted by the Belgian Government for the legitimate purpose of achieving linguistic unity were proportionate to meet that purpose.

8.89   In a series of recent cases, the Grand Chamber of the ECtHR has addressed educational discrimination in the context of placement of Roma children in special schools. In a thorough analysis of the Czech schooling system in *DH v Czech Republic*,[137] the Court held that as a specific type of disadvantaged and vulnerable minority, the Roma required special protection, including in the sphere of education. The placement of Roma in schools for children with mental disabilities meant that they received an education that compounded their difficulties and compromised their subsequent personal development. Although the state did not intend to discriminate, it could not justify the disproportionate adverse effect on the applicants' education. The ECtHR subsequently reached the same conclusion in relation to the Croatian[138] and Greek[139] systems, reiterating the principle that separate does not mean equal.

D. PROTOCOL 1, ARTICLE 3: RIGHT TO FREE ELECTIONS

8.90   By Article 3 of Protocol 1, states that have ratified the Protocol undertake to hold free elections. Although the provision appears to impose an obligation upon the state

---

[134] See, eg *Refah Partisi (the Welfare Party) and ors v Turkey* (2003) 14 BHRC 1, discussed in ch 7, para 7.450.
[135] [2006] UKHL 15, [2007] 1 AC 100.
[136] (1968) 1 EHRR 252.
[137] (2007) 23 BHRC 526.
[138] *Oršuš and ors v Croatia* (2010) 28 BHRC 558.
[139] *Sampanis v Greece* App No 32526/05, 5 June 2008.

rather than conferring a right upon an individual, it was held in *Mathieu-Mohin v Belgium* that Protocol 1, Article 3 does give rise to an individual right and can be the object of a complaint.[140]

The ECtHR in *Mathieu-Mohin* established several general principles. First, it held that Protocol 1, Article 3 extends to the subjective rights of participation—the right to vote and the right to stand for election to the legislature. However, it went on to state that the rights are not absolute. A state could impose conditions on the right to vote and to stand for election, provided that the conditions pursue a legitimate aim, are not disproportionate, and do not thwart the free expression of the opinion of the people in the choice of the legislature. **8.91**

The Grand Chamber has reiterated these principles. It explained in *Zdanoka v Latvia* that the right is akin to Articles 10 and 11, as it guarantees respect for pluralism of opinion in a democratic society.[141] However, unlike Articles 8 to 11, no limitations are specified in the text of the Convention. In their absence, the ECtHR has developed the concept of 'implied limitations', which it has held is of 'major importance for the determination of the relevance of the aims pursued by the restrictions on the rights guaranteed by the provision'.[142] States are 'always free to rely on any legitimate aim' in their justification of restrictions on the right.[143] As the right is phrased in collective terms, the proportionality test will not be strictly applied and there is no test of 'necessity' or 'pressing social need'.[144] **8.92**

Historically, the ECtHR tended to afford states a very generous margin of appreciation in limiting the rights, but the decision in *Hirst v UK (No 2)* signalled a departure from its prior approach.[145] In that case, the ECtHR held that the absolute bar to prisoners voting violated Protocol 1, Article 3. The ECtHR has subsequently indicated that the State retains a wide margin of appreciation in the design of its electoral system,[146] but it is clear that Strasbourg will now conduct a more rigorous review of the justification advanced by states for interference with rights arising under this article, and the older authorities that demonstrate a more 'hands-off' approach are a less reliable guide to its application. **8.93**

The ECtHR has held that positive obligations arise under Protocol 1, Article 3. In *The Communist Party of Russia and ors v Russia*[147] the applicants complained that unequal media coverage of the 2003 national elections detrimentally affected the outcome. The ECtHR found insufficient evidence of any overt manipulation of the media by the Government, but made clear that the requirements of Protocol 1, Article 3 went beyond the negative requirement to desist from such manipulation. First, there needed to be in existence a domestic system to ensure effective **8.94**

---

[140] (1988) 10 EHRR 1.
[141] (2007) 45 EHRR 17, para 115. See also *Yumak and Sadak v Turkey* (2009) 48 EHRR 1.
[142] *Zdanoka v Latvia* (2007) 45 EHRR 17, para 115.
[143] *Georgian Labour Party v Georgia* [2008] ECHR 9103/04, para 124.
[144] See *Zdanoka v Latvia* (2007) 45 EHRR 17.
[145] (2006) 42 EHRR 41. See the discussion in House of Commons library briefing paper SN/PC/01764, 'Prisoner's voting rights'.
[146] Eg in *Scoppola v Italy No 3* App No 126/05, 22 May 2012, GC.
[147] App No 29400/05, 19 June 2012.

examination of individual complaints and appeals in matters concerning electoral rights. Secondly, since there can be no democracy without pluralism, the adoption of certain positive measures to ensure pluralism were required, including an obligation to intervene in order to open up the media to different viewpoints. Finally, the ECtHR contemplated, but did not explicitly lay down, a duty to ensure neutrality of the audio-visual media, noting the complex interrelationship with Article 10 freedom of expression rights.[148]

1. 'Legislature'

8.95   Protocol 1, Article 3 concerns only the choice of the 'legislature'. The term 'legislature' is not confined to the national Parliament and its meaning will vary according to the constitutional structure of the state in question. For example, Belgian regional councils have been held to be constituent parts of the legislature,[149] yet a French regional council has been held not to come within the article.[150]

8.96   The flexibility of the term 'legislature' is demonstrated by the finding in *Matthews v UK* that the European Parliament had the requisite features of a 'legislature' for the residents of Gibraltar.[151] However, the ECmHR decided that other elected bodies, such as the former metropolitan county councils in England, are not 'legislatures' for the purpose of Protocol 1, Article 3.[152]

2. 'Elections'

8.97   While the meaning of 'legislature' may have a degree of flexibility, a tighter approach is taken to the meaning of 'elections'. The ECmHR has ruled that referenda are not subject to Protocol 1, Article 3.[153]

8.98   The ECtHR has also held that presidential elections are not included,[154] although this will depend on the precise political structures in any given state.

8.99   In *R (Barclay) v Secretary of State for Justice and anor*[155] the Supreme Court considered the law governing elections in the Crown Dependency of Sark, one of the Channel Islands. The claimants challenged a new law designed to reform Sark's constitutional arrangements by which the Seigneur (head of state) and the Seneschal (President of the Sark Parliament and chief judge) remained unelected. The claimants contended that this breached their rights under Protocol 1, Article 3.

8.100   The Supreme Court held that there had been no breach of the claimants' rights on the grounds that the Strasbourg cases put 'no narrow focus on one particular

---

[148] See ibid, paras 123–128.
[149] *Mathieu-Mohin v Belgium* (1988) 10 EHRR 1.
[150] *Malarde v France* App No 46813/99, 5 September 2000.
[151] (1999) 28 EHRR 361.
[152] *Booth-Clibborn v UK* (1985) 43 DR 236.
[153] *X v Germany* (1975) 3 DR 98; *X v UK* (1975) 3 DR 165.
[154] *Guliyev v Azerbaijan* App No 35584/02, 27 May 2004; *Boškoski v the Former Yugoslav Republic of Macedonia* App No 11676/04, 2 September 2004.
[155] [2009] UKSC 9, [2010] 1 AC 464.

element of democracy'.[156] The electoral rules needed to be examined in the round and in the light of historical and political factors. Applying those principles, there was no requirement that all members of a legislature be elected. Even if there were such an obligation under Protocol 1, Article 3, the constitutional history of Sark would justify its limitation.

3. Right to vote

Protocol 1, Article 3 contains an implied right to vote. The state may set condi- **8.101** tions on this right, such as minimum age requirements and, in some circumstances, residency.[157] As 'any departure from the principle of universal suffrage risks undermining the democratic validity of the legislature thus elected and the laws which it promulgates', such conditions must not impair the very essence of the right.[158] Exclusion of any groups or categories of the general population must be reconcilable with the article's underlying purposes and its democratic character.[159]

In an illustration of the generous margin of appreciation that the ECtHR still **8.102** affords states in assessing the proportionality of a restriction on the right to vote, the Grand Chamber in *Sitapoulos v Greece* held that a complete absence of provision for expatriates to vote in Greek elections (other than by travelling to Greece to vote) was compatible with Protocol 1, Article 3.[160]

In *Moore v UK* the applicant argued that his right to vote was impaired as men- **8.103** tal health patients were prevented from using a hospital as their residential address in order to register on the electoral roll. The Government reached a friendly settlement with the applicant, agreeing to amend the Representation of the People Act 1983.[161]

In *Hirst v UK (No 2)* the Grand Chamber found that the UK's automatic **8.104** and indiscriminate statutory bar on convicted prisoners voting was an arbitrary and disproportionate restriction on a vitally important Convention right.[162] It fell outside any acceptable margin of appreciation, however wide, and violated Protocol 1, Article 3.[163] The Court went further in the high-water mark case of

---

[156] Ibid at [64].

[157] *Hilbe v Liechtenstein* App No 31981/96, ECHR 1999-VI; *Melnychenko v Ukraine* App No 17707/02, ECHR 2004-X, para 56; *Schindler v United Kingdom* App No 19840/09, 7 May 2013 (upholding a restriction on voting to those who had not been resident in the UK for 15 years).

[158] *Hirst v UK (No 2)* (2006) 42 EHRR 41, para 62.

[159] *Labita v Italy* App No 26772/95, 6 April 2000. See, eg *Alajos Kiss v Hungary* App No 38832/06, 20 May 2010; *Sitaropoulos and anor v Greece* App No 42202/07, 8 July 2010.

[160] App No 42202/07, 13 March 2012, GC.

[161] App No 37841/97, 30 May 2000; cited in Leach, *Taking a Case to the European Court of Human Rights*, 2nd edn (Oxford: Oxford University Press, 2005) 368.

[162] (2006) 42 EHRR 41, para 82. The Registration Appeal Court of Scotland issued a declaration of incompatibility in relation to this point: *Smith v Scott* [2007] CSIH 9. See also *Frodl v Austria* App No 20201/04, 8 April 2010.

[163] The ECtHR reached the same conclusion in respect of a substantially identical blanket ban under Russian law in *Anchugov and Gladkov v Russia* App No 11157/04 and 15162/05, 14 July 2013.

Frodl v Austria, holding that an automatic and general ban on all those serving a sentence of at least a year and whose crime was committed with intent also violated Protocol 1, Article 3 because it lacked the crucial 'discernible and sufficient link between the sanction and the *conduct and circumstances* of the individual concerned'.[164]

8.105   In *Scoppola v Italy No 3* the Chamber reiterated that an automatic ban on voting by particular categories of prisoners without individual consideration was unacceptable: any decision on disenfranchisement should be taken by a court and be duly reasoned.[165] However, when the case came before the Grand Chamber, it adopted a more flexible approach.[166] It held that individual judicial consideration of the proportionality of a ban was not essential and found the Italian system to be compatible with Protocol 1, Article 3. Under the Italian system, prisoners are automatically disenfranchised if they are sentenced to three years' imprisonment or longer. The duration of the ban is for five years for those sentenced to between three and five years, or permanently for those sentenced to longer sentences. There is also provision for earlier remission of the ban for good behaviour.

8.106   As the lone dissenter, Judge Thor Bjorgvinsson, observed, the Grand Chamber's decision not only departed from *Frodl* and the Chamber's decision, but also from aspects of the Grand Chamber's own reasoning in *Hirst No 2*. He observed in particular that:

just like the United Kingdom legislation, Italy's legislation is a blunt instrument stripping of their Convention right to vote a significant number of persons and doing so in an indiscriminate manner and to a large extent regardless of the nature of their crimes, the length of their sentences and their individual circumstances.

8.107   The Government has prevaricated over the implementation of the *Hirst No 2* judgment (as now understood in light of *Scoppola No 3*), and so there has been substantial further litigation both domestically and in Strasbourg. In *Smith v Scott*[167] the Court of Session made a declaration under section 4 of the Human Rights Act that section 3(1) of the Representation of the People Act 1983 was incompatible with Protocol 1, Article 3. The Government, via the Attorney General, subsequently sought to persuade the Supreme Court not to follow the ECtHR's case law in *R (Chester and anor) v Secretary of State for Justice*.[168] A seven-strong Supreme Court unanimously declined to accept the Attorney General's invitation. A majority of the members of the Court also expressed sympathy with the position and reasoning adopted by the ECtHR in response to the UK's blanket ban, remarking on the 'haphazard'[169] and 'arbitrary and discriminate'[170] effects of the ban.[171]

---

[164] (2011) 52 EHRR 5.
[165] App No 126/05, 18 January 2011, para 43.
[166] *Scoppola v Italy (No 3)* (2012) 33 BHRC 126.
[167] [2007] SLT 137.
[168] [2013] UKSC 63, [2014] 1 All ER 683.
[169] See the leading judgment of Lord Mance at [35].
[170] Lady Hale at [98].
[171] See also Lord Clarke at [110].

However, the Court agreed with previous decisions of lower courts that there was no purpose to issuing a further declaration of incompatibility when the matter was already before Parliament and being overseen by the Committee of Ministers of the Council of Europe.

At the Strasbourg level, in *Greens and MT* the ECtHR noted the ongoing vio- **8.108** lation of Protocol 1, Article 3 and issued a pilot judgment. It gave the United Kingdom six months to introduce legislative proposals to amend the blanket ban.[172] This period was subsequently extended, first pending the Chamber decision in *Scoppola v Italy (No 3)*, and then to six months after the Grand Chamber decision in *Scoppola v Italy (No 3)*. Most recently, in *Firth and ors v UK*,[173] the ECtHR has declined to award any compensation by way of just satisfaction for breaches of Protocol 1, Article 3 arising from the prisoner voting ban, and also declined to award legal costs, noting that, following an earlier decision in *McLean and Cole v UK*,[174] applicants need only submit a summary form of application to raise a petition with the ECtHR. The enforcement of the decision in *Hirst No 2* is thus now solely subject to the political process, including enforcement via oversight by the Committee of Ministers.

A Joint Parliamentary Select Committee was established to consider the issue **8.109** and published a report on 18 December 2013 recommending that the Government introduce legislation to allow all prisoners serving sentences of 12 months or less to vote in all UK parliamentary, local, and European elections. The Lord Chancellor and Justice Secretary, Chris Grayling, responded very briefly to the Committee's report on 25 February 2014 without committing the Government to any timescale to introduce legislation.[175] The Government did not bring forward a Bill in the 2014 Queen's Speech. At the most recent Committee of Ministers' meeting on 26 September 2014, the Committee noted the Government's failure to bring forward legislation 'with profound concern and disappointment', urging it to do so 'as soon as possible'.[176] However, it seems unlikely that this will now happen before the general election in 2015.

While, as Laws LJ observed in the Court of Appeal in *R (Chester)*, the issue of **8.110** prisoner voting is one that gives rise to 'philosophical differences of view between reasonable people',[177] it is surely also right, as Lord Mance observed in his leading judgment in the Supreme Court, that it is not a 'fundamental substantive or procedural aspect' of English law.[178] The domestic political resistance to implementation

---

[172] [2010] ECHR 1826, 23 November 2010. See also *Tovey and ors v Ministry of Justice* [2011] EWHC 271 (QB).
[173] App Nos 47784/09, 47806/09, 47812/09, 47818/09, 47829/09, 49001/09, 49007/09, 49018/09, 49033/09, and 49036/09, 12 August 2014.
[174] App Nos 12626/13 and 2522/12.
[175] <http://www.parliament.uk/documents/joint-committees/Draft-Voting-Eligibility-Prisoners-Bill/Grayling-letter-to-Chair.pdf>.
[176] CM/Del/OJ/DH(2014)1208/27, 26 September 2014
[177] [2011] 1 WLR 1436 at [32].
[178] At [35].

of the *Hirst No 2* judgment thus no doubt stems as much from a wider and more fundamental objection to the role of the ECtHR and its modern case law, as implemented in domestic law by the HRA—which the decision in *Hirst No 2* is perceived to epitomize—as from the particular decision itself.

4. Right to stand for election

8.111 Protocol 1, Article 3 also includes a right to stand for election to the legislature.[179] The right has been characterized as the 'passive' aspect of Protocol 1, Article 3, as opposed to the 'active' right to vote. However, the ECtHR has emphasized that 'it is essential to take a holistic approach to the impact which restrictions on either right may have on securing [the right to free elections]'.[180]

8.112 Legislation establishing domestic residence requirements for a parliamentary candidate is not, as such, incompatible with Protocol 1, Article 3. However, the ECtHR has found that, while states have a margin of appreciation as to eligibility conditions of this kind in the abstract, the principle that rights must be effective requires that eligibility procedures themselves contain sufficient safeguards to prevent arbitrary decisions.[181]

8.113 Thus, it found a violation when an individual was denied registration as a candidate on the basis of residence where the domestic law governing proof of residency lacked the necessary certainty and precision.[182] Similarly, in *Podkolzina v Latvia* the disqualification of a candidate on the grounds of lack of competence in Latvia violated Protocol 1, Article 3 because the body that determined competence did not exhibit the necessary procedural safeguards against arbitrariness.[183]

8.114 The right to stand for election includes the right to sit as a member of the legislature once elected. The ECmHR held, in a short admissibility decision, that the contingent right to take up one's seat is not violated by a requirement that elected MPs in the United Kingdom, including Northern Irish Republicans, take the oath of allegiance to the Queen.[184]

8.115 In *R (Barclay) v Secretary of State for Justice and the Lord Chancellor* the Supreme Court considered that the prohibition on aliens standing for election in Sark was justifiable in light of its constitutional history.[185]

8.116 In *R (Woolas) v The Parliamentary Election Court* the High Court upheld the decision of the Election Court, concluding that dishonest statements made by a parliamentary candidate in election campaign literature were aimed at the destruction of the right to free elections and were not protected by Article 10.[186]

---

[179] *Ganchev v Bulgaria* App No 28858/95, 25 November 1996, para 130; *Sadak and ors v Turkey* (2003) 36 EHRR 23, para 33.
[180] *Tanase v Moldova* [2008] ECHR 7/08, para 113.
[181] *Zdanoka v Latvia* (2007) 45 EHRR 17.
[182] *Melnychenko v Ukraine* (2004) 19 BHRC 523.
[183] [2002] ECHR 46726/99. See also *Tanase v Moldova* [2008] ECHR 7/08.
[184] *McGuinness v UK* App No 39511/98, 8 June 1999.
[185] [2009] UKSC 9, [2010] 1 AC 464.
[186] [2010] EWHC 3169 (Admin).

5. Electoral systems

There is no obligation to introduce a specific system of voting, such as proportional **8.117** representation. The state has a wide margin of appreciation in this regard. It does not have to introduce a system of voting which ensures that all votes have equal weight as regards the outcome of the election, or that all candidates have equal chances of victory.

In *Liberal Party v UK* a challenge was made to the system of 'first past the post' **8.118** elections in the United Kingdom, which inevitably disadvantaged smaller political parties.[187] The ECmHR found the complaint inadmissible, stating that the UK system was a fair one overall and that it did not become unfair because of the results that flowed from it.[188]

The ECtHR in *Mathieu-Mohin v Belgium* observed that any electoral system **8.119** must be assessed in the light of the political evolution of the country concerned. Features that would be unacceptable in the context of one system may be justified in another, as long as the chosen system provides for conditions that will ensure the 'free expression of the opinion of the people in the choice of the legislature'.[189]

In *Bowman v UK* the ECtHR examined the relationship of Article 3 of Protocol **8.120** 1 to Article 10 of the Convention (freedom of expression) in the context of electoral laws. The impugned legislation limited the amount of money spent by unauthorized persons on publications during an election period. This limit was found to be a disproportionate infringement on the right of free speech, which was not outweighed by the need to hold free elections.[190]

The ECtHR has rarely been called upon to determine the validity of the result of **8.121** an election. In one such case the ECtHR considered the invalidation of votes in a parliamentary election.[191] It held that the process had been arbitrarily conducted in violation of the right to free elections.

E. PROTOCOL 4

Protocol 4 was opened for signature in September 1963, and, for reasons discussed **8.122** below, although it has been signed by the United Kingdom, it has not yet been ratified.

1. Protocol 4, Article 1

No one shall be deprived of his liberty merely on the ground of inability to fulfil a **8.123** contractual obligation. This provision is almost identical to Article 11 of the United

---

[187] (1980) 4 EHRR 106.

[188] The same position was taken by the ECtHR in *Gitonas v Greece* (1980) 21 DR 211.

[189] (1988) 10 EHRR 1.

[190] (1998) 26 EHRR 1.

[191] *Kovach v Ukraine* [2008] ECHR 39424/02. See also *Kerimova v Azerbaijan* App No 20799/06, 30 September 2010.

Nations International Covenant on Civil and Political Rights (ICCPR), to which the United Kingdom is subject, and it is impossible to find an example of a UK law that would breach it. It applies only to contractual obligations, and does not affect imprisonment for breach of a court order, such as inability to pay a fine. It is limited to an 'inability to fulfil a contractual obligation', thus excluding from its application a refusal to fulfil such an obligation by someone with the means to fulfil it.

8.124 The word 'merely' excludes cases in which the defaulter acts fraudulently or maliciously. Thus, in *X v Germany* this article did not protect a person who was detained for refusing to execute an affidavit in respect of his property at the request of his creditor.[192]

2. Protocol 4, Article 2

8.125 Freedom of movement within a territory applies to 'everyone', including aliens 'lawfully' in a territory. The power of a state to control the entry of non-nationals is preserved by the inclusion of the word 'lawfully'.[193]

8.126 This right of free movement is limited by the restrictions found in Protocol 4, Article 2(3) and (4). All such restrictions are subject to the principle of proportionality, the doctrine of the margin of appreciation, and must be in accordance with law.[194]

8.127 The restrictions in Article 2(3) are familiar (national security or public safety, the maintenance of public order, the prevention of crime, for the protection of health or morals, or for the protection of the rights and freedoms of others). Any restriction is subject to the requirement that it be necessary in a democratic society. These restrictions are similar in content to those found in Articles 8 to 11 of the Convention.

8.128 However, Article 2(4) permits further restrictions based on a criterion not found elsewhere, that of the 'public interest'. This formulation was preferred by the Committee of Experts, a majority of whom rejected a reference to 'economic welfare' being included. However, it is highly likely that their chosen term 'public interest' is broad enough to include consideration of the economic welfare of society in any event.

8.129 The freedom to leave a state applies to nationals and aliens alike, and is subject to the same restrictions that apply to freedom of movement within a state.[195]

8.130 Protocol 4, Article 5, which applies to the Protocol as a whole, provides that if a state that ratifies the Protocol declares that it also applies to an external territory, that external territory is to be treated as separate from the state's metropolitan territory for the purposes of Protocol 4, Articles 2 and 3.

---

[192] (1971) 14 YB 692.

[193] *Omwenyeke v Germany* App No 44294/04, 20 November 2007.

[194] For examples of cases concerning Protocol 4, Art 2, see *X v Belgium* (1981) 24 DR 198; *Schmid v Austria* (1985) 44 DR 195; *Raimondo v Italy* (1994) 18 EHRR 237; *Foldes v Hungary* [2006] ECHR 41463/02; *Gochev v Bulgaria*, App No 34383/03, 26 November 2009.

[195] *X v Germany* (1997) 9 DR 190; *M v Germany* (1984) 37 DR 113; *Piermont v France* (1995) 20 EHRR 301.

3. Protocol 4, Article 3

Protocol 4, Article 3 prohibits expulsion from, and protects entry to, an individual's national territory. **8.131**

An expulsion occurs when 'a person is obliged permanently to leave the territory of the state without being left the possibility of returning later'.[196] Extradition is not within this definition and is outside the scope of this article.[197] **8.132**

Protocol 4, Article 5 applies, so that a state's external territories declared subject to the article are considered separate from the metropolitan territory. This would have allowed the United Kingdom to distinguish between nationals denied entry under the British Nationality Act 1981. **8.133**

4. Protocol 4, Article 4

This article refers to expulsion by a collective measure, as opposed to an expulsion following an individual decision about a particular person.[198] In *A v Netherlands* it was held that it was not a collective expulsion where a number of asylum seekers from the same country had been expelled for similar reasons, as each had received an individual, reasoned decision.[199] In such a case the issue of discriminatory treatment may, of course, arise. **8.134**

In *Hirsi Jamaa and ors v Italy*[200] the Grand Chamber found a breach of Protocol 4, Article 1 arising out of the interception on the High Seas and return of a number of Somali Eritrean nationals who were attempting to reach the Italian coast from Libya by boat. The applicants were taken aboard Italian vessels—thus bringing them within Italy's jurisdiction—and returned to Libya without any individual examination of their circumstances. The Grand Chamber observed that its finding of a violation was not to call into question the right of states to establish their own immigration policies, but rather that problems with managing migratory flows cannot justify having recourse to practices which are not compatible with the state's obligations under the Convention.[201] **8.135**

Most recently, in *Georgia v Russia* the Grand Chamber found a violation of Protocol 4, Article 4, arising out of the expulsion of thousands of Georgian nationals from Russian-controlled territory during the period of political tension between the two states in 2006. Although a summary court decision was made in respect of each Georgian national, the Court considered that the overall conduct of the expulsion procedures during that period had made it impossible to carry out reasonable and objective examination of the particular case of each individual contrary to Protocol 4, Article 4.[202] **8.136**

---

[196] *X v Austria* (1974) 46 CD 214.
[197] *Bruckmann v Germany* (1974) 17 YB 458.
[198] On the meaning of 'expulsion', see para 8.132.
[199] (1988) 59 DR 274. See now also *MA v Cyprus* App No 41872/10, 23 July 2013.
[200] App No 27765/09, 23 February 2012, GC.
[201] Ibid, paras 166–186.
[202] App No 13255/07, 23 July 2014, GC, paras 170–178.

5. Ratification of Protocol 4 by the United Kingdom

8.137   Prior to the passing of the Human Rights Act 1998, the UK Government stated that although Protocol 4 protects 'important rights, and we would like to see them given formal recognition in our law', there were 'potential conflicts' with 'existing laws in relation to different categories of British nationals' which prevented ratification.[203] Concerns that Protocol 4 may confer rights on categories of British nationals who do not currently have that right have prevented ratification.[204]

F. PROTOCOL 6

8.138   Protocol 6 prohibits the death penalty in times of peace and thereby overrides the exception permitting the death penalty under Article 2. The Protocol came into force on 1 March 1985 and all Member States have ratified it except for Russia, which is a signatory and observes a moratorium.

8.139   Protocol 6 was ratified by the United Kingdom in 1999. As originally drafted, the Human Rights Act did not incorporate Protocol 6, but by the time it came into force, it had been inserted into Schedule 1. Protocol 6 has now been superseded by Protocol 13, prohibiting the death penalty in all circumstances.

8.140   As considered in Chapter 6, the ECtHR has held that the Convention has evolved as a result of state practice such that the death penalty violates Articles 2 and Article 3 in all circumstances.[205]

G. PROTOCOL 7

8.141   Following the adoption by the General Assembly of the United Nations of the ICCPR in 1966, the Council of Europe commissioned its Committee of Experts to investigate any problems that could be caused by the coexistence of the European Convention and the ICCPR. The Committee's report[206] on differences between the two documents led to Parliamentary Assembly recommendations,[207] further work, and, eventually, Protocol 7.

8.142   Protocol 7 seeks to bring the Convention into line with the ICCPR. It came into force on 1 November 1988.

8.143   The United Kingdom is the only Member State not yet to be a signatory. The previous Government explained that the United Kingdom would not be in a position to accede to Protocol 7 until legislation to abolish or equalize three rules of matrimonial property law had been passed. Part 15 of the Equality Act 2010 was designed

---

[203] *Rights Brought Home: The Human Rights Bill* (Cm 3782, 1997) paras 4.10–4.11.

[204] Department of Constitutional Affairs, *Report of the Outcome of an Interdepartmental Review Conducted by the Department of Constitutional Affairs* (July 2004) app 6, p 40.

[205] *Al-Saadoon and Mufdhi v UK*, App No 61498/08, 2 March 2010.

[206] Report of the Committee of Experts, Doc H (70) 7 (1969).

[207] Recommendation 683 (1972) and Recommendation 791 (1976).

to achieve this aim. However, there do not currently seem to be any proposals to ratify this Protocol. Nonetheless, the United Kingdom has ratified the ICCPR and it must respect the rights under Protocol 7 as a matter of international law.

The Strasbourg jurisprudence on Protocol 7 is sparse, but the Council of Europe has published an explanatory memorandum which, although not binding upon the ECtHR, is an additional aid to interpretation.[208]   8.144

1. Protocol 7, Article 1

This provision affords a minimum guarantee that the procedural rights speci-   8.145
fied are complied with by a state seeking to expel a lawfully resident alien. The Memorandum stresses that such an individual already benefits from certain guarantees under the Convention and international law, and makes clear that this is a residual article, which 'enables protection to be granted in those cases which are not covered by other international instruments'.[209]

It is a precondition that the person is 'lawfully resident'. The article does not   8.146
therefore apply to an alien who has arrived but not yet passed through immigration control, a person in transit or admitted for a limited period for a non-residential purpose, or those awaiting a decision on a residence application.[210]

The term 'lawfully' refers to domestic law, and it is for that law to determine   8.147
the conditions under which the person's presence is lawful. The provision applies to aliens who enter unlawfully but who have regularized their position, but not to those whose permits have expired or who are in breach of conditions.[211]

Expulsion means any measure compelling the departure of an alien from the terri-   8.148
tory, except extradition, and is a concept independent of any national law definition. A decision to expel must be made in 'accordance with law'.[212] The Memorandum states baldly that 'no exceptions may be made to this rule'.[213] However, in exceptional cases involving public order or national security, an alien may be expelled *before* the exercise of his or her rights. The rights to review must be available after expulsion, and the principles of proportionality should be taken into account.[214]

The sub-paragraphs to Protocol 7, Article 1 set out three specific guarantees,   8.149
namely that the person concerned may submit reasons against his or her expulsion, have the case reviewed, and be represented before the relevant authority.

According to the Memorandum, the right to have the case reviewed does not   8.150
require a two-stage process before different authorities—merely that the 'competent authorities' should review the case in the light of the reasons against expulsion. The alien is not entitled to an oral hearing—a written procedure will suffice.

---

[208] *Text of Protocol No 7 and Explanatory Memorandum*, CE Doc H (84) 5 (Strasbourg: Council of Europe, 1984).
[209] Ibid, paras 6–7.
[210] Ibid, para 9.
[211] See Baroness Royall of Blaisdon, *Hansard*, HL, col 710, 9 February 2010.
[212] *CG and ors v Bulgaria* App No 1365/07, 24 April 2008.
[213] Ibid, para 11.
[214] *Chahal v UK* (1997) 23 EHRR 413; *CG and ors v Bulgaria* App No 1365/07, 24 April 2008.

It does not need to be the authority upon whom the final decision to expel rests, but may have only power of recommendation to the body that does make the final decision.

8.151   The ECmHR has held that a decision to deport does not involve a determination of the person's civil rights or of a criminal charge within the meaning of Article 6 of the Convention.[215] Accordingly, Protocol 7, Article 1 does not affect the interpretation of Article 6. The competent authority does not have to comply with the Article 6 characteristics of a judicial body.

2. Protocol 7, Article 2

8.152   Protocol 7, Article 2 extends the general right to a fair trial provided by Article 6 of the Convention. This article recognizes the right of everyone convicted of a criminal offence to have his or her conviction or sentence reviewed by a higher tribunal. However, it does not require that in every case the individual be entitled to have both his or her conviction and sentence so reviewed. For example, if he or she has pleaded guilty, the right may be restricted to a review of sentence only.[216]

8.153   Where a person has pleaded guilty, the right to appeal may be limited to one against sentence only, and may be satisfied by leave to appeal proceedings where leave is not granted.

8.154   The right is restricted to offences tried by bodies that are 'tribunals' for the purpose of Article 6 of the Convention, and so excludes cases of a disciplinary nature.

8.155   Other limits are found in Article 2(2): offences of a 'minor character' are excluded, as are cases where the person was convicted by the highest tribunal, or following an appeal against acquittal.

8.156   The right to appeal may be satisfied by leave to appeal proceedings where leave is not granted.

8.157   As 'the modalities for the exercise of the right and the grounds on which it may be exercised' are matters to be determined by domestic law, the appeal may be limited to law, or may also include questions of fact.[217]

3. Protocol 7, Article 3

8.158   A right to compensation for miscarriages of justice is established by Protocol 7, Article 3, subject to conditions. Compensation encompasses both pecuniary loss caused by a wrongful conviction and compensation for non-pecuniary damage such as distress, anxiety, inconvenience, and loss of enjoyment of life.[218] The person must have been convicted of a criminal offence by a 'final decision', and suffered punishment as a result. A decision is final where it is irrevocable in that

---

[215] *Agee v UK* (1976) 7 DR 164; see also *Explanatory Memorandum*, 208, para 16.
[216] *Explanatory Memorandum*, 208 para 17.
[217] Ibid, para 18.
[218] *Poghosyan and Baghdasaryan v Armenia* App No 22999/06, para 51.

no further ordinary remedies are available, the parties have exhausted such remedies, or have allowed the time limit to expire without availing themselves of the remedy.[219] Thus, Protocol 7, Article 3 does not apply in cases where a conviction is overturned on an ordinary appeal, or when charges are dismissed in the trial court.

According to the Memorandum, the right to compensation arises only: 8.159

where the person's conviction has been reversed or he has been pardoned, in either case on the grounds that a new or newly discovered fact shows conclusively that there has been a miscarriage of justice—that is, some serious failure in the judicial process involving grave prejudice to the convicted person.[220]

Article 2 operates on a 'clean hands' principle: there will be no right to compensation if it is shown that the non-disclosure of the unknown fact in time was wholly or partly attributable to the convicted person.[221] 8.160

The nature of the procedures to establish a miscarriage of justice is a matter of domestic law or practice for the state (although states are obliged to make provision for compensation in all cases to which Article 3 applies).[222] Once a miscarriage of justice is established, the intention of the article is that compensation should be paid by the state. If it is not, a violation of this article will have occurred. 8.161

In the United Kingdom the relevant provision is section 133 of the Criminal Justice Act 1988. The Supreme Court recently considered Protocol 7, Article 3 in relation to the statutory scheme in *R (Adams) v Secretary of State for Justice*.[223] The court did not consider that it assisted in determining the meaning to be given to the term 'miscarriage of justice' in domestic law. 8.162

4. Protocol 7, Article 4

Article 4 of Protocol 7 incorporates the protection against double jeopardy into the Convention. It is limited to the same national jurisdiction, so that it remains possible to be convicted of the same offence in different jurisdictions. It applies only to criminal proceedings. A 'final' conviction must have been recorded.[224] 8.163

In *Margus v Croatia*, the Grand Chamber considered whether a prosecution of members of the Croat army for offences relating to the killing and serious injury of civilians was compatible with Protocol 7, Article 4 when the applicants had previously been granted an amnesty. The Grand Chamber found that Protocol 7, Article 4 had to be read in light of the state's positive obligations under Articles 2 and 3 to investigate and prosecute such acts, remarking on a growing tendency in international law to regard such amnesties as incompatible with the unanimously 8.164

---

[219] Ibid, para 22.
[220] Ibid, para 32. See *Matveyev v Russia* App No 26601/02, 3 July 2008.
[221] *Explanatory Memorandum*, 208, para 24.
[222] Ibid, para 25.
[223] [2011] UKSC 18. See also *R (Mullen) v Secretary of State for the Home Department* [2004] UKHL 18, [2005] 1 AC 1.
[224] This has the same meaning as under Protocol 7, Art 3.

recognized obligation of states to prosecute and punish grave breaches of fundamental human rights. Accordingly, the prosecutions did not breach Protocol 7, Article 4.[225]

8.165 Article 4(2) allows the reopening of a case in exceptional circumstances, where there is evidence of new or newly discovered facts, or where there has been a fundamental defect in the previous proceedings.

8.166 The Court of Appeal has considered Article 4(2) where a defendant had previously been convicted of wounding with intent and acquitted of attempted murder. The court ruled that a subsequent prosecution for murder following the death of the victim from her injuries did not breach Protocol 7 as the 'new fact' of her death had emerged since the first trial.[226]

8.167 The 'fundamental defect' exception finds effect in domestic law in the Criminal Procedure and Investigations Act 1996, sections 54–56.

8.168 The Criminal Justice Act 2003 has abolished the double jeopardy rule in some circumstances. It makes provision for the quashing of an acquittal and an order for a retrial in respect of certain serious offences where there is 'new and compelling evidence'.[227] These provisions were introduced by Parliament following the Macpherson Report on the Stephen Lawrence Inquiry[228] and a report by the Law Commission.[229] Concerns have been raised as to the Convention-compliance of these measures, although in our view the provisions in themselves appear to be compliant, but their application in an individual case may give rise to a complaint under Protocol 7, Article 4, or even Article 6.

5. Protocol 7, Article 5

8.169 This article places an obligation on the state to provide a system of laws by which spouses have equal rights and responsibilities concerning matters of private law, such as property rights and their relations with their children. It does not apply to areas of law external to the relationship of marriage, such as administrative, fiscal, criminal, social, ecclesiastical, or labour laws.[230]

8.170 It is concerned only with spouses, and specifically precludes the period before marriage. The article is not meant in any way to prevent the state from taking such measures as are necessary in the interests of children; nor is it to prevent the state taking due account of 'all relevant factors' when reaching decisions about the distribution of property upon the dissolution of marriage.[231]

---

[225] App No 4455/10, 27 May 2014, GC, paras 139–140.

[226] *R v Kerry Rena Young* [2005] EWCA Crim 2963.

[227] Criminal Justice Act 2003, s 78.

[228] *The Stephen Lawrence Inquiry: Report of an Inquiry by Sir William Macpherson of Cluny* (Cm 4262-I, 1999).

[229] *Double Jeopardy and Prosecution Appeals* (Law Com No 267, 2001).

[230] This article was the basis for changes made to the common law by Part 15 of the Equality Act 2010, which was drafted by Lord Lester and accepted by the previous Government on the basis that there would then be no obstacle in the way of ratifying the whole Protocol.

[231] *Explanatory Memorandum*, 208, para 38.

This article—as is also the case with Article 12 of the Convention—does not **8.171** include a right to divorce. The Memorandum states that the words 'in the event of its dissolution...do not imply any obligation on a State to provide for dissolution of marriage or to provide any special forms of dissolution'.[232]

H. PROTOCOL 12

Protocol 12 came into force on 1 April 2005. It provides a substantive right to **8.172** equality of treatment in like situations. Unlike Article 14 of the Convention, this is a free-standing equality right, which does not need to 'piggy-back' on an existing Convention right. It applies the expansive grounds of prohibited discrimination in Article 14 (including sex, race, religion, and 'other status') to the exercise of 'any right set forth by law' and to the actions (including the obligations) of public authorities.

The ECtHR has confirmed that, notwithstanding the difference in scope **8.173** between Article 14 and Protocol 12, the meaning of 'discrimination' in Article 1 of Protocol 12 is intended to be identical to that in Article 14, and it has seen no reason to depart from the settled interpretation of this term as developed in its Article 14 case law.[233]

The United Kingdom has not yet signed or ratified Protocol 12. Various con- **8.174** cerns have been raised about the potential breadth of its protection.[234] As the Joint Committee on Human Rights has stated, these concerns are unwarranted.[235] As a signatory to a variety of international human rights instruments concerning equality and non-discrimination, the United Kingdom has already accepted the principles enshrined in Protocol 12. The development of Protocol 12 is effectively stymied by the Government's approach: the United Kingdom will not ratify it until the ECtHR has clarified its parameters, but the ECtHR is hindered in doing so because the most populous Member States, including the United Kingdom, have decided not to ratify it.

I. PROTOCOL 13

Protocol 13 abolishes the death penalty in all circumstances. In so doing, it closes **8.175** the gap left by Protocol 6, which did not exclude the death penalty in respect of acts committed in time of war or of imminent threat of war. Protocol 13 is non-derogable and no reservations may be made in respect of it.[236]

---

[232] Ibid, para 39.
[233] *Zornic v Bosnia and Herzegovina* 3681/06, para 27.
[234] Department of Constitutional Affairs, *Report of the Outcome of an Interdepartmental Review Conducted by the Department of Constitutional Affairs* (July 2004) app 6, p 41.
[235] Joint Committee on Human Rights, 17th Report (2005–2006), HL 99, para 33.
[236] Protocol 13, Arts 2, 3.

8.176   The United Kingdom ratified Protocol 13 on 10 October 2003 and in 2004, Protocol 13, Article 1 was incorporated into the Human Rights Act in place of Protocol 6.[237]

8.177   As considered in Chapter 6, the ECtHR has held that the Convention has evolved as a result of state practice such that the death penalty violates Articles 2 and Article 3 in all circumstances.[238]

---

[237] Human Rights Act (Amendment) Order 2004, SI 2004/1574, Art 2(3).

[238] *Al-Saadoon and Mufdhi v UK* App No 61498/08, 2 March 2010.

9

BEYOND THE DOMESTIC COURTS: TAKING A CASE TO STRASBOURG

A. INTRODUCTION

9.01 The Human Rights Act 1998 did not, and could not, end the practice of taking UK cases to the Strasbourg Court. First, this is because the Human Rights Act 1998 maintains parliamentary sovereignty, so it is likely that there will be cases in which breaches of Convention rights will still arise in primary legislation which cannot be rectified in domestic courts and where Parliament does not legislate to amend the law following a declaration of incompatibility. To date, however, the Government has responded to all such declarations of incompatibility (either by repealing or amending the offending law, or by enacting new legislation).[1] Secondly, domestic courts are more likely than an international body to succumb to local pressure from politicians and the state, and may not always be as robust in their protection of human rights as the Court in Strasbourg. Thirdly, the Strasbourg Court may differ from the domestic courts in its interpretation of particular Convention rights. For example, in *S and Marper v UK*[2] the Grand Chamber took a very different view of the collection and retention of DNA samples and data and Article 8. The Administrative Court,[3] the Court of Appeal,[4] and the House of Lords[5] all rejected the victims' cases and the House of Lords decided that Article 8 was barely engaged, whereas the 17 judges in Strasbourg were unanimous in finding a violation.[6] Fourthly, it is sensible for individuals with the stamina and real issues to test to seek redress there, including those who seek compensation where the domestic court has made a declaration of incompatibility and compensation is not available. Fifthly, since in practice the definitive interpretation of the Convention is

---

[1] However, the Parliamentary Joint Human Rights Committee (JCHR) has expressed real concerns about delays in implementation: see JCHR, *Monitoring the Government's Response to Human Rights Judgments: Annual Report 2008* 31st Report (2007–2008), HL 173, HC 1078 (31 October 2008).

[2] [2008] ECHR 1582, App Nos 30562/04 and 30566/04, 4 December 2008. See an analysis of the different approaches in Brice Dickson, *Human Rights and the United Kingdom Supreme Court* (London: Oxford University Press, 2013).

[3] *R (S) v Chief Constable of South Yorkshire Police and the Secretary of State for the Home Department* and *R (Marper) v Chief Constable of South Yorkshire Police and the Secretary of State for the Home Department* [2002] EWHC 478 (Admin), [2002] EWCA Civ 1275 and *R (LS) v Chief Constable of South Yorkshire and R (Marper) v Chief Constable of South Yorkshire* [2004] UKHL 39.

[4] [2002] EWCA Civ 1275, [2002] 1 WLR 3223.

[5] [2004] UKHL 39, [2004] 1 WLR 2196.

[6] See also *Hirst v UK (No 2)* (2005) 19 BHRC 546, (2006) 42 EHRR 41 where, on the right of prisoners to vote, the Court also took a much stronger pro-rights line and the Government and Parliament have so far refused to implement the judgment.

reserved to the Strasbourg Court, practitioners are likely to want to contribute to this definitive jurisprudence.[7] Sixthly, the next government may amend or abolish the Human Rights Act, perhaps restricting the jurisdiction of the UK courts (see Chapter 1, para 1.59). If that happens, then, depending on what legislation replaces it, Strasbourg may be the only means of directly enforcing Convention rights.[8]

The European Court of Human Rights (ECtHR) is a court of last resort and not 9.02 an appeal court: it has never been permissible to take a case there without exhausting domestic remedies first, and this requirement has been imposed more strictly since the Convention became part of domestic law, and will be increasingly as a result of the implementation of Protocol 15 (see para 9.06). However, a declaration of incompatibility is not regarded as an effective remedy for the purposes of Article 13, although the Court has not closed the possibility of this being the case in future.[9]

Interestingly, the number of cases against the United Kingdom lodged with the 9.03 ECtHR before and after the Human Rights Act came into force seems to have remained roughly the same. The number of allocated cases[10] against the United Kingdom increased considerably in 2010 (2,745), twice that in 2008 or 2009, but has now returned to 912 for 2013.[11] There were 2,519 such allocated cases pending against the United Kingdom at the end of 2013. The Court found only eight violations of the Convention in 2013 (around the usual average) in relation to UK cases (499 violations over the lifetime of the Court), making the United Kingdom in 2013 the 21st 'violator' of the 45 countries subject to the Court's jurisdiction. The number of cases 'communicated' (referred to the Government requiring a response, the initial sifting stage) has reduced from 163 in 2000 to 35 in 2013.[12]

This chapter outlines the procedure for making applications to the European 9.04 Court in Strasbourg. It is included to ensure that those who have exhausted the domestic remedies in the United Kingdom have information on how to proceed further.

Over the last 20 years there has been a huge increase in the number of cases that 9.05 have been dealt with by the Court (partly as a result of the accession of a significant number of countries from Eastern Europe). This increase shows no sign of tailing off and the numbers of cases allocated increased by another 2 per cent between 2012 and 2013.[13] However the Court continues to reduce its backlog of pending cases—particularly at the admissibility stage. At the end of 2010 there were

---

[7] See Lord Bingham in *R (Anderson) v Secretary of State for the Home Department* [2002] UKHL 46, [2003] 1 AC 837 at [18].

[8] See Preface.

[9] See para 9.27.

[10] These are applications which are ready for decision because the file is complete and which have been allocated to a judicial function. Uncompleted applications (that is, cases not allocated) are disposed of administratively because the applicant fails to submit the properly filled in application form and/or necessary supporting documentation within the prescribed time limit.

[11] ECtHR, *Annual Report 2013*. This is probably as a result of a sudden influx of cases from prisoners challenging the continued blanket ban on their voting rights.

[12] ECtHR, *Analysis of Statistics 2013*.

[13] ECtHR, *Analysis of Statistics 2013*.

139,650 allocated cases pending, but at the end of 2013 this had been reduced to 99,900,[14] with most of those cases pending against six countries: Russia (16.8 per cent); Italy (14.4 percent); Ukraine (13.3 per cent); Serbia (11.3 per cent); Turkey (11.0 per cent); and Romania (6.2 per cent); with the United Kingdom in joint seventh place (2.5 per cent). Changes to speed up the Court's procedures and processes and to reduce the number of cases taking up its time (particularly at the admissibility stage) are now already clearly working. Another batch of proposals to deal with the workload problem were, however, agreed at a conference in Brighton during the time that the United Kingdom was chairing the Council of Europe and the 'Brighton Declaration' is now driving further reforms.[15]

9.06   The two sets of amendments to the Convention now set out in Protocols 14 and 15 are designed to make a number of changes to the system to try to solve the Court's problems caused by its 'success'. The Protocol 14 changes and the other internal changes made by the Court itself have already enabled the Court to start to clear its backlog. The stricter process for filing applications themselves, which was implemented by the Court itself at the beginning of 2014 (see para 9.13), is also likely to have an effect on the Court's future workload. The changes set out in Protocol 15 had not yet been implemented at the time of writing. It is likely that they will be in force some time in 2015, and the remainder of this chapter describes the amended system (although any differences with the pre-Protocol 15 system are set out in the text and footnotes).[16] When implemented Protocol 15 will:

- add a new recital to the Preamble to the Convention stressing the margin of appreciation enjoyed by states;
- reduce the maximum age of judges on selection from 70 to 65;
- remove the right of a party to object to a case being dealt with by the Grand Chamber;
- reduce the time for making applications from six months to four months;
- make it easier for specified cases to be declared inadmissible (see paras 9.29 and 9.36).[17]

9.07   For more information on the procedure in the Court, see the amended Convention itself (Appendix 2), the Rules of Procedure of the European Court of Human Rights, April 2014,[18] and the Practice Directions: references to 'rules' in

---

[14] ECtHR, *Annual Report for 2013*.

[15] High Level Conference on the Future of the European Court of Human Right: Brighton Declaration, 20 April 2012, Council of Europe.

[16] The changes made by Protocol 14 came into force on 1 June 2010. For the previous procedure, see the fifth edition of this book.

[17] On 18 December 2013 the Secretary of State for Justice told the UK Parliament: 'We signed Protocol 15 when it was open for signature on 24 June. The UK's ratification of Protocol 15 will be approved by Parliament in the next few months. Some 32 countries have signed it. Five have already ratified it and the rest have not yet. We will do so in due course.' For the transitional arrangements, see *Protocol 15, Explanatory Report*, CETS No 213, Council of Europe.

[18] It is likely that these rules will be amended again once Protocol 15 has taken effect and if so these will be available from the ECtHR's website.

this chapter are to these rules unless otherwise stated.[19] The ECtHR's very helpful website (<http://www.echr.coe.int>) gives access to the amended Convention and all the rules and to the practice directions referred to in this chapter.

The process of reform is far from over, however, and in November 2013 the Council of Europe initiated yet another consultation exercise: **9.08**

holding an open call for information, proposals and views on the issue of the longer-term reform of the system of the European Convention on Human Rights and the European Court of Human Rights. This process follows on from the <u>Brighton Declaration</u>, adopted at a High-level conference in April 2012. It is intended to be open and inclusive, allowing questions to be raised and examined concerning all aspects of the Convention system and the Court.[20]

B. THE STRUCTURE AND JURISDICTION OF THE COURT

The Court consists of one judge nominated by each of the countries belonging to the Council of Europe. These persons act in an individual capacity and cannot be government officials (though they can be ex-government lawyers). The vast majority of decisions in cases will be made by single judges or committees of three. In cases that lead on to substantive judgments the Court will sit in Chambers of seven judges. Reserve judges may also sit, so that the case does not need to be reheard if one judge falls ill, or cannot for some other reason deliberate. Where the Chamber considers that a case raises a serious question affecting the interpretation of the Convention, or where the resolution of a question before it might result in an inconsistency in the Court's case law, it may relinquish jurisdiction to a Grand Chamber of 17 judges, under Article 30 of the Convention. Alternatively, within three months of a decision of a Chamber, any of the parties may request that the case be referred to the Grand Chamber under Article 43. This is an exceptional procedure, and the request will be accepted only if the case raises a serious question affecting the interpretation or application of the Convention or a serious issue of general importance. The first case referred to the Grand Chamber from the United Kingdom under Article 43, *Hatton v UK*,[21] which concerned the Article 8 rights of those in the vicinity of Heathrow Airport, was decided in 2003. **9.09**

The Court can hear applications of alleged violations of the Convention brought by other Member States—as occurred, for example, when the Republic of Ireland complained to the Court about the UK's interrogation practices used in Northern Ireland.[22] But this is rare.[23] In practice the majority of applications are now brought by individuals against states. Negotiations to allow applications against the EU and its institutions are, however, continuing. **9.10**

---

[19] See also Leach, *Taking a Case to the European Court of Human Rights*, 3rd edn (Oxford: Oxford University Press, 2011).

[20] Council of Europe, November 2013.

[21] (2003) 37 EHRR 28.

[22] *Ireland v UK* (1978) 2 EHRR 25.

[23] There are three inter-state cases pending, two by Georgia against Russia and more recently one by Ukraine against Russia.

C. MAKING AN APPLICATION

9.11 Applications should be directed to:

The Registrar of the European Court of Human Rights

Council of Europe

F-67075 Strasbourg-Cedex

France

Tel: 00 33 3 88 41 2018

Fax: 00 33 3 41 27 30

9.12 It is now necessary to make the application on and in the form provided by the Court (available from its website). It is also necessary to ensure that all the questions on the form are answered correctly and all of the documentation required is sent with the form before the expiry of the time limit for applications.[24] The following information is required by the Court:

(a) the applicant's name, date of birth, nationality, sex, occupation, and address;

(b) the name, address, and occupation of anyone acting as the representative;

(c) the respondent country;

(d) a clear and concise statement of the facts, including, of course, the exact dates;

(e) a succinct statement of each and every alleged violation of the Convention and the relevant arguments (this should include the relevant domestic law and any relevant Convention case law);

(f) a succinct statement of compliance with the admissibility criteria, including the four-month[25] rule and the details of all remedies (including any appeal) which have been pursued within the country concerned and, where appropriate, an explanation of why any available remedies have not been pursued (see para 9.27);

(g) the object of the application (for example, the repeal or amendment of certain legislation, or the reversal of a decision and compensation); and

(h) copies of the judgments, decisions, and any other documents relating to the application.[26]

9.13 It used to be possible to write a short initial letter to the Court setting out the details of the application, but this will not be sufficient to interrupt the four-month time.[27] Only a fully completed application along with all the relevant documents

---

[24] Strict rules came into force on 1 January 2014, see *Notes for filling in the application form*, 2014/1, Council of Europe, Rule 47 and Practice Direction: *Institution of Proceedings*.

[25] The time limit will be reduced by Protocol 15 from six months to four months.

[26] Rule 47 and see *Stricter conditions for applying to the European Court of Human Rights*, Press Release, 11 December 2013, ECtHR.

[27] For useful information on how to make an application, see ECtHR, Practice Direction: Institution of Proceedings, 1 January 2014.

will have the effect of instigating a case. It will not be possible to amend or supplement the application after it has been submitted.

1. Urgent cases, interim measures, and the Court's priorities

The Court's full procedures take some time (five years or more in many cases), but it will give priority to very urgent cases (for example, where a person's life or well-being is immediately threatened, as in the case of a motor neurone disease sufferer in *Pretty v United Kingdom*[28]). The Court has now amended its rules allowing urgent and important cases to be dealt with more quickly (see para 9.16 below). The Court can also be asked to implement its interim measures procedure. In rule 39 the Chamber or its President may indicate to the parties interim measures which it considers should be adopted. This will often be a request to refrain from taking action that will prejudice the case—for instance by not deporting someone where the case concerns arguments about the possibility of Article 3 breaches if that person is sent out of the jurisdiction. In such cases, the Court should be contacted directly to ask it to request the Government to refrain from acting until the application has been considered. Telephone contact can be useful to alert the Registry of a request about to be made, which of course then has to be in writing (a telephone call on its own would not be enough). The Court now has a dedicated fax line for such requests and all requests should initially be sent using this line.[29] The Court has expressed its concern about the number of cases wrongly brought under this procedure so it is sensible to get this right.[30]

9.14

The United Kingdom has, generally, always respected requests from the ECtHR for interim measures. However, in one case the Government decided not to comply with a request from the ECtHR to refrain from handing over two people in Iraq to the Iraqi High Tribunal pending their trial for killing two British servicemen.[31] The Secretary of State for Defence stated that:

9.15

This follows the unanimous court of appeal ruling that Mr Al-Saadoon and Mr Mufdhi do not fall within the jurisdiction of the European Convention on Human Rights. After 31 December 2008, the UK had no legal power to detain any individuals in Iraq and continued detention would be a breach of the UK's international law obligations.[32]

The Court in Strasbourg however found that:

In conclusion, the Court does not consider that the authorities of the Contracting State took all steps which could reasonably have been taken in order to comply with the interim measure taken by the Court. The failure to comply with the interim measure and the transfer of the

---

[28] (2002) 35 EHRR 1.

[29] For more details, see Practice Direction: Requests for Interim Measures, 5 March 2003, amended 16 October 2009 and 7 July 2011.

[30] Court press release, 28 July 2011 which also gives a link to the statistics by country for interim measures accepted or refused.

[31] See the judgment of the Court of Appeal, *R (Al-Saadoon and anor) v Secretary of State for Defence* [2009] EWCA Civ 7.

[32] Reported in the *Guardian*, 1 January 2009.

applicants out of the United Kingdom's jurisdiction exposed them to a serious risk of grave and irreparable harm.[33]

In fact the Court now considers interim measures to be binding.[34]

2. The Court's priority policy

9.16 Until 2009 the Court dealt with non-urgent cases as they arrived and were ready for consideration but changed its policy because 'very serious allegations of human rights violations were taking too long to be examined by the Court'.[35] Since then the Court approaches its workload on the basis of the following priorities:

I.   urgent applications—threats to life or health;

II. applications raising questions about the effectiveness of the Convention system: structural or endemic situations or raising questions of general interest (including ones with possible major implications for domestic legal systems or the European system);

III. applications which raise as their main complaint Articles 2, 3, 4, or 5(1) and which have given rise to direct threats to the physical integrity and dignity of human beings;

IV. potentially well-founded applications based on other articles;

V.   applications raising issues already dealt with by pilot or leading judgments;

VI. applications identified as giving rise to a problem of admissibility; and

VII. applications which are manifestly inadmissible.

Obviously the Court will decide which category any particular case fits into, but applicants will wish to ensure that arguments that might push their case up the hierarchy are set out in the application and subsequent correspondence.

3. Court's response to an application

9.17 The Court will register the application and give it a case number and may also request further information or documents.

4. Representation

9.18 Legal representation must be by a lawyer authorized to practice in any Convention country and resident in one of them, unless the President of the Chamber decides otherwise.[36] The Court has the power to direct that an applicant be represented,

---

[33] *Al-Saadoon and Mufdhi v UK* App No 61498/08, 2 March 2010, [2010] ECHR 282, para 165.
[34] *Mamatkulov v Turkey, 4 February 2005*
[35] ECtHR, *The Court's Priority Policy.*
[36] Rule 36.

and at any hearing representation by a lawyer is mandatory unless the President of the Court decides otherwise.[37]

D. ADMISSIBILITY AND MERITS

The Court's jurisdiction is limited and applications can be considered only if they meet the admissibility criteria set out in Article 35 of the Convention, which are rigorously applied and which are set out in turn below. More than 97 per cent of cases are dismissed as being 'inadmissible',[38] and it is therefore critically important to ensure that an application complies with the admissibility requirements, and contains all the facts and arguments of law. To have a real chance of success, it is necessary for the application to set out the facts, the relevant domestic law, and detailed submissions on the law of the Convention. One of the best ways of setting out the application is to model it on a judgment of the Court.[39]   9.19

Article 34 provides that an application under the Convention can be brought by 'any person, non-governmental organization or group of individuals claiming to be the victim of a violation'. Neither individuals nor legal persons have to be citizens of the state concerned, nor of any Member State. They do not have to be resident or physically present in the territory. Applications may not be brought by governmental organizations or other 'emanations of the state'.   9.20

Although applications may be brought by groups of individuals and non-governmental organizations (NGOs), the organization or group must itself be a victim of a violation. Thus, trade unions and NGOs can make applications about an action by the state but only if it was directed towards them. Finally, groups, trade unions, and NGOs can, of course, provide their members with representation, but cannot make applications on behalf of their members. However, in a recent case the Grand Chamber of the Court decided in a case concerning Article 2 and the respondent's responsibility for the death, where no one else could represent the deceased interests an NGO was entitled to do so.[40]   9.21

1. Who is a 'victim'?

An applicant must be one of three types of victim: actual, potential, and indirect. An *actual victim* is someone who is personally affected by the alleged violation. It is not necessary to show that any detriment has been suffered, although this will be relevant to the remedy (but see para 9.36). A *potential victim* is one who is at risk of   9.22

---

[37] Rule 36(2).

[38] Of the 2,000–3,000 applications lodged each year where the UK was the respondent, only about 30 cases were even 'communicated' to the Government, ECtHR, *Analysis of Statistics 2013*.

[39] Practice Direction: *Institution of Proceedings* and see Leach, *Taking a Case to the European Court of Human Rights*, 3rd edn (Oxford: Oxford University Press, 2011), for model applications.

[40] *Centre for Legal Resources on behalf of Valentin Campeanu v Romania*, 17 July 2014. The Court has not set out any criteria for how this exception will operate but the facts of the case suggest that the Court's discretion will be exercised in this way very rarely.

being directly affected by a law or administrative act.[41] An *indirect victim* is one who is immediately affected by a violation which directly affects another, such as a family member of someone imprisoned or killed. Family members of those killed or imprisoned can also successfully include in their cases applications about *direct violations* of their rights—for example Article 3 in disappearance cases. Another example of an indirect victim is a family member of someone deported or facing deportation.[42]

2. Against whom can an application be brought?

9.23   Only states are parties to the Convention (and possibly the EU in the future), and therefore only those states can commit violations. Where there are several state organs involved, it will not be necessary for this purpose to identify which level of the state organization is responsible. Applications cannot be brought against private persons or institutions. However, the application may be based on the state's failure to fulfil positive obligations to ensure that human rights are respected by private persons within the state's jurisdiction.[43]

3. Extent of jurisdiction

9.24   Under Article 1, signatory states are required to 'secure to everyone *within their jurisdiction*' (emphasis added) the rights and freedoms protected by the Convention. This means that states are liable for all events that take place in the territory for which they are responsible, not just those affecting their own nationals, and even if the effects of the events might be felt outside the Council of Europe area. For example, cases have been brought concerning deportation to places where torture might occur, such as in *Chahal v UK*.[44] But the jurisdiction of a state may also extend to the acts of state servants that take place beyond the physical territory of the state.[45] The crucial test for jurisdiction is whether or not the state was exercising de facto control over the events in question. For a general discussion of the principles, see *Bankovic v Belgium and ors*[46] and *Al-Skeini v UK*.[47]

4. The application must concern a Convention issue

9.25   The Court's jurisdiction extends only to applications relating to the rights and freedoms contained in the Convention and the Protocols that the Member State in question has ratified.[48]

---

[41]   See, eg *Dudgeon v UK* (1981) 4 EHRR 149 or *Burden and Burden v UK* (2008) 47 EHRR 38.

[42]   See also n 47.

[43]   See ch 2.

[44]   (1997) 23 EHRR 413.

[45]   See, eg *Loizidou v Turkey* (1997) 23 EHRR 513 concerning the effects of Turkish-sponsored troops in Cyprus.

[46]   (2007) 44 EHRR SE5. See ch 2, para 2.23.

[47]   App No 55721/07 [2011] ECHR 1093.

[48]   The UK has yet to ratify Protocols 4, 7, and 12 (and is unlikely to do so in the near future) so UK claimants cannot found applications on breaches of the rights contained in those protocols.

5. Exhaustion of domestic remedies

The ECtHR has consistently held that it 'may only deal with the matter after all domestic remedies have been exhausted'.   9.26

This rule is applied strictly in practice. It applies only to the remedies that are available, sufficient, and which relate to the breaches alleged. In considering the nature of the remedy, the Court takes into account 'the principles of flexibility and avoidance of undue formalism developed in its case-law on Article 35, in particular that it is sufficient if the applicant has raised the substance of his Convention application before the domestic authorities'.[49] If a potential applicant to the Court is in doubt as to whether alternative remedies have been exhausted, it is usually sensible for the remedy to be pursued, though a 'protective' application to the ECtHR could be lodged simultaneously to avoid falling foul of the four-month[50] time limit should the Court subsequently decide that the remedy was not effective and did not need to be pursued.   9.27

It is most unlikely that a declaration of incompatibility will be regarded as an effective remedy for the purposes of Article 13. This means that, at present, the ECtHR is unlikely to exclude a case at the admissibility stage for failure to exhaust domestic remedies if the only domestic remedy realistically available was a declaration of incompatibility. This was confirmed in *Burden and Burden v UK* where, in a lengthy discussion, the ECtHR held itself not to be satisfied that a declaration of incompatibility could be considered to be an effective judicial remedy.[51] However, the ECtHR did accept that, should evidence emerge at a 'future date' of a 'long-standing and established practice' of the Government giving effect to courts' declarations of incompatibility, this might support a different conclusion.[52] The best advice therefore for the purposes of an application to the Court would be to seek one anyway.[53]   9.28

6. Four-month time limit

Once Protocol 15 is in force, applications to the ECtHR must be made within four[54] months of the final decision of the domestic proceedings (or the date that the victim was informed about the final decision) or, where there are no effective domestic remedies, of the violation of the Convention. This is a reduction from the previous six-month limit. There is very little flexibility for cases brought outside this time limit, though lack of knowledge of the violation may make a later application possible. For example, in *Hilton v UK*[55] a journalist was refused a job within the   9.29

---

[49] See, for instance, the case of *John Shelley v UK* (2008) 46 EHRR SE16, quoting *Cardot v France* (1991) 13 EHRR 853, para 34.

[50] Protocol 15 will reduce the time limit from six months to four months.

[51] (2007) 44 EHRR 51, paras 30–40; confirmed by the Grand Chamber at (2008) 47 EHRR 38.

[52] (2007) 44 EHRR 51, paras 30–40.

[53] See *Carson v UK* App No 42184/05, 16 March 2010 [2010] ECHR 338, where the Art 8 complaint was dismissed as inadmissible on the grounds of non-exhaustion.

[54] Protocol 15 will reduce the time limit from six months to four months.

[55] (1998) 57 DR 108.

BBC, but discovered that this was as a result of a secret vetting process only nine years later.

7. Other inadmissibility grounds

9.30 Under Article 35(2) and (3), the Court may declare an application inadmissible on further grounds, which are dealt with in turn below.

(a) *Anonymity*

9.31 Anonymous applications are inadmissible, although the complainant may request on the application form that he or she wishes his or her identity to be kept confidential (apart from disclosure to the Member State itself).[56]

(b) *Petition is 'substantially the same as' previous applications*

9.32 This restriction prevents successive applications by the same applicant in respect of the same facts, and is not interpreted by the Court to restrict applications in respect of different instances even if the issues are substantially the same. Similarly, the provision does not act to bar a second application where new facts have arisen since the first application.

(c) *Examination by another international body*

9.33 If the matter has already been submitted to, and dealt with by, some other international procedure and contains no new information, it will be inadmissible. This is very unlikely to be an issue, because the only comparable procedures that the United Kingdom has ratified are the petition processes under the United Nations' Convention for the Elimination of All Forms of Discrimination Against Women and the Convention on the Rights of People with Disabilities.

(d) *Incompatible with the provisions of the Convention*

9.34 This ground covers applications which do not concern the rights and freedoms protected by the Convention, as well as situations in which the applicant is not within the jurisdiction of a Member State, or where the application is not directed against the state at all.

(e) *Manifestly ill-founded*

9.35 This is the most difficult criterion to assess. Ostensibly, this term is applied to applications that, on a preliminary examination, do not disclose any possible ground on which a violation could be established. Although the test is a prima facie one used to screen out clearly unmeritorious applications, it is applied very strictly. In effect, the Court's assessment of whether an application is 'ill-founded' is a strict merits test. The Court's assertion that a case is 'manifestly ill-founded' is not the same as

---

[56] Rule 32. See Practice Direction: Requests for Anonymity, 14 January 2010.

saying that it is unarguable. Many cases that are plainly arguable are excluded on this ground.

(f) *No significant disadvantage*

The Court can declare the case inadmissible if 'the applicant has not suffered a significant disadvantage'.[57] If the Court makes this initial assessment it then needs to consider whether or not the application should be examined 'to ensure respect for human rights' before it can declare the case inadmissible. Both of these criteria have to be met before a case can be declared inadmissible:

- the applicant must not have suffered a significant disadvantage; and
- respect for human rights does not require an examination of the application on the merits.

The Court has helpfully set out the principles that can be derived from the cases decided under this provision in its 'Admissibility Guide'.[58]

(g) *Abuse of the right of petition*

The fact that an applicant does not come to the Court with 'clean hands' or for a proper motive will not itself be a reason to reject the application. An inadmissibility ruling on this ground may arise, rather, if the application contains obviously untrue evidence, or where the applicant is demonstrably vexatious.

8. Decision on admissibility

A decision on admissibility will take several months and usually takes much longer. The ECtHR will give its decision on admissibility in writing. Clearly inadmissible cases will go to the Single Judge within a few weeks, but where the issue is less clear the decision will be made by a Committee or the Chamber. This question may be decided without further contact with the applicant or without communicating the case to the government concerned, however, it may seek the Government's observations, and even seek a hearing before deciding the issue of admissibility (although this is very rare). In the majority of cases the inadmissibility decision will be made only on the basis of the application and the material provided by the applicant.[59] The Court is not required to seek any further submissions or alert the applicant that this approach is being taken, and is unlikely to do so. Over 97 per cent of the cases declared inadmissible exit the system at this early stage. No specific reasons will be given for the decision and there is no appeal against decisions on admissibility.

9.36

9.37

9.38

---

[57] Article 35(3)(b). Protocol 15 will remove the third restriction that previously applied before a case could be declared inadmissible under this provision. This third restriction only allowed the Court to declare the case inadmissible if, in addition to the other two conditions set out above, the case had already been rejected on its merits by a domestic tribunal before the application was made to Strasbourg.

[58] 2011. See para 378 onwards. Note that this edition of the Admissibility Guide sets out the law as it applied before the removal of the third restrictions by Protocol 15 (which is likely to come into force some time in 2015).

[59] Article 35 and r 49.

9. Consideration by a Chamber and communication to the Government

9.39 If the case is not declared inadmissible at the initial stage it will be referred to a Chamber of the Court, which will decide on what further action needs to be taken in respect of the application. Often applications are also declared inadmissible by the Chamber at this stage without the opportunity for any further evidence or submissions. Alternatively, the Chamber may decide that further information is required from the applicant and/or state concerned. If this occurs, the application will be formally 'communicated' to the state, which is then invited to make any observations it thinks fit relating to the application.

9.40 In such cases, both parties are sent a statement of the facts of the case, prepared by the Court, together with a series of questions. Both the applicant and the Court then have an opportunity to comment on the account that the Court has produced and respond to the questions. The applicant will be notified of this step and sent a copy. It may take well over 12 months for the case to reach this stage and can easily be two years. For those interested in monitoring pending cases, and for NGOs or others interested in intervening, this is usually the first point at which the Court discloses any details of cases pending in the system.

9.41 Once the Government has replied to the communicated case, the applicant is given a chance to respond in writing.[60] In most cases the Court will want to decide admissibility and merits cases together. In the past, in very rare cases, the Court has invited the parties to make oral submissions on admissibility. In these circumstances the parties will also be asked to make submissions on the merits at the same time (see below for the procedure).

10. Friendly settlements

9.42 Article 38(1)(b) provides that once the Court has declared an application admissible, it shall place itself at the disposal of the parties concerned with a view to securing a friendly settlement. This phase runs in parallel with the Court's investigation of the merits. Thus, after a positive admissibility decision, the Court will write to the parties, asking whether or not they wish to explore the possibility of a settlement and, if so, inviting proposals on the subject. The Court acts as a go-between if the parties do enter into negotiations.

11. Pilot judgments

9.43 The Court has developed a procedure for dealing with large groups of identical cases that derive from the same underlying problem.[61] In such circumstances the Court will select one or more for priority treatment and will use that case or cases to try to achieve a solution that will resolve the issues in all of those other identical cases. The Court will, in such cases, freeze all the other applications pending the

---

[60] For the form for all pleadings, see Practice Direction: Written Pleadings, 1 November 2003 and amended 10 December 2007.

[61] Rule 61; see The Pilot-Judgment Procedure: Information note issued by the Registrar.

resolution of the lead case. The first pilot-judgment case concerned the so-called Bug River cases from Poland.[62]

12. Assessing the merits

Once the Court has made a positive admissibility decision it undertakes an investigation into the merits of the application. In practice, the Court will usually deal with admissibility and merits at the same time. 9.44

The Convention and rules allow a committee of three judges to decide on issues of admissibility and merits of an application where the issues in the case are already the subject of well-established case law from the Court. This provision is designed to deal with repetitive violation cases and cases that all stem from the same fault in a domestic system (for example, primary legislation which has already been held to violate the Convention). 9.45

13. Court's investigative powers

The Court is empowered to obtain any evidence that it considers capable of providing clarification of the facts of the case, either of its own motion or at the request of any party to the application (or a third party—see para 9.47).[63] This can even include deputing its judges, usually three or four for fact-finding hearings, to conduct an inquiry or take evidence in some other way. In practice, however, this occurs only very rarely.[64] 9.46

14. Third-party interventions

According to Article 36 and rule 44, the President of the Court may permit any state, or any natural or legal person, to submit written observations about the application. Such applications can arise because a possible lacuna exists in areas of the argument, which neither the state nor the applicant is willing to fill. The United Kingdom has used the intervention process itself in the case of *Saadi v Italy*.[65] This case concerned deportation and the absolute nature of the prohibition of treatment contrary to Article 3 of the Convention. The United Kingdom was concerned that the Court's jurisprudence meant that the risk of such treatment in the country to which the applicant was to be sent could not be weighed against the reasons (including the protection of national security) put forward by the respondent state to justify expulsion. NGOs often intervene to set out their view of human rights, or because the case raises an issue of particular interest to them. A third party has 9.47

---

[62] *Broniowski v Poland* App No 31443/96, 28 September 2005 [2005] ECHR 647. See also the first pilot judgment against the UK at para. 9.52 below.

[63] Rule 49, see also *Annex to the Rules (concerning investigations)*, 7 July 2003.

[64] See for a recent use of this power the *in camera* evidence session held in the rendition cases against Poland, *Al Nashiri v Poland* and *Husayn (Abu Zubaydah)*, judgment 24 July 2014 (evidence sessions held on 2 December 2013).

[65] (2008) 24 BHRC 123.

12 weeks from the date the notification has been 'communicated' to the state party (see para 9.39 above).[66] The details of selected cases communicated to state parties are now published on the Court's website. Liberty has frequently intervened in cases, as, for example, in *S and Marper v UK*.[67] The Equality and Human Rights Commission can also seek to intervene in cases in the Court, and did so for the first time in February 2009 in the case of *RP v United Kingdom*.[68] It has intervened regularly in UK cases since that time. Businesses also intervene on occasion: for example, in the case of *Hatton v UK*[69] (concerning night flights from Heathrow airport and the effect on the private lives of those living under the flight path), both British Airways and an environmental pressure group, Friends of the Earth, submitted written interventions.

15. Oral hearing

9.48　Hearings, even on the merits of an application, are now extremely rare in relation to the number of cases decided and the vast majority of cases are decided on the papers alone. However, there are still a considerable number of hearings held in the Strasbourg building each year. If a hearing is to take place (whether for an admissibility decision and/or the merits), the applicant will be notified and contacted by the Registry with a date for the hearing (it is difficult to alter the date once it has been fixed). The parties will also be invited to send their final proposed oral arguments in advance to the Court to aid the work of the interpreters. The languages of the Court are English and French.

9.49　Hearings are held in the Human Rights Building in Strasbourg, France. In practice, hearings take approximately two hours, with the parties each being allowed only 30 minutes in all to present their case (followed by a brief period in which to respond to the other party and answer any questions posed by the judges). Hearings are now webcast (via the Court's website) and provide a real insight on the procedure and how advocates might best promote their client's case.

16. Judgment

9.50　Chamber judgments are not read in open court, although the judgment of a Grand Chamber will be read out in summary. In both cases printed copies are made available, and electronic copies are sent to the parties and are published on the website. The judgment of a Chamber does not become final until:

- the parties declare that they will not be requesting a referral of the case to the Grand Chamber;
- three months after the date of the judgment; or

---

[66] See r 44(1)(b).
[67] App Nos 30562/04 and 30566/04, 4 December 2008.
[68] App No 38245/07, 9 October 2012.
[69] (2003) 37 EHRR 28.

- when a panel of five judges of the Court rejects the request for referral to the Grand Chamber.

17. Applications to the Grand Chamber

Under Article 43, either party can seek permission for a referral to the Grand Chamber.[70] In order to gain permission, either party must satisfy a panel of five judges that there exists either a serious question affecting the interpretation of the Convention or the Protocols thereto, or a serious issue of general importance. This request must be made within three months of the Chamber judgment. The process involves a re-examination of the case rather than an appeal as such. It is rare for a case to be referred to the Grand Chamber after a hearing by a Chamber. 9.51

18. Remedies

Where the Court finds that a violation of the Convention has occurred, it is required under Article 41 to consider whether the applicant is entitled to any compensation and/ or costs, under the concept of 'just satisfaction'. Any award is at the complete discretion of the Court and a specific claim must have been made by the applicant. A claim can include pecuniary loss and non-pecuniary loss.[71] The Court has also left open the issue of aggravated damages in a suitable case, but to date has declined to award any form of exemplary or punitive damages: 9.52

The purpose of the Court's award in respect of damage is to compensate the applicant for the actual harmful consequences of a violation. It is not intended to punish the Contracting State responsible. The Court has therefore, until now, considered it inappropriate to accept claims for damages with labels such as 'punitive', 'aggravated' or 'exemplary'.[72]

The Court can order a state to take or refrain from taking specific action and will occasionally include specific proposals for change as part of its declaration of the law. In property cases the Court has ordered the return of property, and in unlawful detention cases the release of the detained person. In the case of *Greens and MT v UK*,[73] which concerned the right of prisoners to vote and the failure of the Government to amend the law, and first decided by the Court in *Hirst v UK*,[74] the Court, in the first pilot judgment decision involving the United Kingdom, decided that the United Kingdom must: 9.53

(a) bring forward, within six months of the date upon which the present judgment becomes final, legislative proposals intended to amend the 1983 Act and, if appropriate, the 2002 Act in a manner which is Convention-compliant; and

---

[70] Rule 73.
[71] See Practice Direction: Just Satisfaction Claims, 28 March 2007, issued by the President of the Court.
[72] Ibid, para 9.
[73] [2010] ECHR 1826, 23 November 2010.
[74] *Hirst v UK (No 2)* (2005) 19 BHRC 546, (2006) 42 EHRR 41.

(b) enact the required legislation within any such period as may be determined by the Committee of Ministers.[75]

The Government sought a reference to the Grand Chamber but the Court rejected this application for a referral.

9.54   It has also been suggested that in the future the Court may be willing to order that a criminal conviction obtained in breach of Article 6 should be quashed or subject to a re-trial.[76]

9.55   Costs cannot be awarded against an applicant.

E. ADVISORY OPINIONS FROM THE EUROPEAN COURT OF HUMAN RIGHTS

1. Requests for advisory opinions by the Committee of Ministers

9.56   The Court may provide advisory opinions if requested to do so by the Committee of Ministers.[77] However the opinions may not deal with the content or scope of the Convention so this procedure has rarely been used.

2. Requests for advisory opinions by a national court

9.57   If implemented, Protocol 16[78] of the Convention will allow the highest court or tribunal of a Member State to request an opinion from the European Court of Human Rights 'on questions of principle relating to the interpretation or application of the rights and freedoms defined in the Convention or the protocols thereto'. At the time of writing it was not clear if or when this protocol might take effect. The UK Government's public position was to wait to see how it was working in practice before considering whether or not to ratify it. If it were to be implemented, it would allow the UK's Supreme Court to seek an opinion from the Strasbourg Court before giving judgment itself (a similar process to obtaining a ruling from the Court of Justice of the European Union).

F. FUNDING FOR CASES IN STRASBOURG

9.58   Funding for cases to Strasbourg is very meagre. However, it is important for potential applicants to be aware that they cannot be held liable to pay the Government's

---

[75] 23 November 2010.

[76] See Leach, *Taking a Case to the European Court of Human Rights*, 3rd edn (Oxford: Oxford University Press, 2011), para 3.49.

[77] Article 47.

[78] The Protocol (see Appendix 2) will come into force once ten Member States have ratified it and it will be for each state (including the UK) to decide whether or not it wishes to ratify and therefore allow its domestic courts to take advantage of this procedure.

costs, and that in the statistically rare case of their application being successful, at least some of their legal costs will be met by the Government.

1. Domestic Legal Services Commission funding

The structure of the Human Rights Act does not make the Convention or its pro-   9.59
cedures part of the law of England and Wales directly and therefore:

Legal help may be used to advise a client of their position under England and Wales law and the options available but may not be used to make an application to ECtHR or for legal aid from that court. This is because the law of ECtHR is not formally part of the law of England and Wales as required by section of the Act.[79]

It might be possible to argue that Convention law could be 'relevant for deter-mining any issue relating to the law of England and Wales', but an applicant will generally have had to exhaust domestic remedies first, and the ECtHR, unlike the European Court of Justice, does not allow interim references to resolve the inter-pretation of a Convention issue.

2. Other sources of funding

Trade unions or pressure groups may fund litigation or provide legal represen-   9.60
tation themselves, or lawyers may act *pro bono* or on a conditional fee basis in important cases.

3. Strasbourg legal aid

The Court itself will provide legal aid (subject to means), but only for those cases   9.61
which reach the stage of being communicated to the Government. As most cases fail before this stage this is a real disincentive for lawyers to take cases. However, legal costs are recoverable where an application is successful.[80] No fees are pay-able to the Court and there is no liability to meet the costs of the Government in any event.

Once the case has been communicated, legal aid will be available for those who   9.62
would qualify on income and capital grounds for civil legal aid in the United Kingdom (even if in an assessment for UK legal aid a contribution would have been required no contribution will need to be made). Legal aid is available from the Court, although the means test for legal aid is carried out by the civil legal aid authorities in the United Kingdom.[81] Legal aid, once granted, will pay a lump sum

---

[79] Section 2.2, *Guidance on authorities and legal aid for cases in courts outside England and Wales*, Legal Aid Agency, August 2013. The Act referred to is the Legal Aid, Sentencing and Punishment of Offenders Act 2012.

[80] Rule 100.

[81] Information on the process is summarized in Section 2.2, *Guidance on authorities and legal aid for cases in courts outside England and Wales*, Legal Aid Agency, August 2013.

to cover all the fees and expenses in the case (currently €850).[82] If the case is never communicated, no legal aid is available.

9.63   Further payments are available to assist in friendly settlement negotiations and to cover representation by one lawyer at any hearing (currently €300), and the travel and accommodation costs of the lawyer and the applicant. In certain circumstances Strasbourg legal aid will stretch to two lawyers.

G. IMPLEMENTATION OF JUDGMENTS

9.64   The Committee of Ministers of the Council of Europe is responsible for ensuring that judgments are implemented by the state concerned.[83] When supervising the implementation of judgments the Committee is concerned to ensure that any just satisfaction awarded has been paid and:

individual measures have been taken to ensure that the violation has ceased and that the injured party is put, as far as possible, in the same situation as the party enjoyed prior to the violation of the Convention; general measures have been adopted, preventing new violations similar to that or those found or putting an end to continuing violations.[84]

Lawyers, NGOs, and others can send submissions to the Committee of Ministers requesting that they urge the state party to implement the judgment in a particular way or can comment on proposals made by a state for implementation. The staff working for the Committee are anxious to hear from those with experience or expertise about the practicalities of implementation, particularly to ensure practical compliance with the Convention in the light of the judgment.

9.65   The Parliamentary Joint Human Rights Committee (JCHR) has also taken a keen interest in implementation and the execution of Court judgments.[85] For instance the JCHR's report of October 2008 expressed serious concerns about the Government's long-standing failure to address the question of prisoners' voting rights after the judgment in *Hirst v UK*.[86] The issue remains unresolved in September 2014, more than eight years after the ECtHR ruled that a blanket denial of prisoners' rights violated Article 3 of Protocol 1. It was unclear whether or not (and if so how) the Government intends to comply with the judgment (see the Preface for more details and the wider political context).

---

[82] Legal aid rates applicable since 1 January 2009.

[83] Article 46 of the Convention; and the Rules of the Committee of Ministers for the Supervision of the Execution of Judgments and of the Terms of Friendly Settlements, 10 May 2006.

[84] Ibid, r 6. For more details see the website of the Committee of Ministers (part of the Council of Europe) <http://www.coe.int/>.

[85] JCHR, *Monitoring the Government's Response to Human Rights Judgments: Annual Report 2008*, 31 October 2008.

[86] *Hirst v UK (No 2)* (2005) 19 BHRC 546, (2006) 42 EHRR 41.

10

RESEARCHING HUMAN RIGHTS JURISPRUDENCE

A. INTRODUCTION

This chapter provides details of the practicalities of conducting research into human **10.01**
rights law. The Strasbourg institutions have taken on an increasing caseload over
the last decade: between the inception of the European Court of Human Rights
(ECtHR) in 1959 and 1998 the Court delivered 837 judgments, whereas in 2013
alone 916 judgments were handed down.[1] Domestic judgments concerning human
rights are now handed down almost daily. The information below provides some
assistance in navigating this daunting jurisprudence to locate the most relevant and
important cases.

The Convention, and the Universal Declaration of Human Rights from which it **10.02**
grew, have been used as models for the written constitutional guarantees of human

---

[1] Registry of the Court, *European Court of Human Rights: Analysis of Statistics 2013* (January 2014).

rights in many Commonwealth constitutions. Not only do UN instruments provide important legal standards that practitioners need to be aware of, but judgments from fora such as the Privy Council, the Constitutional Court of South Africa, and the Supreme Courts of Canada and New Zealand often contain useful and considered guidance on questions involving fundamental rights. Researching international and comparative human rights law is outside the scope of this chapter, but good guidance can be found in the American Society for International Law's *Guide to Electronic Resources for International Law* (<http://www.asil.org/erghome.cfm>), and both the international law (<http://www.asil.org/erghome.cfm>), and the human rights (<http://www.un.org/rights>) sections of the UN website and the home page of the International Court of Justice (<http://www.icj-cij.org>).

B. CONVENTION JURISPRUDENCE

10.03 The European Convention for the Protection of Human Rights and Fundamental Freedoms (Convention) was adopted in 1950, ratified by the United Kingdom in 1951, and entered into force in 1953. To understand the Convention case law, it is necessary to understand the history of how cases were brought in the Strasbourg institutions.

1. Pre-Protocol 11

10.04 Before 1 November 1998 a two-tiered system examined applications lodged in Strasbourg. Initially, the European Commission on Human Rights (ECmHR), an entirely separately staffed body, would examine the facts of the application and deliver an admissibility decision on the case, together with a decision on the merits if the Commission declared the petition admissible. This decision, although critical for determining whether or not a case would go forward to a full hearing, was not binding on the ECtHR itself. Often the ECtHR would deliver a final judgment that was substantially different to the decision reached by the Commission.

10.05 Protocol 11 came into force in 1998 and replaced the old system of adjudication with a new, more streamlined system which abolished the ECmHR. Although the ECmHR no longer exists, its decisions detailing the admissibility or otherwise of applications and opinions on the merits of individual cases are still of relevance to the proper interpretation of the Convention. As with judgments from the ECtHR itself, this jurisprudence 'must be taken into account' under the Human Rights Act by any domestic court or tribunal determining a question involving Convention rights.

2. Protocol 11

10.06 Since 1 November 1998 the two-tier system has been replaced with a single, permanent Court. The Rules of Court of the ECtHR, adopted on 4 November 1998, set out in full the competence of, and procedure before, the new institution. Now, three judges of the ECtHR sit in Committee to determine whether an application is 'admissible'. If it is admissible, seven judges sitting as a Chamber determine the merits of the petition. However, cases involving important questions affecting the interpretation of the Convention may be dealt with by a Grand Chamber of 17 judges, either because the original Chamber cedes jurisdiction, or (rarely) where the Grand Chamber re-hears an important case on a review (Article 43). Judgments of the new Court emerge from each of the different Sections (from I through to IV), which are headed by designated Presidents of Sections and are composed of a varying number of judges. This new system has created the possibility of different Chambers taking different views until an issue is resolved by the Grand Chamber.[2]

The Committee of Ministers plays a supervisory role under Article 46(2). This encompasses not only supervising the execution of judgments, but also ensuring that future violations do not take place with equivalent facts to the ones already dealt with. Reports and resolutions are issued to monitor compliance with judgments and the steps that have been taken to implement the ECtHR's decisions.   **10.07**

3. Weight of authorities

As the Convention is a 'living instrument' and is to be interpreted in the light of present-day conditions, there is no formal doctrine of precedent binding the ECtHR. However, there are a number of factors to be taken into account when considering how much weight should be given to a particular decision from Strasbourg: **10.08**

(a) Court judgments are of more importance than decisions of the ECmHR or the Committee of Ministers. Decisions of the Committee of Ministers are made by politicians, not judges, without the benefit of legal argument, and are less commonly cited than ECtHR or ECmHR judgments.

(b) Judgments of the plenary Court and decisions or opinions of the plenary Commission are the most authoritative. Decisions that are unanimous or have large majorities are more likely to be followed or to be influential than those decided by a narrow majority. A decision of the Grand Chamber on review is a 'second hearing' of an important case and commands greater authority than the previous plenary Court.

(c) Recent decisions are more valuable than decisions made some time ago because the Convention is interpreted as a 'living instrument'. As such, its meaning will develop over time, and new case law will develop in an organic way without old case law being specifically overruled.

(d) Caution is needed where Strasbourg organs have relied on the 'margin of appreciation' in concluding that there was no violation of the Convention, as this doctrine has no direct application in domestic law (see ch 4, paras 4.119–4.130).

(e) Admissibility decisions rarely set out the ECtHR's own views and are less helpful than merits decisions that give an opinion on the law. While cases are often

---

[2] See, eg *Hatton v UK* (2002) 34 EHRR 1.

deemed inadmissible because they are 'manifestly ill-founded', this is not the same as a finding that the point of law involved is unarguable. It may depend on the facts in issue, or application of the margin of appreciation. Nevertheless, a decision that a particular case is inadmissible, on the basis that it is manifestly unfounded, may be the only indication of the view of the Strasbourg organs on the point of law in issue, as such cases never go further. Since the Human Rights Act does not impose a strict doctrine of precedent, these decisions need not prevent a well-founded case on the same point being raised in an English court.

4. Referencing system

10.09　Once lodged, all applications to Strasbourg are given a number commencing with five digits, and then two digits representing the year of the application. Occasionally, the case before the Court involves sensitive issues and demands confidentiality, and so the applicant is referred to by a letter, for example, *W v UK*. These numbers can be found 'attached' to the names of the parties in all ECtHR documentation and are an important aid when searching for case law.

C. FINDING CONVENTION CASE LAW

1. European Court judgments: official reports

10.10　Judgments of the ECtHR before 1996 are published by the Council of Europe in 'Series A' and 'Series B'. Series A contains the full text of the ECtHR's judgments, and from 1985 also contains extracts of the ECmHR's decisions on the merits of applications. Series B contains selective extracts from the pleadings, arguments, and relevant documentation lodged at the ECtHR for individual cases. These reports are cited as 'Series A, no 152' or 'A/152' (or 'Series B, no 123', 'B/123'). Judgments from 1996 onwards are published in the Reports of Judgments and Decisions (RJD) (published by Carl Heymanns Verlag). Every judgment has numbered paragraphs to help locate specific passages. These reports are very specialist and can be difficult to find. However, if a case is reported in either Series A or the RJD, this fact is recorded in the ECtHR's own online database, HUDOC (see para 10.16).

10.11　A widely available domestic alternative is the *European Human Rights Reports* (EHRR) (published by Sweet & Maxwell), although it should be noted that not all judgments of the European Court are reported in this series. The first volume was published in 1979 and references to these reports take the form of year of publication, followed by volume number, and lastly a numbered reference. Prior to 2001, this final number referred to the page at which the judgment was reported, but since 2001 (and volume 34) this number refers to the case itself. For example, *Tolstoy Miloslavsky v United Kingdom* (1995) 20 EHRR 442 refers to the twentieth volume of the EHRR at page 442; whereas *Hatton v United Kingdom* (2002) 34 EHRR 1 refers to the first case printed in the thirty-fourth volume of the EHRR.

Other useful sources of judgments include *Butterworths Human Rights Cases* 10.12 (BHRC) and digests in the *European Human Rights Law Review* (EHRLR).

2. European Commission

The majority of the decisions from the ECmHR are published by the Council of 10.13 Europe in the Decisions and Reports series (DR). These numerical volumes contain cases from 1974 to 1995. There are several indexes (published at 15–20 volume intervals) which contain lists of names, application numbers, and, usefully, summaries of judgments by keyword and article numbers. References to these reports appear as year, volume number, and page number. For example, *Rayner v United Kingdom* (1986) 47 DR 5 refers to the forty-seventh volume of the DRs at page 5. DRs are difficult to locate and are available only in good law libraries or, for some volumes, via The Stationery Office (<http://www.tso.co.uk>).

The EHRR series contains extracts and summaries of some ECmHR decisions. 10.14 In volumes 1 to 14 these are part of the ordinary text, but from volume 15 onwards (approximately 1993) they appear in a separate section at the end of the bound copies of the series. References to these Commission Decisions are abbreviated as 'EHRR CD'.

Other useful sources of judgments include the *Digest of Strasbourg Case Law* and, 10.15 for early, pre-1974 decisions, the *Yearbook of the European Convention on Human Rights* (cited as 'YB'), both of which are published by the Council of Europe.

3. Websites

The ECtHR maintains a free, searchable database of most ECtHR judgments and 10.16 ECmHR decisions. The HUDOC database can be accessed via <http://www.echr. coe.int> and has an online users' guide to help navigate through the search engine. General tips to remember include selecting the appropriate databases to search at the top of the screen (language, type of judgment, and so on) and, if known, using the application number and rough date of judgment to focus searches. The database is comprehensive, constantly updated, and is the best way to locate very recent judgments. It also contains press releases summarizing important judgments. Additionally, the Court publishes Annual Reports containing statistics and developments in the case law over the previous year and has recently started publishing monthly and annual analyses of court statistics. On a monthly basis the ECtHR issues 'Case Law Information Notes' which highlight and summarize important cases. The ECtHR has also started publishing useful handbooks on particular aspects of human rights law addressed by the Court. This information can be found at <http://www.echr.coe.int>.

The ECHR Blog is a useful resource for commentary on ECtHR decisions and 10.17 links to academic articles: <http://www.echrblog.blogspot.com>.

4. Bibliographic resources on Convention case law

10.18 Useful publications on Convention case law are as follows:

European Human Rights Law Review (EHRLR) (London: Sweet & Maxwell, 1996 to date).

Mowbray, *Cases and Materials on the European Convention on Human Rights* (Oxford: Oxford University Press, 2012).

Harris, O'Boyle, and Warbrick, *Law of the European Convention on Human Rights*, 2nd edn (Oxford: Oxford University Press, 2009).

Jacobs, White, and Ovey, *The European Convention on Human Rights*, 4th edn (Oxford: Oxford University Press, 2010).

Reid, *A Practitioners Guide to the European Convention on Human Rights*, 3rd edn (London: Sweet & Maxwell, 2011).

Simor, *Human Rights Practice* (London: Sweet & Maxwell, 2001 to date).

5. *Travaux préparatoires*

10.19 In interpreting the Convention, the ECtHR has very occasionally considered the *travaux préparatoires*, or preparatory documents, relating to the drafting of the Convention. They are published by the Council of Europe in *The Collected Edition of the Travaux Préparatoires of the European Convention on Human Rights* and are available through specialist law libraries. They are also now available online in the ECtHR's increasingly comprehensive electronic library at <http://www.echr.coe. int/Library/COLENTravauxprep.html>. The *travaux préparatoires* are used rarely by the ECtHR, and as a means of confirming its interpretation of a Convention provision only when such an interpretation leaves the meaning ambiguous or obscure, or leads to a result that is manifestly absurd.

D. FINDING HUMAN RIGHTS ACT MATERIALS

10.20 Researching domestic human rights jurisprudence should be carried out in exactly the same way as other domestic legal research. Since the Act specifically provides that 'human rights' cases are not decided by a specialist court or tribunal but can arise in any existing forum, the well-known sets of law reports (Law Reports, Weekly Law Reports, Administrative Court Digest, etc) will contain details of cases raising human rights points and are an important point of reference. However, since the implementation of the Human Rights Act, several series of specialist reports, journals, and books have been published to help lawyers understand the human rights context and locate relevant materials more easily.

1. Law reports, journals, and books

10.21 The *Human Rights Law Reports—UK Cases* (Sweet & Maxwell, 2000 to date) and the *United Kingdom Human Rights Reports* (Jordans, 2000 to date) report the most important decisions on human rights points determined by UK courts.

The *European Human Rights Law Review* (see para 10.18) also contains articles   **10.22**
and commentary on domestic cases raising human rights issues. Other useful publications include the *Human Rights Alerter* (Sweet & Maxwell) and the *Human
Rights Updater* (LexisNexis UK), which cover some Strasbourg decisions as well
as domestic cases. *Public Law* (Sweet & Maxwell), *Criminal Law Review* (Sweet
& Maxwell), *Modern Law Review* (Sweet & Maxwell), and *Judicial Review* (Hart
Publishing) are journals which regularly contain articles and case digests of interest
to those researching human rights points.

Books that provide a good, detailed commentary on the framework and case law   **10.23**
of the Human Rights Act include:

Beatson, Grosz, Hickman, Singh, and Palmer, *Human Rights: Judicial Protection in the United
Kingdom* (London: Sweet & Maxwell, 2008).

Lester and Pannick, *Human Rights Law and Practice*, 3rd edn (London: Butterworths, 2009).

Clayton and Tomlinson, *Human Rights Law*, 2nd edn (Oxford: Oxford University Press, 2009).

2. Electronic and online resources

The main legal publishers provide subscription-based online services incorporating   **10.24**
a mixture of different law reports and texts according to their publishing lists. For
example:

- Westlaw UK's Human Rights subscription package (<http://www.sweetandmax-
  well.co.uk>) offers access to the EHRR, EHRLR, and Simor's *Human Rights
  Practice*.
- LexisNexis Library's online database (<http://www1.lexisnexis.co.uk/lnb/legal/
  legal.html>) indexes a range of human rights materials including the *Butterworths
  Human Rights Cases* reports and the full text of Lester and Pannick.
- Lawtel (<http://www.lawtel.com>) offers a Human Rights Service encompassing
  recent transcripts of judgments from domestic courts and commentary provided
  by experts.

However, there are a growing number of free websites that offer valuable   **10.25**
information on human rights jurisprudence. For locating case law, the British
and Irish Legal Information Institute's database (<http://www.bailii.org>) offers
a good starting point. The webpage of the Parliamentary Joint Committee on
Human Rights (JCHR) (<http://www.parliament.uk/parliamentary_commit-
tees/joint_committee_on_human_rights.cfm>) indexes a number of detailed
reports and evidence taken in support of the JCHR's remit of scrutinizing all
new legislation presented to Parliament and undertaking inquiries on human
rights issues. The JCHR also monitors the Government's implementation of
Strasbourg judgments and response to declarations of incompatibility made by
domestic courts. The JCHR's correspondence with ministers and other officials,
which can be found on the Committee's webpages, often elicits details of the
Government's proposed legislative and policy responses to important human
rights judgments.

10.26   The most exciting development in human rights resources was the launch of the UK Human Rights Blog, which provides excellent summaries of human rights cases from the ECtHR and domestic courts and in-depth articles on current legal issues: <http://ukhumanrightsblog.com/>. The UK Supreme Court blog is also a good resource for commentary on Supreme Court cases and occasional articles on human rights issues: <http://ukscblog.com/>.

3. Use of *Hansard*

10.27   Since the landmark decision of the House of Lords in *Pepper v Hart*,[3] parliamentary statements by ministers may, in certain circumstances, be admissible in order to interpret an Act of Parliament. The principles (set out in the speech of Lord Browne-Wilkinson) indicate that references to *Hansard* may be admissible where:

(a) legislation is obscure or ambiguous, or leads to an absurdity;

(b) the material relied upon consists of one or more statements by a minister or other promoter of the Bill, and such other material as is necessary to understand such statements and their effect; and

(c) the statements relied upon are clear.

10.28   There has rarely, if ever, been a series of parliamentary debates in which Members of Parliament have referred quite so repeatedly and self-consciously to the *Pepper v Hart* principle as during the passage of the Human Rights Bill. Since there are aspects of the Act which could be ambiguous, *Hansard* statements may be admissible in court when arguing regarding its meaning. *Hansard* is accessible online at <http://www.publications.parliament.uk>.[4] It should be borne in mind, however, that some of the *Hansard* statements are controversial, and it is by no means clear that they should be regarded as any more than 'persuasive' by the courts that consider them.

---

[3] [1993] AC 593.

[4] For a detailed examination of the parliamentary debates leading up to the passing of the Human Rights Act, see Cooper and Marshall-Williams, *Legislating for Human Rights: Parliamentary Debates on the Human Rights Bill* (London: Hart Publishing/JUSTICE, 2000).

APPENDIX 1

Human Rights Act 1998

CHAPTER 42
ARRANGEMENT OF SECTIONS

Parliamentary procedure

19. Statements of compatibility.

Supplemental

20. Orders etc. under this Act.
21. Interpretation, etc.
22. Short title, commencement, application and extent.

Schedules

Schedule 1—The Articles.
     Part I—The Convention Rights and Freedoms.
     Part II—The First Protocol.
     Part III—Article 1 of the Thirteenth Protocol.

Schedule 2—Remedial Orders.

Schedule 3—Derogation and Reservation.
     Part I—Derogation (repealed).
     Part II—Reservation.

Schedule 4—Judicial Pensions.

HUMAN RIGHTS ACT 1998
1998 CHAPTER 42

An Act to give further effect to rights and freedoms guaranteed under the European Convention on Human Rights; to make provision with respect to holders of certain judicial offices who become judges of the European Court of Human Rights; and for connected purposes.

[9th November 1998]

BE IT ENACTED by the Queen's most Excellent Majesty, by and with the advice and consent of the Lords Spiritual and Temporal, and Commons, in this present Parliament assembled, and by the authority of the same, as follows:—

Introduction

1. The Convention Rights[1]

(1) In this Act 'the Convention rights' means the rights and fundamental freedoms set out in—
    (a) Articles 2 to 12 and 14 of the Convention,
    (b) Articles 1 to 3 of the First Protocol, and
    (c) Article 1 of the Thirteenth Protocol,
as read with Articles 16 to 18 of the Convention.

(2) Those Articles are to have effect for the purposes of this Act subject to any designated derogation or reservation (as to which see sections 14 and 15).

(3) The Articles are set out in Schedule 1.

(4) The [Secretary of State] may by order make such amendments to this Act as he considers appropriate to reflect the effect, in relation to the United Kingdom, of a protocol.

(5) In subsection (4) 'protocol' means a protocol to the Convention—
    (a) which the United Kingdom has ratified; or
    (b) which the United Kingdom has signed with a view to ratification.

(6) No amendment may be made by an order under subsection (4) so as to come into force before the protocol concerned is in force in relation to the United Kingdom.

2. Interpretation of Convention rights[2]

(1) A court or tribunal determining a question which has arisen in connection with a Convention right must take into account any—
    (a) judgment, decision, declaration or advisory opinion of the European Court of Human Rights,
    (b) opinion of the Commission given in a report adopted under Article 31 of the Convention,
    (c) decision of the Commission in connection with Article 26 or 27(2) of the Convention, or
    (d) decision of the Committee of Ministers taken under Article 46 of the Convention,
whenever made or given, so far as, in the opinion of the court or tribunal, it is relevant to the proceedings in which that question has arisen.

---

[1] This section was amended by the Transfer of Functions (Miscellaneous) Order 2001, SI 2001/3500, art 8, Sch 2, pt I, para 7(a), the Secretary of State for Constitutional Affairs Order 2003, SI 2003/1887, art 9, Sch 2, para 10(1), and the Human Rights Act (Amendment) Order 2004, SI 2004/1574, art 2(1).

[2] This section was amended by the Secretary of State for Constitutional Affairs Order 2003, SI 2003/1887, art 9, Sch 2, para 10(2), and the Transfer of Functions (Lord Chancellor and Secretary of State) Order 2005, SI 2005/3429, art 8, Schedule, para 3.

(2) Evidence of any judgment, decision, declaration or opinion of which account may have to be taken under this section is to be given in proceedings before any court or tribunal in such manner as may be provided by rules.

(3) In this section 'rules' means rules of court or, in the case of proceedings before a tribunal, rules made for the purposes of this section—

    (a) by the Lord Chancellor or the Secretary of State, in relation to any proceedings outside Scotland;

    (b) by the Secretary of State, in relation to proceedings in Scotland; or

    (c) by a Northern Ireland department, in relation to proceedings before a tribunal in Northern Ireland—

        (i) which deals with transferred matters; and

        (ii) for which no rules made under paragraph (a) are in force.

Legislation

3. Interpretation of legislation

(1) So far as it is possible to do so, primary legislation and subordinate legislation must be read and given effect in a way which is compatible with the Convention rights.

(2) This section—

    (a) applies to primary legislation and subordinate legislation whenever enacted;

    (b) does not affect the validity, continuing operation or enforcement of any incompatible primary legislation; and

    (c) does not affect the validity, continuing operation or enforcement of any incompatible subordinate legislation if (disregarding any possibility of revocation) primary legislation prevents removal of the incompatibility.

4. Declaration of incompatibility

(1) Subsection (2) applies in any proceedings in which a court determines whether a provision of primary legislation is compatible with a Convention right.

(2) If the court is satisfied that the provision is incompatible with a Convention right, it may make a declaration of that incompatibility.

(3) Subsection (4) applies in any proceedings in which a court determines whether a provision of subordinate legislation, made in the exercise of a power conferred by primary legislation, is compatible with a Convention right.

(4) If the court is satisfied—

    (a) that the provision is incompatible with a Convention right, and

    (b) that (disregarding any possibility of revocation) the primary legislation concerned prevents removal of the incompatibility, it may make a declaration of that incompatibility.

(5) In this section 'court' means—

    (a) [the Supreme Court];[3]

    (b) the Judicial Committee of the Privy Council;

    (c) the [Court Martial Appeal Court];[4]

    (d) in Scotland, the High Court of Justiciary sitting otherwise than as a trial court or the Court of Session;

    (e) in England and Wales or Northern Ireland, the High Court or the Court of Appeal.

---

[3] Subsection (5)(a) was amended by the Constitutional Reform Act 2005, s 40(4), Sch 9, Pt 1, para 66(1), (2).

[4] Subsection (5)(c) was amended by the Armed Forces Act 2006, s 378(1), Sch 16, para 156.

(f) [the Court of Protection, in any matter being dealt with by the President of the Family Division, the Vice-Chancellor or a puisne judge of the High Court.][5]

(6) A declaration under this section ('a declaration of incompatibility')—

    (a) does not affect the validity, continuing operation or enforcement of the provision in respect of which it is given; and

    (b) is not binding on the parties to the proceedings in which it is made.

5. Right of Crown to intervene[6]

(1) Where a court is considering whether to make a declaration of incompatibility, the Crown is entitled to notice in accordance with rules of court.

(2) In any case to which subsection (1) applies—

    (a) a Minister of the Crown (or a person nominated by him),

    (b) a member of the Scottish Executive,

    (c) a Northern Ireland Minister,

    (d) a Northern Ireland department,

is entitled, on giving notice in accordance with rules of court, to be joined as a party to the proceedings.

(3) Notice under subsection (2) may be given at any time during the proceedings.

(4) A person who has been made a party to criminal proceedings (other than in Scotland) as the result of a notice under subsection (2) may, with leave, appeal to the [Supreme Court][7] against any declaration of incompatibility made in the proceedings.

(5) In subsection (4)—

'criminal proceedings' includes all proceedings before the [Court Martial Appeal Court];[8] and 'leave' means leave granted by the court making the declaration of incompatibility or by the [Supreme Court].[9]

Public authorities

6. Acts of public authorities

(1) It is unlawful for a public authority to act in a way which is incompatible with a Convention right.

(2) Subsection (1) does not apply to an act if—

    (a) as the result of one or more provisions of primary legislation, the authority could not have acted differently; or

    (b) in the case of one or more provisions of, or made under, primary legislation which cannot be read or given effect in a way which is compatible with the Convention rights, the authority was acting so as to give effect to or enforce those provisions.

---

[5] Subsection (5)(f) was inserted by the Mental Capacity Act 2005, s 67(1), Sch 6, Para 43.

[6] The references to the House of Lords in subsections (4) and (5) have been amended by the Constitutional Reform Act 2005, s 40(4), Sch 9, Pt 1, para 66(1), (3). The function under subs (2) is exercisable by the National Assembly for Wales concurrently with any Minister of the Crown by whom it is exercisable, in so far as it relates to any proceedings in which a court is considering whether to make a declaration of incompatibility within the meaning of s 4, in respect of subordinate legislation made, in relation to Wales, by a Minister of the Crown in the exercise of a function which is exercisable by the National Assembly: National Assembly for Wales (Transfer of Functions) (No 2) Order 2000, SI 2000/1830, art 2.

[7] Subsection (4) was amended by the Constitutional Reform Act 2005, s 40(4), Sch 9, Pt 1, para 66(1), (3).

[8] Subsection (5) amended by the Armed Forces Act 2006, s 378(1), Sch 16, para 157.

[9] Subsection (5) was amended by the Constitutional Reform Act 2005, s 40(4), Sch 9, Pt 1, para 66(1), (3).

(3) In this section 'public authority' includes—
    (a) a court or tribunal, and
    (b) any person certain of whose functions are functions of a public nature,
but does not include either House of Parliament or a person exercising functions in connection with proceedings in Parliament.

(4) [. . .]¹⁰

(5) In relation to a particular act, a person is not a public authority by virtue only of subsection (3)(b) if the nature of the act is private.

(6) 'An act' includes a failure to act but does not include a failure to—
    (a) introduce in, or lay before, Parliament a proposal for legislation; or
    (b) make any primary legislation or remedial order.

7. Proceedings¹¹

(1) A person who claims that a public authority has acted (or proposes to act) in a way which is made unlawful by section 6(1) may—
    (a) bring proceedings against the authority under this Act in the appropriate court or tribunal, or
    (b) rely on the Convention right or rights concerned in any legal proceedings, but only if he is (or would be) a victim of the unlawful act.

(2) In subsection (1)(a) 'appropriate court or tribunal' means such court or tribunal as may be determined in accordance with rules; and proceedings against an authority include a counterclaim or similar proceeding.

(3) If the proceedings are brought on an application for judicial review, the applicant is to be taken to have a sufficient interest in relation to the unlawful act only if he is, or would be, a victim of that act.

(4) If the proceedings are made by way of a petition for judicial review in Scotland, the applicant shall be taken to have title and interest to sue in relation to the unlawful act only if he is, or would be, a victim of that act.

(5) Proceedings under subsection (1)(a) must be brought before the end of
    (a) the period of one year beginning with the date on which the act complained of took place; or
    (b) such longer period as the court or tribunal considers equitable having regard to all the circumstances,
but that is subject to any rule imposing a stricter time limit in relation to the procedure in question.

(6) In subsection (1)(b) 'legal proceedings' includes—
    (a) proceedings brought by or at the instigation of a public authority; and
    (b) an appeal against the decision of a court or tribunal.

(7) For the purposes of this section, a person is a victim of an unlawful act only if he would be a victim for the purposes of Article 34 of the Convention if proceedings were brought in the European Court of Human Rights in respect of that act.

(8) Nothing in this Act creates a criminal offence.

---

¹⁰ Subsection (4) was repealed by the Constitutional Reform Act 2005, ss 40(4), 146, Sch 9, Pt 1, para 66(1), (4), Sch 18, Pt 5.

¹¹ This section was amended by the Secretary of State for Constitutional Affairs Order 2003, SI 2003/1887, art 9, Sch 2, para 10(2) and the Transfer of Functions (Lord Chancellor and Secretary of State) Order 2005, SI 2005/3429, art 8, Schedule, para 3.

(9) In this section 'rules' means—

    (a) in relation to proceedings before a court or tribunal outside Scotland, rules made by [the Lord Chancellor] or the Secretary of State for the purposes of this section or rules of court,

    (b) in relation to proceedings before a court or tribunal in Scotland, rules made by the Secretary of State for those purposes,

    (c) in relation to proceedings before a tribunal in Northern Ireland—

        (i) which deals with transferred matters; and

        (ii) for which no rules made under paragraph (a) are in force,

        (iii) rules made by a Northern Ireland department for those purposes,

and includes provision made by order under section 1 of the Courts and Legal Services Act 1990.

(10) In making rules, regard must be had to section 9.

(11) The Minister who has power to make rules in relation to a particular tribunal may, to the extent he considers it necessary to ensure that the tribunal can provide an appropriate remedy in relation to an act (or proposed act) of a public authority which is (or would be) unlawful as a result of section 6(1), by order add to—

    (a) the relief or remedies which the tribunal may grant; or

    (b) the grounds on which it may grant any of them.

(12) An order made under subsection (11) may contain such incidental, supplemental, consequential or transitional provision as the Minister making it considers appropriate.

(13) 'The Minister' includes the Northern Ireland department concerned.

8. Judicial remedies

(1) In relation to any act (or proposed act) of a public authority which the court finds is (or would be) unlawful, it may grant such relief or remedy, or make such order, within its powers as it considers just and appropriate.

(2) But damages may be awarded only by a court which has power to award damages, or to order the payment of compensation, in civil proceedings.

(3) No award of damages is to be made unless, taking account of all the circumstances of the case, including—

    (a) any other relief or remedy granted, or order made, in relation to the act in question (by that or any other court), and

    (b) the consequences of any decision (of that or any other court) in respect of that act,

the court is satisfied that the award is necessary to afford just satisfaction to the person in whose favour it is made.

(4) In determining—

    (a) whether to award damages, or

    (b) the amount of an award,

the court must take into account the principles applied by the European Court of Human Rights in relation to the award of compensation under Article 41 of the Convention.

(5) A public authority against which damages are awarded is to be treated—

    (a) in Scotland, for the purposes of section 3 of the Law Reform (Miscellaneous Provisions) (Scotland) Act 1940 as if the award were made in an action of damages in which the authority has been found liable in respect of loss or damage to the person to whom the award is made;

    (b) for the purposes of the Civil Liability (Contribution) Act 1978 as liable in respect of damage suffered by the person to whom the award is made.

(6) In this section—

'court' includes a tribunal;

'damages' means damages for an unlawful act of a public authority; and

'unlawful' means unlawful under section 6(1).

9. Judicial acts[12]

(1) Proceedings under section 7(1)(a) in respect of a judicial act may be brought only—

    (a) by exercising a right of appeal;

    (b) on an application (in Scotland a petition) for judicial review; or

    (c) in such other forum as may be prescribed by rules.

(2) That does not affect any rule of law which prevents a court from being the subject of judicial review.

(3) In proceedings under this Act in respect of a judicial act done in good faith, damages may not be awarded otherwise than to compensate a person to the extent required by Article 5(5) of the Convention.

(4) An award of damages permitted by subsection (3) is to be made against the Crown but no award may be made unless the appropriate person, if not a party to the proceedings, is joined.

(5) In this section—

'appropriate person' means the Minister responsible for the court concerned, or a person or government department nominated by him;

'court' includes a tribunal;

'judge' includes a member of a tribunal, a justice of the peace or, in Northern Ireland, a lay magistrate and a clerk or other officer entitled to exercise the jurisdiction of a court;

'judicial act' means a judicial act of a court and includes an act done on the instructions, or on behalf, of a judge; and

'rules' has the same meaning as in section 7(9).

Remedial action

10. Power to take remedial action

(1) This section applies if—

    (a) a provision of legislation has been declared under section 4 to be incompatible with a Convention right and, if an appeal lies;

        (i) all persons who may appeal have stated in writing that they do not intend to do so;

        (ii) the time for bringing an appeal has expired and no appeal has been brought within that time; or

        (iii) an appeal brought within that time has been determined or abandoned;

    (b) it appears to a Minister of the Crown or Her Majesty in Council that, having regard to a finding of the European Court of Human Rights made after the coming into force of this section in proceedings against the United Kingdom, a provision of legislation is incompatible with an obligation of the United Kingdom arising from the Convention.

(2) If a Minister of the Crown considers that there are compelling reasons for proceeding under this section, he may by order make such amendments to the legislation as he considers necessary to remove the incompatibility.

---

[12] This section was amended by the Justice (Northern Ireland) Act 2002, s 10(6), Sch 4, para 39.

(3) If, in the case of subordinate legislation, a Minister of the Crown considers—

(a) that it is necessary to amend the primary legislation under which the subordinate legislation in question was made, in order to enable the incompatibility to be removed, and

(b) that there are compelling reasons for proceeding under this section,

he may by order make such amendments to the primary legislation as he considers necessary.

(4) This section also applies where the provision in question is in subordinate legislation and has been quashed, or declared invalid, by reason of incompatibility with a Convention right and the Minister proposes to proceed under paragraph 2(b) of Schedule 2.

(5) If the legislation is an Order in Council, the power conferred by subsection (2) or (3) is exercisable by Her Majesty in Council.

(6) In this section 'legislation' does not include a Measure of the Church Assembly or of the General Synod of the Church of England.

(7) Schedule 2 makes further provision about remedial orders.

Other rights and proceedings

11. Safeguard for existing human rights

A person's reliance on a Convention right does not restrict—

(a) any other right or freedom conferred on him by or under any law having effect in any part of the United Kingdom; or

(b) his right to make any claim or bring any proceedings which he could make or bring apart from sections 7 to 9.

12. Freedom of expression

(1) This section applies if a court is considering whether to grant any relief which, if granted, might affect the exercise of the Convention right to freedom of expression.

(2) If the person against whom the application for relief is made ('the respondent') is neither present nor represented, no such relief is to be granted unless the court is satisfied—

(a) that the applicant has taken all practicable steps to notify the respondent; or

(b) that there are compelling reasons why the respondent should not be notified.

(3) No such relief is to be granted so as to restrain publication before trial unless the court is satisfied that the applicant is likely to establish that publication should not be allowed.

(4) The court must have particular regard to the importance of the Convention right to freedom of expression and, where the proceedings relate to material which the respondent claims, or which appears to the court, to be journalistic, literary or artistic material (or to conduct connected with such material), to—

(a) the extent to which—

(i) the material has, or is about to, become available to the public; or

(ii) it is, or would be, in the public interest for the material to be published

(b) any relevant privacy code.

(5) In this section —

'court' includes a tribunal; and

'relief' includes any remedy or order (other than in criminal proceedings).

13. Freedom of thought, conscience and religion

(1) If a court's determination of any question arising under this Act might affect the exercise by a religious organisation (itself or its members collectively) of the Convention right to freedom of thought, conscience and religion, it must have particular regard to the importance of that right.

(2) In this section 'court' includes a tribunal.

Derogations and reservations

14. Derogations[13]

(1) In this Act 'designated derogation' means any derogation by the United Kingdom from an Article of the Convention, or of any protocol to the Convention, which is designated for the purposes of this Act in an order made by the Secretary of State.

(2) ...

(3) If a designated derogation is amended or replaced it ceases to be a designated derogation.

(4) But subsection (3) does not prevent the Secretary of State from exercising his power under subsection (1) to make a fresh designation order in respect of the Article concerned.

(5) The Secretary of State must by order make such amendments to Schedule 3 as he considers appropriate to reflect—

    (a) any designation order; or

    (b) the effect of subsection (3).

(6) A designation order may be made in anticipation of the making by the United Kingdom of a proposed derogation.

15. Reservations[14]

(1) In this Act 'designated reservation' means—

    (a) the United Kingdom's reservation to Article 2 of the First Protocol to the Convention; and

    (b) any other reservation by the United Kingdom to an Article of the Convention, or of any protocol to the Convention, which is designated for the purposes of this Act in an order made by the Secretary of State.

(2) The text of the reservation referred to in subsection (1)(a) is set out in Part II of Schedule 3.

(3) If a designated reservation is withdrawn wholly or in part it ceases to be a designated reservation.

(4) But subsection (3) does not prevent the Secretary of State from exercising his power under subsection (1)(b) to make a fresh designation order in respect of the Article concerned.

(5) The Secretary of State must by order make such amendments to this Act as he considers appropriate to reflect—

    (a) any designation order; or

    (b) the effect of subsection (3).

16. Period for which designated derogations have effect[15]

(1) If it has not already been withdrawn by the United Kingdom, a designated derogation ceases to have effect for the purposes of this Act at the end of the period of five years beginning with the date on which the order designating it was made.

(2) At any time before the period—

    (a) fixed by subsection (1), or

    (b) extended by an order under this subsection,

comes to an end, the Secretary of State may by order extend it by a further period of five years.

(3) An order under section 14(1) ceases to have effect at the end of the period for consideration, unless a resolution has been passed by each House approving the order.

---

[13] This section was amended by the Human Rights Act (Amendment) Order 2001, SI 2001/1216, art 2, the Transfer of Functions (Miscellaneous) Order 2001, SI 2001/3500, art 8, Sch 2, Pt I, para 7(b), and the Secretary of State for Constitutional Affairs Order 2003, SI 2003/1887, art 1.

[14] [This section was amended by the Transfer of Functions (Miscellaneous) Order 2001, SI 2001/3500, art 8, Sch 2, Pt I, para 7(c). It was further amended by the Secretary of State for Constitutional Affairs Order 2003, SI 2003/1887, art 9, Sch 2, para 10(1).]

[15] This section was amended by the Human Rights Act (Amendment) Order 2001, SI 2001/1216, art 3. It was further amended by the Secretary of State for Constitutional Affairs Order 2003, SI 2003/1887, art 9.

(4) Subsection (3) does not affect—
    (a) anything done in reliance on the order; or
    (b) the power to make a fresh order under section 14(1).

(5) In subsection (3) 'period for consideration' means the period of forty days beginning with the day on which the order was made.

(6) In calculating the period for consideration, no account is to be taken of any time during which—
    (a) Parliament is dissolved or prorogued; or
    (b) both Houses are adjourned for more than four days.

(7) If a designated derogation is withdrawn by the United Kingdom, the Secretary of State must by order make such amendments to this Act as he considers are required to reflect that withdrawal.

17. Periodic review of designated reservations

(1) The appropriate Minister must review the designated reservation referred to in section 15(1)(a)—
    (a) before the end of the period of five years beginning with the date on which section 1(2) came into force; and
    (b) if that designation is still in force, before the end of the period of five years beginning with the date on which the last report relating to it was laid under subsection (3).

(2) The appropriate Minister must review each of the other designated reservations (if any)—
    (a) before the end of the period of five years beginning with the date on which the order designating the reservation first came into force; and
    (b) if the designation is still in force, before the end of the period of five years beginning with the date on which the last report relating to it was laid under subsection (3).

(3) The Minister conducting a review under this section must prepare a report on the result of the review and lay a copy of it before each House of Parliament.

Judges of the European Court of Human Rights

18. Appointment to European Court of Human Rights

(1) In this section 'judicial office' means the office of—
    (a) Lord Justice of Appeal, Justice of the High Court or Circuit judge, in England and Wales;
    (b) judge of the Court of Session or sheriff, in Scotland;
    (c) Lord Justice of Appeal, judge of the High Court or county court judge, in Northern Ireland.

(2) The holder of a judicial office may become a judge of the European Court of Human Rights ('the Court') without being required to relinquish his office.

(3) But he is not required to perform the duties of his judicial office while he is a judge of the Court.

(4) In respect of any period during which he is a judge of the Court—
    (a) a Lord Justice of Appeal or Justice of the High Court is not to count as a judge of the relevant court for the purposes of section 2(1) or 4(1) of the [Senior Courts Act 1981][16] (maximum number of judges) nor as a judge of the [Senior Courts] for the purposes of section 12(1) to (6) of that Act (salaries etc);[17]

---

[16] Subsection (4)(a) was amended by the Constitutional Reform Act 2005, s 59(5), Sch 11, Pt 3, para 6(1),(3).

[17] Subsection (4)(a) was amended by the Constitutional Reform Act 2005, s 59(5), Sch 11, Pt 1, para 4 (1), (3).

(b) a judge of the Court of Session is not to count as a judge of that court for the purposes of section 1(1) of the Court of Session Act 1988 (maximum number of judges) or of section 9(1) (c) of the Administration of Justice Act 1973 ('the 1973 Act') (salaries etc.);

(c) a Lord Justice of Appeal or judge of the High Court in Northern Ireland is not to count as a judge of the relevant court for the purposes of section 2(1) or 3(1) of the Judicature (Northern Ireland) Act 1978 (maximum number of judges) nor as a judge of the [Court of Judicature][18] of Northern Ireland for the purposes of section 9(1)(d) of the 1973 Act (salaries etc.);

(d) a Circuit judge is not to count as such for the purposes of section 18 of the Courts Act 1971 (salaries etc.);

(e) a sheriff is not to count as such for the purposes of section 14 of the Sheriff Courts (Scotland) Act 1907 (salaries etc.);

(f) county court judge of Northern Ireland is not to count as such for the purposes of section 106 of the County Courts Act (Northern Ireland) 1959 (salaries etc.).

(5) If a sheriff principal is appointed a judge of the Court, section 11(1) of the Sheriff Courts (Scotland) Act 1971 (temporary appointment of sheriff principal) applies, while he holds that appointment, as if his office is vacant.

(6) Schedule 4 makes provision about judicial pensions in relation to the holder of a judicial office who serves as a judge of the Court.

(7) The Lord Chancellor or the Secretary of State may by order make such transitional provision (including, in particular, provision for a temporary increase in the maximum number of judges) as he considers appropriate in relation to any holder of a judicial office who has completed his service as a judge of the Court.

(7A) The following paragraphs apply to the making of an order under subsection (7) in relation to any holder of a judicial office listed in subsection (1)(a)—

(a) before deciding what transitional provision it is appropriate to make, the person making the order must consult the Lord Chief Justice of England and Wales;

(b) before making the order, that person must consult the Lord Chief Justice of England and Wales.

(7B) The following paragraphs apply to the making of an order under subsection (7) in relation to any holder of a judicial office listed in subsection (1)(c)—

(a) before deciding what transitional provision it is appropriate to make, the person making the order must consult the Lord Chief Justice of Northern Ireland;

(b) before making the order, that person must consult the Lord Chief Justice of Northern Ireland.

(7C) The Lord Chief Justice of England and Wales may nominate a judicial office holder (within the meaning of section 109(4) of the Constitutional Reform Act 2005) to exercise his functions under this section.

(7D) The Lord Chief Justice of Northern Ireland may nominate any of the following to exercise his functions under this section—

(a) the holder of one of the offices listed in Schedule 1 to the Justice (Northern Ireland) Act 2002;

(b) a Lord Justice of Appeal (as defined in section 88 of that Act).[19]

---

[18] Subsection (4)(c) was amended by the Constitutional Reform Act 2005, s 59(5), Sch 11, Pt 3, para 6(1), (3).

[19] Subsections (7A) to (7D) were inserted by the Constitutional Reform Act 2005, s 15(1), Sch 4, Pt 1, para 278 and the Constitutional Reform Act 2005 (Commencement No 5) Order 2006, SI 2006/1014, art 2(a), Sch 1, paras 10, 11(v). Subsection (4) was amended by the Constitutional Reform Act 2005, s 59(5), Sch 11, Pt 1, para 1(2), Pt 2, para 4(1), (3), and Pt 3, para 6(1), (3).

Parliamentary procedure

19. Statements of compatibility

(1) A Minister of the Crown in charge of a Bill in either House of Parliament must, before the Second Reading of the Bill—
  (a) make a statement to the effect that in his view the provisions of the Bill are compatible with the Convention rights ('a statement of compatibility'); or
  (b) make a statement to the effect that although he is unable to make a statement of compatibility the government nevertheless wishes the House to proceed with the Bill.
(2) The statement must be in writing and be published in such manner as the Minister making it considers appropriate.

Supplemental

20. Orders etc. under this Act[20]

(1) Any power of a Minister of the Crown to make an order under this Act is exercisable by statutory instrument.
(2) The power of the Lord Chancellor or the Secretary of State to make rules (other than rules of court) under section 2(3) or 7(9) is exercisable by statutory instrument.
(3) Any statutory instrument made under section 14, 15 or 16(7) must be laid before Parliament.
(4) No order may be made by the Lord Chancellor or the Secretary of State under section 1(4), 7(11) or 16(2) unless a draft of the order has been laid before, and approved by, each House of Parliament.
(5) Any statutory instrument made under section 18(7) or Schedule 4, or to which subsection (2) applies, shall be subject to annulment in pursuance of a resolution of either House of Parliament.
(6) The power of a Northern Ireland department to make—
  (a) rules under section 2(3)(c) or 7(9)(c), or
  (b) an order under section 7(11),
  is exercisable by statutory rule for the purposes of the Statutory Rules (Northern Ireland) Order 1979.
(7) Any rules made under section 2(3)(c) or 7(9)(c) shall be subject to negative resolution and section 41(6) of the Interpretation Act (Northern Ireland) 1954 (meaning of 'subject to negative resolution') shall apply as if the power to make the rules were conferred by an Act of the Northern Ireland Assembly.
(8) No order may be made by a Northern Ireland department under section 7(11) unless a draft of the order has been laid before, and approved by, the Northern Ireland Assembly.

21. Interpretation etc.[21]

(1) In this Act—
  'amend' includes repeal and apply (with or without modifications);
  'the appropriate Minister' means the Minister of the Crown having charge of the appropriate authorised government department (within the meaning of the Crown Proceedings Act 1947);

---

[20] This section was amended by the Secretary of State for Constitutional Affairs Order 2003, SI 2003/1887, art 9, Sch 2, para 10(2). It was further amended by the Transfer of Functions (Lord Chancellor and Secretary of State) Order 2005, SI 2005/3429, art 8, Schedule, para 3.

[21] This section was amended by the Human Rights Act (Amendment) Order 2004, SI 2004/1574, art 2(2); the Government of Wales Act 2006, s 160(1), Sch 10, para 56(1), (2), (3), (4); and the Armed Forces Act 2006, s 378(2), Sch 17.

'the Commission' means the European Commission of Human Rights;

'the Convention' means the Convention for the Protection of Human Rights and Fundamental Freedoms, agreed by the Council of Europe at Rome on 4th November 1950 as it has effect for the time being in relation to the United Kingdom;

'declaration of incompatibility' means a declaration under section 4;

'Minister of the Crown' has the same meaning as in the Ministers of the Crown Act 1975;

'Northern Ireland Minister' includes the First Minister and the deputy First Minister in Northern Ireland;

'primary legislation' means any—

    (a)   public general Act;

    (b)   local and personal Act;

    (c)   private Act;

    (d)   Measure of the Church Assembly;

    (e)   Measure of the General Synod of the Church of England;

    (f)   Order in Council—

        (i)   made in exercise of Her Majesty's Royal Prerogative;

        (ii) made under section 38(1)(a) of the Northern Ireland Constitution Act 1973 or the corresponding provision of the Northern Ireland Act 1998; or

        (iii) amending an Act of a kind mentioned in paragraph (a), (b) or (c);

and includes an order or other instrument made under primary legislation (otherwise than by the [Welsh Ministers, the First Minister for Wales, the Counsel General to the Welsh Assembly Government], a member of the Scottish Executive, a Northern Ireland Minister or a Northern Ireland department) to the extent to which it operates to bring one or more provisions of that legislation into force or amends any primary legislation;

'the First Protocol' means the protocol to the Convention agreed at Paris on 20th March 1952;

'the Eleventh Protocol' means the protocol to the Convention (restructuring the control machinery established by the Convention) agreed at Strasbourg on 11th May 1994;

'the Thirteenth Protocol' means the protocol to the Convention (concerning the abolition of the death penalty in all circumstances) agreed at Vilnius on 3rd May 2002;

'remedial order' means an order under section 10;

'subordinate legislation' means any—

    (a)   Order in Council other than one—

        (i)   made in exercise of Her Majesty's Royal Prerogative;

        (ii) made under section 38(1)(a) of the Northern Ireland Constitution Act 1973 or the corresponding provision of the Northern Ireland Act 1998; or

        (iii) amending an Act of a kind mentioned in the definition of primary legislation;

    (b)   Act of the Scottish Parliament;

    (ba) Measure of the National Assembly for Wales;

    (bb) Act of the National Assembly for Wales;]

    (c)   Act of the Parliament of Northern Ireland;

    (d)   Measure of the Assembly established under section 1 of the Northern Ireland Assembly Act 1973;

    (e)   Act of the Northern Ireland Assembly;

    (f)   order, rules, regulations, scheme, warrant, byelaw or other instrument made under primary legislation (except to the extent to which it operates to bring one or more provisions of that legislation into force or amends any primary legislation);

    (g)   order, rules, regulations, scheme, warrant, byelaw or other instrument made under legislation mentioned in paragraph (b), (c), (d) or (e) or made under an Order in Council applying only to Northern Ireland;

(h)   order, rules, regulations, scheme, warrant, byelaw or other instrument made by a member of the Scottish Executive, a Northern Ireland Minister or a Northern Ireland department [, Welsh Ministers, the First Minister for Wales, the Counsel General to the Welsh Assembly Government], in exercise of prerogative or other executive functions of Her Majesty which are exercisable by such a person on behalf of Her Majesty;

'transferred matters' has the same meaning as in the Northern Ireland Act 1998; and

'tribunal' means any tribunal in which legal proceedings may be brought.

(2) The references in paragraphs (b) and (c) of section 2(1) to Articles are to Articles of the Convention as they had effect immediately before the coming into force of the Eleventh Protocol.

(3) The reference in paragraph (d) of section 2(1) to Article 46 includes a reference to Articles 32 and 54 of the Convention as they had effect immediately before the coming into force of the Eleventh Protocol.

(4) The references in section 2(1) to a report or decision of the Commission or a decision of the Committee of Ministers include references to a report or decision made as provided by paragraphs 3, 4 and 6 of Article 5 of the Eleventh Protocol (transitional provisions).

[. . .][22]

22. Short title, commencement, application and extent

(1) This Act may be cited as the Human Rights Act 1998.

(2) Sections 18, 20 and 21(5) and this section come into force on the passing of this Act.

(3) The other provisions of this Act come into force on such day as the Secretary of State may by order appoint and different days may be appointed for different purposes.

(4) Paragraph (b) of subsection (1) of section 7 applies to proceedings brought by or at the instigation of a public authority whenever the act in question took place but otherwise that subsection does not apply to an act taking place before the coming into force of that section.

(5) This Act binds the Crown.

(6) This Act extends to Northern Ireland.

[. . .][23]

---

[22] Subsection (5) repealed by the Armed Forces Act 2006, s 378(2), Sch 17.

[23] Subsection (7) repealed by the Armed Forces Act 2006, s 378(2), Sch 17.

SCHEDULES

SCHEDULE 1

Section 1(3)

THE ARTICLES

PART I
THE CONVENTION RIGHTS AND FREEDOMS

Article 2
Right to life

1. Everyone's right to life shall be protected by law. No one shall be deprived of his life intentionally save in the execution of a sentence of a court following his conviction of a crime for which this penalty is provided by law.
2. Deprivation of life shall not be regarded as inflicted in contravention of this Article when it results from the use of force which is no more than absolutely necessary:
   (a) in defence of any person from unlawful violence;
   (b) in order to effect a lawful arrest or to prevent the escape of a person lawfully detained;
   (c) in action lawfully taken for the purpose of quelling a riot or insurrection.

Article 3
Prohibition of torture

No one shall be subjected to torture or to inhuman or degrading treatment or punishment.

Article 4
Prohibition of slavery and forced labour

1. No one shall be held in slavery or servitude.
2. No one shall be required to perform forced or compulsory labour.
3. For the purpose of this Article the term 'forced or compulsory labour' shall not include:
   (a) any work required to be done in the ordinary course of detention imposed according to the provisions of Article 5 of this Convention or during conditional release from such detention;
   (b) any service of a military character or, in case of conscientious objectors in countries where they are recognised, service exacted instead of compulsory military service;
   (c) any service exacted in case of an emergency or calamity threatening the life or well-being of the community;
   (d) any work or service which forms part of normal civic obligations.

Article 5
Right to liberty and security

1. Everyone has the right to liberty and security of person. No one shall be deprived of his liberty save in the following cases and in accordance with a procedure prescribed by law:
   (a) the lawful detention of a person after conviction by a competent court;
   (b) the lawful arrest or detention of a person for non-compliance with the lawful order of a court or in order to secure the fulfilment of any obligation prescribed by law;
   (c) the lawful arrest or detention of a person effected for the purpose of bringing him before the competent legal authority on reasonable suspicion of having committed an offence

or when it is reasonably considered necessary to prevent his committing an offence or fleeing after having done so;

(d) the detention of a minor by lawful order for the purpose of educational supervision or his lawful detention for the purpose of bringing him before the competent legal authority;

(e) the lawful detention of persons for the prevention of the spreading of infectious diseases, of persons of unsound mind, alcoholics or drug addicts or vagrants;

(f) the lawful arrest or detention of a person to prevent his effecting an unauthorised entry into the country or of a person against whom action is being taken with a view to deportation or extradition.

2. Everyone who is arrested shall be informed promptly, in a language which he understands, of the reasons for his arrest and of any charge against him.

3. Everyone arrested or detained in accordance with the provisions of paragraph 1(c) of this Article shall be brought promptly before a judge or other officer authorised by law to exercise judicial power and shall be entitled to trial within a reasonable time or to release pending trial. Release may be conditioned by guarantees to appear for trial.

4. Everyone who is deprived of his liberty by arrest or detention shall be entitled to take proceedings by which the lawfulness of his detention shall be decided speedily by a court and his release ordered if the detention is not lawful.

5. Everyone who has been the victim of arrest or detention in contravention of the provisions of this Article shall have an enforceable right to compensation.

Article 6
Right to a fair trial

1. In the determination of his civil rights and obligations or of any criminal charge against him, everyone is entitled to a fair and public hearing within a reasonable time by an independent and impartial tribunal established by law. Judgment shall be pronounced publicly but the press and public may be excluded from all or part of the trial in the interest of morals, public order or national security in a democratic society, where the interests of juveniles or the protection of the private life of the parties so require, or to the extent strictly necessary in the opinion of the court in special circumstances where publicity would prejudice the interests of justice.

2. Everyone charged with a criminal offence shall be presumed innocent until proved guilty according to law.

3. Everyone charged with a criminal offence has the following minimum rights:

(a) to be informed promptly, in a language which he understands and in detail, of the nature and cause of the accusation against him;

(b) to have adequate time and facilities for the preparation of his defence;

(c) to defend himself in person or through legal assistance of his own choosing or, if he has not sufficient means to pay for legal assistance, to be given it free when the interests of justice so require;

(d) to examine or have examined witnesses against him and to obtain the attendance and examination of witnesses on his behalf under the same conditions as witnesses against him;

(e) to have the free assistance of an interpreter if he cannot understand or speak the language used in court.

Article 7
No punishment without law

1. No one shall be held guilty of any criminal offence on account of any act or omission which did not constitute a criminal offence under national or international law at the time when it

was committed. Nor shall a heavier penalty be imposed than the one that was applicable at the time the criminal offence was committed.

2. This Article shall not prejudice the trial and punishment of any person for any act or omission which, at the time when it was committed, was criminal according to the general principles of law recognised by civilised nations.

Article 8
Right to respect for private and family life

1. Everyone has the right to respect for his private and family life, his home and his correspondence.
2. There shall be no interference by a public authority with the exercise of this right except such as is in accordance with the law and is necessary in a democratic society in the interests of national security, public safety or the economic well being of the country, for the prevention of disorder or crime, for the protection of health or morals, or for the protection of the rights and freedoms of others.

Article 9
Freedom of thought, conscience and religion

1. Everyone has the right to freedom of thought, conscience and religion; this right includes freedom to change his religion or belief and freedom, either alone or in community with others and in public or private, to manifest his religion or belief, in worship, teaching, practice and observance.
2. Freedom to manifest one's religion or beliefs shall be subject only to such limitations as are prescribed by law and are necessary in a democratic society in the interests of public safety, for the protection of public order, health or morals, or for the protection of the rights and freedoms of others.

Article 10
Freedom of expression

1. Everyone has the right to freedom of expression. This right shall include freedom to hold opinions and to receive and impart information and ideas without interference by public authority and regardless of frontiers. This Article shall not prevent States from requiring the licensing of broadcasting, television or cinema enterprises.
2. The exercise of these freedoms, since it carries with it duties and responsibilities, may be subject to such formalities, conditions, restrictions or penalties as are prescribed by law and are necessary in a democratic society, in the interests of national security, territorial integrity or public safety, for the prevention of disorder or crime, for the protection of health or morals, for the protection of the reputation or rights of others, for preventing the disclosure of information received in confidence, or for maintaining the authority and impartiality of the judiciary.

Article 11
Freedom of assembly and association

1. Everyone has the right to freedom of peaceful assembly and to freedom of association with others, including the right to form and to join trade unions for the protection of his interests.

2. No restrictions shall be placed on the exercise of these rights other than such as are prescribed by law and are necessary in a democratic society in the interests of national security or public safety, for the prevention of disorder or crime, for the protection of health or morals or for the protection of the rights and freedoms of others. This Article shall not prevent the imposition of lawful restrictions on the exercise of these rights by members of the armed forces, of the police or of the administration of the State.

Article 12
Right to marry

Men and women of marriageable age have the right to marry and to found a family, according to the national laws governing the exercise of this right.

Article 14
Prohibition of discrimination

The enjoyment of the rights and freedoms set forth in this Convention shall be secured without discrimination on any ground such as sex, race, colour, language, religion, political or other opinion, national or social origin, association with a national minority, property, birth or other status.

Article 16
Restrictions on political activity of aliens

Nothing in Articles 10, 11 and 14 shall be regarded as preventing the High Contracting Parties from imposing restrictions on the political activity of aliens.

Article 17
Prohibition of abuse of rights

Nothing in this Convention may be interpreted as implying for any State, group or person any right to engage in any activity or perform any act aimed at the destruction of any of the rights and freedoms set forth herein or at their limitation to a greater extent than is provided for in the Convention.

Article 18
Limitation on use of restrictions on rights

The restrictions permitted under this Convention to the said rights and freedoms shall not be applied for any purpose other than those for which they have been prescribed.

PART II
THE FIRST PROTOCOL

Article 1
Protection of property

Every natural or legal person is entitled to the peaceful enjoyment of his possessions. No one shall be deprived of his possessions except in the public interest and subject to the conditions provided for by law and by the general principles of international law.

The preceding provisions shall not, however, in any way impair the right of a State to enforce such laws as it deems necessary to control the use of property in accordance with the general interest or to secure the payment of taxes or other contributions or penalties.

Article 2
Right to education

No person shall be denied the right to education. In the exercise of any functions which it assumes in relation to education and to teaching, the State shall respect the right of parents to ensure such education and teaching in conformity with their own religious and philosophical convictions.

Article 3
Right to free elections

The High Contracting Parties undertake to hold free elections at reasonable intervals by secret ballot, under conditions which will ensure the free expression of the opinion of the people in the choice of the legislature.

PART III
ARTICLE 1 OF THE THIRTEENTH PROTOCOL

Abolition of the death penalty

The death penalty shall be abolished. No one shall be condemned to such penalty or executed. [This Part was substituted by the Human Rights Act (Amendment) Order 2004, SI 2004/1574, art 2(3).]

SCHEDULE 2
REMEDIAL ORDERS

Orders

1.—(1) A remedial order may—
- (a) contain such incidental, supplemental, consequential or transitional provision as the person making it considers appropriate;
- (b) be made so as to have effect from a date earlier than that on which it is made;
- (c) make provision for the delegation of specific functions;
- (d) make different provision for different cases.

(2) The power conferred by sub-paragraph (1)(a) includes —
- (a) power to amend primary legislation (including primary legislation other than that which contains the incompatible provision); and
- (b) power to amend or revoke subordinate legislation (including subordinate legislation other than that which contains the incompatible provision).

(3) A remedial order may be made so as to have the same extent as the legislation which it affects.

(4) No person is to be guilty of an offence solely as a result of the retrospective effect of a remedial order.

Procedure

2. No remedial order may be made unless—
   (a) a draft of the order has been approved by a resolution of each House of Parliament made after the end of the period of 60 days beginning with the day on which the draft was laid; or
   (b) it is declared in the order that it appears to the person making it that, because of the urgency of the matter, it is necessary to make the order without a draft being so approved.

Orders laid in draft

3.—(1) No draft may be laid under paragraph 2(a) unless—
   (a) the person proposing to make the order has laid before Parliament a document which contains a draft of the proposed order and the required information; and
   (b) the period of 60 days, beginning with the day on which the document required by this sub-paragraph was laid, has ended.
   (2) If representations have been made during that period, the draft laid under paragraph 2(a) must be accompanied by a statement containing—
   (a) a summary of the representations; and
   (b) if, as a result of the representations, the proposed order has been changed, details of the changes.

Urgent cases

4.—(1) If a remedial order ('the original order') is made without being approved in draft, the person making it must lay it before Parliament, accompanied by the required information, after it is made.
   (2) If representations have been made during the period of 60 days beginning with the day on which the original order was made, the person making it must (after the end of that period) lay before Parliament a statement containing—
   (a) a summary of the representations; and
   (b) if, as a result of the representations, he considers it appropriate to make changes to the original order, details of the changes.
   (3) If sub-paragraph (2)(b) applies, the person making the statement must—
   (a) make a further remedial order replacing the original order; and
   (b) lay the replacement order before Parliament.
   (4) If, at the end of the period of 120 days beginning with the day on which the original order was made, a resolution has not been passed by each House approving the original or replacement order, the order ceases to have effect (but without that affecting anything previously done under either order or the power to make a fresh remedial order).

Definitions

5. In this Schedule—
   'representations' means representations about a remedial order (or proposed remedial order) made to the person making (or proposing to make) it and includes any relevant Parliamentary report or resolution; and
   'required information' means—
   (a) an explanation of the incompatibility which the order (or proposed order) seeks to remove, including particulars of the relevant declaration, finding or order; and
   (b) a statement of the reasons for proceeding under section 10 and for making an order in those terms.

Calculating periods

6. In calculating any period for the purposes of this Schedule, no account is to be taken of any time during which—
    (a) Parliament is dissolved or prorogued; or
    (b) both Houses are adjourned for more than four days.

7.—(1) This paragraph applies in relation to—
    (a) any remedial order made, and any draft of such an order proposed to be made, —
        (i) by the Scottish Ministers; or
        (ii) within devolved competence (within the meaning of the Scotland Act 1998) by Her Majesty in Council; and
    (b) any document or statement to be laid in connection with such an order (or proposed order).

    (2) This Schedule has effect in relation to any such order (or proposed order), document or statement subject to the following modifications.

    (3) Any reference to Parliament, each House of Parliament or both Houses of Parliament shall be construed as a reference to the Scottish Parliament.

    (4) Paragraph 6 does not apply and instead, in calculating any period for the purposes of this Schedule, no account is to be taken of any time during which the Scottish Parliament is dissolved or is in recess for more than four days.

[This Schedule was amended by the Scotland Act 1998 (Consequential Modifications) Order 2000, SI 2000/2040, art 2(1), Schedule, Pt I, para 21.]

SCHEDULE 3
DEROGATION AND RESERVATION

PART I

[The UK's previous derogations from art 5(1) were repealed by the Human Rights Act (Amendment) Order 2001, SI 2001/1216, art 4, and the Human Rights Act 1998 (Amendment) Order 2005, SI 2005/1071, art 2.]

PART II
RESERVATION

At the time of signing the present (First) Protocol, I declare that, in view of certain provisions of the Education Acts in the United Kingdom, the principle affirmed in the second sentence of Article 2 is accepted by the United Kingdom only so far as it is compatible with the provision of efficient instruction and training, and the avoidance of unreasonable public expenditure.

Dated 20 March 1952. Made by the United Kingdom Permanent Representative to the Council of Europe.

[This Schedule was amended by the Human Rights Act (Amendment) Order 2001, SI 2001/1216, art 4. It was further amended by the Human Rights Act 1998 (Amendment No 2) Order 2001, SI 2001/4032, art 2, Schedule.]

SCHEDULE 4
JUDICIAL PENSIONS

Duty to make orders about pensions

1.—(1) The appropriate Minister must by order make provision with respect to pensions payable to or in respect of any holder of a judicial office who serves as an ECHR judge.

(2) A pensions order must include such provision as the Minister making it considers is necessary to secure that —

(a) an ECHR judge who was, immediately before his appointment as an ECHR judge, a member of a judicial pension scheme is entitled to remain as a member of that scheme;

(b) the terms on which he remains a member of the scheme are those which would have been applicable had he not been appointed as an ECHR judge; and

(c) entitlement to benefits payable in accordance with the scheme continues to be determined as if, while serving as an ECHR judge, his salary was that which would (but for section 18(4)) have been payable to him in respect of his continuing service as the holder of his judicial office.

Contributions

2. A pensions order may, in particular, make provision—

(a) for any contributions which are payable by a person who remains a member of a scheme as a result of the order, and which would otherwise be payable by deduction from his salary, to be made otherwise than by deduction from his salary as an ECHR judge; and

(b) for such contributions to be collected in such manner as may be determined by the administrators of the scheme.

Amendments of other enactments

3. A pensions order may amend any provision of, or made under, a pensions Act in such manner and to such extent as the Minister making the order considers necessary or expedient to ensure the proper administration of any scheme to which it relates.

Definitions

4. In this Schedule

'appropriate Minister' means—

(a) in relation to any judicial office whose jurisdiction is exercisable exclusively in relation to Scotland, the Secretary of State; and

(b) otherwise, the Lord Chancellor;

'ECHR judge' means the holder of a judicial office who is serving as a judge of the Court;

'judicial pension scheme' means a scheme established by and in accordance with a pensions Act;

'pensions Act' means—

(a) the County Courts Act (Northern Ireland) 1959;

(b) the Sheriffs' Pensions (Scotland) Act 1961;

(c) the Judicial Pensions Act 1981; or

(d) the Judicial Pensions and Retirement Act 1993; and 'pensions order' means an order made under paragraph 1.

Convention for the Protection of Human Rights and Fundamental Freedoms including the additional substantive Protocols Nos. 1, 4, 6, 7, 12 and 13 and as amended by Protocols Nos. 11, 14, 15 and 16,

The Convention and Protocols below contain both the substantive fundamental rights created by the Convention as well as the provisions dealing with the creation, procedures and workings of the Court. The rights set out in Protocols 4, 7, and 12 have not, however, been ratified by the United Kingdom Government and are not included in the Human Rights Act and therefore cannot form the basis for either applications to the European Court of Human Rights or for breaches of section 6 of the Act.

The amendments to the Convention made by Protocols 15 and 16 are not yet, at the time of writing, in force. The amendments that will be made by Protocol 15 are highlighted in the text below in italics and within brackets [ ] and the changes are dealt with in more detail in Chapter 9. It is likely that Protocol 15 will be in force at some point in 2015, but because it requires the consent of all Member States before it applies the timing is difficult to predict. Protocol 16 (obtaining advisory opinions from the Court) will be found at the end of this appendix. The provision will both need to be ratified by at least 10 Member States to come into force and then, specifically, by the United Kingdom Government to be available to the UK courts.

CONVENTION FOR THE PROTECTION OF HUMAN RIGHTS AND FUNDAMENTAL FREEDOMS

Rome, 4.XI.1950

The governments signatory hereto, being members of the Council of Europe,

Considering the Universal Declaration of Human Rights proclaimed by the General Assembly of the United Nations on 10 December 1948;

Considering that this Declaration aims at securing the universal and effective recognition and observance of the Rights therein declared;

Considering that the aim of the Council of Europe is the achievement of greater unity between its members and that one of the methods by which that aim is to be pursued is the maintenance and further realisation of human rights and fundamental freedoms;

Reaffirming their profound belief in those fundamental freedoms which are the foundation of justice and peace in the world and are best maintained on the one hand by an effective political democracy and on the other by a common understanding and observance of the human rights upon which they depend;

Being resolved, as the governments of European countries which are likeminded and have a common heritage of political traditions, ideals, freedom and the rule of law, to take the first steps for the collective enforcement of certain of the rights stated in the Universal Declaration,

[*Affirming that the High Contracting Parties, in accordance with the principle of subsidiarity, have the primary responsibility to secure the rights and freedoms defined in this Convention and the Protocols thereto, and that in doing so they enjoy a margin of appreciation, subject to the supervisory jurisdiction of the European Court of Human Rights established by this Convention*][1]

Have agreed as follows:

Article 1
Obligation to respect human rights

The High Contracting Parties shall secure to everyone within their jurisdiction the rights and freedoms defined in Section I of this Convention.

SECTION I
RIGHTS AND FREEDOMS

Article 2
Right to life

1. Everyone's right to life shall be protected by law. No one shall be deprived of his life intentionally save in the execution of a sentence of a court following his conviction of a crime for which this penalty is provided by law.
2. Deprivation of life shall not be regarded as inflicted in contravention of this Article when it results from the use of force which is no more than absolutely necessary:
   (a) in defence of any person from unlawful violence;
   (b) in order to effect a lawful arrest or to prevent the escape of a person lawfully detained;
   (c) in action lawfully taken for the purpose of quelling a riot or insurrection.

Article 3
Prohibition of torture

No one shall be subjected to torture or to inhuman or degrading treatment or punishment.

Article 4
Prohibition of slavery and forced labour

1. No one shall be held in slavery or servitude.
2. No one shall be required to perform forced or compulsory labour.
3. For the purpose of this Article the term "forced or compulsory labour" shall not include:
   (a) any work required to be done in the ordinary course of detention imposed according to the provisions of Article 5 of this Convention or during conditional release from such detention;
   (b) any service of a military character or, in case of conscientious objectors in countries where they are recognised, service exacted instead of compulsory military service;

---

[1] Amendment made by Article 1 of Protocol 15, not yet in force.

(c) any service exacted in case of an emergency or calamity threatening the life or well-being of the community;

(d) any work or service which forms part of normal civic obligations.

Article 5
Right to liberty and security

1. Everyone has the right to liberty and security of person. No one shall be deprived of his liberty save in the following cases and in accordance with a procedure prescribed by law:
   (a) the lawful detention of a person after conviction by a competent court;
   (b) the lawful arrest or detention of a person for non-compliance with the lawful order of a court or in order to secure the fulfilment of any obligation prescribed by law;
   (c) the lawful arrest or detention of a person effected for the purpose of bringing him before the competent legal authority on reasonable suspicion of having committed an offence or when it is reasonably considered necessary to prevent his committing an offence or fleeing after having done so;
   (d) the detention of a minor by lawful order for the purpose of educational supervision or his lawful detention for the purpose of bringing him before the competent legal authority;
   (e) the lawful detention of persons for the prevention of the spreading of infectious diseases, of persons of un-sound mind, alcoholics or drug addicts or vagrants;
   (f) the lawful arrest or detention of a person to prevent his effecting an unauthorised entry into the country or of a person against whom action is being taken with a view to deportation or extradition.
2. Everyone who is arrested shall be informed promptly, in a language which he understands, of the reasons for his arrest and of any charge against him.
3. Everyone arrested or detained in accordance with the provisions of paragraph 1(c) of this Article shall be brought promptly before a judge or other officer authorised by law to exercise judicial power and shall be entitled to trial within a reasonable time or to release pending trial. Release may be conditioned by guarantees to appear for trial.
4. Everyone who is deprived of his liberty by arrest or detention shall be entitled to take proceedings by which the lawfulness of his detention shall be decided speedily by a court and his release ordered if the detention is not lawful.
5. Everyone who has been the victim of arrest or detention in contravention of the provisions of this Article shall have an enforceable right to compensation.

Article 6
Right to a fair trial

1. In the determination of his civil rights and obligations or of any criminal charge against him, everyone is entitled to a fair and public hearing within a reasonable time by an independent and impartial tribunal established by law. Judgment shall be pronounced publicly but the press and public may be excluded from all or part of the trial in the interests of morals, public order or national security in a democratic society, where the interests of juveniles or the protection of the private life of the parties so require, or to the extent strictly necessary in the opinion of the court in special circumstances where publicity would prejudice the interests of justice.
2. Everyone charged with a criminal offence shall be presumed innocent until proved guilty according to law.
3. Everyone charged with a criminal offence has the following minimum rights:
   (a) to be informed promptly, in a language which he understands and detail, of the nature and cause of the accusation against him;

(b) to have adequate time and facilities for the preparation of his defence;

(c) to defend himself in person or through legal assistance of his own choosing or, if he has not sufficient means to pay for legal assistance, to be given it free when the interests of justice so require;

(d) to examine or have examined witnesses against him and to obtain the attendance and examination of witnesses on his behalf under the same conditions as witnesses against him;

(e) to have the free assistance of an interpreter if he cannot understand or speak the language used in court.

Article 7
No punishment without law

1. No one shall be held guilty of any criminal offence on account of any act or omission which did not constitute a criminal offence under national or international law at the time when it was committed. Nor shall a heavier penalty be imposed than the one that was applicable at the time the criminal offence was committed.

2. This Article shall not prejudice the trial and punishment of any person for any act or omission which, at the time when it was committed, was criminal according to the general principles of law recognised by civilised nations.

Article 8
Right to respect for private and family life

1. Everyone has the right to respect for his private and family life, his home and his correspondence.

2. There shall be no interference by a public authority with the exercise of this right except such as is in accordance with the law and is necessary in a democratic society in the interests of national security, public safety or the economic well-being of the country, for the prevention of disorder or crime, for the protection of health or morals, or for the protection of the rights and freedoms of others.

Article 9
Freedom of thought, conscience and religion

1. Everyone has the right to freedom of thought, conscience and religion; this right includes freedom to change his religion or belief and freedom, either alone or in community with others and in public or private, to manifest his religion or belief, in worship, teaching, practice and observance.

2. Freedom to manifest one's religion or beliefs shall be subject only to such limitations as are prescribed by law and are necessary in a democratic society in the interests of public safety, for the protection of public order, health or morals, or for the protection of the rights and freedoms of others.

Article 10
Freedom of expression

1. Everyone has the right to freedom of expression. This right shall include freedom to hold opinions and to receive and impart information and ideas without interference by public authority and regardless of frontiers. This Article shall not prevent States from requiring the licensing of broadcasting, television or cinema enterprises.

2. The exercise of these freedoms, since it carries with it duties and responsibilities, may be subject to such formalities, conditions, restrictions or penalties as are prescribed by law and are necessary in a democratic society, in the interests of national security, territorial integrity or public safety, for the prevention of disorder or crime, for the protection of health or morals, for the protection of the reputation or rights of others, for preventing the disclosure of information received in confidence, or for maintaining the authority and impartiality of the judiciary.

Article 11
Freedom of assembly and association

1. Everyone has the right to freedom of peaceful assembly and to freedom of association with others, including the right to form and to join trade unions for the protection of his interests.
2. No restrictions shall be placed on the exercise of these rights other than such as are prescribed by law and are necessary in a democratic society in the interests of national security or public safety, for the prevention of disorder or crime, for the protection of health or morals or for the protection of the rights and freedoms of others. This Article shall not prevent the imposition of lawful restrictions on the exercise of these rights by members of the armed forces, of the police or of the administration of the State.

Article 12
Right to marry

Men and women of marriageable age have the right to marry and to found a family, according to the national laws governing the exercise of this right.

Article 13
Right to an effective remedy

Everyone whose rights and freedoms as set forth in this Convention are violated shall have an effective remedy before a national authority notwithstanding that the violation has been committed by persons acting in an official capacity.

Article 14
Prohibition of discrimination

The enjoyment of the rights and freedoms set forth in this Convention shall be secured without discrimination on any ground such as sex, race, colour, language, religion, political or other opinion, national or social origin, association with a national minority, property, birth or other status.

Article 15
Derogation in time of emergency

1. In time of war or other public emergency threatening the life of the nation any High Contracting Party may take measures derogating from its obligations under this Convention to the extent strictly required by the exigencies of the situation, provided that such measures are not inconsistent with its other obligations under international law.
2. No derogation from Article 2, except in respect of deaths resulting from lawful acts of war, or from Articles 3, 4 § 1 and 7 shall be made under this provision.

3. Any High Contracting Party availing itself of this right of derogation shall keep the Secretary General of the Council of Europe fully informed of the measures which it has taken and the reasons therefor. It shall also inform the Secretary General of the Council of Europe when such measures have ceased to operate and the provisions of the Convention are again being fully executed.

Article 16
Restrictions on political activity of aliens

Nothing in Articles 10, 11 and 14 shall be regarded as preventing the High Contracting Parties from imposing restrictions on the political activity of aliens.

Article 17
Prohibition of abuse of rights

Nothing in this Convention may be interpreted as implying for any State, group or person any right to engage in any activity or perform any act aimed at the destruction of any of the rights and freedoms set forth herein or at their limitation to a greater extent than is provided for in the Convention.

Article 18
Limitation on use of restrictions on rights

The restrictions permitted under this Convention to the said rights and freedoms shall not be applied for any purpose other than those for which they have been prescribed.

SECTION II
EUROPEAN COURT OF HUMAN RIGHTS

Article 19
Establishment of the Court

To ensure the observance of the engagements undertaken by the High Contracting Parties in the Convention and the Protocols thereto, there shall be set up a European Court of Human Rights, hereinafter referred to as "the Court". It shall function on a permanent basis.

Article 20
Number of judges

The Court shall consist of a number of judges equal to that of the High Contracting Parties.

Article 21
Criteria for office

1. The judges shall be of high moral character and must either possess the qualifications required for appointment to high judicial office or be jurisconsults of recognised competence.
   [2. *Candidates shall be less than 65 years of age at the date by which the list of three candidates has been requested by the Parliamentary Assembly, further to Article 22.*][2]

---

[2] Amendment made by Article 2 of Protocol 15, not yet in force. Once the new provision takes effect the next two sub-articles are re-numbered.

2. The judges shall sit on the Court in their individual capacity.
3. During their term of office the judges shall not engage in any activity which is incompatible with their independence, impartiality or with the demands of a full-time office; all questions arising from the application of this paragraph shall be decided by the Court.

Article 22
Election of judges

The judges shall be elected by the Parliamentary Assembly with respect to each High Contracting Party by a majority of votes cast from a list of three candidates nominated by the High Contracting Party.

Article 23
Terms of office and dismissal

1. The judges shall be elected for a period of nine years. They may not be re-elected.
2. [*The terms of office of judges shall expire when they reach the age of 70.*][3]
3. The judges shall hold office until replaced. They shall, however, continue to deal with such cases as they already have under consideration.
4. No judge may be dismissed from office unless the other judges decide by a majority of two-thirds that that judge has ceased to fulfil the required conditions.

Article 24
Registry and rapporteurs

1. The Court shall have a Registry, the functions and organisation of which shall be laid down in the rules of the Court.
2. When sitting in a single-judge formation, the Court shall be assisted by rapporteurs who shall function under the authority of the President of the Court. They shall form part of the Court's Registry.

Article 25
Plenary Court

The plenary Court shall

(a) elect its President and one or two Vice-Presidents for a period of three years; they may be re-elected;
(b) set up Chambers, constituted for a fixed period of time;
(c) elect the Presidents of the Chambers of the Court; they may be re-elected;
(d) adopt the rules of the Court;
(e) elect the Registrar and one or more Deputy Registrars;
(f) make any request under Article 26 § 2.

---

[3] Provision removed by amendment by Article 2 of Protocol 15, not yet in force. Once the provision takes effect the next two sub-articles are re-numbered

Article 26
Single-judge formation, Committees, Chambers and Grand Chamber

1. To consider cases brought before it, the Court shall sit in a single-judge formation, in Committees of three judges, in Chambers of seven judges and in a Grand Chamber of seventeen judges. The Court's Chambers shall set up Committees for a fixed period of time.
2. At the request of the plenary Court, the Committee of Ministers may, by a unanimous decision and for a fixed period, reduce to five the number of judges of the Chambers.
3. When sitting as a single judge, a judge shall not examine any application against the High Contracting Party in respect of which that judge has been elected.
4. There shall sit as an ex officio member of the Chamber and the Grand Chamber the judge elected in respect of the High Contracting Party concerned. If there is none or if that judge is unable to sit, a person chosen by the President of the Court from a list submitted in advance by that Party shall sit in the capacity of judge.
5. The Grand Chamber shall also include the President of the Court, the Vice-Presidents, the Presidents of the Chambers and other judges chosen in accordance with the rules of the Court. When a case is referred to the Grand Chamber under Article 43, no judge from the Chamber which rendered the judgment shall sit in the Grand Chamber, with the exception of the President of the Chamber and the judge who sat in respect of the High Contracting Party concerned.

Article 27
Competence of single judges

1. A single judge may declare inadmissible or strike out of the Court's list of cases an application submitted under Article 34, where such a decision can be taken without further examination.
2. The decision shall be final.
3. If the single judge does not declare an application inadmissible or strike it out, that judge shall forward it to a Committee or to a Chamber for further examination.

Article 28
Competence of Committees

1. In respect of an application submitted under Article 34, a Committee may, by a unanimous vote,
   (a) declare it inadmissible or strike it out of its list of cases, where such decision can be taken without further examination; or
   (b) declare it admissible and render at the same time a judgment on the merits, if the underlying question in the case, concerning the interpretation or the application of the Convention or the Protocols thereto, is already the subject of well-established case-law of the Court.
2. Decisions and judgments under paragraph 1 shall be final.
3. If the judge elected in respect of the High Contracting Party concerned is not a member of the Committee, the Committee may at any stage of the proceedings invite that judge to take the place of one of the members of the Committee, having regard to all relevant factors, including whether that Party has contested the application of the procedure under paragraph 1(b).

Article 29
Decisions by Chambers on admissibility and merits

1. If no decision is taken under Article 27 or 28, or no judgment rendered under Article 28, a Chamber shall decide on the admissibility and merits of individual applications submitted under Article 34. The decision on admissibility may be taken separately.

2. A Chamber shall decide on the admissibility and merits of inter-State applications submitted under Article 33. The decision on admissibility shall be taken separately unless the Court, in exceptional cases, decides otherwise.

Article 30
Relinquishment of jurisdiction to the Grand Chamber

Where a case pending before a Chamber raises a serious question affecting the interpretation of the Convention or the Protocols thereto, or where the resolution of a question before the Chamber might have a result inconsistent with a judgment previously delivered by the Court, the Chamber may, at any time before it has rendered its judgment, relinquish jurisdiction in favour of the Grand Chamber[, *unless one of the parties to the case objects*].[4]

Article 31
Powers of the Grand Chamber

The Grand Chamber shall

(a) determine applications submitted either under Article 33 or Article 34 when a Chamber has relinquished jurisdiction under Article 30 or when the case has been referred to it under Article 43;
(b) decide on issues referred to the Court by the Committee of Ministers in accordance with Article 46 § 4; and
(c) consider requests for advisory opinions submitted under Article 47.

Article 32
Jurisdiction of the Court

1. The jurisdiction of the Court shall extend to all matters concerning the interpretation and application of the Convention and the Protocols thereto which are referred to it as provided in Articles 33, 34, 46 and 47.
2. In the event of dispute as to whether the Court has jurisdiction, the Court shall decide.

Article 33
Inter-State cases

Any High Contracting Party may refer to the Court any alleged breach of the provisions of the Convention and the Protocols thereto by another High Contracting Party.

Article 34
Individual applications

The Court may receive applications from any person, non-governmental organisation or group of individuals claiming to be the victim of a violation by one of the High Contracting Parties of the rights set forth in the Convention or the Protocols thereto. The High Contracting Parties undertake not to hinder in any way the effective exercise of this right.

---

[4] Words in italics removed by Article 3 of Protocol 15, not yet in force.

Article 35
Admissibility criteria

1. The Court may only deal with the matter after all domestic remedies have been exhausted, according to the generally recognised rules of international law, and within a period of six [*four*]⁵ months from the date on which the final decision was taken.
2. The Court shall not deal with any application submitted under Article 34 that
   (a) is anonymous; or
   (b) is substantially the same as a matter that has already been examined by the Court or has already been submitted to another procedure of international investigation or settlement and contains no relevant new information.
3. The Court shall declare inadmissible any individual application submitted under Article 34 if it considers that:
   (a) the application is incompatible with the provisions of the Convention or the Protocols thereto, manifestly ill-founded, or an abuse of the right of individual application; or
   (b) the applicant has not suffered a significant disadvantage, unless respect for human rights as defined in the Convention and the Protocols thereto requires an examination of the application on the merits [*and provided that no case may be rejected on this ground which has not been duly considered by a domestic tribunal*].⁶
4. The Court shall reject any application which it considers inadmissible under this Article. It may do so at any stage of the proceedings.

Article 36
Third party intervention

1. In all cases before a Chamber or the Grand Chamber, a High Contracting Party one of whose nationals is an applicant shall have the right to submit written comments and to take part in hearings.
2. The President of the Court may, in the interest of the proper administration of justice, invite any High Contracting Party which is not a party to the proceedings or any person concerned who is not the applicant to submit written comments or take part in hearings.
3. In all cases before a Chamber or the Grand Chamber, the Council of Europe Commissioner for Human Rights may submit written comments and take part in hearings.

Article 37
Striking out applications

1. The Court may at any stage of the proceedings decide to strike an application out of its list of cases where the circumstances lead to the conclusion that
   (a) the applicant does not intend to pursue his application; or
   (b) the matter has been resolved; or
   (c) for any other reason established by the Court, it is no longer justified to continue the examination of the application.
   However, the Court shall continue the examination of the application if respect for human rights as defined in the Convention and the Protocols thereto so requires.
2. The Court may decide to restore an application to its list of cases if it considers that the circumstances justify such a course.

---

⁵ Period of four months substituted by Article 4 of Protocol 15, not yet in force
⁶ Words in italics removed by Article 2 of Protocol 15, not yet in force.

Article 38
Examination of the case

The Court shall examine the case together with the representatives of the parties and, if need be, undertake an investigation, for the effective conduct of which the High Contracting Parties concerned shall furnish all necessary facilities.

Article 39
Friendly settlements

1. At any stage of the proceedings, the Court may place itself at the disposal of the parties concerned with a view to securing a friendly settlement of the matter on the basis of respect for human rights as defined in the Convention and the Protocols thereto.
2. Proceedings conducted under paragraph 1 shall be confidential.
3. If a friendly settlement is effected, the Court shall strike the case out of its list by means of a decision which shall be confined to a brief statement of the facts and of the solution reached.
4. This decision shall be transmitted to the Committee of Ministers, which shall supervise the execution of the terms of the friendly settlement as set out in the decision.

Article 40
Public hearings and access to documents

1. Hearings shall be in public unless the Court in exceptional circumstances decides otherwise.
2. Documents deposited with the Registrar shall be accessible to the public unless the President of the Court decides otherwise.

Article 41
Just satisfaction

If the Court finds that there has been a violation of the Convention or the Protocols thereto, and if the internal law of the High Contracting Party concerned allows only partial reparation to be made, the Court shall, if necessary, afford just satisfaction to the injured party.

Article 42
Judgments of Chambers

Judgments of Chambers shall become final in accordance with the provisions of Article 44 § 2.

Article 43
Referral to the Grand Chamber

1. Within a period of three months from the date of the judgment of the Chamber, any party to the case may, in exceptional cases, request that the case be referred to the Grand Chamber.
2. A panel of five judges of the Grand Chamber shall accept the request if the case raises a serious question affecting the interpretation or application of the Convention or the Protocols thereto, or a serious issue of general importance.
3. If the panel accepts the request, the Grand Chamber shall decide the case by means of a judgment.

Article 44
Final judgments

1. The judgment of the Grand Chamber shall be final.
2. The judgment of a Chamber shall become final
    (a) when the parties declare that they will not request that the case be referred to the Grand Chamber; or
    (b) three months after the date of the judgment, if reference of the case to the Grand Chamber has not been requested; or
    (c) when the panel of the Grand Chamber rejects the request to refer under Article 43.
3. The final judgment shall be published.

Article 45
Reasons for judgments and decisions

1. Reasons shall be given for judgments as well as for decisions declaring applications admissible or inadmissible.
2. If a judgment does not represent, in whole or in part, the unanimous opinion of the judges, any judge shall be entitled to deliver a separate opinion.

Article 46
Binding force and execution of judgments

1. The High Contracting Parties under-take to abide by the final judgment of the Court in any case to which they are parties.
2. The final judgment of the Court shall be transmitted to the Committee of Ministers, which shall supervise its execution.
3. If the Committee of Ministers considers that the supervision of the execution of a final judgment is hindered by a problem of interpretation of the judgment, it may refer the matter to the Court for a ruling on the question of interpretation. A referral decision shall require a majority vote of two thirds of the representatives entitled to sit on the Committee.
4. If the Committee of Ministers considers that a High Contracting Party refuses to abide by a final judgment in a case to which it is a party, it may, after serving formal notice on that Party and by decision adopted by a majority vote of two-thirds of the representatives entitled to sit on the Committee, refer to the Court the question whether that Party has failed to fulfil its obligation under paragraph 1.
5. If the Court finds a violation of paragraph 1, it shall refer the case to the Committee of Ministers for consideration of the measures to be taken. If the Court finds no violation of paragraph 1, it shall refer the case to the Committee of Ministers, which shall close its examination of the case.

Article 47
Advisory opinions

1. The Court may, at the request of the Committee of Ministers, give advisory opinions on legal questions concerning the interpretation of the Convention and the Protocols thereto.
2. Such opinions shall not deal with any question relating to the content or scope of the rights or freedoms defined in Section I of the Convention and the Protocols thereto, or with any other question which the Court or the Committee of Ministers might have to consider in consequence of any such proceedings as could be instituted in accordance with the Convention.

3. Decisions of the Committee of Ministers to request an advisory opinion of the Court shall require a majority vote of the representatives entitled to sit on the Committee.

Article 48
Advisory jurisdiction of the Court

The Court shall decide whether a request for an advisory opinion submitted by the Committee of Ministers is within its competence as defined in Article 47.

Article 49
Reasons for advisory opinions

1. Reasons shall be given for advisory opinions of the Court.
2. If the advisory opinion does not represent, in whole or in part, the unanimous opinion of the judges, any judge shall be entitled to deliver a separate opinion.
3. Advisory opinions of the Court shall be communicated to the Committee of Ministers.

Article 50
Expenditure on the Court

The expenditure on the Court shall be borne by the Council of Europe.

Article 51
Privileges and immunities of judges

The judges shall be entitled, during the exercise of their functions, to the privileges and immunities provided for in Article 40 of the Statute of the Council of Europe and in the agreements made thereunder.

SECTION III
MISCELLANEOUS PROVISIONS

Article 52
Inquiries by the Secretary General

On receipt of a request from the Secretary General of the Council of Europe any High Contracting Party shall furnish an explanation of the manner in which its internal law ensures the effective implementation of any of the provisions of the Convention.

Article 53
Safeguard for existing human rights

Nothing in this Convention shall be construed as limiting or derogating from any of the human rights and fundamental freedoms which may be ensured under the laws of any High Contracting Party or under any other agreement to which it is a party.

Article 54
Powers of the Committee of Ministers

Nothing in this Convention shall prejudice the powers conferred on the Committee of Ministers by the Statute of the Council of Europe.

Article 55
Exclusion of other means of dispute settlement

The High Contracting Parties agree that, except by special agreement, they will not avail themselves of treaties, conventions or declarations in force between them for the purpose of submitting, by way of petition, a dispute arising out of the interpretation or application of this Convention to a means of settlement other than those provided for in this Convention.

Article 56
Territorial application

1. Any State may at the time of its ratification or at any time thereafter declare by notification addressed to the Secretary General of the Council of Europe that the present Convention shall, subject to paragraph 4 of this Article, extend to all or any of the territories for whose international relations it is responsible.
2. The Convention shall extend to the territory or territories named in the notification as from the thirtieth day after the receipt of this notification by the Secretary General of the Council of Europe.
3. The provisions of this Convention shall be applied in such territories with due regard, however, to local requirements.
4. Any State which has made a declaration in accordance with paragraph 1 of this Article may at any time thereafter declare on behalf of one or more of the territories to which the declaration relates that it accepts the competence of the Court to receive applications from individuals, non-governmental organisations or groups of individuals as provided by Article 34 of the Convention.

Article 57
Reservations

1. Any State may, when signing this Convention or when depositing its instrument of ratification, make a reservation in respect of any particular provision of the Convention to the extent that any law then in force in its territory is not in conformity with the provision. Reservations of a general character shall not be permitted under this Article.
2. Any reservation made under this Article shall contain a brief statement of the law concerned.

Article 58
Denunciation

1. A High Contracting Party may denounce the present Convention only after the expiry of five years from the date on which it became a party to it and after six months' notice contained in a notification addressed to the Secretary General of the Council of Europe, who shall inform the other High Contracting Parties.
2. Such a denunciation shall not have the effect of releasing the High Contracting Party concerned from its obligations under this Convention in respect of any act which, being capable of constituting a violation of such obligations, may have been performed by it before the date at which the denunciation became effective.
3. Any High Contracting Party which shall cease to be a member of the Council of Europe shall cease to be a party to this Convention under the same conditions.
4. The Convention may be denounced in accordance with the provisions of the preceding paragraphs in respect of any territory to which it has been declared to extend under the terms of Article 56.

Article 59
Signature and ratification

1. This Convention shall be open to the signature of the members of the Council of Europe. It shall be ratified. Ratifications shall be deposited with the Secretary General of the Council of Europe.
2. The European Union may accede to this Convention.
3. The present Convention shall come into force after the deposit of ten instruments of ratification.
4. As regards any signatory ratifying subsequently, the Convention shall come into force at the date of the deposit of its instrument of ratification.
5. The Secretary General of the Council of Europe shall notify all the members of the Council of Europe of the entry into force of the Convention, the names of the High Contracting Parties who have ratified it, and the deposit of all instruments of ratification which may be effected subsequently.

Done at Rome this 4th day of November 1950, in English and French, both texts being equally authentic, in a single copy which shall remain deposited in the archives of the Council of Europe. The Secretary General shall transmit certified copies to each of the signatories.

PROTOCOL TO THE CONVENTION FOR THE PROTECTION OF HUMAN RIGHTS AND FUNDAMENTAL FREEDOMS

Paris, 20.III.1952

The governments signatory hereto, being members of the Council of Europe,

Being resolved to take steps to ensure the collective enforcement of certain rights and freedoms other than those already included in Section I of the Convention for the Protection of Human Rights and Fundamental Freedoms signed at Rome on 4 November 1950 (hereinafter referred to as "the Convention"),

Have agreed as follows:

Article 1
Protection of property

Every natural or legal person is entitled to the peaceful enjoyment of his possessions. No one shall be deprived of his possessions except in the public interest and subject to the conditions provided for by law and by the general principles of international law.

The preceding provisions shall not, however, in any way impair the right of a State to enforce such laws as it deems necessary to control the use of property in accordance with the general interest or to secure the payment of taxes or other contributions or penalties.

Article 2
Right to education

No person shall be denied the right to education. In the exercise of any functions which it assumes in relation to education and to teaching, the State shall respect the right of parents to ensure such education and teaching in conformity with their own religious and philosophical convictions.

Article 3
Right to free elections

The High Contracting Parties undertake to hold free elections at reasonable intervals by secret ballot, under conditions which will ensure the free expression of the opinion of the people in the choice of the legislature.

Article 4
Territorial application

Any High Contracting Party may at the time of signature or ratification or at any time there-after communicate to the Secretary General of the Council of Europe a declaration stating the extent to which it undertakes that the provisions of the present Protocol shall apply to such of the territories for the international relations of which it is responsible as are named therein.

Any High Contracting Party which has communicated a declaration in virtue of the preceding paragraph may from time to time communicate a further declaration modifying the terms of any former declaration or terminating the application of the provisions of this Protocol in respect of any territory.

A declaration made in accordance with this Article shall be deemed to have been made in accordance with paragraph 1 of Article 56 of the Convention.

Article 5
Relationship to the Convention

As between the High Contracting Parties the provisions of Articles 1, 2, 3 and 4 of this Protocol shall be regarded as additional Articles to the Convention and all the provisions of the Convention shall apply accordingly.

Article 6
Signature and ratification

This Protocol shall be open for signature by the members of the Council of Europe, who are the signatories of the Convention; it shall be ratified at the same time as or after the ratification of the Convention. It shall enter into force after the deposit of ten instruments of ratification. As regards any signatory ratifying subsequently, the Protocol shall enter into force at the date of the deposit of its instrument of ratification.

The instruments of ratification shall be deposited with the Secretary General of the Council of Europe, who will notify all members of the names of those who have ratified.

Done at Paris on the 20th day of March 1952, in English and French, both texts being equally authentic, in a single copy which shall remain deposited in the archives of the Council of Europe. The Secretary General shall transmit certified copies to each of the signatory governments.

PROTOCOL NO. 4 TO THE CONVENTION FOR THE PROTECTION OF HUMAN RIGHTS AND FUNDAMENTAL FREEDOMS SECURING CERTAIN RIGHTS AND FREEDOMS OTHER THAN THOSE ALREADY INCLUDED IN THE CONVENTION AND IN THE FIRST PROTOCOL THERETO

Strasbourg, 16.IX.1963

The governments signatory hereto, being members of the Council of Europe,

Being resolved to take steps to ensure the collective enforcement of certain rights and freedoms other than those already included in Section I of the Convention for the Protection of Human Rights and Fundamental Freedoms signed at Rome on 4 November 1950 (hereinafter referred to as the "Convention") and in Articles 1 to 3 of the First Protocol to the Convention, signed at Paris on 20 March 1952,

Have agreed as follows:

Article 1
Prohibition of imprisonment for debt

No one shall be deprived of his liberty merely on the ground of inability to fulfil a contractual obligation.

Article 2
Freedom of movement

1. Everyone lawfully within the territory of a State shall, within that territory, have the right to liberty of movement and freedom to choose his residence.
2. Everyone shall be free to leave any country, including his own.
3. No restrictions shall be placed on the exercise of these rights other than such as are in accordance with law and are necessary in a democratic society in the interests of national security or public safety, for the maintenance of ordre public, for the prevention of crime, for the protection of health or morals, or for the protection of the rights and freedoms of others.
4. The rights set forth in paragraph 1 may also be subject, in particular areas, to restrictions imposed in accordance with law and justified by the public interest in a democratic society.

Article 3
Prohibition of expulsion of nationals

1. No one shall be expelled, by means either of an individual or of a collective measure, from the territory of the State of which he is a national.
2. No one shall be deprived of the right to enter the territory of the State of which he is a national.

Article 4
Prohibition of collective expulsion of aliens

Collective expulsion of aliens is prohibited.

Article 5
Territorial application

1. Any High Contracting Party may, at the time of signature or ratification of this Protocol, or at any time thereafter, communicate to the Secretary General of the Council of Europe a declaration stating the extent to which it undertakes that the provisions of this Protocol shall apply to such of the territories for the international relations of which it is responsible as are named therein.
2. Any High Contracting Party which has communicated a declaration in virtue of the preceding paragraph may, from time to time, communicate a further declaration modifying the terms of any former declaration or terminating the application of the provisions of this Protocol in respect of any territory.
3. A declaration made in accordance with this Article shall be deemed to have been made in accordance with paragraph 1 of Article 56 of the Convention.

4. The territory of any State to which this Protocol applies by virtue of ratification or acceptance by that State, and each territory to which this Protocol is applied by virtue of a declaration by that State under this Article, shall be treated as separate territories for the purpose of the references in Articles 2 and 3 to the territory of a State.

5. Any State which has made a declaration in accordance with paragraph 1 or 2 of this Article may at any time thereafter declare on behalf of one or more of the territories to which the declaration relates that it accepts the competence of the Court to receive applications from individuals, non-governmental organisations or groups of individuals as provided in Article 34 of the Convention in respect of all or any of Articles 1 to 4 of this Protocol.

Article 6
Relationship to the Convention

As between the High Contracting Parties the provisions of Articles 1 to 5 of this Protocol shall be regarded as additional Articles to the Convention, and all the provisions of the Convention shall apply accordingly.

Article 7
Signature and ratification

1. This Protocol shall be open for signature by the members of the Council of Europe who are the signatories of the Convention; it shall be ratified at the same time as or after the ratification of the Convention. It shall enter into force after the deposit of five instruments of ratification. As regards any signatory ratifying subsequently, the Protocol shall enter into force at the date of the deposit of its instrument of ratification.

2. The instruments of ratification shall be deposited with the Secretary General of the Council of Europe, who will notify all members of the names of those who have ratified.

In witness whereof the undersigned, being duly authorised thereto, have signed this Protocol.

Done at Strasbourg, this 16th day of September 1963, in English and in French, both texts being equally authoritative, in a single copy which shall remain deposited in the archives of the Council of Europe. The Secretary General shall transmit certified copies to each of the signatory States.

PROTOCOL NO. 6 TO THE CONVENTION FOR THE PROTECTION OF HUMAN RIGHTS AND FUNDAMENTAL FREEDOMS CONCERNING THE ABOLITION OF THE DEATH PENALTY

Strasbourg, 28.IV.1983

The member States of the Council of Europe, signatory to this Protocol to the Convention for the Protection of Human Rights and Fundamental Freedoms, signed at Rome on 4 November 1950 (hereinafter referred to as "the Convention"),

Considering that the evolution that has occurred in several member States of the Council of Europe expresses a general tendency in favour of abolition of the death penalty;

Have agreed as follows:

Article 1
Abolition of the death penalty

The death penalty shall be abolished. No one shall be condemned to such penalty or executed.

Article 2
Death penalty in time of war

A State may make provision in its law for the death penalty in respect of acts committed in time of war or of imminent threat of war; such penalty shall be applied only in the instances laid down in the law and in accordance with its provisions. The State shall communicate to the Secretary General of the Council of Europe the relevant provisions of that law.

Article 3
Prohibition of derogations

No derogation from the provisions of this Protocol shall be made under Article 15 of the Convention.

Article 4
Prohibition of reservations

No reservation may be made under Article 57 of the Convention in respect of the provisions of this Protocol.

Article 5
Territorial application

1. Any State may at the time of signature or when depositing its instrument of ratification, acceptance or approval, specify the territory or territories to which this Protocol shall apply.
2. Any State may at any later date, by a declaration addressed to the Secretary General of the Council of Europe, extend the application of this Protocol to any other territory specified in the declaration. In respect of such territory the Protocol shall enter into force on the first day of the month following the date of receipt of such declaration by the Secretary General.
3. Any declaration made under the two preceding paragraphs may, in respect of any territory specified in such declaration, be withdrawn by a notification addressed to the Secretary General. The withdrawal shall become effective on the first day of the month following the date of receipt of such notification by the Secretary General.

Article 6
Relationship to the Convention

As between the States Parties the provisions of Articles 1 and 5 of this Protocol shall be regarded as additional Articles to the Convention and all the provisions of the Convention shall apply accordingly.

Article 7
Signature and ratification

The Protocol shall be open for signature by the member States of the Council of Europe, signatories to the Convention. It shall be subject to ratification, acceptance or approval. A member State of the Council of Europe may not ratify, accept or approve this Protocol unless it has, simultaneously or previously, ratified the Convention. Instruments of ratification, acceptance or approval shall be deposited with the Secretary General of the Council of Europe.

Article 8
Entry into force

1. This Protocol shall enter into force on the first day of the month following the date on which five member States of the Council of Europe have expressed their consent to be bound by the Protocol in accordance with the pro-visions of Article 7.
2. In respect of any member State which subsequently expresses its consent to be bound by it, the Protocol shall enter into force on the first day of the month following the date of the deposit of the instrument of ratification, acceptance or approval.

Article 9
Depositary functions

The Secretary General of the Council of Europe shall notify the member States of the Council of:

(a) any signature;
(b) the deposit of any instrument of ratification, acceptance or approval;
(c) any date of entry into force of this Protocol in accordance with Articles 5 and 8;
(d) any other act, notification or communication relating to this Protocol.

In witness whereof the undersigned, being duly authorised thereto, have signed this Protocol.

Done at Strasbourg, this 28th day of April 1983, in English and in French, both texts being equally authentic, in a single copy which shall be deposited in the archives of the Council of Europe. The Secretary General of the Council of Europe shall transmit certified copies to each member State of the Council of Europe.

PROTOCOL NO. 7 TO THE CONVENTION FOR THE PROTECTION OF HUMAN RIGHTS AND FUNDAMENTAL FREEDOMS

Strasbourg, 22.XI.1984

The member States of the Council of Europe signatory hereto,

Being resolved to take further steps to ensure the collective enforcement of certain rights and freedoms by means of the Convention for the Protection of Human Rights and Fundamental Freedoms signed at Rome on 4 Nov-ember 1950 (hereinafter referred to as "the Convention"),

Have agreed as follows:

Article 1
Procedural safeguards relating to expulsion of aliens

1. An alien lawfully resident in the territory of a State shall not be expelled therefrom except in pursuance of a decision reached in accordance with law and shall be allowed:
    (a) to submit reasons against his expulsion,
    (b) to have his case reviewed, and
    (c) to be represented for these purposes before the competent authority or a person or persons designated by that authority.
2. An alien may be expelled before the exercise of his rights under paragraph 1(a), (b) and (c) of this Article, when such expulsion is necessary in the interests of public order or is grounded on reasons of national security.

Article 2
Right of appeal in criminal matters

1. Everyone convicted of a criminal offence by a tribunal shall have the right to have his conviction or sentence reviewed by a higher tribunal. The exercise of this right, including the grounds on which it may be exercised, shall be governed by law.
2. This right may be subject to exceptions in regard to offences of a minor character, as prescribed by law, or in cases in which the person concerned was tried in the first instance by the highest tribunal or was convicted following an appeal against acquittal.

Article 3
Compensation for wrongful conviction

When a person has by a final decision been convicted of a criminal offence and when subsequently his conviction has been reversed, or he has been pardoned, on the ground that a new or newly discovered fact shows conclusively that there has been a miscarriage of justice, the person who has suffered punishment as a result of such conviction shall be compensated according to the law or the practice of the State concerned, unless it is proved that the non-disclosure of the unknown fact in time is wholly or partly attributable to him.

Article 4
Right not to be tried or punished twice

1. No one shall be liable to be tried or punished again in criminal proceedings under the jurisdiction of the same State for an offence for which he has already been finally acquitted or convicted in accordance with the law and penal procedure of that State.
2. The provisions of the preceding paragraph shall not prevent the reopening of the case in accordance with the law and penal procedure of the State concerned, if there is evidence of new or newly discovered facts, or if there has been a fundamental defect in the previous proceedings, which could affect the outcome of the case.
3. No derogation from this Article shall be made under Article 15 of the Convention.

Article 5
Equality between spouses

Spouses shall enjoy equality of rights and responsibilities of a private law character between them, and in their relations with their children, as to marriage, during marriage and in the event of its dissolution. This Article shall not prevent States from taking such measures as are necessary in the interests of the children.

Article 6
Territorial application

1. Any State may at the time of signature or when depositing its instrument of ratification, acceptance or approval, specify the territory or territories to which the Protocol shall apply and state the extent to which it undertakes that the provisions of this Protocol shall apply to such territory or territories.
2. Any State may at any later date, by a declaration addressed to the Secretary General of the Council of Europe, extend the application of this Protocol to any other territory specified in the declaration. In respect of such territory the Protocol shall enter into force on the first day

of the month following the expiration of a period of two months after the date of receipt by the Secretary General of such declaration.

3. Any declaration made under the two preceding paragraphs may, in respect of any territory specified in such declaration, be withdrawn or modified by a notification addressed to the Secretary General. The withdrawal or modification shall become effective on the first day of the month following the expiration of a period of two months after the date of receipt of such notification by the Secretary General.

4. A declaration made in accordance with this Article shall be deemed to have been made in accordance with paragraph 1 of Article 56 of the Convention.

5. The territory of any State to which this Protocol applies by virtue of ratification, acceptance or approval by that State, and each territory to which this Protocol is applied by virtue of a declaration by that State under this Article, may be treated as separate territories for the purpose of the reference in Article 1 to the territory of a State.

6. Any State which has made a declaration in accordance with paragraph 1 or 2 of this Article may at any time thereafter declare on behalf of one or more of the territories to which the declaration relates that it accepts the competence of the Court to receive applications from individuals, non-governmental organisations or groups of individuals as provided in Article 34 of the Convention in respect of Articles 1 to 5 of this Protocol.

Article 7
Relationship to the Convention

As between the States Parties, the provisions of Article 1 to 6 of this Protocol shall be regarded as additional Articles to the Convention, and all the provisions of the Convention shall apply accordingly.

Article 8
Signature and ratification

This Protocol shall be open for signature by member States of the Council of Europe which have signed the Convention. It is subject to ratification, acceptance or approval. A member State of the Council of Europe may not ratify, accept or approve this Protocol without previously or simultaneously ratifying the Convention. Instruments of ratification, acceptance or approval shall be deposited with the Secretary General of the Council of Europe.

Article 9
Entry into force

1. This Protocol shall enter into force on the first day of the month following the expiration of a period of two months after the date on which seven member States of the Council of Europe have expressed their consent to be bound by the Protocol in accordance with the provisions of Article 8.

2. In respect of any member State which subsequently expresses its consent to be bound by it, the Protocol shall enter into force on the first day of the month following the expiration of a period of two months after the date of the deposit of the instrument of ratification, acceptance or approval.

Article 10
Depositary functions

The Secretary General of the Council of Europe shall notify all the member States of the Council of Europe of:

(a) any signature;

(b) the deposit of any instrument of ratification, acceptance or approval;

(c) any date of entry into force of this Protocol in accordance with Articles 6 and 9;

(d) any other act, notification or declaration relating to this Protocol.

In witness whereof the undersigned, being duly authorised thereto, have signed this Protocol.

Done at Strasbourg, this 22nd day of November 1984, in English and French, both texts being equally authentic, in a single copy which shall be deposited in the archives of the Council of Europe. The Secretary General of the Council of Europe shall transmit certified copies to each member State of the Council of Europe.

PROTOCOL NO. 12 TO THE CONVENTION FOR THE PROTECTION OF HUMAN RIGHTS AND FUNDAMENTAL FREEDOMS

Rome, 4.XI.2000

The member States of the Council of Europe signatory hereto,

Having regard to the fundamental principle according to which all persons are equal before the law and are entitled to the equal protection of the law;

Being resolved to take further steps to promote the equality of all persons through the collective enforcement of a general prohibition of discrimination by means of the Convention for the Protection of Human Rights and Fundamental Freedoms signed at Rome on 4 November 1950 (hereinafter referred to as "the Convention");

Reaffirming that the principle of non-discrimination does not prevent States Parties from taking measures in order to promote full and effective equality, provided that there is an objective and reasonable justification for those measures,

Have agreed as follows:

Article 1
General prohibition of discrimination

1. The enjoyment of any right set forth by law shall be secured without discrimination on any ground such as sex, race, colour, language, religion, political or other opinion, national or social origin, association with a national minority, property, birth or other status.

2. No one shall be discriminated against by any public authority on any ground such as those mentioned in paragraph 1.

Article 2
Territorial application

1. Any State may, at the time of signature or when depositing its instrument of ratification, acceptance or approval, specify the territory or territories to which this Protocol shall apply.

2. Any State may at any later date, by a declaration addressed to the Secretary General of the Council of Europe, extend the application of this Protocol to any other territory specified in the declaration. In respect of such territory the Protocol shall enter into force on the first day of the month following the expiration of a period of three months after the date of receipt by the Secretary General of such declaration.

3. Any declaration made under the two preceding paragraphs may, in respect of any territory specified in such declaration, be withdrawn or modified by a notification addressed to the Secretary General of the Council of Europe. The withdrawal or modification shall become effective on the first day of the month following the expiration of a period of three months after the date of receipt of such notification by the Secretary General.

4. A declaration made in accordance with this Article shall be deemed to have been made in accordance with paragraph 1 of Article 56 of the Convention.

5. Any State which has made a declaration in accordance with paragraph 1 or 2 of this Article may at any time thereafter declare on behalf of one or more of the territories to which the declaration relates that it accepts the competence of the Court to receive applications from individuals, non-governmental organisations or groups of individuals as provided by Article 34 of the Convention in respect of Article 1 of this Protocol.

Article 3
Relationship to the Convention

As between the States Parties, the provisions of Articles 1 and 2 of this Protocol shall be regarded as additional Articles to the Convention, and all the provisions of the Convention shall apply accordingly.

Article 4
Signature and ratification

This Protocol shall be open for signature by member States of the Council of Europe which have signed the Convention. It is subject to ratification, acceptance or approval. A member State of the Council of Europe may not ratify, accept or approve this Protocol without previously or simultaneously ratifying the Convention. Instruments of ratification, acceptance or approval shall be deposited with the Secretary General of the Council of Europe.

Article 5
Entry into force

1. This Protocol shall enter into force on the first day of the month following the expiration of a period of three months after the date on which ten member States of the Council of Europe have expressed their consent to be bound by the Protocol in accordance with the provisions of Article 4.
2. In respect of any member State which subsequently expresses its consent to be bound by it, the Protocol shall enter into force on the first day of the month following the expiration of a period of three months after the date of the deposit of the instrument of ratification, acceptance or approval.

Article 6
Depositary functions

The Secretary General of the Council of Europe shall notify all the member States of the Council of Europe of:

(a) any signature;
(b) the deposit of any instrument of ratification, acceptance or approval;
(c) any date of entry into force of this Protocol in accordance with Articles 2 and 5;
(d) any other act, notification or communication relating to this Protocol.

In witness whereof the undersigned, being duly authorised thereto, have signed this Protocol.

Done at Rome, this 4th day of November 2000, in English and in French, both texts being equally authentic, in a single copy which shall be deposited in the archives of the Council of Europe. The Secretary General of the Council of Europe shall transmit certified copies to each member State of the Council of Europe.

PROTOCOL NO. 13 TO THE CONVENTION FOR THE PROTECTION OF HUMAN RIGHTS AND FUNDAMENTAL FREEDOMS CONCERNING THE ABOLITION OF THE DEATH PENALTY IN ALL CIRCUMSTANCES

Vilnius, 3.V.2002

The member States of the Council of Europe signatory hereto,

Convinced that everyone's right to life is a basic value in a democratic society and that the abolition of the death penalty is essential for the protection of this right and for the full recognition of the inherent dignity of all human beings;

Wishing to strengthen the protection of the right to life guaranteed by the Convention for the Protection of Human Rights and Fundamental Freedoms signed at Rome on 4 November 1950 (hereinafter referred to as "the Convention");

Noting that Protocol No. 6 to the Convention concerning the abolition of the death penalty, signed at Strasbourg on 28 April 1983, does not exclude the death penalty in respect of acts committed in time of war or of imminent threat of war;

Being resolved to take the final step in order to abolish the death penalty in all circumstances,

Have agreed as follows:

Article 1
Abolition of the death penalty

The death penalty shall be abolished. No one shall be condemned to such penalty or executed.

Article 2
Prohibitions of derogations

No derogation from the provisions of this Protocol shall be made under Article 15 of the Convention.

Article 3
Prohibitions of reservations

No reservation may be made under Article 57 of the Convention in respect of the provisions of this Protocol.

Article 4
Territorial application

1. Any State may, at the time of signature or when depositing its instrument of ratification, acceptance or approval, specify the territory or territories to which this Protocol shall apply.
2. Any State may at any later date, by a declaration addressed to the Secretary General of the Council of Europe, extend the application of this Protocol to any other territory specified in the declaration. In respect of such territory the Protocol shall enter into force on the first day of the month following the expiration of a period of three months after the date of receipt by the Secretary General of such declaration.
3. Any declaration made under the two preceding paragraphs may, in respect of any territory specified in such declaration, be withdrawn or modified by a notification addressed to the Secretary General. The withdrawal or modification shall become effective on the first day of

the month following the expiration of a period of three months after the date of receipt of such notification by the Secretary General.

Article 5
Relationship to the Convention

As between the States Parties the provisions of Articles 1 to 4 of this Protocol shall be regarded as additional Articles to the Convention, and all the provisions of the Convention shall apply accordingly.

Article 6
Signature and ratification

This Protocol shall be open for signature by member States of the Council of Europe which have signed the Convention. It is subject to ratification, acceptance or approval. A member State of the Council of Europe may not ratify, accept or approve this Protocol without previously or simultaneously ratifying the Convention. Instruments of ratification, acceptance or approval shall be deposited with the Secretary General of the Council of Europe.

Article 7
Entry into force

1. This Protocol shall enter into force on the first day of the month following the expiration of a period of three months after the date on which ten member States of the Council of Europe have expressed their consent to be bound by the Protocol in accordance with the provisions of Article 6.
2. In respect of any member State which subsequently expresses its con-sent to be bound by it, the Protocol shall enter into force on the first day of the month following the expiration of a period of three months after the date of the deposit of the instrument of ratification, acceptance or approval.

Article 8
Depositary functions

The Secretary General of the Council of Europe shall notify all the member States of the Council of Europe of:

(a) any signature;
(b) the deposit of any instrument of ratification, acceptance or approval;
(c) any date of entry into force of this Protocol in accordance with Articles 4 and 7;
(d) any other act, notification or communication relating to this Protocol;

In witness whereof the undersigned, being duly authorised thereto, have signed this Protocol.

Done at Vilnius, this 3rd day of May 2002, in English and in French, both texts being equally authentic, in a single copy which shall be deposited in the archives of the Council of Europe. The Secretary General of the Council of Europe shall transmit certified copies to each member State of the Council of Europe

PROTOCOL NO. 16 TO THE CONVENTION ON THE PROTECTION OF HUMAN RIGHTS AND FUNDAMENTAL FREEDOMS[7]

Preamble

The member States of the Council of Europe and other High Contracting Parties to the Convention for the Protection of Human Rights and Fundamental Freedoms, signed at Rome on 4 November 1950 (hereinafter referred to as "the Convention"), signatories hereto,

Having regard to the provisions of the Convention and, in particular, Article 19 establishing the European Court of Human Rights (hereinafter referred to as "the Court");

Considering that the extension of the Court's competence to give advisory opinions will further enhance the interaction between the Court and national authorities and thereby reinforce implementation of the Convention, in accordance with the principle of subsidiarity;

Having regard to Opinion No. 285 (2013) adopted by the Parliamentary Assembly of the Council of Europe on 28 June 2013,

Have agreed as follows:

Article 1

1. Highest courts and tribunals of a High Contracting Party, as specified in accordance with Article 10, may request the Court to give advisory opinions on questions of principle relating to the interpretation or application of the rights and freedoms defined in the Convention or the protocols thereto.
2. The requesting court or tribunal may seek an advisory opinion only in the context of a case pending before it.
3. The requesting court or tribunal shall give reasons for its request and shall provide the relevant legal and factual background of the pending case.

Article 2

1. A panel of five judges of the Grand Chamber shall decide whether to accept the request for an advisory opinion, having regard to Article 1. The panel shall give reasons for any refusal to accept the request.
2. If the panel accepts the request, the Grand Chamber shall deliver the advisory opinion.
3. The panel and the Grand Chamber, as referred to in the preceding paragraphs, shall include *ex officio* the judge elected in respect of the High Contracting Party to which the requesting court or tribunal pertains. If there is none or if that judge is unable to sit, a person chosen by the President of the Court from a list submitted in advance by that Party shall sit in the capacity of judge.

Article 3

The Council of Europe Commissioner for Human Rights and the High Contracting Party to which the requesting court or tribunal pertains shall have the right to submit written comments

---

[7] Protocol 16 (obtaining advisory opinions from the Court) will need both to be ratified by at least 10 member states of the Council of Europe and, specifically, by the United Kingdom Government for this procedure to be available to the UK courts. The Government's intention is to see how it operates in practice before considering whether or not to ratify it.

and take part in any hearing. The President of the Court may, in the interest of the proper administration of justice, invite any other High Contracting Party or person also to submit written comments or take part in any hearing.

Article 4

1. Reasons shall be given for advisory opinions.
2. If the advisory opinion does not represent, in whole or in part, the unanimous opinion of the judges, any judge shall be entitled to deliver a separate opinion.
3. Advisory opinions shall be communicated to the requesting court or tribunal and to the High Contracting Party to which that court or tribunal pertains.
4. Advisory opinions shall be published.

Article 5

Advisory opinions shall not be binding.

Article 6

As between the High Contracting Parties the provisions of Articles 1 to 5 of this Protocol shall be regarded as additional articles to the Convention, and all the provisions of the Convention shall apply accordingly.

Article 7

1. This Protocol shall be open for signature by the High Contracting Parties to the Convention, which may express their consent to be bound by:
   (a) signature without reservation as to ratification, acceptance or approval; or
   (b) signature subject to ratification, acceptance or approval, followed by ratification, acceptance or approval.
2. The instruments of ratification, acceptance or approval shall be deposited with the Secretary General of the Council of Europe.

Article 8

1. This Protocol shall enter into force on the first day of the month following the expiration of a period of three months after the date on which ten High Contracting Parties to the Convention have expressed their consent to be bound by the Protocol in accordance with the provisions of Article 7.
2. In respect of any High Contracting Party to the Convention which subsequently expresses its consent to be bound by it, the Protocol shall enter into force on the first day of the month following the expiration of a period of three months after the date of the expression of its consent to be bound by the Protocol in accordance with the provisions of Article 7.

Article 9

No reservation may be made under Article 57 of the Convention in respect of the provisions of this Protocol.

Article 10

Each High Contracting Party to the Convention shall, at the time of signature or when depositing its instrument of ratification, acceptance or approval, by means of a declaration addressed to the Secretary General of the Council of Europe, indicate the courts or tribunals that it designates for the purposes of Article 1, paragraph 1, of this Protocol. This declaration may be modified at any later date and in the same manner.

Article 11

The Secretary General of the Council of Europe shall notify the member States of the Council of Europe and the other High Contracting Parties to the Convention of:
    (a) any signature;
    (b) the deposit of any instrument of ratification, acceptance or approval;
    (c) any date of entry into force of this Protocol in accordance with Article 8;
    (d) any declaration made in accordance with Article 10; and
    (e) any other act, notification or communication relating to this Protocol.

In witness whereof the undersigned, being duly authorised thereto, have signed this Protocol.

Done at Strasbourg, this 2nd day of October 2013, in English and French, both texts being equally authentic, in a single copy which shall be deposited in the archives of the Council of Europe. The Secretary General of the Council of Europe shall transmit certified copies to each member State of the Council of Europe and to the other High Contracting Parties to the Convention.

Index